GUDEA'S TEMPLE BUILDING
The Representation of an Early Mesopotamian Ruler in Text and Image

CUNEIFORM MONOGRAPHS 17

Edited by

T. Abusch, M. J. Geller, Th. P. J. van den Hout
S. M. Maul and F. A. M. Wiggermann

STYX
PUBLICATIONS
GRONINGEN
2000

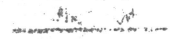

CUNEIFORM MONOGRAPHS 17

GUDEA'S TEMPLE BUILDING

The Representation of an Early Mesopotamian Ruler in Text and Image

by

Claudia E. Suter

STYX
PUBLICATIONS
GRONINGEN
2000

ISBN 90 5693 035 4
ISSN 0929-0052

100335252X

STYX Publications
Postbus 2659
9704 CR GRONINGEN
THE NETHERLANDS
Tel. # 31 (0)50–5717502
Fax. # 31 (0)50–5733325
E-mail: styxnl@compuserve.com

T

Contents

Du bist aus Stein, ich aber singe,
Du bist das Denkmal, und ich fliege.

Marina Zvetajeva

Acknowledgements

This book is a revised version of my University of Pennsylvania dissertation from 1995. During the writing of my dissertation and its revision I have received encouragement and assistance from many people. Irene Winter encouraged me to work on the Gudea stelae, aware of my interest in bringing text and image together. This study has much benefited from her patient and critical reading of earlier drafts. Richard Zettler and Holly Pittman have contributed to the progress of the work as supervisors of my dissertation. I first read Gudea's Cylinder Inscriptions in class with Åke Sjöberg, and he graciously granted me access to his "Zettelkasten." My understanding of this fascinating text has enormously profited from discussions of difficult passages with Miguel Civil. He also was to no small part responsible for the timely completion of my dissertation by discouraging me from endless "perfecting." The late Hermann Behrens generously let me use a manuscript of *Neusumerische Bau- and Weihinschriften*, and Evi Braun-Holzinger one of her *Mesopotamische Weihgaben*, before they were published. In the preparation of this book I received many valuable suggestions from Frans Wiggermann, Evi Braun-Holzinger, Karen Wilson, Julia Asher, and Markus Hilgert.

Several museum curators assisted me during my visits: Annie Caubet, Françoise Tallon, and Elizabeth Le Breton in the Louvre; Evelyne Klengel-Brandt and Joachim Mahrzahn in the Vorderasiatische Museum; Edibe Uzunoğlu in the Archaeological Museum of Istanbul; and Julian Reade and Dominique Collon in the British Museum. I am grateful to Alex Silber for his assistance in photographing Gudea material in Istanbul, and to Phoebe Adams for providing me with a practicable plan and method for the illustration of the "conceivable scenarios."

I am indebted to Ann Guinan for making my thoughts more readable, and to Jennifer More for improving my English. Last but not least I would like to thank Frans Wiggermann and Geerd Haayer for their interest in publishing my study. Without their invitation I might not have had the courage to revise my dissertation.

Abbreviations

Abbreviations for periodicals and cuneiform sources follow the *Pennsylvania Sumerian Dictionary*, Volume 1 (1992), the *Chicago Assyrian Dictionary*, Volume 17 (1989), and the *Reallexikon der Assyriologie*, Volume 7 (1987–90). Additional abbreviations used are:

BNYPL	Bulletin of the New York Public Library.
CHT	Chicago Hypertext, Sumerian Corpus (Oriental Institute, Chicago).
DC	de Sarzec, *Découvertes en Chaldée*.
FT	de Genouillac, *Fouilles de Tello*.
JRGS	Journal of the Royal Geographical Society.
MNB	Siglum of the Louvre, Paris.
NPEPP	New Princeton Encyclopedia of Poetry and Poetics.
OMRO	Oudheidkundige mededeelinge uit het Rijksmuseum van Oudheden te Leiden.
VA	Siglum of the Vorderasiatisches Museum, Berlin.
ZVO	Zapiski Vostoćnago Otdelentija Russkago Archeolgićeskago Obšćestva.

Tables

Illustrations

I. INTRODUCTION

A. Text and Image

1. *As Media of Communication*

Text and image share the common purpose of communicating a message. The act of communicating can be analyzed according to the information theory formulated by Shannon in 1948.[1] This theory provides a mathematical and philosophical view of the transmission of information. Although its practical applications are concerned mainly with engineering, it embeds human activities in an essentially social context, and therefore is applicable to linguistic and artistic expressions. In Mesopotamian studies, information theory has been applied to the analysis of writing systems and the interpretation of written text,[2] and it has served as a background for the examination of the historical relevance of visual imagery.[3]

In an act of communication one can distinguish the source (sender, author, etc.) of the message, the channel through which the message is transmitted (medium), and the receiver (addressee, reader, audience, etc.). The process can be sketched as follows:

source → encoding → channel of transmission → decoding → receiver

Miguel Civil formulated the following guidelines based on information theory and on the logic of conversation, which are relevant for the interpretation of ancient texts and can be extended to that of ancient images as well.[4] First, for the best possible communication, sender and receiver must share a common knowledge of their world. The background is assumed and not included in the message. This is a major source of limitations for the modern scholar, since he is not the intended receiver. Second, according to the degree to which sender and receiver share previous knowledge of particular events, the message can omit explicit mention of sub-events which can be considered present by implication or presupposition, and therefore need not articulate fundamental aspects that contextualize the explicit message. Third, the message will normally include what is "new" or unknown to the receiver, and omit what is already known. The more unexpected a piece of information, the more probable its inclusion in the message. If the information transmitted is already known or is being repeated, the message is not simply informative, but rather has didactic, rhetoric, or aesthetic purposes.

---

[1] For a simple but scientific overview see Raisbeck *Information Theory*; for a more anecdotal presentation of background and applications see Campbell *Grammatical Man*.

[2] Civil *Or* 42 (1973), 22–26, and "Limites," 226–228.

[3] Asher-Greve *Cahiers du Centre d'Etude du Proche-Orient Ancien* 5 (1989), 175 note *.

[4] "Limites," 226–228. The rebuttal of these guidelines by Hallo *JAOS* 110 (1990), confuses the inescapable psychological and material limitations of the interpretation of ancient sources with a voluntary assertion of skepticism.

A. Text and Image

In narrative messages, considerations of economy of time and materials oblige the poet or the artist to compress the message by eliminating the parts that the intended receiver can supply from his/her personal knowledge, or that are implied or presupposed by the nature of the events themselves. In selecting the parts to be included, the author will naturally pick the ones that are either more essential for identifying an event or more unusual or striking. A narrative is not a mechanical succession of events of equal importance, but can be analyzed as a tree of events with a core event at its root. The core is successively elaborated upon by making explicit more and more episodes and circumstances. This is not unlike the expansion of a grammatical sentence by relative and adverbial clauses, and by the coordination or subordination of other sentences.

Before and after being "sent" through the channel, the message is transferred from one system of symbols to another. This encoding is vital, and entails a main difference between written and pictorial expressions. In a written message, the speech component is encoded in visual symbols; in a pictorial message, a mental content is encoded in shapes and colors. These systems have to be decoded by the receiver. In terms of structure, a distinction can be made between discrete and nondiscrete qualities.[5] In a verbal communication the units are clearly distinguishable and discrete; in a visual communication, on the other hand, they are less well-defined and more continuous. Text is discontinuous and marked by gaps, while images are more dense in terms of syntax and semantics. The structure of text is a key to its decipherment, while images do not impose the same kind of rigid ordering. In other words, "the image has many possibilities of construction and perception, whereas the text has a single mode of formulation and reading."[6]

As a consequence, there is a major difference between verbal and visual transmission: the first is done one bit at a time, and requires a stretch of time to be transferred, while the second is transferred all at once. This is corroborated by clinical cases which show that verbal and visual recognition memory systems are functionally and topographically distinct.[7] A verbal medium cannot transmit simultaneous events as such, but is suitable to describe time sequences. A visual medium, on the other hand, can directly represent simultaneous events, but requires "redrawing" the events to encode a time sequence. The redrawing results in a "strip" representation, as, for example, in medieval panels representing the life of Christ.[8] To circumvent the time frame limitation, the artist may "compress" two or more actions in one scene, or leave aspects of time ambiguous.

Each mode of representation has specific limitations rooted in the nature of the senses that perceive it: the eye or the ear.[9] Words cannot directly represent shapes, sizes, and colors, while images by themselves cannot identify by name, show mental or psychological conditions, or accurately represent physical movement. In contrast to the

---

[5] Lotman *New Literary History* 6 (1975); Nelson Goodman as discussed by Mitchell *Iconology*, 53–74; Davis *Masking the Blow*, 242–248.

[6] Miller "Maya Image and Text," 182; this author labels the distinction as one of linear versus multivariate. In the quotation above, the accent is on mode; the obviously multiple interpretations are not excluded.

[7] Cohen *New Literary History* 7 (1976), 519.

[8] The space-time difference was first systematically formulated by Lessing, see Mitchell *Iconology*, 95–115.

[9] On eye and ear from a philosophical perspective see Mitchell *Iconology*, 116–149.

verbal, the visual cannot avoid ekphrastic specification. Verbal narrative can compensate for the difficulty of representing physical properties of characters, objects, or places by description.[10] Visual narrative, on the other hand, can circumvent its limitation only by including written labels and/or inscriptions, although the addition of symbolic attributes and gesture can up to a point replace the naming. The opposite strategy – adding images to text – is limited in ancient Mesopotamia to sporadic figures on astronomical and mathematical tablets, and a few sketchy plans of buildings or fields.

"Description is so much a part of narrative that there really is no narrative which does not include a degree of it."[11] In a verbal narrative, description can be distinguished from narration in the type of verb used. Passages with the verbs "to be" (and various types of copulative sentences, including comparative phrases ending in -gin₇ and -àm) and "to have" are descriptive, while passages with action verbs are narrative. In the case of images, one can formulate an empirical rule by analogy, and identify description if a verbal account of the image necessitates the verbs "to be" or "to have," narration if verbs of action are needed. By this definition, a single scene can very well be narrative.[12] A representation of a hero killing a lion can stand for a long story of epic dimensions. By showing, for instance, the birth and childhood of the hero, his antagonisms with other heroes, etc., the artist can make the story more and more explicit.

2. *In Mesopotamian Studies*

For millennia, text and image were circumscribed by the limits imposed by the channel of dissemination. The invention of the printing press brought about a first revolution. A series of further innovations from still photography, to film, to television, to computers, to everything encompassed by present-day multimedia have marked a dramatic turning point. Text and image have become infinitely reproducible and all-pervasive. Partly as a result of this accelerating cascade of discoveries, we have witnessed the arts develop rapidly in new directions: expressionism, cubism, futurism, the Russian avant-garde, abstract painting, and many other new forms of visual, verbal, and musical expression. At the same time, academia has developed a whole array of new theories and methods which scrutinize our ways of perception: psychoanalysis, structuralism, semiotics, information theory, gender studies, narratology, post-structuralism, and deconstruction. The study of the transmission of information in the ancient world, the interplay of verbal and visual channels under different conditions, the role of tradition in the choice of forms of expression have become increasingly attractive subjects of research.

The new insights and outlooks described above have generally had little impact on the methodology in ancient Mesopotamian studies. Piotr Michalowski has noted the lack of interest in non-traditional approaches among Assyriologists,[13] which can be extended to students of other facets of the ancient Mesopotamian legacy. Methodology

---

[10] See also Davis *Masking the Blow*, 248.
[11] Blanchard *Semiotica* 22 (1978), 236.
[12] Compare Davis *Masking the Blow*, 235–239.
[13] "Orality and Literacy," 228; see now also "Sailing to Babylon."

is rarely discussed. Too often presumptions are left unexamined or are not even made explicit. This may be due in part to the relative youth of the field, which is still in need of the most basic compilation and treatment of its material. Perhaps it is also due in part to the problems presented by the data which consists of an overwhelming number of texts and relatively few and fragmented pictorial monuments in contrast to, for example, the legacy of ancient Egypt. Yet, Mesopotamian studies have not been entirely unaffected by new approaches, and the interest is growing in recent years. To give a few examples: Mario Liverani, Piotr Michalowski, and Norman Yoffee have challenged traditional approaches to the reconstruction of history from ancient texts.[14] Miguel Civil has contributed an important non-traditional interpretation of the Sumerian writing system.[15] The Groningen Group has offered new perspectives for the perception and interpretation of Mesopotamian literary works, discussing issues such as orality and poetry in light of contemporary literary criticism.[16] Irene Winter has opened stimulating new vistas on Mesopotamian royal monuments using current anthropological and art historical concepts.[17]

A notorious problem of ancient Mesopotamian studies for those interested in the interplay of verbal and visual channels in the transmission of information concerns the traditional separation of assyriologists who study the texts, archaeologists who study the artifacts, and art historians who study the images. This division of labor impedes a comprehensive investigation into the thoughts and perception of the human beings who produced these cultural remains. As Jean Bottéro remarked,[18] "both the archaeologist and philologist have access to only half of the total object of historical research: the complete human of the past." Text and image are often combined on the same monument, and complement each other in their communicative function. Royal rhetoric, for example, is manifest not only in texts, but also in images. In 1964 Leo Oppenheim wrote: "The battle for synthesis is the battle he is to fight, and this battle should be considered his *raison d'être*."[19] Yet, *he* refers only to the Assyriologist. Oppenheim saw in the visual record only an illustration of the "factual" information contained in texts.[20] The visual record, however, is, as Winter demonstrated,[21] "a highly-developed system of communication in its own right," and it contributes in its own way to our reconstruction of ancient Mesopotamia. A plea for a holistic approach and more interdisciplinary work was voiced at the Albright Centennial Conference in Baltimore in 1991, entitled "The

---

[14] Liverani *Or* 42 (1973), and *HANE* 5 (1993); Michalowski *JAOS* 103 (1983), and "Charisma and Control;" Yoffee *Economic Role of the Crown*, *JCS* 30 (1978), and "Late Great Tradition."

[15] *Or* 42 (1973).

[16] *Mesopotamian Epic Literature* and *Mesopotamian Poetic Language*, both edited by Vanstiphout and Vogelzang, with useful bibliographies. See also Abusch *History of Religions* 26 (1986), and "Gilgamesh's Request."

[17] See especially *Studies in Visual Communication* 7 (1981), "Throneroom of Assurnasirpal II," "After the Battle," *BiMes* 21 (1986).

[18] *Mesopotamia*, 43.

[19] *Ancient Mesopotamia*, 28.

[20] Oppenheim *Ancient Mesopotamia*, 10: "the texts on clay tablets are far more valuable, far more relevant, than the monuments that have been discovered, although the latter, especially the famous reliefs on the walls of Assyrian palaces and the countless products of glyptic art, offer welcome illustration to the wealth of factual information contained on clay tablets, stelae, and votive offerings."

[21] *CRRA* 33 (1987), 201.

I. Introduction

Study of the Ancient Near East in the Twenty-First Century,"[22] and a similar plea for "increased cross-frontier awareness" was made by Nicholas Postgate in a conference on cognitive archaeology.[23]

Although there are hardly any studies primarily dedicated to the investigation of text-image relationships in ancient Mesopotamia, comparisons between these two media have been made with varying degree of success. Jerry Cooper considered the correspondences between text and image a "notoriously difficult problem in Mesopotamian art."[24] I would classify the problem not so much one of art, but rather of the modern scholar interpreting both texts and images of a now dead civilization. Interpretation presupposes some knowledge about the intentions and circumstances of the message, and this is where the difficulty resides. More often texts do not simply explain images, and images do not simply illustrate texts. Acknowledging that there are "match and missmatch," Postgate proposed that we "direct our attention quite deliberately to the reasons why the match is good in some and bad in other cases, since this will expose more of the discrete identity of the two classes."[25] The analysis of good matches, and an attempt at understanding "bad" matches, will also lead to a more careful consideration of what can be compared and why.

Figurines used in magic are a case in point for an optimal correspondence between text and image. Ritual texts give detailed instructions for the making and use of such figurines. They specify the material(s) of which the figurine is to be made, its posture and attributes, the textual label to be inscribed on it as, for example, "go out evil, come in good," and prescribe the place (and time) where the figurine is to be used. Figurines matching these descriptions have been found in excavations.[26] Based on the ritual texts, Frans Wiggermann succeeded in identifying various magical figures in the visual record which have previously puzzled scholars.[27] In this case, the comparison of text and image helps identify and contextualize the image, and it also informs the text by confirming that the rituals were indeed performed as prescribed, and that the texts thus present accurate ritual instructions. This latter fact explains the good match.

Marie-Thérèse Barrelet studied the correlation of text and image of a different type of figure. She compared actual images of kings to their description in texts.[28] Her visual data includes statues and figures in relief which form part of the official representation of the king. Her textual data includes year names and royal inscriptions which commemorate the fabrication or installation of royal images, and which belong, like the actual images, in the realm of the official representation. Also under consideration are scribal annotations concerning the visual representation on royal monuments the inscriptions of which were copied, and factual administrative records such as offering lists and delivery receipts in which the recipients are royal images. Since her inquiry is concerned with concrete

---

[22] For instance, Zettler "Written Documents," who discussed the integration of texts and archaeological data.
[23] Postgate "Text and figure."
[24] "Mesopotamian Historical Consciousness," 45.
[25] "Text and figure," 180.
[26] Rittig *Assyrisch-babylonische Kleinplastik*; Postgate "Text and Figure," 176–179.
[27] *JEOL* 27 (1981–82), and 29 (1985–86); *Protective Spirits*, 186–187; *RlA* 8 (1994): 222–246 s.v. Mischwesen.
[28] *CRRA* 19 (1974).

physical images that exist(ed) in reality, incongruity of genre is irrelevant. Barrelet did not include poetic images of kings which occur, for example, in royal hymns. A comparison of the latter with actual images is likely to yield interesting results of a different sort, contributing to the distinction between concepts manifest in both media, and streams of tradition which are confined to one or the other.[29]

In general, one can observe one major discrepancy between the images and texts Barrelet compared, and that concerns their chronological distribution:[30] the number of actual royal images decreases from the Early Dynastic to the Old Babylonian periods, while that of texts describing them, beginning only in the Akkad period, increases dramatically in the Old Babylonian period. In part, this result certainly reflects the chance of finds in archaeology, in part, a change in the materials used; indestructible stone prevalent in the early periods is replaced by reusable metal in later periods. Another explanation, as Barrelet suggested,[31] is that the verbal description is a later development which arose only with the canonization of visual images. A particular case of uneven distribution concerns the image of the kid carrier which occurs frequently in verbal descriptions of royal images, but is rare among the identified visual representations of kings.[32] Barrelet is probably correct in assuming that at least some of the numerous unidentified images of kid carriers in statuary, glyptic, and terra cotta do represent a king.[33] If a verbal description does not match any preserved image, there are two possible explanations: either no visual representation of this particular image has survived, or it has not been discovered in our data. As Barrelet showed for the "running king,"[34] a careful study of texts describing royal images helps identify and understand significant details in the visual record.

Barrelet lamented a lack in the visual record of certain aspects and attributes of kingship known from more poetic texts, and mentioned as an example, like other scholars before and after her, the royal insignia.[35] One should keep in mind, however, that in contrast to Egypt, for instance, royal insignia were not strictly canonized in Mesopotamia. Written sources mention a number of objects which can be identified as royal insignia from the context, and they usually occur together, but the composition of the group slightly varies from text to text. They include a headgear (aga or men), a throne (^{giš}gu-za), a "scepter" (gidri), a measuring rod (gi-ninda), and a rope (éš). Although in visual representations the king does not seem to be systematically associated with these insignia, it is not quite true that they are entirely absent. One may identify the headgear with the brimmed cap worn exclusively by ruler figures;[36] the throne with the stool on which kings sit in presentation scenes in which they receive their subjects;[37] and the "scepter" possibly with the palm

---

[29] A first step in this direction was made by Winter "Body of the Able Ruler."
[30] *CRRA* 19 (1974), 31.
[31] *CRRA* 19 (1974), 34.
[32] Barrelet *CRRA* 19 (1974), 34–35.
[33] On the kid carrier see also Suter *JCS* 43–45 (1991–93).
[34] *CRRA* 19 (1974), 35.
[35] Barrelet *CRRA* 19 (1974), 38–40; Strommenger *RlA* 4 (1972–75), 347 s.v. Herrscher; Krecher *RlA* 5 (1976–80), 112 s.v. Insignien; Cooper "Mesopotamian Historical Consciousness," 46.
[36] See chapter IV.D.1.a.
[37] See Winter "The King and the Cup," 255.

frond which Gudea carries on some stela fragments.[38] As for the measuring rod and rope, it is true that they are seen only in the hands of deities, yet always in scenes in which they are pointed toward an approaching king.[39] In this case, the emphasis lies on the transfer from deity to king, and this is the context in which these particular insignia play a role in the texts as well. In sum, royal insignia are attributes that characterize royalty, but the king need not be associated with all of them at all time.

This example shows that one should not accept an apparent discrepancy too soon, but rather look harder for the missing link. The identification of concrete objects or details in the imagery with concepts known from texts naturally adds significance, and invariably improves the preception of the image. It is this background shared by the sender and receiver of the message which allows the modern scholar to proceed from the pre-iconographic to the iconographic analysis in Panofsky's terminology.[40]

As we move from single figures to narrative scenes, the correlation between text and image becomes more complex. The interpretation of the rich repertoire depicted on Akkadian seals, for example, continues to cause difficulty. Henri Frankfort laid the groundwork for its interpretation in 1939. He observed that their "strong inclination towards the concrete which we have found to underlie the stylistic innovations of the period led to an efflorescence of designs depicting actuality as was never equalled before or afterwards."[41] Noticing that "it is through their attributes, positions or actions that we must recognise the personalities involved,"[42] he proposed an approach which remains valuable and is worth citing in extenso:[43]

> For if the meaning of the Akkadian seals is no longer self-evident, there are indirect methods by which it may be discerned. It should be possible systematically to collect and compare the extant versions of a given subject, and thus to distinguish the accidental from the essential, and to elucidate obscure details by examining variations which may be complementary. We should, moreover, scan such texts as have come down to us with a view to relevant allusions.
>
> It is, of course, with the first of these two steps that we are particularly concerned. Hitherto almost all interpretations of seal designs have been based on one or two cylinders discussed in isolation. It is evident that such an approach can only be haphazard. Just as the literary form of certain myths has been preserved in more than one copy of the same text or even in more than one version, so certain myths have found pictorial expression on a number of seals in identical or slightly varying renderings, and again on others which show dissimilar versions. We must therefore first establish the pictorial equivalent of a standard text: next we must consider the variants as sources of additional information; and only then are we in a position to search the literary tradition for parallels with the pictorial stories.
>
> There are a number of texts referring to subjects dealt with by the seal cutters of Sargon's age. These texts are later than the seals, but though this difference in age may be a source of error, it would be exceedingly unwise to deny the irrelevancy *a priori*. We already know that numerous religious usages and beliefs have come down from very ancient times, though we

---

[38] See chapter V.C.5.
[39] See Figs. 25–26, and compare also the Hammurabi Stela = Börker-Klähn *Bildstelen*, no. 113.
[40] *Studien zur Ikonologie*, 41.
[41] *Cylinder Seals*, 91.
[42] *Cylinder Seals*, 92.
[43] *Cylinder Seals*, 93–94.

happen to know them only form late documents. If we refuse to countenance any combination, however prudent, of texts of the First Millennium B.C. with seals of the Third, we are destroying the only bridge between the literary and the pictorial expression of Mesopotamian religion.

The results obtained by these comparisons seem, moreover, to justify the method. It is interesting that ritual texts rather than purely literary works supply parallels to the seal designs, and this circumstance should guide further research. Nor is it hard to explain. The literary form of a myth, even when it is rich in metaphor, retains nevertheless a more general character than the acts of a ritual. These acts possess, in fact, the same degree of definition as an image, and a ritual thus uses symbolism in the same manner as pictorial art. It is for these reasons that the description of a ritual, or a commentary on it, supplies us more often with a clue to the Akkadian seal designs than the literary description of gods and events in the great epics of Babylonia. ... If the scenes are bound to become more comprehensible as a result of such research, the interpretation of the texts is equally certain to profit by a fuller utilisation of the illustrated encyclopedia constituted by the Sargonid seals."

Although not all of Frankfort's interpretations can be supported today, and there are many more seal images and texts to consider, his methodology still stands. The first step especially deserves more attention than it has received in the past. Other approaches proposed have failed to produce positive results. No one today would defend Anton Moortgat's notion of the all-encompassing Tammuz motif, nor is Pierre Amiet's concept of a "cosmological mythology" construed independent of textual tradition convincing.[44] Despite the considerable chronological gap between the images and texts Frankfort used, I would defend the search for texts to compare with the images, looking not so much for perfect matches, but rather seeking a mental background. The difficulties we still have today finding these texts may, in part, be explained by a now lost oral tradition. The writing down of mythological stories in a largely illiterate society should surprise us, and one wonders whether this activity reached its peak at a time when the oral tradition was vanishing. This would explain why some comparable texts come to us from a much later period. Contrary to earlier views, the excavations at Ebla have shown that Semitic literature goes back to the third millennium, and Piotr Steinkeller suggested that it may be these stories, still insufficiently known, that inspired Akkadian seal images.[45]

Not all Akkadian seal images, however, need to reflect a particular story. Inspired by their concrete nature, like Frankfort, and based on Francastel's thesis that an image is "constituée par un assemblage d'éléments réorganisés à partir du réel et liés ensemble par un rapport symbolique," Barrelet set out to explore different levels of the figurative imagination, and the mechanisms involved in the creative process.[46] As possible sources of inspiration that guided the Akkadian seal cutter, she conceived of several categories depending on whether the artist worked in the precincts of a palace or temple, or outside of the abodes of power and learning.[47] In the first case, the seal cutter would have had access to the intelligentsia of his time, and his production would be more likely to visualize complex concepts reflecting the values of a restricted elite. In the second case,

---

[44] Amiet *Glyptique mésopotamienne*. For a critique see Bernbeck *BaM* 27 (1996), 165.
[45] "Early Semitic Literature," 244–247.
[46] *Or* 39 (1970), 213–224.
[47] *Or* 39 (1970), 219–220.

he would have been on his own, and his production could have been influenced by three categories of sources: stories from the common pool of oral tradition, as for Greek vase painters; visual experience occasioned by festivals that included some sort of spectacles along the lines of those performed in fifteenth century Italy or the *pasos* of the *Semana Santa* in today's Spain; and the store of imagery depicted in other media subservient to the official representation in palace and temple. She concluded from a detailed analysis of the seals pertaining to the Ea/Enki cycle that most scenes centering around the god associated with flowing water were produced outside of the centers of power, and were most likely inspired by festivals during which actual images of the god could be seen. For two particular seal images, distinctly different from all others, however, she showed convincingly that they must have been made for members of the elite.[48]

Although little documentary evidence has survived of such festivals, the assumption is supported by cross-cultural comparison. Barrelet's study merits more attention, for it demonstrates that inquiries about the source of inspiration and the creative process involved in artistic production make an important contribution to the interpretation of imagery. These issues have hardly been considered before and are still neglected.

The one example most often cited as evidence for the mythological background of Akkadian seal images – and believed by some to be the only one – is the story of Etana, who ascended to heaven on the back of an eagle.[49] Two recent studies have scrutinized this motif. Both operate on the basic assumption that the visual representation of a man on the back of an eagle ascending to heaven reflects in one way or another a story about Etana. Piotr Steinkeller used the imagery in combination with the textual evidence in an attempt to reconstruct an original story, now lost.[50] Although, in the absence of written documentation, his scenario cannot be proven, it makes perfect sense in terms of the creative process at the origin of a story, and is not contradicted by any detail of the extant data. If correct, the image freezes the most dramatic moment of the story – its turning point – which is, at the same time, best fit for visual representation. It epitomizes the essence of the story. This study confirms Frankfort's contention that the interpretation of texts can profit from a fuller utilization of the images.

Reinhard Bernbeck took a different approach.[51] Although crediting Barrelet for having opened new possibilities for the interpretation of Akkadian seals, he unjustly accused her study of having as an end in itself the reconstruction of "rites" from images, of denying any relation between the images and the preserved texts, and of not going beyond the pre-iconographic level of interpretation. His approach presupposes that myth and rite are interdependent. This thesis goes back to Frazer's *Golden Bough*, and has found surprisingly many followers in anthropology. The alleged interdependence has never been adequately proven, and G. S. Kirk in his study of myth has convincingly demonstrated that "there is neither logic nor other virtue in trying to confine the term

---

[48] *Or* 39 (1970), 240–249.
[49] For earlier literature see Bernbeck *BaM* 27 (1996), 174 note 68.
[50] "Early Semitic Literature," 248–255.
[51] *BaM* 27 (1996), 164–171.

'myth' to tales associated in some way with sacred ritual."[52] Nor is there evidence in Mesopotamia for the enactment of myths. The recital of *Enuma Eliš* at the New Year Festival in the late first millennium B.C. is but a small episode in this twelve-day religious festival, and its inclusion can be explained on grounds other than the interdependence of myth and rite.[53] Moreover, the Etana story is a narrative with universal folktale motifs,[54] and can hardly be called a "social drama." Bernbeck's analysis of the Etana scene takes the written version of the story too literally,[55] and his interpretation of the pictorial motif of the "bull of heaven" as a rendition of the "social drama" is not convincing.[56]

Two other motifs, the banquet scene and the presentation scene, have been assumed to represent rites, and in both cases this presumption has undermined the possibility of a reasonable interpretation. Both motifs were extremely popular in early Mesopotamian art, and exist in many variations. They occur in different media, including stone monuments dedicated by the ruler in temples, luxury items of the palace, and seals used in the administration. Depending on the medium, they appear in isolation or in the context of an extended narrative. The banquet scene has been interpreted variously as a rite for the deceased or a rite epitomizing the New Year festival.[57] Gudrun Selz dedicated a monograph to this motif, in which she documented its chronological development in early Mesopotamian art.[58] On the assumption that all banquet scenes depict the same event, she presupposed a cultic meaning which could be gained only from textual sources. These did not receive a comprehensive discussion, however.[59] Selz's failure to differentiate between the various media which depict banquet scenes distorts her typology,[60] and is in part responsible for her unwarranted assessment of the motif. This is obvious in her rejection of Amiet, whose conclusions I accept: "la cérémonie du banquet a dû être célébrée en de multiple circonstances, par des particuliers, par diverses collectivités et enfin par des rois, à l'occasion de leurs victoires et probablement aussi lors des fêtes liturgiques au nombre desquelles celle du Nouvel-An a fort bien pu être comptée."[61] The same picture emerges from the different contexts in which banquets occur in verbal narratives.[62]

Not unlike Selz, Martha Haussperger, who produced the only monograph on the presentation scene, aimed at a chronological typology rather than an interpretation of the motif. She advised against "speculating about the rite depicted in the presentation scene, if it indeed renders one, as long as corresponding textual data and other archaeological

---

[52] *Myth*, 12–29.
[53] Kirk *Myth*, 14.
[54] Steinkeller "Early Semitic Literature," 255.
[55] *BaM* 27 (1996), 174–180. He divorced the Etana motif from the shepherd's background, in which he saw another episode, and concluded that disparate levels of time and space were combined in one image.
[56] *BaM* 27 (1996), 181–196. Nor is the answer he provides ibidem, 196–204, satisfactory for the question formulated by Postgate "Text and figure," 182: "why was a scene like this suitable to feature on the seals, almost uniquely in its human narrative, and why did this only happen in the Akkad period."
[57] See Selz *Bankettszene*, 1–11.
[58] *Bankettszene*, 11–12.
[59] Selz *Bankettszene*, 581–584.
[60] See chapter IV.C.2.b.
[61] Quoted in Selz *Bankettszene*, 10. See also Asher-Greve *BiOr* 44 (1987), 794-795.
[62] See Vanstiphout *Res Orientales* 4 (1992), 9–12.

implications are lacking." Yet, based on her dating the origin of the motif to Enheduanna, she proceeded to conjecture that it rendered a rite of Nanna.[63] Neither the date nor
the assumption that the scene rendered a rite, much less of Nanna, can be supported.
Haussperger's exclusion of media other than the glyptic art and her confinement to two
compositional versions of the scene cannot do justice to the motif. Moreover, unaware
of basic principles in the composition of Mesopotamian imagery such as the distinction
between culminating and episodic scenes, and the recognition of core and expansion in
the representation of an event,[64] the author erroneously interpreted these two versions
as two different moments of the same event.[65]

A consideration of the function of cylinder seals and of the context in which presentation
scenes occur in other media, together with an elementary art historical background and
an awareness of basic concepts of the society that produced the image would have
precluded such errors. It is unfortunate that Irene Winter's important contributions to our
understanding of the presentation scene[66] had no influence on Haussperger's discussion,
although they are listed in her bibliography. The presentation scene is a typical example
of a conceptual image. It can be elucidated only with a methodologically sound analysis
of its components in all its variations together with a search for its mental background.
This background shared by sender and receiver is reflected in texts, though not in a
literal way.[67] As Irene Winter has pointed out:[68]

> We do not have a cultural situation in which monolithic religious/mythological/heroic texts
> stand behind the very fabric of society – as the Bible does for the Judeo-Christian West,
> the Odyssey and the Iliad for the classical world, or the Ramayana and the Bhagavad Gita
> for the Indian subcontinent. Nor do we have a tradition of inscriptions directly associated
> with and therefore identifying mythological/religious images. Through juxtaposition with
> text, as in illustrated books or through labeling, as on Greek vases, for example, images in
> later Western art at least are far more likely to be accurately identified; and these identifiable
> images then provide a basic corpus from which to argue for the unknown. The problem is
> further exacerbated by the tendency in the art of the ancient Near East ... to be 'allusive'
> rather than explicit, with the 'culminating scene' of a given story standing for the whole. We
> often find the story behind the image, therefore, demanding the viewer's prior knowledge
> and correct identification of the scene – a process of 'matching' rather than 'reading' of the
> imagery itself qua narrative.

There is only a small corpus of narrative poems in Mesopotamia that has deities and
heroes as actors (small if compared with the Odyssey, Iliad or the Bhagavad Gita), and
there are hardly any extant visual representations. Two episodes from the Gilgameš
epic, perhaps the most popular and wide-spread story in ancient Mesopotamia, are
notable exceptions: the killing of Huwawa and the killing of the Bull of Heaven.[69] The

---

[63] *Einführungsszene*, 77.
[64] See chapters IV.C.2.a-b.
[65] *Einführungsszene*, 69.
[66] "The King and the Cup;" "Legitimation of Authority."
[67] For further discussion see chapter IV.B.7.
[68] "After the Battle," 11–12.
[69] As Wilfred G. Lambert "Gilgamesh in Literature and Art," has excellently documented, they are depicted
in the *Kleinkunst* through several centuries and across geographical borders.

bulk of ancient Mesopotamian images, and especially more extensive visual narratives, pertain to the official representation of the ruler, which is also documented in texts. Since royal monuments often combine text and image, they are preconditioned subjects for a comparison of the two media. The division into different disciplines within the field of ancient Mesopotamian studies, however, has hampered research in this area. The recent compilation of all inscribed dedicatory objects from the Early Dynastic to the Old Babylonian periods by Eva Braun-Holzinger,[70] which includes careful descriptions of the objects and imagery sculpted on them along with a transliteration and translation or summary of their inscription, has made a positive contribution, one which will hopefully encourage more comparative work, and lead to a fuller understanding of these objects.

Irene Winter has contributed pioneering analyses of royal monuments that combine text and image. In two examples from different periods she detected different degrees of interrelation between the two media. The throne room of the Neo-Assyrian king Assurnasirpal attests to "an extraordinary degree of correspondence between the organization of the decorative scheme and that of the text accompanying it," and the relationship is manifest "both in structural organization and in content."[71] In this case, Winter did not answer the question about whether the "correspondence reflects a conscious translation of the text into visual terms, or an unconscious cultural ordering that underlies text and image equally." In contrast, on the stela of the Early Dynastic king Eannatum of Lagaš, the correspondence of text and image is not exact:[72]

> The visual imagery has its own agenda. ... the reliefs detail the immediate action(s), while the text emphasizes the longer-range antecedents and consequences. In fact, the text and the imagery come from different traditions. The text derives from a combination of known celebratory proclamations and legalistic documents that include background, current intervention, resolution, and proscriptions. ... The imagery ... has developed out of a visual tradition representing sequences surrounding, or culminating in, a single event. ... text and imagery differ not only in content but also in intent: the text serving the legal case of the legitimacy of Lagash's claims over Umma and the Gu'eden at the highest (literate) levels, its audience both internal and external; the visual portion addressed more to an internal (not necessarily literate) audience, its message related to the hierarchy and power of the state itself.

Her studies demonstrate that in order to analyze the relationship of text and image, in addition to an analysis of their content and structure, one must study them in terms of messages, and inquire about their sender, receiver, and the traditions of their channel.[73]

3. Gudea: A Case Study

Gudea was a ruler of the southern Mesopotamian city-state of Lagaš at the end of the third millennium B.C. His material legacy exceeds that of most other early Mesopotamian rulers in quantity. The corpus consists of a variety of inscribed and sculpted artifacts

---

[70] *Weihgaben.*
[71] "Throneroom of Assurnasirpal," 27.
[72] "After the Battle," 22–23.
[73] See also Cooper "Mesopotamian Historical Consciousness," 45–48.

which were elements in or equipment of temples, and commemorate this ruler's dedication to a particular deity or his (re)construction of the deity's temple. The most extensive written building account is the long text inscribed on two large clay cylinders, which pertains to the construction of Eninnu, the temple of Lagaš's divine patron Ningirsu. Detailed pictorial accounts of temple construction were sculpted on several limestone stelae. Due to their poor preservation, the assignment of individual fragments to particular stelae remains problematic, though it is clear that the surviving imagery forms parts of various scenes which can be interpreted as episodes of the construction of a temple, and at least one stela did pertain to Eninnu. This study will investigate and compare the written and pictorial accounts of Gudea with special emphasis on the cylinders and stelae. Although text and imagery clearly relate the same type of events, their correlation has hardly been considered, nor has the remaining material of Gudea received a comprehensive treatment in the context of these accounts.

The Gudea material is suited to the investigation of text-image relationships for several reasons. It forms a substantial and uniform corpus of an early Mesopotamian ruler's manifestation in verbal and visual media – substantial because of the large amount and variety of inscribed and sculpted objects, and uniform in regard to the ultimate source of the message and its main subject. The material has already received basic treatment. The artifacts of interest to archaeologists and art historians have been catalogued, and the inscriptions have been compiled and edited by philologists. Moreover, the corpus promises to be interesting in regard to the history and development (tradition and innovation) of royal representation in Mesopotamia. Gudea could look back at the history of his own city-state, several hundred years old, and, at the same time, witness the rise of the powerful Ur III state as it established far-reaching military and bureaucratic control over other Mesopotamian cities as well as some foreign lands. With a detailed analysis of Gudea's cylinders and stelae and a comparison of their messages to one another and to the remaining Gudea material, I hope to elucidate the interrelations and correspondences of text and image in the rhetoric of a Sumerian city-state ruler, and to contribute to an improved and more comprehensive understanding of this important body of royal representation.

The comparison of text and image first requires a sound understanding of the comparanda and their context. The material other than cylinders and stelae is presented in part II which includes an overview of the types of artifacts and their provenance, an analysis of contents and structure of the inscriptions, and a description and interpretation of the imagery. A catalogue of these artifacts is provided in Appendix A. Parts III and IV are dedicated to the Cylinder Inscriptions and the stela fragments, respectively. They aim at a comprehensive understanding of these narratives in terms of contents, narrative structure, composition, and communicative function. A catalogue of the stela fragments based on personal examination is provided in Appendix B. Selected passages of the cylinder inscriptions are translated in Appendix C. In view of the enormous size of the text and the philological difficulties still inherent in many details, which require a philological discussion, a full translation is outside the limits of the present study. Part V compares the verbal and visual narratives in terms of their communicative context and narrative components, and examines correspondences and differences between the two

13

media as well as their interrelation. Before plunging in *media res*, a few words about Gudea's reign are necessary.

B.   Gudea's Reign

Knowledge of Gudea's reign is limited. Neither its length nor its precise dates can be established with any certainty. The numerous inscribed artifacts commissioned by him and the names given to his regnal years pertain to cultic activities in his city-state. Aside from these official documents issued by the ruling power, there are hardly any sources that furnish additional information or relate his reign to contemporary events outside Lagaš. The extent of his sphere of influence remains open to speculation. This chapter presents a synopsis of the facts presently known and the problems still unsolved.

1.   *Chronology*

Gudea was a member of what scholars have conventionally termed the Second Dynasty of Lagaš, distinguishing the rulers of the late third millennium from their Early Dynastic predecessors.[74] The number of Lagaš II rulers, their sequence, and the length of their reigns remains problematic.[75] Probably for political reasons, Lagaš is not included in the Sumerian King List,[76] and the Lagaš King List is a satirical answer to the former.[77] It can therefore not be considered for historical reconstruction. The sources for the Lagaš II chronology are confined to royal inscriptions which mention kin affiliations or synchronisms with rulers of other city-states, and administrative documents which provide year names as well as prosopographic data.

Most Lagaš II inscriptions do not mention the filiation of the rulers. Exceptions are some inscriptions of Urningirsu and Pirigme, the son and grandson of Gudea, respectively. In the case of Urningirsu, the filiation seemingly served to distinguish this ruler from an earlier namesake.[78] Other kinship relations are apparent in inscriptions of female members of the royal family who identify themselves as wives and/or daughters of known rulers. This evidence seems to indicate that the succession was not from father to son, but followed a different kin-based system. Unfortunately Renger's efforts to elucidate this system, and with it the sequence of the Lagaš II rulers,[79] remain hypothetical due to the lack of conclusive evidence and an adequate understanding of Sumerian kin terminology.

About thirty-five year names from administrative tablets are attributed to this period.[80]

---

[74] Although two distinct dynasties are not substantiated in the ancient sources and may prove to be a simplification, the terms Lagaš I and II are retained here due to the lack of a more adequate terminology.

[75] Compare the lists given by Sollberger *AfO* 17 (1954–56), 32; Bottéro *FWG* 2 (1965), 117; Falkenstein *Einleitung*, 6; Maeda *ASJ* 10 (1988), 24; and Monaco *ASJ* 12 (1990), 101.

[76] For the political nature (dynastic legitimization) of the Sumerian King List see Michalowski *JAOS* 103 (1983), esp. 242, and Wilcke "Genealogical and Geographical Thought."

[77] Sollberger *JCS* 21 (1967).

[78] See Maeda *ASJ* 10 (1988), 20–22.

[79] *AOAT* 25 (1976).

[80] They have been compiled by Sollberger *AfO* 17 (1954–56), 31–35, and again by Falkenstein *Einleitung*, 6–11, and are further discussed by Maeda *ASJ* 10 (1988), 25–31, and Steinkeller *JCS* 40 (1988), 51 note 14. Sigrist *Catalogue*, 317f. includes a list with some changes, yet lacks sources as well as comments. A reexamination of the presently available sources for the year names of the Lagaš II rulers, and along with it

Their usefulness for the internal chronology of Lagaš II, however, is diminished by the rare mention of the ruler to whose reign they pertain, and by the absence of a coherent date list for this period. Although recent studies of administrative texts from Lagaš have shed new light on the sequence of the Lagas II rulers, there is no unambiguous solution.[81] The material has not been fully published, nor has it been exhausted.[82] What can be said with certainty is that Urbaba, whose daughter Gudea married, preceded him, and that Urningirsu II and Pirigme, his son and grandson, ruled after him.

The only synchronism between a Lagaš II ruler and a dynast of another city-state is the mention of Namhani[83] of Lagaš in the Law Code of Urnamma,[84] who founded the Third Dynasty of Ur. In accordance with Kramer's understanding of the relevant passage in this text, Lagaš II had generally been assigned a place in the interval between the hegemonies of the kings of Akkad and those of the Third Dynasty of Ur. Urnamma's alleged victory over Namhani, however, which supposedly brought about the end of the Second Dynasty of Lagaš, is not supported by the text, which informs us of little more than the contemporaneity of the two rulers.[85] Furthermore, the conventional historiography attributing complete control over southern Mesopotamia to the dynasties of Akkad and Ur III from day one to their fall, broken only during the period in which the Guti[86] controlled the northern part of southern Mesopotamia and Lagaš II the southern part, may prove to be too simplistic. Competing city-states rather than hegemonies were the norm throughout most of the third and early second millennia B.C. in Mesopotamia. Hegemonic power never lasted more than a few generations,[87] and the control over other city-states fluctuated.[88]

The time between Šarkališarri, the last powerful king of Akkad, and the rise of the Third Dynasty of Ur under Urnamma, initially estimated to be about eighty years, has been reduced by recent studies to a mere forty years or even less.[89] It seems more than likely that the combined reigns of the Lagaš II rulers exceeded this span of time. On prosopographic grounds, Steinkeller demonstrated that Gudea's reign, in particular,

---

those of Urnamma, is a desideratum.

[81] The importance of prosopographic data for the elucidation of the Lagaš II chronology was noted already by Diakonoff in *MIO* 15 (1969), 525. The recent progress and present situation is well summarized by Lafont *BiOr* 50 (1993), 677f. Cf. Carroué's highly hypothetical interpretation of the data in *ASJ* 16 (1994).

[82] For the administrative tablets from Tello in general see Jones *AS* 20 (1976), 41–46; for the present state of publication see Lafont and Yildiz *Tablettes cunéiformes de Tello*, 1–8.

[83] Monaco's distinction of two rulers of this name based on the different spellings – Nammahni in the royal inscriptions, and both Namhani and Nammahni in administrative documents – in *ASJ* 12 (1990), is not convincing, see Maeda *ASJ* 15 (1993).

[84] As Geller *ZA* 81 (1991), 145f., has demonstrated, the attempt to attribute this text to Šulgi, which has become fashionable in recent years, is unfounded and most unlikely.

[85] Already Steinkeller *JCS* 40 (1988), 47 note 2. A possible alternative for the sign in line 78 read ug$_5$ by Kramer *Or* 52 (1983), 455 note 12, would be íl in which case Urnamma installed Namhani in his office; see Roth *Law Codes*, 15, and RIME 3/2.1.1.22. Unfortunately the present condition of the text, which is protected by a heavy coating, does not permit a decision.

[86] On the problem of the Guti see Hallo *RlA* 3 (1957–71), and Gragg *Keš Temple Hymn*, 162.

[87] Michalowski *Charisma and Control*, 56ff.

[88] See Maeda *ASJ* 10 (1988), 23.

[89] Hallo *RlA* 3 (1957–71), 713f.; Boese *WZKM* 74 (1982), 33–35; Dittmann *BaM* 25 (1994), 97–101. Glassner *NABU* (1994), no. 9, counted with thirty years only.

overlapped with that of Urnamma.[90] While the Lagaš II chronology cannot be solved at present, Gudea's overlap with Urnamma is indisputable.[91] This overlap is further supported by striking similarities in the cultural remains of these rulers. In general, one can observe a new orientation in the visual and verbal arts during this period.[92] The stelae of Gudea and Urnamma are comparable in iconography and style.[93] Foundation figurines representing a basket carrier with a human lower body are evidenced for Gudea and Urnamma only, whereas the figurine with a peg-shaped lower body, apparently developed late in Urnamma's reign, becomes standard thereafter.[94] The orthography and grammar of Gudea's inscriptions have close affinities with Ur III literary texts such as the Copper and Silver debate, which mentions Urnamma,[95] and are quite different from the short-lived orthographic reforms evidenced in certain Šulgi hymns.[96]

2. *Recorded Events*

According to Steinkeller,[97] eleven year names can assuredly be assigned to Gudea. However, considering the quantity of monuments and artifacts attributable to Gudea, and the many construction activities recorded in his inscriptions, it is likely that his reign lasted longer. The year names commemorate the (re)construction of certain temples or their equipment with dedicatory gifts, events which are also documented in his inscriptions.[98] Exceptions are the name of the first regnal year which records Gudea's installment in office, and the fragmentary name of year "8" which seems to refer to the installment of a nin-dingir priestess. From the cursory mention of a military campaign to Elam in the context of Eninnu's equipment with gifts (Statue B 6:64-69), we learn that Gudea's reign was not solely dedicated to the maintenance of the cult in Lagaš. It appears that the incentive for mentioning this event was not the campaign itself, but was rather due to the fact that the booty which resulted from it was presented as a gift to the god for whom Gudea had rebuilt his temple. The oblique way in which this military exploit is reported indicates that Gudea had no interest in commemorating events other

---

[90] *JCS* 40 (1988), 47–53. His suggestions in regard to the sequence of the Lagaš II rulers conflict with the results of the studies by Maeda in *ASJ* 10 (1988) and Monaco in *ASJ* 12 (1990). Especially Monaco's results, however, are arrived at on the basis of a number of assumptions which require further substantiation, see Maeda *ASJ* 15 (1993).

[91] See Lafont *BiOr* 50 (1993), 678. Vallat's scenario recently suggested in *NABU* (1997), no. 1, according to which Gudea's accession to the throne falls in Urnamma's second year, is based on several assumptions which cannot be substantiated.

[92] For example, the contents and strict composition of building inscriptions, see Falkenstein *Einleitung*, 173; or the iconography and style of cylinder seals, see Dittmann *BaM* 25 (1994), 101.

[93] Börker-Klähn *Bildstelen*, §§ 25f., 47, 172. But see also chapter IV.C.3.b.

[94] Rashid *Gründungsfiguren*, pl. 39. Steible's attribution of the peg-shaped figurine of Urningirsu to Urningirsu I (no. 4) is not beyond doubt, see Suter *JCS* 50 (1998), 71.

[95] Civil *Sumerian Debates and Dialogues*, forthcoming.

[96] Klein *Three Šulgi Hymns*, 64–70 and 131–134, which, however, is at variance with his opinion expressed in "From Gudea to Šulgi," 290, where he argued for a dependence of Šulgi's hymns on Gudea's literary works, and suggested that Šulgi employed scribes who had formerly worked for Gudea. The affinities shared between Gudea and Šulgi are better explained as arising from a common literary tradition.

[97] *JCS* 40 (1988), 51 note 14.

[98] This coincidence is not surprising, since both were issued by the same source. The commemoration of the same events in regnal year names, royal inscriptions and royal hymns is common practice in Mesopotamia, see Hallo *CRRA* 17 (1970), 118f., and Frayne *CRRA* 28 (1982).

than those concerned with his service for the gods. The same picture emanates from the visual arts: with one possible exception,[99] Gudea is never represented as victorious warrior, like some of his Early Dynastic predecessors at Lagaš or the kings of Akkad.

In an attempt to assess the scope of Gudea's construction program I offer here a survey of the buildings recorded in his inscriptions. It is ordered by sites, and lists, in addition to the divine beneficiary and designation of the building, the sources according to the catalogue in Appendix A,[100] references to the temple lists compiled by Falkenstein and George,[101] and comments concerning problematic identifications or locations. The type and number of records for each construction and its history are presented in Tables I.B.1 and 2.

Girsu:

1. Ningirsu: é-50:
CN.17–21; BS.12–16; DS.3–16; DT.1; FT.16–30; FG.3, 4?, 5, 7–9?, 10, 11–18?, 21?, 22–27, 28?, 29, 33?; FK.2; SV.6; Statues B, D, W; UI.2; UI.5.
Falkenstein 116–143; George no. 897.
Comments: 16+ bricks (BS.12) refer to this building with its epithet é-ánzu^mušen-bábbar only. Some inscriptions add parts built therein, namely a-ga-eren (BS.12) and gi-gunu$_4$ (DT.1 and Statues B, D); UI.5 records but the construction of Ningirsu's gi-gunu$_4$.

2. Ningirsu: é-PA:
CN.16; BS.10–11; DS.2, 20; FT.15; Statues D, G.
Falkenstein 131–133 no. 32; George nos. 393 (é-gidru), 1155 (é-ub-imin).

3. Ningirsu: abul-ká-sur-ra:
CN.22; GL.2; UI.4.
Falkenstein 137f. no. 43.

4. Baba: é-sila-sír-sír.[102]
CN.1–2; BS.1–2; FT.1–4; DP.2; Statues E, H.
Falkenstein 147f. no. 10 (é-tar-sír-sír); George nos. 1085 (é-tar-sír-sír), 1198 (é-uru-kù-ga).
Comments: Esilasirsir is usually referred to as Baba's house of Urukug (é-uru-kù-ga), only Statues E and H provide its proper name. I have included here Baba's wall of Urukug (bàd-uru-kù-ga-ka: CN.1, FT.1), since it must refer to this building.

5. Igalim: é-me-huš-gal-an-ki:
CN.6; FT.7–11; FG.1–2.
Falkenstein 153 no. 20; George no. 755.

---

[99] SO.5 in Appendix A; see chapter II.C.3.c.
[100] Only inscriptions in which the divine name and the building designation are either entirely preserved or believably restored are included.
[101] Falkensten *Einleitung*, 116–170; George *House Most High*.
[102] For the reading of this temple name see Selz *Götterwelt*, 26 note 73.

6. Šulšaga: *é-ki-tuš-akkil-lí*:
CN.29; FT.37–39; FG.6; FK.1.
Falkenstein 152 no. 14; George no. 618.

7. Gatumdug: *é-uru-kù-ga*:
CN.5; BS.3–4; FT.5; GL.1; Statue F.
Falkenstein 146 no. 6; George no. 1314.
Comments: The é-gír-su^ki^ on the fragmentary foundation tablet (FT.5) rests on Steible's reconstruction (Gudea 14); if correct, this house was probably identical with the one in Urukug. The Lagaš I attestations listed by George pertain to Gatumdug's temple in Lagaš.[103]

8. Inanna: *é-an-na-gír-su^ki^*:
CN.7–9; BS.5, 22; FT.12; FB.1–2; Statue C.
Falkenstein 149 no. 1; George no. 77.
Comments: In some inscriptions this building is designated as Inanna's é-gír-su^ki^ (CN.9, BS.5) or her é only (BS.22).

9. Dumuziabzu: *é-gír-su^ki^*:
CN.3.
Falkenstein 150 no. 4; George no. 1298.

10. Geštinanna: *é-gír-su^ki^*:
Statues M, N, O.
Falkenstein 150f. no. 7; George nos. 975 (é-sag-ug$_5$), 1315.

11. Meslamtaea: *é-gír-su^ki^*:
CN.10; BS.6.
Falkenstein 153 no. 19; George no. 1359.

12. Ninazu: *é-gír-su^ki^*:
CN.30.
George no. 1370.

13. Nindara:[104] *é-gír-su^ki^*:
CN.14; BS.9; FT.41.
Falkenstein 154 no. 22; George no. 1371.

14. Ningišzida: *é-gír-su^ki^*:
CN.23–24; BS.18–20; DS.19; FT.32–35; DP.3; Statue I.
Falkenstein 154f. no. 25; George no. 1379.
Comments: The door plaque (DP.3) seems to refer to this building as Ningišzida's é only.

---

[103] See Selz *Götterwelt*, 134–136.
[104] For the reading nin-dar-a see Civil "Šulgi-ki-ur$_5$-sag$_9$-kalam-ma," 50.

15. Ninhursag: *é-gír-su*^{ki}:
CN.25–26; Statue A.
Falkenstein 155 no. 26; George nos. 716 (é-mah), 1381.
Comments: Two clay nail (CN.25), both from Tello, refer to this building as Nin-hursag's é only, while Statue A designates it as her house of the city of Girsu (1:8: é-uru-gír-su^{ki}-ka-ni), and later refers to it as her great house (2:5: é-mah), which I understand as a descriptive term rather than a temple name (contra George no. 716 and Steible *Neusumerische Bau- und Weihinschriften* 2, 71).

16. Ninšubur: *é*:
CN.28; FT.36.
Falkenstein 155 no. 28; George no. 757 (é-me-kìlib-ba-sag-íl).
Comments: Falkenstein located this temple in Girsu where the six clay nails (CN.28) were found. George's suggestion that Gudea's unnamed temple be identical with Rimsin's é-me-kìlib-ba-sag-íl, the location of which remains uncertain, is not convincing.

Lagaš:

17. Ningirsu: *é-ba-gára*:
BS.17; DS.17–18; FT.31.
Falkenstein 157f. no. 3; George no. 96.

Ningin:[105]

18. Nanše: *é-sirara*₆:
CN.11–12; BS.7–8; DS.1; FT.13; FB.3.
Falkenstein 163f. no. 5; George no. 992.
Comments: One unprovenienced clay nail (CN.12) refers to Nanše's é only.

19. Hendursag: *é*:
FT.6.
Falkenstein 162 no. 1; George no. 1323.
Comments: Since Hendursag belongs to Nanše's circle, Falkenstein located this building in Ningin. This location is also suggested by the provenance of the record, which was purchased in Zurghul. George's suggestion that Gudea's Hendursag house was the same as that built by Enannatum I in Urukug (En. I 29 4:3) is doubtful. During the Lagaš I period Hendursag was worshipped in Urukug as well as in Ningin and Guabba.[106]

---

[105] The reading of this GN follows Krecher "Phonem /g/," 53.
[106] See Selz *Götterwelt*, 144 § 10.

20. Nindub: é:
CN.15.
Falkenstein 154 no. 23; George no. 1372.
Comments: Falkenstein mistakenly read é-gír-su^ki^, and located this building in Girsu. George wondered whether its location was in Uruk, where three clay nails were found, or in Zurghul, where a fourth clay nail was found. A closer examination of the findspots of the records from Uruk reveals them as secondary deposits.[107] Since Nindub belongs to Nanše's circle,[108] his temple was probably located in Ningin.

Guidigna:

21. Enki: é-gú-^id^idigna:
CN.4.
George no. 1306.

Zulum:

22. Nanše: é-an-gur₂₂-zú-lum^ki^:
CN.13.
George no. 250 (é-engur-ra).[109]

Kiessa:

23. Nindara: é-làl-túm-ki-ès-sá^ki^:
FT.14.
Falkenstein 168 no. 20; George no. 699.

GuabbaTUR:

24. NinmarKI:[110] é-gú-ab-ba-TÙR^ki^:
CN.27.
George no. 273 (èš-gú-tùr).
Comments: The text records the construction of the wall (bàd) of GuabbaTUR and the temple within it. GuabbaTUR obviously refers to the town quarter of Guabba, perhaps its temple district, where NinmarKI's temple was located.[111]

The number of divine houses Gudea claims to have built is remarkable. The term é used in temple names designates an inhabitable architectural structure regardless of its

---

[107] Braun-Holzinger *ASJ* 19 (1997), 11f. nos. 6–8.
[108] Falkenstein 89 no. 41.
[109] Falkenstein, to whom this text was not available, had mistaken the name of this building for the full name of Esirara (163f. no. 5), based on Lagaš I attestations which omit the place determinative.
[110] For the controversy concerning the reading of this divine name see Attinger *NABU* (1995), no. 33.
[111] Steible *Neusumerische Bau- und Weihinschriften 1*, 336 note 1. In Gudea's time Guabba designated the capital of the province Guabbagula within the state of Lagaš, while in Early Dynastic times it designated this province, and its capital was simply named after NinmarKI's temple; see Selz *Götterwelt*, 257 note 1228.

function or size, and by extension can refer also to the grounds belonging to it.[112] Thus it can designate an entire estate as well as a single room or room compartment (shrine in the case of a temple) of it. For an assessment of Gudea's construction program one would like to know the size of the various buildings, and, in view of the tradition of cult places, whether Gudea built them anew or merely restored existing ones. Since no substantial architecture of Gudea has survived,[113] only textual information can elucidate these questions. Table I.B.1 shows that Gudea's construction program was concentrated on the capital city, Girsu, and in particular on Eninnu. Seventy-three percent of the records pertain to this temple complex, twenty-four to houses of thirteen different deities in the same town, and less than five percent to temples in Lagaš, Ningin, and various smaller places within the city-state.

Eninnu was the abode of the divine patron of Girsu and the state of Lagaš. According to the Cylinder Inscriptions, it incorporated various quarters with different functions.[114] Several buildings in Girsu are likely parts of this temple complex. The é-PA, which is mentioned in close conjunction with Eninnu (Statue D 2:6–12; Statue E 1:14–17), was probably a separate building within it. The Kasurra, where several objects were set up for Ningirsu in connection with the construction of Eninnu, was apparently one of its gates, or perhaps a gate house.[115] The house of Ningirsu's consort Baba must have been part of the complex as well, since its name (Silasirsir) occurs in reference to Eninnu's place of assignments (CA 26:9). Finally, one could imagine as shrines within Eninnu the houses of Igalim and Šulšaga, the children of Ningirsu and Baba, who are mentioned among Eninnu's staff.

In addition, Falkenstein tentatively placed some of the "houses of Girsu" in Eninnu, because their patrons' main cult places were not original in Girsu.[116] This applies also to Inanna's house, while Ninšubur plays only a minor role in Lagaš. Since there is no obvious connection between Ningirsu and the patrons of these buildings, they could be conceived of equally well as small shrines within the sacred district called Urukug,[117] which included both the Eninnu complex and Gatumdug's temple. The houses of Gudea's personal god Ningišzida and his consort Geštinanna are the only divine houses known to have been located elsewhere in Girsu.[118]

Ebagara and Esirara were the temples of the patron deities of Lagaš and Ningin, respectively, the two other larger towns within the state. Hendursag and Nindub, who both belonged to Nanše's circle, may have been worshipped in her Esirara, named after the

---

[112] Compare Edzard "Names of Sumerian Temples," 159.

[113] See chapter II.A.2.a, p. 34.

[114] See chapter III.C.1.e.

[115] At Kasurra Gudea set up a stela (CA 23:13–18), a gate lion (GL.2), and a trophy of Ningirsu (CA 26:6–8), and at its quay he moored wood shipments from the cedar mountains (CA 15:19–35), and anchored the boat which he presented to Ningirsu (Statue D 3:3–12).

[116] Falkenstein *Einleitung*, 148f.

[117] In contrast to previous reconstructions, Urukug was always located in Girsu; see Selz *Götterwelt*, 5f. §§ 14–18.

[118] Falkenstein *Einleitung*, 143f. See also chapter II.A.2.a.

temple district of Ningin.[119] The remaining four buildings were located in smaller towns or hamlets: Guidigna evidently on the shore of the Tigris,[120] Zulum in the area bordering the state of Ur,[121] Kiessa near the city of Lagaš,[122] and Guabba, the sea port of the state, near Ningin.[123]

Table I.B.1: Number and Type of Records for Gudea's Constructions[124]

	CN	BS	DS	FT	FF	GL	DP	SV	St	UI	Total
Girsu:											
1. Ningirsu: é-50	1456	122	15	15	11			1	3	2	1625
2. Ningirsu: é-PA	63	3	2	1					1		70
3. Ningirsu: abul-ká-sur-ra	14				1					1	16
4. Baba: é-sila-sír-sír	29	8		4					2		43
5. Igalim: é-me-huš-gal-an-ki	36			5	2						43
6. Šulšaga: é-ki-tuš-akkil-lí	24			3	2						29
7. Gatumdug: é-uru-kù-ga	41	6		1	1				1		50
8. Inanna: é-an-na	18	3		1	2				1		25
9. Dumuziabzu: é-gír-su^{ki}	35										35
10. Geštinanna: é-gír-su^{ki}									3		3
11. Meslamtaea: é-gír-su^{ki}	31	1									32
12. Ninazu: é-gír-su^{ki}	1										1
13. Nindara: é-gír-su^{ki}	151	7		1							159
14. Ningišzida: é-gír-su^{ki}	113	7	1	4			1		2		128
15. Ninhursag: é-gír-su^{ki}	9								1		10
16. Ninšubur: é	6			1							7
Lagaš:											
17. Ningirsu: é-ba-gára		33	2	1							36
Ningin:											
18. Nanše: é-sirara$_6$	38	13	1	1	1						54
19. Hendursag: é				1							1
20. Nindub: é	5										5
Other Sites:											
21. Enki: é-gú-^{id}idigna	1										1
22. Nanše: é-an-gur$_{22}$-zú-lum^{ki}	3										3
23. Nindara: é-làl-túm-ki-ès-sá^{ki}				1							1
24. NinmarKI: é-gú-ab-ba-TÙR^{ki}	1										1

[119] Black *Sumer* 46 (1989–90) 71–74.
[120] RGTC II 268 s.v.
[121] RGTC I 147 s.v. Sulum.
[122] RGTC I 88 s.v.
[123] RGTC I 61 and II 63–65 s.v.
[124] Object categories are abbreviated as in Appendix A: CN = clay nail; BS = brick; DS = door socket or threshold; FT = foundation tablet; FF = foundation figurine; GL = gate lion; DP = door plaque; SV = stone vessel; St = statue; UI = unidentified object.

Table I.B.2: Gudea's Constructions in Historical Perspective[125]

	built by Lagaš I rulers or Situation in Lagaš I	*desecrated by Lugal-zagesi*	*(re)built by Urbaba*
Girsu:			
1. Ningirsu: é-50	Ent. 80; Ukg. 1:3:8′; etc.		1:3:6; etc.
2. Ningirsu: é-PA	located in Lagaš		
3. Ningirsu: abul-ká-sur-ra			
4. Baba: é-sila-sír-sír	Urn. 18 (é-sila); Ukg. 1:1:10; etc. (é-DN)		1:4:6; etc.
5. Igalim: é-me-huš-gal-an-ki	Ukg. 1:2:2; etc.		
6. Šulšaga: é-ki-tuš-akkil-lí	Ukg. 1:2:5; etc.		
7. Gatumdug: é-uru-kù-ga	DN's temple in Lagaš		
8. Inanna: é-an-na	located in Lagaš		
9. Dumuziabzu: é-gír-su^{ki}	DN's temple in Kinunir		1:6:11
10. Geštinanna: é-gír-su^{ki}	DN's temple in Sagub		1:6:7
11. Meslamtaea: é-gír-su^{ki}	MesanDU worshipped in Girsu, Ningin		
12. Ninazu: é-gír-su^{ki}	DN worshipped in Enegi		
13. Nindara: é-gír-su^{ki}	DN's main temple in Kiessa; see no. 23		
14. Ningišzida: é-gír-su^{ki}			
15. Ninhursag: é-gír-su^{ki}	DN's temple in tir-kùg		1:4:1
16. Ninšubur: é	DN worshipped in Girsu, Lagaš, Ningin		
Lagaš:			
17. Ningirsu: é-ba-gára	Urn. 25:5:2; etc.	Ukg. 16:3:3	
Ningin:			
18. Nanše: é-sirara_6	Ukg. 1:3:10′		
19. Hendursag: é	DN worshipped in Ningin, Girsu, Guabba		
20. Nindub: é	DN worshipped in Ningin		
Other Sites:			
21. Enki: é-gú-^{id}idigna	DN worshipped in various other places		
22. Nanše: é-an-gur_{22}-zú-lum^{ki}	Ent. 1:2:7; etc.	Ukg. 16:6:6	
23. Nindara: é-làl-túm-ki-ès-sá^{ki}	En. I 20:2:2 (é+DN)	Ukg. 16:5:4	1:5:3 (é+DN)
24. NinmarKI: é-gú-ab-ba-TÙR^{ki}	Urn. 26:3:2; etc. (é-DN)		1:5:11 (èš-gú-tùr)

---

[125] If the construction or desecration of the building is documented in a royal inscription, reference is given to the text. The comments concerning the situation in Lagaš I rely on Selz *Götterwelt*.

In his inscriptions Gudea frequently states that "he restored it (the mentioned building) to its former state."[126] Indeed, the major temples already occur in the records of his Early Dynastic predecessors, as shown in Table I.B.2. UruKAgina,[127] the last Early Dynastic ruler of Lagaš, informs us that Lugalzagesi, his rival from Umma, destroyed or desecrated a number of temples in the state of Lagaš (Ukg. 16), though Girsu was seemingly spared.[128] Urbaba rebuilt at least one of the desecrated temples outside Girsu, and, at the same time, initiated the cult of a large pantheon in the capital city.[129] Keeping in mind that this historical perspective is based on the surviving royal inscriptions only, the picture that emerges suggests that Gudea carried out minor repairs on already existing temples, especially those rebuilt by his immediate predecessor, and, following his example, continued to build a number of small shrines for deities not previously worshipped in Girsu. The large quantity of records for Eninnu together with the Cylinder Inscriptions, which give the impression that Gudea built this temple from scratch, may indicate that he added a substantial building to this complex – perhaps the é-PA which is conspicuously absent in the Cylinder Inscriptions.

The remaining inscribed objects do not add much new information. Most of them are dedicated to deities whose temples are evidenced in the building records, as the following list shows:[130]

Baba:	Statue BB
Enlil:	SV.2
Gatumdug:	UI.1
Hendursag:	SO.1
Igalim:	MH.1–2
Inanna:	SV.3
Meslamtaea:	Statue X
Ninizimua:	SV.12
Nindara:	SV.4; MH.3, 5–6
Ninegal:	SV.5
Ningirsu:	DP.1; SV.7–8; MH.7–8; Statues K, Y; UI.3
Ningišzida:	SO.4; SV.9–10; Statue Q

Notable exceptions are the stone vessels for Enlil, Ninizimua, and Ninegal. The one dedicated to Enlil was made for his main sanctuary in Nippur, where it was found. Ninizimua can be equated with Ninazimua, Ningišzida's consort. Gudea syncretized her with the old Lagašite goddess Geštinanna,[131] who had her shrine in Girsu. Ninegal occurs only once more in Lagaš, namely as beneficiary of a female statue dedicated for

---

[126] See chapter II.B.2.c § 3.h.

[127] The reading of this name remains a matter of dispute; see Edzard *AulaOr* 9 (1991), and Lambert *AulaOr* 10 (1992).

[128] Selz *ASJ* 12 (1990), 118.

[129] See Falkenstein *Einleitung*, 115f.

[130] The sources are cited according to the catalogue in Appendix A.

[131] In Statue M/N/O 1:1–2 nin-a-izi-mú-a is Geštinanna's epithet; see Steible *Neusumerische Bau- und Weihinschriften* 1, 350 note 1. One wonders whether ᵈnin-izi-mú-a is the second rather than the first line of the now fragmentary inscription on the vessel under discussion, and stood in apposition to Geštinanna, like in the statue inscriptions. Unfortunately the side with the beginning of female inscription has never been reproduced.

Gudea's life in her temple (Gudea 41). She also had a temple built by Urnamma in Ur.[132] Since Ninegal occurs as an epithet of various goddesses, and of Inanna in particular, Gudea's vessel, as well as the female statue, may have been destined for Inanna's temple in Girsu.[133]

Despite the large number of records and buildings, Gudea's construction activity was limited in scope. All buildings were located within the city-state borders,[134] and the majority in the capital itself. With the exception of a few large complexes, notably Eninnu, and perhaps also Esirara and Ebagara, they seem to have been limited in scale. The large complexes, as well as some of the smaller buildings, were previously established, and Gudea probably only restored, or perhaps enlarged them. Yet, the large number of deities that received their own shrines in Girsu is remarkable. This must have led to an expansion of the sacred district. The only addition to the Lagašite pantheon introduced by Gudea is that of his personal deity Ningišzida. The stone vessel for Enlil, the one object dedicated outside the state borders, pays respect to the chief god of the Sumerian pantheon, the ultimate source of royal power,[135] and attests to Gudea's adherence to Sumerian tradition.

3. Sphere of Influence

In the interval between the Akkad and Ur III periods, Lagaš II is generally assumed to have played a major, if not hegemonic, role in southern Sumer, with the Guti controlling the northern cities of the southern alluvium. Although Lagaš appears to have been prosperous under the rules of Urbaba and Gudea, the claim for hegemony is difficult to substantiate with the available sources. The role of Lagaš II may have been overestimated because so little is known of contemporary history.

The Lagaš II rulers clearly wanted to be seen and understood as traditional Sumerian city-state rulers. In contrast to most kings of Akkad and the Third Dynasty of Ur, they do not claim control over territory other than their own titulature city-state. They use the title ensí lagaš^ki, which was already traditional in the Early Dynastic period.[136] Similarly, the deities mentioned in their epithets almost exclusively belong to the Lagašite pantheon. The administrative records from Lagaš pertaining to this period indicate that most Lagaš II rulers were independent, except for short intervals which coincide with powerful kings of Akkad or Ur. There are no indications in administrative records from other city-states that Lagaš claimed control over them. Like Gudea's inscriptions and year names, those

---

[132] Urnammu 18–19; see George *House Most High*, no. 1373. The temple attested in Ur III administrative documents mentioned by Falkenstein *Einleitung*, 89f. no. 42, was probably that of Urnamma in Ur.

[133] Another less likely possibility would be that Gudea's scribes misspelled Ninegal for Ninagal for whom Urbaba built a temple in Urukug (Urbaba 1 5:4–7, 8 3:8–11); see George *House Most High*, no. 1368.

[134] Vallat *NABU* (1997), no. 1, reported a new source according to which Gudea built a temple in Adamdun in the Susiana, yet did not reveal what kind of text it is, nor what precisely it says.

[135] For the role of Nippur and Enlil regarding royal power in the Sumerian world, see Tinney *Nippur Lament*, 55–62.

[136] Apparently the title ensí GN was a generic royal title in Lagaš before the Ur III period, when it came to designate city-state governors installed by kings with hegemonic claims. Therefore I translate it simply as "ruler," rather than "governor" which implies subjection to a suzerain. See now also Jacobsen "Ensí."

of other Lagaš II rulers are exclusively concerned with temple constructions and/or equipment within their state borders.

That Lagaš was a center of royal economic importance in the Akkad period may explain its prosperity in the period immediately following.[137] Both Urbaba and Gudea had ambitious construction programs which required the import of precious material from foreign lands. Urbaba's daughter held the prestigious office of the en-priestess of Nanna in Ur.[138] Gudea campaigned against Elam, and was posthumously venerated. This evidence, however, does not permit the conclusion that Urbaba or Gudea controlled southern Mesopotamia. If Gudea had had political control beyond his city-state, one would expect him to have made use of it. However, the labor force levied for the construction of Eninnu, for example, is comprised of people from Lagašite districts,[139] rather than recruits from other city-states.

The inscriptions on Gudea's statues made of diorite and on two limestone objects (SV.7, MH.7) say that the stone for the fabrication of these objects was imported from abroad. In addition, Statue B (5:28–6:63) and Cylinder A (14:28–16:24) contain long lists of woods, stones, and metals which Gudea claims to have imported from various distant places for the construction of Eninnu. These lists, together with Urnamma's claim to have regained control over the sea trade (Urnammu 26, 47, and year 4), led Falkenstein to conclude that prior to Urnamma, Ur and the sea trade were in Lagaš's hands.[140] Gudea's access to foreign material, however, need not imply a monopoly over trade routes, and his boasts, at least in part, can be explained as literary fancy.[141] On the basis of the overlap of Gudea with Urnamma, and the fact that Urnamma, too, is known to have campaigned against Elam early in his reign, Steinkeller's scenario that this campaign was a co-venture of the two rulers in their common quest to reopen trade routes is more likely.[142] Lafont has convincingly argued for friendly relations between Lagaš and Ur during the formative stage of the Ur III hegemony.[143]

Falkenstein saw further evidence for his thesis that Gudea controlled southern Mesopotamia in the building records either found in or said to come from Sumerian cities outside of Lagaš; in the mention to Ningirsu's trip to Eridu in Cylinder B; and in Gudea's posthumous fame.[144] Upon a closer examination, however, these arguments cannot be supported. The building records presently available from outside Lagaš territory exclusively commemorate the construction of buildings in this city-state.[145] Falkenstein's assumption that Gudea used them for constructions in other Sumerian cities, since the latter were too minor for the drafting of individual texts, would undermine any hegemonic claim, and is unlikely in view of the ardent boasts of Mesopotamian rulers regarding

---

[137]   Foster *Iraq* 47 (1985), 29.
[138]   Urbaba 11f; see also Sollberger *AfO* 17 (1954–56), 23–29.
[139]   See chapter III.B.4.2.
[140]   *Einleitung*, 44.
[141]   Compare Hurowitz *Temple Building*, 171–223, and in particular 205–223.
[142]   *JCS* 40 (1988), 52f.
[143]   *BiOr* 50 (1993), 678 and 681.
[144]   *Einleitung*, 42–45, and *RlA* 3 (1957–71), 677f. s.v. Gudea.
[145]   See chapter II.A.2.b.

their deeds. Furthermore, the regularly excavated records from these cities were usually found in secondary first millennium B.C. contexts, and had apparently been displaced in antiquity.[146] Ningirsu's trip to Eridu should be viewed in the context of divine journeys in myth and cult, rather than as reflecting political history.[147] Gudea's posthumous fame is limited to Lagaš, and though it speaks to this ruler's popularity, need not be based on hegemonic power.[148]

Gudea wanted to be remembered as a traditional city-state ruler, under whose relatively long and stable reign Lagaš enjoyed independence and apparent prosperity. He was seemingly not ambitious for territorial expansion, but rather for economic wealth gained through trade and diplomatic relations, and only exceptionally by means of military campaigns. One wonders whether this was a conscious reaction to the very different attitude of the kings of Akkad, which may have been unpopular at this time.

---

[146] See chapter II.A.2.b with note 31.
[147] See chapter III.B.7.3 with note 129.
[148] This fame has two facets. First, Ur III administrative documents reveal that Gudea was posthumously deified, and received regular offerings in Lagaš during this period, see Falkenstein *Einleitung*, 45, and Sallaberger *Kultischer Kalender*, 94 with table 28. Second, Gudea is mentioned or alluded to in literary compositions which are most likely the product of Lagaš, see chapter III.F.1 with notes 317–319.

II. MINOR SOURCES

A. The Artifacts and their Provenance

1. The Corpus

Aside form the cylinders and some stela fragments, two thousand four hundred and forty-five artifacts bear inscriptions which identify Gudea, the ruler of Lagaš, as their commissioner. A catalogue of this material is provided in Appendix A. The corpus as defined in the Appendix includes the following numbers and categories of artifacts:

2075	Clay Nails
203	Brick Stones
20	Door Sockets
1	Stair Step
41	Foundation Tablets
33	Foundation Figurines representing a Kneeling God
5	Foundation Figurines representing a Basket Carrier
3	Foundation Figurines representing a Bull
2	Gate Lions
3	Door Plaques
5	Pedestals or Stands
13	Stone Vessels
12	Mace Heads
21	Statues representing Gudea
1	Cylinder Seal
7	Unidentified Objects

While the cylinder seal was used within the administration, all other objects were destined for the temples Gudea built or restored. They served structural, decorative, magical, or ritual purposes: bricks, door sockets, and stair steps were elements of the structure; clay nails decorated the walls;[1] door plaques served as shutter devices;[2] gate lions magically protected the building; foundation deposits magically anchored the building;[3] stone vessels were used as instruments in the cult; mace heads were accouterment of warrior deities and recipients of offerings; pedestals and stands supported other objects; and statues perpetually represented their donor in attendance and received offerings.

---

[1] Donbaz and Grayson *Clay Cones from Ashur*, 1–3. English authors have dubbed these objects knobs, bosses, pegs, or cones. Since the same terms are used also for other categories of object, I prefer the term clay nail, basically a translation of the German *Tonnagel*.

[2] Hansen *JNES* 22 (1963), 147–153; Zettler *JCS* 39 (1987), 210ff. and figs. 3–4; Braun-Holzinger *Weihgaben*, 306.

[3] Ellis *Foundation Deposits*, 3.

A. The Artifacts and their Provenance

In terms of quantity, the clay nails by far outnumber all other artifacts. They are made of easily available and cheap material, and large numbers were needed to create decorative patterns. More surprising at first sight is the comparatively small number of clay bricks. The fact that only those bricks that made it into a museum or private collection were recorded, and that bricks are bulky and aesthetically unappealing objects, may explain this circumstance. The next largest group comprises the copper figurines and stone tablets which were buried together in foundation boxes at crucial points under the building. The remaining identifiable objects are carved in stone, and encompass between one and twenty-one exemplars per category. The large number of statues of the ruler is unparalleled in Mesopotamian history.

The door plaques, gate lions, foundation figurines, stone vessels, stands, pedestals, and statues as well as the seal bear imagery that either relates to their function or conveys a message concerning the ruler who commissioned them. While the text inscribed on the seal simply identifies its owner, all other inscriptions are commemorative in nature. The texts written on elements used in the structure of the temple usually record its construction, and those on movable objects their dedication by the ruler,[4] though statue inscriptions may add the construction of the temple for which they were destined. Together with the imagery, these texts are intended to perpetuate the memory of Gudea whose prosperous reign allowed him to make use of his royal privileges, in this case to build temples and equip them, and thus fulfill his duties *vis-à-vis* the gods, for which he received in return their approval in his office as the city-state ruler. Before discussing the inscriptions and imagery in more detail, I will review the provenance of the artifacts.

2. Provenance

Provenance is understood as the place where an artifact was found by modern explorers. It does not always coincide with the place for which an artifact was destined according to its inscription or with its original location in antiquity. Archaeological evidence shows that commemorative artifacts could be carried off as booty by enemies, reinstalled by later generations in reverence of their ancient predecessors, or simply reused in later buildings, perhaps because the memory of their commissioner had vanished.[5]

Because most of the Gudea material was discovered over a hundred years ago when Near Eastern archaeology was still in its beginnings, its provenance poses a problem. Findspots were recorded only for works of art that seemed of importance to the early explorers, and find contexts often remain dubious in the absence of adequate excavation techniques and recording methods. In addition, uncountable artifacts were looted by illicit diggers and sold off the art market. These objects are sometimes published as coming from the site the dealer had indicated to his client, or simply attributed to

---

[4] However, DS.17 and 18 bear dedicatory inscriptions, and SV.6 a building inscription. These irregularities can be explained with the suggestion made by Braun-Holzinger *Weihgaben*, 16f., that the type of text depended on the circumstance of the dedication, i.e. whether the object was made in connection with the (re)construction of the temple, or deposited there at a later time.

[5] Wilcke "Geschichtsbewusstsein," 39.

Tello where large quantities of Gudea material had been discovered.[6] As a result, the provenance of many artifacts is impossible to verify today, especially in the case of the thousands of clay nails.

Table II.A.1: Number and Type of Artifacts according to their Provenance[7]

	CN	BS	DS	DT	FT	FF	GL	DP	SO	SV	MH	St	CS	UI	Total
Tello	1591	125	15	1	18	28	1	3	2	11	10	16	1	4	1824
al-Hiba	5	35	2												42
Zurghul	24	4			1	1									30
Uruk	7				1		1								9
Ur	7				1										8
Nippur										1					1
Larsa	1	1													2
Tell Jidr		2													2
Medain	1														1
Umm Chatil	1														1
Tell Hammam												1			1
Unknown	438	36	3		20	12		3	1	2	4			3	524

a. Tello

As Table II.A.1 shows, the vast majority of Gudea artifacts were found at or are said to come from Tello, ancient Girsu. Girsu was a large, flourishing town from the Early Dynastic into the Ur III period. The meager textual and archaeological evidence after year 6 of the Ur III dynast Ibbi-Suen implies that it thereafter became an insignificant provincial town.[8] In the third century B.C. the otherwise unknown Aramaic ruler, Adad-naddin-ahhe, built a palace there. Traces of fire and the demolition of monuments antedating the end of the Ur III period, such as the decapitation of most Gudea statues and the mutilation of his stelae, suggest that the site had been sacked. Those most likely responsible for the destruction are the Elamites in their war against Ibbi-Suen.

Tello was excavated in two phases, from 1878 to 1909, and from 1929 to 1933.[9] The early excavations were conducted by Ernest de Sarzec and then Gaston Cros, both members of the French diplomatic corps with an amateur knowledge of archaeology. Their finds were divided between the French government and the Ottoman authorities, and are housed today in the Louvre or the Archaeological Museum in Istanbul. The supervisors during the second phase were first Henri de Genouillac, a philologist acquainted with the tablets from the early excavations, and in the last two seasons André Parrot, an archaeologist. Their finds were divided between the excavators and the Iraqi Department of Antiquities, and are housed today in the Louvre or the Iraq Museum. During absences

---

6 Sollberger *Syria* 52 (1975), 76 note 10.
7 Object categories are abbreviated as in Appendix A: CN = clay nail; BS = brick stone; DS = door socket; DT = stair step; FT = foundation tablet; FF = foundation figurine; GL = gate lion; DP = door plaque; SO = pedestal or stand; MH = mace head; St = statue; CS = cylinder seal; UI = unidentified object.
8 Falkenstein and Opificius *RlA* 3 (1957–71), 385–401 s.v. Girsu, especially 390.
9 For a history of the excavations, see Parrot *Tello*, 14–33.

of the official excavators the site was repeatedly looted by locals who had realized the value Western museums and collectors attributed to their booty.[10] There is hardly any institution collecting antiquities which does not possess at least a clay nail of Gudea. The French excavators were confronted with superimposed remains from different periods of the untill then unknown Sumerian culture. They were inexperienced in excavating sun-dried brick architecture and lacked adequate recording techniques. Moreover, their work was repeatedly interrupted by upheavals in the region forcing them to evacuate the site, as well as illicit digs during their absences. As a result, they recovered only scanty architectural remains. The location on the site of the many buildings commemorated in Gudea's inscriptions is impeded by the fact that the findspots of inscribed architectural elements found in large numbers, such as bricks, clay nails, and foundation deposits, were not recorded individually.[11]

The following structures can be attributed to Gudea (Fig. 1): a twelve meter long niched wall with an entrance, a double basin, a platform, a well, and an exedra on Tell A (tell du palais);[12] a staircase with foundation deposits, and a construction associated with three brick pedestals between Tell A and B;[13] a pillar made of bricks (BS.12) recording the construction of Eninnu's place of judgment, four foundation deposits,[14] and parts of an enclosing wall on Tell I (tell des piliers).[15] The remains on Tell A have generally been interpreted as part of Gudea's Eninnu, based not only on the niched wall, but also on the accumulation of Gudea objects there, especially bricks pertaining to Eninnu. Falkenstein suggested that the remains between Tell A and B and the wall on Tell I were its North and South Eastern confines, resulting in a NW-SE extension of 460 meters, and a SW-NE extension of 300–320 meters.[16]

According to Parrot,[17] Gudea's clay nails and bricks were found all over the site (Fig. 2). Many from Tell A were reused in the palace of Adad-naddin-ahhe.[18] Several door sockets pertaining to Eninnu (DS.3–5, 10–11) were found on Tell A, one on Tell J (DS.8), and another on Tell G (DS.9).[19] Whether they were found *in situ* remains uncertain. Foundation boxes were found in the triangle between Tell A, B, and K, which is in more or less the same area as the door sockets.[20] Most boxes were empty. Others belonging to a single group contained figurines and tablets commemorating different buildings, which suggests that they were reburied in later times.[21]

---

[10] Parrot mentioned three pillages: one before 1877 that produced a torso, a head of a statue, and a tablet, all of Gudea (*Tello*, 16); another in 1902 that produced 1600 tablets (ibidem, 22f.); and a third one in 1924 which produced a number of statues of Gudea and one of his son Urningirsu (ibidem, 26).

[11] Opificius *RlA* 3 (1957–71), 391–393 s.v. Girsu.

[12] Parrot *Tello*, 151–155 fig. 33.

[13] NFT 65–67, 279–383; see also chapter IV.A.2.

[14] NFT 156–158 fig. 34.

[15] NFT 148; see also chapter III.A.1.

[16] Falkenstein *Einleitung*, 121, and *RlA* 3 (1957–71), 387f. s.v. Girsu; see also Börker-Klähn *Bildstelen*, §§ 119–130.

[17] *Tello*, 206.

[18] For the excavations on Tell A and their interpretation see Parrot *Tello*, 151–155.

[19] Parrot *Tello*, 201.

[20] Van Buren *Foundation Figurines*, 13–15, and 18f.; Parrot *Tello*, 202–204; and Rashid *Gründungsfiguren*, 18f.

[21] Ellis *Foundation Deposits*, 61f.

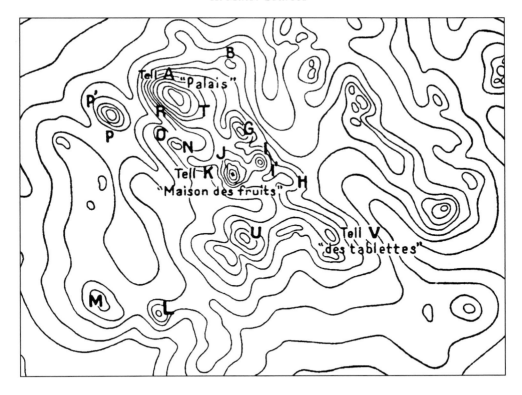

Fig. 2: Map of Tello, the "Tells."

The two door plaque fragments dedicated to Ningirsu and Baba or Gatumdug, respectively (DP.1–2); fragments of two sculpted limestone basins (SV.6–7), both dedicated to Ningirsu; and a mace head (MH.8), also dedicated to Ningirsu, were discovered on Tell A. These sculptures seem to have been reused as fill in the late palace.[22] Another mace head with lion heads (MH.12) came from nearby between Tell A and B. The fragments of a pedestal depicting prisoners (SO.5) were found between Tell I and J, seemingly out of context. The third plaque fragment (DP.3) and the famous libation vessel (SV.9), both dedicated to Ningišzida, were found on Tell V.

The discovery of the famous statues of Gudea remains problematic. De Sarzec claimed to have excavated the first lot consisting of Statues A-H in the palace on Tell A.[23] According to the dealer Géjou, who was involved in trading finds from illicit digs at Tello, these statues were found before de Sarzec's arrival on the site.[24] If Statues A-C, and E-H were found in the courtyard of Adad-naddin-ahhe's palace, they must have been

---

[22] Heuzey's contention that fragments of SV.7 were found *in situ* (DC 216f.) is incorrect, see Unger *AOTU* II,3 (1921), 27–36. According to Unger ibidem, 34, some fragments were found between Tell A and B.

[23] DC 4, and Heuzey *Catalogue*, 7f. De Sarzec reported to have started excavations at Tello because of a huge statue (Statue D) sticking out of the ground, which he had seen during a visit to the site.

[24] See FT II, 13 note 3, and Parrot *Tello*, 16.

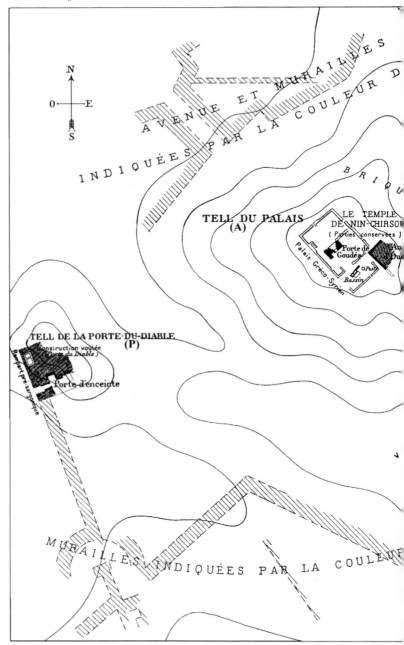

Fig. 1: Map of Tello, Central Past of Excavations.

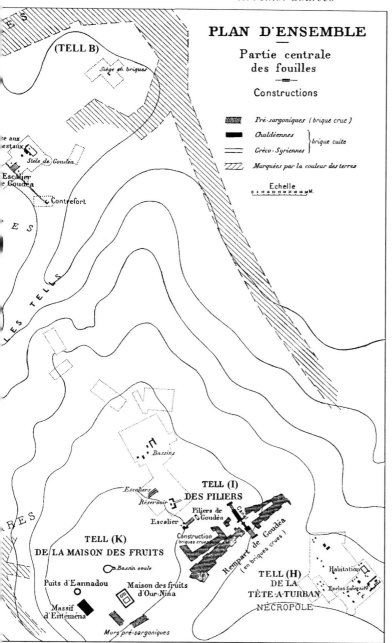

PLAN D'ENSEMBLE
—
Partie centrale
des fouilles
—
Constructions

Pré-sargoniques (brique crue)
Chaldéennes ⎫
Gréco-Syriennes ⎬ brique cuite
Marquées par la couleur des terres

Echelle

(TELL B)

Siège en briques

re aux
estaux

Stèle de Goudéa

Escalier
e Goudéa

Contrefort

LES TELLS

Bassins

TELL (I)
DES PILIERS

Escaliers

Réservoir

Piliers de
Goudéa

Escalier

TELL (K)
DE LA MAISON DES FRUITS

Construction
briques crues

Bassin ovale

Rempart de Goudéa
(en briques crues)

Habitation

Puits d'Eannadou

Maison des fruits
d'Our-Nina

TELL (H)
DE LA
TÊTE-A-TURBAN
NÉCROPOLE

Enclos funéraire

Massif
d'Entéména

Murs pré-sargoniques

set up there by this ruler.[25] In any case, those reported from the palace (Statues A-H, K, and W) were apparently not found *in situ* – they are dedicated to different deities, and must have originally stood in different shrines. Statue I, dedicated to Ningišzida, was found on Tell V, and Statue S on Tell H.

Statues M-Q were acquired in the twenties, and are believed by some to be fakes and by others to come from illicit digs at Tello.[26] All these statues are dedicated either to Ningišzida or to his consort Geštinanna. According to de Genouillac, they were pillaged from Tello in 1924, together with two statues of Gudea's son Urningirsu also dedicated to Ningišzida, and acquired at the same time as the former.[27] Their findspot South East of Tell V, he reported, was shown to him by local diggers. Statue I and the libation vase SV.9, both dedicated to Ningišzida, previously found on Tell V, may have inspired the locals to dig there. When de Genouillac subsequently excavated the site, he found more objects associated with Ningišzida (including the door plaque DP.3), scanty architectural remains which he interpreted as the temple of Ningišzida, and a tablet showing a plan of the temples of Ningišzida and Geštinanna located on either side of a street.[28] It is possible, therefore, that the above mentioned objects came from these two temples.

In summary, there was a concentration of Gudea material on Tell A, most of which was apparently reused in Adad-naddin-ahhe's palace, but may originally have belonged to Gudea's Eninnu. A group of objects pertaining to Ningišzida, some of them excavated South East of Tell V, seems to come from Gudea's temple for this deity. Other objects were found within the area Falkenstein assigned to Gudea's Eninnu.

b. Other Sites

Ninety-six artifacts of Gudea originate from sites other than Tello. Most of them were found in the other two important cities in the state of Lagaš: al-Hiba, ancient Lagaš, and Zurghul, ancient Ningin. Only twenty-three stem from sites in other southern Mesopotamian city-states. Except for the artifacts from al-Hiba, the archaeological context of the objects either remains unknown, or they were not found *in situ*.

Most artifacts from al-Hiba – thirty-two bricks (BS.17) and two door sockets (DS 17–18) – record the construction of Ningirsu's Ebagara some remains of which have been excavated at this site.[29] Similarly, most artifacts from Zurghul, twenty-three clay nails (CN.11, 15), four bricks (BS.7), a foundation tablet (FT.13), and a foundation figurine (FB.3), record the construction of temples known or likely to have been located at that site, namely Nanše's Esirara and the temple of Nindub.[30] The remaining architectural

---

[25] Heuzey DC, 405; Parrot *Tello*, 155.

[26] While the case is quite clear for Statue P, which has to be excluded as a fake (see Appendix A), the authenticity of the others remains disputable. Johansen's evidence in favor of their being fakes (*Statues of Gudea*) was discussed by Colbow *Rundplastik*, 76–89, who concluded that none of his arguments are proof beyond doubt; her discussion includes an updated bibliography on the controversy.

[27] FT II 17–19; see also Parrot *Tello*, 158f.

[28] For the architectural remains see FT II pl. XXI; for the temple plans (AO 13022) see ibidem pl. LIII, and Foster and Polinger Foster *Iraq* 40 (1978), 61.

[29] Hansen *Sumer* 34 (1978), 82.

[30] See chapter I.B.2. nos. 18–20. Zurghul, though visited by several explorers, remains largely unexcavated.

elements are reported from sites other than the buildings they record. In most cases the buildings are known from a much larger number of records reported from their original location, as Table II.A.2 shows. The records scattered at sites other than those for which they were destined must have been displaced in later times, either as booty, since they bear royal inscriptions, or as building material for reuse.[31] They may also have been published with an incorrect provenance.

Only two dedicatory objects[32] stem from sites other than Tello: Statue U was found at Tell Hammam, and the stone basin SV.2 at Nippur. Statue U is dedicated to Nanše for whom Gudea (re)built temples in Ningin and Zulum, and was apparently displaced in antiquity. The stone basin SV.2, on the other hand, is dedicated to Enlil, the patron deity of Nippur, and was destined for his temple there.

In summary, the artifacts not found at Tello include mainly building records from Lagaš and Ningin, i. e. within the borders of Lagaš, and one object dedicated to Enlil in Nippur, the pan-Sumerian religious center. The small number of remaining artifacts reported from other sites record Gudea's construction of temples in his city-state, and were either not found at their original location, or published with an unreliable provenance.

Koldewey spent twelve days excavating in 1887, and published the results in *ZA* 2 (1887). After that the site was surveyed by Dougherty *AASOR* 7 (1925–26), 56f., Jacobsen *RA* 52 (1958), and by the excavators of al-Hiba, see Biggs *BiMes* 3 (1976), 12.

[31] Braun-Holzinger *ASJ* 19 (1997), 3–5, showed that those recorded during regular excavations were found in first millennium B.C. levels.

[32] I am using the term *dedicatory* rather than the conventional *votive*, since there is no evidence that these objects implied a vow, as Grayson *JAOS* 90 (1970), 529, observed. See also van Driel *JAOS* 93 (1973), 67–69. While Grayson "Marginalia," 264–265, revised his earlier view based on one Middle Assyrian royal inscription which expresses a vow, I maintain it for third millennium B.C. objects.

Table II.A.2: Records with a Provenience not Corresponding with their Inscription[33]

Construction recorded	Original Location	Number & Type of Records	Other Proveniences	Number & Type of Records
Ningirsu: é-50	Tello:	1310 CN; 96+ BS; 14 DS; 1 DT; 7 FT; 5 FF; 1 SO; 1 SV; 3 St; 1 UI	al-Hiba:	1 CN
			Zurghul:	1 CN
			Ur:	1 CN
			Tell Jidr:	1 BS
			Medain:	1 CN
Ningirsu: abul-ká-sur-ra	Tello:	13 CN	al-Hiba:	1 CN
			Uruk:	1 GL
Baba: é-sila-sír-sír	Tello:	20 CN; 3 BS; 1 FT; 2 St	al-Hiba:	1 CN
			Tell Jidr:	1 BS
Gatumdug: é-uru-kù-ga	Tello:	28 CN; 2 BS; 1 FT; 1 GL; 1 St	al-Hiba:	3 BS
Dumuziabzu: é-gír-su^{ki}	Tello:	12 CN	Uruk:	1 CN
			Ur:	1 CN
Nindara: é-gír-su^{ki}	Tello:	69 CN; 4 BS	Uruk:	2 CN
			Larsa:	1 CN
Ninšubur: é	Tello:	6 CN	Uruk:	1 FT
Nanše: é-sirara$_6$	Zurghul:	22 CN; 4 BS; 1 FT; 1 FF	Tello:	2 CN; 4 BS
			al-Hiba:	2 CN
			Uruk:	1 CN
			Ur:	2 CN
			Umm Chatil:	1 CN
			Larsa:	1 BS
Nindub: é	Zurghul:	1 CN	Uruk:	3 CN
Enki: é-gú-^{id}idigna	Guidigna		Ur:	1 CN
Nanše: é-an-gur$_{22}$-zú-lum^{ki}	Zulum		Ur:	2 CN
Nindara: é-làl-DU-ki-ès-sá^{ki}	Kiessa		Ur:	1 FT

---

[33] Object categories are abbreviated as in Appendix A: CN = clay nail; BS = brick stone; DS = door socket; DT = stair step; FT = foundation tablet; FF = foundation figurine; GL = gate lion; SO = pedestal or stand; St = statue; UI = unidentified object.

B.   The Inscriptions

Among the two thousand four hundred and forty-four commemorative inscriptions of Gudea, there are only one hundred and six different texts. Multiple copies of the same text frequently occur on structural elements, especially clay nails and bricks, while dedicatory objects rarely bear the same inscription.[34] Overall the texts are repetitive and rigid in their formulation. They consist of basic components and optional complements composed in varying combinations according to a strict scheme. Their contents and structure has been briefly described by Falkenstein,[35] who had a considerably smaller number of texts at his disposal. This chapter examines the larger corpus now available, which will be compared to the Cylinder Inscriptions in chapter III.E.

1.   Core Components

With three exceptions,[36] all texts contain three indispensable components in the following order: name of a deity (DN); name and title of Gudea (gu-dè-a ensí lagaš^{ki}); one or a contiguous series of three transitive verb(s) with its (their) object(s). The deity is the beneficiary (dative), and Gudea the agent of the verbal phrase(s) through which they are set in relation. On the basis of the verbs three types of records can be distinguished: building inscriptions which commemorate the construction of a temple (é), gate (abul), or wall (bàd) using the verb "to build" (dù); dedicatory inscriptions which commemorate the dedication of the inscribed object using the verb "to dedicate" (a – ru); and statue inscriptions which commemorate the fashioning (alan tu), naming (mu-šè sa$_4$), and induction into the temple (é-a ku$_4$) of the inscribed statue.[37] In all verbal phrases the divine beneficiary is referred to with a possessive pronoun in the dative. A sample of each type is given below with the core components in bold face:

1) *Building Inscription* (*Gudea 51*):

^{d}nin-gír-su	For Ningirsu,
ur-sag kal-ga ^{d}en-líl-lá	the strong hero of Enlil,
lugal-a-ni	his master,
gù-dé-a ensí lagaš^{ki}-ke$_4$	Gudea, the ruler of Lagaš,
níg-ul-e pa mu-na-è	made appear an everlasting thing;
é-50 anzú^{mušen} babbár-ra-ni	his Eninnu, the white Anzu,
mu-na-dù	he (re)built for him;
ki-bé mu-na-gi$_4$	restored it to its former state for him.

---

[34] Exceptions are MH.1–2; MH.3–5; MH.6 and SV.4; SV.9–10 and SO.4.

[35] *Einleitung*, 171–177.

[36] The seal inscription (CS.1) which contains only Gudea's name and title; Gudea 76, inscribed on three bricks (BS.21), which contains Gudea's name, title, and one epithet characterizing him as temple builder; and Gudea 54, inscribed on an agate cone (UI.3), which contains a speech to Ningirsu comparable to Lagaš I inscriptions, see Steible *Neusumerische Bau- und Weihinschriften*, Gudea 54 with note 1.

[37] The terminology used here is purely formal; it does not imply that building or statue inscriptions are not dedicatory in nature.

B. The Inscriptions

2) *Dedicatory Inscription* (*Gudea 20*):

^dig-alim	For Igalim,
dumu ki-ág ^dnin-gír-su-ka	the beloved son of Ningirsu,
lugal-a-ni	his master,
gù-dé-a ensí lagaš^{ki}-ke₄	Gudea, the ruler of Lagaš,
nam-ti-la-ni-šè	for his life
a mu-na-ru	dedicated it (the inscribed object) for him.

3) *Statue Inscription* (*Statue A*):

^dnin-hur-sag	For Ninhursag,
nin uru-da mú-a	the lady grown with the city,
ama-dumu-dumu-ne	the mother of all children,
nin-ani	his lady,
gù-dé-a ensí lagaš^{ki}-ke₄	Gudea, the ruler of Lagaš,
é uru gír-su^{ki}-ka-ni	(re)built for her
mu-na-dù	her temple of the city Girsu.
dub-šen kù-ga-ni	He fashioned
mu-na-dím	her pure treasure chest for her;
^{giš}dúr-gar mah nam-nin-ka-ni	fashioned
mu-na-dím	the great throne of her ladyship for her;
é mah-ni-a mu-na-ni-ku₄	entered them into her great temple for her.
kur má-gan^{ki}-ta	From the foreign land Magan
^{na₄}esi im-ta-e₁₁	he imported diorite;
alan-na-ni-šè mu-tu	created her statue with it for her;
nin an-ki-a nam-tar-re-ne	named it for her "The lady of the ones
^dnin-tu ama dingir-re-ne-ke₄	who decree destiny in the universe,
gù-dé-a lú é dù-a-ka	Nintu, the mother of all deities,
nam-ti-la-ni mu-sù	has made long the life of
mu-šè mu-na-sa₄	Gudea, the temple builder;"
é-a mu-na-ni-ku₄	entered it in the temple for her.

2. *Optional Complements*

Each core component is amplified with more or less extensive optional complements. Like the core components, these consist of building blocks in the form of formulaic phrases and sentences or members of a lexical or semantic set. I will first review the complements of the core beneficiary and agent of all inscriptions, and then those of the core verbs with their objects for each record type. Tables II.B.1–2 provide schematized overviews of all components and their distribution in the well-preserved texts. The paragraph numbers in the following discussion refer to the numbers of the complements in these tables.

a. Beneficiary

1.b. In most texts the name of the divine beneficiary is followed by epithets which characterize the deity in terms of status and aspect. Their number ranges from one up to eight. The same epithets recur with the same deities; in the eight texts addressed to Baba, for example, she is always the "daughter of An" (dumu an-na), seven times the "beautiful woman" (munus sag$_9$-ga), six times the "lady of Urukug" (nin uru-kù-ga), twice the "lady abundance" (nin hé-gál), and once she receives four additional epithets (Statue E 1:6–9). Identical or similar divine epithets occur also in the Cylinder Inscriptions, as well as in other texts, which shows that they are drawn from a commonly shared repertoire.

1.c. In addition to or instead of epithets, almost all texts express the relation between the agent and the divine beneficiary with the appositional phrase: "his lord/lady" (lugal/nin-a-ni), or "his deity" (dingir-a-ni) in the case of Gudea's personal god Ningišzida and his father Ninazu.[38]

b. Agent

2.b. Gudea can be characterized by epithets which follow his name and title. While the building and dedicatory inscriptions occasionally use only one epithet out of a choice of four, the statue inscriptions may contain up to nine out of a choice of sixteen. Like the divine epithets, these royal epithets are drawn from a common repertoire.[39] Three semantic categories can be distinguished in Gudea's inscriptions: one which stylizes him as the minion of a deity, another which characterizes him as a temple builder, and a third which states his qualities as an ideal ruler. In the first category Gudea is frequently related to Gatumdug, who appears as his mother in the Cylinder Inscriptions (CA 3:6–8), but occasionally also to other deities:

ur ^{d}gá-tùm-dùg-ke$_4$ (Gudea 15:7, 15a:6, 23:7, 25:7, 67:6); ur ^{d}gá-tùm-dùg árad ki-ág-zu (Statue F 1:6–7); dumu tu-da ^{d}gá-tùm-dùg-ke$_4$ (Statue B 2:16–17 = D 1:17–18).[40] Sipa šà-ge pà-da ^{d}nin-gír-su-ka (Statue B 2:8–9 = D 1:11–12); igi zi bar-ra ^{d}nanše (Statue B 2:10–11); agrig kal-ga ^{d}nanše (Statue D 1:13–14); á sum-ma ^{d}nin-dar-a (Statue B 2:12–13); lú inim-ma sè-ga ^{d}ba-ba$_6$ (Statue B 2:14–15 = D 1:15–16); nam-nir-gál gidri sum-ma ^{d}ig-alim-ka (Statue B 2:18–19 = D 1:19–2:1); zi šà-gál-la šu dagal dùg-ga ^{d}šul-šà-ga-ka (Statue B 3:1–2 = D 2:2–3); sag zi ukkin-na pa-è-a ^{d}nin-giš-zi-da dingir-ra-na-ke$_4$ (Statue B 3:3–5). In addition to these Lagašite deites, Gudea is related to Enlil, the chief of the Sumerian pantheon: má-gíd ^{d}en-líl-lá (Statue D 1:9–10); má-gíd é-kur-ra (Gudea 12:8–9).

Most often he is characterized as the builder of Eninnu, but twice also as that of Esirara:

---

[38] While Ningišzida frequently occurs in Gudea's texts, in which he is always characterized as "his deity" (Gudea 64–68; Statue B 3:4–5, 9:4; C 1:1–6; E 8:11–12; G 2:8–9; I 3:7–8; Q 1:1–2; CA 5:20, 18:15; CB 23:18), Ninazu is addressed but in one clay nail inscription (CN.30 = Gudea 92), and only once more mentioned in his capacity as Ningišzida's father (Statue I 1:4–5). The single occurrence of the epithet dingir-a-ni for Ninazu in the mentioned clay nail inscription should be explained with his relation to Ningišzida, rather than interpreted as evidence for Ninazu being Gudea's second personal deity, as Kobayashi *Orient* 30–31 (1995), suggested.

[39] See Seux *Epithètes Royales.*

[40] The meaning of the element ur in ur-DN, a frequent type of personal name, is controversial, see Edzard "Private Frömmigkeit," 202 with bibliography. Civil (personal communication) believes that it is simply the Sumerian counterpart of Akkadian (*w)arad-*, "servant," and has the same meaning.

lú é-50 ^{d}nin-gír-su-ka in-dù-a (Gudea 4 rev. 1–3, 45:7–9, 46:8–10, 56:7–9, 64:6–8, 76:4–6, 87:4′–6′, 93:4′–6′, 94 1:8–2:1, Statue B 8:3–5, C 2:8–10, G 1:8–10, Q 1:6–2:1); lú é-50 ánzu^{mušen} bábbar ^{d}nin-gír-su-ka mu-dù-a (Gudea 88 2:1–4, 95:1′–3′); lú é-50 ^{d}nin-gír-su-ka é-PA é ub 7-a-ni mu-dù-a (Gudea 6 rev. 1–4, 96:4′–7′, Statue E 1:14–17); lú níg-ul-e pa bí-è-a é-50 ánzu^{mušen} bábbar ^{d}nin-gír-su-ka mu-dù-a (Statue F 1:8–11); lú é-sirara$_6$ é-nanše in-dù-a (Gudea 34:7–9); [...] é-na[nše] mu-dù-[a] (Gudea 97:1′–2′).

The third category, confined to the statue inscriptions, qualifies him as mu gi$_{16}$-sa, "one of eternal name" (Statue B 2:5, C 2:5, D 1:8),[41] or as lú si-sá uru-ni/dingir-ra-ni ki-ág-e, "righteous man who loves his city/god" (Statue D 2:4–5, I 2:6–8).

All these epithets, especially those of the first category, serve to underline Gudea's legitimacy as ruler of Lagaš. The deity or building in the epithet does not necessarily coincide with the divine beneficiary or building of the core sentence.

Table II.B.1: Components and their Distribution in the Complete Building and Dedicatory Inscriptions

	1. Beneficiary			*2. Agent*		*3. Building*										*4. Dedication*			
	a	*b*	*c*	*a*	*b*	*a*	*b*	*c*	*d*	*e*	*f*	*g*	*h*	*i*	*j*	*a*	*b*	*c*	*d*
04	Baba	3	x	x	x		b		U		x	x							
05	"	3	x	x			b		U		x	x							
06	"	3	x	x	x		e		U			x							
07	"	2	x	x			e		U		x	x							
08	"	3	x	x			e		U		x	x							
09	"	1	x	x			e		U		x	x							
10	Dumuziabzu		x	x			e		G		x	x							
11	Enki	2	x	x			e		I		x	x							
12	Enlil	1		x	x											x	x	x	
13	Gatumdug	1	x	x			e		U		x	x		x					
15	"	1	x	x	x		e		U		x	x							
15a	"		x	x	x		e		U		x	x							
17	Hendursag		x	x			e				x	x							
19	Igalim	1	x	x			e	x			x	x							
20	"	1	x	x												x	x		
23	Inanna	1	x	x	x		e		G		x	x							
24	"	1	x	x			e	x	G		x	x							
25	"	1	x	x	x		e	x	G		x	x							
26	"	1	x	x			e		G		x	x							
27	"	1	x	x												x	x		
28	Meslamtaea		x	x			e		G		x	x							
29	Nanše	2	x	x		x	e	x	N	x	x	x							
30	"	2	x	x		x	e	x	N	x	x	x	x						
31	"	2	x	x		x	e	x	N	x	x	x	x	x					

---

[41] The term gi$_{16}$-sa can denote the two semantically related ideas of "treasure" or "long duration;" see also Falkenstein *ZA* 58 (1967), 6.

	1. Beneficiary			2. Agent		3. Building										4. Dedication			
	a	*b*	*c*	*a*	*b*	*a*	*b*	*c*	*d*	*e*	*f*	*g*	*h*	*i*	*j*	*a*	*b*	*c*	*d*
32	"	1	x	x			e				x	x							
33	"	2	x	x			e	x	Z		x	x							
34	Nindara	1	x	x	x													x	x
35	"	1	x	x														x	x
36	"	1	x	x			e		G		x	x							
37	"	1	x	x			e	x	K	x	x	x							
39	Nindub		x	x			e				x	x							
40	Ninegal	1	x	x														x	x
44	Ningirsu	1	x	x												x		x	x
45	"	1		x	x		e	x			x	x	x						
45a	"	1		x		x	e	x			x	x	x						
46	"	1	x	x	x		e	x			x	x	x						
47	"	1	x	x			e				x	x	x	x					
48	"	1		x		x	e	x			x	x	x	x					
49	"	1		x			e	x			x	x	x						
49a	"	1		x			e	x			x	x	x	x					
50	"	1		x		x	e	x			x	x	x						
51	"	1	x	x		x	e	x			x	x	x	x					
52	"	1	x	x			e	x			x	x	x						
53	"	1	x	x		x	e	x			x	x	x						
55	"	1		x														x	x
56	"	1		x	x		a	x			x		x	x					
57	"	1	x	x		x	e	x			x	x	x		x				
58	"	2	x	x			e	x			x	x							
59	"	1	x	x			e	x			x	x							
61	"	1	x	x												x		x	x
64	Ningišzida		x	x	x		e		G		x	x							
65	"		x	x														x	x
66	"		x	x			e				x	x							
67	"		x	x	x		e		G		x	x							
68	"		x	x			e		G		x	x							
69	Ninhursag		x	x			e				x	x							
70	"	3		x			e		G		x	x							
72	NinmarKI	2	x	x			b		A		x	x		x					
73	Ninšubur	1	x	x			e				x	x							
74	"		x	x			e				x	x							
75	Šulšaga	1	x	x			e	x			x	x							
91	Inanna	1	x	x			e				x	x							
92	Ninazu		x	x			e		G		x	x							
94	Ningirsu	1	x	x	x		a	x		x	x	x	x			x			

B. The Inscriptions

The texts numbers are those of Steible's edition of the Gudea texts in *Neusumerische Bau- und Weihinschriften*. The components are the following:

1. Beneficiary:	a: **DN**		f: -a-ni
	b: epithet(s)		g: **mu-na-dù**
	c: **lugal/nin/dingir-a-ni**		h: ki-bé mu-na-gi₄
2. Agent:	a: gù-dé-a ensí lagaš^ki		i: 2ⁿᵈ construction
	b: epithet		j: function of inscribed object
3. Building:	a: níg-ul-e pa mu-na-è	*4. Dedication*:	a: fabrication of object
	b: **é/bàd/abul**		b: locative
	c: name		c: nam-ti-la-ni-šè
	d: of GN		d: **a mu-na-ru**
	e: epithet		e: name of object

X marks the presence of an element. Numbers indicate quantity. Lower case letters stand for the following objects: a = abul, b = bàd, and e = é; upper case letters for the following geographical names: A = GuabbaTUR, G = Girsu, I = Guidigna, K = Kiessa, N = Ningin, U = Urukug, and Z = Zulum. As far as preserved, the fragmentary texts do not deviate from the scheme given in this table; their preserved elements are considered in the following discussion.

c. Building Inscriptions

3.a. In a number of texts the core action is preceded by the phrase "he (Gudea) made appear an everlasting thing for him/her (deity)" which shares beneficiary and agent with the core verb.[42] This formulaic phrase introduces the core action in generic terms, and points out the durability of the future construction.

3.c-f. Like the agent, the object (b) of the core verb is usually linked to the divine beneficiary with the possessive pronoun "his/her" (f). It may be named (c), and/or specified in terms of its location by a geographic name in the genitive case designating either a city or a particular area of a city (d).[43] The two buildings given an epithet (e) are é-50, which is often characterized as ánzu^mušen bábbar, "white Anzu;" and é-PA, which is always characterized as é ub-7, "house with 7 'corners.'" While none of the specifications of the object (c-f) are indispensable, each text uses at least one.

3.h. The core verb is sometimes followed by the phrase: "he (Gudea) restored it (the aforementioned object) to its former state for him/her (deity)."[44] This formulaic phrase, which shares agent, beneficiary, and object with the core, specifies the building in terms of its historical tradition. Most temples Gudea claims to have built existed already;

---

[42] The reading níg-ul should be preferred over níg-du₇ (cf. Falkenstein *Grammatik* II, 123, and again Steible *Neusumerische Bau- und Weihinschriften* 2, 16f.), since it has auslaut -l in other texts, including royal inscriptions of the Lagaš I and Ur III dynasties in which it is combined with the same verb (pa – è), and therefore hardly differs in meaning from the Gudea texts; see Cooper *Return of Ninurta*, 139 commentary to line 193. The verb pa – è means "to appear" in the sense of becoming a reality visible to all. The introduction of a person, object, or action in generic terms before specifying it, is common in Sumerian literary texts.

[43] For the names and geographical location, see the list of Gudea's constructions in chapter I.B.2. In the case of Nanše's Esirara (Gudea 29–31) the city (Ningin) precedes the object in the form of a locative, while the temple district (Sirara) follows as a genitive. In this case, the city is given an epithet.

[44] Gudea 82 uses this phrase as its main and only verb.

they were restored rather than built anew by him.[45] The verb "to build" (dù) does not necessarily imply creation in Sumerian. This phrase removes the ambiguity in regard to creation or restoration. Its absence, however, does not allow the conclusion that the construction did not exist before, since the phrase does not occur in all texts pertaining to the same building. It is simply an optional element.

3.i. Four texts commemorate a second construction in an additional clause which repeats the core verb, and shares agent and beneficiary with it. A city wall can be built in conjunction with a temple (Gudea 31, 72),[46] or a specific building (a-ga-eren/gi-gunu₄) built within (šà-ba) the temple commemorated in the core sentence (Gudea 47, 57). The object of this second construction can be specified in terms similar to the first object (3.c-f).

3.j. The two texts inscribed on gate lions (GL.1–2) specify the function of the inscribed object: ^{giš}ig-kam, "it (the inscribed lion) belongs to the (temple's) door" (Gudea 13:9, 94 2:7).

d. Dedicatory Inscriptions

4.a. The object of the core verb in dedicatory inscriptions is assumed to be that on which the text is inscribed. Only two texts – one on a mace head (MH.7), the other on a basin (SV.7) – specifically name it, and relate its fabrication, including the provision of the material of which it is made:

[...-t]a [x im]-ta-e₁₁ [ŠI]M mah-[šè] mu-na-dím, "From [...] he (Gudea) imported [...], and fashioned it for him into a large basin (?)" (Gudea 43 1:1′–3′); hur-sag ur-in-gi₄-rí-az a-ab-ba igi-nim-ka ^{na4}nu₁₁-gal-e mu-ba-al im-ta-e₁₁ šita ur-sag-3-šè mu-na-dím, "In the mountain lands of Uringiriaz at the upper sea he quarried alabaster, imported it, and fashioned it for him into a mace with three lion heads" (Gudea 44 2:2–3:4).

4.b. The location for which the object is destined is named in two texts – one on a basin (SV.2), the other on two door sockets (DS.17–18) – in the form of a temple name in the locative or locative/terminative case: èš nibru^{ki} dur-an-ki-šè (Gudea 12:3f.); é ba-gará-ka (Gudea 61:8).[47]

4.c. The cause of the dedication is specified in most dedicatory records by means of the adverb "for his (Gudea's) life."

4.e. One text inscribed on a libation vessel (SV.12) mentions the name given to the dedicated object: dùn-lá-ba dingir arhuš-sù-mu ki-ša-ra ba-an-zi-ge mu-bi, "the name of this dùn-lá (is) 'my compassionate deity raised me to the horizon' " (Gudea 89:2′–5′).[48]

---

[45] See Table I.B.2.

[46] In Gudea 31 the temple is mentioned before the wall, while Gudea 72 mentions the wall first and has the temple built therein (šà-ba).

[47] In the latter case the door sockets (DS.17–18) are "set up" (gub) there, rather than "dedicated" (a – ru).

[48] On dùn-lá and this type of libation vessel see Braun-Holzinger *ZA* 79 (1989), and Selz *NABU* (1997) no. 36.

e. Statue Inscriptions

Gudea's statue inscriptions each exist in only one copy. In one instance, however, three texts (Statues M, N, O) vary only in regard to the name. Overall they differ considerably in length: the shortest text (Statue Q) comprises fourteen cases, the longest (Statue B) three hundred and sixty-six. The amount of information or specificity varies accordingly. Furthermore, the building blocks are less rigidly structured than in the other inscriptions.

3.a. Preceding the information concerning the statue itself, most texts describe in more or less detail the construction of the temple for which the statue is destined. For the construction proper they use the same clause(s) as the building inscriptions (6 and 8, corresponding to elements 3.a-i of the building inscriptions).[49] In Statue H this information appears in the form of a temporal clause subordinate to the core action, thus confirming its subordination to the core, and the logical order of temple construction before consecration of the statue. In addition, Statues B, C, E, and F detail preceding events. Six building blocks, some of which consist of several phrases, clauses, or sentences can be distinguished. The first block consists of a temporal clause specifying the reason for Gudea's construction, namely his appointment by the deity for whom the temple is built and the statue made (1):

"when Ningirsu, looking approvingly at his city, had appointed Gudea as good shepherd in the country, had taken his hand from the midst of 216,000 people" (Statue B 3:6–11); "when Inanna had looked at him with her life(-giving) eyes" (Statue C 2:11–13); "when Baba, his lady, had appointed him in her heart" (Statue E 1:18–20); "(when) Gatumdug, his lady, had given birth to him in the sparkling banquet hall in her beloved city Lagaš" (Statue F 1:12–2:1).

The parallel of Statue B in Lagaš I inscriptions noted by Steible,[50] leaves no doubt that these clauses are stereotyped formulae.[51] The second block describes Gudea's qualification for it (2):

"Gudea, the ruler of Lagaš, being of vast intelligence, being a servant loved by his lady" (Statue C 2:14–19); "(Gudea), being a prudent servant of his lady, was going to make the excellence of his lady known, and take care of the cult of Baba, his lady" (Statue E 2:1–8); "(Gudea) did not let pleasant sleep enter his eyes in order to build the temple of Gatumdug, his lady. Being of vast intelligence, being a prudent servant of his lady" (Statue F 2:2–11).[52]

---

[49] Statue A 1:8f., B 5:12–20, C 3:11–13, D 2:6–12, E 3:16–4:2, F 3:6f., G 1:11–18, H 2:1–4, M 2:5f., W 4′–6′. Statue D accounts not only for the construction of the beneficiary's temple, but also for that of his consort (3:13–4:1) which may have been part of the former. Statue I summarizes several constructions: the divine house of Ningirsu, that of Nanše, that of the great gods of Lagaš, and finally that of Ningišzida who is the beneficiary of the statue (Statue I 2:14–3:10). This text seemingly stands in the tradition of Gudea's predecessor Urbaba, whose statue commemorates the construction of a number of different temples (Urbaba 1). Alternatively, the mention of the other constructions could be explained with Gudea's introduction of Ningišzida into the Lagašite pantheon.

[50] *Neusumerische Bau- und Weihinschriften* 2, 10 note 14.

[51] A variation is found in Statue I in which the temporal clause occurs at the very beginning of the text, and consists of two statements: first that Ningirsu appointed Ningišzida (1:1–2:2), and second that Gudea built Ningirsu's Eninnu (2:3–13). Typologically, the first one resembles the temporal clauses just discussed, while the second resembles the temporal clause in Statue H, though beneficiaries and agents are not always identical with those of the core sentences. This modification is partly due to the fact that the text summarizes several constructions, partly perhaps also to the fact that Ningišzida was introduced in Lagaš by Gudea. The information concerning the statue (4.a.3–5) is phrased as in Gudea's other statue inscriptions.

[52] In addition, Statue E (2:9–20) interposes between qualification and construction account a comitative stating that Gudea built Baba's temple like he built Ningirsu's Eninnu.

Table II.B.2: Components and their Distribution in the Complete Statue Inscriptions

	A	B	C	D	E	F	G	H	I	M-O	Q
1. Beneficiary:											
a. **DN**	NH	NG	IN	NG	BA	GA	NG	BA	NZ	GE	NZ
b. epithet(s)	2	1	1	1	8	1	1	5	1	2	
c. lugal/nin/dingir-a-ni	x		x	x	x		x	x	x	x	x
2. Agent:											
a. **gù-dé-a ensí lagaš**^{ki}	x	x	x	x	x	x	x	x	x	x	x
b. epithet(s)		9	2	9	1	4	1		1		1
3. Concerning the Temple:											
a. Construction:											
1. divine appointment		x	x		x	x			x		
2. Gudea's qualification			x		x	x					
3. city purified		x			x						
4. bricks made		x	x		x	x					
5. social conditions		x									
6. níg-ul(-e) pa – è		x		x	x						
7. foundation purified			x		x	x					
8. temple built	x	x	x	x	x	x	x	x	x	x	
b. Equipment:											
1. u_4 é-... mu(-na)-dù-a	x			x		x					
2. dedicatory gifts:											
a. materials imported		x		x							
b. objects fashioned	x	x		x	x	x					
c. objects installed	x	x		x	x						
3. Baba's bridewealth				x	x		x				
4. livestock						x					
5. Gudea's achievements		x									
6. petition for blessings							x				
4. Concerning the Statue:											
a. Creation and Consecration:											
1. šà mu-ba-ka					x		x				
2. stone imported	x	x	x	x	x		x	x			
3. **alan-na-(ni)-šè mu-tu**	x	x	x	x	x		x	x	x	x	x
4. **[name] mu-šè mu-na-sa_4**	x	x	x	x	x			x	x	x	x
5. **é(-...)-a mu-na-ni-ku_4**	x	x	x	x	x			x	x	x	x
b. Provisions:											
1. label	x			x	x	x	?	?		x	
2. curse		x	x		x				x		
3. offerings		x									
4. speech order		x	x[?]								

B. The Inscriptions

The abbreviations for the names of the deities are: BA = Baba, GA = Gatumdug, GE = Geštinanna, IN = Inanna, NG = Ningirsu, NH = Ninhursag, NZ = Ningišzida. X marks the presence of an element. Numbers indicate quantity. As far as preserved, the fragmentary texts contain the same components: Statue K has 4.a.2–5, and b.2; Statue S has 4.b.2; Statue U has 1–2.a, 3.a.8, and 4.b.1; Statue W has 3.a.8; Statue X has 1–2.a; Statue Y has 1–2.a; Statue Z has 4.a.2–3; Statue BB has 1–2, and 4.a.3.

The remaining four building blocks concern the purification of the city (3); that of the foundations (7); the making of the bricks (4); and a description of special social conditions imposed during this period (5).[53]

3.b. As a natural corollary of the construction, several texts account for the temple's equipment with dedicatory gifts and/or economic products. At times such an episode is introduced with a temporal clause that sets it in relation to the temple construction: "when he (Gudea) had built the ... temple (for ...)" (1).[54] The dedicatory gifts involve one or a combination of the following actions: the import of building material (2.a), the fashioning of the object(s) (2.b), and its (their) installation (2.c).[55] Each object is usually linked to the core beneficiary with a possessive pronoun. The economic products can consist of the provision for Baba's bridewealth for the New Year festival (6), or of livestock with its caretakers (5).[56] In Statue B the information concerning the temple concludes with a reiteration of Gudea's achievement (6), in Statue E with a petition for blessings (7).[57]

4.a. The three core actions (3–5) may reflect rituals of making and consecration which endowed the human-made artifact with a cultic life.[58] The names of the statues (4) consist of a wish, order, or statement that the divine beneficiary bless(ed) Gudea with long life.[59] Immediately preceding the statue's fashioning, most texts inscribed on statues made of diorite account for the importation of this material (2): kur/hur-sag má-gan^{ki}-ta ^{na_4}esi im-ta-e$_{11}$, "from the mountain land Magan he (Gudea) imported diorite." Statue E and G begin this section with the temporal adverb "in this year" (1) referring to the year in which Gudea augmented Baba's bridewealth.

---

[53] They are discussed in detail in chapter III.E.2.c.

[54] Statue B 5:21f., 6:70–75, E 6:5–17, G 4:21–5:12.

[55] Statue A 2:1–5, B 5:28-6:63, D 3:3–12, E 4:3–15, F 3:8–11. The passage in Statue B, which provides the most extensive list of objects, is introduced with a statement concerning the circumstances of Gudea's imports (5:23–27), and succeeded by the bestowal of war booty at which occasion the temporal clause (3.b.1) is repeated (6:64–76). A similar statement concerning the imports occurs also in Statue D (4:2–14). For further discussion see chapter III.E.2.d.

[56] These components are quoted in chapter III.E.2.e.

[57] Statue B 6:77–7:9, E 7:22–8:15; for the latter see also chapter III.E.2.f.

[58] Winter *Journal of Ritual Studies* 6 (1992) 21–24; Selz *ASJ* 14 (1992), 255 § V; idem "Holy Drum," 176f. §§4.1.1. Statue G lacks the naming and induction (4.a.4–5), and Statue F lacks all core verbs (4.a.3–5). An explanation for this oddity may be found in the empty space of approximately 7–10 cases at the proper place for the missing elements, namely after the creation of the statue (4.a.3) in Statue G, and at the end of column 4 in Statue F. It seems that the two texts were never finished. For a different explanation based on the contents of the inscription, but ignoring the nature of the carrier of the text, cf. Steible *Neusumerische Bau- und Weihinschriften* 2, 53 note 10, and 57f. note 14; idem *MDOG* 126 (1994), 94–96.

[59] See chapter III.E.2.f. The two exceptions, Statue M 3:2 (nam-šita-e ba-DU), and Q 2:4 (é mu-ni-túm), follow Lagaš I prototypes, see Steible *Neusumerische Bau- und Weihinschriften* 2, 75 note 4, and 78 note 4.

4.b. Some texts provide information pertaining to the statue's life and function in the temple. Several statues bear a label on the shoulder identifying them as images of Gudea; the label contains his name, title, and an optional epithet relating him to the deity to whom the statue is dedicated (1). A number of statues are protected from violation by a curse at the end of the main text (2).[60] In addition, Statue B provides a list of offerings for the statue protected by a curse in the first column of text which is separated from the main text by indentation (3). Furthermore, it contains a speech order (4) subsequent to the core verbs (7:21–48) instructing the statue to tell Ningirsu that Gudea built Eninnu according to the conditions society required. The first column of text in Statue C may be understood as an exclamation, too.[61] It is indented from the main text, and states that "Ningišzida (is) the god of Gudea, the man who built Eanna."

3. Conclusions

All texts contain a core and a number of optional complements consisting of stereotyped building blocks. They can be formulaic phrases (lugal-a-ni, nam-ti-la-ni-šè, níg-ul-e pa mu-na-è, uru izi im-ta-lá ..., kur má-gan^{ki}-ta ^{na_4}esi im-ta-e$_{11}$), or members of a set (DN, epithet, GN, locative, divine appointment, curse). When composing a text the scribe could choose and arrange these elements within the limits of certain guidelines which were in part dependent on the type of object on which it was inscribed. Not a single text contains all optional complements, and only the corpus in its entirety provides a complete account of all known details.

Each text commemorates basically one event: the construction of a temple, gate, or city wall, or the consecration of a dedicatory object.[62] The basic information – agent, beneficiary, verb – is contained in the core. Most optional complements elaborate upon the core components. The nominal components are expanded with descriptive appositions (1.b-c, 2.b, building inscriptions 3.c-f), the verbal component with adverbs specifying place (dedicatory inscriptions 4.b), time (statue inscriptions 4.a.1), or cause (dedicatory inscriptions 4.c) of the core action, or with additional clauses which share agent and beneficiary with the core verb. Such additional clauses either introduce the core action in generic terms (building inscriptions 3.a), specify an aspect of it (building inscriptions 3.h), or detail preceding events implied in it (dedicatory inscriptions 4.a, statue inscriptions 4.a.2).

---

[60] The curse may contain from six (Statue E) to one hundred and ten cases (Statue B). It consists of recurrent elements, like the main text. Only Statue B contains unparalleled passages. For an overview of these elements in Mesopotamian monumental inscriptions see Michalowski and Walker "New Sumerian 'Law Code'," 391–394. In Statue I the curse precedes the information concerning the statue, and concerns the aforementioned temple of Ningišzida (I 3:11–4:7).

[61] So Braun-Holzinger *Weihgaben*, St 109, contra Steible *Neusumerische Bau- und Weihinschriften* 2, 3 note 1.

[62] Two of three texts mentioned in note 36, which do not contain any of the common core verbs, can be understood as an allusion to one such event: the brick inscription Gudea 76 refers to a temple construction in Gudea's epithet, while the speech order Gudea 54, like the one in Statue B, specifies the function of the object, and thus alludes to its dedication.

B. The Inscriptions

Supplementary information concerns either the life and functions of the inscribed object (building inscriptions 3.j, statue inscriptions 4.b), or a second event related to the core event. Some building inscriptions combine two related constructions, while most statue inscriptions combine the consecration of the inscribed object with the construction of the temple for which it is destined. The second event either succeeds or precedes the core event, and has the same agent and beneficiary. In the building and dedicatory inscriptions, as well as the shorter statue inscriptions, agent and beneficiary are referred to only by pronouns after their initial introduction, while the longer statue inscriptions may repeat their name and characterization.[63]

The construction account in the statue inscriptions may consist of the same elements as the building inscriptions (3.a.6 and 8). More often, however, it is more detailed. In these cases several episodes preceding (3.a.1, 3, 4, 7) and/or succeeding (3.b.3–5) the construction are related, usually in consecutive order.[64] Each episode encompasses one or more clauses. If it encompasses several clauses, the passage may relate consecutive actions, contain generalizations or specifications of certain actions, or enumerate a number of similar actions.[65] The order of episodes can be emphasized with a time reference to a preceding event (3.b.1, 4.a.1). In addition to the core agent, the divine beneficiary may become active,[66] or Gudea's personal god Ningišzida may act on his behalf.[67] Rarely is the chain of events interrupted by a description of Gudea's qualification (3.a.2), his achievement (3.b.5), or a description of special conditions (3.a.5). These either conclude an episode or set the stage for the next one.

---

[63] In some construction summaries (3.a.6/8), for example, the beneficiary is reintroduced by name and epithet(s) (Statue B 5:12f., E 3:16–19, G 1:11f.), while in some temporal clauses (3.b.1) Gudea's name and title are repeated (Statue B 6:70ff., E 6:5ff.).

[64] Statue D, however, shows that the different complements need not always occur in the same order: the provision of Baba's bridewealth (3.b.3) precedes the bestowal of the dedicatory boat (3.b.2.b-c) which precedes the import of wood for the latter's fabrication (3.b.2.a). Note the nice transition to the next part (4) which begins with the import of stone for the statue (4.a.2). In Statue G, the augmentation of Baba's bridewealth (3.b.3) succeeds the core verbs (4.a.3–5), while its delivery is mentioned before (4.a.1).

[65] The purification of the foundation (3.a.7), for example, is introduced with a generic statement (he purified the foundation) which is then specified in two consecutive actions (he cleaned it with fire; sprinkled its perimeter with clarified butter). The temple's equipment with livestock (4.b.4) consists of an enumeration of similar pairs of consecutive actions (Statue F 3:12–4:13); that with dedicatory gifts (4.b.2) in Statue B (5:28–6:63) of an enumeration of similar series of several consecutive actions. See chapter III.E.2.c-e.

[66] In the divine appointment (3.a.1) the deity appoints Gudea; in the introduction to the imports (3.b.2.a) in Statue B (5:21–27) Ningirsu opens the trade routes for Gudea, while in the similar passage in Statue D (4:2–14) Gudea receives materials through the power (á-...-ta) of Ningirsu and Nanše.

[67] In the presentation of Baba's bridewealth (Statue G 2:8–10), and in the petition for blessings (Statue E 7:22–8:15). The description of the special conditions imposed during the construction (3.a.5) consists of an enumeration of legal regulations in which people of the city are involved. The analogous passage in the Cylinder Inscriptions (CA 12:20–13:15) reveals that Gudea imposed these conditions. He can thus be considered the ultimate agent. The same applies to verbal forms with the prefix ba-, in which the focus is on the object rather than the agent as, for example, in Statue B 4:7–9: é-^{d}nin-gír-su-ka eridu-gin$_7$ ki sikil-la bí-dù, "the temple of Ningirsu was built in a pure place like Eridu."

Fig. 3: Gudea Statue A at scale 1:10.

Fig. 4: Gudea Statue B at scale 1:10.

Fig. 5: Gudea Statue N at scale 1:10.

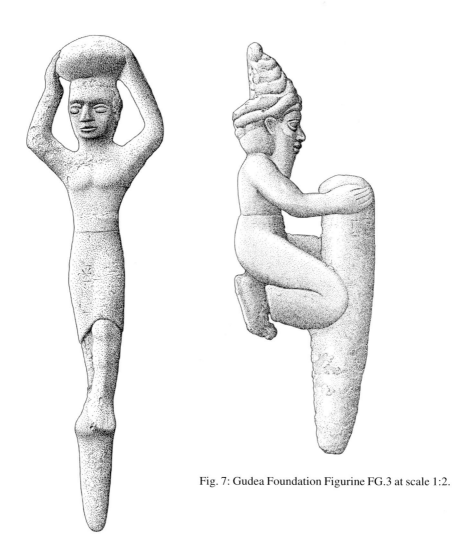

Fig. 7: Gudea Foundation Figurine FG.3 at scale 1:2.

Fig. 6: Gudea Foundation Figurine FK.3 at scale 1:2.

Fig. 8: Gudea Basin SV.7.

Fig. 9: Gudea Seal CS.1 at scale 2:1.

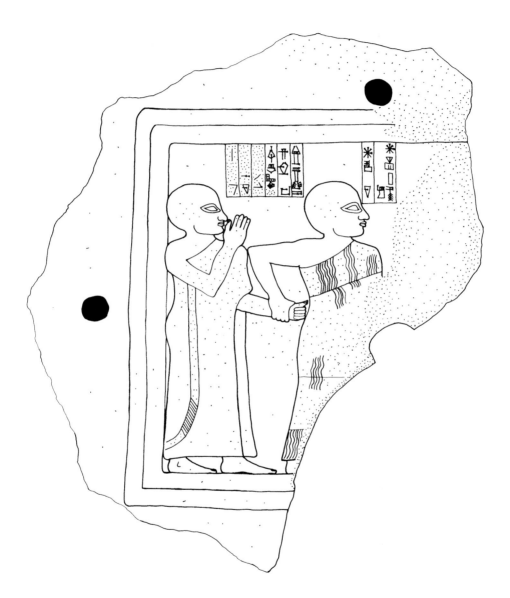

Fig. 10: Gudea Door Plaque DP.3 at scale 1:3.

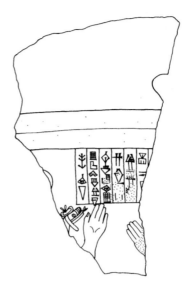

Fig. 11: Gudea Door Plaque DP.2 at scale 1:3.

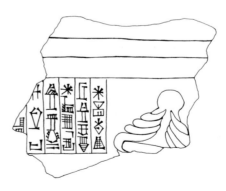

Fig. 12: Gudea Door Plaque DP.1 at scale 1:3.

C. The Imagery

The corpus defined in Appendix A includes artifacts which are sculpted in the round or carved in relief. Their imagery expresses a visual message in addition to the inscribed verbal message. The figures represented include the ruler, a few other human beings, deities, hybrid creatures, and animals. They occur either in isolation, in groups of a heraldic nature, or in a narrative context consisting of no more than one scene. This chapter reviews the repertoire of figures and scenes, and discusses their identification and meaning.

1. Anthropomorphic Figures

a. The Statues Representing Gudea (Figs. 3–5)

All statues represent Gudea dressed in garments typically worn by rulers in this period:[68] a long fringed mantle, and the head, if preserved, covered with a brimmed cap.[69] In addition to the dedicatory inscription, a label on the shoulder of most statues removes any doubt that "Gudea, the ruler of Lagaš" is represented. Realistic portraiture did not exist in ancient Mesopotamia.[70] The Gudea statues belong to those images of rulers that combine the representation of an actual person with a symbolic type.[71] Stylistic features such as their massiveness, the pronounced muscled arms, and the large eyes function as signifiers of rulership appropriate to the socio-political context of Gudea's Lagaš.

All statues are made of stone. This durable material, difficult to reuse for the fabrication of other objects, may account for their large quantity compared with the surviving statues of other Mesopotamian rulers. Statue B (7:49–54) specifically states that: "nobody will (re)work this statue which is made neither of silver nor lapis lazuli, nor copper, nor tin, nor bronze, but of diorite."[72] The size of the statues ranges from over life-size to mere statuettes.[73] Azarpay observed that the life-size statues were conceived as tiers of superimposed units which were reduced on the vertical axis only in small-scale statues. She suggested that the principal factor in the determination of the height/width ratio was the difference in dimension of the imported blocks of diorite.[74]

---

[68] See chapter IV.D.1.a.

[69] Only the reconstructed Statue S is bareheaded. Unfortunately many statues do not preserve the head.

[70] See Strommenger *BaM* 1 (1960), 92; Winter *JCS* 36 (1984) 107f., who speaks of "signature elements."

[71] Winter "Body of the Able Ruler," 583.

[72] The original understanding of this passage (Falkenstein *AnOr* 28 (1949), 56) is to prefer over Steible's new interpretation in *Neusumerische Bau- und Weihinschriften* 2, 32 note 95. The application of metal, let alone lapis lazuli, to a diorite statue makes much less sense than the assumption that these materials could be reworked in the future and thus result in the destruction of the object made of them, a fate which must have afflicted many statues now lost, as the quantitative comparison of extant metal statues with their documentation in texts indicates.

[73] The seated Statue D was over life-size; the standing Statues A, C, E, G, K, and U with an average height of 155 cm, and the seated Statues B, F, and H with an average height of 105 cm are about life-size; the standing Statues M-O have an average height of 56 cm, and the seated Statues I and Q of 37.5 cm.

[74] Azarpay "Canon of Proportions," 99 and 101; see also idem "Neo-Sumerian Canon," 166f., and *JAOS* 110 (1990), 660–665. For a different view cf. Colbow *Rundplastik*, 98.

Ten statues render Gudea standing, while seven show him seated. Like other early Mesopotamian representations of human beings dedicated to deities in their temples, they hold their hands folded on their body. Based on the context in narrative scenes, this gesture is best understood as signifying passive attendance or attentiveness.[75] The seated Statues B (Fig. 4) and F exhibit a tablet on the lap with a ruler and a stylus. While the tablet of Statue F is blank, that of Statue B shows an architectural plan of an enclosure with six gates. Since Statue B is dedicated to Ningirsu and records the construction of his temple in its inscription, the enclosure is probably that of Eninnu.[76] These two statues represent Gudea as temple architect, and emphasize his personal involvement in the construction. The standing Statue N (Fig. 5) holds a vase from which four streams of water flow down on each side of the dress into identical vases depicted on the pedestal, which are equally overflowing with water. Little fish swim up the streams to the vase held by Gudea. This statue evidently shows the ruler in possession of prosperity symbolized by the overflowing vase.[77] As will become clear, prosperity is received in return for the good services the ruler performes for the gods.

Several stylistic and chronological groupings of the Gudea statues have been proposed, although none is convincing. Schlossman and Spycket approached the sculptures from an insufficiently defined Western notion of portraiture which does not apply.[78] Based on the proportions of the statues and on two hundred and twenty-four minute iconographic and stylistic markers, Colbow distinguished three workshops. Following Azarpay's above mentioned observations, the proportions of the Gudea statues cannot be taken as stylistic indicators, and the validity for stylistic analysis of the two hundred and twenty-four markers, which obscure any relation to the works as a whole, remains dubious.[79] Steible attempted to establish a chronological order for the statues,[80] but this hinges on several improbable assumptions,[81] and is contradicted by the very texts that he used as evidence.[82]

---

[75] See chapter IV.D.1.d, p. 261f.

[76] See now Heisel *Bauzeichnungen*, 19f.

[77] So already Unger *AfO Beiheft* 1 (1933), 132f. (erroneously Statue S). The overflowing vase is usually held by deities, and only rarely by deified kings replacing the enthroned deity in Ur III presentation scenes on seals, see Buchanan *Early Near Eastern Seals*, no. 642. There is, however, another diorite fragment from Tello (AO 39), published in DC pl. 8bis:6, which preserves part of a fringed mantle with two engraved wavy lines, and must have belonged to a statue of a ruler holding the overflowing vase. The overflowing vase is further discussed in chapter II.C.1.d below.

[78] Schlossman *AfO* 26 (1978–79), 56–60; Spycket, *Statuaire*, 194.

[79] See the review by Braun-Holzinger in *ZA* 79 (1989), 302–305.

[80] First presented in a series of lectures in the United States, and now published in *MDOG* 126 (1994). An oral version of his thesis was followed by Azarpay *JAOS* 110 (1990), 660–665, who attempted to corroborate it with arguments pertaining to the scale and proportion of the statues.

[81] The assumed development of ever larger statues dedicated to ever higher-ranked deities is somewhat naive; moreover Ninhursag was not important anymore in Gudea's time. Neither material and size of the statue nor divine beneficiary and formulaic components of its inscription are valid criteria for a chronology. There is no evidence to corroborate that Gudea's access to materials from Magan was restricted at any time, much less for its timing within his reign. The text component mentioning the import of diorite from Magan (see chapter II.B.2.e § 4.b.2) is a building block the inclusion of which is optional, as the two statues made of diorite but lacking this component (Statues I and Q) show; moreover it cannot be expected in inscriptions of statues made of other materials. See now also the critique by Braun-Holzinger in *ASJ* 19 (1997), 6–10.

[82] Statues B, D, and K with mention of Magan record the construction of Eninnu, while Statue I without mention of Magan records the construction of several buildings which are specifically said to have been built after Eninnu.

According to their inscriptions, the statues are dedicated to various deities, and were to be set up in the temples that Gudea (re)built. The use of the verb tud – to give birth – for the making of the statues, and the name-giving suggest that not unlike other cult objects, they assumed a life of their own in the temple.[83] At the same time they represented the ruler *vis-à-vis* a deity. Winter suggested that the standing statues were placed "in attendance upon divine images," while the seated ones were themselves "the object of cultic attention."[84] Offerings for the seated Statue B are indeed determined in the first column of its inscription. Offerings, however, are also mentioned for the standing Statues E and K in the curse of their inscriptions (Statue E 9:11–12; Statue K 3':7–10). The context in which the latter occur, together with the wish in the curse of Statue B (7:55) that this seated statue be set up at the ki-a-nag, where the deceased received offerings,[85] may indicate that, regardless of their posture, the offerings for Gudea statues were meant for the future after the death of their donor. This seems to be corroborated by Braun-Holzinger's observation that the first column of Statue B, which prescribes the offerings for the statue, may have been inscribed later than the main text, since it is indented, written in a smaller script, and encroaches the fringe of Gudea's dress.[86] In her treatment of Early Dynastic to Old Babylonian dedicatory gifts, she further observed that offerings for royal statues usually relate to deceased rulers.[87]

Where in the temple such statues were set up when dedicated, and whether they confronted divine images, remains problematic. The extant statues of the Akkad to the Ur III period were not found *in situ*. In Early Dynastic Mari, standing and sitting statues were found in temple cellae where they received offerings.[88] The Northern Mesopotamian temples, however, exhibit lay-outs different from those in the South – their cellae, for example, lack altars – suggesting a difference in cultic practices. Colbow observed that seated statues are hard to imagine in the cella of the temple, since the ruler never confronts a deity sitting in presentation scenes.[89] Yet, Statue B communicates a message, given verbatim in its inscription (7:21–48), from its human donor to its divine beneficiary.[90] Moreover, the standing statues are not portrayed in the posture that usually is assumed in the presence of an enthroned deity in presentation scenes.[91] It would seem therefore, that the statues did not assume the same approach toward the deity as

---

[83] See chapter II.B.2.e § 4.a.3–5.

[84] *Journal of Ritual Studies* 6 (1992), 26. Ibidem 25, Winter observed that the standing statues are usually inscribed on the back, the seated ones on the front, which could indicate from which side the statues were seen by those approaching them, an idea expressed already by Barrelet *CRRA* 19 (1974), 52. The placement of the inscription, however, may as well have been a question of practicability.

[85] Gomi *Orient* 12 (1976), and Michalowski *Or* 46 (1977), 222.

[86] *Weihgaben*, 229.

[87] *Weihgaben*, 228f. There is only one exception: the statue of Šaša, the wife of the Early Dynastic ruler UruKAgina; see now Selz *ASJ* 14 (1992).

[88] Mayer-Opificius *AOAT* 220 (1988), 259–261.

[89] *Rundplastik*, 90f.

[90] This phenomenon is attested elsewhere, see Braun-Holzinger *Weihgaben*, 228.

[91] According to Braun-Holzinger (personal communication) this may have been due to technical reasons, since raised arms were more difficult to realize in monumental stone sculpture than, for example, in metal works where they are attested; see, for example, Braun-Holzinger *Figürliche Bronzen*, nos. 37 and 169. Yet, the raised arm of a petitioner could have been sculpted aligned with the body in stone sculpture, if the kir_4 šu – gál was to be signified; on the latter see chapter IV.D.1.d, p. 260f.

the animate human beings they represented,[92] and/or were not set up in front of divine images.

Textual evidence from the Ur III and Isin-Larsa periods indicates that the courtyard of the temple was a place where royal statues were installed.[93] This seems also to be the case for the statue of the Lagaš II queen NinKAgina, which was to bring offerings (sizkúr) to Baba in her courtyard.[94] That stone statues were placed at the ki-a-nag, as Statue B seems to suggest, is difficult to substantiate. The context of the relevant statement in Statue B, its curse section, and the verbal form ha-ba-gub, an optative, may indicate that this statue was not originally set up there. Since there is no evidence of stone statues receiving offerings at the ki-a-nag,[95] the text may simply imply that Gudea wished this statue to be attended after his death, not necessarily that it was ever going to stand at such a place in reality. Yet, the composition known as *Lugal* states that images of the rulers were set up precisely there. When determining the destiny of diorite, Ninurta says to this stone:[96]

475	lugal u_4 sùd-rá mu-ni ì-gá-gá-a	After the king, who established his name in remote days,
476	alan-bi u_4 ul-lí-a-aš à-mu-un-dím-ma	has made this image for the future, and
477	é-50 é-kiri$_4$-zal sùd-gá	after he placed it at the ki-a-nag of Eninnu, the house full
478	ki-a-nag-ba um-mi-gub-bé me-te-aš hé-em-ši-gál	joy, may you (Diorite) be placed there as a suitable ornament."

Rather than viewing this passage as a confirmation of the statement in Statue B and as evidence for royal statues being set up at the ki-a-nag, it may simply be a reflection of the former, perhaps blended with later traditions. For the Ur III king Šulgi, for instance, the situation may already have differed, since he was deified during his life-time and worshipped in temples of his own in the provinces. Although we know that Eninnu had a ki-a-nag, its location remains enigmatic. In the Cylinder Inscriptions it is mentioned in relation to the trophies of Ningirsu, i.e. his former foes. They are set up at seven distinct locations in the temple complex (CA 25:24–26:14), and at the same time:

CA 26:15	ur-sag ug$_5$-ga ì-me-ša-ke$_4$-éš	Since they were dead warriors,
CA 26:16	ka-bi ki-a-nag-šè mu-gar	he set their mouths toward the ki-a-nag.
CA 26:17	mu-bi mu-ru dingir-re-ne-ka	Gudea, the ruler of Lagaš,
CA 26:18f.	gù-dé-a énsi lagaš^{ki}-ke$_4$ pa-è ba-ni-a	had their name appear in the midst of the deities.

---

[92] I disagree with the general view that all statues dedicated in temples are represented praying. As Mayer-Opificius *AOAT* 220 (1988), 252, observed, this interpretation betrays the modern viewer in whose culture folded hands designate praying. On this gesture see chapter IV.D.1.d, p. 261f. The message Statue B was to bring to the deity is by no means a prayer. This is not to exclude, however, that some statues were represented thus, as Isin-Larsa and Old Babylonian description of statues indicate, see Braun-Holzinger *Weihgaben*, 228.

[93] Braun-Holzinger *Weihgaben*, 238. Two of the four examples, however, are statues of deceased predecessors. For stelae set up in courtyards see chapter IV.F.3.

[94] Nammahni 1 2:2–7. Sizkúr – dug$_4$/e does not *per se* imply a prayer; see Civil *Farmer's Instructions*, 92 §87.

[95] Braun-Holzinger *Weihgaben*, 229, contra Selz *ASJ* 14 (1992), 247.

[96] For the text see van Dijk *Lugal* I, 112f.

One wonders whether the ki-a-nag was simply any location where the deceased could receive offerings, rather than a physical part of the temple. The term suspiciously lacks the é which usually precedes the names of distinct rooms or quarters of a temple. The connection of the ki-a-nag with establishing one's fame in both texts seems to imply that it is the provision of regular offerings for the deceased (and, by extension, for his/her representation) that keeps alive his/her memory. In any case, *Lugal* leaves no doubt that, aside from being cult objects and representing the ruler *vis-à-vis* deities, royal statues were intended to perpetuate his memory after death.

b. The Basket Carrier (Fig. 6)
Five foundation figurines (FK.1–5) represent a bareheaded, bare-chested male figure wearing a short skirt like workmen and carrying a basket on his head. This figurine type first appears under Gudea, but becomes standard in Ur III times and thereafter. In contrast to Gudea's figurines, the lower bodies of those of his son Urningirsu and the Ur III rulers are peg-shaped, except for one of Urnamma which wears a long skirt.[97] Two door plaques of the Lagaš I ruler Urnanše (Fig. 37)[98] depict him in this same posture wearing a ceremonial dress. They record temple constructions as the foundation figurines do, and thus leave no doubt that the latter, too, represent the ruler as construction worker.[99] Basket carriers are a common feature in construction scenes;[100] one could even say that they signify construction work, and are an important marker in identifying such scenes. Like the architect, the royal basket carrier manifests the ruler's personal involvement in the temple construction.

c. The Kneeling God Holding a Peg (Fig. 7)
The majority of foundation figurines (FG.1–33) represent a half-kneeling god holding a huge peg. The figure is identified as a god by his horned crown. Like other male gods of this period, he wears his hair in a chignon, and is bearded. A similar foundation figurine, though slightly larger and more carefully modeled, is otherwise attested only for Gudea's predecessor Urbaba.[101] The same figure is depicted on a pedestal of the Elamite ruler Puzur-Inšušinak,[102] a contemporary of Gudea.[103] On this sculpture his dress can be clearly identified as the short skirt of workmen. He approaches a huge crouching lion, and is followed by a Lamma goddess with raised arms. The scene recalls presentation scenes in which a king approaches a deity. The unusual configuration of a deity approaching a lion may be due to the adaptation of Mesopotamian iconography to an Elamite monument, in which the figures assumed new meaning in the process. The precise identity of the peg figure in Lagaš as well as the meaning this image was

---

[97] Rashid *Gründungsfiguren*, pl. 39; see also chapter I.B.1 note 94.
[98] Braun-Holzinger *Weihgaben*, W 1 and 4.
[99] Ellis *Foundation Deposits*, 23–24.
[100] See chapter IV.B.3.
[101] Rashid *Gründungsfiguren*, no. 80. Steible's assignment of this figure to Gudea is incorrect, see Appendix A note 3.
[102] Braun-Holzinger *Weihgaben*, Sockel 2. The figurine presented to an enthroned god on an Akkadian seal (Amiet *Glyptique susienne*, no. 1565), is probably not a foundation figurine, as van Driel *JAOS* 93 (1973), 71, suggested, since no peg is visible. For the representation of a foundation figurine on a stela fragment of Gudea see ST.55 in Appendix B.
[103] See Dittmann *BaM* 25 (1994), 100.

to convey remain open to speculation.[104] Rashid suggested that the image reflects the belief that gods participate in the construction of temples.[105] If it was to epitomize a specific sub-event, like the basket carrier, it may have evoked the driving in of pegs in the course of measuring out the construction site, done under divine guidance.[106]

d. The Goddesses with Overflowing Vases (Fig. 8)

The large limestone basin (SV.7) restored by Unger from twenty-six fragments[107] is carved in relief on its outside. It shows a row of goddesses walking on a stream of water. Between them they are holding vases from which water flows down into the stream. These, in turn, are fed with water poured from vases which are held by smaller-scale goddesses hovering above. All goddesses wear long pleated dresses, and crowns with a single horn pair. There are remains of at least six standing and four hovering goddesses. Considering the importance the number seven plays in Gudea's inscriptions, Unger's reconstruction of seven goddesses of each type is credible.[108]

The inscription on the basin, which relates its fashioning, designates it as a large ŠIM,[109] a relatively rare and only vaguely understood term, perhaps to be read $agarin_x$. The fashioning of one or more ŠIM is also related in the Cylinder Inscriptions, and the finished artifact is mentioned again in the description of the temple:

CA 23:6	ŠIM-ŠIM-šè mu-dím-dím	(From the stones' sides) they made basins.
CA 23:7	é-a mu-ni-šu₄-šu₄	They (the stairs and basins) stand in the house.
CA 29:5	ŠIM[na4] é-a šu-ga-bi	The stone basin which stands in the house
CA 29:6	é-gudu₄ kù a nu-silig₅-ge-dam	is (like) the pure house of the gudu never lacking water.

Since the metaphor paraphrasing the basin refers to the ceaseless flow of water, it is possible that the basin(s) mentioned in the account of Eninnu's construction is (are) identical with the fragmentary remains of the one (perhaps two?) actually found within the area of Gudea's Eninnu, as Unger presumed.[110]

Several similar and somewhat intuitive identifications of the goddesses with the over-

---

[104] Ellis's propositions in *Foundation Deposits*, 81, were based on the assumption that the Lagaš I peg figurines represent the ruler's personal god, which was convincingly rebuked by van Driel in *JAOS* 93 (1973), 70 and Kobayashi in *Orient* 24 (1988).

[105] *Gründungsfiguren*, 42f.

[106] Fields and building areas were marked off on the ground by a set of pegs around which a rope was fastened. The marking of the construction site of a temple and of its ground-plan is described in Gudea's Cylinder Inscriptions, see chapter III.B.4.4 and 5.2, and repeatedly referred to with the term temen – si(g), for which see Dunham *RA* 80 (1986).

[107] *Istanbul Asariatika Müzerleri Neşriyati* 8 (1933), 12.

[108] These numbers were already suggested by Heuzey *Origines*, 154. Although Unger's reconstruction seems correct overall, not all details are beyond doubt. The order of the fragments with inscriptions, for example, was rearranged by Steible *Neusumerische Bau- und Weihinschriften* I, 296 note 1, though I wonder whether lines a) 1'–4' are better inserted between lines b) 6' and 7', rather than preceding lines b) 1'–8'.

[109] Gudea 43 1:2'; see chapter II.B.2.d § 4.a.

[110] *AOTU* II,3 (1921), 84–87.

flowing vases have been proposed: Heuzey saw personifications of the Euphrates and Tigris;[111] Unger saw personifications of sources and rain clouds that form the Tigris, and identified them with Ningirsu and Baba's seven daughters;[112] van Buren saw personifications of higher white clouds and lower rain clouds, whom she assigned to Ea's circle.[113] Neither are the seven (not fourteen!) daughters of Ningirsu and Baba ever associated with water,[114] nor can fourteen personified clouds be made out in Ea's circle.

As van Buren observed, the dress and headgear of the goddess suggest that she was a minor deity. Considering her multiplication as well, she may personify a concept rather than portraying an individual deity, not unlike Lamma who signified divine protection.[115] The clue must be the overflowing vase which van Buren correctly interpreted as a symbol of abundance and prosperity.[116] This interpretation is corroborated by the *Göttertypentext* which states that the image of Kulullû is blessing with one hand (*ikarrab*) and holding abundance (HÉ.GÁL) in the other.[117] The protective spirit Kulullû is usually associated with abundance and divine benevolence,[118] and may be reminiscent of the god bestowing the overflowing vase upon a human petitioner in much earlier presentation scenes.[119]

The narrative context in which the goddess with the overflowing vase occurs is confined to presentations of a human petitioner to a deity. The Akkadian seal of the scribe Ili-Eštar[120] shows her accompanying the petitioner, not unlike a Lamma. On the Urnamma Stela (Fig. 33)[121] she is hovering over the offering of flowing water to the ruler by the enthroned deity. In this scene the goddess underlines the gift bestowed on the ruler, and figures as a personification of it, while on the seal she may have implied and guaranteed that the petitioner who offers an antelope(?) is pleading for and will receive blessings of abundance in return. The basin of Gudea is dedicated to Ningirsu, and may be understood as a plea for prosperity as well as a boast of its successful outcome.

2. Animals and Hybrid Creatures

a. Lions

Two partially preserved sculptures in the round are shaped in the form of crouching lions ready to attack (GL.1–2).[122] According to their inscriptions, they were set up at the gate of the temples of Ningirsu and Gatumdug, respectively. Lions are common guardians of

---

[111] *Catalogue*, 146–148.
[112] *AOTU* II,3 (1921), 114–117, and *Istanbul Asariatika Müzerleri Neşriyati* 8 (1933) 15f.
[113] *Flowing Vase*, 65–67.
[114] Falkenstein *Einleitung*, 75 no. 18.
[115] See chapter II.C.3.a, p. 67.
[116] *Flowing Vase*. That the overflowing vase was exclusively an attribute of Ea/Enki and his circle, however, as expressed in her study, which remains the only comprehensive one on this subject, needs revision.
[117] Köcher *MIO* 1 (1953), 106 vi 7–8. I owe this reference to Wiggermann.
[118] Wiggermann *Protective Spirits*, 182f. no. 9.
[119] See chapter II.C.3.a.
[120] Collon *Cylinder Seals* II, no. 213. See also the low quality post-Akkadian seal Porada *Corpus*, no. 260.
[121] Discussed in chapter IV.C.2.a, p. 217–220.
[122] A lion head (AO 71) and an unpublished front piece of a lion (AO 68), both from Tello, may have belonged to GL.1, see DC 230f. pl. 24:1; Parrot *Tello*, 195f. fig. 42m; Spycket *Statuaire*, 221 notes 193f.

buildings.[123] The wide open mouth of GL.2 evidently was to inspire fear and keep out unwanted visitors.

Lions are also carved on a basin fragment (SV.6) and a mace head (MH.7), both dedicated to Ningirsu. The basin shows a crouching lion with the body seen in profile, while the head, sculpted nearly in the round, confronts the viewer full face. From the mace head three lion heads are looking out at the beholder. Lions are associated with Ningirsu elsewhere,[124] and are here best understood as a symbol of prowess in the context of his warrior aspect.[125]

b. Bulls

Three foundation figurines take the shape of a bull on a platform on top of a peg. Two bulls are recumbent (FB.1–2), while the third one stands grazing amidst tall reeds (FB.3), recalling the famous gold and lapis lazuli sculpture from the royal cemetery in Ur and representations of similar images on Akkadian cylinder seals.[126] In contrast to the basket carrier and the kneeling god with the peg, these bull figurines are dedicated to female deities: the former two to Inanna, the latter to Nanše. Only one other example of a bull-shaped foundation figurine is known.[127] It was found at Tello, and records Šulgi's construction of Nanše's Ešeššešegara in Girsu (Šulgi 13B). This bull is recumbent like two of Gudea's, but, unlike them, its head is lifted up and it is mounted on a longer and slimmer peg. Since it was deposited in Girsu, it was most certainly inspired by Gudea's bulls. There is no apparent link between the bull and the two goddesses or the temple construction.

c. The Human-Faced Bison

One stand (SO.1) is sculpted in the shape of a recumbent human-faced bison who turns his head toward the beholder. He wears a horned crown and his face is flanked by long curly plaits. Similar stands are known from other Lagaš II rulers, and one exemplar was found at Ur.[128] While Gudea's stand is dedicated to Hendursag, the other two inscribed stands are dedicated to Baba.[129] No relation is apparent between these Lagašite deities and the human-faced bison, who is originally associated with Utu.[130] The image of the recumbent bison with a human face goes back to Early Dynastic times.[131] Obviously a mythical being, it is apparently related to the bison-man, who is originally associated

---

[123] Braun-Holzinger *Weihgaben*, 7 and 319f.

[124] See chapter IV.B.7, p. 198 with note 205.

[125] For this aspect see chapter III.C.1.b.

[126] Strommenger *Fünf Jahrtausende*, no. 80 pl. XIV, and no. 113 4th row.

[127] MNB 1371, see Rashid *Gründungsfiguren*, no. 132.

[128] Huot *Sumer* 34 (1978), and Boehmer *IBK* 24 (1986). For their use as stands see Braun-Holzinger *Weihgaben*, 321.

[129] Urningirsu I 2 and Urgar 3. Urgar 3:2 is perhaps better restored [ᵈba-ba₆] based on Urningirsu I 2:2; cf. Steible *Neusumerische Bau- und Weihinschriften* 1, 372 note 2.

[130] Wiggermann *Protective Spirits*, 174–179. Ibidem 179, Wiggermann mentioned clay plaques representing erect bison-men which were found in the context of the Old Babylonian chapel of Hendursag in Ur. These were of an apotropaic nature, and not necessarily related with Hendursag.

[131] Boehmer *BaM* 9 (1978). His contention that the ancient images depict a bull with an attached beard rather than a real bison was convincingly rebutted by Braun-Holzinger *Figürliche Bronzen*, 29 note 10.

with Utu as well.[132] The bison-man is represented with an identical human face, but in erect position.

The Sumerian term for bison is alim, which occurs with or without the determinative gud, "bovine." Following Landsberger, Boehmer suggested identifying the occurrences with determinative as the mythical bison, and those without as the real animal.[133] Wiggermann identified the former (Akk. *kusarikku*) with the bison-man, and the latter (Akk. *alimbû*) tentatively with the human-faced bison.[134] The Sumerian terms, however, seem to be exchangeable in context, and Heimpel's distinction – alim for bison in general and gud-alim for male bison in particular – may come closer to the native denotation, if there was one.[135] Whether the ancients clearly distinguished between real and mythical sphere is not beyond doubt. Among the defeated foes of Ningirsu which have become his trophies, and as such assumed apotropaic functions, Gudea lists:

CA 26:4	šu-nir ᵈutu sag-alim-ma	the standard of Utu: bison's head
CA 26:13	má-gi₄-lum gud-alim-bi-da	the Magilum and the bison-bull

d. Serpents and Serpent-Dragons

The entirely preserved libation cup dedicated to Ningišzida (SV.9) exhibits relief carving of superb quality. Around the fine spout, which tapers toward the bottom of the cup, two snakes are entwined, followed on either side by an erect serpent-dragon holding a gate post.[136] The serpent-dragons combine the head of a serpent with the body and forelegs of a panther, the wings and hind legs of an eagle, and their tail ends in a scorpion's sting. They wear single-horned crowns combined with a pair of goat's horns. Similar dragons, though without wings, are represented on Akkadian seals.[137] The wings may have been left out for a practical reason: on all these representations a deity is sitting or standing on the dragon. One seal depicts behind this party, and evidently belonging to it, a gatepost alongside which a snake rears up.[138] The analogous combination of dragon, snake, and gatepost suggests that the two serpent creatures on this seal are identical with those on Gudea's cup.

The serpent-dragon can be identified with Mušhuš, who is associated with several snake-gods.[139] The association with both Tišpak and Ninazu is documented in texts and images, though the identification of Ninazu on images is not completely certain.

---

[132] Wiggermann *Protective Spirits*, 176 note 10. Ibidem 174, Wiggermann thought that they were originally identical, but then separated into two figures. This must have been before the Early Dynastic period, since they are visually distinguished by then, and do appear side by side in the same image.

[133] *Glyptik*, 44 note 185.

[134] *RlA* 8 (1994), 242 § 7.3, and 243 § 7.17.a.

[135] *Tierbilder*, 77 note 1. See also Behm-Blancke *Tierbild*, 51 note 333.

[136] The same scene was depicted on another libation cup from Tello (AO 25609, formerly AO 306) of which only the foot is preserved, see DC 236; Parrot *Tello*, 199; de Miroschedji *DAFI* 3 (1973), fig. 3.

[137] Boehmer *Glyptik*, figs. 565–572. Instead of the ears (?) of Gudea's serpent-dragons, the Akkadian ones seem to have a goat's beard. Whether they had a scorpion's sting, like Gudea's, is difficult to determine based on the reproductions of the seal images.

[138] Boehmer *Glyptik*, fig. 572.

[139] Wiggermann *RlA* 8 (1995), 455–462 s.v. Mušhuššu.

As Wiggermann observed,[140] Tišpak apparently appropriated Mušhuš from Ninazu, his predecessor at Ešnunna, who was also worshipped at Enigi and in Lagaš. In contrast, the association of Mušhuš with Ningišzida is manifest only in Gudea's art. This cup and the recurrent representation of Ningišzida with serpent-dragon heads protruding from his shoulders on Gudea's seal and stelae leave no doubt about this relationship.[141] It can be explained with Ningišzida being Ninazu's son as well as a snake-god.[142] The snake must be Muššatur who is often paired with Mušhuš in texts.[143] Their apotropaic nature is well documented, especially at gates, and thus explains the gateposts in visual representations. In Gudea Cylinder A they are described thus:

CA 26:24	si-gar-bi-ta muš-šà-tùr	From its (Eninnu's) bolt Muššatur and
	muš-huš	Mušhuš
CA 26:25	am-šè eme è-dè	are sticking out their tongues at a
		wild bull.

3. Narrative Scenes

a. Presentation Scenes (Figs. 9–12)

The cylinder seal and the door plaques carved in relief show presentation scenes of the ruler to a deity. Although the seal itself has not survived, its image is preserved in two ancient sealings (CS.1) which allow us to redraw it in its entirety (Fig. 9). A bareheaded male in a long fringed mantle is led by a god into the presence of an enthroned god. Behind them follow a goddess with raised arms and a winged serpent-dragon. The goddess wears the same pleated dress and single-horned crown as the goddesses with the overflowing vases, while both gods wear flounced garments and multiple-horned crowns. The enthroned god holds a vase in his left from which water flows into another vase in his right which he offers to the approaching god, who gestures its reception by holding its bottom. Streams of water flow down both vases into overflowing vases on either side of the god's throne, two of which serve as his footstool. The throne itself is decorated with three more overflowing vases. This god is obviously in possession of prosperity, and about to bestow it on the approaching petitioner.

The inscription on top of the dragon identifies the seal owner as "Gudea, ruler of Lagaš." He is represented by the human petitioner with a raised right arm.[144] The god leading Gudea by the hand must be his personal god Ningišzida.[145] His depiction with heads of

---

[140] Ibidem 457.

[141] CS.1 and DP.2 in Appendix A, and ST.1, 6, 32, 39, 44 in Appendix B. Wiggermann *RlA* 8 (1995), 458, mentioned in addition an Ur III seal from Tello (Delaporte *Catalogue Louvre*, T.111) which is dedicated to Ningišzida, and depicts a god enthroned on a Mušhuš from whose shoulders protrude snakes. The shoulder emblems were probably inspired by Ningišzida's representation under Gudea, though one wonders whether the differences in their rendering was intentional, considering the short period of time that separates this seal from Gudea's images.

[142] For all these snake-gods see now Wiggermann "Transtigridian Snake Gods."

[143] Wiggermann *RlA* 8 (1995), 462.

[144] On this gesture see chapter IV.D.1.d, p. 260f.

[145] On Ningišzida as Gudea's personal god see chapter III.C.1.d, p. 112.

serpent-dragons growing from his shoulders was introduced by Gudea's artists.[146] Thus the serpent-dragon under the seal inscription must also be assigned to Ningišzida. The minor goddess is identified as Lamma by her gesture,[147] which appears for the first time under Gudea, but becomes standard from the Ur III period onward.[148] The identification of the enthroned god has been controversial, though hardly discussed in detail. Some scholars identify him with Enki, presuming that overflowing vases belong to the realm of this god only.[149] Others favor an identification with Ningirsu, which I assume is because he is a more likely candidate to bless Gudea with prosperity.[150] He was the patron deity of Lagaš, while Enki played only a minor role in this state. Moreover, as Wiggermann observed,[151] the analogous scene on a stela of Gudea (Fig. 17)[152] which includes the minister of the enthroned deity argues against Enki. The figure who carries the signature staff of ministers cannot be Enki's minister because he is not represented with the typical double-face of Isimud.[153] Therefore his enthroned lord must be another god.

On Akkadian seal images the overflowing vase seems to be an attribute and marker of the water god, usually identified with Enki, whose residence was in Abzu, the fresh water lake. He occurs in various contexts, one being the enthroned deity to whom a human petitioner is presented.[154] On the nine seal images of the Lagaš II and Ur III periods known to me to include a god holding the overflowing vase, he is enthroned and, in contrast to the Akkadian images, offers the flowing water to an approaching human petitioner. Eight images, including the seal of Gudea, are impressed on tablets from Tello;[155] one seal belongs to a certain Girsu-Kidug, who must be from Girsu;[156] the other is recut, probably from an Akkadian seal, and exhibits an unusual attitude of the petitioner reminiscent of the Gudea statues.[157] Except for the latter, there are no markers other than the overflowing vase which would commend an identification with the water god. On the contrary, lion and lion-headed eagle on some of them, in combination with their provenance, clearly point to Ningirsu.[158] This evidence suggests to me that at Lagaš during the Lagaš II and Ur III periods, the overflowing vase was appropriated from the water god of earlier images, and used by the city-god Ningirsu instead.

---

[146] See chapter II.C.2.d above. The same characterization of a snake-god with serpent-dragon heads protruding from the shoulders was later adopted for Tišpak in Ešnunna; see OIP 72 pl. 66 no. 709.

[147] The identification is based on a Kassite stela which depicts such a figure, and names it Lamma in its inscription, see Foxvog et al. *RlA* 6 (1980–83), 446–455 s.v. Lamma, especially 452f.

[148] In the Akkad period, Lamma wears the same garment and crown as on Gudea's monuments, the outfit of minor goddesses, but is represented with only one arm raised, see Spycket *RA* 54 (1960), 80f.

[149] Heuzey *RA* 5 (1902); Ward *Seal Cylinders*, 23 no. 14; van Buren *Flowing Vase*, 64f.; Delaporte *Catalogue Louvre*, T.108; Frankfort *Cylinder Seals*, 143; and Parrot *Tello*, 201f.

[150] Meyer *Sumerier*, 46f.; Jeremias *Handbuch*, 388; Amiet "Mythological Repertory," 41; and Collon *First Impressions*, no. 531; Wiggermann *RlA* 8 (1995), 458.

[151] *JEOL* 29 (1985–86), 8 note 14.

[152] ST.1–2 in Appendix B.

[153] For the latter see Boehmer *RlA* 5 (1976–80), 179–181 s.v. Isimud.

[154] Boehmer *Glyptik*, 87–93 figs. 491–526.

[155] Delaporte *Catalogue Louvre*, T.108, 116, 117 (= ITT 3 pl. IV no. 6641 = ITT 5 pl. III no. 9870), 119; ITT 2 pl. II no. 4262; ITT 3 pl. I no. 5963; Buchanan *Early Near Eastern Seals*, no. 608.

[156] Collon *Cylinder Seals* II, no. 439.

[157] Collon *Cylinder Seals* II, no. 440.

[158] See chapters IV.B.4, p. 187f. and IV.B.7 p. 198 with note 205.

None of the door plaques is complete. It is clear, however, that they contained one single scene extending over a rectangular relief surface circumscribed by a raised double band. Holes for attachment are left in the center as well as on the surplus surface beyond the double band (Fig. 10–11). The largest fragment (DP.3) preserves the left side of the scene with two figures heading to the right: Gudea, in the same outfit and posture as on the seal, is led by a slightly taller, bareheaded figure wearing a flounced garment (Fig. 10). By analogy with other presentation scenes, one expects them to approach an enthroned deity on the lost right side. This must have been Ningišzida, since he is the beneficiary in the inscription,[159] and because the fragment was found in the presumed Ningišzida temple of Girsu. Such a restoration explains further why the figure leading Gudea deviates from that in other presentations of this ruler. If the plaque depicted Gudea's presentation to his personal god Ningišzida, he cannot be leading his human protégé at the same time. Braun-Holzinger convincingly argued that the bareheaded god introducing Gudea to Ningišzida on this plaque is the latter's minister Alla.[160]

The other two plaque pieces only preserve parts of their upper edges. DP.2 has an inscription dedicated to Baba or Gatumdug below the worn double band, and depicts two hands and the head of a serpent-dragon (Fig. 11). The hand pointing to the right and the head of the serpent-dragon can be attributed to a Ningišzida figure, the hand pointing to the left must have belonged to the enthroned goddess. DP.1 preserves the beginning of an inscription addressed to Ningirsu, and depicts a horned crown of a deity facing left (Fig. 12). The horned crown thus probably belonged to an enthroned Ningirsu.

b. A Review of Captives?

Seven relief fragments, all slightly curved, can tentatively be attributed to a pedestal depicting a war-related scene (SO.5).[161] The inscription mentioning Ningirsu's temple is very fragmentary (AO 26428a), and the attribution to Gudea not completely certain. Below it are carved the upper bodies of three male figures facing right. They are bareheaded, bare-chested, and bound by ropes around their necks as well as their upper arms. They were doubtless part of a row of captives as depicted on Akkadian victory stelae (Fig. 30–32). Three more fragments can be attributed to this row: one with part of a bare head next to a rope (AO 26428c), and two preserving naked legs facing right (AO 26428d and g); war captives are usually represented naked. Another fragment (AO 26428b) shows the upper bodies of two bearded male figures facing left: one with short curly hair grabs the other by his long hair. The latter has a rope around his neck. This captive, differentiated from the others by his hair style, may have been an enemy leader escorted by a Lagašite soldier. Another piece (AO 26428f) preserves a fragmentary head with a brimmed cap and facing right; behind it remains a bird's wing which could have been part of a standard as depicted on some stela fragments (ST.23, 24, 28). Because

---

[159] Already Hansen *JNES* 22 (1963), 149f.
[160] "Bote des Ningišzida," 41f. Compare Spycket *Statuaire*, 187 note 19.
[161] The fragments inventoried under number AO 26428 have hardly been treated coherently in the literature. Only two (a-b) are published with photos. Börker-Klähn *Bildstelen*, no. 92, incorrectly identified b as a stela fragment. Braun-Holzinger *Weihgaben*, Sockel 6, already suggested that a, b (her AO 52), d and g (her b-c) belonged together. Since two pieces were on exhibit, the rest in storage during my visit to the Louvre, I could not verify whether some of the fragments join.

the brimmed cap was worn exclusively by rulers in this period,[162] this head probably belonged to a Lagašite ruler receiving the captives, not unlike the ruler on the Standard of Ur (Fig. 26). The last fragment (AO 26428e) depicts part of the pleated skirt with knot of a figure facing right, which may be attributed to a soldier escorting captives or to a standard carrier. If this monument was commissioned by Gudea, it is the only one which visually commemorates a military event, and one is tempted to connect it with his Elam campaign.[163]

4. Conclusions

The icons and scenes discussed above have symbolic value. They personify concepts rooted in society or allude to an event in an abbreviated way. The ruler is represented in attentiveness, as petitioner *vis-à-vis* a deity, as temple builder drafting the plan or carrying the basket, or as recipient of the god-given prosperity that the overflowing vase symbolized. Other human beings appear only in the review of captives; they are anonymous soldiers and war prisoners, though the latter may have included an enemy leader identified in the now lost part of the inscription. High-ranked deities such as Ningirsu and Baba are depicted enthroned, and receive and/or bless the ruler. Ningišzida appears as mediator between his royal protégé and the latter, but once also in their place, in which case his minister Alla takes his usual role. Other minor deities include the protective spirit Lamma, the goddess with the overflowing vase, and the god with a peg. They each exhibit an attribute (overflowing vase, peg) or gesture (both arms raised) signifying or alluding to the concept which they personify. The hybrid creatures (Mušhuš, Muššatur, and the human-faced bison) and the animals (lions and bulls) fulfill apotropaic and/or decorative purposes. Mušhuš once appears in a narrative scene (on Gudea's seal), yet as part of the setting rather than as a participant.

Most of the figures are known since Early Dynastic or Akkadian times. These include the ruler in attentiveness or as petitioner, the enthroned deity, the mediator between them, the minister of the enthroned deity, the goddess with the overflowing vase, the basket carrier, soldiers and captives, the serpent-dragon together with the snake, the recumbent bison with a human face, apotropaic lions, and the bull grazing amidst reed. The composition of groups and scenes, too, have Early Dynastic or Akkadian precursors, namely the row of figures for the goddesses with overflowing vases, the antithetical arrangement for the serpent-dragons and snakes, the presentation scene, and the review of war captives. The kneeling god holding a peg is known from Gudea's predecessor Urbaba. For the first time attested are the royal architect, the ruler in possession of prosperity, the adaptation of the basket carrier as a foundation figurine, the representation of Ningišzida with serpent-dragons protruding from his shoulders, that of Lamma with both arms raised, and that of the recumbent, human-faced bison with a horned crown and its adaptation as a stand. While the two new royal images do not seem to have been integrated into the pool of imagery, the bison-stand is evidenced under Gudea's successors in Lagaš,

---

[162] See chapter IV.D.1.a.
[163] See chapter I.B.2 p. 17.

C. The Imagery

the representation of Ningišzida was adopted for Tišpak in Ešnunna, and that of Lamma as well as the foundation figurine in the shape of a basket carrier became standard in Mesopotamia for the next several hundred years. In sum, Gudea's artists made use of traditional figures and compositions, but also reshaped known motifs and compositions into new images and media, as well as introducing a few new types.

III. THE CYLINDERS

A. Introduction

1. Discovery

The two large clay cylinders which bear the most detailed account of Gudea's construction of Eninnu were discovered by de Sarzec during the first excavation season at Tello in 1877.[1] They were found in a survey trench on Tell I′ "dans l'intérieur du chemin tournant."[2] Excavated the following year, the "chemin tournant" turned out to be a drain which passed under a Gudea period enclosing wall later excavated by Cros (Fig. 13).[3] Although the cylinders were not found *in situ*, they were found in the context of Gudea period architectural remains. The enclosing wall was adjoined by remains of a building associated with four empty foundation boxes and a brick pillar.[4] The inscription on the bricks of this pillar records Gudea's construction of Agaeren within Eninnu, and identifies it as Ningirsu's place of judgment.[5]

The proximity of the findspot of the cylinders to a building of Eninnu together with the fact that they commemorate Gudea's construction of Eninnu suggests that they were originally kept in this temple, whether in the Agaeren or elsewhere. They probably ended up in the drain, when Eninnu was destroyed, only a few generations after Gudea's reign.[6] In 1878 the cylinders were shipped to Paris, and entered the collection of the Louvre where they are still displayed today.[7]

2. Description

The cylinders were labeled A and B, and will be referred to subsequently as CA (Cylinder A) and CB (Cylinder B). CA measures 61 cm in height and 32 cm in diameter, CB 56 cm in height and 33 cm in diameter (Fig. 14). They are hollow, and their bases are pierced in the center. Their clay shells are 2,5–3 cm thick, and the perforations measure about 3 cm in diameter. When de Sarzec found the cylinders, their insides were filled with plaster ("plâtre"), and the perforations were closed with clay plugs ("bouchons").[8] Expecting

---

[1] DC 5, and Parrot *Tello*, 16.

[2] DC 65f.

[3] DC 433 with pl. 60:2; NFT 305–308; Parrot *Tello*, 148.

[4] Parrot *Tello*, 156–158 with fig. 34; Rashid *Gründungsfiguren*, 18.

[5] BS.12 in Appendix A. Agaeren seems to be a compound of a-ga, "rear" as opposed to front or interior (see PSD A I 68f.) and eren, "cedar." According to CA 8:6–7 (compare also 22:21f., 23:25, 26:1), Eninnu's place of judgment was located at the Šugalam Gate. To pass judgment at gates was common practice in the ancient Near East.

[6] DC 66; see chapter II.A.2.a, p. 31.

[7] AO 13300.

[8] DC 66. The exact nature of this "plaster" is unknown. The mentioned clay plugs were obviously not kept for conservation.

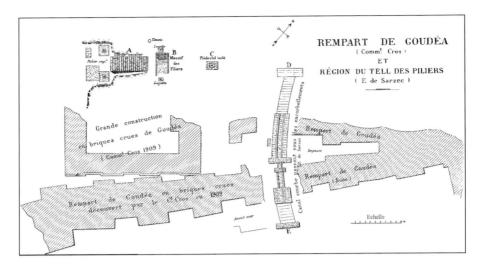

Fig. 13: Map of Tello, Tell I.

to find precious objects, he removed the plaster, but it did not contain anything. Both cylinders are cracked, and partially pieced together.[9] CA is complete except for a crevice at the top base, while CB has a more substantial lacuna. The Louvre possesses twelve additional cylinder fragments from Tello, some of which can be restored in the lacuna of CB.[10]

The inscribed text is arranged in columns parallel to the axis of the cylinder. CA contains thirty columns, CB twenty-four. All columns, except for the last one, extend over the entire height of the cylinder. Each column is divided into cases, ranging from sixteen to thirty-five per column. Each case contains from one to six lines of signs which are generally transliterated as one line of text. While some cases correspond to an average line in the Sumerian scribal tradition, most are shorter.[11] Together, the two cylinders contain approximately one thousand three hundred and sixty-three cases, which makes them one of the longest Sumerian literary compositions. The direction of the text indicates that the normal position of the cylinders was horizontal.[12]

The paleography, ductus, and sign forms of the Cylinder Inscriptions correspond to those of the Lagaš II inscriptions written on clay objects. In the development of cuneiform writing, they occupy a place between the Old Akkadian and Ur III inscriptions, though

---

[9] Since their find condition is not further documented, it remains unclear whether they were found cracked, or broke in the course of removing the plaster or during the transport to Paris.

[10] Possible restorations are discussed in chapter III.B.10.4.

[11] See also chapters III.D.3 and F.3, p. 157.

[12] Compare the direction of text on Gudea objects which are oriented in space as, for example, the statues. In the Louvre the Cylinders are displayed vertically in accordance with the modern direction of reading cuneiform. The latter conforms with the ancient writing after the 90° rotation of signs which did not take place before the early second millennium, as Picchioni *Or* 49 (1980) showed; for a different opinion cf. Edzard *RlA* 5 (1976–80), 546–548.

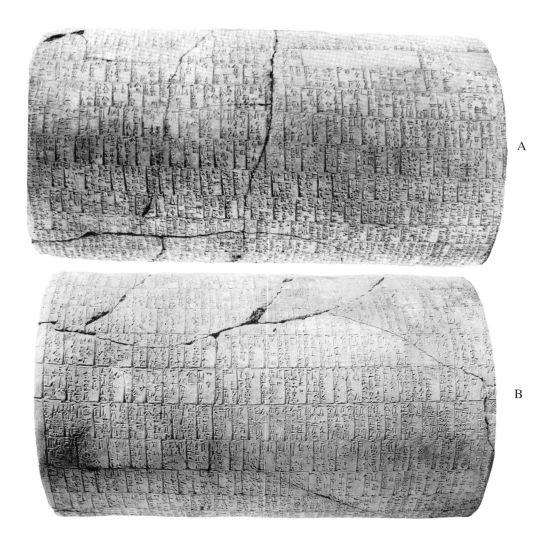

Fig. 14: Gudea Cylinders at scale 1:4.

they are closer to the latter.[13] The orthography is comparable to that of the Ur III inscriptions.[14] Slight differences in the shape of certain signs between CA and CB may indicate that they were written by different hands.[15]

3. Cylinders as Carriers of Text

Clay cylinders, though less common than clay tablets, are not exceptional as carriers of text in ancient Mesopotamia.[16] The oldest known cylinders date to the Akkadian period and bear literary texts of a mythic nature.[17] A cylinder fragment attributable to the Ur III dynast Urnamma was found in the Inanna temple in Nippur; it contains a narrative royal inscription which mentions military campaigns.[18] Until late Old Babylonian times cylinders continued to be used for literary and lexical texts.[19] The same text types are more often written on clay tablets or prisms, which differ from the cylinders only in cross-section. Since an average tablet has less writing surface than an average cylinder or prism, one reason for the use of the latter may have been merely a question of size. Converting the text inscribed on CA to a square surface inscribed on both sides would result in a gigantic tablet measuring fifty-five by fifty-five centimeters.

Gudea's cylinders are most akin to the Urnamma fragment, which apparently commemorates royal deeds and was also found in a temple. They are, however, considerably bigger than the latter[20] or any other Mesopotamian cylinder. It has been suggested that they were mounted on wooden axles introduced through their perforations for rotation.[21]

---

[13] Note, for example, the KU$_4$ sign discussed by Watson *Catalogue Birmingham*, 79–85.

[14] See Falkenstein *Grammatik* II, §§ 2 and 6. Although the orthography is quite homogenous throughout the text, there are some inconsistencies. If we had several copies of the text, it seems likely that they would exhibit the orthographic variants typical of Sumerian compositions preserved in several copies.

[15] E, for example, looks like UD-*gunû* in CB. Moreover, CB exhibits more sign omissions and other orthographic irregularities than CA.

[16] A comprehensive study which establishes a valid typology of written documents in terms of their shape and function is needed. Cuneiformists rarely pay attention to the carriers of their texts, and their terminology for geometrical forms such as cylinders, prisms, or cones is often incompatible with actual geometry. Shape and function of such objects have been discussed by Ellis *Foundation Deposits*, 108–125; the Presargonic clay cones also by Cooper *RA* 79 (1985). The terminology for cylinders and prisms proposed by Ellis op. cit., 108f., however, uses shape designations in a typology based on the orientation of writing, and, thus, confuses the issue of a clear classification.

[17] For example, the "Barton Cylinder" edited by Alster and Westenholz in *ASJ* 16 (1994), and the one from Adab published in OIP 14 no. 53.

[18] Civil *Or* 54 (1985). If Cooper's speculation that three slightly curved inscribed clay fragments from Lagaš belonged to cylinders rather than cones or vessels in *RA* 79 (1985), 99 (referring to table 1 nos. 13, 14, and 21) is correct, cylinders were used for the commemoration of royal deeds already in Presargonic times.

[19] For a lexical example, see the cylinder from Abu Harmal cited in Ellis *Foundation Deposits*, 113. The so-called barrel cylinders, attested from Samsu-Iluna to Seleucus II (ibidem, 114) are excluded from the discussion here, since they are not geometric cylinders and have the text oriented perpendicular to the axis rather than parallel. Moreover they had a clearly definable function almost certainly different from real cylinders: they were inserted in the walls of buildings the construction of which they commemorate, and are thus comparable to other commemorative building records.

[20] Civil *Or* 54 (1985), 27, calculated its original diameter at 10.6 cm, i.e. one third of that of Gudea's cylinders.

[21] Price *Cylinder Inscriptions*, v, suggested that they were rotated for reading, while Ellis *Foundation Deposits*, 114 note 3, considered the rotating more suitable for writing.

Such a mounting has been proposed for other perforated cylinders.[22] Gudea's cylinders, however, were filled with plaster, and their perforations were closed with plugs. Since they are unusually large, they are likely to have been filled after firing to reinforce their stability.[23] The plugs could then have served as handles in some sort of mounting device not unlike the alleged stick. Considering their impressive appearance, one is tempted to imagine them on display in the temple.[24]

4. The Subscripts

The Cylinder Inscriptions present the longest and most detailed Mesopotamian temple building account in the form of past tense narration by a third person. The composition has two parts, each inscribed on one cylinder: CA contains the events culminating in the construction of Eninnu, CB its inauguration. Each part concludes with a subscript consisting of a doxology and a colophon. The term doxology, borrowed from Christian hymnology, designates a liturgical expression of praise. A large number of Sumerian literary compositions of various contents conclude with an expression consisting of the term "praise" (zà-mí) combined with a name, usually that of the central figure – most frequently a deity – or central object of the composition, which may be expanded in different ways.[25] The doxologies of the Cylinder Inscriptions (CA 30:14 = CB 24:15) extol Ningirsu (ᵈnin-gír-sú zà-mí), and include an acclamation of his temple Eninnu with more emphasis on its physical appearance in CA (30:6–13), and on its fame in CB (24:9–14).

Colophons are scribal notations at the end of the main text and are physically set apart from it. They identify the composition, and may contain other information relevant to scribes.[26] The colophons of the Cylinder Inscriptions are anticipatory genitive constructions which differ only in the last term:

CA 30:15f: é-ᵈnin-gír-sú-ka dù-a zà-mí mu-ru-bi-im
CB 24:16f: é-ᵈnin-gír-sú-ka dù-a zà-mí egir-bi

Both refer to the composition as the "Praise of the Built House of Ningirsu." Colophons and literary catalogues usually designate the works by their incipit, although thematic titles, like the one in the cylinders, also occur.[27] CA is then identified as "its middle"

---

[22] See Cooper *RA* 79 (1985), 108 note 11.

[23] Ellis *Foundation Deposits*, 109, observed that cylinders and prisms can be wheel made and that their being hollow or solid is partly a matter of size. Considering that perforated objects are easier to fire than solid ones, the perforations of Gudea's cylinders could simply be a by-product of their fabrication, though their horizontal orientation speaks in favor of a mounting.

[24] According to Edzard *RlA* 5 (1976–80), 567, cones and cylinders were made for public display. Although the idea is attractive, there is to my knowledge no evidence to confirm it; see also chapter III.F.3, p. 157.

[25] See Wilcke *AS* 20 (1976), 246–248, and Black "Structural Features," 74f. For a list of known compositions ending in a doxology see Edzard *RlA* 7 (1987), 36–48 s.v. Literatur.

[26] Hunger *RlA* 6 (1980–83), 186f. s.v. Kolophon with further literature.

[27] For example, the doxology of *Enki's Journey to Eridu* 123–129, as noted by Hurowitz *Temple Building*, 35 note 3.

(mu-ru-bi-im), CB as "its continuation" (egir-bi).[28] This reference to the parts of a literary composition is unparalleled. Whether the terms are to be analyzed as nouns or as adjectives modifying zà-mí remains ambiguous. Nouns could designate the middle and end of a bi-partite composition, while adjectives could imply a tri-partite composition. Some scholars have assumed a now lost first part.[29] A comparison with other ancient Near Eastern building accounts, however, suggests that no integral part of the narrative is missing,[30] and the subject matter of such a first part remains mere speculation.[31] Moreover, the beginning of CA is reminiscent of opening passages of other literary compositions,[32] and therefore is more than likely to be the very beginning of the composition. The cylinder fragments from Tello, which do not fit either cylinder, cannot be taken as evidence for a now lost part, since there is no reason to assume that they belonged to the same composition.[33] Thus the unusual colophons are best interpreted as "middle" and "continuation," respectively, "of the praise of the built house of Ningirsu,"[34] and their uniqueness is explained by the unusual circumstance that one composition did not fit on a single cylinder because of its extraordinary length.[35]

5. Previous Studies

The Cylinder Inscriptions were first published in de Sarzec's excavation report in the form of high quality heliographs which show all segments of both cylinders.[36] These reproductions remain the best to this day. Since then, the text has been repeatedly copied, transliterated, and translated into various modern languages. In 1905 Thureau-Dangin offered a transliteration and the first, still insightful translation.[37] Twenty years later he published the now standard copy of the cuneiform text in which he included the additional cylinder fragments known to him.[38] Only a few years later, the American scholar Price published a comprehensive edition of the Cylinder Inscriptions including a copy, a transliteration, and an English translation of the text, as well as philological notes, a glossary, and a sign list.[39] This edition has been outdated by more recent studies, though the glossary and sign list are the only ones available. Witzel's annotated German

---

[28] Egir has two basic meanings: it can designate the "back" in contrast to a "front" (for example, in CB 2:9f.), or posteriority, i.e. continuation, in a sequence. The latter seems more suitable in this case.

[29] Kramer *Sacred Marriage*, 141f.; van Dijk *Lugal* I, 11 note 25; Jacobsen *Harps*, 386; and Hurowitz *Temple Building*, 33–38.

[30] Also Hurowitz *Temple Construction*, 34.

[31] For conceivable but not very likely subject matters see Hurowitz *Temple Construction*, 35–38.

[32] See Black "Structural Features," 73f. with appendix B.

[33] There may have existed similar compositions for other temples Gudea claims to have built, not unlike the stelae and statues made for different temples.

[34] See also Falkenstein *Grammatik* II, 14 § 85, *Einleitung*, 178f., and Thomsen *Sumerian Language*, 276.

[35] The identical designation of the composition in both colophons leaves no doubt that the two parts were conceived as one work, not two separable compositions, as suggested by Averbeck *Ritual and Structure*, 262.

[36] DC pls. 33–36. Single view photos are reproduced in Kramer *Sacred Marriage*, 24f., and one of CB in Tallon *Asian Art* 5 (1992), 35.

[37] SAKI 88–141. This corpus of Sumerian and Akkadian royal inscriptions, originally published in French, was translated into German two years later. Since the German edition (SAKI) is more widely available than the French, the former has been used here.

[38] TCL 8. This copy replaced an earlier one prepared by Toscanne (*Cylindres de Gudea*) in 1901.

[39] *Cylinder Inscriptions*.

Table III.A.1: Comparison of Previous Outlines

Falkenstein	Averbeck	Hurowitz	Klein
Introduction CA 1:1–9	First Dream CA 1:1–7:8	Divine Decision (CA 1:1–21)	Commissioning CA 1:1–12:20
Commission CA 1:10–7:8		Clarification (CA 1:22–12:12)	
Preparations 1 CA 7:9–12:20	Second Dream CA 7:9–12:19		
Preparations 2 CA 12:21–17:1?	Construction CA 12:20–25:21	Preparations (CA 12:13–20:12)	Preparations & Construction CA 12:21–29:12
Construction CA 17:2?–29:12	Outfitting CA 25:22–30:16	Construction (CA 20:13–30:14)	
Praise CA 29:13–30:14			Praise CA 29:13–30:14
Praise CB 1:1–11	Preparations CB 1:1–2:6	Gods assemble	Dedication CB 1:1–20:12
Preparations CB 1:12–4:24	Induction CB 2:7–13:10	Induction	
Induction CB 5:1–6:10			
Equipment CB 6:11–17:16	Celebrations CB 13:11–24:17	Gifts	
Celebrations CB 17:17–24:8		Destinies	Blessings CB 20:13–24:8
Praise CB 24:9–15			

translation of CA in 1922, followed by a copy of the cuneiform in 1932, and Barton's English translation of 1929, are out of date, too.[40] The annotated French translation by Lambert and Tournay of 1948 still offers several original suggestions.[41]

A milestone in the philological understanding of the text was Falkenstein's publication of a detailed grammar of all Gudea inscriptions, followed by an introduction containing comprehensive overviews of the history, pantheon, and cult topography of Lagaš in his time as well as a classification of the inscriptions.[42] Falkenstein translated the Cylinder Inscriptions for a German anthology of Sumerian and Akkadian hymns and prayers.[43] He was working on a new scholarly edition which remained unfinished when he died in 1966. In 1971 Baer published a hitherto unknown cylinder fragment in the Louvre, and, for the first time, discussed the relation of the now twelve additional fragments to the

---

[40] Barton *Royal Inscriptions*; Witzel *Keilschriftliche Studien* 3 (1922), and *Gudea Inscriptiones*.
[41] *RB* 55 (1948).
[42] *Grammatik*, and *Einleitung*.
[43] SAHG 138–182.

Cylinder Inscriptions.[44] He showed that some fragments cannot be part of either cylinder for physical reasons, and proposed to restore others in the lacuna in CB. His restoration proposal, used only in part by later translators, remains tentative due to the lack of clear physical joins.[45] Four new translations have appeared since then,[46] though none includes a substantial commentary. Most notable among them is Jacobsen's English translation from 1987, which offers many inspiring new vistas.[47] Those of Castellino, Averbeck, and Wilson do not represent a significant progress in the understanding of the text.[48] Since its first publication, selected passages and single lines have been quoted and discussed in various studies.[49]

Several scholars have offered outlines of the text.[50] The differences among them are a question of labels rather than of the understanding of the contents.[51] To illustrate this point, four recent outlines are compared in Table III.A.1.[52] Their division of the text reflects approaches differing in emphasis. Falkenstein's is based on the development of the plot as well as formal characteristics, Averbeck's solely, and in my mind inappropriately, on one recurrent statement.[53] Hurowitz and Klein approached the text in comparsion with ancient Near Eastern building accounts and Sumerian "building and dedication hymns," respectively.

While there is consensus on a rudimentary understanding of the text, many details remain problematic. The difficulties are not so much specific to this text, but rather are common to the study of Sumerian texts, or ancient texts on the whole. Culture-specific knowledge assumed by the ancient source often escapes the modern reader.[54] Our understanding of Sumerian grammar and lexicon is still limited.[55] The present translations of the cylinders often diverge in their analysis of verbal phrases as well as the syntactic relationship of

---

[44] *RA* 65 (1971).

[45] Possible restorations are discussed in chapter III.B.10.4.

[46] Edzard's translation in *RIME* 3/1 appeared after this manuscript was completed. [See my review in JCS 50 (1998).]

[47] *Harps*, 386–444. Jacobsen was preparing a commentary to his translation when he died in 1992. Inquiries about the manuscript have revealed that it had been sent to California for posthumous publication, but was stolen by a student who disappeared thereafter.

[48] Castellino *Testi*, 215–264; Averbeck *Ritual and Structure*, 589–712; Wilson *Cylinders of Gudea*.

[49] For example: Gudea's dreams by Oppenheim *Dreams*, 211f., 224; the brick making by Heimpel *JNES* 46 (1987); Ningirsu's trophies by Cooper *Return of Ninurta*, 141–154, and van Dijk *Lugal* I, 10–16; metaphoric descriptions of Eninnu by Edzard "Skyscrapers and Bricks." For grammatical analyses see Falkenstein *Grammatik*; Thomsen *Sumerian Language*; and Attinger *Eléments*. An index of the lines quoted in Falkenstein's grammar was provided by Edzard et al. *Ergänzungsheft*.

[50] Price *Cylinder Inscriptions*, xiiif., Falkenstein *Einleitung*, 179–181; Castellino *Testi*, 216f; Averbeck *Ritual and Structure*, 335–352; Klein *ASJ* 11 (1989), 63; Hurowitz *Temple Building*, 50–57.

[51] Summaries of the contents were given by Kramer *Sacred Marriage*, 137–140, and *Temple*, 2–7; Falkenstein *Einleitung*, 118–120; Jacobsen *Harps*, 386f.; and Hurowitz *Temple Building*, 38–46.

[52] For lack of space I have simplified the titles given by the authors and limited the detailed outlines of Falkenstein and Averbeck to their main sections.

[53] Averbeck's contention that the linear outline of the text hinges on this formula (*Ritual and Structure*, 264–266) is supported neither by its contents, a very general assertion of Gudea's competence, nor by its occurrence in other texts. In the cylinders and other texts it occurs either once or several times at irregular intervals and functions at best as a pause between events, see chapter III.D.2.c with note 286.

[54] On this problem see Civil "Limites," 225–232, esp. 226f.

[55] A state of the art including summaries and discussions of problems was presented by Thomsen *Sumerian Language*.

arguments within a sentence. Whether a dative infix refers to Gudea or Ningirsu, for instance, can make a significant difference in the interpretation of a passage. In regard to the lexicon, rare technical terms relating to the process of the temple construction require more study. These difficulties, together with the extraordinary length of the text, may explain the lack of an up-to-date edition, and, in part, may account for the absence of proficient analyses of its narrative and poetic structure.[56]

In the following I will first discuss the contents of the Cylinder Inscriptions in linear sequence, and give the reasons for my understanding of the text (chapter III.B). The next chapter (III.C) scrutinizes its narrative components (event participants, place, time), and analyzes the structure of the narrative from a multidimensional perspective. I will then discuss in selected examples poetic features and devices that the text employs (chapter III.D). The recognition of poetic traits elaborates on the nature of the composition and on its representation of events. The following chapter compares the contents of the Cylinder Inscriptions with that of Gudea's other inscriptions (chapter III.E). It expounds on the issue of core and expansion in the recording of the same or similar events, and elucidates some mechanisms underlying the composition of all these texts. In the final chapter of this part (chapter III.F), I will address the message of the Cylinder Inscriptions, and examine the source and possible receivers as well as the circumstances of transmission. Before turning to the detailed description of the contents, a synoptic outline is given below.

6.   *Outline of the Text*

PART I: THE CONSTRUCTION

	1. The Project
CA 1:1–9	1.1. Predestination
CA 1:10–16	1.2. Preview
CA 1:17–21	1.3. Commission

	2. Verification of the Revelation
CA 1:22–2:3	2.1. Gudea's Immediate Reaction
	2.2. Visit to Lagaš
CA 2:4–6	2.2.1. Journey
CA 2:7–22	2.2.2. Prayer to Ningirsu
CA 2:23	2.2.3. Ešeš-festival
CA 2:24-4:2	2.2.4. Prayer to Gatumdug
	2.3. Visit to Ningin
CA 4:3–4	2.3.1. Journey
CA 4:5–5:10	2.3.2. Prayer to Nanše

---

[56] The "ritual structure" has been studied by Averbeck *Ritual and Structure*. His definition of ritual extends to many episodes which I would simply interpret as narrative events of the story, while his "structural analysis" does not proceed beyond a very detailed description of the linear sequence of the text.

PART II: THE INAUGURATION

B.   The Text in Linear Sequence

1.   The Project (CA 1:1–21, see Appendix C.1)

The first section lays out the initial circumstances of Gudea's construction of Eninnu. It is established that the project is predestined (1.1), its realization is previewed (1.2), and finally it is launched (1.3). Grammatically the first sub-section is dominated by affirmatives (with na prefix), the second by *marû*-forms, and the third by *ḫamṭu*-forms.

1.1: Predestination (CA 1:1–9)
The story begins with the determination of destinies (CA 1:1). From the all encompassing universe the narrator moves to the place of the story, the city-state Lagaš, which is being allotted its share of cultural institutions (me) (CA 1:2).[57] Enlil, the ultimate authority concerning destinies, approves of Ningirsu, the divine patron of Lagaš (CA 1:3).[58] As a result, an "everlasting thing," an allusion to Eninnu, is announced (CA 1:4).[59] Enlil's favorable disposition is further described in a metaphor equating his satisfaction (overflowing heart) with the riverine flood (CA 1:5–9).

1.2: Preview (CA 1:10–16)
The focus shifts to Ningirsu who is responsible for the fulfillment of the mes of his predestined house, Eninnu, which is named here for the first time (CA 1:10–11). The mes of Eninnu must be included in those allotted to Lagaš. Next the ruler is introduced as the human agent willing and capable of carrying out the project (CA 1:12–16). While the predicted action of the owner of the house (CA 1:11) anticipates the effect of the construction, those of the ruler (CA 1:13–16) anticipate its accomplishment.[60]

This section may be understood as a speech of Ningirsu in which he promotes the ruler as agent for the project in the divine assembly.[61] It would be perceived from the perspective of Ningirsu, in contrast to the previous one perceived from that of Enlil. The

---

[57] For the Sumerian term me, left untranslated in Appendix C due to the lack of an English term encompassing its complex concept, see Farber *RlA* 7 (1987–90), 610–613 s. v. me with previous literature. *Keš Hymn* 1–9 implies that Enlil allotted destinies concerning me to all Sumerian city-states at the beginning of time; our story seems to allude to this event.

[58] Enlil's approval of Ningirsu is expressed with the same compound verb (igi zi – bar) which is used in royal epithets to express the divine approval of a ruler. It may denote a general approval of the patron of Lagaš. More likely this line implies Enlil's approval of the project alluded to in the following verse, since Enlil's role to give or deny permission for a temple construction is a well known topos; see Cooper *Curse of Agade*, 240 commentary to line 57.

[59] Compare the concluding statement CB 17:12–14: níg-ul uru-na-ke₄ pa bí-è gù-dé-a é-50 mu-dù me-bi šu bí-du₇ "The everlasting thing of his city appeared. Gudea built Eninnu. Its mes were perfected." Like in this summary statement, the clause "to have the everlasting thing appear" often precedes the construction predicate in Gudea's building inscriptions; see chapter II.B.2.c § 3.a. The "everlasting thing" appears also in the context of the making of the bricks (CA 18:25), the basic element of the construction.

[60] Lines CA 1:10–11 are parallel to the remainder of this sub-section in that each passage introduces the respective agent in the first verse by title (master/ruler), who then is predicted to perform one or a series of analogous action(s) in the future. If the restoration in CB 23:8′, however, is correct (see 10.4 below), line 1:11 may refer to Enlil rather than to Ningirsu.

[61] So the translations Lambert and Tournay *RB* 55 (1948), 408; Falkenstein SAHG, 138; Averbeck *Ritual and Structure*, 593f.; and Edzard "Skyscrapers and Bricks," 18.

speech would then form a frame with Ningirsu's speech during the inauguration banquet in which he promotes Eninnu and its builder for divine blessings (section 10.4.2).

1.3: Commission (CA 1:17–21)

The agent of the project – the ruler of Lagaš – is finally identified by name. Gudea receives the commission to build Eninnu from Ningirsu through a dream. The chain of authority from Enlil to city god to ruler reflects the cosmic hierarchy, well attested in other compositions. If we look at the second sub-section from Ningirsu's perspective, the narration moves from the highest level of divine authority (Enlil) in the first sub-section (1.1), to the level of local divine authority (Ningirsu) in the second (1.2), to the level of human authority (Gudea) in the third (1.3). The focus has shifted to the human protagonist.

2. *Verification of the Revelation (CA 1:22–7:8)*

In response to his dream, Gudea sets out to verify it. For this purpose he travels to the divine dream-interpreter Nanše, who resides in Ningin. The journey involves a stopover at Bagara, Ningirsu's temple in the city Lagaš. The verification of the revelation thus takes place in the three major cities of Lagaš and involves Gudea's interaction with Lagašite deities. Three sub-sections are generated by the change of place from Girsu (2.1) to Lagaš (2.2) to Ningin (2.3). The second and third sub-sections can be further subdivided on the basis of formulaic repetition patterns and narration-speech alternation.

2.1: Gudea's Immediate Reaction (CA 1:22–2:3)

Gudea's immediate reaction to the obviously unexpected revelation[62] is expressed in an inner monologue,[63] in which he decides to bring the dream to Nanše so that she may reveal its "heart" (CA 2:3 = 3:28) which he does not know (CA 1:27). Gudea's incentive for a dream interpretation is not his lack of understanding the message – he promises Ningirsu that he will build his house, before he gets to Nanše (CA 2:14) – but his need to dispel the enigma inherent in every divine communication by separating the message from the medium of its transmission.[64] Thus the "heart" here refers to the authenticity of the revelation, rather than the meaning or contents of the dream message.

2.2: Visit to Lagaš (CA 2:4–4:2)

A brief account of the first part of the journey follows (2.2.1). At Bagara, Gudea addresses first Ningirsu, then Gatumdug in prayer, enlisting their support for a successful journey. The prayers are rendered in direct speech. The speeches are framed by a formulaic introduction and response. These two parallel prayer blocks (2.2.2 and 2.2.4) are separated by the celebration of the Ešeš-festival, which is summarized in one sentence (2.2.3).[65]

---

[62] The dream is referred to as maš-gi₆ (CA 1:27) as well as ma-mu (CA 1:29). The latter term is a general term for dream, the former seems to connote unexpected revelation, see Oppenheim *Dreams*, 225f.

[63] On inner monologue in Sumerian literature see Edzard *HSS* 37 (1993).

[64] See Oppenheim *Dreams*, 219.

[65] The term èš-èš usually designates the moon holidays (the four quarters of the moon in the lunar calendar), though in Girsu the same term is also used for other holidays; see Sallaberger *Kultischer Kalender*, 38–41 and

The prayer introductions consist of a clause indicating the location (CA 2:7 and 24), two parallel clauses relating to the offering of bread and water (CA 2:8 and 25), and two parallel clauses introducing the speech (CA 2:9 and 26).[66] The prayers contain an address, a message, and a petition, all of which are interrelated.[67] In the first prayer Gudea addresses Ningirsu's relation with Eridu, the seat of the primeval temple, and Nippur, the traditional cult center of Sumer (CA 2:10–12). He assures him that he will build his house (CA 2:13–15), and pleads for the support of his sister Nanše (CA 2:16–19).

In the prayer to Gatumdug, the petition is developed step by step moving from general to specific. The introductory address underlines Gatumdug's power as daughter of An, her independence, and her main function as birth goddess (CA 2:28–3:2). Then Gudea addresses her as the founder of Lagaš, as a source of life, and links her to himself as his parent (CA 3:3–9). Next he addresses her as his protector, and pleads for her protection (CA 3:10-17). Finally he specifies this last aspect, i.e. relates the purpose of his journey, and pleads for her protection during this journey (CA 3:18–28).

The last part of the prayer to Gatumdug repeats parts of Gudea's inner monologue. Thus both prayers conclude with the wish that Nanše might confirm the authenticity of the revelation (CA 2:19 and 3:28). A formulaic phrase stating that the prayer was heard and accepted by the deity (CA 2:20–22 and 3:29–4:2) succeeds each prayer. The audience now anticipates the continuation of the journey, and, in particular, the verification of the dream revelation.

2.3: Visit to Ningin (CA 4:3–7:8)

The second part of the journey (2.3.1) is narrated in the same way as the first (section 2.2.1). Again Gudea addresses the patron deity immediately upon arrival (2.3.2). The speech is preceded by a formulaic introduction analogous to the previous ones (CA 4:5–7). Gudea addresses Nanše in her capacity as fate determiner and diviner (CA 4:8–13), and proceeds to relate the contents of his dream which consisted of seven images (CA 4:14–5:10). The petition, namely that Nanše establish the authenticity of the revelation, is not stated, perhaps because it is implied in the message, or because the audience is already familiar with the purpose of Gudea's prayer to Nanše.

In response to his prayer, Nanše replies to Gudea in direct speech (CA 5:11). First she interprets his dream, identifying its images one by one (CA 5:12–6:13),[68] and thus dispelling the enigma of the divine communication. Then she instructs him to fashion

---

285. Although it is likely that Gudea's visit coincided with a regular holiday, it is not clear which particular holiday this Ešeš-festival refers to.

[66] The first element is phrased individually depending on the situation, the second identical, and the third analogous.

[67] The address characterizes the deity with epithets that praise those aspects of the deity which will enable him/her to grant the petition, while the message introduces the purpose of the petition. This structure is traditional in Mesopotamian prayers.

[68] Gudea saw Ningirsu commanding him to build his house; Ningišzida supporting him during the project; Nidaba consulting the stars for it; Nindub drafting the plan; the utensils for making the brickwork; chirping birds signifying his eagerness; and himself as a donkey pawing the ground, an allusion to the digging of the foundation.

and consecrate a chariot for Ningirsu so that the god will reveal the plan of his house (CA 6:14–7:8). The chariot was probably meant as a gift to ensure Ningirsu's continued favor, and may also have been needed for him to leave his temple during the construction. While Nanše's interpretation of the dream establishes the authenticity of the revelation, her instruction leads to the verification of the message – the commission to build Eninnu.

3. Verification of the Commission (CA 7:9–12:19)

The verification of the commission involves Gudea's communication with Ningirsu, which is sought by means of a dream incubation. This main event takes place in Girsu. Three sub-sections can be distinguished on the basis of the alternation of agents: Gudea (3.1), Ningirsu (3.2), Gudea (3.3). The entire section is set between two occurrences of a recurrent phrase stating Gudea's competence (CA 7:9f. and 12:20).[69]

3.1: Preparations for a Dream Incubation (CA 7:9–9:4)

The preparations include the fashioning and consecration of a chariot for Ningirsu (3.1.1), and a prayer to Ningirsu (3.1.3) preceded by food offerings (3.1.2). The first sub-section stands out as anticipated realization of a foregoing instruction, the second as narration of new information, and the third as a direct speech.

Gudea's realization of Nanše's instruction concerning the chariot for Ningirsu (see Appendix C.2) begins with a summary statement (CA 7:11–12) which is followed by a full account of the event, repeating all the prescriptions given as they are realized (CA 7:13–29). Then Gudea enters the temple himself (CA 7:30), seemingly at the end of the induction procession,[70] and exits again (CA 8:1). These actions link the chariot episode to the following event. The next statement (CA 8:2f.) may refer to Gudea's uninterrupted care for the project, or simply describe the passing of time. It is followed by an indication of night-time (CA 8:4f.),[71] when Gudea offers animals and incense at Šugalam (CA 8:6–12), one of the gates of Eninnu.[72]

The ensuing prayer takes place in the Ubšukkina (CA 8:14), an assembly hall within the temple where the gods are thought to determine destinies,[73] and thus alludes to the fate of Gudea's project. Both the preceding offerings and the prayer introduction formula (CA 8:13f.) are more elaborate than those of the previous prayers, and may have been the required ritual introduction for a dream incubation. If so, they would have prepared the audience for the upcoming communication between ruler and god. Gudea addresses Ningirsu as his master, relates him to Enlil (CA 8:15f.), and informs him that he will build his house, but lacks a sign (CA 8:18f.). The "young man with not (enough) acclaim" (šul ka-tar nu-tuk) in line CA 8:17 could be an apposition to Ningirsu in the address, or refer to Gudea who is the agent in the following line. In any case it indicates

---

[69] See chapter III.D.2.c.
[70] A procession is implied by the accompaniment of music (CA 7:24–25).
[71] The same statement recurs in CB 4:15–16 as part of a description of the night just before Ningirsu and Baba enter the new house.
[72] Falkenstein *Einleitung*, 140f. no. 49.
[73] Falkenstein *Einleitung*, 141 no. 12.

why Eninnu should be built: for the fame of its future inhabitant or builder, respectively. Gudea then states that he does not know the "heart" of the message (CA 8:20–22), which is now equated to the raging heart of Ningirsu himself (CA 8:23–9:3, see CA 4:21), and ends the speech with the question: "How am I able to know it?" (CA 9:4).

3.2: Ningirsu's Response (CA 9:5–12:11)

Ningirsu responds to Gudea by transmitting a message through a dream (3.2.1).[74] The dream message is related in the form of a direct speech. The speech begins with the affirmation that he, Ningirsu, is giving Gudea the sign to build his house and instructions concerning his cult (3.2.2), and ends with the words: "May you know my sign" (CA 12:11). This framing confirms that Ningirsu's message complies with Gudea's petition.

The core of the message consists of two parts (3.2.4 and 6), each preceded by a description of Eninnu (3.2.3 and 5). In the first part Ningirsu portrays himself, describing his functions as warrior of Enlil (CA 9:20–10:6), and išib of An (CA 10:7–13), and his roles in four temples in the city-state of Lagaš, namely Tiraš (CA 10:15–18), Ehuš (CA 10:19–23), Ebabbar (CA 10:24–26), and Ebagara (CA 10:27–29).[75] In the second part he foresees Gudea's construction of Eninnu.[76] This part consists of two analogous passages, each introduced with the same temporal clause (CA 11:6 = CA 11:19): "When you (Gudea) will act for it (Eninnu)."[77] In the first passage Ningirsu promises agricultural surplus as a general prerequisite for the project (CA 11:7–17), in the second he promises ideal working conditions and the provision of building materials (CA 11:20–12:9). The first promise is induced by his call for rain (CA 11:7), the second by his call upon the North Wind (CA 11:20–23).[78]

The speech ends with the frame theme of the sign (CA 12:11). The preceding sentence (CA 12:10), literally, "Then fire will touch your side" (u₄-bi-a á-zu izi bí-tag), can be understood as a manifestation of the sign,[79] or as an allusion to the cleaning of the construction site with fire, the first event related in the following section (4.1.1).[80] In the latter case, it would indicate to Gudea what to do next, as did Nanše's instruction for this section. Ningirsu's indications and promises regarding the project anticipate future events. Similar descriptions of Eninnu recur at various points throughout the text.[81] His two main functions will be considered by Gudea in the presentation of dedicatory gifts (section 9.1). Abundance is mentioned in conjunction with Gudea's accomplishment of

---

[74] For the idiom expressing this divine activity compare Eannatum 1 6:25–32, and Sin-Iddinam's prayer to Nininsina 20–22, see Hallo *AOAT* 25 (1976), 223, and Jacobsen ibidem, 253. For a visual representation of a dream incubation see Asher *CRRA* 33 (1987), 27–32.

[75] The first three temples were apparently situated in minor towns, see Falkenstein *Einleitung*, 169 no. 28, 167 no. 14, and 166 no. 8.

[76] The first clause of the second part starts, like the members of the preceding section, with the name of a temple, Eninnu, followed by a row of epithets (CA 11:1–4).

[77] The second time the phrase is preceded by a parallel temporal clause (CA 11:18).

[78] The call for rain and wind may imply a reference to spring rains and summer during which only wind from the north can ease the heat, respectively.

[79] So Landsberger *WO* 3 (1964), 72, and Civil "Epistolary of the Edubba."

[80] So Jacobsen *Harps*, 403 note 56.

[81] See chapter III.C.1.e.

the project.[82] The mention of foundation (CA 11:10) and perimeter (CA 11:18), and the promises concerning work force and building materials anticipate the upcoming events (sections 4–5).

3.3: Gudea's Immediate Reaction (CA 12:12–19)

Gudea's immediate reaction to Ningirsu's speech concludes the verification of the commission. Four incidents are related: Gudea wakes up remembering the dream (CA 12:12f.),[83] he heeds Ningirsu's words (CA 12:14f.; see CA 7:11f.), performs an extispicy successfully (CA 12:16f.), and Ningirsu's "heart" becomes clear to him (CA 12:18f.). The first confirms that Gudea received the dream, the second that he received its message, the third confirms the authenticity of the divine communication by another type of divination, and the last incident describes the result. Gudea is now ready to initiate the project.

4. *Construction Preparations (CA 12:20–20:12)*

Before starting the actual construction Gudea carries out a series of preparations. Each step concludes with the recurrent statement: "Joyfully he (Gudea) established it for him (Ningirsu)," which occurs only in this section and generates its sub-sections.[84] Girsu is at the center of all activity: the events either take place there, or are directed hither. The actors include Lagašites and foreigners on the human level, as well as deities from Lagaš, Sumer, and foreign lands.

4.1: Preparations in City (CA 12:20-14:6)

The first unit of actions takes place in Girsu. It includes the purification of the city (4.1.1) and construction site (4.1.3), between which the preparation of the brick mold and loam pit is interposed (4.1.2). The juxtaposition of information concerning purification activities and brick mold preparation in CA and some statue inscriptions confirms that they were conceived as one unit of preparations.[85]

Gudea's "purification" of the city (4.1.1) involves the suspension of all contentious legal activity, including a general amnesty, and the expulsion of certain "unclean" people. The entire passage is introduced with a summary statement that Gudea gave instructions, and the people were in agreement (CA 12:21–23). The suspension of legal activity consists of a passage detailing Gudea's instructions (CA 12:24–13:2), and one detailing

---

[82] CA 11:9 = CB 19:14. This repetition does not necessarily imply that Ningirsu's promise is fulfilled only at the very completion of the project, as Averbeck *Ritual and Structure* suggested. Abundance is not only a result of, but also a prerequisite for the project. For abundance mentioned in CA 11:8 and 11 see CB 5:18. Compare also CA 11:12–13 and CB 11:15–17.

[83] For the formalized phrasing of the waking from a dream see Oppenheim *Dreams*, 190f.; Falkenstein *CRRA* 14 (1966), 58 with note 9; and Alster *Dumuzi's Dream*, 88f. commentary to lines 17f.

[84] For this phrase see also chapter III.D.2.c. The transitions between the recruitment of the Lagašite districts (4.2) and the import of materials from foreign countries (4.3), and between the latter and the measuring out of the construction site (4.4) are lost in the break at the top base of CA affecting several cases at the beginning of columns 15–17. In both instances there is enough room to assume the concluding statement in the break. Since the three sections relate different events involving different geographical spheres, I have treated them as individual units.

[85] See Table III.E.2.

its effect, i.e. the people's obedience (CA 13:3–11). The expulsion of "unclean" people (CA 13:14f.), expressed in one sentence, is preceded by the general statement that Gudea "purified" the city (CA 13:12f.).[86]

Preparing the brick mold and loam pit (4.1.2) Gudea verifies the designed brick mold and the loam pit by extispicy, and marks or protects the place with a standard of Anzu.[87] Next he purifies and cleans a specific area in the city which must be the construction site (4.1.3). The event is first summarized (CA 13:24f.),[88] and then specified as the burning of a fire spiced with incense (CA 13:26–27), and accompanied by prayers (CA 13:28f.), in which the Anunna of Lagaš participate (CA 14:1–4).

4.2: Recruitment of Work Force (CA 14:7–15:3?, see Appendix C.3)

Like the previous section, the account of the recruitment of the Lagašite districts begins with a summary statement (CA 14:7): "At that time the ruler made a conscription in his country." The temporal adverb marks the beginning of a new section. The following two analogous sentences specify where the levy was imposed, i.e. in Ningirsu's Guedinna (CA 14:8–10) and Nanše's Gugišbarra (CA 14:11–13), presumably the estates of their temples.[89] The following passage describes the mobilization of three districts, and their parade led by standards (CA 14:14–27), according to the following scheme: X mobilized for him in DN's district;[90] Y, DN's standard, marched at its head. Element X seems to be the name or slogan characterizing the work teams[91] and may allude to the equipment of the districts. The districts are those of Ningirsu, Nanše, and Inanna.[92] Their emblems (Y) are Lugalkurdub, the sacred gull (u_5 ku), and the disc (aš-me).[93]

---

[86] Similar special conditions are described in Statue B 3:15–5:11, in which the expulsion of "unclean" people precedes the legal instructions, which shows that the two were conceived as parts of the same event. The purification statement (CA 13:12f.) occurs as the first construction preparation in Statue B 3:12 and E 2:21–22. The fact that the same statement occurs before the last detail of the people's obedience in CA, and precedes the brick mold preparation in the statue inscriptions, suggests that it summarizes the event of imposing special social conditions. If so the purification denotes an abstract ethical act, rather than a concrete action; see also chapter III.E.2.c. Its practical purpose may have been to gather as many men for the construction work as possible.

[87] See Heimpel *JNES* 46 (1987), 206 and 210, and compare the abbreviated version of this event related in some statue inscriptions, see Table III.E.2.

[88] Read: u_5 24 (iku)-šè uru mu-na-kù-ge, u_5 mu-na-sikil-e, "He purified an area of 24 iku in the city for him, cleaned the area for him." U_5 originally means high ground near river or canal banks, or even an island; see Civil *Farmer's Instructions*, 131f. The context here suggests that it refers to the ground of the construction site which stands out like a high ground. The ground need not be a mound, as suggested by Jacobsen *Harps*, 404 note 61. There is no mention of the digging of earth; rather it is cleaned by fire. Therefore I interpret u_5 as a surface and the measurements as an indication of area rather than volume. The extension of the area would be approximately 294 by 294 meters, a reasonable size for the construction site, and not far off from the dimensions proposed by Falkenstein for the extension of Eninnu, see chapter II.A.2.a, p. 34.

[89] Falkenstein *Einleitung*, 87 and 96f.

[90] It is not clear whether Gudea or the particular district is the agent of the sentence: in the first case the dative infix would refer to Ningirsu, in the second to Gudea. Since Ningirsu does not occur in this entire section, and because the pattern of Gudea giving an instruction which the people obey occurs elsewhere, the second possibility is preferred here.

[91] For similar slogans designating clans or districts in Africa see Vansina *Oral Tradition*, 145f.

[92] If the districts of Ningirsu and Nanše were identical with the aforementioned Guedinna and Gugišbarra, one wonders why Inanna's district was not mentioned there, too.

[93] For a discussion of these emblems in relation to the standard procession depicted on the stelae fragments see chapter IV.B.1.

The text continues with the phrase "to build Ningirsu's house" (CA 14:29), and, after five damaged cases (CA 15:1–5), resumes with the account of the import of building materials.[94] The phrase "to build Ningirsu's house" may have been part of a last statement concerning the recruitment followed by the recurrent statement concluding this event, or the very beginning of the account of the imports. The first reconstruction is preferable for two reasons: first, there is a change of topics involving a change of the place of action: the recruitment takes place in Lagaš, while the building materials are shipped from foreign countries; second, the phrase "to build Ningirsu's house" occurs two more times at the end of a passage: in the last statement concerning the purification of the construction site (CA 14:1–4), and in the summary statement concluding the first passage of imports (CA 15:6–10).

4.3: Provision of Materials (CA 15:4?–17:4?)

The section concerning the building materials[95] consists of five passages stylized by repetition patterns. The first four passages list the import of materials: tribute from the people of Elam, Susa, Magan, and Meluhha whom Gudea gathers in his city (CA 15:6–10); copper and wood shipments sent from Dilmun in cooperation with the local deities (CA 15:11–18); wood shipments from the cedar-, cypress-, and juniper-mountains (CA 15:19–16:2), and stone shipments from the Magda mountains (CA 16:3–12) which Gudea has accessed with Ningirsu's help;[96] and finally copper from Kimaš (CA 16:13–17), gold and silver from its mountains (CA 16:18–21), carnelian from Meluhha (CA 16:22f.), and alabaster from its mountain (CA 16:24).

The fifth passage moves on to the processing of the materials. Gudea employs various artisans (CA 16:25–30). The following two lines describe their work in metaphors (CA 16:31–32). After six damaged cases (CA 17:1–6) the text resumes with a description of Gudea's zeal (CA 17:7–9). The description of the craftsmen's work probably continued, if only for a few more lines. The remains of an u_4 at the beginning of CA 17:5 may have been part of the adverbial expression "at that time" (u_4-ba) introducing a new line of thought (compare CA 14:7). It is tempting, therefore, to restore the recurrent concluding statement in the previous, entirely broken case (CA 17:4), and assume the beginning of a new sub-section in CA 17:5.[97]

---

[94] The remains in CA 15:4f. seem to belong to this passage.

[95] Since raw materials needed for a temple construction such as timber, stone, and metals are scarce or nonexistent in southern Mesopotamia, they have to be imported from foreign countries. The boast of receiving materials from all over the then known world is a topos common in royal inscriptions, and occurs also in Gudea's Statue B 5:21–6:76, and D 4:2–14, see chapter III.E.2.d.

[96] For a transliteration and translation of CA 15:19–16:12 see Appendix C.4, and for further discussion chapter V.C.1. The break at the beginning of column 16 can be restored on the basis of the parallelism of the two passages.

[97] Jacobsen's restoration in *Harps*, 409, does not comply with the remains of CA 17:5. His understanding of CA 17:6, on the other hand, provides an ingenious solution preferable to previous translations, which had to assume the unlikely writing gi_{25} for gi_6. His restoration can be modified by using a less space-consuming referent for the assumed agent (Ningirsu) to fit in CA 17:5 after the adverbial expression, for example: "[At that] time [his master] did ..., he condensed for him the clouds." The first action (the preserved prefix mu presupposes a finite verb) would have been parallel to the second. If so, the introduction to section 4.4 takes up one of the promises Ningirsu made to Gudea in section 3.2.6.

90

4.4: Measuring Out of Construction Site (CA 17:5?–28)

The fourth preparation begins with a description of agent and object: Gudea's zeal for the project is evoked (CA 17:7–9), and his divine support for the upcoming event delineated, first in general (CA 17:10–14), and then in particular: "Nidaba opened the 'House of Wisdom' for him; Enki directed the plan of the house for him" (CA 17:15–17). Eninnu is described in terms of its future greatness (CA 17:18f.), and that of its future inhabitant (CA 17:20f.). The text then specifies that Gudea surveyed the construction site for Eninnu (CA 17:22–25),[98] and personally marked its perimeter with a rope fastened around pegs at its edges (CA 17:26f.).[99]

4.5: Fabrication of Bricks (CA 17:29–20:4)

Next Gudea makes one brick symbolizing the entire process of the fabrication of the bricks.[100] In preparation for this event he soothes Ningirsu's heart in the "old house" (CA 17:29–18:2), takes a (ritual?) bath the following morning (CA 18:3f.), and offers animals and prayers in Urukug at noon (CA 18:5–9). With basket and brick mold, he proceeds to the place where the bricks are made, escorted by Lugalkurdub, Igalim, and Ningišzida (CA 18:10–16).

First he wets the frame of the brick mold (CA 18:17), and drums are played (CA 18:18).[101] Then he mixes clay of the loam pit with honey, butter, oil and various aromatic essences in a basket, and fills the brick mold (CA 18:19–24). The accomplishment of this first step is described as the "appearing of the everlasting thing" (CA 18:25),[102] and the people sprinkle oil and cedar essence and rejoice with the ruler (CA 18:26–19:2).

Next Gudea removes the brick from the mold and sets it down to dry (CA 19:3). While the brick is drying (CA 19:8–9), he prepares the clay mixture for the remaining bricks (CA 19:4–7), and Enki determines its fate (CA 19:10f.). The following verse (CA 19:12) is damaged. When the text resumes, Gudea raises the brick and publicly displays it (CA 19:13–15), which is further described in two metaphors (CA 19:16–18). He brings it

---

[98] The compound verb u₅ – dug₄ in CA 17:24f. is unusual. Sjöberg apud Averbeck *Ritual and Structure*, 650 note 300, suggested to equate it with u₆ – dug₄ "to admire," and translate it here with "to inspect." Attinger *Éléments*, § 897, listed it under the verb ù-u₈(-a), u₂₋₅/₈(-a), ù-wa-wa, GIŠGAL (u₁₈/ùlu) du₁₁/e/di "to lament," but noted also its similarity with *Lugal* 289f. listed under u₆ – du₁₁ (see his footnotes 2144 and 2178); see also Jacobsen "Asakku," 229 note 11. A connection between u₅ here and u₅ referring to the construction site in the account of its purification (CA 13:24–25), as noted by Averbeck, op. cit., seems likely, and may explain the unusual compound, which I would tentatively translate "to survey an area" in accordance with the context.

[99] The expression gána éš–gar (CA 17:26) usually refers to the annual survey or subdivision of agricultural fields in the first month of the year (see Cohen *Cultic Calendars*, 201f.); in this context the expression á giš – gar (CA 17:27a) can then mean "to assign tasks" to the workmen who work a particular field. Gudea's measuring activity could thus refer to the measuring out of the fields of Eninnu's estate. Since the estate does not play any role during the construction, I prefer to understand this section as the measuring out of the construction site, and interpret á-ba giš bí-gar as "he drove in pegs at its edges. Ní-te-ni mu-zu (CA 17:27b), literally "he knew/learned it himself," seems to indicate that Gudea directed the aforementioned action personally.

[100] This section has been discussed in detail by Heimpel *JNES* 46 (1987), 206–211, and Edzard "Skyscrapers and Bricks," 18–20. For the well known topos of the fabrication of the first brick, compare also *Nippur Lament* line 3, and Ellis *Foundation Deposits*, 26–29.

[101] Jacobsen *Harps*, 410, understood the playing of drums as a metaphor for the pouring of water.

[102] See chapter III.B.1.1 with note 59 above.

to the construction site (CA 19:19), and reviews the layout of the building (CA 19:20), which is compared to Nidaba's calculations (CA 19:21). The following description of Gudea's zeal (CA 19:22–27) may concern the layout or the project in general.

The section concludes with three statements about the present state of the project (CA 19:28–20:3), followed by the recurrent concluding statement (CA 20:4). The first statement reiterates that Ningirsu's "heart" has become clear to Gudea (CA 19:28; see CA 12:18f.). The second, which mentions Ningirsu's word (CA 20:1), seems to express that Gudea obeyed Ningirsu's instruction and successfully accomplished the preparations for the project. And the third alludes to an auspicious oracle (CA 20:2–3), which may refer to Gudea's verification of the incubation dream (section 3.3), or more likely anticipate the upcoming verification of the preparations, and in particular the third dream message.

4.6: Verification (CA 20:5–12)
In the last sub-section ending with the recurrent conclusion (CA 20:12), the preliminary preparations are verified by three types of divination: first an extispicy (CA 20:5), then a method involving barley and water (CA 20:6),[103] and finally a dream incubation performed by a professional (CA 20:7–11).[104] The results of the first two are positive, and the dream envisions the completion of the building. Gudea is ready for the actual construction.

5.   The Construction (CA 20:13–30:14)

The scene is the construction site in Girsu. The actors are Gudea and anonymous construction workers on the human level, and Lagašite deities on the divine. Passages in which Gudea figures as the only agent (5.2, 5.4, 5.6) alternate with passages in which he is assisted by human workers or deities (5.1, 5.3, 5.5, 5.7). The former each relate a specific event, and are structured by similar repetition patterns, while the latter are for the most part descriptive.

5.1: Divine Collaboration (CA 20:13–23)
The construction account begins with divine collaboration. Preparations already undertaken by Gudea are repeated in the divine realm, namely by Enki, Nanše, Gatumdug, and Baba (CA 20:15–20). This passage is framed by statements concerning cult personnel (CA 20:14 and 20:21),[105] which are in turn framed by the mention of me (CA 20:13 and

---

[103] Although this method is to my knowledge not attested in other cuneiform texts, the context leaves no doubt that it was a type of divination. The sprinkling of barley grains together with the rite of hand-washing and prayers are the preparations for a bull sacrifice in the Odyssey III 440-460.

[104] Falkenstein *CRRA* 14 (1966), 55f.

[105] The priests mentioned are usga in CA 20:14, and en and lagar in CA 20:21. The usga (who occur in the same function also in CA 28:9) are a type of lustration priests, see Michalowski *Lamentation*, 104f. commentary to line 447. En is one of the highest priestly offices serving one deity, and in charge of the temple estate, see Renger *ZA* 58 (1967), 114–34. If male, the en usually serves a goddess, if female a god. Since lagar and en appear side by side in literary as well as administrative texts from the Akkadian through Old Babylonian times (see Goodnick Westenholz *CRRA* 35 (1992) 310), lagar may be an alternative writing for lukur (Civil personal communication), a priestess who had, like the en, a special relation with a deity of the opposite sex, see Renger, op. cit. 175f. In Girsu several lukur served Ningirsu, see section 8.2.12 below.

20:22).[106] The cult personnel assigned to the temple here may have been employed to take care of the cult during the upcoming construction. The section concludes with the admiration of the Anunna (CA 20:23).

5.2: The Foundation (CA 20:24–21:12, see Appendix C.5)

The construction starts with a description of the ruler well-known from visual representations that epitomize the builder:[107] "Gudea, the temple-builder, put the basket for the house (like) a pure crown on (his) head" (CA 20:24f.). Thus equipped he proceeds to lay the foundation (CA 20:26).[108] He then marks a square on it with a chalk line (CA 20:27).[109] This action is repeated six more times, each time followed by a different metaphor (CA 21:1–12). Thus Gudea delimits seven squares, probably the outline for the stepped platforms on which the temple was to be built.

5.3: Construction Begun (CA 21:13–22:23)

Three passages can be distinguished in this section, each concluding with a generic statement (CA 21:25, 22:9f., 22:22f.). First the gate frame (CA 21:13–16) and a wooden structure (CA 21:17f.) are set up; the following metaphors (CA 21:19–24) presumably refer to the raising of the walls along this structure. The mention of reed lattice (gi-guru$_5$), summit (sa-dú), and upper drains (ÉxU-an-na) in the next passage (CA 21:26–22:8) seems to imply the construction of the roof. The last passage concerns the temple's surroundings: Gudea marks the "perimeter of Abzu" (CA 22:11–13), presumably a pond, and the "outer perimeter" (CA 22:14–15),[110] presumably that of the temple area; he plants pillars and trees (CA 22:16–19),[111] and installs Ningirsu's weapon Šarur (CA 22:20f.).[112]

5.4: The Stelae (CA 22:24–24:7, see Appendix C.6)

The fourth sub-section relates how Gudea made and consecrated several stelae. The stone slabs were imported and carved in one year and then installed in seven days around the temple (CA 22:24–23:4). The stones' sides, which he laid down as stairs and fashioned into basins (CA 23:5–7), may designate the sides of the slabs which remained

---

[106] Gudea seems to be the agent of these sentences, although he remains unnamed. If ba-ra in gu mu-ba-ra (CA 20:13a) stands for barà "to spread," which can be said of strings (gu), the action could refer to Gudea's marking the place for the walls with strings, and thus allude to the upcoming event described in the next section.

[107] See chapter II.C.1.b.

[108] I assume that the second action in this line (á-gar ki im-mi-tag) paraphrases the first (uš mu-gar), and read with Thureau-Dangin SAKI 110, and evidently also Jacobsen *Harps*, 413, á-gar for é-gar$_8$ "wall."

[109] For a detailed discussion of this line crucial for the meaning of the entire section see Suter *ZA* 87 (1997).

[110] The heroes surrounding the house and drinking water at the ki-a-nag must refer to the trophies of Ningirsu which are set up around the temple at the same places as the stelae surrounding the house (CA 23:4 and 29:1), and whose mouths are equally set to the ki-a-nag, see section 5.6.

[111] Jacobsen *Harps*, 416 note 113, followed by PSD A II 176 § 5, interpreted ábgal in CA 22:17 as "wizzard," and associated it with foundation figurines. This interpretation is not support by any corroborating evidence. In the third millenium, abgal is the name of a profession, while later it comes to designate sages and mythical figures used for apotropaic purposes; see Wiggermann *Protective Spirits*, 76f. What ábgal, interposed between pillars (dim) and poplars (^{giš}ásal), means, remains uncertain.

[112] For the Šarur see also chapter V.C.4.

after the stelae had been carved out, and which were then used for other stone items, i.e. stairs and a basin.[113]

The consecration of the stelae is stylized according to the following scheme: the stone that he erected in place X, he named Y (CA 23:8–24:7). The places of installment (X) seem to be outdoor places in the temple area of Eninnu.[114] The names (Y) given to them are reminiscent of royal epithets of the type which express divine approval of a ruler.[115] In the first five the deity named is Ningirsu and in the sixth it is Baba.[116]

5.5: Construction Continued (CA 24:8–25:21)

The construction account continues with a passage that describes Gudea's building activity using similes according to the following scheme: Gudea/He had (his master's/Ningirsu's) house/it(s X) do Y like Z (CA 24:8–25). A metaphoric description of the temple facade follows, moving from the overall aspect (CA 24:26–25:4)[117] to the gate and its parts (CA 25:5–13);[118] this passage is styled according to the scheme: its X is (like) Y. From the outside the narrator moves to the inside, and relates the construction (or installation) of the dining hall and sleeping quarters (CA 25:14–19). The concluding statement conveys the end of Gudea's construction: "He built it. After he finished working (lit. "took hands off"), the deities' hearts were satisfied" (CA 25:20f.).

5.6: The Trophies of Ningirsu (CA 25:22–26:19)

Next Gudea installs the trophies of Ningirsu.[119] The event is introduced with a recurrent phrase stating Gudea's competence (CA 25:22f.).[120] The account of the installation follows the scheme: at X he (Gudea) was installing Y (CA 25:24–26:14). One or two trophies (Y) are installed at each of seven different places (X), some of which coincide with those places where stelae were set up.[121] The section concludes with a summary statement concerning their function and name (CA 26:15–19).[122]

5.7: Construction Completed (CA 26:20–30:5)

A rather long sub-section describes in great detail the completed Eninnu inside and out. The description is interrupted twice by a pair of actions concerning finishing

---

[113] The same items recur next to the stelae in the description of the finished temple in CA 28:19 and 29:5, see chapter II.C.1.d.

[114] For further discussion see chapter IV.F.3.

[115] See chapter II.B.2.b § 2.b, and compare the names of the Gudea statues quoted in chapter III.E.2.f.

[116] One wonders why only six stelae are named here, since seven seem to be alluded to in CA 23:4, and are mentioned in CA 29:1f. One explanation might be that only six were actually made, but seven mentioned later because it is a magical number, but see also chapter III.F.3 p. 157 note 360.

[117] The four features of the facade described are dub-lá "gate-house" (also in CA 24:18, see Dunham *Foundations*, 432–450); giš gar-ra, literally "wooden parts" (Jacobsen *Harps*, 419, suggested "scaffolding"); suhur "tent" (see Civil *RA* 61 (1967)); and buru₆ (KID) mah "reed mat" (also in CA 21:16).

[118] The parts of the gate are ^{giš}ti "vault," literally "arrow"; giš-ká-an-na "gate frame" (also CA 21:13); and sig₇-igi "arch" (see Civil *BiOr* 40 (1983), 564 note 1). The last item, traditionally read bára bábbar "white dais," does not fit in a description of the facade; Jacobsen *Harps*, 420, translated "sparkling fresh water" (mir bábbar), and interpreted it as the water supply system.

[119] For a discussion of Ningirsu's trophies see Cooper *Return of Ninurta*, 141–154; Black *SMS Bulletin* 15 (1988); Wiggermann *Protective Spirits*, 153f.

[120] See chapter III.D.2.c.

[121] So the Šugalam, the East front, the Kasurra, and Baba's rear chamber; in addition occur the armory, the front toward the city, and the Silasirsir.

[122] For a translation see chapter II.C.1.a, p. 60.

touches. Several passages can be isolated as thematic and stylistic units. The first passage describes the doors inside the building with their parts (CA 26:20–27) and their locking devices (CA 26:28–27:1).[123] A general description of Eninnu's greatness follows (CA 27:2–10). The next passage describes the building from all sides in and out (CA 27:11–19), and then relates how Gudea painted the walls with colors (CA 27:20–28:2). Next, the inside structures of the house are detailed in terms of function (CA 28:3–18), and the outdoor installations are described (CA 28:19–29:9). Again Eninnu's greatness is evoked (CA 29:10–18) and, in conclusion, its construction is credited to Ningirsu, Ningišzida, and Gudea together (CA 30:1–5).

6. *Inauguration Preparations (CB 1:1–19)*

The second part of the composition relates Gudea's consecration of Eninnu. The first section prepares the audience for this major event. At the new temple where people and gods have assembled, Gudea carries out preliminary preparations. Three sub-sections can be distinguished: a hymnical description of Eninnu (6.1); a summary stating the arrival of people and deities (6.2); and an account of Gudea's preparations (6.3).

6.1: Praise to Eninnu (CB 1:1-9)
The praise of Eninnu extols its greatness in phrases similar to previous descriptions.

6.2: Gathering at Eninnu (CB 1:10–11)
There the people as well as the deities (Anunna) gather to admire the new construction. Together with the first sub-section (6.1) this sets the stage for the upcoming events.

6.3: Preliminary Preparations (CB 1:12–19)
The focus shifts to the protagonist. Gudea accumulates food provisions, first fresh fruits to accompany prayers (CB 1:12–15),[124] and then the supplies for the evening meal (CB 1:16–19). The first provision anticipates Gudea's prayer to Ningirsu and Baba in which he will ask them to enter their new house (section 7.2), the second anticipates the reception meal upon their entry (section 7.5).[125]

---

[123] Pegs are nailed into beams, and ropes tied to the doors; the door can then be closed by fastening the rope to the peg. Remains of such locking devices were recovered at different sites in Mesopotamia, see Zettler *JCS* 39 (1987), 197ff. with further literature.

[124] For the verb in CB 1:13 (ki im-mi-zu-zu), I follow Thureau-Dangin SAKI 123, operating with the literal meaning of ki "place" and zu "to know," and interpreting the statement as a prerequisite for the following action. In CB 1:14 I read nì-sáh-a for nì-sa-ha, Akk. *muthummu* "fruit (of a garden or orchard)" (see CAD M 2 298 s.v.) used in prime offerings (see *Nanše Hymn* 15f.). Thus I translate CB 1:12–15: "Being wise and expert in words (kù – zu ka – zu is probably a wordplay), the ruler knew the place of the divinity. For prayers and pleas he was spreading the prime offerings on the ground. The ruler was going to say a plea to his city-god."

[125] CB 1:15 implies that the fresh fruit (nì-sáh-a) was a preparation for the upcoming prayer to Ningirsu, though a dish with fruits is also prepared for the induction (CB 3:18–24), which is preceded by prayers (CB 4:22). The evening meal (kin-sig$_x$ [SAR]) consisting of sheep is prepared before the induction (CB 3:25–27), and served at the reception meal (section 7.5); yet, meat and wine are also served at the inauguration banquet (section 10.3). Thus the preliminaries may anticipate not only the immediately upcoming events, but the entire inauguration.

7. Induction of Ningirsu and Baba (CB 1:20–6:3)

Section seven relates the events leading to and culminating in Ningirsu's and Baba's entry into the new temple. The place of action alternates between the new and old house.[126] Besides the protagonist Gudea and the entering divine couple, the deities in general (Anunna) and certain deities of the Eridu pantheon are involved. Five events or units can be distinguished: a prayer to the Anunna (7.1); one to Ningirsu and Baba (7.2); an account of various other preparations (7.3); a description of the entry of the divine couple (7.4); and an account of the reception meal (7.5).

7.1: Prayer to the Anunna (CB 1:20–2:6)

Gudea's prayer to the Anunna is introduced by a simple prayer introduction formula (CB 1:20–21a). The speech consists of an address (CB 1:21b–2:4), a message (CB 2:5), and a petition (CB 2:6). Gudea addresses the Anunna in their capacity as protective spirits (Lamma), and as eloquent and "life lengtheners," alluding to their role as transmitters of the ruler's petition to a higher deity. The message is that Gudea has completed Eninnu, and it now requires an inhabitant. The Anunna are implored to support Gudea's induction of Ningirsu and Baba, or, more precisely, his upcoming petition for their entry.[127]

7.2: Prayer to Ningirsu and Baba (CB 2:7–3:4)

Gudea invites Ningirsu and Baba to enter their new house. The section starts with a recurrent phrase stating Gudea's competence (CB 2:7f.).[128] Then the effect of Gudea's prayer to the Anunna is described: the protective spirits Lamma and Udug escort Gudea to the old house where Ningirsu dwells and where Gudea will make him the greatest gift, an allusion to the "new" house (CB 2:8–13). As are the prayers to Ningirsu and Gatumdug in sections 2.2.2 and 2.2.4, this prayer is introduced with a simple prayer introduction formula (CB 2:14f.) and followed by an acceptance formula (CB 3:2–4).

While the introduction and acceptance formulae mention only Ningirsu, the prayer also addresses his consort Baba. It consists of two parts, each containing the usual address, message, and petition. Gudea addresses Ningirsu as lord whose words are preeminent (CB 2:16–18), assures him that he obeyed his words and built his house (CB 2:19–21), and implores him to enter (CB 2:22). Baba is addressed simply by name, informed that her quarters are ready (CB 2:23), and implored to inhabit them (CB 3:1).

7.3: Preparations (CB 3:5–4:21)

Before Ningirsu and Baba arrive, further preparations are carried out. The section starts with an elaborate time indication which places the event at the beginning of the fourth day of a new year, the day on which Ningirsu is supposed to return from Eridu (CB 3:5–

---

[126] See chapter III.C.2.a.

[127] Thus the prayer functions like Gudea's prayers to Ningirsu and Gatumdug in sections 2.2.2 and 2.2.4 with respect to his petition to Nanše in section 2.3.2. In contrast to the latter, however, this prayer is not preceded by offerings nor followed by an acceptance formula. Furthermore, the Anunna are referred to in the third person in the address. Could this prayer be an inner monologue of Gudea rather than spoken out loud? If so, it would parallel Gudea's inner monologue in section 2.1; as that monologue introduced the verification process, this one would introduce the induction of the temple's inhabitant(s).

[128] See chapter III.D.2.c.

12).[129] In preparation for the induction of its divine inhabitants, Gudea ensures that the house is ready and all attendant magic rites have been performed. He casts carnelian and lapis lazuli into the corners (CB 3:13f.),[130] and sprinkles clarified butter on the ground (CB 3:15); the masons, having finished their work, leave (or have left?) the house (CB 3:16f.). Then he prepares food: fruits, butter, honey (CB 3:18–24), and the evening meal for the arriving deity (CB 3:25–27).[131] The next passage describes the magic rites for the cleaning of the house performed by deities of the Eridu pantheon: Asar, Ninmada, Enki, Nindub, and Nanše (CB 4:1–12). Finally, Gudea orders humans and beasts to rest and be silent for the night (CB 4:13–15), and the effect is described in a poetic passage (CB 4:16–21). The stage is set for Ningirsu's arrival.

7.4: Entry of Ningirsu and Baba (CB 4:22–5:18)
The entry of the master of the house is introduced with a summary statement (CB 4:22–5:1) including a time indication, the late night moon (CB 4:23: ì-ti níg-u$_4$-zal-la-ke$_4$). Then four subsequent aspects of Ningirsu's (CB 5:2–9) and three of Baba's (CB 5:10–15) entry are described in poetic language. The section concludes with the mention of destinies and abundance for Lagaš (CB 5:16–18), doubtlessly an effect of the gods' entry, and, at the same time, anticipating the blessings pronounced later (in section 10.4.3).[132]

7.5: Reception Meal (5:19–6:3)
Upon his arrival, Ningirsu is offered a meal at which he is joined by the deities of Lagaš. Like the previous two sub-sections, this one is introduced with a time indication, the sunrise (CB 5:19). Meat and wine are served (CB 5:20–6:2). The section concludes with a metaphor evoking the noise of the banquet (CB 6:3).

8. *Induction of the Divine Staff (CB 6:4–13:10)*

The induction of the divine household staff takes place on the following morning in the newly inhabited Eninnu and is staged in a divine realm. The main event, a parade of the staff members before Ningirsu (8.2), is preceded by their appointment (8.1) and

---

[129] Ningirsu's return from Eridu seems to allude to a periodic cult festival, since it is mentioned in the context of a calendar date. Although such a festival is not documented in the extant administrative records, the mention of Ningirsu's going to and coming from Eridu in the description of Lugalsisa's functions (section 8.2.5) points in the same direction; so also Green *Eridu*, 269. For two mythical journeys to Eridu of Ninurta, with whom Ningirsu was syncretized (see chapter III.C.1.b), see Green ibidem, 171–173. At the same time, Ningirsu's return from Eridu could relate to the story, since Eridu is the seat of the primeval temple. On this matter see also Averbeck *Ritual and Structure*, 370–374, and Hurowitz *Temple Building*, 42.
[130] According to Hansen *RlA* 6 (1980–83), 427, bits of semi-precious stones, including carnelian and lapis lazuli, together with pieces of gold foil, copper, flint, mother of pearl, and shells, were found immediately below the first course of bricks of the foundation of the platform of the temple in area B at al-Hiba. Considering this archaeological evidence, one wonders whether the present line retrospectively refers to the rites that were performed while laying the foundation.
[131] The food preparations seem to be those for which provisions were made earlier (section 6.3). Gudea is explicitly mentioned as agent at the beginning and end of the passage (CB 3:13–27).
[132] The determination of destinies stands parallel to the sunrise (CB 5:16), previously compared to Ningirsu's entry (CB 5:8–9), while the state of abundance stands parallel to Baba's entry (CB 5:17–18). At the same time the sunrise may be understood literally, since the deities arrive during the last quarter of the night. Their taking possession of their new house may have been purposely planned to coincide with sunrise.

followed by divine approval (8.3). The actors are Ningirsu in the first sub-section, his divine staff in the second, and the chief deities of the Sumerian pantheon in the last.

8.1: Appointment of Ningirsu's Divine Staff (CB 6:4–10)

Bread and milk are brough to Ningirsu, who then rouses from sleep (CB 6:4–7).[133] He proceeds to appoint his divine staff (CB 6:8–10).[134]

8.2: Entry of Ningirsu's Divine Staff (CB 6:11–12:25)

Twenty-two deities characterized as functionaries of Ningirsu's household parade before their master. The entry of each deity is described in a frame consisting of an enumeration of the member's office functions (mes) in complement phrases (ending in -a-da), followed by the main clause: "DN paraded with his office functions (mes) before lord Ningirsu." Ningirsu's staff parallels that of a royal court and estate.[135] The functionaries include Igalim, chief prosecutor (gal$_5$-lá gal: 8.2.1);[136] Šulšaga, master of lustration (en šu$_4$-luh: 8.2.2); Lugalkurdub, war general (šagin: 8.2.3); Kuršunaburuam, vice war general (šagin min-kam: 8.2.4); Lugalsisa, counselor (ad-gi$_4$-gi$_4$: 8.2.5); Šaganšegbar, minister (sukkal: 8.2.6); Kindazi, sort of a *valet de chambre* (lú é-dùg-ga: 8.2.7);[137] Ensignun, assherd (sipa anše: 8.2.8); Enlulim, goatherd (sipa máš-lulim: 8.2.9); Ušumkalamma, musician (nar: 8.2.10); Lugaligihušam, personified drum (balag: 8.2.11);[138] the seven children of Baba who transmit the ruler's petition to Ningirsu (8.2.12);[139] Gišbare, farmer (engar: 8.2.13); Lamma, fishery inspector (enku: 8.2.14); Dimgalabzu, herald (nimgir: 8.2.15); and Lugal, guard (en-nu: 8.2.16). With all these offices (mes) brought into the temple, Eninnu receives the prerequisites to function as a temple estate.

8.3: Divine Approval (CB 12:26–13:10)

The five highest-ranked deities of the Sumerian pantheon (An, Enlil, Ninhursag, Enki, Suen), followed by Ningirsu and Nanše, each perform one action (CB 12:26–13:8). Their actions express their approval of everything accomplished up to this point.[140] The section concludes with the following statement (CB 13:9f.): "The deity, seed of everything good, built the house. Its name appeared."

---

[133] This passage refers to a regular offering, as implied by the description of Šulšaga's duties in CB 7:5–8.

[134] The mention of mes in CB 6:8 must relate to the mes with which the staff members parade in section 8.2. Ningirsu may have received them from Enki, the keeper of mes, during his visit to Eridu. CB 6:9 remains problematic; only Jacobsen *Harps*, 430, offered a full translation.

[135] See the respective entries in Falkenstein *Einleitung*, 58–114, and the glosses in Jacobsen *Harps*, 430–436.

[136] See Civil "Mesopotamian Jails," 74 commentary to line 96.

[137] His name means literally "the good barber."

[138] That the Sumerian term balag designated a drum in Gudea's time is certain, see the discussion by Black *AulaOr* 9 (1991), 28 note 39. Whether it had the same meaning in all periods and contexts is not clear; CAD is noncommittal, and PSD does not mention drum as a possible meaning.

[139] This is the only unit which deviates from the stylistic scheme of this section.

[140] Enlil's action (CB 13:1): sag-ba gur bí-dar remains enigmatic; the same action is performed by Gudea in CB 18:14. Enki's action is identical with that which he performed at the beginning of the construction, compare CA 20:15.

9. Inauguration Presents (CB 13:11–16:2, see Appendix C.7)

The next section, introduced by a recurrent statement concerning Gudea's competence (CB 13:11–13),[141] switches back to the human realm.[142] Gudea presents two kinds of gifts: dedicatory gifts (9.1) and economic products (9.3). One night passes between these two events (9.2). The presentations are each stylized with a different poetic device, while the night is described metaphorically.

9.1: Dedicatory Gifts (CB 13:11–14:18)

Gudea bestows two sets of dedicatory gifts on the temple. After identical introduction statements (CB 13:14–17 and 14:9–12), the items of each set are enumerated. The first set includes a chariot drawn by donkey stallions together with various weapons (CB 13:18–14:8); the second consists of precious metals and stones along with cult vessels for the sá-dug$_4$-offerings to be carried on an offering table to An (CB 14:13–17). The two sets of gifts correspond to Ningirsu's two main functions described in his self-portrait: the chariot and weapons enable him to assume his office as warrior of Enlil (CA 9:20–10:6), while the cult vessels enable him to assume his office as išib of An (CA 10:7–14).[143]

9.2: Rest (CB 14:19–24)

The following passage consists of three statements. The mention of a pleasant place in the first (CB 14:19f.), and of rest in the second (CB 14:21f.) and third (CB 14:23f.), leaves no doubt that this passage represents a pause between the presentation of dedicatory gifts and that of economic products.[144] Since Gudea is the agent of these two events, he could also be the agent in the transitional passage. Alternatively, the transitional passage could be understood as a reaction of Ningirsu, who after receiving the gifts makes Lagaš his permanent residence by resting there. If so, it would corroborate the second part of Ningirsu's self-portrait which describes his functions in other temples (CA 10:15–29), and, in the ensuing description of Eninnu, emphasizes that this temple is his permanent residence (CA 11:1–4).

9.3: Economic Products (CB 14:25–16:2)

Gudea's presentation of economic products is formulated in one extensive sentence. The main clause, stating that Gudea presented them for Ningirsu (CB 15:23–16:2), is preceded by twenty-one similar complement clauses which list the presented items (CB 14:25–15:22). The first eighteen items pertain to four economic spheres: fishery (CB 14:25–15:1); grain cultivation (CB 15:2–4); animal husbandry (CB 15:5–11); and the

---

[141] See chapter III.D.2.c.

[142] Gudea is referred to by epithets linking him to Ningirsu and Nanše just mentioned in the previous section.

[143] Chariots, weapons, and cult vessels are common dedicatory gifts; for weapons and cult vessels of stone dedicated to Ningirsu by Gudea see Appendix A. Note that the formulaic introduction to the list of gifts refers to Gudea by name and title (CB 13:15f. and 14:10f.) as in the dedicatory inscriptions.

[144] See Jacobsen *Harps*, 438. Averbeck *Ritual and Structure*, 381, suggested that the passage related the presentation of a bed as one of the gifts. This is unlikely in view of the structure as well as the fact that the dedicatory gifts correspond to Ningirsu's offices, where a bed would be out of place. Moreover, the temple has already been furnished, see section 5.

processing of these products (CB 15:12–18).[145] The remaining three items pertain to a musical performance (CB 15:19–22), evidently referring to the accompaniment of a procession.[146] Such a procession is also implied by the mention of functionaries in charge of some products (CB 15:1; 11; 14).

10.   Inauguration Banquet (CB 16:3–24:15)

Four sub-sections can be distinguished in this last section: preparations for the banquet (10.1), a description of the social conditions imposed for the inauguration (10.2), an account of the festivities (10.3), and divine speeches culminating in the blessing of temple and builder (10.4). In addition to Gudea, who is present in all four sub-sections, the first and fourth involve deities, while the second and third involve people of Lagaš.

10.1: Preparations (CB 16:3–17:16)

This section comprises four passages. The first and last each relate a preparation carried out by Gudea, presumably for the upcoming celebrations: he installs a tent in the temple (CB 16:5f.)[147] and provides the temple with butter, cream, and bread (CB 17:15f.). Each preparation is preceded by a general statement about Gudea's achievements, including the mention of me (CB 16:3f. and 17:12–14),[148] which may anticipate the blessings pronounced during the divine banquet (section 10.4.3). The central two passages are (anticipatory?) descriptions of the divine banquet hosts and of their banquet meal: Ningirsu is pictured on his chariot (CB 16:7-16) and in the sleeping quarters with Baba (CB 17:1–3);[149] the nesag-offering is cooking (CB 17:4–6) and the drinking bowls and goblets in the banquet hall are overflowing (CB 17:7–11).

10.2: Social Conditions (CB 17:17–18:13)

For the inauguration of Eninnu Gudea imposes special social conditions for a seven day period starting with Ningirsu's entry (CB 17:17–19).[150] They are detailed in a description (CB 17:20–18:9)[151] which resembles the description of the special conditions imposed for the construction (section 4.1.1). A summary of their effect concludes this section (CB 18:10–13).

---

[145] For Ningirsu's house of young women mentioned in CB 15:16f. see Jacobsen *Harps*, 438 note 51. Note that the first two spheres are described each in three lines, the latter two each in seven lines.

[146] Courtyard and music are linked in the description of the temple (CA 28:18) as well as in the functions of Ningirsu's musician (section 8.2.10). The last item (CB 15:21f.) also accompanied Gudea's presentation of a chariot in CA 7:24.

[147] Read: má-gur₈-gin₇ MUNSUB im-[dù/si] dím sa-bi im-ak "like on a magur-boat he [built] a tent, made its stanchions." For CB 16:5, which recurs in a description of Eninnu in CB 22:7, see Civil *RA* 61 (1967), 64 § 2.1.4.

[148] A similar frame of action and mention of me was encountered in section 5.1, the central part of which equally involved deities.

[149] Baba, who is grammatically the agent, is associated with this action already in Gudea's prayer (CB 3:1). Frankfort *Kingship*, 330, correctly observed that the cohabitation of Ningirsu and Baba described their occupation of the temple in terms of divine level reality, not as a human ritual enactment. Thus, this passage is at best an allusion to the sacred marriage rite, not a description of it. Alternatively, it may describe the divine hosts reclining at the banquet.

[150] For CB 17:17f. see Steible *Neusumerische Bau- und Weihinschriften* 2, 29f. note 86.

[151] The text is restored on the basis of the almost verbatim parallel in Statue B 7:29–48; both texts are quoted in chapter III.D.3.

10.3: Festivities (CB 18:14–19:15)

The next section seems to describe the festivities: Gudea enters Eninnu (CB 18:14–18),[152] sacrifices bulls and kids (CB 18:19), pours out wine (CB 18:20f.), and has music played (CB 18:22–19:1). He then stands on a buttress of the temple and is admired by his city (CB 19:2–4). The following lines, approximately seven cases of text, are broken. The text resumes with a description of the abundance which the ruler enjoys with his city-state (CB 19:13–15).

Falkenstein understood this section as the consumption of the banquet in the human realm, as opposed to an ensuing banquet in the divine realm (section 10.4).[153] Since the food and drinks mentioned are typical offerings for deities, and because the following section does not mention any food and drinks, this section is better understood as the festivities taking place in both the divine and human realms at the same time.

10.4: "After-Dinner Speeches" (CB 19:16–24:8)

A considerable part of this section is affected by the lacuna in CB.[154] The remains and possible restorations leave no doubt that it contained an account of the "after-dinner speeches" held at the divine banquet, the topic of which was the praise and blessing of the house and its builder.[155] An introductory statement states that Gudea gave the banquet for Ningirsu (CB 19:16f.). Then the divine guests are enumerated according to their order at table, which corresponds to their rank in the Sumerian pantheon. The list which is only partly preserved includes An, Enlil, and Ninmah (CB 19:18–21). After four broken cases, the text resumes in the middle of a speech. The break must have contained the end of the guest list as well as an introduction to the speech. The former probably included Enki, since he is present later, and perhaps Suen, since he occurs in the apparently identical list of gods who approved of the induction (section 8.3).

In the first speech, restored from fragments 5i+3i, Ningirsu seems to laud Gudea for his achievement (CB 20:5′–13′).[156] After a gap of two cases, he is described determining Eninnu's destiny (CB 20:14–19), followed by the beginning of a description of Eninnu (CB 20:20f.). Part of this passage is repeated when the text resumes (CB 21:17–19), and is again followed by the beginning of a description of Eninnu (CB 21:20). The gap in column 21 can be restored in part with additional fragments. The end of column 20 and the remains on fragment 2i suggest that the description of Eninnu continued

---

[152] The phrase sag gur–dar in CB 18:14 was said of Enlil in the context of the divine approval of the state of affairs in CB 13:1. Here it may express Gudea's approval of the effect of his establishment of special conditions. Alternatively, it may describe his appearance entering the temple, as suggested by Jacobsen *Harps*, 440, who understood the previous statement (CB 18:12f.) as Gudea coming out into the city, rather than the city coming out, a possibility which cannot be excluded since the grammar remains ambiguous. Depending on the interpretation of 18:14, the following statement (CB 18:15f.) either elaborates on the approval motif (see CA 24:5 where the same statement occurs in the name of a stela expressing the divine approval of the ruler), or on Gudea's appearance (in the sense that it was such, that he was recognized even by An). His appearance is then expressed in a metaphor (CB 18:17).

[153] *Einleitung*, 181.

[154] See chapter III.A.2.

[155] For the connection of divine banquet and fate determination see Vanstiphout *Res Orientales* 4 (1992), 11f.

[156] So also Jacobsen *Harps*, 441f.

(CB 21:1′–6′). A passage restored from fragments 5ii+3ii+4i describes Ningirsu in his warrior aspect (CB 21:7′–13′).[157] Ningirsu's name also appears on fragment 12i, which fits just before the preserved end of column 21 (CB 21:16′). Thus Ningirsu was also the agent in the second passage concerning Eninnu's destiny. These two analogous passages do not recount the actual fate determination for Eninnu, but rather Ningirsu's wish for it, as will become clear from what follows.[158] The repetition of this wish creates an atmosphere of expectation.

Large parts of the gap in column 22 can also be restored. On fragment 2ii the description of Eninnu ends with the statement that it is destined to long life (CB 22:1′f.). Then Ningirsu praises Eninnu in a direct speech (CB 22:3′–16′).[159] While the middle of the speech on fragments 9i and 5iii+4ii is mostly damaged, its beginning and end are well preserved on fragments 2ii and 12ii. The speech ends like this: "I am lord Ningirsu. Who will build for me?" (CB 22:16′). Fragment 12ii also preserves the introduction formula to a responding speech by Enki (CB 22:17′f.).

Enki responds to Ningirsu with blessings for the temple which will make its inhabitant famous (CB 22:19–23:1). These blessings continue in the gap which can be restored with fragments 2iii and 9ii (CB 23:2′–8′).[160] The last line on fragment 9ii may have concluded the blessing of Eninnu: "The [mes] of the shrine Enin[nu I will make visible] in heaven and on earth [for you]" (CB 23:8′, see CA 1:11). One more line can be restored with fragment 4iii: it mentions Silasirsir, Eninnu's place of assignment (CB 23:10′). The remainder of the text preserved in this sub-section describes the blessing of Gudea with long life (CB 23:17–24:8, see Appendix C.8). The mention of the location Silasirsir seems a possible beginning for the switch from the blessing of Eninnu to that of Gudea, which may have also involved a change of speakers. The most likely candidate would be Enlil who made the construction of Eninnu possible in the first place (see section 1.1.). An and Ningirsu must be excluded, since they are mentioned in the speech.

If the proposed restorations, which remain uncertain, are correct, this sub-section consisted of three parts: an introduction mentioning the host of the banquet and enumerating the divine guests; a second part in which Ningirsu promoted the builder and the building in front of the divine assembly; and a third part in which Enki, and possibly Enlil, blessed the building and the builder, respectively, in reaction to Ningirsu's speeches.

---

[157] Also Jacobsen *Harps*, 442. His understanding of this passage as a praise of Ningirsu by Enki, however, is not supported by the remains.

[158] Therefore I analyze the verbal prefix hé with Falkenstein SAHG 181, as a precative rather than an affirmative.

[159] Also Jacobsen *Harps*, 443.

[160] In part also Jacobsen *Harps*, 443.

C.   Analysis of the Narrative

1.   *Event Participants*

In narrative theory, analysis of character revolves around their relation with the plot.[161] In light of modern narratives in which "the contemplation of character is the predominant pleasure,"[162] the position of Aristotle that characters are subservient to the plot, defended by formalists and structuralists, needs modification. But it is precisely the comparison with modern literature that confirms its validity in regard to ancient narratives. Distinguishing between plot-centered and character-centered narratives, as does Todorov,[163] the narrative of the Cylinder Inscriptions belongs at the extreme end of the first group. All characters fulfill their function in the events centered around the temple construction. No character undergoes a psychological process. The protagonist is simply competent in the accomplishment of his task, and receives his reward in return.

The event participants in the narrative under discussion include both divine and human beings. Deities are named, while humans, with the exception of the ruler, remain anonymous. The deities and the ruler are assumed to be known to the audience, since they are not formally introduced. Only two characters are crucial for the plot: Gudea who builds Eninnu, and Ningirsu who inhabits it. Since the inanimate temple is crucial to the plot and can assume the grammatical role of an agent, it can to some degree be conceived as an event participant. Like Gudea and the deities, it is named and assumed to be known. An overview of the acting characters in each section of the linear outline is given in Table III.C.1. The following discussion examines the referents and characterization of these event participants, and their role in the narrative.

a. The Agent: Gudea

Grammatically, the name gù-dé-a is a passive participle of the Sumerian verb gù – dé, meaning "the one who is/was called." Other occurrences of this name are confined to some officials from Lagaš,[164] whose names were probably inspired by Gudea's memory, and a governor of Gudua in the Ur III period.[165] The Akkadian equivalent *nabû* is a frequent component of names, and occurs in particular in royal names which express the ruler's nomination by a deity.[166] Sumerian compounds composed with verbs of the same semantic group serve as royal epithets; for example, sipa šà-ge pà-da DN-ke₄ "shepherd chosen in heart by DN." There are only two texts in which the verb gù – dé is used in such an epithet: the Cylinder Inscriptions, undoubtedly a pun on Gudea's name,[167] and a Hammurabi text translated from Akkadian.[168] Gudea is evidently an abbreviation of

---

[161]   See the discussions by Chatman *Story and Discourse*, 107–116, and Martin *Theories of Narrative*, 116f.
[162]   Chatman *Story and Discourse*, 113.
[163]   Todorov *Poetics of Prose*, 66.
[164]   Limet *Anthroponomie*, 424, and Fischer *BaM* 27 (1996), 223 notes 44–45.
[165]   RGTC II 66f. Gudea of Gudua could be a pun.
[166]   See Seux *Epithètes Royales*, 175–79; Stamm *Namengebung*, 141f. § 17.5; CAD N/1 p.31.
[167]   CB 6:17: sipa ᵈnin-gír-su-ke₄ gù-dé-a, "shepherd called by Ningirsu." Compare also CA 2:20 = 3:29 = CB 3:2: gù-dé-a-ni giš ba-tuk-àm, "his call was heard."
[168]   Seux *Epithètes Royales*, 408: gù-dé-a-an-na.

such a compound – perhaps construed under Akkadian influence – and could therefore be a throne name.[169]

In addition to his name, Gudea is referred to as ensí "the ruler," or sipa "the shepherd." These designations identify him in terms of his office: ensí is the title officially used by the Lagaš II rulers; sipa a common Sumerian term describing the royal office in a metaphor.[170] The latter can be expanded to identify the source of the office as well, like in the royal epithets mentioned above.[171] The protagonist's name occurs sixty times, his title twenty-four times, and the shepherd epithet fourteen times. The secondary designations are used not only anaphorically, but occasionally occur in apposition to the name. Such combinations emphasize the protagonist at crucial points in the narrative. Name and full title (gù-dé-a ensí lagaš^{ki}), which is obligatory in the other inscriptions,[172] is used when Gudea installs Ningirsu's trophies (CA 26:18); when the text reiterates his marking of the perimeter (CA 30:4); and when he presents the dedicatory gifts (CB 13:15 and 14:10). Seven times the name is immediately preceded by the shepherd epithet which in these cases only is qualified as good[173] (sipa zi gù-dé-a): in the recurrent statements underlining Gudea's competence (CA 7:9, 25:22, CB 2:7) or achievements (CA 14:5); in Ningirsu's address to Gudea (CA 11:5); in the construction (CA 24:9); and in the description of Lugalsisa's function as conveyor of the ruler's petition to Ningirsu (CB 8:18). According to Hallo,[174] the attributive position implies that the ruler was addressed as "good shepherd PN" by his subjects.

As befits a Mesopotamian ruler, Gudea claims divine parentage.[175] Postulating an intimate relationship with deities serves to legitimate the ruler in his office. Gudea addresses Gatumdug explicitly as his birth mother (CA 3:6–8, 17:13f.)[176] and Nanše simply as mother (CA 1:29 = 3:25, 4:13, 5:11). In addition, in the blessing (CB 23:19, 24:7) Ninsun and Ningišzida are mentioned as his mother and father, respectively. Gatumdug, as Lagaš's mother, and Nanše, as Ningirsu's sister, link Gudea to the Lagašite dynastic tradition. Ninsun, the mother of Lugalbanda, links him to the mythic kings of Uruk, who are claimed as relatives also by the contemporary Ur III dynast Urnamma and his

---

[169] For the existence of throne names in the ancient Near East see Gelb *Rocznik Orientalistyczny* 17 (1953); for possible throne names of Sumerian and Old Akkadian kings in particular see Sjöberg *OrSuec* 21 (1972), 112.

[170] Hallo *Royal Titles*, 147–149. Note that Gudea identifies himself as "shepherd" in the first occurrence of this term (CA 1:26).

[171] CA 13:19: "shepherd nominated by Nanše;" and CB 13:12: "prudent shepherd of Ningirsu." These deities address Gudea as shepherd (CA 5:12, 11:5). A similar epithet is composed with agrig: "strong steward of Nanše" (CB 13:11).

[172] See chapter II.B.2.b.

[173] The term zi, sometimes translated as "faithful" or the like, can be said not only of human beings, but also of animals (for example, cows) and inanimate things (for example, bricks). It has the connotation of someone or something that performs as expected. The translation "good" not only fits persons as well as things, but is also traditional in combination with "shepherd."

[174] *Royal Titles*, 147.

[175] In general see Sjöberg *Or Suec* 21 (1972). Like his predecessor Urbaba and the Ur III kings, Gudea not only never mentions his human parents, but explicitly states that he does not have any.

[176] Compare the epithets in Statue B 2:16f. = D 1:17f., and F 1:12–2:1. Falkenstein *Einleitung*, 2, interpreted this evidence as an indication that Gudea was the son of a priestess of Gatumdug. The epithet dumu tu-da ^{d}gá-tùm-dùg-ke$_4$, "child born by Gatumdug," is perhaps better understood as a traditional epithet of the rulers of Lagaš, since it occurs already in Lagaš I inscriptions, see Entemena 25:9-10.

successor Šulgi.[177] Ningišzida is Gudea's personal god.[178]

While the designations discussed so far, as well as his relation with the gods, define Gudea in terms of his office in general, further characterizations highlight the one aspect of the ruler which is the focus of the present narrative: the temple builder. In the form of an apposition, the temple builder epithet occurs in varied form nine times throughout the text.[179] In addition, recurrent phrases state Gudea's competence and achievement,[180] and assert his ceaseless endeavor for it: "for the sake of building his master's house, night after night he did not sleep, at noon he did not rest." (CA 17:7–9).[181]

Gudea is present in all major events, except for Ningirsu's appointment of his staff (section 8), which plays in a purely divine realm. Except for the very last episode (10.4) in which he receives divine blessings in return for the successful accomplishment of his task, he usually is the agent. His function is determined at the beginning when he is given the divine commission (section 1.3), after having been introduced as the ruler apt for it and eager to carry it out (section 1.2).[182] The association of Gudea with the ruler who will build Eninnu reveals that it is his office which entitles and obliges him to the task.[183] His office also determines his relation with the other characters in the story. The human beings, his subjects, assist him according to his orders, while the deities collaborate in accordance with the destiny decreed for Lagaš (section 1.1).

Table III.C.1: Actors, Places of Action, and Time of the Events in Linear Sequence

	Actors	*Place of Action*	*Time*
01.01	Enlil	universe>Lagaš>Girsu	beginning of time
01.02	Ningirsu	(Girsu)	
01.03	Gudea, Ningirsu	(Girsu)	one day in Gudea's reign
02.01	Gudea	(Girsu)	(one day, continued)
02.02	Gudea, Ningirsu, Gatumdug	(Girsu)>(Lagaš-city): Ebagara	(one day & night)
02.03	Gudea, Nanše	Ebagara>Ningin: Esirara	(one day)
03.01	Gudea	(Girsu): Eninnu: Šugalam>Ubšukinna	several days

---

[177] Sjöberg *Or Suec* 21 (1972).

[178] See chapter III.C.1.d.

[179] Gù-dé-a lú é dù-a in CA 15:13, 20:24, CB 13:14, 14:9; énsi é-50 dù-ra in CA 13:10, 15:17, 16:13; énsi é-50 mu-dù-a in CB 15:23; and lú é-lugal-na dù-dam in CA 16:18.

[180] See chapter III.D.2.c.

[181] His persistency is predicted already in the first dream (CA 6:9–11). See also CA 19:22–27: "Like a young man building a house anew he did not fall asleep. Like a cow keeping an eye on her calf he stood to the house in ... Like someone 'placing little bread in the mouth' he did not get tired of coming and going" and the boast that the stelae were made and installed in the shortest possible time (CA 22:24–23:4).

[182] The introduction of a character first in generic terms (ruler), and then in specific ones (Gudea) is a constant stylistic device in Sumerian literary compositions.

[183] Compare CB 2:5: "I am the shepherd. I built the house."

	Actors	Place of Action	Time
03.02	Ningirsu	(Ubšukinna)	(one day)
03.03	Gudea	(Ubšukinna)	(one day, continued)
04.01	Gudea, people & deities of Lagaš	Girsu>construction site	several days
04.02	Gudea, work force of Lagaš	Lagaš>Girsu	(several days)
04.03	Gudea, Ningirsu, people & deities of all lands	foreign lands>Girsu	(several months)
04.04	Gudea, Enki, Nidaba	(Girsu): construction site	(one day)
04.05	Gudea, Lugalkurdub, Igalim, Ningišzida, people of Lagaš, Utu, Enki	(Girsu): Girnun>Urukug: (construction site)	one day
04.06	Gudea, diviner	(Girsu: construction site)	(one day, continued)
05.01	Gudea, priests, Enki, Nanše, Gatumdug, Baba, Anunna	(Girsu: construction site)	(one day)
05.02	Gudea	(Girsu: construction site)	(seven (?) days)
05.03	Gudea, workmen	(Girsu: construction site)	(several months)
05.04	Gudea	(Girsu: construction site)[184]	seven days
05.05	Gudea, workmen	(Girsu: construction site)	(several months)
05.06	Gudea	(Girsu: construction site)[185]	(seven (?) days)
05.07	Gudea, workmen, Ningirsu, Ningišzida	(Girsu: construction site)	(several weeks)
06.01	Eninnu	(Girsu: rebuilt) Eninnu	(1st day of a new year)
06.02	people, deities	(Girsu: rebuilt Eninnu)	(1st day, continued)
06.03	Gudea	(Girsu: rebuilt Eninnu)	(1st day, continued)
07.01	Gudea	(Girsu: rebuilt Eninnu)	(2nd day of a new year)
07.02	Gudea, Udug, Lamma, Ningirsu	(Girsu): previous Eninnu	(3rd day of a new year)
07.03	Gudea, Asar, Ninmada, Enki, Nindub, Nanše	(Girsu: rebuilt) Eninnu>Girsu>Lagaš	4th day of a new year
07.04	Ningirsu, Baba	(Girsu: rebuilt) Eninnu	(4th day): late night moon
07.05	Gudea, Ningirsu, deities of Lagaš	(Girsu: rebuilt) Eninnu	(4th day): day time
08.01	Ningirsu	(Girsu: rebuilt) Eninnu	(5th day): morning
08.02	Ningirsu's staff	(Girsu: rebuilt Eninnu)	(5th day, continued)
08.03	Ningirsu, Nanše, An, Enlil, Ninhursag, Enki, Suen	(Girsu: rebuilt Eninnu)	(5th day, continued)
09.01	Gudea	(Girsu: rebuilt) Eninnu	(6th day of a new year)
09.02	Gudea, Ningirsu, all lands	(Girsu: rebuilt) Eninnu & all lands	(6/7th day): night

---

[184] The places where the stelae are installed are: the large courtyard, the Kasurra, the East front, the front facing the Šugalam, the front facing the EURUga, and Baba's rear chamber.
[185] The places where Ningirsu's trophies are installed are: the armory, the front facing the city, the Šugalam, the East front, the Kasurra, the Silasirsir, and Baba's rear chamber.

	Actors	Place of Action	Time
09.03	Gudea, temple estate employees	(Girsu: rebuilt) Eninnu	(7th day of a new year)
10.01	Gudea, Ningirsu, Baba	(Girsu: rebuilt) Eninnu	(7th day, continued)
10.02	Gudea, people of Girsu	Girsu	seven days
10.03	Gudea, people of Lagaš	(Girsu: rebuilt) Eninnu	(7th day, continued)
10.04	Gudea, Ningirsu, An, Enlil, Ninmah, [Enki, Suen]	(Girsu): rebuilt Eninnu	(7th day, continued)

b. The Beneficiary: Ningirsu

Ningirsu's name literally means "the lord of Girsu."[186] He is the patron of the state of Lagaš, and resides in its capital Girsu. His name appears already in the Abu Salabikh god lists.[187] Ningirsu belongs to the second generation of gods in the Sumerian pantheon of historical time. In Gudea's time, he was considered a son of Enlil, though there are hints that he may originally have been a son of Enki.[188] His mother is Enlil's consort Ninhursag, and his wife is Baba, the eldest daughter of An.[189] As Enlil's son, Ningirsu was syncretized with Ninurta at the latest in Gudea's time, when local mythology began to be interpreted in national terms.[190] Ningirsu/Ninurta has two main aspects: he is the warrior of Enlil who fights against monsters and the foreign land (kur), but also the patron of agriculture.[191]

In the present text, Ningirsu is mentioned more than any other character. In addition to his name, he is called "lord" (en), "master" (lugal), "warrior" (ur-sag), or "son of Enlil" (dumu ᵈen-líl-lá).[192] His name occurs almost a hundred times, en fifty times, lugal forty-two times, ur-sag twenty-four times, and dumu ᵈen-líl-lá eight times. The secondary designations are used both anaphorically and in apposition to the name. En and lugal are titles commonly shared by gods and kings.[193] In reference to Ningirsu en is used predominantly in apposition, yet also anaphorically in direct speeches,[194] while lugal occurs almost exclusively as anaphora, and is then usually linked to either Gudea or Eninnu with a possessive suffix. Lugal seems to imply Ningirsu's role as Lagaš's patron,

[186] Falkenstein *Einleitung*, 90. The reading of GÍR in GÍR-su is not confirmed. If read *irsu (see Civil *BiOr* 40 (1983) 562), nin-*irsu-a(k) and nin-urta would be simply two dialectical writings, both irsu and urt(a) being derived from Semitic *ard/ṣ* "earth." Ningirsu/Ninurta would then mean "Lord of the Earth."
[187] OIP 99 83.
[188] Falkenstein *Einleitung*, 90f.; Sjöberg *Temple Hymns*, 10.
[189] Falkenstein *Einleitung*, 91f.
[190] Cooper *Return of Ninurta*, 11 with note 3, and Wiggermann *Protective Spirits*, 162.
[191] The first aspect is the topic of several mythical tales, for example, *Angim* edited by Cooper *Return of Ninurta*, and *Lugal* edited by Van Dijk *Lugal*. For the latter, documented mostly in hymns, see Civil *Farmer's Instructions*, 98 commentary to line 108.
[192] In addition, the following allusive designations occur each once: ú-a lagašᵏⁱ, "provider/caretaker of Lagaš" (CA 22:23); dingir uru-na, "his (Gudea's) city-god" (CB 1:15), and dingir numun zi-zi-da, "deity, seed of everything good" (CB 13:9).
[193] In the Cylinder Inscriptions en occurs as a component in epithets of Šulšaga (CB 7:9) and Suen (CB 13:4), and in the names of Ningirsu's shepherds Ensignun and Enlulim (CB 10:1 and 7); lugal as a title in apposition to Enki (CA 19:11, CB 4:3, 13:3), and as component in the names of Lugalkurdub (CA 14:18, 18:13, CB 7:22) and Lugalkisalsi (CA 23:9). In the human sphere, en designates a priestly profession (CA 20:21), and lugal the master of a servant (CA 13:7, CB 17:21).
[194] For example, CA 8:15f., 9:22f., CB 2:17f.

not unlike the way ensí implies Gudea's role in respect to Lagaš, while en, like sipa for Gudea, is more poetic. Ur-sag defines Ningirsu in his warrior aspect, and the filiation implies his rank in the Sumerian pantheon.[195] The use of these designations is not context-specific.[196]

Ningirsu's kinship with Enlil is apparent not only in the filiation, but also in speeches and descriptions throughout the text. Gudea alludes to it when addressing Ningirsu as "excellent in Nippur" (CA 2:12), or "semen ejaculated by Great Mountain" (CA 8:16).[197] Ningirsu claims Enlil as his biological father (CA 10:1). He is called warrior, deluge, or storm of Enlil (CA 9:21, 10:2, 4, 23:14, 20), and associated with Enlil's symbol Anzu (CA 4:17 = 5:14f., 9:14, CB 14:16).[198] The original relation with Enki is apparent in the fact that Enki's daughter Nanše figures as Ningirsu's sister (CA 2:16, 5:17), and perhaps also in the frequent reference to Abzu, and the mention of Ningirsu's trip to Eridu.[199] Ningirsu's mother is mentioned twice, though she remains unnamed (CB 10:5, 21:9' = fragment 5 ii 4).

In his self-portrait, Ningirsu explains his offices in the divine world: his father invested him as warrior (CA 10:1–6), his father-in-law as išib (CA 10:12–14).[200] He fulfills these duties not only in Eninnu, for which Gudea provides the necessary implements (CB 13:18–14:8 and 14:13–18), but also in the secondary temples of Lagaš (CA 10:15–29). While his cultic duties are not mentioned again, the warrior aspect is manifest throughout the text. He is a "lord without rival" (CA 9:22 = 23:21), "expert in battle" (CA 17:21), and has a fierce glare which the enemy cannot bear.[201] His temple is equipped with trophies, a chariot, and weapons. In epithets and descriptions his strength is frequently compared or equated with the force of nature: Gudea saw Ningirsu "surpassing like heaven and earth, a deity as to his head, an Anzu as to his arms, a deluge as to his lower

---

[195] In the cylinders ur-sag is also used in reference to Nindub (CA 5:2 = 6:3), to defeated foes of Ningirsu (CA 25:25, 28, see 26:15), and to Ningirsu's weapon Šarur (CB 7:19). Ur-sag kal-ga ᵈen-líl-lá, "mighty warrior of Enlil" is the most common epithet of Ningirsu in Gudea's dedicatory inscriptions (Gudea 42–60, 62–63, 94, Statue B, D, G). "Warrior of Enlil" is Ningirsu's traditional epithet in Early Dynastic Lagaš, while the filiation "son of Enlil" is not attested at that time.

[196] Gudea, for example, addresses Ningirsu not only as his master, but also with other designations, and Ningirsu can be referred to with any designation regardless of his function in a particular context.

[197] Compare also CB 21:8'= fragment 5 ii 3.

[198] Anzu is frequently associated with Ningirsu in texts and images from the Early Dynastic to the Neo-Sumerian period, though it can be associated also with other deities. For visual representations in Gudea's art see chapter IV.B.4. Wiggermann *Protective Spirits*, 159–161, suggested that Anzu was originally Enlil's symbol, and when associated with other deities represents the general power (= Enlil) under which they operate. The association with Ningirsu is not surprising, since Ningirsu is Enlil's warrior.

[199] Abzu occurs almost exclusively in the construction account (CA 21:22, 26f., 22:6, 11, 24:20f., 26f., 25:18f., 26:30, 29:3f.; see also CA 10:15f., CB 5:7); once Eridu occurs in its place (CA 29:9). More specific is the address in Gudea's first prayer to Ningirsu which calls him "high-ranking in Abzu" (CA 2:11), before mentioning his relation with Enlil. The frequent mention of Abzu as well as Ningirsu's journey to Eridu (see chapter III.B.7.3), may be linked to either the fact that Enki's abode, Abzu in Eridu, was traditionally the primeval temple, and thus a prototype for all other temples, or to a special relation between Ningirsu and Enki. The rivalry of Enki and Enlil may have played a role, too.

[200] Išib was a cultic office which also human kings could assume. CAD I/J p. 242f. translates its Akkadian equivalent *išippu* with "purification priest."

[201] CA 9:13–15, 25, 10:3, 17:20, see also 28:21f. For other mentions of Ningirsu's enemy see CA 10:21–23, and the descriptions of his war generals in CB 7:12–8:9. The enemy of Ningirsu is the kur = "mountains, foreign lands" (see CB 7:17), like in *Angim* and *Lugal*.

body, and with panthers at his sides" (CA 4:14–19);[202] his raging heart is "uprising like the ocean, set up like the esi-tree (?), roaring like overflowing water, destroying towns like a deluge, dashing upon the rebels like a storm, ... untiring (like) overflowing water, ... vast like heaven" (CA 8:23–9:2).[203] Some of these metaphors (deluge, storm, panther) are then associated with his war implements, and with his residence Eninnu.[204] The agricultural aspect, which Ningirsu probably inherited through the syncretism with Ninurta, is apparent only in his promises to call for rain which will bring agricultural surplus (CA 11:7–17).

Ningirsu is introduced in the context of Enlil's determination of the fate of Lagaš (section 1.1). Once approved as patron of Lagaš, he commissions the ruler with the construction of his residence (section 1.3) and, thus, becomes the beneficiary of Gudea's actions. Ningirsu's actions are restricted to his role as Eninnu's inhabitant (lugal é-50). Aside from commissioning his temple, he provides specific instructions for its realization (section 3.2); enters and inhabits the newly built temple (sections 7.4, 10.1); and promotes its builder for blessings in the divine assembly (section 10.4.2). All actions subsequent to the commission are instigated by Gudea's prayers and/or offerings (sections 3.1, 7.2, 9, 10.3). While instructions and promotion are related through direct speech, entry and inhabitation are described in metaphors. Although Ningirsu hardly participates in the construction (sections 4–5), he is credited with it as well (CA 30:1).[205] His relation with other characters is determined by his rank and status in the pantheon: as Enlil's son he interacts with higher-ranked deities of the Sumerian pantheon, as patron of Lagaš with Gudea, his proxy in the human world, and as master of Eninnu with his wife and household staff.

c. Other Human Beings

The human beings other than Gudea remain anonymous. If not entirely generic, they are specified typologically as members of a social group or inhabitants of a geographic area. Generic people (un)[206] are present at Gudea's second prayer to Ningirsu (CA 8:13), during the brick making (CA 19:15), in the inauguration (CB 1:10), and also occur as beneficiaries of prosperity and vital force in Ningirsu's promises (CA 11:9, 24). An equally undefined collective, apparent only in the plural forms of finite verbs, assists Gudea in the construction (CA 21:13–26:30).[207]

---

[202] As Falkenstein *Einleitung*, 95, noted, this description is metaphoric, rather than pictorial; the deities in Gudea's art are usually anthropomorphic.

[203] See also CA 10:21–23, CB 10:19–23. His heart can be soothed with presents or prayers, see CA 7:5, 18:2, CB 10:16.

[204] The deluge metaphor is used for Ningirsu (CA 10:2, 23:14, CB 9:22, 10:21), and his weapon Šarur (CA 15:24, CB 8:2, see also 7:14); the storm metaphor for Ningirsu (CA 23:20, CB 5:5), one of his weapons (CB 7:24), the donkeys of his chariot (CB 13:19), and Eninnu (CA 25:9); the panther metaphor for Ningirsu (CA 2:10, CB 9:21), one of his weapons (CB 13:23), the donkeys of his chariot (CA 7:20f., CB 9:16), and Eninnu (CA 21:6, 26:26f., 27:3f.).

[205] He plays an active role only in one sub-event in the provision of building materials (CA 15:19–16:12), yet he is mentioned in one or another way in almost every sub-section.

[206] In the Cylinder Inscriptions the signs for "people" (un) and "country" (kalam) are not paleographically distinguished, as in later texts. The signified, not always unambiguous, is either indicated by the auslaut (kalam is followed by -ma, un by -gá or -e) or to be guessed from the context (CA 3:4, 21:12, CB 1:10).

[207] In addition, some of the widely used verbal forms with ba prefix may be understood as having anonymous people as agent.

Social groups are defined by gender, kin, class, or profession. Members of a specific gender, kin, and/or class heed Gudea's promulgation of special conditions for the construction (CA 13:3-13:15) and the inauguration (CB 17:20–18:9). The professionals include a diviner who receives the third dream for Gudea (CA 20:7f.); artisans, specifically silversmiths and stone cutters, who process the imported building materials (CA 16:25–27); and priests, namely usga (CA 20:14), en and lagar (CA 20:21), who are assigned to the temple before the actual construction.

Inhabitants of geographic areas[208] occur in the construction preparations: three distinct Lagašite districts mobilize for the labor (section 4.2) and various foreign countries (Elam, Susa, Magan, Meluhha, and Kimaš) dispatch building materials (section 4.3). In addition, inhabitants of more generic spheres, namely the city (Girsu), the city-state (Lagaš), the home country (kalam), and the foreign lands (kur), are present in various events. The fact that they are often paired in the same event, indicates that they function mainly as a setting, much like the generic people. The geographical horizons of these people will be discussed below.

d. Other Deities
The deities other than Ningirsu appear individually or as a collective named Anunna. The number of individually named deities is impressive. The following review examines only their functions in the events of the narrative.[209]

An, the leader of the Sumerian pantheon, approves of the newly inhabited Eninnu (CB 12:26) and presides over the inauguration banquet (CB 19:18). He is said to have founded Eninnu (CA 9:11, 27:8, CB 20:20), and determined the fate of Lagaš (CB 24:11). He is also mentioned as father of Gatumdug (CA 2:28: dumu an kù-ge tu-da), Baba (CA 20:19: dumu-sag an-na; CB 5:15: dumu an kù-ge), and forefather of Ningišzida (CB 23:18: dumu-KA an-na); as authority in relation to Ningirsu (CA 10:7–14, compare CB 14:16–18), Eninnu (CA 24:5), and Gudea (CB 18:15f., 24:5); and in a metaphor (CB 16:18).

Enlil makes the construction of Eninnu possible through his determination of Lagaš's destiny (section 1.1; see also CA 4:9, CB 1:3, 24:11). Subsequent to An, he and his wife **Ninhursag** approve of the newly inhabited Eninnu (CB 13:1f.) and also participate in the inauguration banquet (CB 19:19–21), during which Enlil may have blessed Gudea.[210] Enlil is mentioned innumerable times in relation to Ningirsu[211] and once in relation to Gudea (CA 17:11).

---

[208] Sumerian rarely distinguishes between territory and inhabitants of a geographical area. The latter can be designated as "sons of GN." In the Cylinder Inscriptions this distinction is not made at all. Thus only context can determine whether the inhabitants or the territory itself is signified; more often it is the former.
[209] For a detailed description of these deities see Falkenstein *Einleitung*, 55–115. The following deities are mentioned only in similes or descriptions: Iškur (CA 26:21), Ištaran (CA 10:26), Nirah (CA 27:1), and Ninsun (CB 23:19f.).
[210] See chapter III.B.10.4.
[211] See chapter III.C.1.b.

Enki plays a more active role, presumably because he is the god of wisdom and technology, the inhabitant of the primeval temple, and a helper of humankind. He supervises the plan (CA 17:17); determines the fate of the clay for the bricks (CA 19:11); marks the perimeter of the house (CA 20:15; compare CA 22:12f. and CB 13:3); collaborates in the preparations for Ningirsu's entry (CB 4:3); and finally blesses Eninnu at the banquet (CB 22:17ff.). Minor deities of his circle collaborate at his side or independently. **Nidaba** opens the "House of Wisdom" for the plan (CA 17:15f.). **Asar**, **Ninmada**, and **Nindub** participate in the preparation for Ningirsu's entry (CB 4:1–2, 4:4f.; compare CB 6:3); only in this event they are referred to as a collective with an anonymous plural verb (CB 4:11f.). Nidaba and Nindub appear also in Gudea's revelation dream as astromancer and architect of the construction project, respectively (CA 5:21–6:5).

Suen, the Moon, participates in the approval of Eninnu (CB 13:4f.) and probably also in the inauguration banquet.[212] Once he is mentioned in a description of the night (CB 3:10–12). **Utu**, the Sun, appears only in his celestial manifestation: he dries the bricks (CA 19:9), and is mentioned in time indications (CA 18:5, CB 5:19), as well as in many similes and metaphors.[213]

Nanše plays a major role in the verification process by interpreting Gudea's first dream and advising him on how to proceed from there (CA 5:11–7:8). While Ningirsu remains distant and fearsome, Nanše converses directly with Gudea who confidentially calls her "mother." Together with Enki and other Lagašite deities, Nanše collaborates in the construction (CA 20:16); with Enki's circle she participates in the preparations for Ningirsu's entry (CB 4:6); and with her brother Ningirsu and the chief gods of the Sumerian pantheon she joins in the approval of Eninnu (CB 13:7f.). Furthermore, her district mobilizes for the construction work (CA 14:19–23; compare 14:12f.), and she is mentioned as legislator of Lagaš at her brother's side (CB 18:4f.). Her prominence in the story may be due to her affiliation with both Ningirsu and Enki.

Gatumdug and **Baba**, the other two Lagašite goddesses, both daughters of An (CA 2:28; 20:19, CB 5:15), play minor roles. As mother of Lagaš, Gatumdug accepts Gudea's petition for a successful journey to Ningin (CA 4:1f.), and as birth-giving goddess, she gives birth to the bricks (CA 20:17f.). Baba sprinkles these bricks (CA 20:19f.) and, at her husband's side, enters (CB 5:10–15) and inhabits (CB 17:1–3) the newly built Eninnu, where she has her own quarters (CA 26:12, CB 2:23f.) and a stela (CA 24:4–7).

The **staff of Ningirsu** consists of eighteen minor deities. They enter the temple on Ningirsu's directive by virtue of their offices (section 8.2). Only Igalim, Lugalkurdub, Lamma, and Ušumkalamma occur elsewhere, all as escorts of Gudea: the protective spirit Lamma, together with her counterpart **Udug**, escort him on his way to invite Ningirsu into the newly built house (CB 2:9f.; compare CA 3:20f.); Igalim and Lugalkurdub guide him on his way to fashion the bricks (CA 18:13f.); and Ušumkalamma, the drum,

---

[212] See chapter III.B.10.4.
[213] His name often serves as a synonym for the sun. His yoke team is mentioned in the name of Inanna's district (CA 14:25), and in a metaphor (CA 19:16f.), and his emblem occurs among Ningirsu's trophies (CA 26:4).

acts as escort during the presentation of a chariot in the verification process (CA 7:24f.) and of economic products in the inauguration (CB 15:21f.), and performs during the festivities (CB 18:22).

Ningišzida participates in his role as Gudea's personal god. In the revelation dream he appears as the rising sun, perhaps a metaphor for support (CA 5:19–20); together with Igalim and Lugalkurdub he leads Gudea on his way to fashion the bricks (CA 18:15f.); and he is, like Ningirsu, credited for the construction of Eninnu, retrospectively (CA 30:2f.). Except for the last occurrence, his name is followed by the term dingir and a possessive pronoun relating it to Gudea, like in all its occurrences in Gudea's other inscriptions.[214] Moreover, the deity who blesses Gudea states: dingir-zu en ᵈnin-giš-zi-da dumu-KA an-na-kam, "Your (personal) deity is lord Ningišzida, the offspring of An" (CB 23:18).

Ninzaga and **Ninsikila**, the patrons of Dilmun, deliver copper and timber for the construction (CA 15:11–18).

Nintukalamma, obviously a patron of artisans, oversees the production of bronze implements and/or artifacts for the construction (CA 16:28–30).

Anunna includes all deities of the Sumerian pantheon who are not specifically mentioned as active participants.[215] They are present at the construction (CA 20:23) as well as at the inauguration (CB 1:11). In the context of the induction of Ningirsu Gudea pleads for their support (section 7.1). The deities of the Lagašite pantheon in particular (ᵈa-nun-na ki lagaš^{ki}) join Gudea in prayer after the purification of the construction site (CA 14:1) and participate in the reception meal for Ningirsu (CB 5:22). The newly built Eninnu provides an assembly hall for them (CA 27:14f.).

e. The Object: Eninnu

The name Eninnu is a compound of the noun "house" (é) and the number fifty (ninnu). É is a common component in Mesopotamian temple names, and is often translated as temple, though it designates any residential building or estate, regardless of whether its inhabitants are divine, royal, or common. Fifty is the number allocated to Enlil, and seems to be related to the fifty mes which Enlil invests upon Ningirsu (CA 10:1–6).[216] In the text under discussion, Eninnu is referred to by its name sixty-four times, and designated simply as "house" innumerable times. The name may be preceded by the appositions sig₄ "brick" in the sense of "brickwork" or èš "shrine." Both appositions can be nominally expanded, and rarely the expanded form is used as anaphora.[217] Both are common terms referring to temples: sig₄ highlights the physical aspect as an architectural structure, èš the cultic aspect as a place of worship. The generic designation "house" is often linked to

---

[214] Gudea 64–68; Statue B 3:5, 9:4; E 8:11; G 2:8; I 3:8; Q: 1:2.

[215] The concept has been discussed by Falkenstein *AS* 16 (1965).

[216] See Edzard "Names of the Sumerian Temples," 160 note 6.

[217] Èš occurs five times in apposition (CA 5:18, 22:8, CB 6:10, 10:6, 18:8), and èš numun i-a, "the shrine of sprouting seed" once as anaphora (CB 13:6). Sig₄ occurs six times in apposition in Ningirsu's speech at the banquet (CB 20:15–18 and 21:17–19), sig₄ zi, "good brickwork" twice (CA 6:8, CB 1:3), and "brickwork of Sumer" once (CA 21:25), while "brickwork of Lagaš" is once used as anaphora (CB 13:7).

its owner, i.e. followed by his name (é-ᵈnin-gír-su-ka) or his epithet "master" in genitive (é-lugal-ak), or by a possessive pronoun referring to him. The importance of "house" as a focus of attention is reflected in the syntax; an inverted genitive construction puts it almost always at the beginning of the sentence.

"White Anzu" (anzuᵐᵘˢᵉⁿ-babbár) is Eninnu's standard epithet in Lagaš II inscriptions including the cylinders.[218] The association of Anzu with Eninnu is inspired by the relationship of Anzu with its inhabitant.[219] Thus, name as well as epithet affiliate the temple with its divine inhabitant. Eninnu is described in general terms at various points throughout the text, while its parts are described as it is built (section 5). The general descriptions emphasize the temple's majestic appearance in figures of speech common to temple descriptions in Sumerian literary texts.[220] The Mesopotamian ziggurats dominated the flat landscape, and were visible from afar. The descriptions of the various parts are metaphorical, which obscures the meaning of rare technical terms for parts of the structure, and impedes a modern visualization of Eninnu's physical appearance. Moreover, the enumeration of the parts does not seem to follow a logical sequence.

What can be determined from the text in regard to the general arrangement and components of Eninnu's structure conforms with our knowledge of Mesopotamian temples. It incorporated a complex of buildings arranged around courtyards and may have included a ziggurat.[221] The temple area was enclosed by an outer perimeter (CA 22:14) and its main entrance had an impressive facade (CA 24:26–25:11). The interior contained public and residential quarters as well as household tracts and storerooms. The former include a throne room (CA 25:12), a banquet hall (CA 25:14), and sleeping quarters (CA 25:17); the latter a cowbarn, bakery, butchery, kitchen, wine cellar, brewery, treasury, carriage house, music room (CA 28:3-18), and an armory (CA 25:24). Seven stelae were installed outdoors, presumably in courtyards (CA 23:8–24:7, 29:1f.), along with Ningirsu's trophies (CA 25:24–26:14), and his main weapon, the Šarur (CA 22:20f.). There was also a garden (CA 28:23) and a pond (CA 22:11). Gudea's presentation of economic products (section 9.3) as well as the fact that Ningirsu's divine staff includes shepherds (sections 8.2.8–9), a farmer (section 8.2.13), a fishery inspector (section 8.2.14), and a tax-collector (section 8.2.15) confirm that Eninnu had its own estate. The only features not necessarily shared by other Mesopotamian temples are the armory, trophies, and weapons which reflect the warrior aspect of Eninnu's inhabitant.

---

[218] This epithet is first attested in Urbaba 1; compare also Gudea 47–53, 57, 61, Statue B 5:15, D 2:7, I 2:11 = P 2:12, W 5′. Jacobsen's translation of Anzu as Thunderbird (*Tammuz*, 339 note 27) is based on an ethymology of the outdated reading IM.DUGUD.
[219] "White Anzu" or "Anzu" not only follows the temple's name as an epithet (CA 7:2, 7:28, 17:22), but can also be equated or compared with it (CA 11:3, 21:4, CB 1:8). Once the temple is referred to as "House Anzu" (CB 23:1). Anzu occurs consequently also as an emblem on standards (CA 13:22, 27:18f.). For the association of Anzu with Ningirsu see note 198 above.
[220] The temple is compared to the brightness and splendor of sun and moon (CA 21:10, 12, 24:10, 14, 23, 30:8f., CB 1:7, 3:12); like a mountain it or its radiance abuts with heaven (CA 9:16, 17:18, CB 1:6, 24:9); it is grown between heaven and earth (CA 24:9, CB 1:2, 24:14, see CA 17:19, 20:10, 21:23); its awe overlays all lands (CA 9:17, 27:6, 29:14, 18); its fame reaches the end of the world (CA 9:18, 24:11, 29:16). For similar descriptions in other texts see *Temple Hymns* edited by Sjöberg, and Edzard "Skyscrapers and Bricks."
[221] See chapter III.B.5.2.

Eninnu is linked to Lagaš's destiny (section 1.1), since the state cannot exist without a divine patron who resides there. This is evident, for example, in lamentations over the destruction of cities in which the divine patrons are forced to leave their doomed cities.[222] Its name is introduced in the context of its inhabitant and builder (section 1.2). When Ningirsu commissions Gudea with the temple construction (section 1.3), Eninnu becomes the main object of the story. Its construction results in the acclaim of its inhabitant as well as its builder: Ningirsu's excellence is made known in all lands (CB 24:12f.), and Gudea is blessed with a stable rule, fame, and long life (CB 23:17–24:8). Thus, Eninnu ultimately serves to glorify its divine inhabitant and to immortalize its royal builder.

f. Conclusions

All event participants in the narrative are types. They act according to their role in the Sumerian world. Gudea fulfills a task expected of a ruler, the people participate as his subjects and are defined in terms of rank and profession, the deities act according to their rank and function in the pantheon, and Eninnu figures as a typical Mesopotamian temple. Depending on their role, some participants are more active than others. Enki and Nanše, for example, help at several stages, while the divine patrons of Dilmun appear only once. Similarly, generic people act repeatedly throughout the construction, while the professional dreamer appears only once. Any character trait exhibited, such as the warrior aspect of Ningirsu, is presupposed and predictable in the context of the Sumerian world. There remains little to fill in, except for culture-specific knowledge which permits a recognition of the closed constructs of characters and object.

Only Gudea and Ningirsu are required for the completion of the main events: to build and inhabit Eninnu. The importance of Gudea, Ningirsu, and Eninnu in the narrative is evident in the multiple referents used for them. It is understood that "ruler" and "shepherd" always refer to Gudea; "lord," "master," "hero," and "son of Enlil" always refer to Ningirsu; and "house" always refers to Eninnu. The role of Gudea as agent, Ningirsu as beneficiary, and Eninnu as object, is presumed to the point that, without mention of the corresponding name in immediate vicinity, "he" can be used to refer to Gudea, "for him" to Ningirsu, and "it(s)" to Eninnu. All secondary characters can be perceived as an extension of either Gudea or Ningirsu, or simply as background setting. Ningirsu's wife and staff, who inhabit the temple with him, are an extension of Ningirsu. Most other characters assist or support Gudea in his actions and can be conceived as an extension of the protagonist. Human beings act on his command, deities collaborate. Divine and human collectives serve mainly as background setting. Their role, and especially that of the Anunna, is comparable to that of the chorus in Greek drama.

---

[222] See, for example, the *Curse of Agade* edited by Cooper, and the *Lamentation over Sumer and Ur* edited by Michalowski.

2. Space

a. Place of Action

At the very beginning, the spatial focus shifts immediately from the all encompassing universe (CA 1:1) to the city-state Lagaš (CA 1:2), and from there to "our city," i.e. Girsu, and the "everlasting thing," an allusion to Eninnu (CA 1:4). After that, explicit place indications are almost exclusively confined to the context of prayers or of events which play outside of Girsu.

All prayers are performed in specific temples: the first one to Ningirsu and that to Gatumdug in the Ebagara in Lagaš (CA 2:7–9); the one to Nanše in the courtyard of her Esirara in Ningin (CA 4:4–7);[223] the second and third prayers to Ningirsu in his Eninnu in Girsu: the text mentions the Ubšukinna (CA 8:14) for the second, and Eninnu (CB 2:14f.) for the third, and presumes the knowledge that the Ubšukinna is the divine assembly hall of this temple. The Eninnu in these prayers must be the one which existed before Gudea's reconstruction, since they precede Ningirsu's induction into the new temple. In the context of the third prayer the text specifically mentions that Ningirsu was dwelling in é ul é libir – "the ancient, previous house" (CB 2:11). The "previous house" was mentioned once before in reference to a prayer preceding the brick making (CA 17:29–18:2), while é gibil – "the new house" is specifically mentioned in relation to the inauguration banquet (CB 19:16). Since Gudea's immediate predecessor Urbaba also claims to have built Eninnu, and because remains of both constructions were found in immediate vicinity at Tello,[224] it is unlikely that Gudea actually rebuilt the entire temple.[225] The terms "previous" and "new" in reference to Eninnu seem to be consciously chosen to give the illusion that Gudea built an entire temple.

Gudea's journey to Nigin in order to verify his revelation dream is the only event in which Gudea leaves the capital. The journey's final destination is identified twice: at the outset (CA 2:4–6), and after the stopover at Lagaš (CA 4:3–4). Rather than to the name of that town, the text refers to its main temple (Bagara) where Gudea spends his time during the stopover (CA 2:7 and 23). Neither is the port of departure mentioned, nor the return trip related, a clear indication for the Girsu-centric perspective of the narrative.

When place indications are lacking, the place of action can be inferred from the context. The tentative overview in Table III.C.1 shows that most events play in Girsu, and more specifically at the site of Eninnu, regardless of whether the acting characters are human or divine. The initial circumstances (section 1) focus on Lagaš, and more precisely on Eninnu, and Gudea evidently receives the dream in Girsu. For the verification of the revelation (section 2) he travels to Ningin. The verification of the commission (section 3) occurs for the most part, if not entirely, in the old Eninnu.[226] Some construction

---

[223] The temple names here are not preceded by é, like in the building inscriptions (chapter II.B.2.c), and the location of Ebagara in Lagaš is not specifically mentioned.

[224] Parrot *Tello*, 151–155 with fig. 33.

[225] See chapter I.B.2, p. 25.

[226] The storehouse (CA 7:13) was probably that of the temple (compare the metaphor in CA 11:1). If the temple had its own workshop, the chariot for Ningirsu (section 3.1.1) was not only presented to him in Eninnu

preparations (section 4) take place in the entire city (sections 4.1.1, 4.2, 4.3),[227] others at the construction site (sections 4.1.2–3, 4.4, 4.5, 4.6). The actual construction (section 5) naturally takes place there, too. The inauguration (sections 6–10) plays entirely at the newly built temple, except for Gudea's prayer to Ningirsu in the old Eninnu (section 7.2).

b. Geographical Horizon

Although the events take place in (or focus on) Girsu or the state of Lagaš, the geographical horizon is not limited to these spheres. Apart from Girsu (gír-su^{ki}), usually referred to as the city (uru), and the state of Lagaš (ki lagaš^{ki}, or simply lagaš^{ki}), there is mention of the home country (kalam) and the foreign lands (kur or kur-kur). Two or more spheres are often paired in the same event: city and Lagaš, for instance, are mentioned in the purification of the city (CA 12:21–23); the two together with all lands during the brick making (CA 18:27–19:2); city and country in the night of Ningirsu's arrival (CB 4:13f.).[228] The way spheres are contrasted and the rare mention of other Sumerian cities confined to divine epithets or figures of speech[229] give the impression that kalam refers to the state of Lagaš, rather than Sumer in its entirety. Sumer (ki-en-gi), however, is mentioned once (CB 22:23) and deities of the Sumerian pantheon who have their main residence outside of Lagaš (for example, An, Enlil, Suen) participate in the events. Therefore kalam must refer to Sumer, like in other texts.[230] Thus the narrative conceives of four geographical spheres: the capital city, the city-state, the Sumerian world, and the foreign lands.

The sphere of the main characters is the city-state of Lagaš: Gudea is its earthly ruler, Ningirsu its divine patron. The events either take place at the center of their sphere – the capital city Girsu – or are perceived from that perspective. The journey to Ningin is the only event which takes us outside of Girsu. This rupture in the unity of the place of action is explained by the well-known topos of the journey for the purpose of finding a solution to a problem.[231] While Gudea's destination is indicated upon departure and arrival there (sections 2.2.1 and 2.3.1), the place of departure and the return to Girsu is silently assumed: being the capital of Lagaš, Girsu is Gudea's place of residence and the mention of "his storehouse" (CA 7:13) in the section following the journey is sufficient to imply that we are back there. The other two events which involve other spheres, the

---

(CA 7:28), but also made there. The ensuing sacrifices (section 3.1.2) and prayer (section 3.1.3) take place in specific parts of Eninnu, namely the Šugalam (CA 8:6) and the Ubšukinna (CA 8:14). Ningirsu's response (section 3.2) as well as Gudea's reaction to it (section 3.3) can be assumed to have taken place there, too.

[227] Although the work force is recruited in Lagašite districts presumably outside of Girsu (section 4.2), and the building materials are obtained from foreign lands (section 4.3), these events are staged in Girsu, see below.

[228] Not in subsequent lines, but still in the same event, the city is paired with Lagaš in the account of the special social conditions for the inauguration (CB 18:1 and 12f.), and in the banquet (CB 19:4 and 14f.), and the two together with all lands in the description of the rest between Gudea's presentation of dedicatory gifts and economic products (CB 14:19f. and 23).

[229] Nippur (CA 2:12f.), Keš and Aratta (CA 27:2), and Eridu (CA 29:9); the latter also in the mention of Ningirsu's trip tither (CB 3:9, 8:13, 15).

[230] The royal title lugal-kalam-ma used by kings of Uruk, Akkad, etc. implied the rule over Sumer; see Hallo *Royal Titles*, 18–20.

[231] Compare, for example, *Inanna's Journey to Eridu*, *Inanna's Descent*, and *Gilgameš*. The topos is universal in folk tales, see Propp *Morphology*, function XI.

recruitment of work force in three Lagašite districts (section 4.2) and the provision of materials from foreign lands (section 4.3), are perceived from the perspective of the capital. Gudea does not leave the city, but simply delegates the conscription from Girsu, reviews the parade of the districts there, and receives the building materials there where they are further processed.

In conclusion we can say that the spatial point of view of the narrator concurs with that of the main characters.[232] This is corroborated by the initial reference to Girsu as "our city" (CA 1:4).[233] The ambiguous use of kalam may be explained as the narrator's ambition to make his city-state the center of the Sumerian world.

3. Time

a. Time Indications
Although Gudea is a historical figure, and his reconstruction of Eninnu is substantiated in the inscribed remains of the temple, the events recounted in the present text do not correlate to actual historical incidents.[234] Rather, they are tied to a mythical event: the beginning of time, when destinies were determined (CA 1:1). Eninnu is built to last forever (CA 1:4, 18:25, CB 17:12). Time indications remain vague. For some events only the day is mentioned (u_4);[235] other events are assigned a specific time of day.[236] Only one event, Ningirsu's entry, is dated to a particular calendar date, i.e. the fourth day of a new year (CB 3:5–12).

Similarly, indications concerning the duration of events are few, and usually vague. Gudea apparently spends a night in Lagaš on his way to Ningin, since he is setting up his bed in the Ebagara (CA 2:24; compare 3:10f.). Several days and nights are spent in preparation for the incubation dream (CA 8:2f.). The purification of the construction site involves prayers lasting one day and one night (CA 13:28f.). Time is spent for the bricks to dry (CA 19:1f.). Ningirsu's awakening from sleep before appointing his staff (CB 6:4–7) implies that a night was spent between his entry and that of the staff. A night's rest is described between the presentation of dedicatory gifts and economic products (section 9.2). Only one event in each part of the composition is related to a more specific span of time: the stelae are fashioned in one year, and installed in seven days (CA 22:24–23:4), and the special social conditions imposed for the inauguration of the rebuilt temple are in effect for seven days (CB 17:19). The latter is tied to Ningirsu's

---

[232] For the concurrence of the spatial point of view of narrator and character see Uspensky *Poetics of Composition*, 58f. Chatman *Story and Discourse*, 96f., speaks of "story and discourse space."
[233] For a possible parallel of the use of "our city," see Šulgi F 27.
[234] This is not unusual in ancient Near Eastern building accounts; compare, for example, Lackenbacher *Roi bâtisseur*, 8.
[235] Gudea's reception of the revelation dream (CA 1:17), his telling Nanše his dream (CA 4:13), Ningirsu's giving the requested sign (CA 12:10), Gudea's levy of work force (CA 14:7), and possibly also the measuring out of the construction site (CA 17:5).
[236] Three preparations for the brick making (CA 17:29, 18:3, 18:5), and three events around Ningirsu's entry (CB 3:26, 4:23, 5:19). A particular season of the year, the spring, may have been implied in the metaphor for Enlil's approval (CA 1:5–9), and spring and summer in Ningirsu's promises (CA 11:7–9 and 20–23). The abundance of water could be understood also as a prerequisite for a great project.

entry (CB 17:18) which took place on the fourth day of a new year (CB 3:5–12). The duration of the other events can only be estimated. Table III.C.1 provides an overview of the indicated and estimated (in parentheses) timing of the events.

The rounding of numbers in reference to the duration of events is not unusual in Mesopotamian accounts of royal deeds.[237] Nevertheless, the numbers in Gudea's account are not unrealistic: seven days is a reasonable time for the installation of the stelae and the inauguration festivities, respectively, and one year for the fashioning of the stelae which includes, of course, the import of stone from foreign lands. The absence of other time frames make one wonder whether the one year in the first part, and the seven days in the second, could be applied to the entire construction and inauguration, respectively. Since the seven days in the second part include Ningirsu's induction, they may have included the previous preparations (sections 6–7.2) as well. Neither other time indications nor a reasonable estimate of the duration of the events contradict this assumption. Moreover, the application of a time frame to part of an event as *pars pro toto* for the entire event is evidenced in other building accounts.[238] The fact that the story exhibits unity of place (Girsu) further supports the idea that it also had a unity of time.

In addition to the indication of points in time and of the duration of events, some events are interrelated by temporal clauses: Nanše foresees Ningirsu's willingness to communicate crucial information to Gudea after he presents him with a chariot (CA 6:15–7:2); Ningirsu promises ideal conditions for the construction after Gudea starts the project (CA 11:6 and 18f.);[239] Ningirsu's entry is anticipated in Gudea's preparations for it (CB 3:25), while the special social conditions for the inauguration are retrospectively linked to this event (CB 17:18).[240] The three anticipations foreshadow upcoming events, while the retrospective account of the special social conditions is a clear analepsis, since Gudea imposed it before he prepared the banquet in which context it is recounted.[241]

b. Narrated versus Narrative Time
Narrated time refers to the time of that which is narrated, while narrative time refers

---

[237] Samsu-Iluna, for example, achieves eight victories in one single year, and builds Ebabbar in that same year (RIME 4 E.4.3.7.3). For a discussion of stereotype time frames, especially in Assyrian accounts, with further references, see Tadmor *Iraq* 35 (1973), 143.

[238] Samsu-Iluna, for example, claims to have made the bricks for six fortresses in two months (RIME 4 E.4.3.7.5), and those for Ebabbar in one year (ibidem E.4.3.7.3).

[239] In the first case Gudea's anticipated actions are expressed with prospective clauses (with ù prefix), in the second with when-clauses (with u₄). Prospective clauses as in Nanše's instruction occur frequently in descriptions of deities: CA 3:4, 10:22, CB 8:4–6, 10:23, 11:21, 12:1f.

[240] Both are expressed with when-clauses with u₄. Some relative clauses, constructed with a finite or non-finite verb to which a possessive pronoun is suffixed, contain a temporal notion, and may be translated with a when-clause as well; see Gragg *JNES* 32 (1973), 124–134. These, however, occur only at lower levels of the hierarchy of events, namely in the preparation of the brick mold and loam pit (CA 13:20f.), in the brick making (CA 19:8), and in the descriptions of the functions of Ningirsu's staff (CB 8:13, 10:19–23). After-clauses (ta suffix) also occur only at low levels of the hierarchy: in the journey from Girsu to Lagaš (CA 2:7), and in the completion of the construction (CA 25:20).

[241] Analepsis and prolepsis are discussed in detail by Genette *Figure III*, 90–115; see also Chatman *Story and Discourse*, 64. Section 10.4.1 could be another analepsis, and ur-sag é gibil-na ku₄-ra-àm (CB 19:16) an equivalent of a temporal clause, since the festivities of the banquet have been described in the previous section (10.3).

to the time of the narration; the distinction is between signified and signifying time.[242] If narrative time coincides with narrated time, the result is a scene; if it is shorter, the result is a summary; if it is longer, the result is a pause; if it is zero, the result is an ellipsis.[243] The time covered in the narrative is ideally one year and seven days. Most events are summarized in more or less detail in third person past tense narration. Ellipses are rare; an example is the return trip from Ningin. Scenes appear in the form of inner monologues and direct speeches; they dominate in the verification process (sections 1.2, 2.1, 2.2.2, 2.2.4, 2.3.2, 2.3.3, 3.1.3, 3.2), and also occur in the induction (section 7.1, 7.2), and at the banquet (section 10.4). Pauses appear in the form of descriptions, usually of Gudea, Ningirsu, or Eninnu. These descriptions can encompass longer passages (for example, in the case of Eninnu: CA 24:26–25:13, 26:20–27, 27:2–19, 28:3–29:18; or Gudea: 17:7–14, 19:22–27), or short intermezzos (for example, the recurrent statements about Gudea's competence: CA 7:9f., 12:20, 25:22f., CB 2:7f., 13:12f.).

4. The Relation of Events

a. Sequence

In verbal narratives, the order in which events are presented is normally assumed to correspond to their temporal sequence unless other temporal relations are indicated.[244] With the exception of one analepsis,[245] no anachronisms are indicated in the text. Generally, the narration complies with the logical order of the narrated events. Yet, not all sections follow a simple sequence of events. Section 4 recounts, one after another, a number of thematically related events, namely construction preparations, which do not necessarily follow one another, but most of which can be conceived as parallel events. It does not seem significant, for example, whether the work force was recruited before the building material was provided or vice versa. That the order in which some preparations are recounted bears no significance is corroborated by comparison with the different sequence of these events in some statue inscriptions.[246] Section five, on the other hand, interposes the installation of stelae and trophies (sections 5.4 and 6) between different stages of the construction (sections 5.3, 5.5, 5.7). These anomalies will become clear when considering the hierarchy of events.

b. Hierarchy

An event is defined as any part of the story which can be expressed or summarized in one sentence.[247] This unit can be an essential part of the whole or part of a subordinate unit, which may be parsed into yet smaller units until one reaches the level of single actions and happenings. The importance of a sequence of events can be determined

---

[242] The terminology used here is inspired by the German terms "erzählte Zeit" and "Erzählzeit" corresponding to the French terms "temps de l'histoire" and "temps du récit;" see Genette *Figure III*, 77f.
[243] This scheme follows closely that of Genette *Figure III*, 122–144; see also Chatman *Story and Discourse*, 67–79, and Martin *Theories of Narrative*, 124.
[244] On the order of events see Genette *Figure III*, 78–121.
[245] See chapter III.C.3.a.
[246] See chapter III.E.2.c.
[247] See Prince *Grammar of Stories*, 17.

only in relation to the whole. Every narrative has its hierarchy of events.[248] A six-level hierarchy of the events narrated in Gudea's Cylinder Inscriptions is illustrated on Table III.C.2. The story is parsed into three main branches: the initial circumstances, the construction of Eninnu, and its inauguration. Each branch can be parsed into smaller units on different levels.

The first branch (sections 1–3) can be summarized thus: Ningirsu commissioned Gudea with the construction of Eninnu. This event consists of two main parts: the commission itself (section 1) and its verification (sections 2–3). Since divine communication requires verification, the latter is a consequence of the former, and thus subsumed in it. Ningirsu's commissioning Gudea with the temple construction includes not only the communication itself (1.3), but elaborates on the circumstances which led to it, namely the predestination of Eninnu (1.1), and the qualification of Gudea (1.2). Gudea's verification of the commission consists of two parts, one concerning the medium of the divine communication (section 2), and another concerning its precise message (section 3). Each part is further subdivided into smaller units on several levels, usually three on one level, which follow the sequence of the text.[249]

The second branch (sections 4–5) can be summarized as: Gudea built Eninnu for Ningirsu. Construction is a process of creation by transformation; according to a plan, materials are transformed into a structure by some work force. Therefore, construction implies not only the physical assembly of building units (section 5), but also the provisions necessary for the transformation (section 4). In this story the latter comprise four specific preparations (4.1–5), and their ensuing verification (4.6). The preparations include ritual purification of the city, recruitment of the work force, preparation of the building materials, and preparation of the construction site. These preparations, which are parallel rather than sequential, can each be perceived as twofold events. Purification (4.1.1) and recruitment (4.2) consist each of an action of Gudea (promulgation/conscription) and a reaction of people (observance/mobilization). Two kinds of building materials are provided and transformed into building units: woods, metals, stones are imported from foreign lands, and prepared in Girsu (4.3), while the bricks are locally made (4.5) with clay and brick mold prepared beforehand (4.1.2). The construction site is first purified (4.1.3), and then measured out (4.4). While the purification and the verification by divination pertain to temple building in particular, the other preparations are common to any house construction. The transformation of the prepared materials into the planned structure (section 5) includes three main events: the designation of the foundation (5.1–2); the construction of the main structure in three phases (5.3, 5.5, 5.7); and the installation of stelae (5.4) and trophies (5.6).

The third branch (sections 6–10) can be summarized as: Gudea inaugurated Eninnu. The inauguration of a man-made object is a rite of passage which puts the object to its use, and usually includes festivities. The temple houses deities and serves as a place of worship. In addition, Mesopotamian temples incorporate an estate with its own economy.

---

[248] This approach follows in the line of Tomaševsky and Barthes; see Martin *Theories of Narrative*, 111–115.
[249] See chapter III.B.2–3.

Table III.C.2: Hierarchy of the Events in a Tree-Structure

① commission
- commission
  - predestination
  - qualification of builder
  - transmission
- verification of
  - medium
    - immediate reaction
    - journey to Ningin
      - Lagaš
        - prayer
        - èš-èš
        - prayer
      - Ningin
        - prayer
        - response
  - message
    - preparations
      - chariot
      - ritual
      - prayer
    - response
      - reaction
        - waking
        - extispicy

② construction
- preparations
  - preparations
    - social conditions
      - promulgation
      - observance
    - labor
      - recruitment
      - parade
    - materials
      - bricks
        - mold
        - clay
        - fabrication
      - other
        - import
        - processing
  - verification
    - site
      - purification
      - measuring
- assembly
  - foundation
  - structure
    - walls & roof
    - facade
    - interior
  - installations
    - pond & trees
    - stelae
    - trophies

③ inauguration
- preliminaries
  - public's arrival
  - food provisions
- induction of deities
  - chief couple
    - prayers
    - rituals
    - entry
    - reception
    - meal
  - their staff
    - appointment
    - entry
    - approval
- presentation of gifts
  - dedicatory gifts
  - economic produce
- banquet
  - preparations
  - festivities
  - speeches
    - guest list
    - promotion
    - blessings
      - temple
      - builder

C. Analysis of the Narrative

In this story the inauguration entails four main events: preliminary preparation (section 6), entry of the divine inhabitants (sections 7–8), presentation of gifts (section 9), and a banquet (section 10). The first event which initiates the inauguration is twofold: people and deities gather (6.2), and Gudea provides for food offerings to come (6.3). The entry of the deities proceeds in two steps: first Ningirsu and Baba enter (section 7), and then their staff (section 8). The entry of the divine couple (7.4) includes preparations consisting of two prayers (7.1–2) and other rituals (7.3), and the ensuing reception meal (7.5). The entry of the staff members (8.2) is preceded by Ningirsu's organizing their offices (mar-za) (8.1), and concludes with general divine approval (8.3). Gudea's presentation of gifts is again twofold: he presents dedicatory gifts which let Ningirsu assume his functions (9.1), and economic products of the now prosperous land which will assure the good functioning of the temple's economy (9.3). The banquet contains three events: preparation (10.1), festivities (10.3), and the "after-dinner speeches" which culminate in the blessing of the temple and its builder (10.4).

The preceding description shows that there are certain types of relations among events which can be united into a larger unit, regardless of their level in the hierarchy. An action may require certain circumstances (commission); preceding preparation (construction, inauguration, induction, banquet); or an ensuing reaction or effect (observance, mobilization, verification, approval, reception, blessing). Alternatively, an event may include two or several similar actions (verification of medium and message, entry of divine couple and staff, presentation of dedicatory and economic gifts, construction preparations), or a sequence of actions all serving one purpose (assembly of building units, inauguration). The commission and the inauguration of the temple may be perceived as circumstance and consequence, respectively, of the construction. Thus the three main events can be united on a higher level, and the entire narrative summarized in the sentence: Gudea built Eninnu for Ningirsu. This sentence conveys the essence of the message in terms of information, and can be viewed as its core. The core of the Cylinder Inscriptions is thus identical with the core of the majority of Gudea's building inscriptions (ᵈnin-gír-sú-ra gù-dé-a é-50 mu-na-dù).[250]

The grammatical role of agent, object, beneficiary, and verb in the core sentence corresponds largely to the role of the main characters, object, and action in the story. Gudea is the agent, Ningirsu the beneficiary, Eninnu the object, and the verb "to build" the main action. These roles are assumed at the beginning of the narrative, and constantly actualized throughout it. The core components are mentioned in one way or another in almost every section of the text. The nominal components (Gudea, Ningirsu, Eninnu) are the only entities referred to by several different referents. Wherever they are mentioned, they usually appear grammatically in the same role as in the core sentence, so much so that they can be referred to by the respective pronouns without having been named in the immediate context.[251] All other characters can be perceived as an expansion of

---

[250] See Table I.B.1 no. 1, and chapter II.B.2.c. This is not to say that there are not critical differences between these documents; see chapter III.F.2.
[251] Occasionally, however, the roles of Gudea and Ningirsu are switched, a phenomenon also encountered in the statue inscriptions, and Eninnu also appears as intransitive subject in descriptions or as beneficiary of actions.

the core or mere background. While the event participants have been discussed in detail above, the core action requires further study.

The verb dù is a transitive verb.[252] In almost all its occurrences in the present text in which the meaning is "to build,"[253] the object is Eninnu.[254] Together with this object the verb occurs forty-five times; thirty-five times in the first part of the composition, with an expected concentration in sections 4 and 5, and ten times in the second. In other words, the core event is actualized throughout the text. Nine finite forms anticipate the construction, four appear in the construction process, and eight retrospectively.[255] The anticipations are either *marû*-forms or volitive; all other occurrences are *hamṭu*-forms. Thus in its process the construction is perceived from a past perspective, rather than as an ongoing event. The finite forms appear in sentences which are identical to the core sentence. Gudea is usually their agent, though Ningirsu and Ningišzida are credited together with Gudea for it, retrospectively.[256] If the beneficiary is mentioned, it is always Ningirsu. Non-finite forms govern either complement or relative clauses. All thirteen complement clauses (for example, "in order to build the pure house") occur before the physical construction in sentences anticipating it (sections 1–3), or in construction preparations (section 4).[257] The relative clauses are governed by either Gudea (who was building/built Eninnu), or Eninnu (which is built). The former are builder epithets of Gudea which occur throughout the text;[258] the latter occur after the construction.[259] While the recurrent builder epithet emphasizes the agent of the core action, some complement clauses have other agents who act on Gudea's behalf. "To build" is obviously the key verb in the narrative. It not only actualizes the core action, but also summarizes it, much like the other inscriptions of Gudea.

c. Narrative Anaphora

The orientation in the sequence and hierarchy of events is facilitated by anticipations of future events and recollections of past events at various points in the text. Only exceptionally are they temporally linked to the "story-now." More often they take the

---

[252] It belongs to the transitive verbs that do not take the b infix before the root, and to the class of regular verbs which do not change their basic stem. Yoshikawa's suggestion that the *marû*-form is marked by the suffix e, and thus distinguished from the *hamṭu*-form is followed here. For a discussion of this and other interpretations see Thomsen *Sumerian Language*, §§ 232f.

[253] The following other meanings of dù occur in the Cylinder Inscriptions: to plant plants or trees (CA 3:12, 22:8); to erect standards, posts, stelae (CA 20:1, 22:17, 23:3, CB 22:4); to mount in reference to animals (CB 15:6); and the compound verbs ì-bí–dù (CA 8:12, 13:27), KA–dù (CA 13:4), and sag–dù (CA 17:9).

[254] Only two occurrences do not explicitly mention the object (CA 25:20, CB 22:16); in both cases the context leaves no doubt that Eninnu is meant. Twice the object is a part of Eninnu, its sleeping quarters (CA 25:17), or its cattle pen and sheepfold (CB 15:5). Only four times dù "to build" occurs with another object: twice in the expression uru dù-a "fortified city" (CA 14:11, CB 8:16); in a description of Ehuš, one of Ningirsu's places of worship (CA 10:19); and in a metaphor describing Gudea's eagerness to construct (CA 19:22).

[255] CA 2:14, 8:18, 9:7f., 12:1; 21;17, 22:9, 24:8, 25:20; 30:1f., CB 2:5, 2:21, 13:9f., 17:13.

[256] Ningirsu and Ningišzida in CA 30:1–3, and Ningirsu again in CB 13:9f.; compare also CB 22:16. Once, in Ningirsu's promises, days and nights are agents in a metaphoric way (CA 12:1f).

[257] CA 1:16, 19, 4:20, 5:18, 6:1, 11, 9:9; 14:2, 28, 15:9, 17:7, 20:2, 9.

[258] Only some of these epithets include a relative head (lú), in which case they may also include a genitive, see note 179 above.

[259] In the colophons in CA 30:15 and CB 24:16, and in a description of the temple in CB 20:20f.

Table III.C.3: Graph Illustrating Narrative Anaphora

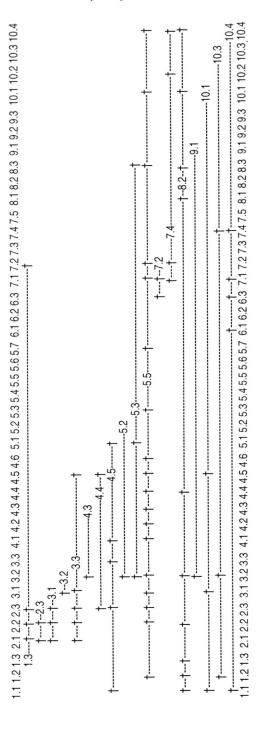

The numbers refer to the sections of the outline; † indicates in which other section the event is anticipated or recollected. The text references, arranged by the section in which the event occurs, are as follows:

1.3: the revelation dream: CA 1:17<1:27<1:29<3:25<4:13<5:12.

Ningirsu's speaking about building the house: CA 1:19>2:13<4:20<5:18<CB 2:19.

2.3: telling the dream to Nanše: 1:24>1:29>3:22f>3:25>4:13.

Nanše's interpretation: CA 2:3>2:19>3:28>5:12.

3.1: following Nanše's instruction: CA 1:25>3:24>6:14>CA 7:11f.

3.2: elucidating the sign (gizkim): 8:19>9:9>12:11.

3.3: elucidating the "heart" of the dream/Ningirsu: CA 1:27>2:3>3:28>4:21>7:4f.>8:22-9:4>12:18f.<19:28.

4.3: arrival of building materials: CA 12:3-12:9>15:6-16:24.

4.4: laying out the plan of the house: CA 6:5>7:6>17:17<19:20.

4.5: sacrificing perfect bulls and kids: CA 1:14>18:7.

making the bricks: CA 1:15>5:7>6:7>13:17>18:17-19:19<20:18.

5.2: laying the foundation: CA 11:10>20:26

5.3: marking the perimeter: CA 11:18>20:15>22:11-15<CB 13:3.

5.5: "acting well": CA 2:13>11:6>11:19>(25:20)<CB 2:20.

building the house: CA 1:16>19>2:14>4:20>5:18>6:1>11>8:18>9:7-9>12:1>14:2>28>15:9>17:7>20:2>9>

21:17>22:9>24:8>25:20<30:1-3<13<CB 2:5<21<13:10<17:13<20:7.

7.2: praying for Ningirsu's induction: CB 1:15>2:6>2:14f.<3:3.

7.4: Ningirsu's entry: CB 2:5>2:22>5:1<17:18<19:16.

8.2: Eninnu's mes: CA 1:2>1:11>1:20>2:15>9:11f>17:19>CB 6:8>6:23—7:11—23—8:9—22—9:4f.—14—

10:2—8—15—11:2—26—12:6—17—25<13:5<16:3<17:14<[20:8]<[23:8].

9.1: Ningirsu assuming his offices: CA 9:20-10:13>CB 13:14-14:18.

10.1: appearing of the everlasting thing (níg-ul): CA 1:4>8:20>18:25>CB 17:12.

10.3: sacrificing perfect bulls and kids: CA 1:14>CB 18:19.

arrival of abundance for Lagaš: CA 11:8-11>CB 5:18>19:14f.

10.4: determination of Eninnu's destiny: CA 1:1-2>CB 1:3>13>5:16>20:15-19>21:17-19>22:17-24:8<24:11.

blessing of Gudea with long life: CB 2:3f.>24:8.

form of independent phrases or clauses comparable to anaphora in poetic language.[260] Table III.C.3 illustrates the use of narrative anaphora in the cylinders. The linked events can be higher or lower in the hierarchy and more or less far apart from each other. In the verification of the revelation (section 2), Gudea's telling of the dream to Nanše, as well as her interpretation, are mentioned two or three times, respectively, before they actually take place. The anticipations are identical or similar phrases: "I want to speak to someone, I want to speak to someone" (CA 1:24=3:22f.); "I shall bring my dream to my mother" (CA 1:29=3:25); "May my Nanše, sister, deity from Sirara, reveal its heart for me/pave its way for me" (CA 2:2f.=3:27f./2:18f.). The "heart" of the dream or Ningirsu, alternatively, is a key term in the verification process (sections 2–3), and is recollected at the accomplishment of the last construction preparation (section 4.5). On a higher level, Ningirsu's speaking about building the house recounted in section 1, is harkened back to several times in the course of the verification of the revelation (section 2) and mentioned again in the inauguration of the newly built temple when Gudea pleads for Ningirsu's entry (section 7). Ningirsu's entry, a major event which has its story-now in section 7.4, is anticipated twice (sections 7.1 and 7.2) and recollected twice (sections 10.2 and 10.4). As these examples show, narrative anaphorae can create tension or suspense. I see their main function in leading the audience through the story as announcing and recalling important events, comparable to flags that serve as points of reference in orientation.

---

[260] The term anaphora is used here also for anticipatory anaphora, i.e. cataphora.

D. Poetic Traits

Poetry, defined as verbal art, is a heightened mode of discourse which can be achieved by various means, a basic characteristic being its rhythmic structure.[261] This structure is achieved mainly by means of repetition patterns which manifest "the projection of the principle of equivalence from the axis of selection to that of combination, resulting in a heightened quotient of self-reference."[262] Repetition can occur in different aspects of language (phonology, lexicon, grammar) and on different levels of the structure (verse, stanza, strophe).[263] In addition to repetition patterns, Sumerian literary texts exhibit a particular vocabulary, phraseology, figures of speech, and certain grammatical peculiarities.[264] These features are not unique to such texts, yet they occur with more frequency in them. The distinction between poetic and non-poetic texts is a question of degree. The Cylinder Inscriptions are not highly poetic, but they do exhibit poetic traits. In view of the length of this text an exhaustive analysis of these traits is beyond the scope of the present study. The following presentation intends to point out examples which illustrate the nature of the text. They support and enhance the linear outline proposed in this study and set a background for the comparison with other inscriptions of Gudea and for a classification of the cylinders within Sumerian literature.

1. General Features

Falkenstein pointed out the frequent mention in the Cylinder Inscriptions of religious concepts that are typical of literary texts.[265] Examples of phraseology are the opening "When destinies had to be determined in the universe" (CA 1:1);[266] "Let me instruct you. May you follow my instruction" (CA 6:14);[267] "Nidaba opened the 'House of Wisdom' for him" (CA 17:15f.).[268] Related to phraseology is the use of word pairs[269] such as heaven & earth, day & night, south & north, lord/lady & male servant/female servant, perfect oxen & perfect sheep, bread & water.[270]

---

[261] NPEPP 938–942 s.v. poetry.
[262] NPEPP 1035–1037 s.v. repetition.
[263] The definition and classification of such patterns in Sumerian poetry is still in its beginnings. In general see Wilcke *AS* 20 (1976), 212–219; Krecher "Sumerian Literature," 122f. and 128–132; Vanstiphout "Repetition and Structure;" and NPEPP 1233f. s.v. Sumerian poetry. Some poetic devices in the Cylinder Inscriptions have been pointed out already by Falkenstein *Einleitung*, 181–183.
[264] See Wilcke *AS* 20 (1976), 207–212, and Krecher "Sumerische Literatur," 117–123.
[265] Falkenstein *Einleitung*, 185f.
[266] See Black "Structural Features," 73f. with appendix B.
[267] See Alster *Proverbs*, 29f.
[268] See *Enmerkar and the Lord of Aratta* 321f.
[269] On word pairs in Sumerian see Alster *Proverbs*, 31f., and Krecher "Sumerische Literatur," 123. Word pairs have been studied exhaustively in the Bible, see Berlin *UF* 15 (1983), 7–16. Berlin ibidem, 16, pointed out that word pairs are a window into language behavior, rather than literary tradition. They are activated by literary devices, rather than being a literary device in themselves, since they exist potentially in all languages. In Sumerian, word pairs are also used to designate collectives, see Civil *RA* 61 (1967), 64 note 2.
[270] an & ki: CA 1:1, 1:11, 17:9, 20:16, 21:23, 24:9, 25:13, CB 1:2, 13:5, 24:14; u_4 & gi_6: CA 8:2f., 12:1f., 13:28f., CB 4:22, 6:5, 7:6; sig & nim: CA 12:3–5, 17:23–25, CB 24:2; lugal/nin & arád/gemé: CA 13:6–9, CB 17:20f.; gu_4 du_7 & máš du_7: CA 1:14, 18:7, CB 7:4, 18:19; ninda & a: CA 2:8, 2:25, 4:6.

Figures of speech occur in the form of similes and metaphors. Similes are recognizable by the use of the equative "like" (-gin$_7$) suffixed to the nominal phrase or by the use of an enclitic copula (-ám), whereas metaphors are not morphologically marked.[271] Metaphors can be missed if taken literally; they can also be mistakenly assumed when the ancient Sumerian had something concrete in mind.[272] Since most metaphors in Sumerian literary texts use imagery similar or identical to similes in the same texts, they can usually be detected as such. In the Cylinder Inscriptions figures of speech are frequent in descriptions of Eninnu, but also occur in descriptions of deities, or Gudea.[273]

Grammatical peculiarities concern mainly unusual word order.[274] In the Cylinder Inscriptions the names and anaphorae referring to Eninnu and Ningirsu are noticeably placed at the beginning of a line, regardless of the syntax which would often assign them a different place in normal word order. Another example of unusual word order are the prayer acceptance formulae which refer to the divine agent with a nominal referent twice in the same sentence: first with a generic term (lugal/nin/ursag) linked to Gudea by a possessive pronoun (-a-ni), then with the personal name immediately preceding the verb.[275]

2. Repetition Patterns

a. Phrase Reduplication
A phrase, usually not longer than one line of text, is repeated identically and contiguously.[276] Phrase reduplication is analogous to intensive reduplication in grammar. This device is used sparingly in the Cylinder Inscriptions; two examples are: "I want to speak to someone, I want to speak to someone" (CA 1:24=3:22f.); "Again, for the one lying down, for the one lying down" (CA 9:5).

b. Narrative Repetition
Rather than referring to a previous passage by anaphoric means, the entire passage is repeated verbatim, or with only minor adjustments of tense or person.[277] Narrative repetition is frequent in narrative poems with an oral background. It often occurs in

---

[271] For the various grammatical constructions of metaphors see Wilcke *AS* 20 (1976), 210–212. His type d (nominal predicate without copula) is basically a simile, for example, in CA 12:18f.: "For Gudea Ningirsu's heart, being the sun, emerged," i.e., "for Gudea Ningirsu's heart emerged like the sun." See also the detailed discussion of figures of speech by Heimpel *Tierbilder*, 11–72.

[272] Berlin *Enmerkar* 28.

[273] For Eninnu see CA 21:13–24, 24:8–25, 24:26–25:13, 26:20–27:1, 28:19–29:9, 30:6–12, and chapter III.C.1.e; for deities CA 3:11, 14f., 10:23; for Gudea CA 19:22–27. See also Falkenstein *Einleitung*, 186.

[274] In general see Wilcke *AS* 20 (1976), 208–210; for a compilation of unusual word order in Gudea's inscriptions see Falkenstein *Grammatik* II, §§ 83–85.

[275] CA 2:21f.: lugal-a-ni sízkur rá-zu-ni gù-dé-a-áš, en ^{d}nin-gír-sú-ke$_4$ šu ba-ši-ti; compare CA 4:1f., and CB 3:3f.

[276] Wilcke *AS* 20 (1976), 214, accounted for this type of repetition under the heading "ornamentale Wiederholung (R-5)" which also includes types of parallelism; Vanstiphout "Repetition and Structure," 251–254, under the heading "serial repetition" which also includes other poetic devices. See also Berlin *Enmerkar*, 24f.

[277] Wilcke *AS* 20 (1976), 212f., called this type of repetition "epische Wiederholung;" Krecher "Sumerische Literatur," 131f., "erzählerische Wiederholung;" and Vanstiphout "Repetition and Structure," 248–251, "wholesale repetition."

the context of speeches. A speech can be repeated by another speaker or to another listener, or an instruction or prediction given in a speech can be realized or come true. The three instances of narrative repetition in the Cylinder Inscriptions all occur in the verification process (sections 2–3) which is permeated with speeches. First, Gudea's inner monologue (CA 1:24–2:3), except for two lines (CA 1:24f.), is repeated verbatim in the petition of his prayer to Gatumdug (CA 3:22–28). The repetition restates the purpose of the impending trip and, thus, underlines its importance, and, at the same time, delays it creating tension.

The second instance is of a special type in that the repeated passage is interrupted several times, and enhanced with new information. Gudea tells Nanše his dream consisting of seven images (CA 4:14–5:10). When Nanše interprets the dream, she repeats each image as described by Gudea, with the pronouns changed from first to second person, and adds her identification (CA 5:13–6:13). This phenomenon also occurs in Dumuzi's Dream.[278] In both texts the dream incident is vital to the plot; it foreshadows coming events and sets the mood for them.[279] The third instance is the realization of an instruction. Nanše advises Gudea to fashion a chariot and present it to Ningirsu (CA 6:16–7:2), which he does (CA 7:13–29). The verbal forms and pronouns are changed from second to third person, the tense from future to past, and minor details are altered.[280] Again, the repetition creates tension, this time in regard to the verification process by delaying Ningirsu's response.

c. Recurrent Formulae

A formulaic sentence or clause is repeated at regular or irregular intervals throughout the text or through part of it. The formula, first defined by Parry in 1928, is a hallmark of oral literature.[281] With regard to the narrative context, two types of recurrent formulae can be distinguished: first, events repeated in the story, and second, self-contained descriptive statements which function as a pause and transition between two events. Examples of the first type in the Cylinder Inscriptions are the recurrent prayer introduction and acceptance;[282] obedience of a divine instruction;[283] extispicy;[284] or the description of

---

[278] Alster *Dumuzi's Dream*, 33–40.

[279] Oppenheim *Dreams*, 212.

[280] Three verses concerning details of the chariot in Nanše's instruction (CA 6:19–21) are unparalleled in Gudea's execution, and a strophe elaborating on the building material in the latter (CA 7:15–18) did not occur in the instruction. Furthermore, the dative object in CA 6:17 is reduced to a pronoun in CA 7:19, while the donkeys in CA 6:18 are given an epithet in CA 7:20f. None of these details alter the event; rather they are expansions or reductions of a particular action.

[281] NPEPP 422f. s.v. formula. Alster *Dumuzi's Dream*, 15–27, the first and only application of the Parry-Lord theories to Sumerian literature, is not accurate concerning the definition of formula, and has met with criticism; for a recent stand on this matter see Michalowski "Orality and Literacy." Both, Wilcke *AS* 20 (1976), 214–217, and Krecher "Sumerian Literature," 128–131, include examples of recurrent formulae in Sumerian literary texts under the heading "refrain." This term, however, applies only to sentences set at regular intervals, and they need not be formulaic; for a definition see NPEPP 1018f. s.v. refrain. Vanstiphout "Repetition and Structure," 254f., on the other hand, lists refrains and irregularly set recurrent statements under the heading "formulaic repetition," though his examples are not formulae.

[282] CA 2:8f., 2:25f., 4:6f.; CA 2:20–22, 3:29–4:2, CB 3:2–4.

[283] CA 7:11f., 12:14f.

[284] CA 12:16f., 20:5.

night-time.[285] The second type is represented by two formulae expressing the competence and expertise of the protagonist; both are attested also in other texts. "He knows great things, and also accomplishes great things" occurs at irregular intervals throughout the text (CA 7:9f., 12:20, 25:22f., CB 2:7f., 13:12f.);[286] "He joyfully established it for him" concludes the sub-sections of section 4 (CA 14:5f., 17:28, 20:4, 20:12).[287]

d. Semantic Parallelism

Parallelism can be considered a subtype of repetition: identical or similar syntactic patterns are repeated in contiguous clauses and may then activate repetitions on the level of lexicon or phonology.[288] A repetition can have one or several equivalencies of various types and degrees on a scale ranging from verbatim repetition to faint semantic similarity. While repetition on the phonological level (rhyme, meter) is rare in ancient Near Eastern poetry, that on the lexical level, i.e. semantic parallelism, is a driving force in cuneiform literature and the Bible.[289] It occurs frequently in the Cylinder Inscriptions. A few simple, small-scale examples are quoted here:

1) CA 21:19–22

é hur-sag-gin₇ im-mú-mú-ne — They were making the house grow like a mountain,

dugud-gin₇ an-šà-ge im-mi-ni-íb-diri-diri-ne — were making it float like a cloud in the midst of the sky,

gu₄-gin₇ si im-mi-íb-íl-íl-ne — were making it raise (its) horns like a bull,

ᵍⁱˢgána-abzu-gin₇ kur-kur-ra sag ba-ni-íb-íl-ne — were making it outstanding in all lands like the gana of Abzu.

2) CA 3:6f.

ama nu-tuku-me ama-mu zé-me — I do not have a mother; you are my mother.

nu-tuku-me a-mu zé-me — I do not have a father; you are my father.

3) CA 11:26f.

gi₆-a-na ì-ti ma-ra-é-é — At midnight the moon(light) will always emerge for you.

e-bar₇-GANA u₄-ma-dam ma-ra-é-é — At noon pleasant sun(light) will always emerge for you.

4) CA 12:12f.

gù-dé-a ì-zi ù-sa-ga-àm — Gudea rose; it was sleep.

ì-ha-luh ma-mu-dam — He shuddered; it was a dream.

---

[285] CA 8:4f., CB 4:15f.
[286] This formula occurs in variant versions in various literay texts since the Early Dynastic period; see Falkenstein *Einleitung*, 183 note 5, and Alster "Interaction," 63.
[287] This formula also occurs in *Gilgameš and Huwawa* 46f., and *Samsu-Iluna B* 27f., as noted by Averbeck *Ritual and Structure*, 640 note 264.
[288] Alternatively, repetition can be considered a subtype of parallelism, see NPEPP 877–879 s.v. parallelism.
[289] Sumerologists have dealt only briefly with this subject, see Wilcke *AS* 20 (1976), 217–219. Berlin *Enmerkar*, applied the biblical studies approach to a Sumerian text; see also her *Dynamics of Biblical Parallelism*.

5) CA 7:17f.

giš mes-e sag bí-sag₉	The mes-wood was hewed,
giš ha-lu-úb-ba gín bí-bar	the oak-wood was split with an ax.

6) CA 9:20–22

gá ᵈnin-gír-sú a huš gi₄-a	I (am) Ningirsu who stops the fierce waters,
ur-sag gal ki-ᵈen-líl-lá-ka	the great warrior of Enlil's realm,
en gaba-ri nu-tuk	the lord without adversary.

7) CA 17:10–14

igi zi-bar-ra ᵈnanše-kam	He is the one looked at approvingly by Nanše.
ᵈen-líl-lá lí šà-ga-na-kam	He is the one of Enlil's choice.
énsi [...] x x [...] ᵈnin-gír-sú-kam	He is the [...] ruler of Ningirsu.
gù-dé-a unu₆ mah-a tu-da	Gudea is the one born in the huge banquet hall
ᵈgá-tùm-dùg-ga-kam	by Gatumdug.

Each parallelism usually involves several equivalencies. On the grammatical level, the equivalencies in the above examples are identical nominal or verbal chains; on the lexical level, they are synonyms, word pairs, different referents for the same character or object, or terms of the same lexical set (for example, deities, actions expressing divine approval).

The enumeration of the members of a lexical set is a favorite device in Sumerian poetry, which can extend to passages of considerable length.[290] If combined with syntactic and verbatim repetitions rigid frames are generated. The parallel clauses can contain several lexical equivalencies. In the Cylinder Inscriptions such frames are frequent. Shorter enumerations occur, for example, for the recruitment of work force: "In his [word pair for geographical area], in [DN]'s [GN], he made a conscription" (CA 14:8–13); and the ensuing mobilization: "[name of clan] mobilized for him in [DN]'s district; its [name of standard ([DN]'s standard)], marched at its head" (CA 14:14–27); or in the provision of materials: "(In accord) with [DN = name of male/female patron of Dilmun] he (Gudea) gave orders; [type(s) of building material] he/she sent for Gudea, [builder epithet]" (CA 15:11–18). The rigidity of such frames can be loosened by minor deviations – for example, in the appointment of artisans: "[referent for Gudea] was building [referent for Eninnu] with [type of building material], and employed [class of artisan]" (CA 16:25–30), in which the last phrase differs in the third member.

Examples of longer enumerations are the installation and naming of the stelae: "The stone which he erected in [name of location in Eninnu], that stone he named [name of stela]" (CA 23:8–24:7); the installation of Ningirsu's trophies: "At [name of location in Eninnu], its [function of location], he was installing [name(s) of trophie(s)]" (CA 25:24–26:14); and the entry of Ningirsu's staff: "[functions: to do x, y, z] [DN + epithet(s)] was

---

290 Wilcke *AS* 20 (1976), 219; Krecher "Sumerische Literatur," 128–131; and Civil *AOS* 67 (1987). It is related to the compilation of lists of classified items, be they animals, materials, implements, or other entities, which was a specialty of the Sumerian scribes. For the Sumerian perception of abstract concepts see Farber-Flügge *AulaOr* 9 (1991).

parading with his mes before Ningirsu" (CB 6:11–12:25). The last example contains an enumeration within an enumeration: that of the staff members who enter, and that of the functions of each staff member. A similar enumeration of items combined with a single verb also occurs in Gudea's presentation of economic products (section 9.3). Enumerations without verbatim repetition but with more or less rigid syntactical frames occur, for example, in the description of special social conditions (sections 4.1.1, 10.2), the descriptions of Eninnu (for example, CA 28:3–18), or the divine approval (section 8.3).

Thematically similar passages forming a semantic unit without syntactic parallelism are often linked by the repetition of a sentence or clause at their beginning or end. "When you will act well for it," for example, introduces each of two lists of Ningirsu's promises (CA 11:6 and 11:19). A slightly varied statement introduces two analogous passages which form a sub-unit of the importations in section 4.3: "In [foreign country] lord Ningirsu established roads for Gudea" (CA 15:19–21 and 16:3–5). Other examples are: "The one/ruler building the house, Gudea, the ruler of Lagaš, is going to offer gifts for the house/it" heading each of two sets of gifts (CB 13:14–17 and 14:9–12) in section 9.1; "It was the Sun coming forth" (CB 5:9 and 16) which concludes the two parallel sub-sections of section 7.4 describing Ningirsu's and Baba's entry; and "Eninnu's awe covers all the lands like a cloth" (CA 27:6f. and 29:18f.) in section 5.7.

e. Chiasmus
Chiasmus is defined as the inversion of two terms. Like repetition, chiasmus occurs on different levels of the text.[291] It is rather rare in Sumerian literature,[292] and examples are difficult to come by in the Cylinder Inscriptions:[293]

1) CA 13:3f.

ama-a dumu-da gù nu-ma-da-dé No **mother** had words with (her) **child**.

dumu-ù ama-ni-ra ka dù-a No **child** spoke rebelliously to his/her **mother**.

2) CA 17:20f.

Lugal-bi en igi huš íl-íl **Its master** (is) a fiercely glaring **lord**.

ur-sag ᵈnin-gír-sú mè gal-zu-bi **Warrior** Ningirsu (is) **its expert** in battle.

f. Ring Composition
In ring compositions two terms are repeated at the beginning and end of a passage, thus binding it together. The framed passage can be of varying size.[294] Two small-scale examples in the Cylinders are:

---

[291] NPEPP 183f. s.v. chiasmus.

[292] Wilcke *AS* 20 (1976), 218f., and Berlin *Enmerkar*, 26f.

[293] See also CA 26:20–27: the ... its ... its ... the ... ; CB 13:6–12: Ningirsu ... Nanše ... Nanše ... Ningirsu. I would not consider truly chiastic the examples given by Hurowitz *Temple Building*, 50, and 65f.

[294] For a definition see NPEPP 1072f. s.v. ring composition; for examples in other Sumerian texts see Berlin *Enmerkar*, 26.

1) CA 11:1–4

é-mu é-sag kal kur-kur-ra	**My house**, the store house of all lands,
á zi-da lagaš^{ki}	the right side of Lagaš,
ánzu^{mušen} na-šár-ra šeg$_{12}$ gi$_4$-gi$_4$	the Anzu howling in the wide sky,
é-50 é-nam-lugal-mu	Eninnu, **my royal house**.

2) CA 3:10–15

gi$_6$-a ma-ni-ná	**At night (when) I lay down**,
giš-ul$_4$ gal-mu-me zà-mu mu-ús	you are my great ul-tree (?); you stand by my side.
li$_9$-bar a gal-la dù-a-me	You are the one who planted the wild grain in plenty of water.
zi-šà mu-ši-ni-gál	You let life's breath be there.
an-dùl dagal-me gizzu-zu-šè	You are a large awning.
ní ga-ma-ši-íb-te	**Beneath your shade let me rest**.

On a larger scale, ring compositions are generated by the mention of me in sections 5.1 and 10.1 (CA 20:13–22; CB 16:3–17:14);[295] by the mention of the sign (gizkim) in Ningirsu's speech in response to Gudea's incubation (sections 3.2.2 and 3.2.7); by the reaction of Gudea in the verification process (sections 2.1 and 3.3); by the analogous description of Eninnu in the second part of the composition (section 6.1 and doxology of CB); and by the theme of divine fate determination on the level of the entire composition (sections 1.1 and 10.4).

g. Combinations

Different patterns can be combined, as in the following examples:

1) CA 9:7–10

ma-dù-na ma-dù-na	That which you will build for me, which you will build for me,
énsi é-mu ma-dù-na	ruler, my house which you will build for me,
gù-dé-a é-mu dù-da gizkim-bi ga-ra-ab-sum	Gudea, the sign of my house to be built let me give to you;
garza-gá mul-an kù-ba gù ga-mu-ra-a-dé	the pure tablets of my cult let me read out to you.

2) CA 17:22–25

é-50 ánzu^{mušen} bábbar-šè	For Eninnu, the white Anzu,
gù-dé-a sig-ta ba-ši-gin, nim-šè u$_5$ bí-dug$_4$	Gudea went from south to north, surveyed (?) the area;
nim-ta ba-ši-gin, sig-šè u$_5$ bí-dug$_4$	went from north to south, surveyed (?) the area.

3) CA 3:16–21

š[u m]ah-za sa-ga á zi-da-bi	May your huge hands, the right side of ...,
nin-mu ^{d}gá-tùm-dùg gá-ra ha-mu-ú-ru	milady Gatumdug, watch over me.

---

[295] Section 5.1 has a second ring, the mention of priests in CA 20:14 and 21.

uru-šè ì-du-e gizkim-mu hé-sa$_6$	I shall go to the city; may my sign be favorable.
kur a-ta íl-la ningin$_6$(AB×HA)^{ki}-šè	Toward Ningin, the land rising above the water,
ú-dug$_4$ sag$_9$-ga-zu igi-šè ha-ma-du	may your good Udug walk in front of me,
^{d}lamma sag$_9$-ga-zu gìri-a ha-mu-da-du	may your good Lamma walk behind me.

The first example combines phrase reduplication and semantic parallelism, the second phrase reduplication and chiasmus, and the third semantic parallelism and ring composition. In addition, parallel frames can be combined with a concluding and/or introductory statement to form a section as, for example, in sections 4.1.1, 4.2, 5.2, 5.4, 5.6, 7.4, 8.

3. Overall Structure

The Cylinder Inscriptions lack rubrics as well as graphic divisions beyond that of the case-ruled lines which wrap around in columns. Although the repetition patterns just discussed generate certain units, the text does not exhibit an overall poetic structure resulting from a division into stanzas and strophes.[296] In comparison with other Sumerian literary texts, its line division, though tending towards short-lines, is not always consistent.[297] That line division is originally a question of syntax, rather than semantics, can be demonstrated by the following comparison:

CB 17:17–18:9:	Statue B 7:29–46:
géme nin-a-né mu-da-sá-àm	géme nin-a-né mu-da-sá-àm
árad-dè lugal-e zag mu-da-gub-àm	árad-dè
	lugal-e zag mu-da-gub-àm
uru-na uzug$_x$-ni zag-bi-a mu-da-a-ná-àm	uru-na uzug$_x$-ni
	zag-bi-a mu-da-a-ná-àm
eme níg hul-da dug$_4$ ba-da-kúr	
níg-érim é-ba im-ma-an-g[i$_4$]	níg-érim é-bi-a
	im-mi-gi$_4$
níg g[i-gi-na] ^{d}[nanše] ^{d}nin-[gír-sú]-k[a-šè]	níg gi-gi-na
	^{d}nanše
	^{d}nin-gír-sú-ka-šè
èn [im]-ma-[ši-tar]	èn im-ma-ši-tar
nu-siki [lú níg-tuk] nu-m[u-na-gar]	nu-siki lú níg tuk nu-mu-na-gar
nu-m[a-su] lú [á-tuk] nu-na-[gar]	na-ma-su lú á tuk nu-na-gar
é ib[ila] nu-[tuk]	é ibila nu-tuk
dumu-mu[nus-bi ì-bí]-lu-[ba mi-ni-ku$_4$]	dumu-munus-bi ì-bí-la-ba
	mi-ni-ku$_4$

This passage of the Cylinder Inscriptions, duplicated in Statue B, enumerates legal regulations each consisting of one full sentence. In both texts one item of the set tends

---

[296] Such divisions occur in shorter, more lyrical Sumerian compositions, see Wilcke *AS* 20 (1976), 233–239; Berlin *Enmerkar*, 10–12; Vanstiphout "Verse Language," 323–328.

[297] The same phrase reduplication, for example, can be written in one line once (CA 1:24), but in two another time (CA 3:22–23). See also Falkenstein *Einleitung*, 185. On line division and the relation of line and verse see Wilcke *AS* 20 (1976), 220–224; Berlin *Enmerkar*, 22–24; and Vanstiphout "Verse Language," 311–323.

to be written in one line. Larger sentences, however, are split into smaller syntactic units that are written in two or three lines. This happens only twice in the Cylinders, but five times in Statue B. The segments of text in one line are generally larger in the Cylinders than in other inscriptions of Gudea. The Cylinders thus show a tendency for not only syntactic but also semantic unity in one line.

In addition, a few passages exhibit a metric structure. Heimpel detected one instance in which the number of syllables is kept constant by the insertion of the "filler" -àm (CA 21:1–12).[298] Such instances, however, are few and scattered. In conclusion, we can say that one line of text in the Cylinder Inscriptions tends to correspond to a syntactic unit which may coincide with a semantic unit, and sometimes also with a rhythmic one. In a conservative definition the text does not qualify as a poem written in verse.

---

[298] Heimpel *Or* 39 (1970), 492–495. Further examples are offered by Wilcke *AS* 20 (1976), 224–231; see also Edzard *RlA* 8 (1993), 148f. s.v. Metrik. In other compositions Civil "Sumerian Poetry," 1233f., observed lines of 8+5 syllables.

E.   Comparison with the Other Inscriptions

1.   General Observations

All inscriptions of Gudea commemorate one main event in which the ruler acts for a deity. In the Cylinder Inscriptions and the building inscriptions the core event is the construction of a temple, while in the dedicatory and statue inscriptions it is the consecration of a dedicatory object. The statue inscriptions are often combined with an account of the construction of the temple in which the statue is consecrated. In contrast to most other inscriptions, which summarize the core event in basically one sentence, the Cylinder Inscriptions detail and actualize the core event, elaborate and extend the core characters (Gudea and Ningirsu) and object (Eninnu), and add information on circumstances and consequences.

In the Cylinder Inscriptions, agent, beneficiary, and object are introduced in a narrative context (the initial circumstances), referred to with several different referents (name, title, or epithets) throughout the text, and described variously at different points. In addition, numerous other deities and human beings participate in the events. Similarly, the core verb recurs many times and in different forms throughout the text, and the core action is expanded in various aspects and implications. In the other inscriptions the event participants are limited to agent and beneficiary. They are identified once in their grammatical role, referred to afterwards by pronouns only, and their characterization is restricted to epithets. The same applies to the object in the building inscriptions. The core verbs occur only once in finite forms, except for some building inscriptions which add a second construction in which the same verb is repeated. In the building inscriptions the expansion of the core action is restricted to two formulaic phrases generalizing or specifying the action; in the dedicatory and statue inscriptions to a brief account of the preceding fabrication of the object in not more than three clauses, if it is not already included in the core, or an adverbial indication of place or cause.

An exception is the construction account in some statue inscriptions, which elaborates on circumstances, details preparations, and specifies natural conclusions. The divine beneficiary or Gudea's personal god Ningišzida may act on his behalf. Furthermore, other deities may occur in the curse, and human beings in the descriptions of special social conditions. Consequently the names of agent and beneficiary can be repeated, and Gudea's qualification and achievement described in finite clauses at the beginning or end. These detailed construction accounts may use poetic devices such as semantic parallelism and enumeration. The statue inscriptions can thus be considered a link between building and dedicatory inscriptions on one hand, and the Cylinder Inscriptions on the other. The remainder of this chapter investigates the correspondences between the cylinders and the statue inscriptions in more detail. It illustrates how thin the boundary between factual royal inscription and a more poetic and narrative text concerning the ruler can be in terms of contents and form, and further elucidates the mechanisms of the composition of such texts, especially how a core message can be expanded by making explicit more and more events and circumstances implied in it.

2. The Construction in the Cylinder and Statue Inscriptions

a. Overview

Most components of the construction account in the statue inscriptions correspond to certain sections in the Cylinder Inscriptions. Table III.E.1 provides a synopsis.[299]

Table III.E.1: Correspondences between Cylinder and Statue Inscriptions

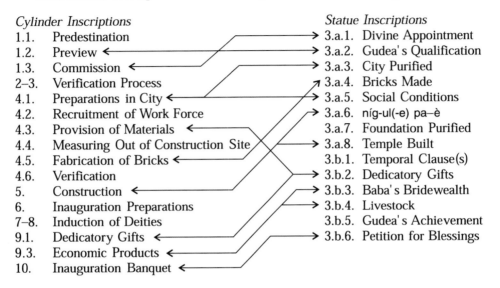

Cylinder Inscriptions
1.1. Predestination
1.2. Preview
1.3. Commission
2–3. Verification Process
4.1. Preparations in City
4.2. Recruitment of Work Force
4.3. Provision of Materials
4.4. Measuring Out of Construction Site
4.5. Fabrication of Bricks
4.6. Verification
5.   Construction
6.   Inauguration Preparations
7–8. Induction of Deities
9.1. Dedicatory Gifts
9.3. Economic Products
10.   Inauguration Banquet

Statue Inscriptions
3.a.1. Divine Appointment
3.a.2. Gudea's Qualification
3.a.3. City Purified
3.a.4. Bricks Made
3.a.5. Social Conditions
3.a.6. níg-ul(-e) pa–è
3.a.7. Foundation Purified
3.a.8. Temple Built
3.b.1. Temporal Clause(s)
3.b.2. Dedicatory Gifts
3.b.3. Baba's Bridewealth
3.b.4. Livestock
3.b.5. Gudea's Achievement
3.b.6. Petition for Blessings

b. Initial Circumstances

The divine appointment and the short description of Gudea's qualifications in the statue inscriptions (components 3.a.1–2) are reminiscent of the divine commission in the cylinders (section 1). The former state in a general way that the deity for whom the temple will be built appointed Gudea and detail his qualifications,[300] while Cylinder A makes explicit that Ningirsu commissioned Gudea with the construction of his temple (section 1.3), after his qualifications for this task have been described (section 1.2). The statue inscriptions contain the divine appointment in a when-clause, and the qualifications in appositions or short sentences without further context, while the cylinders embed this event in a mythical context (section 1.1). The verification process triggered by the divine communication (sections 2–3) is not narrated in the statue inscriptions.

---

[299] The section and component numbers are the same as in chapter III.A.6 and Table II.B.2, respectively.
[300] See chapter II.B.2.e § 3.a. The description of Gudea's qualification (component 3.a.2) as well as that of his achievement (component 3.b.5) are comparable not only to section 1.2 in the Cylinder Inscriptions, but also to other characterizations of Gudea throughout that text, see chapter III.C.1.a. They interrupt the action in order to focus on its agent. Only Statue B, when reiterating Gudea's achievement (6:77–7:9), refers to a commission (7:7–9): inim dug₄-ga ᵈnin-gír-su-ka-ke₄ šu zi im-mi-gar, "He (Gudea) fulfilled Ningirsu's command."

c. Construction

In Cylinder A the account of Eninnu's construction expands over two main sections, one detailing preparations (section 4), the other describing the assembly of the structure (section 5). The statue inscriptions, like the building inscriptions, summarize the construction of the temple in one sentence (component 3.a.6), often introduced with the formulaic phrase referring to the appearing of an everlasting thing (component 3.a.8).[301] Only Statues B, C, E, and F specify preceding preparations. Some of these, however, are related in as much or more detail as their counterparts in Cylinder A. The relevant passages are translated in Table III.E.2.

Table III.E.2: The Construction Account in the Cylinder and Statue Inscriptions[302]

	Cylinder A		*Statues B, C, E, and F*	
12:20	He knows great things, and also accomplishes great things.			—
12:21–23	The ruler gave instructions in his city, equally for everyone. Lagaš, like the children of one mother, agreed unanimously.			— —
12:24–26	He opened manacles, lifted fetters,[303] established ... The "spoken words" were revoked. He suspended capital offenses.			— –
13:1	He loosened the tongue of whip (and) goad.	B 4:10f	No whip was wielded; no strap was wielded.	5.d
13:2	He placed wool of a pregnant sheep into the (overseer's) hands.	B 4:13–19	In the hands of generals, intendants, and overseers of the working conscripts he put combed wool for control.	5.f
13:3	No mother had words with (her) child.	B 4:12	No mother threw anything at her child.	5.e
13:4f	No child spoke rebelliously to his/her mother.			—
13:6–9	Concerning a male servant who had ... wages, his master did not smash (his) head. Concerning a female servant who acted evil (?) against her, her mistress did not throw anything at her face.			— –

---

[301] The appearing of the everlasting thing (níg-ul) is mentioned several times in the Cylinder Inscriptions: first, at the outset (CA 1:4), then in Gudea's first prayer to Ningirsu (CA 8:20), next in the context of the brick making (CA 18:25), and finally after Gudea bestowed the inauguration presents (CB 17:12), where it precedes the core verb, like in the other inscriptions; see chapter III.B.1.1 note 59, and Table III.C.3 under 4.5.

[302] The numbers given to the components of the statue inscriptions in Table II.B.2 are annotated on the right.

[303] For CA 12:24–26 see Civil "Mesopotamian Jails," 76.

Cylinder A		Statues B, C, E, and F		
—		B 5:1–4	No grave was dug in the city; no corpse was buried; no lamentation priest brought the drum, uttered a lament; no wailing woman wailed.	5.g
13:10f	To the ruler building Eninnu, to Gudea no one filed a claim about it.	B 5:5–11	Within the borders of Lagaš no defendant stood at the place of oaths, no creditor entered a man's home.	5.h
13:12f	The ruler purified the city, cleansed it with fire	B 3:12 E 2:21f	He purified the city, cleansed it with fire.	3
13:14f	The ... (various "unclean" persons) were expelled from the city.	B 3:15–4:4	The ... (various "unclean" persons)[304] he expelled from the city.	5.a
—		B 4:5f	No woman carried her basket; the eunuchs did the building work for her.	5.b
—		B 4:7–9	Ningirsu's house was built in a place as clean as Eridu.	5.c
—		B 3:13	He set down the brick mold.	4.a
13:16f	Toward the frame of the brick mold a kid was laid down. The brick (mold) was chosen by extispicy.	B 3:14	The brick (mold) was chosen by extispicy.	4.b
13:18f	Its loam pit was looked at approvingly. The shepherd nominated by Nanše established it primarily.			—
13:20	When the frame of the brick mold was designed,	C 2:20f E 3:1f F 2:12f.	The frame of the brick mold was designed.	4.c
13:21–23	when he had established the loam pit primarily, the Anzu, the emblem of his master, was shining (there) on a standard.	C 2:22f E 3:3f F 2:14	At the loam pit the standard was shining.	4.d
17:29–20:4	(section 4.5)	C 3:1–5 E 3:5–9 F 2:16ff	He mixed its clay in a pure place. He molded its brick in a clean place. [E only:] He placed the brick in the brick mold.	4.e
18:25	An everlasting thing appeared.	B 5:12ff E 3:10	For Ningirsu, his master, he had an everlasting thing appear. / An everlasting thing appeared.	6

---

[304] For these unclean persons designated here and in CA 13:14f. by terms whose exact meaning is not easy to ascertain, see Behrens *Enlil and Ninlil* 150–159.

Cylinder A		Statues B, C, E, and F		
13:24f	He purified the city, an area of 24 iku, for him, cleaned the area for him.	C 3:6f E 3:11f F 3:1f	He purified its foundation, cleansed it with fire.	7.a
13:26f	Juniper, a clean mountain plant, was set on fire; he had build up cedar aroma, a fragrance for deities.	C 3:8ff E 3:13ff F 3:3ff	He treated its perimeter with perfume.	7.b
13:28– 14:4	He had the day (go by) in prayer for him, spent the night in appeal for him. To build Ningirsu's house, the Anunna of Lagaš prayed and pleaded with Gudea.			—
14:5f	The good shepherd Gudea joyfully established it for him.			—
20:13– 30:5	(section 5)	B 5:15ff C 3:11ff E 3:16ff F 3:6f	He built his/her temple <name> for him/her/DN+epithet (E adds: in a pure place in GN; B adds: restored it for him. In it he built his TN with cedars ...)	8

The first construction preparation in all statue inscriptions concerns the purification of the city recounted in two standard sentences (component 3). Cylinder A, however, begins with the establishment of special social conditions (lines 12:21–13:15), and accounts for the purification of the city between the penultimate and the last detail of the latter (lines 13:12f.). In Statue B similar social conditions (component 5) are described after the account of the brick making (component 4). The association of special social conditions with the purification of the city in Cylinder A and the absence of the former in Statue C, E, and F may indicate that the standard sentences referring to the purification of the city summarize the effect of the special social conditions.

The detailed description of the special social conditions in Statue B and Cylinder A entails an enumeration of legal regulations which Cylinder A introduces with a generic statement (lines 12:21–23). Some regulations are almost identical in both accounts, although each account also contains regulations not recorded in the other. The comparison shows that for the author's purposes the list need not be complete, and that the regulations can be formulated accordingly and ordered differently without changing the information about Gudea's promulgation of special social conditions.

A similar phenomenon can be observed in regard to the brick making. Statue B, on one hand, and Statues C, E, and F, on the other, each mention two different sub-events concerning the preparation of the brick mold (components 4.a-b and 4.c-d, respectively), while Cylinder A presents a slightly expanded account which includes all four of them. The statue inscriptions evidently use two distinct sub-events as *pars pro toto*. Statues C, E, and F then summarize the brick making in three sentences (component 4.e), while Cylinder A relates this event in a long, much more detailed passage (section 4.5). Again, the three activities accounted for in the statue inscriptions stand for the event as a whole.[305]

The recruitment of the work force (section 4.2), the provision of materials (section 4.3), the measuring out of the construction site (section 4.4), and the verification of the preparations (section 4.6) are skipped in the statues' construction account.[306]

The comparison of the temple construction narrated in sections 4–5 of the cylinders to the similar events recounted in the statue inscriptions confirms the hierarchy of events proposed in chapter III.C.4.b. Some statue inscriptions summarize these events in one sentence, others specify particular preparations. The absence of preparations in the former confirms that they are not required to represent a temple construction, but are optional expansions. They are implied in the core action of building a temple. Not all of them need to be included. The events can be ordered freely, unless they are bound by a logical sequence (for example, making of brick mold before making of brick). Each event can be detailed into smaller units (for example, the brick making). Again, not all sub-events implied in this event need to be made explicit. A selection is sufficient to represent the entire sub-event. Such sub-events may be introduced with a generic statement (for example, that introducing the establishment of special social conditions in CA 12:21–23). Only by putting all texts together does the modern reader obtain a comprehensive, if not complete, picture of all activities implied in the construction.

d. Dedicatory Gifts
Several statue inscriptions continue the construction account with the equipment of the temple with various gifts before they resume with their core, the consecration of the statue. These events are comparable to section 9 in Cylinder B. While the latter is embedded in the context of the inauguration of the temple, following the induction of the divine inhabitants (sections 6–8) and preceding the banquet (section 10), the analogous passages in the statue inscriptions lack such a context, perhaps because their core event concerns the statue rather than the temple. Consequently, the remaining sections of Cylinder B have no parallel in the statue inscriptions, except for the petition for blessings in Statue E which will be discussed below.

Both general categories of gifts encountered in Cylinder B (section 9.1 and 9.3) occur also in the statue inscriptions: dedicatory objects (component 3.b.2) and economic products (components 3.b.3–4). Compared with the construction preparations, the accounts concerning these gifts are less standardized. The type of gift is conditioned by the gender of the divine beneficiary, and the formulation of similar events exhibits more variation.

---

[305] The first sentence in the statues' account is comparable to CA 18:20–22, the second to CA 18:23f., and the third to CA 19:8f.
[306] The provision of materials for the fabrication of dedicatory objects is related in Statue B and D in the context of these gifts; see below.

In the statue inscriptions, female deities receive thrones (Statue A, F), treasure chests (Statue A, F), and drums (Statue A, E, F) as dedicatory gifts, while Ningirsu receives a boat (Statue D), or weapons (Statue B), as in Cylinder B. In contrast to section 9.1 in Cylinder B which simply enlists two sets of dedicatory gifts after a statement expressing Gudea's bestowal of them (CB 13:11–14:18), the statue inscriptions also mention the fabrication of the gifts which may include the importation of the material of which they are made, an event that is recounted in the context of the construction preparations in the cylinders (sections 4.3). These actions are expressed by a small number of recurrent verbs which may be repeated for each gift generating semantic parallelisms or enumeration.[307] The gifts for female deities will serve as an example:

Statue E

1	4:03f	He fashioned the great throne of her ladyship for her,
2	4:06f	(and) set it up at her place of judgment.
3	4:08f	He fashioned her pure treasure chest for her,
4	4:10f	(and) entered it into her great house.
5	4:12f	He fashioned the drum (called) "Lady preeminent with An,"
6	4:14f	(and) set it up in her large courtyard.

Statue A

3	2:01f	He fashioned her pure treasure chest for her,
1	2:03f	fashioned the great throne of her ladyship for her,
4	2:05	(and) entered them into her great house.

Statue F

1	3:08f	He fashioned the great throne of her ladyship for her,
3	3:10f	fashioned her pure treasure chest for her.[308]

Similarly, several actions, including the import of material, are described for a number of weapons for Ningirsu and some other items used for the construction of Eninnu in Statue B 5:28–6:63. This much more extensive passage is introduced with a reference to the circumstances relating how Gudea acquired the materials (5:21–27). A similar statement concerning Gudea's acquisition of materials occurs in Statue D 4:2–14, although it is independent from the account of the presentation of the dedicatory boat (3:3–12). These statements are reminiscent of two introductory statements in the account of imports in Cylinder A 15:19–21 and 16:3–5; all indicate that Ningirsu enabled Gudea to acquire the materials. A comparison of the imports in Statue B and Cylinder A reveals some interesting discrepancies. Tables III.E.3–4 list origin, entity, and the verbs used in each text.

---

[307] The most common verbs are e_{11} for the import of material; dím for the fashioning of dedicatory objects; gub or ku_4 for the installation or induction into the temple. In addition, the following verbs occur in Statue B: ad-šè – ak-ak, DU, bal-bal, má-a – si-si in the context of imports; dù, DU.DU, gar, si-si in the context of the installation of weapons. Ningirsu's boat, after being made, is moored (ús), rigged (ka-kéš), and offered (sag-rig$_7$) (Statue D 3:3–12).

[308] For dub-šen "treasure chest," see Civil *AulaOr* 5 (1987), 20f. commentary to line 2.

Table III.E.3: Importation of Building Materials and their Use in Statue B

	origin	*entity*	*verb(s) for import*	*use for material*
5:28–52	ama-a-núm hur-sag eren	^{giš}eren	ad-šè mu-AK.AK	šar-ùr
		^{giš}taškarin	im-ta-e$_{11}$	šar-gaz
				^{urudu}kak dur$_{10}$-da
				^{urudu}kak dur$_{10}$-al-lub
				ig-gal é-50-a
				giš-ùr-šè é mah-a
5:53–6:2	^{uru}ur-su^{ki} hur-sag eb-la	^{giš}za-ba-lum	ad-šè mu-AK.AK	giš-ùr-šè é-50-a
		^{giš}ù-suh$_5$		
		^{giš}tu-lu-bu-um		
		giš-kur		
6:3–12	ù-ma-núm hur-sag me-nu-a	^{na_4}na-gal	im-ta-e$_{11}$	na-rú-a kisal
	ba$_{11}$-sa-la hur-sag mar-dú			é-50-a
6:13–20	ti-da-num hur-sag mar-dú	nu$_{11}$-gal lagab-bi-a	mi-ni-túm	ur-pad-da
				sag-gul é-a
6:21–25	abul-at^{ki} hur-sag ki-maš	urudu	mu-ni-ba-al	šita ub-e nu-íl
6:26–32	kur me-luh-ha	^{giš}esi	im-ta-e$_{11}$	<?>
		lagab-nìr	im-ta-e$_{11}$	šita ur-sag-3
6:33–37	hur-sag ha-hu-um	kù-sig$_{17}$ sahar-ba	im-ta-e$_{11}$	šita ur-sag-3
6:38–44	kur me-luh-ha	kù-sig$_{17}$ sahar-ba	im-ta-e$_{11}$	é-mar-uru$_5$
		ÁB.RI	im-ta-e$_{11}$	
6:45–50	gu-bi-in^{ki} kur ^{giš}ha-lu-úb	^{giš}ha-lu-úb	im-ta-e$_{11}$	mušen šar-ùr
6:51–58	ma-ad-ga^{ki} hur-sag íd-lú-ru-da	ésir-gú-REC 214	im-ta-e$_{11}$	ki-sá é-50-a
		^{im}ha-um		
6:59–63	hur-sag bar-me	^{na_4}na-lu-a	má gal-gal-a	úr é-50-a
			im-mi-si-si	

Most entities occur in both accounts, though some are listed only in one or the other. Their order and grouping differs. The comparison in Table III.E.5, arranged by entities, shows that the geographical origin of the materials is more specific in Statue B, which furnishes distinct geographical names of cities and regions, often in combination, while Cylinder A indicates only regions and usually in a poetic-descriptive way such as "land of oak" or "land of cedar." The latter occurs once also in Statue B, but is preceded by the geographical name of this region. The verbs are more varied in Cylinder A. Statue B uses for almost all entities simply ta-e$_{11}$ "to import," which, in the case of lumber, can be preceded with or replaced with ad-šè AK.AK "to make rafts." Cylinder A uses ta-e$_{11}$ only twice, and, in addition to two other verbs that occur in Statue B (túm, ba-al), it employs more poetic terms such as kar ús "to moor at the quay" or šu – peš "to spread before." In terms of mode, it is interesting that Statue B uses mostly *hamṭu*-forms, and Cylinder A mostly *marû-forms*. This can be explained by the context: Statue B lists the imports retrospectively when relating the equipment of Eninnu with gifts, while in Cylinder A they are accounted for together with other preparations for its construction.

In part, the composer of Cylinder A may have wanted to actualize this event, and tell it in a mode which is more likely to catch the attention and involve the audience, much like an English story teller might switch into present tense when reaching a particularly thrilling or crucial moment in the narrative. Moreover, the verbal forms in Cylinder A include dative infixes, while none of those in Statue B do. Whether the dative refers to Ningirsu or to Gudea is not that clear, and perhaps deliberately left ambiguous. In sum, this comparison clearly reveals that the statue inscriptions are more factual in nature, and the cylinders more poetic.

Table III.E.4: Importation of Building Materials in Cylinder A

	origin	*entity*	*verb(s)*
15:6–10	elam šušin^{ki} má-gan me-luh-ha	(not specified)	mu-na-gin mu-na-gin gú giš mu-na-ab-gál gír-su^{ki}-šè gú mu-na-si-si
15:11–14	[Dilmun]	urudu	Ninzaga mu-na-ab-ús-e
15:15–18	[Dilmun]	^{giš}ha-lu-úb ^{giš}esi ^{giš}ab-ba	Ninsikila mu-na-ab-ús-e
15:19–16:2	kur ^{giš}eren hur-sag ^{giš}eren hur-sag ^{giš}šu-úr-me hur-sag ^{giš}za-ba-lum	^{giš}eren ad ^{giš}eren ad ^{giš}šu-úr-me ad ^{giš}za-ba-lum ^{giš}ù-<suh$_5$ ^{giš}tu-lu-bu-um ^{giš}e-ra-núm	ad gal-gal-bi ... kar mah ká-sur-ra-ke$_4$ [... -ús]
16:3–12	[kur ...]	na gal-gal lagab-ba ha-ù-na na-lu-a esir im-babbar	mi-ni-túm má ... im-ma-na-ús
16:15–17	ki-maš hur-sag urudu	urudu gi-si-a-ba	mu-ni-ba-al
16:18–20	kur-bi	kù-sig$_{17}$ sahar-ba	mu-na-túm
16:21	kur-bi	kù-NE-a	u-na-ta-e$_{11}$-dè
16:22–23	me-luh-ha	gug-gi-rin	šu mu-na-peš-e
16:24	kur nu$_{11}$	u$_{11}$	mu-na-ta-e$_{11}$-dè

Table III.E.5: Comparison of Origin and Verbal Forms in Cylinder A and Statue B

entity	Cylinder A		Statue B	
	origin	*verbal form*	*origin*	*verbal form*
ÁB.RI	—	—	kur me-luh-ha	im-ta-e$_{11}$
esir	[kur ...]	má ... im-ma-na-ús	ma-ad-ga^{ki} hur-sag íd-lú-ru-da	im-ta-e$_{11}$
giš-kur	—	—	^{uru}ur-su^{ki} hur-sag eb-la	ad-šè mu-AK.AK
^{giš}ab-ba	(Dilmun)	Ninsikila mu-na-ab-ús-e	—	—
^{giš}e-ra-núm	[kur ^{giš}eren]?	ad gal-gal-bi ... kar ... [ús]	—	—
^{giš}eren	kur/hur-sag ^{giš}eren	ad gal-gal-bi ... kar ... [ús]	ama-a-núm hur-sag eren	ad-šè mu-AK.AK im-ta-e$_{11}$
^{giš}esi	(Dilmun)	Ninsikila mu-na-ab-ús-e	kur me-luh-ha	im-ta-e$_{11}$
^{giš}ha-lu-úb	(Dilmun)	Ninsikila mu-na-ab-ús-e	gu-bi-in^{ki} kur ^{giš}ha-lu-úb	im-ta-e$_{11}$
^{giš}šu-úr-me	hur-sag ^{giš}šu-úr-me	ad gal-gal-bi ... kar ... [ús]	—	—
^{giš}taškarin	—	—	ama-a-núm hur-sag eren	ad-šè mu-AK.AK im-ta-e$_{11}$
^{giš}tu-lu-bu-um	[kur ^{giš}eren]?	ad gal-gal-bi ... kar ... [ús]	^{uru}ur-su^{ki} hur-sag eb-la	ad-šè mu-AK.AK
^{giš}ù-suh$_5$	[kur ^{giš}eren]?	ad gal-gal-bi ... kar ... [ús]	^{uru}ur-su^{ki} hur-sag eb-la	ad-šè mu-AK.AK
^{giš}za-ba-lum	hur-sag ^{giš}za-ba-lum	ad gal-gal-bi ... kar ... [ús]	^{uru}ur-su^{ki} hur-sag eb-la	ad-šè mu-AK.AK
gug-gi-rin	me-luh-ha	šu mu-na-peš-e	—	—
im-babbar	[kur ...]	má ... im-ma-na-ús	—	—
^{im}ha-um	[kur ...]	má ... im-ma-na-ús	ma-ad-ga^{ki} hur-sag	im-ta-e$_{11}$ íd-lú-ru-da
kù-NE-a	kur-bi	mu-na-ta-e$_{11}$-dè	—	—
kù-sig$_{17}$	kur-bi	mu-na-túm	hur-sag ha-hu-um	im-ta-e$_{11}$ kur me-luh-ha
^{na_4}na-lu-a	[kur ...]	má ... im-ma-na-ús	hur-sag bar-me	má gal-gal-a im-mi-si-si
^{na_4}na(-gal)	[kur ...]	mi-ni-túm	ù-ma-núm hur-sag me-nu-a ba$_{11}$-sa-la hur-sag mar-dú	im-ta-e$_{11}$
nìr	—	—	kur me-luh-ha	im-ta-e$_{11}$
nu$_{11}$(-gal)	kur nu$_{11}$	mu-na-ta-e$_{11}$-dè	ti-da-num hur-sag mar-dú	mi-ni-túm
urudu	(Dilmun) ki-maš hur-sag urudu	Ninzaga mu-na-ab-ús-e mu-ni-ba-al	abul-at^{ki} hur-sag mar-dú	mu-ni-ba-al

e. Economic Products

Like the dedicatory gifts, the economic products are simply listed in the Cylinder Inscriptions, followed by the statement that Gudea presented them to Ningirsu (section 9.3). They are the products of fishery, grain cultivation, and animal husbandry and include the personnel in charge of them. The products of the animal husbandry, together with its caretakers, are listed in a slightly modified and enlarged enumeration in Statue F 3:12–4:13. The comparison of the relevant passages illustrates how the same event can be cast in different schemes:

Statue F

1	3:12f	The oxen were directed under the yoke,
2	3:14f	(and) he had their farmer and ox-driver follow them.
3	3:16f	In the good cows he multiplied the good calves,
4	3:18f	(and) their cowherds were made to follow them.
5	4:01f	In the good ewes he multiplied the good lambs,
6	4:03f	(and) had their shepherds follow them.
7	4:05f	In the good goats he multiplied the good kids,
8	4:07f	(and) had their shepherds follow them.
9	4:09f	The mature jennies gave birth to the swift donkeys,
10	4:12f	(and) their assherds were made to follow them.

Cylinder B

11	15:05	the (newly) built cattle pens, the (newly) built sheepfold,
5	15:06	the good ewes producing lambs,
12	15:07	the rams mounting (?) their good ewes,
3	15:08	the good cows putting down calves,
13	15:09	the seed bull roaring in their midst,
1	15:10	the oxen directed under the yoke,
2	15:11	farmer and ox-drivers in charge of them,
		(... Gudea presented to lord Ningirsu.)

Statues D, E, and G account for a special type of gift: the bridewealth of Baba. This consists mostly of food provisions, but also includes livestock and other agricultural products, which were regularly offered on the New Year's festival.[309] The comparison of the three accounts is instructive for the expansion of the core of a subordinate event.

Statue D 2:13–3:2:

In it (temple) he (Gudea) provided for the bridewealth of Baba, his lady.

Statue E 5:1–7:21 = G 3:5–6:19:

On New Year's day, the festival of Baba, on which to provide the bridewealth, [list of items with their amounts] were the bridewealth of Baba in the old house in former times. When Gudea, the ruler of Lagaš, had (re)built his beloved house Eninnu for Ningirsu, his master, had (re)built her beloved house Esilasirsir for Baba, his lady, [list of items with their

---

[309] On bridewealth (níg-mí-ús-sá) see Greengus *HUCA* 61 (1990).

increased amounts] were the bridewealth of Baba in the new house which Gudea, ruler of Lagaš, the house builder, increased.

Statue G 2:1–16

Ningirsu put together a bridewealth, which rejoices the heart, for Baba, the daughter of An, his beloved bride. His (Gudea's) god Ningišzida followed behind it. Gudea, ruler of Lagaš, congratulated (him/them), from Girsu to Urukug.

Statue D summarizes the event in one sentence. The basic elements of this sentence can be interpreted as the core of this event: Gudea provides for the bridewealth of Baba. It includes only two micro expansions: the epithet of Baba (his lady), which links the agent to the divine beneficiary, and the location (in it) which links the event to the temple construction. Statues E and G expand on the object and circumstances of the provision. They enlist all items of the offering, and introduce the information that Gudea increased their quantities. In both texts this is done identically in the form of two statements, each linked to a list of items[310] resembling formally the presentation of gifts in Cylinder B. In addition, Statue G accounts for the delivery of the offerings, a natural corollary of their provision. The involvement of additional characters is inherent in this event, since bridewealth is offered by the groom to the bride for the wedding festivities and is usually delivered by a friend or servant of the groom.[311] The roles of Ningišzida and Gudea evoke a presentation scene in which a petitioning Gudea follows his personal god Ningišzida into the presence of Baba, delivering the bridewealth on behalf of Ningirsu. This is confirmed by the ensuing petition for blessings in Statue E, discussed below.

f. Inauguration Banquet

Two components of the statue inscriptions are reminiscent of distinct parts of the inauguration banquet in section 10 of the Cylinder Inscriptions: the speech order (component 4.b.4) and the petition for blessings (component 3.b.6). Although they are perceived from a different perspective. The speech which Statue B is to transmit to its divine beneficiary asserts the latter that a series of special regulations were observed during a period of seven days when Gudea built Eninnu (Statue B 7:26–46). These regulations are identical to those imposed for the inauguration banquet in Cylinder B 17:17–18:9.[312] Cylinder B embeds the observance of special regulations in the narrative, while Statue B recounts this event as a detached message of its carrier.

The blessings for which Ningišzida petitions the divine beneficiary of Statue E on Gudea's behalf (Statue E 7:22–8:15):

To restore the house of Baba,

---

[310] The only differences in the lists concern numbers: compare Statue E 5:21 with G 4:15, and Statue E 7:6 with G 6:4.

[311] Greengus *HUCA* 61 (1990). The fact that Ningišzida delivers the bridewealth for Ningirsu is noteworthy, since Ningišzida is not traditionally related with Ningirsu, but was introduced into the Lagašite pantheon by Gudea. Falkenstein *Einleitung*, 101–104, already observed that Gudea used every opportunity to establish his personal god. By having him act on Ningirsu's behalf, Gudea not only integrates Ningišzida in a traditional cult event, the festival of Baba, but also links himself to a mythic event, the delivery of bridewealth in the divine realm.

[312] For a transliteration of these passages see chapter III.D.3.

to make its abundance appear,
to make firm the base of Lagaš's throne,
to keep a scepter of firm words in the hands of Gudea, ruler of Lagaš,
to lengthen the days of his life,
(these petitions) his god Ningišzida presented to Baba
in her house of Urukug.

are very similar to those pronounced at the inauguration banquet in Cylinder B 23:10?–24:8.[313] While the former are only wished for, and the statue may have been meant as their mediator, those in the cylinders are related as an event which happened in actuality. They are addressed to the ruler in direct speech out of the mouth of a deity. To some degree, the names of the statues (component 4.a.4) reflect the same event, since they express the beneficiary's blessing of the ruler with long life in return for his temple construction in an even more abridged version:

Statue A
3:4–4:2
nin an-ki-a nam tar-re-ne, ᵈnin-tu, ama-digir-re-ne-ke₄, gù-dé-a, lú é dù-a-ka, nam-ti-la-ni mu-sù

The lady of the ones who decree destiny in the universe, Nintu, the mother of all deities, has made long the life of Gudea, the one who built the temple.

Statue B
7:14–17
lugal-mu, é-a-ni mu-na-dù, nam-ti níg-ba-mu

I built his temple for my master; (long) life (be) my gift.

Statue C
3:18–4:1
gù-dé-a, lú é dù-a-ka, nam-ti-la-ni hé-sù

May the life of Gudea, the one who built the temple, be long.

Statue D
5:2–7
lugal á dugud-da-ni, kur-e nu-íl-e, ᵈnin-gír-su-ke⁴, gù-dé-a-ar, lú é dù-a-ra, nam-mu mu-ni-tar

The master, whose heavy arm the foreign lands cannot bear, Ningirsu, has decreed a favorable destiny for Gudea, who built the temple.

Statue E
9:1–3
nin-mu ba-zi-ge, nam-ti ba, u₄ dug₄ -ga-ba ì-dù

My lady: I am ready; give me life, (and) I will build on time.[314]

Statue H
3:1–5
nin dumu ki-ág an kù-ga-ke₄, ama ᵈba-ba₆, é-sila-sír-sír-ta, gù-dé-a, nam-ti mu-na-sum

The lady, beloved child of holy An, mother Baba, has given (long) life to Gudea from the Esilasirsir.

Statue I
5:3–6
gù-dé-a, lú é dù-a-ka, nam-ti-il! mu-na-sum

To Gudea, the one who built the temple, he (Ningišzida) has given (long) life.

Statue K
2':6'–8'
[lú? l]ugal-ni, [ki]-ág-me, [nam]-ti-mu hé-sù

I am the one loved by his master; may my life be long.

Statue N
3:4–5
ᵈgeštin-an-na-ke₄, nam-ti mu-na-sum

Geštinanna has given him (long) life.

---

[313] For a transliteration and translation see Appendix C no. 8.

Statue O ^dgeštin-an-na-ke₄, igi zi mu-ši-bar   Geštinanna has looked at him approvingly.
3:2–3

It is interesting that some names treat the blessing as an event in the past, like the Cylinder Inscriptions, while others treat it as a wish, like the passage in Statue E.

---

[314] For a similar name which alludes to the divine commission in the first part, see Gudea 81.

F. The Message

Looking at the text in terms of its message raises the questions of who communicates
what to whom, and, secondarily, why, when, where, and how. Knowledge of the socio-
cultural context of the communication is vital for answering these questions. This
context largely escapes the modern reader not only in the case of Gudea's cylinders,
but in Sumerian literary works in general, since he/she is not the intended receiver and
has no informants available. Because the context was obvious to the ancient source and
receiver of the message, there is little information about it extant. Much of the ensuing
discussion must remain speculative.

1. Source

It is generally assumed that Gudea commissioned the Cylinder Inscriptions, and is thus
the ultimate source of the message. Although there is no solid evidence to confirm this
assumption, it is the most probable one. Based on paleography and orthography, the
time range allows for a date of the text in the Lagaš II or early Ur III periods.[315] That
a later Lagašite ruler wanted to commemorate the deeds of his predecessor seems less
likely,[316] since royal inscriptions and hymns were usually commissioned by the ruler to
whom they pertain. Collected songs of Gudea (èn-du ka-kéš-rá-mu) are mentioned in the
curse of his Statue B (8:21–23), where they are protected against fraud. Further evidence
of Gudea's patronage of literary works are a short hymn to Baba which mentions his
appointment by this Lagašite goddess,[317] and perhaps also the *Nanše Hymn*, which
portrays him in ritual activity (37–41).[318] Both hymns are evident products of Lagaš.[319]

The author of the text remains anonymous as in most Mesopotamian literary works,
especially Sumerian ones.[320] As a notable exception, scholars have repeatedly pointed
out Sargon's daughter Enheduanna, high-priestess in Ur, who claims to have compiled
(ka-kéš) the *Temple Hymns* (ibidem, line 543f.), and "created" (tu-ud) a hymn to Inanna
called *Ninmešarra* (ibidem, line 138). Other compositions have been attributed to her,

---

[315] See chapter III.A.2.

[316] It is noteworthy, however, that Gudea's son Urningirsu who, unlike other Lagaš II rulers, persistently
uses his filiation in his inscriptions, usually characterizes his father as the builder of Eninnu, see Urningirsu
II 1–10.

[317] STVC 36, see Falkenstein *SAHG*, 85ff.

[318] Heimpel *JCS* 33 (1981). Ibidem 67, Heimpel considered as possible patron either Gudea or Urningirsu,
the late Ur III en of Nanše, who may be the more likely candidate.

[319] Gudea is mentioned also in the fable *Heron and Turtle* line 19, whose transmission is known only in the
Nippur tradition; see Gragg *AfO* 24 (1973). Hallo's tentative attribution to Gudea of several compositions
centering on Ninurta, including *Angim* and *Lugal*, which supposedly allude to this ruler or his deeds (*AS* 20
(1976), 183–185), remains doubtful. That *Angim* is a mythical version of Gudea's Elam campaign is mere
speculation. *Lugal* contains a passage (463–78) which is part of Ninurta's blessing of the diorite, and refers
to statues of the king (lugal) being placed at the ki-a-nag of Eninnu; see chapter II.C.1.a, p. 60. Because
Gudea Statue B, which is made of diorite and dedicated to Ningirsu in the Eninnu, is wished to be placed at
the ki-a-nag (Statue B 7:49–55), van Dijk *Lugal* I, 2, in accord with Hallo and other scholars, maintained that
this passage alluded to Gudea in particular. This need not be the case, since Gudea's predecessor Urbaba as
well as his son Urningirsu equally dedicated diorite statues to Ningirsu; see Urbaba 1 and Urningirsu II 6–7,
10. The choice of Eninnu must have been governed by the fact that the composition praises Ningirsu/Ninurta.

[320] On anonymity and authorship in cuneiform literature see Lambert *JCS* 11 (1957), and Michalowski
"Sailing to Babylon," 183–193.

though without firm evidence.[321] Whether she can be considered the author, in a modern sense, of the compositions mentioned remains doubtful.[322] Similarly, it is difficult to determine in what measure Šulgi's claim to authorship of literary works is empty boasting.[323] As Michalowski observed,[324] "the uniqueness of these claims of authorship only serves to underline the anonymity of Sumerian literature." One should bear in mind that originality and artistic inspiration were most certainly viewed in a different light than in our society.

What do we know about the anonymous authors of Sumerian literary works? The Šulgi Hymns, which constitute practically the only Sumerian source of information on this issue, mention singer-musicians (nar) and scribes (dub-sar) in the context of various types of compositions which can be subsumed under the general heading of songs (èn-du), although who actually composed the works remains ambiguous.[325] The evidence can be interpreted in the sense that the singer-musician was the composer who dictated the text to a scribe for written transmission, or that the scribe was the composer who read it to the singer-musicians for oral transmission.[326] The mention of um-mi-a in a similar context in two royal hymns has been taken as an argument for the first scenario.[327] Um-mi-a, however, need not be a literate scholar, as is generally assumed, but can also be a craftsman. The term is better understood as a generic for "master" or "expert" of whatever art or craft the context indicates. Alster's contention that the Cylinder Inscriptions must be a "genuine pen-composition"[328] cannot be substantiated. Whether scribe or singer-musician, and regardless of whether the evidence presented above is representative of the composition of Sumerian "songs" in general,[329] the composers of works such as the Šulgi Hymns or Gudea's Cylinder Inscriptions probably belonged to the intelligentsia of the royal court.[330]

The text under discussion is a narration by a third person. This raises the question of the relation between narrator and author.[331] The narrator reports on events in both the divine and human realms in mythical as well as historical time, and never directly addresses his audience. He is omnipresent and remains covert. His geographical sphere as well as

---

[321] See Alster "Interaction," 43 note 80, and Goodnick Westenholz "Enheduanna," 540 and 548f., who took a more positive view in favor of Enheduanna's authorship.

[322] Civil "Limites," 229, and Michalowski "Sailing to Babylon," 184.

[323] Black *AfO* 29–30 (1983-84), 111.

[324] "Sailing to Babylon," 184.

[325] Šulgi B 309–314; E 240–253; see Alster "Interaction," 45–49.

[326] The second scenario is maintained by Klein *Royal Hymns*, 20f., Ludwig *Hymnen des Išme-Dagan*, 43, Cooper "Babbling," 113f., and apparently also Alster "Interaction," 45–50. The first scenario is favored by Black *AfO* 29–30 (1983–84), 112f., who conceived of singer-musicians talented enough to compose versus singer-musicians who interpreted the compositions of others. In chapter III.A.2, I considered the possibility that CA was written by a different hand than CB. If indeed two scribes were involved, it seems less likely that they were identical with the composer, though one cannot exclude the possibility of a plurality of composers.

[327] Šulgi E 20–22; Išme-Dagan V$_a$ 18–20; see Ludwig *Hymnen des Išme-Dagan*, 41f., and Alster "Interaction," 47f.

[328] Alster "Interaction," 64, without discussion.

[329] See Alster "Interaction," 46.

[330] Compare Komoróczy cited in Cooper "Babbling," 114.

[331] In addition to narrator and author, modern narratology distinguishes implied or dramatized authors; see Chatman *Story and Discourse*, 147–151; Martin *Theories of Narrative*, 153–156; Prince *Grammar of Stories*, 16. These entities, however, are difficult to detect in ancient texts for obvious reasons.

that of his audience, however, is centered in Lagaš: at the beginning of his account he refers to Girsu as "our city" (CA 1:4), and the events are clearly perceived from that perspective.[332] His spatial point of view concurs with that of his protagonists: Gudea and Ningirsu, the ruler and divine patron of Lagaš, respectively. Without explicitly glorifying him, he endeavors to depict a positive image of Gudea who was evidently his patron. Except for his omnipresence, the narrator can be said to coincide with the author. Omnipresence implies a super-human narrator, and is no doubt consciously chosen. Like anonymous authorship, it averts any inquiry into the individual human creativity behind this composition.

In addition to the royal patron and the author, one could conceive of a third party intermediary between them, namely from among the ranks of high officials of the entourage of the ruler. It is noteworthy that most *arad-zu* seals which mention Gudea belong to scribes, and that two of them are further designated as his sons.[333] It seems, therefore, that Gudea had educated confidants at his disposal, some recruited from his own family, who might have had some influence on governmental affairs and, perhaps, also on the image of the ruler for royal rhetoric. If Gudea entrusted someone with the commemoration of his construction of Eninnu in the form of a literary work, one could imagine his confidants suggesting suitable individuals for this task, and possibly providing this skilled personnel with some guidelines concerning the desired product. This, however, remains speculation.

2. Contents

The core message of the Cylinder Inscriptions is that Gudea built Eninnu for Ningirsu. This information is also recorded in the majority of Gudea's building inscriptions and some statue inscriptions. The difference between the factual building and statue inscriptions on one hand, and the cylinders on the other lies in part in the minute detailing and poetic elaboration of the message in the latter, but more importantly in the *Sitz im Leben* of the obviously different documents. The former are inscribed on immediate parts of the building or dedicatory objects which all had a distinct function within the temple, while the latter is written on a carrier used for the transmission of literary texts, and may have had a life independent of it.

Despite of the extensive expansion of the core in the Cylinder Inscriptions, the text does not account for every event of the story in the same detail. As pointed out above,[334] some events are abbreviated or entirely excluded, while others –prayers, for example – are described in full length. The reasons for the choice of sub-events to be included and/or detailed must have been in part dictated by what the intended receiver was expected to fill in based on his personal knowledge of the described event and his familiarity with native tradition and convention in contrast to new or spectacular information. In part

---

[332] See chapter III.C.2.b.
[333] For a bibliography see Porada *Andrews University Seminary Studies* 6 (1968), 141 note 17f. These seals are insufficiently published and their evaluation is subject to revision.
[334] See chapter III.C.3.b.

the choice must have been governed by the intention to repeat certain information for aesthetic or rhetoric purposes.

3. *Circumstances*

The circumstances of the composition and transmission of the Cylinder Inscriptions are closely linked to the *Sitz im Leben* of the text. Thus, a brief consideration of genre seems in place. Correct generic classification can provide a key to the understanding of the intentions of the message of a given communication, since it directs the author when composing, and facilitates the decoding of the message by the receiver. One should bear in mind, however, that genre is a fluid phenomenon rather than a set of fixed types and its classification should consider multiple criteria based on different aspects of the text. Only few Assyriologists have addressed this issue in depth,[335] and many commonly used designations for particular text groups (for example, royal hymns or royal inscriptions) remain unsatisfactory.

From the perspective of conventional Assyriological classification of Sumerian literary texts it is difficult to assign the Cylinder Inscriptions to any particular group, although the composition does not stand isolated within Mesopotamian tradition. It has been classified as a temple hymn[336] as well as a royal hymn,[337] but was also grouped with royal inscriptions as an "improper" dedicatory inscription.[338] Some descriptive passages are reminiscent of the Temple Hymn Collection[339] and poetic accounts of royal deeds do occur in narrative passages of royal hymns. Yet the composition in question has little in common with a typical hymn.[340] It is primarily a narration of "historical" events, and lacks emphatic exaltations as well as hymnic rubrics. Its narrative mode (third person past tense narration including some direct speech) and its (relatively moderate) use of poetic devices is more akin to narrative poems such as those of the Enmerkar-Lugalbanda cycle. In contrast to these, however, it lacks the folktale elements so typical of the latter and is more historical in content. Its core message is a common topic in royal inscriptions and certain passages indeed parallel Gudea's own statue inscriptions.[341] Yet the Cylinder

---

[335] Vanstiphout *CRRA* 32 (1986), 1–11; Edzard *RlA* 7 (1987), 35–48 s.v. Literatur; Longman *Autobiography*, 3–21; Tinney *Nippur Lament*, 11–25. A symposium volume on the subject has been announced by the Mesopotamian Literature Group, see Vanstiphout et al. *Mesopotamian Poetic Language*, xi. For a good overview of the present state of genre discussion in other fields see NPEPP 456-459 s.v. genre.

[336] Wilcke "Sumerische Kultlieder," 2129; Hallo *CRRA* 17 (1970), 120; Edzard *RlA* 7 (1987), 42 s.v. Literatur; Alster "Interaction," 38. Wilcke seems to revise his classification in *RlA* 4 (1972–75), 539–544 s.v. Hymne, where he silently excluded Gudea's cylinders. Note Falkenstein's more cautious designations "Tempelbau-Hymne" in SAHG 137, and "Bau-Hymne" in *Einleitung*, 178.

[337] Klein "From Gudea to Šulgi," 301. In *ASJ* 11 (1989), and "Šulgi and Išmedagan," he specified it as a "building and dedication hymn," which he defined as a sub-type of royal hymns. Black's observation in *AfO* 29–30 (1983–84), 113, that a systematic study of the whole group of royal hymns from a literary point of view remains a desideratum, is still valid.

[338] Krecher "Sumerische Literatur," 138, called it *eine uneigentliche Weihinschrift*. For the problems in defining "royal inscription" see Edzard *RlA* 6 (1980–83), 59f. s.v. Königsinschriften.

[339] The general phraseology of temple descriptions must go back to a shared tradition, while the description of Eninnu in Temple Hymn 20 (lines 247–54) may be indebted to Gudea's Cylinder Inscriptions (compare especially CA 25:15f. and 26:1f.), as Wilcke observed in *ZA* 62 (1972), 48 note 27.

[340] For a definition of hymn in Sumerian literature see Wilcke *RlA* 4 (1972–75), 539–544 s.v. Hymne.

[341] See chapter III.E.2.

Inscriptions do not conform to the format of a typical royal inscription, and each of its two parts concludes with a doxology and a colophon. While the former is typical of compositions of a more poetic nature,[342] the latter testifies to the document character of its written transmission.

The classifications described above consider almost exclusively contents and form. Ancient subscripts, catalogues of literary works, and certain statements in the Šulgi Hymns seem to indicate that a native classification would have been made more along the lines of the circumstances of the composition and transmission of the text. Wilcke contended that subscripts cannot denote a generic classification, since texts of different "attitude" were given the same subscript.[343] The criteria with which he approached Sumerian literature, however, are those of Western literary criticism dating back to ancient Greek thinkers, who classified literature according to its lyric, epic, or dramatic mode. This approach is anachronistic.[344] A useful distinction between critical genre and ethnic genre in Sumerian compositions was made by Tinney.[345] Although a straightforward analysis of the latter is impeded by the fact that we are bereft of native informants, some observations are permissible. A number of literary subscripts are identical to the names for musical instruments (for example, adab, balag, tigi, zamzam), others are compounds of the term šìr "song," with various abstract nouns, for example, song of the liturgist's craft (šìr-nam-gala), war-song (šìr-nam-érim-ma), heroic song (šìr-nam-ur-sag-ga).[346] The latter may include terms which seem to define the topic of the composition (war-song, heroic song). The larger number of literary subscripts which designate musical instruments or intimate a performer (song of the liturgist's craft), on the other hand, seem to be indicative of the performance aspect of the work rather than its contents or form.

Tinney conceived of the following candidates for such performative criteria: performance participants, time of performance, type of event, and scope and composition of audience.[347] He further speculated that èn-du lugal, "royal songs," for example, referred to compositions in the performance of which the king was a participant, rather than to "royal hymns" *per se*. This would explain why an Ur III literary catalogue[348] includes under the heading en₈-du lugal compositions seemingly diverse to Assyriologists who classified them as "royal hymns" on the one hand, and "divine hymns with or without mention of a king" on the other.[349] In addition to performative criteria one could conceive of criteria pertaining to the circumstances of the composition, distinguishing, for example, whether a song was commissioned by a king, was recasting an oral tradition, was an ad hoc improvisation, etc. If such a criterium existed, one could explain why not a

---

[342] Note, however, the very last statement in Statue B, immediately following the long curse section, which is somewhat reminiscent of a doxology (9:27–30): gaba gal dingir-re-ne-ka, en ᵈnin-gír-su-ka, nam-mah-a-ni, un-e hé-zu-zu, "Let everybody know the greatness of lord Ningirsu, the champion of the gods."

[343] *AS* 20 (1976), 262.

[344] See Volk *Inanna und Šukaletuda*, 3 note 1.

[345] *Nippur Lament*, 11–18.

[346] For an overview of Sumerian literary subscripts, see Wilcke *AS* 20 (1976), 258; Ludwig *Hymnen des Išme-Dagan*, 29.

[347] *Nippur Lament*, 18.

[348] Hallo JAOS 83 (1963), 168–174; Ludwig *Hymnen des Išme-Dagan*, 40.

[349] See Ludwig *Hymnen des Išme-Dagan*, 27.

single one of the song types said to praise Šulgi's great achievements in Šulgi E (16–38) occurs as a subscript in "royal hymns." The names of those songs which are attested as subscripts in known literary compositions occur in hymns which praise a deity and may, but need not, mention a king. Ludwig suggested that in the latter, the king was equated with the deity, and concluded that a "royal song" may be hidden in every hymn praising a deity.[350] I would suggest that èn-du lugal designated either compositions in which the king acted as a participant or which the king commissioned.

In such a definition Gudea's Cylinder Inscriptions would qualify as a "royal song." That the text was perceived as a "song" rather than a factual record, such as most building and dedicatory inscription, is suggested also by the doxology. Doxologies cannot be considered indicative of a particular genre,[351] since they occur in a large number of diverse compositions with differing literary subscripts.[352] Longman considered them indicative of mode, i.e. "characteristics of emotional or tonal nature that transect various genres or forms,"[353] and Black noted their function as "a form of 'flag' to indicate the approaching end of a composition."[354] If not a particular genre, they may have designated a larger category of texts. In Šulgi E, zà-mí is mentioned side by side with šùd under the heading šìr:

14 lugal mu šì-ra hé-du₇-me-en	I am the king, I have a name fit for songs.
15 šul-gi-me-en šùd zà-mí-gá silim-éš ga-dug₄	I am Šulgi, I want to congratulate (myself) in my blessings and praises.

Ludwig tentatively interpreted these lines as evidence for a twofold classification of songs into "blessings" and "praises."[355] In any case, this passage shows that "praises" were included among songs which makes them candidates for performance. Sumerian uses two very general terms for song: šìr and èn-du. A differentiation between them, if it existed, is hard to detect. Their exchangeable use as heading for a number of identical types of songs in Šulgi E rather suggests that they were synonyms.[356] As a working hypothesis, I would suggest then that the Cylinder Inscriptions were included in Gudea's collection of songs (èn-du), and were considered a royal song (èn-du lugal) as well as a praise song (zà-mí) for Ningirsu, two still rather broad categories of texts.

Turning to the particular occasion for the composition of the Cylinder Inscriptions, one could imagine that the text was composed to celebrate the completion of Gudea's reconstruction of Eninnu and was first performed during its inauguration celebrations. The text informs us that songs accompanied by music were performed on this occasion.[357] The place of performance would naturally be Eninnu.[358] What shape such a performance

[350] *Hymnen des Išme-Dagan*, 35–39.
[351] Cf. Hallo *AS* 20 (1976), 181–203.
[352] See Cooper *Return of Ninurta*, 4 with note 8; Ludwig *Hymnen des Išme-Dagan*, 33f.
[353] *Autobiography*, 10 and 14.
[354] "Structural Features," 74f.
[355] *Hymnen des Išme-Dagan*, 34f.
[356] Copare Šulgi E 16–38 and 53–56; see Ludwig *Hymnen des Išme-Dagan*, 35–38.
[357] CB 18:22–19:1 mentions the performance of a tigi to the accompaniment of the drum called Ušumkalamma, and the playing of ala drums; see also chapter IV.B.5.
[358] Based on his interpretation of Statue B 8:21–26, Klein "From Gudea to Šulgi," 297, concluded that

may have taken, remains, of course, mere speculation. Sauren's suggestion of a mystery play[359] may take the issue too far. I would rather conceive of a recitation accompanied by musical instruments which may have involved several voices, perhaps including a choir, and probably also involved the participation of the ruler. Given the persistence of the veneration of ancestral statues and other cult objects in Lagaš, a periodic recitation thereafter can seriously be considered.

In contrast to the "royal songs" of Šulgi and other kings succeeding Gudea, his cylinders present the only extant copy of this composition. We cannot be sure whether the text was written down to be read to the performers who would then learn it by heart, or whether it was written down so that the memorable occasion would not be forgotten, or both. What the *Sitz im Leben* of the document itself was remains unclear. One could conceive of mere storage in the temple, the construction of which it records; of a display, considering that the document, being the two largest known cylinders, was impressive in itself; or of a draft for a monumental inscription.[360] At least from the Isin period on there is evidence that "songs" were inscribed on stelae, which then assumed functions similar to other dedicatory objects.[361] In this context it is interesting to recall that the Cylinder Inscriptions are case-ruled and tend towards short-lines, like inscriptions engraved in stone rather than typical literary compositions written on clay.[362] The text lacks a curse, but then by far not all dedicatory records set up in temples include one. If the cylinders were a draft, one would have a good explanation why the text is preserved in one copy only.

4. Receiver

As possible receiver of the message of the Cylinder Inscriptions one must consider, even if in a rhetorical way, deities, and Ningirsu in particular. He is the object of praise in the doxologies. It is well known that Mesopotamian gods were "entertained" and kept well disposed by the performance of songs, and that they were informed about the great achievements of the rulers, their proxies in the human sphere.[363] In keeping with this tradition, Gudea's Statue B was to "speak" to Ningirsu, and orally transmit a message given word for word in its inscription (7:21–48). Ludwig considers the

---

Gudea's collected songs were performed in Ningirsu's courtyard during the Ešeš-festival. As attractive as this thesis is, it has to be dismissed: first, the single èš for èš-èš is unparalleled, and in conjunction with gar may simply be a different reading for éš-gàr, "daily duties," which are not to be neglected and kept in mind (igi-šè tuku) in the temple courtyard; second, the object of the last two verbs are the "daily duties" rather than the collected songs mentioned earlier, i.e. lines 8:24–26 form a new unit independent of the previous one consisting of lines 8:21–23.

[359] *CRRA* 20 (1975).

[360] This last possibility was suggested to me by Miguel Civil, who maintains that this would explain why only six stelae occur in the section of the Cylinder Inscriptions which relates their installment, while seven are mentioned in total; see chapter III.B.5.4. The Cylinder Inscriptions would be the draft of the seventh stela.

[361] Ludwig *Hymnen des Išme-Dagan*, 67–69. Tinney *Nippur Lament*, 25, speculated that "certain types of monumental text are simply a sub-case of literary production geared to ritual needs."

[362] For a preliminary overview of texts written in short-line, see Tinney *OLZ* 90 (1995), 10–14.

[363] For example, in letters to gods, see Borger *RlA* 3 (1957–71), 575f. s.v. Gottesbrief.

Rechenschaftsbericht or *apologia* an important aspect of hymns which relate or praise royal deeds.[364]

It is too restrictive to suppose that the composition inscribed on the cylinders of Gudea was addressed to Ningirsu only. Yet human receivers of the message are more difficult to identify, if only because our sources do not specifically mention them. Furthermore, there are factors to consider in regard to them which are irrelevant in the case of a divine audience. Whereas deities are assumed to be able to comprehend a message in poetic Sumerian, whether oral or written, in the human world only scribes could read, and the language of Sumerian poetic compositions was not necessarily understood by the population at large.[365] Whether Sumerian still was the vernacular language of the majority of Lagaš's citizens during Gudea's reign, is by no means clear.[366] For the Neo-Assyrian period it can be demonstrated that the language used for the commemoration of royal deeds (Standard Babylonian) was not the vernacular and was not understood by the population at large, and that the written messages which formed part of royal rhetoric were mainly addressed to a small circle of high officials in an effort to foster their loyalty to the crown.[367] As attractive as this comparison is, one should keep in mind that the Neo-Assyrian kings ruled over an empire of considerable extension, while Gudea was a city-state ruler.

Language aside, the text assumes the receiver's familiarity with the characters and places of the story, as well as with certain religious concepts of the Sumerian world. While Lagaš's citizens can be assumed to have known who Gudea and Ningirsu were, what Eninnu was, and where Girsu, Lagaš and Ningin were, the knowledge of other less well known deities and places mentioned in the text may have been restricted to the educated upper echelons of the society. Specialized knowledge of religious concepts was probably required to understand, for example, that the "excellent in Nippur" (CA 2:12) or the "semen ejaculated by Great Mountain" (CA 8:16) refer to Ningirsu. Whether the rich repertory of figures of speech, especially all the metaphors for the temple and its parts, were common knowledge is questionable. However, this does not necessarily preclude that less knowledgeable segments of the population were *a priori* excluded as receivers, since the core of the message that Gudea, the ruler of Lagaš, built the temple of his city god, can easily be grasped without specialized knowledge.

If the text was performed, as suggested above, the only likely place for this event in Gudea's time was the temple, and in particular the main courtyard of Eninnu. I do not think that we can extrapolate from Išme-Dagan's songs, which were performed not only

---

[364] *Hymnen des Išme-Dagan*, 54–65.

[365] See Michalowski "Charisma and Control," 63; idem "Orality and Literacy," especially 238; and Cooper "Babbling," 188f.

[366] An examination of the onomasticon in the Lagaš II administrative texts may shed some light on the ethnic composition of the population of Lagaš at that time, though one cannot exclude that a Semite would be given a Sumerian name, and vice versa. Unlike the names of Ur III dynasts, those of the Lagaš II rulers are good Sumerian. Given the preceding rule of the kings of Akkad over large parts of the Sumerian-speaking area, however, multi-ethnicity is very likely in the Lagaš II period.

[367] See Michalowski "Charisma and Control," 244, and Russell *Sennacherib's Palace*, 254f.

in the temple but in the entire country,[368] to the different socio-political situation in Gudea's Lagaš. As audience for such a performance the ruler's family and the temple personnel are natural candidates. If the presence of "Lagaš" in the inauguration festivities in Cylinder B (19:13–15) refers to the population of the city-state at large, it suggests an audience beyond the scope of upper echelons of the society, at least for the inaugural performance.

As a document, the cylinders are in themselves a demonstration of power, since literacy was restricted and writing was a tool of the ruling class. If they were on display in the temple, and located in the Agaeren near which they were found, and if Agaeren was a public court area,[369] they may have been seen by most visitors to the temple. If they were a draft for a stela, we can be sure that the stela was on display, probably in the main courtyard, and therefore visible to visitors of the temple beyond its personnel.[370]

---

[368] Išme-Dagan Va 20–30; see Ludwig *Hymnen des Išme-Dagan*, 53.
[369] See chapter III.A.1.
[370] See chapter IV.F.3.

IV.   THE STELAE

A.   Introduction

1.   The Corpus

The stelae of Gudea have survived only in fragments. The find circumstances of the excavated pieces leave no doubt that the monuments to which they belonged were mutilated in antiquity.[1] The delimitation of the corpus must remain imprecise due to the present condition. The catalogue in Appendix B includes all bas-relief fragments that are potential candidates for stelae of Gudea and were accessible for examination. In the description of their imagery in chapter IV.B I will question the attribution of some fragments to a stela, and that of a few others to Gudea. Six unpublished fragments in the Archaeological Museum of Istanbul were not accessible for detailed examination. Nor were the eleven boxes of approximately two hundred small relief chips from Tello in the same museum. The exclusion of the latter will not greatly diminish the results of this study, since their extremely poor preservation leaves their imagery often indistinct and their attribution to stelae of Gudea indeterminate.

The sixty-four bas-relief fragments considered in this study are all made of limestone, and none is known from a site other than Tello. Six fragments preserve part of a dividing band, a characteristic of registered stelae, together with imagery that includes a figure identified by a written label as "Gudea, the ruler of Lagaš." Twenty-five additional fragments preserve characteristics of registered stelae, i.e. part of a dividing band or an edge, together with iconographic and stylistic affinities which makes an attribution to Gudea possible. Five of the remaining thirty-three pieces can be atttributed to Gudea based on their label inscription, the rest share the above mentioned iconographic and stylistic affinities. These thirty-three pieces pieces do not preserve a formal characteristic of a registered stela. Some may have belonged to a door plaque or a flat-sided pedestal. The majority, however, depict figures which are compatible in size and iconography with the imagery carved on the stela fragments.

The imagery depicted on the fragments can be identified as parts of scenes representing various episodes of Gudea's temple constructions. The recurrence of motifs and subtle differences in size and proportions of the represented figures and objects indicate that the fragments belonged to several stelae similar in shape and composition. Their number cannot be determined with precision.

---

[1]   So also Heuzey NFT 283.

2. Find Circumstances

All stela fragments which were discovered during regular excavations originate from Tello. The remaining pieces are likely to have come from the same site. They were purchased between 1906 and 1926,[2] when illicit digs at Tello were at their peak.[3] Moreover, no Gudea stela fragments are reported from any other site in southern Mesopotamia. With two exceptions, all excavated fragments were found within the area attributable to Gudea's Eninnu, yet not *in situ*. Table IV.A.1 provides an overview of the "tells" at Tello where they were found.

Table IV.A.1: Stela Fragments according to Excavation Areas at Tello[4]

Tell A:	ST.7, 10, 16, 21[?], 36, 37, 47[?], 48[?], 50[?], 51[?], 52, 53
Tell A/B:	ST.4, 5[?], 6[?], 8[?], 9, 11, 12[?], 13, 18, 20, 23, 24, 25, 26, 27, 28[?], 29, 30[?], 31[?], 34, 35, 39, 42, 43, 45, 46[?], 49, 54, 55, 60, 61, 62[?], 63.
Tell H:	ST.17
Tell Y:	ST.22

Most fragments were exposed by Cros between Tell A and B during his third and fourth campaigns in 1905 and 1909.[5] In this area (Fig. 15) lay two successive terraces linked by a stairway (A).[6] The stairway consisted of nine steps said to be made of tufa stone, and was situated at a distance of about one hundred meters from the remains of Eninnu on Tell A. It can be attributed to Gudea's Eninnu on the basis of the inscription on its second step.[7] The stela fragments were dispersed between this stairway and the wall of the inferior terrace, approximately ten meters to the northeast (E-F), which is also attributed to Gudea.[8] Three pedestals made of brick (C, C', D) abutted that wall, and

---

[2] Ten fragments were purchased by the Vorderasiatische Museum in Berlin, six of which (ST.1, 2, 14, 38, 40, 41, 44, 64) were published in 1906; the four remaining ones (ST.32, 57, 58, 59) have inventory numbers in the same range, and were therefore probably acquired at the same time. The one fragment purchased by the British Museum (ST.33) was published in 1923. Two fragments were purchased by the Louvre in 1925 (ST.15, 56), and a third one in 1926 (ST.3), all from a dealer (Géjou) known to have traded in objects illicitly dug at Tello. The fragment in the Iraq Museum (ST.19) was published in 1936, together with the restored Gudea Statue Q, which was acquired by confiscation from an illicit dealer, and almost certainly stems from Tello.

[3] See chapter II.A.2.a, note 10.

[4] Question marks indicate that the assignment to an excavation area at Tello is tentatively based on the campaign from which the fragment stems, which in turn is based on museum file cards or inferred from the sequence of museum numbers. Fragments from de Sarzec's 1881 campaign are most likely to come from Tell A, those from Cros' campaigns from Tell A/B.

[5] Not all fragments from Cros's campaigns were found in 1905, as reported by Börker-Klähn *Bildstelen*, § 57. Heuzey's instructions for the 1909 campaign include the search for more stela fragments where the previous ones had been found (see Parrot *Tello*, 316), and Cros was successful, see NFT 308; Parrot *Tello*, 25.

[6] Cros NFT 66f., and Heuzey ibidem, 279–283, 298–300. See also van Buren *Foundation Figurines*, 14, and Rashid *Gründungsfiguren*, 18.

[7] DT.1 in Appendix A. The only information on the foundation deposits associated with the stairway is Heuzey's indication in NFT 282, that the figurines were kneeling gods. This is not sufficient for an assignment to a particular building, see Appendix A note 23.

[8] The "curieux édifice" (NFT 282) has been identified as the wall of the inferior terrace by Seidl *Or* 55 (1986), 324. It was associated with a foundation deposit consisting of a tablet attributed to Gudea, and a figurine of the basket carrier type. Unfortunately, the inscription of the only basket carrier of Gudea mentioned

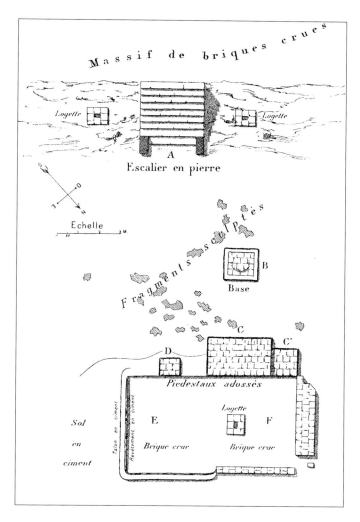

Fig. 15: Map of Tello, Area between Tell A and B.

a fourth one stood between those and the stairway (B). The surfaces of these pedestals measure in meters: B ca. 1.6 x 1.6; C 3 x 1.85; C' ca. 1.3 x 1.3; and D ca. 0.9 x 0.9.[9]

The excavators followed by Börker-Klähn assumed a relationship between these pedestals and the original monument(s) to which the fragments belonged.[10] Yet, the preserved lower ends of early Mesopotamian stelae exhibit bottom zones left unpolished and de-

---

by Cros (FK.4 in Appendix A) has vanished.

[9] The measurements of C are given by Cros NFT 66, those of the other pedestals are computed based on Fig. 15. For different dimensions, cf. Börker-Klähn *Bildstelen*, § 57.

[10] Cros NFT 67; Heuzey ibidem, 283 and 296; Parrot *Tello*, 177; Börker-Klähn *Bildstelen*, §§ 57 and 133f.

void of representation,[11] and this also appears to be the case for two fragments of Gudea (ST.11 and 12). If such stelae were mounted on pedestals, the latter must have had a cavity for fitting in and hiding their unworked end. Only one of the four pedestals in question (B) has a cavity, but it is circular,[12] and therefore not an appropriate mounting for a stela. Moreover, the dimensions of pedestals C' and D are too small for such monuments. Thus the pedestals must have carried other dedicatory gifts, perhaps royal statues or maces for which pedestals (ki-gal) made of bricks are attested in texts.[13]

Another consideration speaks against a relationship of the stela fragments with the pedestals. A comparison of the fragments in terms of size and iconography of their representation shows that they belonged to several stelae. If we are to believe the Cylinder Inscriptions, according to which Gudea erected each of the seven stelae of Eninnu at a different location within the temple complex,[14] one would not expect more than one stela at this location during his reign. The accumulation in a small area of a large number of fragments of several different stelae suggests to me that this was the location where the remains of destroyed monuments were collected for reuse in the foundation of new buildings. That this location coincided with the original location of one stela in Gudea's time cannot be entirely ruled out.

Twelve fragments were exposed by de Sarzec on Tell A in 1881. Two are known to have been reused in the palace of the Aramaic ruler Adad-naddin-ahhe, the rest are likely to have had the same fate.[15] Heuzey conjectured that these fragments were removed in antiquity from the findspot of the other fragments found by Cros, since the latter was at a short distance from the palace.[16] Alternatively, the builders of Adad-naddin-ahhe's palace may have found them in the immediate vicinity of their construction site, since remains of Gudea's Eninnu lay under that palace.[17] One of the two remaining pieces was found by Cros near Lagaš II period tombs on Tell H, the other by Parrot in a residential area on Tell Y which dates to the Ur III and Isin-Larsa periods.

Since all fragments excavated by the French expedition, with the exception of the two from Tell H and Y, were found in immediate proximity of architectural remains of Gudea's Eninnu, it is conceivable that they belonged to stelae originally dedicated in this temple. Their location within the temple complex, however, cannot be determined on the basis of their find circumstances.

---

[11] See Table IV.C.1.

[12] Heuzey NFT 283.

[13] Braun-Holzinger *Weihgaben*, 345. A mace head and a basin found nearby, both of Gudea, are likely candidates; see MH.12 and SV.7 in Appendix A. In addition, Heuzey NFT 296, mentioned a large curved fragment with a badly preserved inscription which I am not able to identify.

[14] Appendix C no. 6; see also chapter IV.F.3.

[15] De Sarzec mentioned only two fragments in his report: ST.7 served as a door socket in gate M (DC 37), and ST.57 as fill under the main courtyard (DC 48). The remaining fragments are described by Heuzey without reference to their find location (DC 211–222, 353–385). According to the Louvre inventory, they were all found in 1881, and must therefore have been discovered in the Aramaic palace on Tell A on which de Sarzec excavations were focused during this campaign; see Parrot *Tello*, 18, and compare ibidem, 172.

[16] Heuzey NFT 283 and 285.

[17] See chapter II.A.2.a, p. 34.

3. Inscriptions

Fifteen fragments bear inscriptions. Two types of texts can be distinguished: labels which function as a caption to the imagery and commemorative inscriptions. Eleven labels identify a ruler figure as "Gudea, the ruler of Lagaš" (ST.1, 5, 12, 19, 30, 32, 42, 43, [44], 46, 47). The twelfth label is inscribed next to the representation of a raft (ST.11), and reads ad ^{giš}er[in], "raft of cedar."[18] The three commemorative inscriptions are very fragmentary:

ST.20	*ST.21*	*ST.22*
1′ da-[x x]	1′ i[m-mi-lu]	1′ [ama-laga]š$^{?ki}$
2′ ⌜x-x⌝-ma-ni	2′ si[g₄-bi ki-sikil-a]	2′ [kù g]á-tùm-dùg-ge
3′ énsi in-⌜x⌝	3′ im-m[i-du₈]	3′ [da-r]í-šè mu-i-i
4′ gú-[...]	4′ [u]š-bi m[u-kù]	4′ [laga]š^{ki}-⌜šè⌝
(broken)	5′ [iz]i im-ta-[lá]	5′ [...]⌜x⌝-SI
	6′ [teme]n-[bi]	6′ [...] A
	(broken)	(broken)

The inscription on ST.21 is restored on the basis of a parallel passage in Gudea Statue C 3:2–10;[19] it relates preparations for the construction of a temple, namely the making of bricks, and the purification of the foundations. The text inscribed on ST.20 mentions a ruler, that on ST.22 states that someone praised Gatumdug.[20] That Gatumdug was the beneficiary of the stela to which ST.22 belonged can neither be confirmed nor ruled out.[21] Although the latter two inscriptions are too poorly preserved to determine their contents, it is clear they are not compatible with the same rigid scheme as Gudea's building and dedicatory inscription, nor is ST.21.[22] These fragmentary stela inscriptions must have belonged to more elaborate texts. By analogy with the more elaborate statue inscriptions and based on the remains of ST.21, one can expect them to have included an account of both the dedication of the stela and of the construction of the temple for which it was destined.

4. The Stela as Monument

Stela is a Greek term which originally designated a vertical stone boulder or slab, but was then used in a more restricted sense in reference to carved stone monuments such as grave stones, border stones, or victory monuments. The Sumerian term which corresponds largely to the Greek term, and is used by Gudea himself, is na-rú-a.[23] The

---

[18] Thureau-Dangin read the third sign šu, see NFT 296 note 2, followed by Börker-Klähn *Bildstelen*, no. 58, and Braun-Holzinger *Weihgaben*, Stele 21. A collation of the remains of the sign, however, favors the reading erin which makes better sense in this context.
[19] Steible *Neusumerische Bau- und Weihinschriften*, Gudea 80, and Braun-Holzinger *Weihgaben*, Stele 17.
[20] For previous transliterations of the inscription on ST.20 see Braun-Holzinger *Weihgaben*, Stele 22, and for that on ST.22 Steible *Neusumerische Bau- und Weihinschriften*, Lagaš 39, and Braun-Holzinger ibidem, Stele 18. The text on ST.20 is clearly not a building inscription for Eninnu, as Heuzey NFT 296, reported, followed by Börker-Klähn *Bildstelen*, no. 60.
[21] Börker-Klähn *Bildstelen*, no. 87, spoke of a dedication to Gatumdug.
[22] See Table II.B.1.
[23] Braun-Holzinger *Weihgaben*, 330.

oldest known Mesopotamian exemplar, the Lion-Hunt Stela,[24] dates to the end of the fourth millennium B.C. Mesopotamian stelae are by and large royal monuments.[25] They commemorate royal deeds in imagery and text. These deeds can be military victories, or they can be of a more civilian nature such as construction activities or the promulgation of laws. Like most royal monuments, they were dedicated to deities[26] and stood in their temples.[27] Textual evidence suggests that victory and law stelae were produced in duplicates or even multiple copies as early as the late Early Dynastic period. The copies were set up at the boundaries determined by a military victory, at the places of victorious battles, or, in the case of law stela, in other cities of the empire. The Eannatum Stela which commemorates Lagaš's victory over Umma, for example, stood in Ningirsu's temple in Girsu, and its inscription specifically states that other version(s) stood in the field between Umma and Lagaš.[28]

Like other dedicatory objects, stelae could be named and thus endowed with life and made fit to receive offerings.[29] The curse formulae in a number of their inscriptions, together with textual and archaeological evidence of mutilations, deportations, and restorations, show that stelae were not mere cult objects. They were also destined to glorify the ruler whose deeds they commemorate in present and future, perpetuating his memory, and thus served as vehicles for royal rhetoric.[30] This is supported by the fact that the rulers always appear successful – at times even heroic – and accords well with the fact that some stelae were produced in more than one copy.

Both text and imagery can be more or less detailed. The text may consist of a simple building inscription, a short account of a victory followed by a dedication, a long war report including resulting legal specifications, or an entire law code. The imagery may consist of a single scene which stands for an entire story, such as the king triumphing over an enemy, or it may specify various episodes in a series of different scenes. Text and imagery do not correspond in the sense that one illustrates or explains the other, but complement each other, each growing out of its own tradition.[31]

5. *Previous Studies*

Although the stela fragments of Gudea were found nearly one hundred years ago, and some even earlier, they have not yet been published in their entirety. The state of publication of individual fragments varies. While some have been repeatedly reproduced and discussed in various surveys and studies of Mesopotamian art and history,[32] oth-

---

[24] Börker-Klähn *Bildstelen*, no. 1.
[25] Exceptions are the so-called Kudurrus, legal contracts recorded on pillar-shaped stones which may also bear pictorial representation. They are considerably smaller than royal stelae. For the Early Dynastic examples see Gelb et al. *Land Tenure*, for the Kassite ones Brinkman *RlA* 6 (1980–83), 268–77 s.v. Kudurru.
[26] Braun-Holzinger *Weihgaben*, 330f.
[27] Börker-Klähn *Bildstelen*, §§ 34–52.
[28] See Winter "After the Battle," 23–25, and for more examples Börker-Klähn *Bildstelen*, §§ 332–337.
[29] See Gelb *Names* 4 (1956), and Selz "Holy Drum," 173f. §§ 23f. no. 1.
[30] Winter "After the Battle," and Börker-Klähn *Bildstelen*, §§ 166–168, 338–340.
[31] Winter "After the Battle," 22f.
[32] For a nearly exhaustive bibliography see Börker-Klähn *Bildstelen*, nos. 35–90 in conjunction with my Appendix B.

Fig. 16: Istanbul Reconstruction of Gudea Stela Top ST.4–5 at scale 1:8.

ers have received little or no attention. The reports of the French excavations at Tello reproduce and/or describe only little more than half of the excavated fragments.[33] Nor have all the fragments of unknown provenance been published immediately upon their acquisition. The information provided in these various publications is not entirely satisfactory: findspots of excavated pieces have not always been recorded, descriptions and measurements are often incomplete, and some museum numbers were never indicated. In 1982, Börker-Klähn provided a catalogue and illustrations of most of the fragments presently known, and, thus, made this corpus accessible for further studies.[34]

Several scholars have undertaken restorations or reconstructions of Gudea's stelae. During his term as a curator at the Archaeological Museum in Istanbul, Unger joined a number of fragments from Cros' campaigns, in many cases with casts of pieces housed in Paris, and also restored and partially reconstructed two top registers (Fig. 16).[35] In

---

[33] DC includes ten of the twelve pieces presently known from de Sarzec's campaigns, only six of which are reproduced. NFT includes twenty-five of the thirty-four pieces presently known from Cros' campaigns, with twenty-three reproduced. Heuzey NFT 283, mentioned more than one hundred fragments found in 1905; see also Parrot *Tello*, 172 and 177. Some of the extra ones are probably identical with the twenty-six pieces later joined with fragments from Cros' campaigns; the rest must be sought among the unpublished material in Istanbul. In the final report, Parrot *Tello*, 172–186, catalogued the bas-relief fragments attributed to Gudea without distinguishing between stela and door plaque. His catalogue does not include fragments which were not already published or mentioned in previous reports, and even ignores some of those; only five of the purchased fragments are included though twelve had been published by then.

[34] Börker-Klähn *Bildstelen*, nos. 35–90. Note, however, that the information for some entries in this catalogue was not updated; previously unpublished Istanbul pieces, for example, lack museum numbers, measurements, and findspot indication.

[35] Only one restored top register (ST.4+5) and one join (ST.12) were published by Unger himself; most other restoration (ST.6+7+8) and joins (9, 13, 18, 20, 23, 27, 28, 29, 34, 60, 61, 62) were published by Börker-Klähn. The joins in ST.9 had been proposed already by Heuzey NFT, 285 fig. 2.

Fig. 17: Berlin Reconstruction of Gudea Stela Top ST.1–2 at scale 1:8.

Berlin three fragments have been combined to form another, almost complete top register (Fig. 17). Heuzey was the first to attribute particular fragments to particular monuments. Assuming that the stelae of Gudea stood on the brick pedestals near which Cros had found the majority of the fragments, he assigned most of the then published fragments to one large stela which he envisioned on the largest pedestal; and two other fragments, because of their finer grain, to two "less important" stelae on the adjacent pedestals.[36] He then allocated a number of fragments to specific registers of his large stela, based partly on two fragments which preserve an edge and/or imagery of two registers, partly on the association of motifs. A slightly modified version of this proposal was illustrated by Parrot in the final excavation reports (Fig. 18);[37] the drawing encompasses only one broad and one narrow side of the stela. Parrot proposed reading the imagery on the five registers from bottom to top as follows: battle scene, enumeration of prisoners, procession of standards, cortege of drummers, Gudea's gratitude to Ningirsu.[38]

---

[36] Heuzey NFT 283–298. An earlier version of basically the same proposal was published in *Monuments et Mémoires* 16 (1909), 5–24.

[37] Parrot *Tello*, 181 fig. 37. Parrot assigned a figure of Gudea to the top register (ST.42) which Heuzey did not assign to any register, but excluded other fragments of standards in the third register (ST.23, 26, 63) which Heuzey had mentioned there.

[38] Parrot *Tello*, 179–182.

Because of various inaccuracies relating to size and proportions of figures as well as associations and interpretations of motifs, this proposal was justly refuted by Börker-Klähn.[39] In her own extensive reconstruction, she assigned a large part of the presently known fragments a place on four different stelae, and partly restored some of their registers, completing broken figures as well as adding motifs (Fig. 19).[40] Although she claims to have taken into account various criteria, including contents, composition, proportions, and carving peculiarities,[41] her reconstruction is not convincing overall.[42] Several fragments are not drawn to scale, a number of details of the imagery are misunderstood, and the new joins are unacceptable. The fragments are grouped in an unsystematic, nearly random way with little consideration for the formal characteristics of the original monuments or the composition of imagery in Mesopotamian art. The obsession with mirror images, for example, only obscures the meaning of the represented, and is ill-suited for stelae carved on four sides. Moreover, the reading of the reconstructed imagery is not discussed, and would indeed pose problems.

Interpretation of the imagery on Gudea's stelae, occasionally with reference to the events related in the Cylinder Inscriptions, has been limited to some well known fragments. This explains why issues regarding the message of the stelae have not been seriously addressed. This study attempts a comprehensive analytical investigation of all the fragments from a narratological point of view. Although the present preservation of the stelae is extremely frustrating, the fragments present a wealth of unparalleled motifs that deserve more attention and can be brought to life with recourse to the pool of Mesopotamian imagery and text. In the following chapters I will first describe the imagery depicted on the fragments grouped by themes, and discuss it in light of both pictorial parallels and textual information drawn mainly from the Cylinder Inscriptions (IV.B). Although any reconstruction of the stelae must remain hypothetical, some observations can be made if one scrutinizes the guidelines underlying the composition of imagery in Mesopotamia. The next chapter (IV.C), therefore, offers an analytical review of early Mesopotamian monuments in terms of form and composition before proposing conceivable scenarios for the imagery on Gudea's stelae. It follows an analysis of the components of the visual narrative represented on the stelae and its organization as far as the fragmentary condition permits (chapter IV.D). A comparison of this narrative with the imagery depicted on other sculpted objects of Gudea expounds upon the issue of expansion and reduction in the visual representation of events (chapter IV.E). The last chapter (IV.F) explores the stelae in terms of their message, and discusses source, receiver, and the circumstances of transmission.

---

[39] Börker-Klähn *Bildstelen*, § 118.

[40] Börker-Klähn *Bildstelen*, §§ 53–136 with pls. A-F. This reconstruction replaces her previous proposal of the reconstruction of one stela in *PKG* 14 (1975), 199–201 with fig. 36.

[41] Börker-Klähn *Bildstelen*, § 53.

[42] Compare the reviews by Invernizzi *Mesopotamia* 18–19 (1983–84), 242–243; Seidl *Or* 55 (1986), 321f.; Spycket *WO* 14 (1983), 247f.; and Tallon *Syria* 62 (1985), 188f.

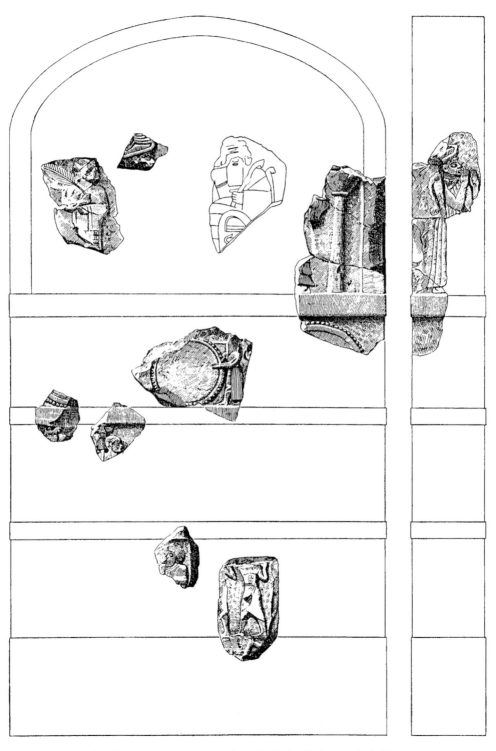

Fig. 18: Heuzey's Reconstruction of a Gudea Stela at scale 1:12.

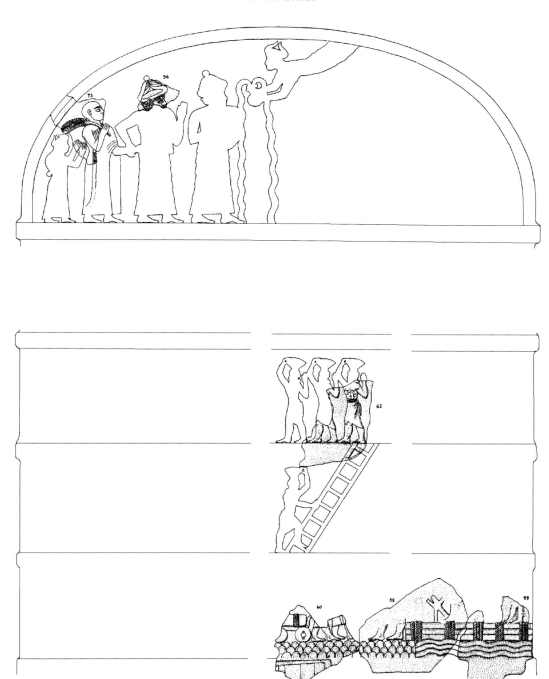

Fig. 19b: Börker-Klähn's "Eninnu Stela," Front, at scale 1:12.

Fig. 19a: Börker-Klähn's "Eninnu Stela," Back, at scale 1:12.

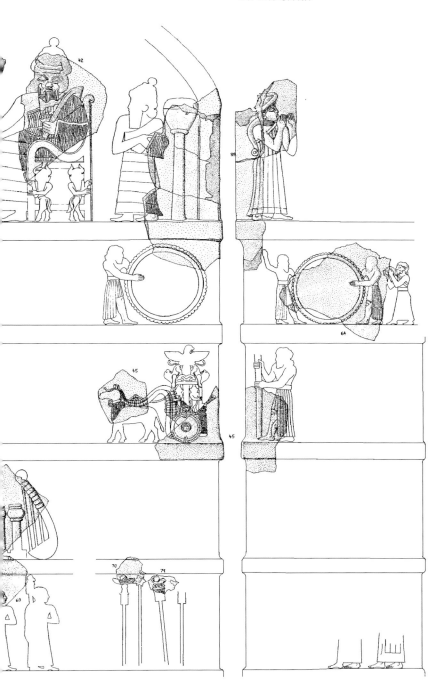

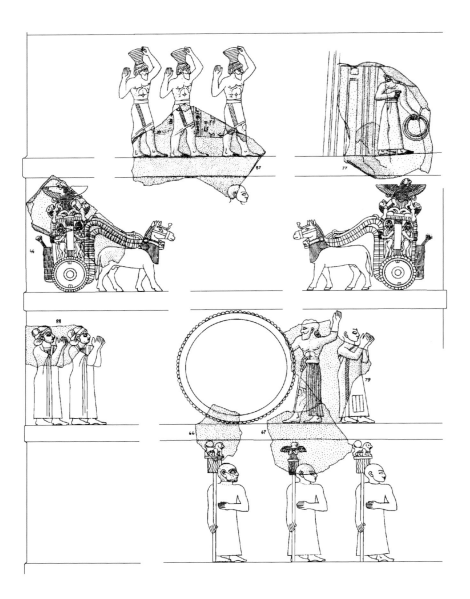

Fig. 19c: Börker-Klähn's "Eninnu Stela," Fragments, at scale 1:12.

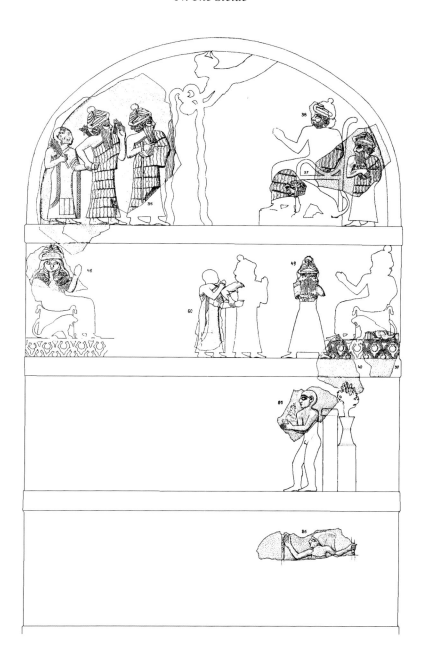

Fig. 19d: Börker-Klähn's "Enki Stela" at scale 1:12.

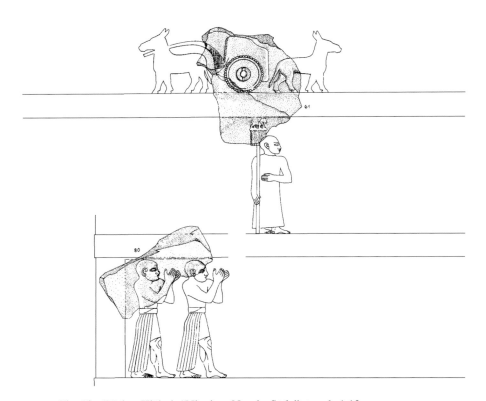

Fig. 19e: Börker-Klähn's "Ningirsu-Nanshe Stela" at scale 1:12.

B.   The Imagery

1.   *Standard Parades (ST.23–28, 63)*

Several fragments show standards usually carried by male figures. The largest fragment with this motif, ST.28, has a somewhat worn surface. It depicts a row of three identical looking male figures, each carrying a standard. The heads and faces of the carriers are shaved. They wear a long cape, apparently fastened by two bands across their chest, over what seems to be an ankle-length skirt.[43] These garments are reminiscent of the outfit of parading soldiers on Early Dynastic and Akkadian monuments (Fig. 26, 28, 30, 32).[44] The men are facing right, and hold the standard in their right hand with the arm extended and pressed against the body. The left hand, apparently formed to make a fist, rests on the chest. While the shaft of the standard extends down to the ankle, its top reaches beyond their head. The two partly preserved tops remain indistinct, though one can make out an outstretched bird's wing on the right.

The fragments ST.23 and 24 show below a dividing band the upper part of a standard with the same emblem behind the shaved head or scalp of a carrier facing right. Their surfaces are less worn, and they clearly show the emblem placed on a small platform from which a streamer hangs. That the rectangle inscribed with wavy lines represents a streamer and not a brick mold[45] is evident by analogy with the more realistically rendered standards on the Naramsin Stela (Fig. 28): the object inscribed with parallel lines below the emblem curves to the left of the pole as if streaming in the wind. Ur III texts which record the distribution of sheep's wool for standards may suggest that such streamers were made of wool.[46] The emblem depicted on ST. 23 and 24 has been described as a bird, yet it is a hybrid creature with the head and outstretched wings of a bird and the torso of a human figure holding a staff against its chest. Its long bill faces the same direction as the standard carrier. By analogy with these fragments the better preserved standard emblem on ST.28 can be interpreted as such a bird-man. This hybrid creature remains without parallel.

Another standard emblem is depicted on ST.63 and in the lower registers of ST.25 and 27. In each case only the emblem and (part of) the streamer of the standard are preserved. A lion carrying a circular disc on its back stands on the platform. All three lions face right and show their teeth. The image on a stamped brick from Tello, probably of Early Dynastic date,[47] is, to my knowledge, the only parallel for a lion with a disc on its back. That lion is couchant, seems to show its teeth, and the disc on his back has a short stick-like support. While the standards on ST.25 and 27 could have been carried like those on ST.23, 24, and 28, that on ST.63 is preceded by the remains of another object on the right with no room for a carrier. This object can no longer be identified.[48] In view of

---

[43] The rendition of this garment by Börker-Klähn *Bildstelen*, pl. C (Fig. 19a) no. 68, is inaccurate.
[44] See Strommenger *APAW* 2 (1971), 41f. no. 3, and 44 no. 7.
[45] Cf. Börker-Klähn *Bildstelen*, § 85.
[46] See Civil *Farmer's Instructions*, 150 note 6.
[47] NFT 309, fig. 19.
[48] Börker-Klähn *Bildstelen*, pl. C (Fig. 19a) no. 71 (erroneously for no. 70), saw a bird's wing. If anything,

an unpublished fragment in Istanbul which presumably shows a "forest" of standards,[49] it may have belonged to another standard emblem.

In addition to these standards, Heuzey identified a small fragment (ST.26) depicting the upper part of a lion-headed eagle with outstretched wings as part of a standard.[50] His interpretation has generally been accepted, although the streamer characteristic of these standards is not preserved, and none of the other standards has this emblem. Unlike the emblems of the other standards, the lion-headed eagle faces left. To its right abuts an obscure object which Börker-Klähn interpreted as another standard emblem in the form of a star.[51] On the original, however, the object is less regular in shape. Moreover, there is not enough room for a streamer or an animal carrying the emblem. The obscure object may instead have been related to the lion-headed eagle. The only other lion-headed eagle on Gudea's stela fragments appears on top of a chariot (ST.61). Unfortunately the fragment is broken at its left wing, and leaves unresolved whether the obscure object on ST.26 could have been part of a similar chariot. Although standards with lion-headed eagles are attested in presentation scenes on seals,[52] I think it less likely that the lion-headed eagle on ST.26 belonged to a standard because of the obscure object linked to it.

In the Cylinder Inscriptions, three different standards (šu-nir) are mentioned marching at the head of the Lagašites recruited for the temple construction. Lugalkurdub marches at the head of Ningirsu's district, the sacred gull (u_5) at the head of Nanše's district, and the disc at the head of Inanna's district.[53] Landsberger linked the fragments described above with this passage. He proposed identifying the disc carried by a lion with Inanna's standard and the lion-headed eagle with Ningirsu's standard, the latter based on the well-documented association of Anzu with this god.[54] Because the Sumerian term u_5 had then been interpreted as part of a ship (Akk. hinnu), Nanše's standard remained obscure to him. The same term, however, can also designate a water bird, perhaps a seagull, which is frequently associated with Nanše.[55] This led Pongratz-Leisten to identify the standard emblem depicted on ST.23, 24, and 28, which she identified as a simple bird following older descriptions, with Nanše's standard.[56]

The association of standards with team formations is more than plausible. Visual representations in Mesopotamia (Fig. 28) as well as Egypt[57] show standard carriers usually in military contexts. Two Early Dynastic texts already mention military levies in which

---

the remains look more like the claw of a bird of prey.

[49] Börker-Klähn *Bildstelen*, § 84.

[50] NFT 290.

[51] *Bildstelen*, no. 71 (erroneously no. 70 on pl. C = Fig. 19a).

[52] For example, Delaporte *Catalogue Louvre*, no. T.116; Fuhr-Jaeppelt *Löwenadler*, fig. 206. Anzu occurs on a standard also in CA 13:22 and 27:18f.; see also chapter IV.B.4.

[53] Appendix C no. 3.

[54] Landsberger *WZKM* 57 (1961), 17 note 64.

[55] See especially *Nanše and the Birds* 1–22, according to which that bird lives in the canebrake and the sea shore, and flies around Nanše.

[56] Pongratz-Leisten *BaM* 23 (1992), 303. So also Steinkeller in a lecture held at the Jacobsen Memorial in London 1994, in which he suggested identifying the bird as a cormorant, darter, or pelican (personal communication).

[57] *Lexikon der Aegyptologie* 5 (1984), 1255f. s.v. Standarten.

the troops are recruited by districts.[58] The three soldiers behind the ruler on the Standard of Ur (Fig. 26) may have carried standards, the emblems of which are lost today.[59] Standards appear also in the context of temples and deities. An Uruk period seal depicts three figures directed toward a temple.[60] The first wears a skirt and carries a staff, while the other two are nude and carry a standard-like object, a pole topped by what looks like an Egyptian sign, H on the left and KA on the right.[61] In Lagaš II and Ur III presentation scenes standards are stuck in the ground next to the enthroned deity or held by that deity or by his/her attendant.[62] The seal images accord with the association of standards with deities in the Cylinder Inscriptions and the resemblance between the outfit worn by the carriers on Gudea's stelae with that of team formations by districts. If the standards were brought to a particular place, as the unpublished fragment in Istanbul suggests, this may have been the loam pit for the fabrication of the bricks, since Gudea's cylinder and statue inscriptions mention standards there.[63]

Some of the above equations of the standards depicted on the stelae with those mentioned in the Cylinder Inscriptions, however, are disputable. Only the identification of the disc with the disc of Inanna, who is traditionally also associated with lions, is beyond doubt. The equation of the lion-headed eagle with Lugalkurdub is problematic because Anzu and Lugalkurdub exist independently in the text,[64] and the lion-headed eagle did not necessarily belong to a standard. It is equally possible to associate the bird-man standard with Lugalkurdub, since he is the "falcon of the rebels."[65] Should this association be correct, Nanše's bird must have looked different. The preserved part of the damaged emblem on the left standard on ST.28, which bears little resemblance to the better preserved ones, could be interpreted as the lower part of a bird in profile. Images of birds seen in profile occur on top of poles or standards in presentation scenes on seals from Tello and Ur.[66] Of course, there need not be a perfect match between the standards in the text and those depicted on the stelae.

---

[58] Deimel Fara II no. 40 and OIP 99 no. 282. These texts were brought to my attention by M. Civil.
[59] The reconstruction of one on the Mari Standard, however, is incorrect, as noted by Calmeyer *CRRA* 15 (1967), 166.
[60] Amiet *Glyptique mésopotamienne*, pl. 46 no. 658.
[61] A different interpretation of the emblems was suggested by Boehmer *BaM* 22 (1991), 229, while Mayer-Opificius "Feldzeichen," 216, recently considered the seal a fake. The unusual features she observed might be better explained with Egyptian influence.
[62] For standards with the lion-headed eagle, see note 52 above; for standards with a seated bird in profile, see note 66 below; for standards with a lion, see Buchanan *Early Near Eastern Seals*, nos. 618–620, of which nos. 618–619 have also a streamer.
[63] CA 13:20–23, and Statue C 2:20–23 = E 3:1–4 = F 2:12–15 in Table III.E.2.
[64] That Anzu and Lugalkurdub cannot be identical is substantiated by a passage in *Angim* (lines 51–68) in which Anzu is the chariot emblem (61), and Lugalkurdub the escort following behind that chariot (67f.), see Wiggermann *Protective Spirits*, 160. See also chapter IV.B.4 below.
[65] CB 7:12–23. The stick-like object in the visual representation could be linked to his role as Ningirsu's leading war general as well as that of Gudea's escort in CA 18:13. Note that in these two passages Lugalkurdub is written with a divine determinative, in contrast to the passage in which he occurs as a standard. Selz "Holy Drum" 177 § 34, suggested that Lugalkurdub is a name or epithet for Ningirsu's weapon called Šarur. Yet again, Lugalkurdub and Šarur both occur in the Cylinder Inscriptions without any obvious connection.
[66] ITT 3, pl. IV no. 5974; 5, pl. IV nos. 10015 and 10056; UE X no. 247.

2.   Shipment of Materials (ST.11, 12, 20, 58)

Three fragments in Istanbul (ST.11, 12, and 20) contain parts of scenes depicting the shipment of building materials. They do not physically join, as suggested in Börker-Klähn's reconstruction (Fig. 19b nos. 58–60), though two of them (ST.11 and 12) almost certainly belonged to the same scene. They contain parts of "a raft of cedar" of the same dimensions rendered by three logs fastened together by a triple rope at several points. Its right side floats on water rendered by three wavy lines, its left abuts a mountainous area rendered by several rows of scales. The legs of three figures facing left remain on the fragments; one stood on the rear end of the raft, another on its forepart in front of what looks like an oarlock holding a steering oar, while the third stood on land in front of the raft.

The scene depicted on ST.20 takes place in a mountainous area indicated by three rows of scales similar to those on ST.11, but of larger dimensions.[67] It shows part of a cart on which lies what appears to be a stone slab fastened by a rope and in front of it the lower bodies of two figures. They wear knee-length skirts. The rope leading from the cart toward the figures suggests that they were pulling it. It is unlikely that carts, like the one depicted on this fragment, could endure the weight of stone slabs over long distances. The scene presumably depicted the transportation of the slab from the quarry to a river so it could be shipped to Girsu.

It is not until the first millennium that one encounters imagery comparable to that depicted on these fragments. The quarrying and transport of a huge stone slab for the fabrication of a winged bull is depicted in great detail on the reliefs in court IV of Sennacherib's palace at Nineveh,[68] while the transport of timber occurs on reliefs in court VIII of Sargon's palace at Khorsabad.[69] Unger, who first published the three Istanbul fragments, associated their imagery with the provision of building materials for a temple construction,[70] probably inspired by Gudea's written accounts.

The Cylinder Inscriptions and Statue B contain long passages describing the importation of various woods, stones, and metals from all over the then known world for the construction of Eninnu.[71] They mention cedar rafts as well as stone slabs. Cedars for the fabrication of weapons, doors, and supporting beams were sent downstream, probably on the Euphrates, in the form of rafts from the Amanus mountains (today's Lebanon). Stone slabs for the fashioning of stelae were shipped from Umanum and Basalla, places in the mountain lands of the Meneans and the Mardu (to the northeast of southern Mesopotamia). The imagery depicted on the stela fragments described above doubtless belongs in the context of these events. The scenes, however, cannot be reconstructed in their entirety in the absence of comparable imagery in early Mesopotamian art.

---

[67] The scale of the drawing in Börker-Klähn *Bildstelen*, pl. B (Fig. 19b) no. 60, is inaccurate. In her catalogue entry, the author mentions an unpublished fragment in Istanbul which shows a similar mountainous area, and may have belonged in the same thematic context as the three Istanbul fragments discussed here.
[68] Russell *Sennacherib's Palace*, 94–116.
[69] Ibidem, 199 fig. 107.
[70] *Sumerische und Akkadische Kunst*, 44. Börker-Klähn *Bildstelen*, no. 60, identified the stone slab as a stela.
[71] CA 14:28–16:24, and Statue B 5:28–6:63; see Tables III.E.3–5.

In addition to these fragments, Börker-Klähn assigned the small fragment ST.58 in Berlin to the same context because of the scanty remains of scales depicting a mountainous area.[72] On these scales one can make out the lower legs of a figure dressed in a pleated skirt. The left foot rests on the ground, the right is slightly pointed forward. The knees are bent, as indicated by the pleats, and suggest that the figure was either sitting or falling backwards. Neither the posture nor the dress of this figure seem to fit a shipment scene. One would expect a figure involved in transporting materials to be in a standing position and wearing a short skirt, like workmen or soldiers in action.[73] On the stelae of Gudea and Urnamma, the pleated skirt is worn by drummers and men involved with dedicatory objects, both possibly temple employees.[74] On Akkadian cylinder seals, this skirt is worn exclusively by deities.[75] The puzzling posture could fit a deity defeated in combat, and such divine combats often take place in the mountains.[76] If this fragment belonged to a shipment scene on a stela of Gudea, and if the figure represented a temple employee, it could have depicted a scribe registering the inventory of the shipment (Pl. A). This, however, must remain mere speculation.

3. Construction Work (ST.10, 18, 22, 34, 48, 56)

Several fragments of Gudea's stelae can be assigned to scenes which depicted construction work, even if these remain scanty. Comparable imagery is confined to an unprovenienced Akkadian seal in Jerusalem, and two registers on the front of the Urnamma Stela.[77] The scene on the seal (Fig. 20) evolves around a structure reminiscent of a temple gate, and involves six laboring gods.[78] One sits on what appears to be a heap of rubble and holds a basket upside down. Since he is the only one dressed, he is likely to have carried out work less heavy and dirty than the others, perhaps making or fixing baskets which were used for carrying mortar or dirt. Another god holds a hoe over a large container, apparently mixing mortar. A third one carries a basket on his head, and climbs a ladder leaning against the structure. He was probably providing the workers on top of the structure with the mortar made by the god behind him. The god facing left on top of the structure bends forward, and seems to verify the left edge of the structure with a plumb line. Another god kneels on the right top edge of the structure and points with one arm in the direction of the sixth god who, standing on the ground below, stretches his arms in opposite directions, nearly touching the side of the structure with his hands.

---

[72] *Bildstelen*, no. 53 and § 109.

[73] For workmen, see chapter IV.D.1.b; for soldiers in action, see Figs. 26 and 30.

[74] See chapter IV.D.1.b.

[75] See Strommenger *APAW* 2 (1971), 40 with fig. 12.

[76] Compare Boehmer *Glyptik*, figs. 300–306, 316–18, 332, 343, 350.

[77] For possible Early Dynastic representations of construction work, see chapter IV.C.2.b, p. 222.

[78] The seal was first published by Opitz *AfO* 6 (1930), 61f. pl. III:2. See also Frankfort *Cylinder Seals*, 131f. pl. XXIIk; Amiet *Glyptique mésopotamienne*, no. 1485; Boehmer *Glyptik*, 118 pl. XXIX no. 353; Muscarella *Ladders to Heaven*, no. 44 with the best reproduction; and now *Bible Lands Museum*, 50. According to Borowski "Seal Collection," 112f., the seal was acquired in southern Mesopotamia from a peasant woman who wore it on her necklace. She had apparently used it as a spindle. This explains the indentation around the center of the seal. Unexplained remain the two vertical lines above the crouching god which are reminiscent of an inscription box, and the pot-like object in front of the tall god in the middle which is disconnected. For its composition see chapter IV.D.3.a, p. 265.

Fig. 20: Akkadian Seal in Jerusalem at scale 3:2.

The latter may have been handling a tow-rope by means of which building material was lifted up to the former, unless each of them carried out a different activity.

The scene on the Urnamma Stela is fragmentary. Woolley, Börker-Klähn, Becker, and Canby have engaged in restorations which differ in detail (Fig. 33b-f).[79] What is certain is that the scene extended over two registers separated only by a raised line and linked by a ladder. The ladder is leaning to the left, and seen on the background of a brick wall. Legs at its bottom and top indicate that one figure was climbing the ladder, another followed behind, and a third one facing the opposite direction stood at its top. The head of a basket carrier on the right edge of the lower register, and the raised arm of another, both facing left and seen against the same brick wall, suggest that a row of identical figures were approaching the ladder. Although their precise place remains uncertain, a few smaller fragments with a brick wall background, including one which seemingly contained part of a recessed temple gate, can be assigned to this register. Two small fragments, each with part of a foot on top of the brick wall, must be assigned to the upper register. One of them also preserves a forearm reaching to the ground which must have belonged to a workman in action. On the right side of this register the upper bodies remain of three distinct figures facing left: a god with raised forearm, the king equipped with building tools, and a servant supporting the weight of the tools on the king's shoulder. The god was probably leading the king to the construction site, just as Lugalkurdub and Igalim accompanied Gudea on his way to make the bricks.[80] The tools Urnamma carries – a reed basket, a hoe, and an ax – are fit for making bricks. The god may have been Kulla, the god of brick making.[81] In any case, the presence of a deity manifests the divine approval and guidance of the king's construction. As the Cylinder Inscriptions indicate, these are required not only at the beginning of the project, but also at several stages in the course of its execution.[82]

---

[79] Woolley UE 6, pl. 43b; Börker-Klähn *Bildstelen*, pl. H; Becker *BaM* 16 (1985), 314f. fig. 6a-b; Canby *Expedition* 29 (1987), 61 fig. 13, and *IstM* 43 (1993), 148 fig. 1.
[80] CA 18:13–16; for a translation see chapter V.C.2.
[81] For this god see Lambert *JNES* 46 (1987).
[82] Both positive extispicy (CA 13:17, 20:5–11) and divine collaboration (CA 14:1–4, 16:29f., 17:10–18, 18:13–16, 19:28f., 20:15–20) must be considered as divine approval and guidance.

The Gudea fragment ST.34 is reminiscent of the construction scene on the Urnamma Stela. It preserves parts of two registers separated by a fine line and linked by a ladder. The upper register shows parts of a row of three figures facing left. The best preserved one is bare-chested, and wears a knee-length skirt. He has short curly hair, of which only a few curls at his neck remain. His left arm is bent in such a way that his hand reaches his neck, while his right arm, now lost, must have been raised over his head. The legs, scanty remains of a skirt, and the left arm of the figure in front of him are identical. Only part of a foot remains of the third figure. Börker-Klähn identified these figures as construction workers, and restored them with baskets carried on their heads (Fig. 19b no. 62). Her reconstruction is based in part on the Urnamma Stela, in part on an unpublished fragment in Istanbul which shows a basket held by a hand agreeing in size with the figures on ST.34.[83] This unpublished fragment supposedly preserves a dividing band beyond the basket, and traces on the upper register of two figures in long garments facing right. Börker-Klähn interpreted them as a party of the king analogous to that on the Urnamma Stela. On the Gudea stela, however, these figures occur above the two-register construction scene. The figures on ST.34 doubtless belonged to a construction scene because of the presence of the ladder. Whether they carried baskets, however, is not certain. Their arm posture differs from that of the basket carriers on the Urnamma Stela, and they are not in the lower but in the upper register of the scene.

The upper register of ST.22 shows the lower bodies of three figures facing right. The middle one wears a short skirt, and so probably did the others of whom only bare lower legs remain. Their dress suggests that they were workmen. Börker-Klähn restored them carrying baskets (Fig. 19c no. 57). They could have been approaching a ladder leaning to the right, but it could not have been the one on ST.34, since the figures are larger in size.

ST.56 shows the upper body of a bare-chested male figure between two vertically suspended ropes. He is wearing what looks like a conical hat and faces left. With his left hand he grasps the rope to his left, while the right hand is seen open and only touches the rope in front of him. His hat as well as his gesture remain unparalleled. Börker-Klähn thought that he may have performed an acrobatic act.[84] Alternatively, I suggest placing this fragment in the context of construction work. The man may be handling a tow-rope, as probably did the divine builder on the right side of the structure on the Jerusalem seal (Fig. 20). The conical hat could be a predecessor of our hard-hat.

ST.18 depicts a male figure turning its back to a recessed gate. His garment is not clearly discernible, but probably was a long skirt bound around the waist. He seems to wear his hair in a chignon. He holds two large coils of rope in front of him.[85] A rope of the same thickness emerges from his right hand which is held against his chest and runs along his lower arm over to the gate.[86] Faint remains on the figure's right shoulder seem to

---

[83] *Bildstelen*, § 73. Heuzey NFT 292, followed by Parrot *Tello*, 180f., mistook the ladder for a weapon, and interpreted the figures as war prisoners or tributaries.

[84] *PKG* 14 (1975), no. 108a.

[85] Correctly identified by Börker-Klähn *Bildstelen*, no. 77. Heuzey NFT 294, had wondered whether the object was an oversize bracelet for a goddess.

[86] Börker-Klähn *Bildstelen*, pl. E (Fig. 19c) no. 77, saw a short stick instead.

indicate that this rope originated in the coil held in the left hand, and was led over the shoulder to the other hand. Although the precise activity of this figure remains uncertain, the use of the rope implies surveying or construction work. Furthermore, a recessed gate apparently occurred in the construction scene on the Urnamma Stela (Fig. 33e-f), and an architectural structure also on the Jerusalem seal (Fig. 20).

Two more fragments show parts of a scene involving a rope. The broad side of the middle register of ST.10 depicts a row of four male figures facing right, whose size increases from left to right. They are followed by a considerably taller figure on the adjoining left side of the stela, apparently a ruler. All are dressed in ceremonial gowns. The ruler has curly hair and a beard, the other men are shaved.[87] The former holds his hands on the chest, while the others carry different objects. The figure on the right holds a round object in his left hand, and a peg or small mallet in his right, while the figure behind him carries a metal hoe, similar to the one on Urnamma's shoulder (Fig. 33). The objects of the others are not discernible. This procession, often reproduced and described, has been understood as a scene of worship in which the figures either pray or bring offerings.[88] Hoes and pegs or mallets, however, would be unusual offerings, and the round object carried by the first figure is not an omphalos bowl. This is evident by comparison with an until now unpublished fragment in Istanbul (ST.48).

ST.48 shows a row of three similar figures facing right. The best preserved one holds an object of the same contour as the alleged omphalos bowl, but which, thanks to the well preserved surface of this fragment, can be identified as a rolled up rope. The arm gesture of the figure behind him parallels that of the third figure on ST.10. All that remains of the figure in front is the elbow of its bent arm. The tools carried by the figures in these two evidently similar scenes are appropriate for measuring out a field or construction site. In the Cylinder Inscription, Gudea marks the perimeter of the construction site by means of a rope stretched around wooden pegs.[89] The hoe could have been used to clean or loosen the soil where the pegs were to be driven in, and the mallet to drive in the pegs. The figure with raised forearms and closed hands may have held a tablet to record the measurements. Thus, these fragments most likely belonged to a scene depicting the measuring of the construction site.[90]

The attribution of ST.10 to a stela of Gudea, however, is doubtful. The carving is cruder, and the height of the registers, of the dividing bands, and of the represented figures exceeds the size of all other fragments considerably. Furthermore, the ruler figure on the left deviates from the usual representations of Gudea, which show him shaved and in some cases wearing the brimmed cap.[91] Beards are worn by the kings of Akkad and again those of the Third Dynasty of Ur.[92] While the former are portrayed with long hair, which may be bound in a chignon at the neck, the latter usually wear the brimmed cap over

---

[87] The small figure in front of him may have had the same hair style.

[88] For a bibliography and the most recent description see Börker-Klähn *Bildstelen*, no. 90 and §§ 106–108.

[89] CA 17:22–26; see chapter III.B.4.4.

[90] Alternatively, it could be linked to the marking of the stepped platforms described in CA 20:27–21:12, which is done in a similar way; see chapter III.B.5.2.

[91] See chapter IV.D.1.a.

[92] For example, Sargon (Fig. 30), Naramsin (Fig. 28), the Akkadian royal head form Nineveh (Strommenger *Fünf Jahrtausende*, pl. XXIII), Urnamma (Fig. 33), the ruler on the Susa Stela (Fig. 34).

short curly hair visible along the brim. Uncovered short curly hair is worn by non-royal figures on Akkadian monuments,[93] and has been identified as the Akkadian hairdo.[94] Combined with a beard, this hairstyle is worn also by a scribe of Gudea on his seal,[95] and by other non-royal figures on the stelae of Gudea (ST.49–50) and Urnamma (Fig. 33). The authenticity of the one statue which represents Gudea's son Urningirsu with this hairdo is doubtful;[96] the other statue shows him shaved and wearing the brimmed cap, like his father.[97] Urbaba is also represented beardless.[98] Could the mysterious ruler figure on ST.10 represent a governor of Lagaš when this state was under Akkadian rule?

4. Temple Equipment (ST.14, 27, 29, 55, 59, 60, 61, 62, 64)

A number of fragments depict objects dedicated to the gods in their temples, including a gate lion, a foundation deposit, divine chariots and weapons, and a stela. With the exception of the chariots made of wood, actual examples of these types of gifts were found in Tello. Their representation in other media, however, is either entirely unparalleled or only attested in different contexts. Although little remains of the scenes in which these objects occur, it seems that they are depicted being brought to the temple.

The upper register of the much-eroded fragment ST.29 shows the hind legs of a lion on the rear of a low wheel-cart in front of what looks like the stool of the seated Gudea statues.[99] A curved line leading from the foot of the lion to that object suggests that the two were linked.[100] Unlike Gudea's stools, a lion's head protrudes from the side of the object. Its broken top leaves open the question whether it was a stool or another similar looking piece of furniture. Scanty remains of an apparently identical object can be made out at the left end. Börker-Klähn interpreted the entire installation as part of a lion throne.[101] Mesopotamian representations of lion thrones,[102] however, and the two on the stelae of Gudea in particular (ST.2 and 17), look quite different. Lions were common gate guardians, and fragments of two such sculptures set up at temple gates by Gudea have survived.[103] The lion on the cart is therefore better envisioned in a scene depicting the transport of such a sculpture to the temple gate.[104]

---

[93] For example, on Sargonic stelae (Figs. 30–31), and on the Tello Stela (Börker-Klähn *Bildstelen*, no. 21). The bearded soldiers on the Akkadian stelae Figs. 28 and 32 probably wear this hairdo under their helmets. Several statuettes of the Akkad period show the same hairdo, see Amiet *Art d'Agadé*, nos. 7, 18, 41. Since they are minor works of art compared with the royal statuary of this period, they probably represent officials and not kings.

[94] Börker-Klähn *RlA* 4 (1972–75), 3f. s.v. Haartracht.

[95] Parrot *Tello*, fig. 43a.

[96] Braun-Holzinger *Weihgaben*, St 137, pointed out several unusual and suspicious features: the inscription, the treatment of the eyes, and the beard.

[97] Braun-Holzinger *Weihgaben*, St 136.

[98] Braun-Holzinger *Weihgaben*, St 135.

[99] See Appendix A Statues B, D, F, H, I, Q. Compare the seal of a cup-bearer of Gudea: Fischer *BaM* 27 (1996), 228 fig. 12.

[100] The surface in the thus created triangular between the lion's hind leg and the stool-like object is raised from the background, though less high than that of the lion.

[101] *Bildstelen*, no. 78 and § 99.

[102] Metzger *Königsthron und Gottesthron*, pl. 65 and 72, and Haussperger *Einführungsszene*, 96 note 509, and 104 note 618.

[103] GL.1–2 in Appendix A.

[104] A miniature sculpture of a lion on an identical cart, together with a hedgehog on a cart, were buried as

ST.55 shows the upper body of a bare-chested, shaved male who carries a foundation deposit. Since the ruler is never represented bare-chested, the carrier cannot be Gudea,[105] but must be a servant, probably wearing a skirt.[106] The deposit consists of a figurine in the shape of a kneeling god with a peg placed on an object of oblong rectangular shape.[107] The kneeling god with peg is the most common type of foundation figurine from Gudea's reign.[108] The rectangular object probably represents the foundation tablet which was buried together with the figurine. Behind the shoulder of the carrier are the remains of another oblong rectangular object and of a hand holding it.[109] The figure following behind may have carried the box for the foundation deposit or another dedicatory object.

Parts of a similar, if not identical, chariot seen in side-view are preserved on four different fragments (ST.14, 27, 61, and 62). Although all four chariots are fragmentary, enough remains to construct a relatively complete composite image.[110] The chariot had two wheels, and was drawn by two equids, as shown by the overlapping mane and pair of ears of a second equid on ST.14. The wheel shows a hub with a linch pin, and a metal tire made in two segments with clamps at either end. A stylized palm tree emerges from the center of the wagon, and is flanked by bison-men.[111] These are seen upper body frontal and lower body in profile, and hold with both their hands a frame which emerges from behind the wheel on either side and passes over their heads in front of the palm. On the crown of the palm hovers a lion-headed eagle with spread wings, which clenches its claws into the back of flanking lions. The lions turn their heads back up toward him, and place their hind legs on the palm crown and their fore legs on the frame. The lion-headed eagle was probably double-headed, since the one preserved head, beyond which the fragment is broken, is off center in relation to the body, and faces the opposite direction of the equids.[112] A massive double draught pole ending in a lion-head protome ties the equids to the chariot, and a large quiver filled with arrows is attached to its back.[113] The reins, which pass through a terret ring on the pole (ST.14), seem to lead

---

part of a deposit in the Middle Elamite Inšušinak Temple at Susa; see Harper *Royal City*, no. 101. What their original function was, and with what intent they were buried remains open to speculation. Were they toys of the elite, or models of a sculptural decoration of the temple later dedicated to the god, or were they simply made for the purpose of the dedication?

[105] Cf. Heuzey NFT 294, followed by Boehmer *Or* 35 (1966), 358.

[106] That he was entirely nude, as suggested by Börker-Klähn *Bildstelen*, pl. A (Fig. 19d) no. 89, is less likely, since he does not perform a ritual act.

[107] The figurine was correctly identified by Heuzey NFT 294f. fig. 8, followed by Parrot *Tello*, 178 fig. 36f, Boehmer *Or* 35 (1966), 358 pl. LII no. 15, and Ellis *Foundation Deposits*, 79 fig. 15. Börker-Klähn *Bildstelen*, no. 85, mistook the figurine for a statuette of a seated deity.

[108] See chapter II.C.1.c.

[109] Börker-Klähn *Bildstelen*, no. 85 and § 69, apparently did not see the hand, and interpreted the remains as an offering stand as depicted on ST.4. The latter, however, is shaped differently, and there are no offerings depicted on ST.55.

[110] For a detailed description of the chariot on ST.14 see Littauer and Crouwel *Wheeled Vehicles*, 39 and 44f.

[111] For this creature see chapter IV.B.8.

[112] The lion-headed eagle with two heads facing opposite directions occurs from the Akkad to the Ur III periods; see Braun-Holzinger RlA 7 (1987), 95f. § 1.c. A good example is depicted on the seal of UrDUN from Lagaš (Fig. 21).

[113] The structure at the back of the chariot on ST.27 cannot be the draught pole, as Börker-Klähn *Bildstelen*, no. 61 and pl. D (Fig. 19e), suggested. There are no traces of a draught animal on the left of the fragment, but very clearly on the other side of the wagon. Although one cannot make out the arrows as well as on ST.14,

up toward the lion-headed eagle (ST.61–62). No driver is visible. On the adjoining side of ST.14, a male figure, of whom only the lower body is preserved, follows behind the chariot. He wears a long pleated skirt on top of a short skirt, and is apparently holding the shaft of an object, perhaps a large mace,[114] in front of him.

Compared with the extant early Mesopotamian representations of chariots, the fancy elaboration of this chariot is unique. No representations of contemporary or Ur III chariots have survived, and most earlier representations depict chariots of humans either in warfare, as on the obverse of the Standard of Ur (Fig. 26) and side B of the Eannatum Stela (Fig. 27), or in the ensuing victory celebrations, as on a number of door plaques (Figs. 35–36).[115] The closest parallel in terms of shape is found on an Akkadian seal representing a libation in front of the weather god.[116] He rides a chariot pulled by a winged dragon on which his consort stands. This two-wheeler has a quiver at the back and a rather tall cage-like casing topped by what may be a stylized palm crown. Its rider stands astride the pole casing, and leads the reins with his right arm raised over the casing, while holding a whip in his left. By analogy, the chariots on Gudea's stelae are best interpreted as similar straddle cars.[117] The driver would have stood between the elaborate casing and the quiver. On ST.14 there is a small space between the legs of the right-facing bison-man and the quiver just big enough for a leg. Like the Akkadian chariot, those on the stelae of Gudea are evidently destined for the divine world. This explains the lavishly decorated casing which appears to be too high for actual use, as well as the mythical creatures on it.

In Gudea's inscriptions all chariots are associated with Ningirsu. Both chariots Gudea presents to him had this god's emblem (šu-nir) on it,[118] which, in another passage, is identified as Anzu.[119] Anzu's association with Ningirsu/Ninurta is well-documented. The Akkadian Anzu myth relates how Ningirsu defeated this mythical creature, and Sumerian literary texts refer to Anzu as Ningirsu's defeated foe and trophy. According to *Angim* (54–62) Ningirsu's trophies, including Anzu, decorated his chariot.[120] Gudea's Cylinder Inscriptions are inconsistent regarding Ningirsu's relation with Anzu. On the

---

the general shape of the structure is similar to that of the quiver with arrows on ST.14, and the pattern of the quiver (rows of vertical lines) is the same as on ST.14, while the draught poles on ST.14 and 61 exhibit a distinctly different pattern.

[114] Börker-Klähn *Bildstelen*, no. 45, wondered whether the shaft belonged to a standard. The clearly identifiable standards, however, have a much less massive shaft, and are carried close to the body by differently dressed figures, see chapter IV.B.1.

[115] Boese *Weihplatten*, nos. AG 2, AG 5, CT 2, CT 1, U 1. They are discussed in chapter IV.C.2.b. Compare also a scarlet ware vessel from Khafaje: OIP 63 pl. 138.

[116] UE IX no. 92 = Boehmer *Glyptik*, fig. 372 = Collon *First Impressions*, no. 726.

[117] Littauer and Crouwel *Wheeled Vehicles*, 45, identified the chariot remains on ST.14 as a straddle car, and their only other example of this type for the late third millennium is the Akkadian seal described above, see ibidem 39.

[118] CA 7:22, and CB 16:11.

[119] CA 13:22, see Table III.E.2. See also CA 27:18–19. In CA 13:22f. šu-nir and urì are juxtaposed, while CA 27:18 uses the term urì. Both terms can be translated "standard," and a differentiation between them is difficult. For the sources see Pongratz-Leisten *BaM* 23 (1992), 302–308. šu-nir occurs in literary as well as administrative texts, while urì is confined to the former. Could urì refer to the standard as a whole, and šu-nir to its characterizing emblem, which is then used as *pars pro toto*? This would accord with the fact that šu-nirs are made of metal, while the materials for urì include also reed.

[120] In general see Cooper *Return of Ninurta*, 143 and 153f.

one hand, Anzu is omnipresent in the text because of its association with Ningirsu, and twice occurs as his standard emblem.[121] On the other hand, Anzu is absent from the list of Ningirsu's trophies, and once Lugalkurdub is mentioned as his emblem instead.[122] This opposition may be explained with a change in the conception of Anzu taking place in Gudea's time.[123] In visual representations the lion-headed eagle is generally identified with Anzu because of its bird component. Braun-Holzinger called attention to the slim evidence for this equation, and cautioned against generalization.[124] The identification is suggested by and can be accepted only for the representations of the lion-headed eagle with spread wings, usually over lions, from Lagaš, which are dedicated to Ningirsu, its divine patron.[125] They date from the late Early Dynastic to the Ur III period. Thereafter the lion-headed eagle is relegated to the periphery,[126] and the visual representation of Anzu in Mesopotamia took a different shape.[127]

The Sumerian term for bison ($^{(gud)}$alim) always refers to a mythical creature.[128] Whether all bison-men in the visual record can be identified with this particular creature is not beyond doubt.[129] In the case of the chariot on Gudea's stelae, however, the equation can be considered certain, since ^{gud}alim is mentioned among the trophies of Ningirsu which Gudea installs in Eninnu, and which according to *Angim* decorated Ninurta's chariot.[130] Two other trophies of Ningirsu mentioned in Gudea's list of trophies seem to be represented on the chariots on the stelae: Palm (gišimmar) and Lion (ur-mah).[131] All these correspondences, together with Ningirsu being the most likely candidate in Gudea's Lagaš for receiving a chariot, strongly suggest that the chariots represent dedicatory gifts for this god.

In the Cylinder Inscriptions, Ningirsu receives a chariot in the course of the verification of the divine command,[132] another among the inauguration presents,[133] and is described as standing on one during the banquet.[134] Aside from the emblem, the text mentions a quiver with arrows, and donkeys as draught animals, which accords well with the visual representation. For several reasons the chariots on the stelae occurred most likely in a scene depicting their bestowal, together with other gifts, during the inauguration of the temple. A human figure follows behind the chariot on ST.14, and he probably was carrying a dedicatory mace. The procession of human figures bringing gifts – usually

---

[121] See chapters III.C.1.b and e.

[122] See chapter IV.B.1.

[123] So already Landsberger quoted in Cooper *Return of Ninurta*, 154.

[124] *RlA* 7 (1987), 96.

[125] Interestingly, the Anzu that occurs as a standard emblem in CA 27:18–19 is described as spreading its wings: urì é-da si-si-ga-bi, ^{d}anzu^{mušen} kur-muš-a da hé-bad-rá-àm "the standard which he (Gudea) erected in the temple (Eninnu) is Anzu spreading its wings in Kurmuš."

[126] Wiggermann *Protective Spirits*, 161.

[127] Braun-Holzinger *RlA* 7 (1987), 96, and Wiggermann *RlA* 8 (1994), 243 no. 14.

[128] See also chapter II.C.2.c.

[129] For a critical discussion see Wiggermann *Protective Spirits*, 174–179.

[130] CA 26:13 and *Angim* 57; see Cooper *Return of Ninurta*, 141 and 148f.

[131] CA 26:3 and 7; lugal ^{giš}gišimmar is mentioned also in *Lugal* 132; so also Wiggermann *Protective Spirits*, 162.

[132] CA 7:11–29, see Appendix C no. 2.

[133] CB 13:18-20, see Appendix C no. 7.

[134] CB 16:7–16, see chapter III.B.10.1.

food supplies – to a temple is well attested in Mesopotamian imagery.[135] It regularly occurs in the context of banquets, and thus fits well with Gudea's inauguration of the temple for which a banquet was held. There are no indications that the verification of the dream was translated into images, and Ningirsu cannot be depicted on the chariot, since no driver is represented.

ST.60 shows the display of what appears to be a stela flanked by various weapons in antithetical arrangement. The stela has a curved top, like most Mesopotamian stelae, and is left blank, probably because the general shape was sufficient for recognizing the object, and the available space did not allow for enough detail to inscribe figurative representation. A similar self-reference to the monument occurs on the Uruk Vase (Fig. 23). Of the three fragmentary weapons on the left of the stela, enough is preserved to confirm that they parallel those on the right. These include a staff with five balls, which surpasses the stela in height; three maces, and an ax with a curved blade, all of the same height as the stela and planted on pedestals; and a higher fragmentary object at the right end. The two maces on either side of the ax have a smaller head than the third, and the ax is decorated with a lion head. Börker-Klähn identified the object on the far right as a harp, though she noted that the remains on its upper left, shaped like a cane turned upside down, could not belong to it.[136] Furthermore, the strings seem too thick, and the instrument would have had only two, which is unlikely.[137] In view of the assembly of weapons preceding it, one is tempted to think of a bow with two arrows, or perhaps a quiver.

The representation of a stela is unparalleled in early Mesopotamian imagery, while the ball staff, maces, and the curved blade lion ax are well attested as attributes of various warrior deities.[138] However, they do not occur in such a display anywhere else. The most likely recipient for these dedicatory gifts in Lagaš is again Ningirsu, whose warrior aspect is well documented.[139] In the Cylinder Inscriptions, he receives, together with the chariot, a number of weapons as gifts on the occasion of the inauguration of Eninnu. They include a seven-headed mace, a lion-headed mace, sword blades, a bow, arrows, and a quiver.[140] A slightly different assemblage of weapons for Ningirsu's Eninnu is listed in Statue B:[141] the weapons called Šarur and Šargaz, which are also attested for Ninurta;[142] two types of axes, one with a curved blade;[143] two maces, one with three lion heads; and a quiver. The installation of several stelae at different locations in Eninnu is

---

[135] Selz *Bankettszene*, 122–125, 196–198, 312–316, 406f., 465, 558. Compare also the Uruk Vase (Fig. 23) with good reproductions in Strommenger *Fünf Jahrtausende*, figs. 19–22, and the booty processions on side B of the Ur Standard (Fig. 26), and on the Nasiriya Stela (Fig. 32).
[136] *Bildstelen*, no. 63; her drawing on pl. F (Fig. 19a) is imprecise.
[137] For a well-preserved Akkadian harp see Rashid *Musikgeschichte*, fig. 44.
[138] For the ball staff see Solyman *Götterwaffen*, 35–3-8, 97–100, 117; for the mace ibidem 19–31, 65–86, 116f.; and for the lion ax ibidem 53f., 104–107, 117.
[139] See chapter III.C.1.b.
[140] CB 13:14–14:8, see Appendix C no. 7.
[141] Statue B 5:37–44, and 6:21–44.
[142] *Angim* 129f.; CT 25 17; K 9336+13558:9 (see Cooper *Return of Ninurta*, pl. VIII); see also chapter V.C.4.
[143] Statue B 5:43: $^{urudu}dur_{10}$-al-lub$_5$, see Civil Farmer's Instructions, 150.

described during its construction.[144] The display depicted on ST.60 may have been the focal point of a procession of figures bringing other dedicatory gifts to the temple.

Two additional fragments depict divine weapons. ST.59 shows part of the lower body of a figure facing left. It is dressed in a long pleated skirt. In front of the skirt appears a large mace in horizontal position, held either by this figure, if his arm was bent backwards, or by a figure following behind. The mace together with the garment, which is also worn by the figure following behind the chariot on ST.14, make this fragment a candidate for a gift procession. Alternatively, it may have belonged to a divine combat scene on an Akkadian monument.[145] ST.64 preserves only a bundle of seven maces. Börker-Klähn is certainly correct in attributing this weapon to Ningirsu:[146] a seven-headed mace is mentioned in the Cylinder Inscriptions among the weapons bestowed upon the temple,[147] and the seal of UrDUN (Fig. 21) depicts it in the hand of the enthroned Ningirsu.[148] On the stela, it may have been held by an enthroned Ningirsu, as Börker-Klähn suggested (Fig. 19a no. 43), or carried among other weapons in the procession of figures bringing gifts to the temple.

5. Percussion Instruments and Musical Performances (ST.9, 13, 15, 23, 25, 53, 54)

Five fragments depict parts of large drums and/or drummers similar to those in the more complete scene on side B of the Urnamma Stela (Fig. 33). The left half of the fourth register shows two figures playing a drum, and a third one apparently playing cymbals. The huge drum, seen frontal, is nearly as high as its players. The semicircular bosses along its edge must be the pegs by means of which the membrane was fastened to the frame, and the instrument tuned. The drummers have curly hair and beards, and wear long pleated skirts. They apparently beat the front of the drum in alternative movements, while holding it by its rear. One man touches with his right hand the membrane, while the other raises his left arm over the head for the next beat; both have the other arm disappearing behind the drum.[149] The fragmentary figure behind the drummer on the right wears a long dress and holds his arms in front of his face. By analogy with a stela fragment in Jerusalem,[150] he can be restored as a cymbalist.

The Jerusalem fragment shows the upper body of a cymbal player facing right in front of an arm raised like that of the drummer on the Urnamma Stela. Behind remains the lower arm of a third figure in vertical position. Its hand is closed, and seems to be holding an object, perhaps a sound stick or sistrum. Börker-Klähn, followed by Becker, attributed the Jerusalem fragment, together with two additional fragments from Ur – one showing

---

[144] CA 22:24–24:8, see Appendix C no. 6, and compare Statue B 6:3–12.

[145] In the Akkadian period this skirt is worn by deities, and in divine combats on Akkadian seals the mace is often held in this position; see notes 75–76 above.

[146] *Bildstelen*, no. 43.

[147] CB 13:21. In CB 7:12 the seven-headed mace is mentioned in relation to Ningirsu's second war general during the parade of the divine temple staff. In *Angim* 138 this weapon is associated with Ninurta.

[148] For other bundles with between four and nine maces see Solyman *Götterwaffen*, 35, 93–97, 117, 123.

[149] This makes it unlikely that the drum was two-sided, as suggested by Stauder in Rashid *Musikgeschichte*, 70.

[150] Rashid *Musikgeschichte*, 73 fig. 56.

a segment of another drum, the other the head of a drummer – to a mirror image of the scene described above on the right side of the same register (Fig. 33b-c). Although Börker-Klähn's reconstruction is plausible in view of the existence of another drum and the tendency toward mirror images on the Urnamma Stela, the attribution of the Jerusalem fragment to it is unlikely. Its carving is much cruder than that of the Urnamma Stela, and the cymbalist wears a fringed mantle and his hair in a double chignon.

A comparable drummer scene is represented on a high-quality stone vase fragment of Ur III or slightly later date.[151] Two male figures play a drum similar to the one on the Urnamma Stela, but smaller in relation to its players. In contrast to the latter, this drum was apparently two-sided. Both players raise their right arm for a beat; the one on the right touches with his left the front membrane, while the left arm of the other disappears behind the drum where it must have touched the back membrane. The drummers wear the same pleated skirt and short curly hair as those on the Urnamma Stela, yet they are shaved and have a necklace. On the drum stands a ram-headed figurine in a long dress holding a vase in front of its chest. This musical scene is subordinate to another scene. A female figure on the left and two male figures on the right of the drummers turn their backs to them. They are directed toward the lost side of the vase where one expects the focal point of the primary scene. The male figures are shaved and wear a fringed mantle. The one next to the drummer raises his left hand to his nose in the typical gesture of a petitioner in presentation scenes, while his right arm rests on his waist. The other wears a necklace, like the drummers, and carries a band with fringes in his right hand held against his waist, while his left grabs the wrist of that hand. The female, dressed in a plain garment, holds her arms with open hands in front of her breast, like a Lamma: the left hand is seen from inside, the right from outside. Her long hair is loose, and she wears a many-layered necklace. Her hairdo, her necklace, and especially the ribbon around her head are, as Strommenger observed, reminiscent of the seated female on the Ninsun Plaque.[152] She is, therefore, likely to be an en priestess, and perhaps the dedicator of this vase.

The Gudea fragment ST.54 shows a scene almost identical to that on the Urnamma Stela. Only the drummers' roles are reversed. The one on the right is beating the drum, while the one on the left, now largely damaged, must have raised his arm for the next beat. Their other arms disappear behind the drum. On the right remain sections of the superimposed cymbals of a cymbalist.[153] In contrast to the Urnamma Stela, the drum slightly exceeds the players in height, and the drummers wear the pleated skirt more open and their hair in a double chignon.

---

[151] The fragment was first published by Heuzey in NFT 287–90. For its date and the best reproduction of its imagery see Strommenger *Fünf Jahrtausende*, no. 128, and for further discussion Rashid *Musikgeschichte*, 68 fig. 49.

[152] AO 2761. For a good photograph see Strommenger *Fünf Jahrtausende*, pl. 129; for further bibliography see Braun-Holzinger *Weihgaben*, W 27.

[153] Also Börker-Klähn *Bildstelen*, pl. F (Fig. 19a) no. 64, whose drawing, however, is inaccurate regarding a small detail: the outer circle of the object is not the hand of the cymbal player, but the edge of the second cymbal.

A drummer raising his arm for a beat is depicted on ST.23, as Börker-Klähn recognized.[154] Like the drummers on ST.54, he wears a pleated skirt over a short plain skirt and his hair in a double chignon. His head and legs are seen in profile, while his upper body with the abdominal muscles is seen frontal. Back to back stands a male figure dressed in a fringed mantle, whose shaven head and lower body are lost. The posture of his arms indicates that he held both his hands close to his face. While his gesture and his outfit are reminiscent of the third figure from the right in the procession on ST.10, his position in relation to the drummer recalls the scene on the vase fragment described above. This indicates that he belonged to a scene only marginally related to the musical performance. Börker-Klähn's reconstruction showing him clapping his hands (Fig. 19c no. 79) is not convincing, and if he represented Gudea,[155] as she suggested by reconstructing a label on his dress, one would expect him to be taller than the drummer.

The torso preserved on the left side of ST.13 could have belonged to a drummer dressed in a pleated skirt, and placing his left hand on the membrane of a drum, as reconstructed by Börker-Klähn (Fig. 19a no. 65).[156] Yet, the imagery on the adjoining side suggests a different scenario. A bare-chested figure with a beard and a double chignon holds a large drum by its right edge with both his hands.[157] The way the drum is held, together with the absence of a second drummer on its left side, make it clear that this drum is not played. It looks as if the figure in the outfit of a drummer is rolling his instrument along in a procession or parade, following behind another figure on the adjoining side, who may, for all that is left, have carried a dedicatory object in front of him. Taking into account the weight of such a huge drum as represented on the stelae of Gudea, its transport by way of rolling can seriously be considered. The metal bosses around its edge, which resemble the tires of the chariots on ST.14 and 27, would have facilitated the transport.

Segments of two more drums are preserved in the lower register of ST.9 and in the upper register of ST.25. That on ST.9 is placed at the right edge of the image field with no room for a drummer on that side, and may have belonged to a mirror image of the scene component on the right side of ST.13.[158] Nothing can be said about the context of the drum on ST.25.

Large framed drums, as represented on the above described Lagaš II and Ur III monuments, are rare in earlier Mesopotamian imagery. The only two examples known to me are on the Bedre Stela (Fig. 38) and on an Early Dynastic seal.[159] Both drums reach only to the chest of their players. The one on the Bedre Stela is played by one man, that on

---

[154] *Bildstelen*, no. 79, correcting Heuzey NFT 295, followed by Parrot *Tello*, 182, who misunderstood the drummer's chignon for the muzzle of a lion genie protecting the figure on the right.
[155] See already Heuzey NFT 295.
[156] *Bildstelen*, § 82.
[157] The description and drawing of this so-far unpublished side of the fragment by Börker-Klähn *Bildstelen*, § 82 and pl. F (Fig. 19a) no. 65 are inaccurate.
[158] Börker-Klähn *Bildstelen*, § 82 and pl. F (Fig. 19a) no. 89, reconstructed a drummer beating the drum on the left. Her reconstruction, however, is based on the incorrect rendition of the drummer on the right side of ST.13, see note 157 above.
[159] Rashid *Musikgeschichte*, 50f. fig. 26, and 68f. fig. 50.

the seal by two. Both occur in a scene subordinate to the larger context of a banquet, as is common for musical performances in Mesopotamian imagery.[160]

In Gudea's Cylinder Inscriptions several percussion instruments are played on different occasions. The balag-drum called ušumgal kalam-ma, "Dragon of the Country," accompanies two gift processions to the temple: the chariot given to Ningirsu in the verification process, and the economic products presented to him before the banquet.[161] Two other percussion instruments (si-im and á-lá) accompany the performance of an adab-song during the brick making, and, together with the former, the presentation of economic products.[162] "Dragon of the Country" and á-lá are also played at the banquet.[163] All these instruments evidently belonged to the temple's equipment, since they are mentioned in the description of Eninnu, the balag having a special room therein.[164]

The match of the large number of Sumerian terms which are thought to designate musical instrument with instruments in visual representations is problematic, in part because it is not clear whether the Sumerian terms designate concrete instruments or particular tunes or sounds after which the instruments were named.[165] Administrative texts which list materials for their fabrication, on the other hand, speak for concrete objects. Balag-drums must have been of some importance, since kings commemorated their fabrication,[166] and numerous texts attest to the attention they received in the cult.[167] Gudea's fifth regnal year is named after the fabrication of the balag-drum called "Dragon of the Country."[168] In the Cylinder Inscriptions, "Dragon of the Country" is characterized as Ningirsu's beloved drum, his famous roaring instrument and consultant, and figures as the musician (nar) of his staff.[169] In addition, Ningirsu's staff includes a personified balag-drum called lugal igi huš, "Master with Fierce Eyes."[170] As mentioned above, the balag-drum "Dragon of the Country" occurs in several major events in the course of the construction and inauguration of Eninnu. This evidence, together with the use of large ox hides for their fabrication,[171] make it likely that the large drums depicted on the stelae were balag-drums.[172] The sim and ala usually appear as a pair. They can be preceded by the determinative for leather (kuš), copper (urudu), bronze (zabar) or wood (giš), and ox sinews are used for their fabrication; in literary texts they occur in the context of

---

[160] Selz *Bankettszene*, 463f., 503, 556–558.

[161] CA 7:24–28, and CB 15:21f. For the balag being a drum see chapter III.B.8.2 note 138.

[162] CA 18:18, and CB 15:20.

[163] CB 18:22–19:1.

[164] CA 28:17f.

[165] See Hartmann *Musik*, 57.

[166] For example, Ibbi-Suen year 21, see Black *AulaOr* 9 (1991), 28 note 40; the copy of a dedicatory inscription of Išbierra according to which this king made and dedicated a balag-drum for Enlil, see RIME 4 I.4.1.1. As a dedicatory object, the balag-drum has tradition in Lagaš itself; it occurs frequently in Lagaš I offering lists.

[167] Selz "Holy Drum," 178 §§ 8–39.

[168] Sollberger *AfO* 17 (1954–56), 33f.

[169] CA 6:24f. = 7:24f., and CB 10:14.

[170] CB 11:1.

[171] See PSD B 75–77 s.v. balag A.1.

[172] Black *AulaOr* 9 (1991), 28 with note 41.

cultic festivals or banquets.[173] They were probably smaller percussion instruments such as cymbals, sistra, or sound sticks.

The scene on the stelae of Gudea in which a large drum and cymbals are played together fits best in the context of the inauguration of the temple. The instruments are played in place, and musical scenes have a tradition in the context of banquets in Mesopotamian imagery. The large drums which apparently are rolled along could have been part of a procession of people bringing gifts to the temple.

Two more fragments are likely parts of musical performances. They depict figures clapping their hands. ST.15 shows the upper bodies of two identically dressed females facing right at the left edge of an image field. The ladies wear a pleated dress and a fringed mantle covering their shoulders. They have their hair tucked up in a double chignon, and covered by a thin cloth fastened with a ribbon. The figure whose arms are preserved holds her hands open in front of her face, placing one palm at a slight angle on the other. Based on the position of her shoulder, the other woman may have performed the same gesture. Börker-Klähn correctly identified this gesture as hand clapping.[174] It corresponds precisely to the *sordas* in Flamenco, which produce a muffled sound. ST.53 shows parts of upper bodies of three figures facing right. The figure in the middle claps his hands, like the lady on the previous fragment. On its right remains but a shaved scalp which must have belonged to a male figure, on its left barely an outline of nearly vertically raised forearms.[175] The badly eroded surface of this fragment makes it difficult to identify the clapper's outfit. Heuzey saw a bare head with a ribbon around its front, which to him seemed bound at the neck,[176] Börker-Klähn simply a bare head.[177] The combination of a bare head with a ribbon is unlikely, while the bare head alone ignores the outline of what looks like a chignon at the neck. If Heuzey is correct about the ribbon, the combination of a ribbon with a chignon suggests a similar lady as depicted on ST.15. The outline of the back, which looks more like that of a dress than that of a bare shoulder, supports this interpretation.

The gesture of hand-clapping is rarely attested in early Mesopotamian art, though two Early Dynastic seals seem to render female clappers in the context of a musical scene forming part of a banquet.[178] They are accompanying players of lyres, flutes, and sound sticks. Neo-Assyrian palace reliefs depict clappers repeatedly, usually together with

---

[173] PSD A II 80–82 s.v. á-lá A; for si-im (written also šèm or šem$_4$) see Hartmann *Musik*, 98–100.

[174] *PKG* 14 (1975), 202 no. 112b. Parrot *Tello*, 185, interpreted it as a prayer gesture. According to Börker-Klähn *Bildstelen*, no. 88, there is a similar fragment unpublished in Istanbul.

[175] Although Börker-Klähn *Bildstelen*, no. 80, mentions the contour of a third figure on the left in her catalogue, the drawing on pl. D (Fig. 19e) shows only two figures, and gives the false impression that the fragment preserves the left edge of the stela.

[176] DC 221, and NFT 292 note 1, followed by Parrot *Tello*, 177. Heuzey interpreted the clapper's gesture as one of submission, and wrongly attributed the fragment to a military scene. This may have influenced his seeing a bare male head.

[177] *Bildstelen*, no. 80.

[178] Selz *Bankettszene*, 309f. figs. 254f. = Rashid *Musikgeschichte*, 50 figs. 23–24. The two men on an inlay of a harp from Ur which Rashid *Musikgeschichte*, 48f. fig. 17, identified as female clappers, are holding small objects, as Dolce *Intarsi Mesopotamici*, U.176f., recognized. Two identical inlay figures were found in Tello, see ibidem, pl. XVII T.20f.

musicians, in various ceremonial contexts.[179] The Sumerian term for hand clapping has not been identified. Börker-Klähn assigned the clappers on the stelae of Gudea to musical scenes with percussion instruments on the assumption that the figure behind the cymbalist on the Jerusalem fragment, as well as the figure turning its back to the drummer on ST.23, were clapping their hands.[180] Although her assumption is incorrect in the first case, and unlikely in the second, the association of clapping with a musical performance is convincing.

6. *Libation Scenes (ST.4, 5, 30, 33, 35)*

ST.4 depicts a libation scene. An offering stand is placed in what must have been the center of the scene. It consists of two oblong supports, the left one step higher than the right. Both are incised with a pattern reminiscent of a recessed temple gate. Three flat elliptical shapes, which may represent loaves of bread, lie on the left support.[181] They are topped by what looks like a bird-shaped container and a small bowl from which very fine wavy lines, probably meant to render vapor, emerge.[182] Although the precise nature of these objects remains ambiguous, their place on the stand leaves no doubt that they represent offerings. The right support carries a tall conical vase[183] with what looks like a bushy plant.[184] On the right a shaved male figure pours a liquid rendered by three wavy lines from a spouted jug into the vase. Only the upper body and part of one foot of the libator remain. He was probably nude,[185] since libators with this kind of jug are always seen nude. The large open hand to the left of the bushy plant must have belonged to the deity to whom the offerings were directed. This deity was probably seated, and pointed with a raised forearm toward the libator. Above the offering stand was a star of which two points remain. This is enough to recognize that it was identical to those depicted in the top center of the Naramsin Stela (Fig. 28), the Urnamma Stela (Fig. 33), and the stela from Susa dated to late Ur III or Isin-Larsa (Fig. 34). Unger, who joined the many fragments of which ST.4 consists, placed ST.5, two fragments with a Gudea figure facing left, behind the libator (Fig. 16).[186] Gudea, identified by a label next to his

---

[179] See Rashid *Musikgeschichte*, figs. 139f.; 149f.; Volk "Improvisierte Musik," 167 with fig. 11.

[180] *Bildstelen*, § 81.

[181] Similarly, Gressmann *Altorientalische Bilder*, no. 441, who identified them as "cakes."

[182] Gressmann *Altorientalische Bilder*, no. 441, followed by Unger *ZDPV* 77 (1961), 81, and Seidl *Or* 55 (1986), 322, interpreted the animal-shaped container as an oil lamp. Börker-Klähn *Bildstelen*, no. 81–84, mentioned an animal sculpture and an incense bowl.

[183] The lower part of such a vase made of gypsum and dedicated for Gudea's life was found at Tello, see Braun-Holzinger *Weihgaben*, Ständer 4.

[184] Seidl *Or* 55 (1986), 322, rightly questioned Börker-Klähn's new interpretation of smoke evaporating from the vase (cf. *Bildstelen*, no. 81–84 and § 103), and argued in favor of the traditional reading as a plant, which is supported by analogy with other libations poured on tree-like plants as, for example, on an Early Dynastic door plaque from Tello (Boese *Weihplatten*, T 10), the Eannatum Stela (Fig. 27), the Urnamma Stela (Fig. 33a), and the Susa Stela (Fig. 34).

[185] So already Gressmann *Altorientalische Bilder*, no. 441, followed by Contenau *Manuel* II, 738 fig. 519, and *Monuments mésopotamiens*, 21 pl. XIId, and Börker-Klähn *Bildstelen*, § 103 and fig. 81–84. Unger's restoration (Fig. 16) shows him dressed in a long mantle. When I examined the piece, I was under the impression that there were traces of pleats under his left arm and a line across his chest, which may have inspired Unger's restoration. These traces are perhaps better interpreted as irregularities in the surface, since they are not compatible with any known dress, and because of the well-documented nudity of the libator.

[186] Several scholars erroneously identified the libator with Gudea: Jastrow *Bildermappe*, no. 83, Contenau *Manuel* II, 738 fig. 519, idem *Monuments mésopotamiens*, 21 pl. XIId, Parrot *Tello*, 179, and again Barrelet

head, is shaved, and wears the fringed mantle. He stands on a small platform, and holds his hands folded on his chest.

Two other fragments show scanty remains of a libation scene in a lower register, without adding any new details. ST.30 preserves the shaved head of a libator facing left and the upper end of his jug from which liquid flows.[187] ST.33 preserves the tip of a bushy plant like the one emerging from the conical vase on ST.4, but with coarser leaves. In addition, some of the fragmentarily preserved divine figures could have been recipients of a libation. Their attribution to a particular scene remains problematic, since enthroned deities are also an essential part in presentation scenes. It is interesting, however, that all identifiable presentations of Gudea are directed to the right side, while the libations on ST.4 and 30 are directed to the left. If the direction of the two scenes was consistent, the goddess on ST.35, who raises her left forearm, would be a likely candidate for a libation scene. The fragment preserves only her bust, which is seen frontal. She wears a multiple-horned crown and a flounced garment covering her shoulders. Her wavy hair is separated into four strands ending in a curl, two on the side falling on her shoulders, and two along the face falling on her breast.

Libation scenes are amply documented on early Mesopotamian stone reliefs and cylinder seals. Early Dynastic images show a nude priest pouring a liquid from a spouted jug into a conical vessel from which a bushy plant sprouts,[188] while Urnamma and other kings after him perform the libation personally, pouring liquid from a goblet over a date-palm shoot in a conical vase (Figs. 33–34).[189] Stepped altars with the same offerings as those depicted on the higher support on ST.4 occur on Akkadian seals.[190] If combined with a libation, however, the liquid is poured on the ground. The spouted jug commonly used by the nude libator on Early Dynastic images also appears on the Enheduanna Disc,[191] and is still used by UrDUN (Fig. 21), a contemporary of the Ur III kings Amar-Suen and Šu-Sin from Girsu,[192] perhaps because he is a priest and not a king.[193] The libation goblet is first attested on Akkadian seals, where it is used by male and female figures dressed in

---

CRRA 19 (1974), 90 no. F74. Unger's restoration as well as the fact that no trace of a fringed mantle is visible on the left arm of the libator speak against this interpretation.

[187] Börker-Klähn Bildstelen, § 114, mentioned an unpublished fragment in Istanbul which preserves a complete libation jug.

[188] Compare side B ot the Eannatum Stela (Fig. 27), a plaque from the Giparu at Ur (Boese Weihplatten, U.4), and one from Tello (ibidem, T 10). On other door plaques and seals, the nude priest is represented just holding the jug in front of a deity, as if an abbreviation of such a libation scene. A bushy plant in a conical vessel is represented in front of the goddess on a plaque from Nippur (ibidem, N 11).

[189] Compare many seals predominantly from Ur, but also from Tello: UE IX nos. 259–276; Parrot Glyptique, nos. 42–52. Most of these seals are of low quality, and show abbreviated scenes. A beautiful parallel to the scene on the Urnamma and Susa Stelae is found on a seal belonging to a governor of Nippur in Šulgi's time: Tallon Asian Art 5 (1992), 39 fig. 9.

[190] Boehmer Glyptik, figs. 373, 387, 546, 646.

[191] UE IV, pl. 41d, and Winter CRRA 33 (1986), 191 fig. 1. Like Gudea, Enheduanna attends a libation performed by a priest in front of her. Unfortunately this figure is so badly-preserved that its attire can be determined.

[192] Fischer BaM 27 (1996), 222 with note 43. Note the discrepancy between main text and footnote regarding the dating of the other seals of UrDUN.

[193] It also occurs as an abbreviation for a libation or as an attribute or filling motif on some lower-quality Ur III seals, for example, Collon British Museum II, nos. 330, 357, 447, 466.

Fig. 21: Seal of UrDUN at scale 2:1.

fringed mantles,[194] and one example is attributable to Gudea.[195] In sum, Gudea's libation scenes combine Early Dynastic and Akkadian elements in a new composition which prefers the Early Dynastic nude priest with the spouted jug over the Akkadian novelty of the direct libation with a goblet, but includes an Akkadian stepped altar.

Textual sources inform us about various occasions for libations.[196] A problem with their interpretation is the definition of the term libation. Can all sorts of liquid offerings be considered libations, or only specific pourings? The latter seems more likely, yet the nouns and verbs designating a libation as distinct from other liquid offerings have not clearly been identified. In Gudea's Cylinder Inscriptions, the pouring (dé) of liquids occurs in two different contexts. Gudea's prayers during the verification process are introduced with an offer (giš-tag) of bread and the pouring of water.[197] Since all verbs have ba-prefixes, Gudea did not necessarily perform the act personally. At the reception for Ningirsu after his entry into the new temple, and again at the inauguration banquet, animals are offered and Gudea pours wine into bowls.[198] I would consider the latter offerings and the former libations, since they function as a ritual frame for the prayers and may have been poured by a priest. If so, the libation scenes on Gudea's stelae can be related to the verification of the divine commission necessary for any temple building project.[199] In more general terms, the prayer signifies a petition, and libations could therefore also occur as introductions to other petitions of the ruler.

7. *Presentation Scenes (ST.1, 2, 3, 6-9, 17, 32, 33, 36, 37, 41, 44)*

A number of stela fragments of Gudea contain parts of presentation scenes. The most

---

[194] Boehmer *Glyptik*, figs. 373, 384, 646, 648.
[195] SV.9 in Appendix A, see chapter II.C.2.d.
[196] See Heimpel *RlA* 7 (1987–90), 1–5 s.v. Libation.
[197] CA 2:8 = 2:25 = 4:6.
[198] CB 5:20f. and 18:19–21.
[199] Naramsin and Amar-Suen were refused a positive oracle when verifying a temple construction project, see Cooper *Curse of Agade*, 27f.

substantial such scene is preserved on ST.1, which shows three figures facing right. Gudea, identified by a label on his fringed mantle, is bareheaded, and carries a palm branch in his right hand.[200] He is led by his personal god Ningišzida, identified by the serpent-dragon heads protruding from his shoulders.[201] Ningišzida wears the flounced garment and the multiple-horned crown, and raises his left open hand to his nose. They are preceded by another god in the same outfit as Ningišzida, who holds a staff in his left hand on the chest, while the right hand grasps the wrist of the left. The staff characterizes this god as a minister.[202] In front of him are the remains of a vertical water jet rendered by four wavy lines. If ST.2 belonged to this scene, as suggested by the restoration in Berlin (Fig. 17), the three figures faced a deity who is dressed in a flounced garment and seated on a lion throne.[203] Behind the throne stands a smaller figure in the same outfit as the approaching gods and the same arm posture as the minister. He is doubtless the divine attendant of the enthroned deity.

By analogy with Gudea's seal image (Fig. 9) and other sealings from Tello,[204] one expects the source of the water jet on ST.1 to be an overflowing vase held in the enthroned deity's right hand and offered to the approaching party. In addition, one could imagine a goddess with an overflowing vase hovering above the seated deity from whose vase more water flows into the vase below, as she is depicted on Gudea's basin (Fig. 8) and in the presentation scenes in the top registers of the Urnamma Stela (Fig. 33). As argued in the case of Gudea's seal, the most likely deity to bestow prosperity signified by the overflowing vase upon Gudea is Ningirsu. In the case of the stela, this is corroborated by the lion throne, since Ningirsu is often associated with lions. The seal of UrDUN (Fig. 21), for example, represents a nude priest libating before an enthroned god from whose shoulders protrude lion heads, and whose throne and foot-rest are decorated with lions.[205] Since UrDUN is identified as Ningirsu's išib-priest in the seal inscription, the god must be Ningirsu and the libator UrDUN himself. The fact that the minister on ST.1 is not the double-faced Isimud speaks against Börker-Klähn's identification of the enthroned deity on ST.2 as Enki.[206] If the enthroned god on ST.2 is Ningirsu, then the minister and the attendant can tentatively be identified with Šaganšegbar and Kindazi, who occur as minister (sukkal) and sort of a *valet de chambre* (lú é-dùg-ga), respectively, in the enumeration of Ningirsu's staff in the Cylinder Inscriptions.[207]

---

[200] Next to the palm branch seems to emerge another object from behind Gudea's hand, which, together with what might be its other end below Gudea's hand, looks somewhat like the adze held by the god in the second register on side A of the Urnamma Stela (Fig. 33). This shape, however, could be an irregularity in the surface, the piece below Gudea's hand the end of the palm branch, and the diagonal line from the palm branch to Gudea's neck the seam of his dress.

[201] See chapter II.C.3.a.

[202] See Wiggermann *JEOL* 29 (1985–86), 7–16.

[203] For this throne type with back and arm supports see Metzger *Königsthron und Gottesthron*, 290 and pl. 77.

[204] See chapter II.C.3.a with notes 155–157.

[205] For the god seated on a lion throne and with lion heads protruding from his shoulders on other seals from Tello see Delaporte *Catalogue Louvre*, T.113 = ITT V pl. V no. 10044; Buchanan *Early Near Eastern Seals*, no. 617; Fischer *BaM* 27 (1996), 228 fig. 8. Lions or lion heads are sculpted also on objects Gudea dedicated to Ningirsu, see chapter II.C.2.a.

[206] So observed by Wiggermann; see chapter II.C.3.a.

[207] Wiggermann *JEOL* 29 (1985–86), 8 note 14. Note, however, that the deity holding the shepherd's staff in KAR I 19:5, mentioned by Wiggermann in this context, is not Šaganšegbar but Sumuqan. For Šaganšegbar

Two other fragments depict a Gudea figure led by his personal god. ST.6 preserves a Ningišzida figure, with serpent-dragon heads protruding from his shoulders, leading a figure dressed in a fringed mantle of whom only the torso remains. This figure can only be Gudea, since Ningišzida is not attested as the personal god of any other ruler. Both Gudea and Ningišzida raise one hand to their nose. The fragment thus combines the posture of the Gudea figure from the seal with that of the Ningišzida figure from ST.1. The other fragment, ST.44, shows a headless figure dressed in a fringed mantle with the same arm gesture as Gudea on the seal and on ST.6, and being led by a figure of whom only the right shoulder and arm remains. Traces of the case of a label inscription on the fringed mantle suggest that this figure was a ruler.

It is tempting to identify both fragments as parts of presentation scenes, since the motif of one figure leading another by the hand is attested only in such scenes. The Cylinder Inscriptions, however, mention Ningišzida holding Gudea by the hand on his way to make the bricks.[208] In view of this passage and the scarce comparative material for extensive visual narratives as represented on the stelae of Gudea, one cannot exclude the possibility that this motif could also occur in other contexts. ST.6 is a likely part of a presentation scene, since the large size of its figures speak for its belonging to a top register, and presentation scenes occur in the top register on the stelae of both Gudea and Urnamma. In contrast, the figures on ST.44 are much smaller. Because this fragment does not preserve any characteristic element of the original monument it belonged to, it may as well have been part of a door plaque.

Another top register fragment, ST.3, preserves the upper body of a shaved male figure dressed in a fringed mantle. He is holding a palm branch, as does the Gudea figure on ST.1. Behind him appear two open hands side by side. The hand on the left is seen from the outside, the other from the inside. This gesture is attested only for the Lamma goddess.[209] A Lamma follows Gudea in the presentation scene depicted on his seal (Fig. 9). In contrast to the latter, the one in this top register was apparently much smaller than Gudea. A complete and bigger Lamma is depicted at the left end of the right side of ST.9. She wears the pleated dress and a single-horned crown, like that on Gudea's seal. Her hair falls over her shoulder down to her waist, and her neck is adorned with a necklace consisting of several rings. Since Lammas are widely attested in presentation scenes, and because this fragment as well as ST.3 belong to top registers, both are likely parts of presentation scenes.

ST.32 shows remains of three lower bodies facing left: the first of a deity dressed in a flounced garment, the second of a Gudea figure with a fragmentary label inscription on a plain garment, and the third of a figure wearing a pleated dress. Börker-Klähn interpreted them as part of a presentation scene by analogy with ST.1 and 44.[210] Although the pleated

---

and Kindazi see also chapter V.C.2.

[208] CA 18:15f.; see chapter V.C.2.

[209] See chapter II.C.3.a. with note 147. Parrot *Tello*, 185f., followed by Börker-Klähn *Bildstelen*, § 72, identified this figure as "Galalim" based on CA 18:14. Galalim, however, is an outdated reading for Igalim, whom we know as Ningirsu's son, see chapter III.C.1.d.

[210] *Bildstelen*, no. 51.

(not flounced) garment of the third figure probably belonged to a Lamma figure, like the one depicted on Gudea's seal (Fig. 9),[211] her interpretation is not beyond doubt. The party faces the opposite direction of all identifiable presentations of Gudea, and the proportions of the figures are too small for a top register. The fragment could have shown Gudea heading to the construction site under divine guidance.

Moving from the party of Gudea to that of the seated deity, the assignment of fragments to a particular scene becomes less certain, since deities are not limited to presentation scenes. If all presentation scenes had the enthroned deity on the right side, the divine figures on ST.7, 36, and 37, as well as the lion throne of which parts are preserved on ST.17 and 33, are candidates for the enthroned deity in such a scene, those on ST.8 and on the left side of ST.9 for his/her attendant.

ST.36 depicts a god seen full-face, who holds an object with a long shaft in his left hand on the chest, and probably gestured toward an approaching party with his now broken right arm. He wears the flounced garment typical for gods, and a multiple-horned crown of which only traces are left. He has a long beard, and his hair is bound in a chignon on either side, perhaps in an attempt to render a frontal view of a single chignon at the neck. His throne has back and arm supports, like the one on ST.2. Only the left end of a single-horned crown remains of the mythical creatures which decorated the throne. Börker-Klähn convincingly attributed this crown to a bison-man.[212] Heuzey identified the object held by the god as a scepter,[213] while most other scholars saw a weapon,[214] which Solyman specified as a curved sword.[215] Unfortunately the shaft breaks off just at the shoulder of the god, and a line on the much eroded surface gives the deceiving impression that there was a curved end to it. This weapon was more likely a curved blade ax as seen on the shoulder of the enthroned god on the seal of UrDUN (Fig. 21) and several other sealings from Tello.[216] The ax has a long shaft held exactly like the one on ST.36. Its blade, which may end in a lion-head, like the one on ST.60, is clearly beyond the shoulders of the god, where the surface of our fragment is broken. On two sealings this god is further characterized with a seven-headed mace and a lion-headed eagle, and there can be no doubt that he represents Ningirsu. If Börker-Klähn's reconstruction of ST.64 in the hand of the god on ST.36 is correct, he too held a seven-headed mace. The

---

[211] It cannot be the pleated skirt worn by male figures, since the preserved leg is the one which would be seen nude protruding from the slit of the skirt.

[212] *Bildstelen*, no. 42 and pl. F (Fig. 19a). In contrast to these bison-men, those on the chariot on ST.61 wear multiple-horned crowns. Meyer *Sumerier*, 54, suggested that the single-horned crown on this throne belonged to a lion, which would be without parallel, and is, therefore, not convincing. The figures wearing the single-horned crown in Gudea's art are the Lamma on Gudea's seal (Fig. 9) and on ST.9, and Ningišzida's serpent-dragon on Gudea's seal and on the libation vase SV.9 (see Appendix A). Neither of these figures is attested on thrones, while the bison-man occurs on a throne on an Old Babylonian cylinder seal from Mari: Metzger *Königsthron und Gottesthron*, no. 800 A. This creature is, therefore, the most likely candidate for this throne.

[213] DC 212, followed by Meyer *Sumerier*, 54.

[214] Jastrow *Bildermappe*, no. 10; Meissner *Grundzüge*, 45; Parrot *Tello*, 173; and Börker-Klähn *Bildstelen*, no. 42.

[215] *Götterwaffen*, 109. Note his erroneous designation of our fragment as a terra cotta.

[216] Buchanan *Early Near Eastern Seals*, no. 673; Fischer *BaM* 27 (1996), 228 fig. 9. See also Solyman *Götterwaffen*, 53f., 104–107.

postulated bison-men on his throne accord with a Ningirsu figure, since they are this god's trophies, and occur also on his chariot on ST.14 and ST.61.[217]

ST.7 depicts the upper body of a goddess seen full-face. She holds an overflowing vase in front of her with her left hand. Her right arm is broken, but probably gestured toward an approaching party on the left.[218] She wears a multiple-horned crown and a flounced garment with an elaborately decorated neck and a shawl, as well as two necklaces, one consisting of several rings, the other with three beads in the center. Her hair falls in wavy lines onto her shoulders. Because of her dress and crown, and also because she was probably enthroned and receiving a petitioner, this goddess cannot be the minor deity associated with the overflowing vase on Gudea's basin.[219] In presentation scenes in Gudea's art, the overflowing vase is a generic symbol of prosperity, and therefore does not provide a clue to her identity. In view of several features which this fragment shares with ST.36 – both show a deity full-face, are of about the same proportions, relief height, and similar execution in details – one is tempted to see in her the counterpart to the god on ST.36,[220] and tentatively identify her as Ningirsu's consort Baba.[221] The bestowal of prosperity would certainly befit the highest goddess of the Lagašite pantheon.

ST.37 shows the lower body of an enthroned deity dressed in a flounced garment and sitting on an apparently cubic seat; its precise shape remains ambiguous. This throne is placed on several roughly cut steps, which have been interpreted as the representation of a rock.[222] A slim support for this interpretation might be found in an Akkadian seal, which shows an enthroned Šamaš on two similar, though thicker steps,[223] since Šamaš can also be enthroned on mountains represented by the common scales.[224] If these steps indeed signify mountain lands, the enthroned deity might have been Ningirsu's mother Ninhursag, the lady of the mountain lands. It is probably this goddess that is represented seated on mountain scales on an Early Dynastic door plaque from Tello.[225] The preserved imagery on ST.37 is clearly too small for a top register. Whether the piece belonged to a stela at all is doubtful. It does not preserve any characteristic elements of the original monument and may well have been part of a door plaque.[226] Its attribution to Gudea remains uncertain as well. If the steps represent mountains it is, in fact, unlikely, since mountains are rendered as scales in Gudea's art.

---

[217] See chapter IV.B.4. Already Heuzey DC 211, identified this god with Ningisru, though without discussion. It is perhaps no coincidence that the god on ST.36 is represented full-face, like the warrior god on Akkadian seals, see Boehmer *Glyptik*, 70.

[218] So also Unger's reconstruction in Istanbul, see Börker-Klähn *Bildstelen*, fig. 41b.

[219] See chapter II.C.1.d.

[220] So also Börker-Klähn *Bildstelen*, no. 42.

[221] Jastrow *Bildermappe*, no. 19, saw a Baba, too. Van Buren *Flowing Vase*, 67, and Börker-Klähn *Bildstelen*, § 97, identified the goddess with Nanše, based on their too narrow interpretation of the overflowing vase. A door plaque dedicated to Baba for Gudea's life (DC pl. 25:5 = Braun-Holzinger *Weihgaben*, W 24) shows a goddess seated on the lap of an enthroned god, and gesturing to the left where one expects the petitioner. The upper body of the goddess, doubtless Baba, is seen frontal.

[222] Heuzey DC 215f.; Parrot *Tello*, 174; Boese *Weihplatten*, 206.

[223] Collon *British Museum* II, no. 162.

[224] Boehmer *Glyptik*, figs. 456, 461.

[225] Boese *Weihplatten*, T 10.

[226] So Boese *Weihplatten*, 206. Börker-Klähn did not include it in her *Bildstelen*.

ST.17 and 33 show a frieze of two rows of overflowing vases of the same proportions, and must have belonged to the same scene. ST.17 preserves the right edge of a register field. On top of the frieze one can make out the remains of the hind part of a lion in front of a recessed structure. A fraction of a lion's mane is left on the continuation on ST.33,[227] which, in addition, shows a foot facing right with a piece of the hem of a long dress in front of the overflowing vases. Together these are the remains of a throne seat in the shape of a recessed temple gate, like the ones on the Urnamma Stela (Fig. 33) and Ur III seals.[228] It was flanked by lions, and stood on a pedestal decorated with overflowing vases. Placing the two fragments as close together as the balanced continuation of the frieze allows, makes it unlikely that the mane on ST.33 belonged to the lion on the throne. Rather, it must have belonged to a foot-stool also decorated with a lion.[229] The indistinct remains in front of the lion's mane may then be part of the lion rather than the heel of the enthroned deity.[230] The foot on the same level as the pedestal must have belonged to a figure approaching the throne from the left.

ST.41 shows the bare upper body of a god with two bearded faces in profile under one multiple-horned crown. He doubtless represents Isimud, the double-faced minister of Enki well attested on Akkadian seals. Börker-Klähn proposed placing this fragment in a presentation of Gudea to Enki, the deity she assumed to be on the throne depicted on ST.17+33.[231] Akkadian representations associate Enki with the overflowing vase, but never with lions.[232] By analogy with Gudea's seal (Fig. 9) and the combination of ST.1 and 2, the lions and the overflowing vases on ST.17+33 can also be associated with Ningirsu. The attribution of ST.41 to a stela of Gudea, however, is doubtful. First, Isimud is never mentioned in the Gudea texts, and his master Enki, though participating in the construction of Eninnu recounted in the Cylinder Inscriptions,[233] plays a very minor role in the cult of Lagaš during Gudea's reign.[234] Second, ST.41 would be the only representation of an Isimud during this and the Ur III period. On Akkadian seals, Isimud usually occurs in scenes of mythological content, and only rarely in presentations of humans to Enki.[235] After the Akkadian period, his representation is relegated to peripheral regions, except for two anomalous Old Babylonian seals that evidently derived their imagery from Akkadian seals.[236] The Isimud on ST.41 is smaller in size than most figures on the Gudea fragments discussed so far, and the relief is flatter. If he did belong

---

[227] Börker-Klähn *Bildstelen*, no. 40, saw a claw of a wild cat in addition to fur.

[228] So already van Buren *Flowing Vase*, 69.

[229] A lion-decorated foot-stool occurs, for example, on UrDUN's seal (Fig. 21).

[230] Börker-Klähn *Bildstelen*, § 66, mentioned in this context a badly eroded fragment in the Louvre which supposedly shows a lion throne combined with a lion foot-stool, yet did not integrate this consideration in her reconstruction drawing on pl. A (Fig. 19d) no. 40. This fragment is doubtless AO 28543, a fragment of a door plaque, which was so eroded when I examined it that I could not make out the foot-stool.

[231] *Bildstelen*, § 67 and pl. A (Fig. 19d) no. 49.

[232] That lions flanked his temple in Eridu is not enough evidence, since lions are common guardians of temples of many deities.

[233] See chapter III.C.1.d.

[234] The only inscription addressed to Enki is on a clay nail recording Gudea's reconstruction of a temple for this god in a small hamlet of the state, see CN.4 in Appendix

[235] Boehmer *RlA* 5 (1976–80), 179–181 s.v. Isimud; Nunn "Mehrgesichtigkeit," 145f.

[236] al-Gailani Werr *Chronology*, 52 no. 322; Collon *British Museum* III, no. 103. Contrary to Boehmer and Nunn (see note 235 above), I doubt that the double-faced master of animals on Kassite and Nuzi seals is really meant to represent Isimud.

to a stela of Gudea, however, he is best imagined in connection with his master in a lower register which may have visualized Enki's participation in the construction.

The left side of the top register of ST.9 depicts a huge mace behind the remains of a standing figure facing left. The figure wears a flounced garment, and probably held his left arm on his chest. Maces as tall as human and divine figures appear in presentations to warrior deities on seals.[237] They are usually stuck into the ground, rather than mounted on pedestals, like the ones flanking a stela on ST.60. The best candidate for the enthroned deity associated with this mace in Lagaš is Ningirsu. The standing figure was most likely the divine attendant behind his throne.[238] ST.8 shows most of the right side of a god facing left. He wears a flounced garment, a horned crown of which only a part remains,[239] a beard, and a chignon. His left arm rests on his chest. The large size of the figure speaks in favor of his belonging to a top register, and there the most likely role would be the divine attendant behind the throne.[240]

The origins of the presentation scene go back to the Early Dynastic period. From the Lagaš II through the Old Babylonian period, it is the most popular subject on royal monuments as well as on seal images. There are variations in its components and composition, some specific to a certain period, others depending on the context. These, however, do not affect the underlying concept. At their basis, all presentation scenes render an official or ceremonial encounter between two parties of different status and rank, usually a petitioner and his/her grantor. As Winter convincingly argued,[241] the presentation scene manifests a relationship of authority rooted in the structure of society. In the case of Gudea, it is his interaction with the Lagašite pantheon on behalf of the people of Lagaš which establishes his position in this city-state.

The core components of Gudea's presentation scenes are a standing Gudea in front of an enthroned deity. Usually Gudea is led by his personal god Ningišzida. Only when the latter is in the position of the enthroned deity himself, is he led by another minor god.[242] The Lamma, who may accompany him, as well as the minister and attendant of the enthroned deity are optional complements. Lamma is not present on ST.1+2, while the minister and the divine attendant are absent on the seal (Fig. 9). On the stela fragments and on the seal the enthroned deity is either Ningirsu or his consort Baba. The higher status and rank of the chief couple of the Lagašite pantheon *vis-à-vis* the other scene participants is expressed in their enthroned position and their role as bestowers of prosperity, signified by the overflowing vase. Gudea's role as a petitioner *vis-à-vis* them is implied in his gesture of holding his hand to the nose.[243] If he carries a palm branch, his personal god performs the petition gesture for him. Similarly, his personal god may receive the overflowing vase for him. Statue N (Fig. 5) renders Gudea in the possession

---

[237] See Solyman *Götterwaffen*, figs. 310, 312, 337, 338. For this mace see also chapter V.C.4.
[238] So already Heuzey NFT, 285.
[239] The Istanbul restoration with a single-horned crown illustrated in Börker-Klähn *Bildstelen*, fig. 41b, is unlikely, since all other divine attendants had a multiple-horned crown.
[240] So also Unger's restoration, see Börker-Klähn *Bildstelen*, fig. 41b.
[241] *BiMes* 21 (1986), and "Legitimation of Authority."
[242] DP.3 in Appendix A, see chapter II.C.3.a.
[243] See chapter IV.D.1.d.

of this prosperity. The bestowal of prosperity upon Gudea by Ningirsu or Baba signifies the blessing of the ruler by the highest divine order in his state. It legitimizes Gudea in his office.

In the context of a temple construction, the bestowal of prosperity can be associated with the divine blessings Gudea receives as a reward for his successfully completed project in the Cylinder Inscriptions.[244] The blessings are conferred in the form of a direct speech, and Gudea may be imagined standing in front of the deity who pronounced them. Note, however, that the deity in the written account was probably not Ningirsu but a higher-ranked deity of the Sumerian pantheon. Rain and abundance from heaven are promised by Ningirsu already for the construction,[245] and a metaphor alluding to abundance as a prerogative for the project occurs at the very beginning of the text.[246] Abundance and prosperity are not only a reward but also a prerogative for the temple construction. That both these aspects are epitomized in the presentation scene accords with its conceptual nature.

8. *A Divine Combat (ST.38)*

The fragment ST.38 in Berlin shows an unusual combat. A bare-chested, bearded god with a chignon grabs a bison-man by his beard, and cuts his throat with a dagger. Only the upper bodies of the figures are left. From the preserved right shoulder of the victorious god protrudes the head of a serpent-like creature, similar to the serpent-dragon heads of Ningišzida on Gudea's libation cup and stela fragments.[247] Whether it wore a horned crown like the latter is unclear, since the fragment breaks just at that point. While the bison-men on the chariot (ST.61) wear multiple-horned crowns, this one has simply two animal horns. The human hair and beard, and the bull's ears, however, are the same.[248] His head, seen in profile and facing his enemy, is attached to a frontal body turned to the side. The carving quality is rather crude.

The divine combat is a typical theme of the Akkad period, and the defeat of an anthropomorphic god over a bison-man well attested on Akkadian cylinder seals.[249] The anthropomorphic god is sometimes characterized by rays protruding from his shoulder, but never by serpent-dragons. He usually holds the bison-man by his tail and one horn, only once he attacks the beast with a dagger. The god with serpent-dragon heads protruding from his shoulders does not occur before Gudea, and is nowhere else attested in combat.

---

[244] CB 23:10?–24:8, see Appendix C no. 8.
[245] CA 11:8–11, see chapter III.B.3.2.
[246] CA 1:5–9, see chapter III.B.1.1.
[247] Compare SV.9 described in chapter II.C.2.d, and ST.2. Slight differences seem to occur in the rendering of the neck, and of its lower jaw.
[248] Wiggermann's identification of the figure as the "bull-eared god" in *RlA* 8 (1994), 235 s.v. Mischwesen, known mainly from Old Bablylonian terra cottas, is not convincing, especially since bull's ears are combined with several different types of gods; see Wrede *BaM* 21 (1990), 251f. nos. 59–60.
[249] Boehmer *Glyptik*, 49–59.

Opitz, who first published the fragment, identified the victor with Ningišzida, and dated the fragment to Gudea's reign.[250] He assumed that it represented a specific myth, now lost. Hymns addressed to Ningišzida describe him as a warrior, though this was not his main aspect.[251] According to textual sources, the subduer of the bison-man, who is essentially a monster or personification of distant mountain lands, is traditionally Utu, the overseer of the mountain lands, but from Gudea's time onward also Ningirsu, probably as a by-product of his dealings with the mountain lands.[252] Was Ningirsu's defeat appropriated by Gudea's personal god Ningišzida?

Wiggermann observed that textual sources exhibit a fundamental lack of precision concerning combats of gods with monsters, which also partly applies to Akkadian seals in regard to the subduers. He has come to the conclusion that such combats do not represent specific myths, but are "examples of the general scheme with one or several variable players on both sides."[253] Thus, texts as well as images are not meant to represent specific combats, but rather the common struggle with the forces of evil and may reflect upon historical events. As Börker-Klähn observed,[254] such a topic has no place in the context of temple construction on Gudea's stelae and must have belonged to another monument.

9. Other Fragments (ST.12, 16, 19, 21, 22, 29–31, 39–40, 42–43, 45–47, 49, 50–52, 57)

The remaining fragments represent parts of bodies of human or divine figures which are too deficient to be assigned to specific scenes. Seven fragments must be attributed to Gudea, since they contain a label identifying this ruler. ST.42 and 43 each preserve a nearly complete Gudea figure with the label on his fringed mantle. Both wear a brimmed cap, and face right. On ST.43 Gudea holds the hands folded on his chest, on ST.42 he holds a palm branch in his right hand, while the left forms a fist on his chest. Neither fragment could have belonged to a presentation or libation scene, since Gudea never wears the brimmed cap in these scenes.[255] Furthermore, one would expect him to be led by the hand in a presentation scene, and facing left in a libation scene. Since he holds his hands on his chest, these fragments must have belonged to other scenes in which Gudea participated in a passive way.

The right side of ST.12 shows the lower body of a Gudea following another figure in a long dress to the right. The surface is very eroded. Only traces of Gudea's label are left on his mantle. The position of the fringe indicates that Gudea held the left arm on his chest. Between the figures there are remains of an object clearly indicated by the higher relief.[256] The preserved part recalls a shaft, though it is now somewhat shapeless due to the broken surface. Since the figures turn their back to the importation scene depicted on

---

[250] *AfO* 5 (1928–1929), 87f.

[251] See van Dijk *Götterlieder* II, no. 4, and Sjöberg *StOr* 46 (1975).

[252] Wiggermann *Protective Spirits*, 174–179. Note the bison-men depicted on Ningirsu's chariot on ST.14 and 61, and perhaps also on his throne on ST.36.

[253] *Protective Spirits*, 154f.

[254] *Bildstelen*, § 110.

[255] Also Börker-Klähn *Bildstelen*, nos. 74–75 and § 72.

[256] Not indicated by Börker-Klähn *Bildstelen*, pl. C (Fig. 19a) no. 59.

the left side, they probably belonged to another scene which continued on the adjacent right side.

The upper register of ST.30 depicts the lower body of a Gudea facing an obscure object on the right. The fringe of his mantle is positioned as on the previous fragments, indicating that he held the left arm on his chest. The object, of which only the lowest part is preserved, looks like the giant foot of a piece of furniture. It may have been similar to the equally obscure object depicted on ST.31, which shows part of a "leg" in addition to the "foot." Nothing else remains of the scene.

ST.19 preserves only the head of a Gudea figure identified by a label in front of it. Gudea wears the brimmed cap, and faces right. ST.45 preserves a head with the same cap facing right. It must have belonged to a ruler figure, since the brimmed cap is reserved for kings throughout the Ur III period.[257] ST.46 and 47 preserve only a fraction of the fringed mantle with Gudea's label inscription.

ST.49 depicts the upper body of a male figure with neck-length curly hair and a short beard stylized by parallel zig-zag lines. He wears the fringed mantle, and holds his arms on his chest in the same position as the divine attendant on ST.2. His outfit and posture are reminiscent of the ruler figure on ST.10. In contrast to the latter, the male on ST.49 faces the opposite direction, and is compatible in size with the other Gudea fragments. A similar figure, though with raised forearms, occurs on an isolated fragment of the Urnamma Stela, which has been placed in the lowest register on side B (Fig. 33). This figure is clearly not a ruler figure, and ST.49 probably was not either.

ST.50 and 51 preserve each a fragmentary head with neck-length curly hair. Börker-Klähn considered attributing them to musicians by analogy with the Urnamma Stela.[258] The drummers on Gudea's stelae (ST.13, 23, and 54), however, wear chignons. ST.50 and 51 may have belonged to workmen instead, since the workman on ST.34 has this hairdo.

ST.52 preserves a complete shaved head. Börker-Klähn's attribution to a standard carrier – that of the standard on ST.25 – is feasible.[259] To whom the broken shaved head in the lower register of ST.22 belonged remains unresolved. That the relief remains on the lower register of ST.29 are scalps of human figures, as suggested by Börker-Klähn,[260] is not beyond doubt.

ST.57 shows a bare flexed left arm with its shoulder and part of the chest. This fragment can belong only to a bare-chested male figure. Women have covered shoulders, and the flounced garments of gods as well as the fringed mantles of men always cover the

---

[257] See chapter IV.D.1.a.
[258] *Bildstelen*, § 112.
[259] *Bildstelen*, § 93 and pl. E (Fig. 19c) no. 66. Heuzey's attribution to ST.10 in DC 221, is not possible due to size.
[260] *Bildstelen*, § 98 and pl. D (Fig. 19e) no. 78.

left shoulders no matter which direction they face.[261] The arm may have belonged to a workman or a gift carrier.

The relatively large head of a god facing right on ST.39 can be attributed to a Ningišzida figure, since part of a serpent-dragon head protruding from the right shoulder is still visible. Its size as well as its direction allow an attribution to a presentation scene in a top register. ST.40 depicts the head of a god facing left. This head could have belonged to a seated god[262] or his divine attendant in a presentation scene, or to a god leading Gudea in another scene.

The last two fragments preserve but feet: two facing opposite directions on ST.21, one facing left on ST.16. On both fragment the feet stand on a very narrow band which separates the imagery from an inscription in the case of ST.21, and from an overflowing vase, probably the remains of a frieze, carved in shallow relief in the case of ST.16. In contrast to other overflowing vases on Gudea's monument, this has a plant in it, and fish swimming upstream, like on Statue N.

---

[261] Compare, for example, ST.1 and 5. It can, therefore, not have belonged to a Gudea figure, as Börker-Klähn *Bildstelen*, no. 52, suggested.

[262] Börker-Klähn *Bildstelen*, pl. A (Fig. 19d) no. 36.

C. About the Reconstruction

Due to the precarious preservation of the stelae of Gudea, their reconstruction must remain conjectural. The fragments are insubstantial compared, for example, with those of the stelae of Eannatum and Urnamma, and belong to an unknown number of monuments. The recurrence of motifs, together with variances in size of the represented figures and objects, leave no doubt that they belonged to several similar monuments, though their attribution to particular stelae remains difficult. Börker-Klähn already observed that neither the provenance nor color and erosion of the stone are valid criteria.[263] Although the imagery of many fragments can be identified as part of distinct scenes, hardly any of these scenes is complete. Nor can their sequence be firmly established. The reconstruction and organization of scenes on the original monuments is hampered by the scarcity and fragmentation of comparative material. Only presentation and libation scenes are well documented in early Mesopotamian art. An equally detailed visual narrative concerned with royal construction work is attested only once more on the Urnamma Stela. This monument is incomplete and its imagery and composition differ in a number of details from the stelae of Gudea.

In view of this situation, I cannot offer more than conceivable scenarios.[264] Any such attempt requires first a clear idea of the formal characteristics of the extant early Mesopotamian stelae, and of the principles underlying the composition of imagery on early Mesopotamian monuments. With these guidelines established, I will review the fragments which preserve formal characteristics of the original monument and attempt to determine the shape and composition one would expect of the stelae of Gudea. In a next step I will consider the compatibility of the fragments in terms of imagery, size, and stylistic peculiarities, and propose some conceivable scenarios.

1. Formal Characteristics of Early Mesopotamian Stelae

Table IV.C.1 provides a synopsis of the pertinent formal characteristics of Mesopotamian stelae from the Early Dynastic to the Ur III periods. Since many stelae are incomplete, one has to turn to different monuments for different characteristics. Yet, enough is preserved to show that the stelae were neither uniform in terms of form and proportions, nor do they lend themselves to a clear typology. Rather than identifying a "classical registered stela" that underwent a process of standardization culminating in the stelae of Gudea and Urnamma, as Börker-Klähn did without clearly defining its form or prototypes and despite the formal differences between the stelae of Gudea and Urnamma,[265] I see each stela exhibiting individual traits as well as characteristics shared with others, though in different combinations. In part, this is probably due to the shape and proportions of the blocks of stone that were available.

---

[263] *Bildstelen*, §§ 53–56.
[264] Technical resources such as photogrammetry, or petrographic analysis of the fragments, which might improve the work on the reconstruction of the fragments, were beyond the limits of this study.
[265] *Bildstelen*, §§ 25 and 61.

C. About the Reconstruction

In general, Mesopotamian stelae have an oblong body and a curved top, with the possible exception of the Naramsin Stela, which was apparently elliptical, like the mountain depicted on it.[266] The preserved bottoms consist of an unpolished zone below the imagery and/or inscribed text, which may have been originally embedded in a pedestal or in the ground. The height of the stela tends to approximate twice its width. Only that of the Eannatum Stela is less than one and a half its width. The width always exceeds the depth, though the ratio between them varies considerably from 1:12 (Eannatum) to 1:1.5 (Sargon), and may have largely depended on the proportions of the stone block from which the stela was cut. The less flat stelae tend to have rounded edges as opposed to sharp ones.[267] The monuments can be carved in relief on one, two, three or four sides. There is not necessarily a pattern between the width-depth ratio and the number of sides carved: the Eannatum Stela with a ration of 1:12, for example, has imagery on three sides, while the Naramsin Stela with a ratio of 1:4 is one-sided.

Table IV.C.1: Formal Characteristics of Early Mesopotamian Stelae

Fig.		H	W	D	Top	Bot	Edg	Sid	Mar	Reg	HRT	HRO
	Early Dynastic:											
	Tello (7)	*350	200	20		+	s	1?	?	1		*50
38	Bedre (12)	90+	45	22		+	r	4	+	2		*25
24	Urnanše (15)	25	25	12	r		r?	3	–	1	25	
25	Urnanše (16)	91	47	17	r	+	r	4	+	0		
27	Eannatum (17)	*180	*130	11	r		s	4	–	2/5	*110/20	*70/40
	Akkad:											
30	Sargon (18)	91+	60	45		+	r	4?	–	2		30
28	Naramsin (26)	200+	105	25	r		s	1	+	0		
32	Nasiriya (22)	70+	*100	8+			s	4?	+	3		22
	Tello (21)[268]	34.5+	27+	11	r		s	2	–	3		12
	Ur III:											
33	Urnamma (94)	*300	154	36	r		s	2	–	5	82	40
34	Susa (100)	76+	62	14	r		s	1?	+	1	70	

The numbers in parentheses following the stela designations are those of the catalogue in Börker-Klähn *Bildstelen.* H = complete height; W = complete width; D = complete depth; Bot = bottom zone; Edg = edges; Sid = sides which are carved with relief and/or inscribed; Mar = margin band; Reg = number of preserved registers; HRT = height of top register; HRO = height of other registers; r = rounded; s = sharp; * = restored or estimated.

---

[266] Unless this is an optical illusion due to the breakage.

[267] Börker-Klähn *Bildstelen,* §§ 1–33, distinguished between "Plattenstele" and "Pfeilerstele." There is, however, no clear pattern between these two types regarding other formal characteristics that would commend such a typology.

[268] My discussion considers only the sculpted fragment AO 2678, not the inscribed fragment AO 2679 which has been attributed to the same stela on uncertain grounds (see most recently Foster *Iraq* 47 (1985), 17 fig. 1), since the combination of the two fragments is unlikely in view of the different contents of text (distribution of land to royal dependents) and images, see Gelb et al. *Land Tenure,* no. 24.

Regardless of how many sides are carved, some have margin bands along the edges. Most stelae have several horizontal registers separated by dividing bands. Exceptions are the stelae of Urnanše and Naramsin. The two preserved registers of the Bedre Stela are of equal height, and identical on all four sides. The same seems to apply to the rectangular registers of the Akkadian stelae with two or more carved sides (Sargon, Nasiriya, Tello). On the Eannatum Stela, on the other hand, the registers have not only different heights, but differ also in number on opposing sides: one broad side has two registers whereby the top one is twice as high as the other; the other broad side and the narrow side carved with imagery share the same five registers, four of which are similar in height, while the top one is much narrower. The two carved sides of the Urnamma Stela have the same number of registers; the top registers are about twice as high as the other four rectangular registers, which among them are of similar height. Although neither of the latter two stelae have the bottom preserved, they do not seem to be missing any additional registers. They have well-balanced proportions, and there are no fragments extant for additional registers. If the Sargonic fragment (Fig. 29) belonged to the Sargon Stela, or to another Akkadian stela of the same scale, that stela had the same ratio of top register to other registers as the Urnamma Stela. On all the stelae the height of the registers corresponds more or less to the height of the figures or objects in them.

Written labels identifying human figures are attested since the Early Dynastic period. On one stela and the plaques of Urnanše (Figs. 25 and 37) not only the ruler, but also members of the royal family and high officials, are thus identified.[269] Since the time of Eannatum the labels are almost exclusively reserved for ruler figures. On Akkadian victory monuments they also identify defeated rulers and certain objects in the representation.[270] On the stelae of Eannatum and Sargon the labels are placed next to the head of the ruler, while on the Urnamma Stela the label is on the lower part of his garment. Commemorative inscriptions are originally carved in the same field as the imagery, but gradually become separated from it: on the Eannatum Stela the text is placed in the blank space between figures; on the Sargon Stela in the lower half on one side of the bottom register; on the Naramsin Stela beyond the head of the king; and on the Urnamma Stela on a broad band between registers. In some cases inscriptions may also have been inscribed on the pedestal of the monument.[271]

2. *The Composition of Imagery on Early Mesopotamian Monuments*

a. Culminating Scene versus Episodes.

In a short but fundamental study on narrative in early Mesopotamian art, Perkins distinguished two basic "methods:" one allusive, "employing the culminating scene – one group of figures, one moment of time, at the climax of a series of events – to stand

---

[269] Braun-Holzinger Weihgaben, W 1-4 and Stele 5. The texts next to Urnanše are short building inscriptions, while the labels of the other figures contain only name and/or filiation and/or profession. Several high officials are identified by labels also on the Ušumgal Kudurru, see Gelb et al. *Land Tenure*, no. 12.

[270] These labels are known only in copies of texts originally inscribed on now lost monuments, see Braun-Holzinger *Weihgaben*, 281–290. Buccellati "Through a Tablet Darkly," offered a reconstruction of such a monument which is hard to accept.

[271] Braun-Holzinger *Weihgaben*, 331.

for the entire story;" the other more explicit, showing "successive episodes of a story, often juxtaposed without clear delimitation."[272] She observed that the more explicit method rarely includes all episodes of a story, but only a selection with the climax in view, and, thus betrays a tendency toward the allusive. There is neither a thematic nor a chronological distinction between them, and both "methods" can be combined on the same monument. Perkins characterized the difference between them as one of emphasis, placed on either the development of action, or on its completion. The former "encourages concrete realism," the latter "lends itself especially to symbolism."[273]

One of the oldest examples of the "episodic method" is found in the Lion-Hunt Stela from Uruk (Fig. 22).[274] The roughly cut boulder is polished and carved on one side only. Two scenes of hunting are superimposed: an identically looking male figure attacks lions once with a lance, another time with a bow. The male figure wears the skirt, beard and ribbon that characterize the ruler in this period. This stela doubtless represents two episodes of a royal hunt, in which "sheer concrete vigor" conveys the "challenging statement of this ruler's power."[275]

The Uruk Vase (Fig. 23)[276] exemplifies the "culmination method:" it shows the encounter of a ruler, almost entirely lost in the break, with the divine in the form of a female figure – who probably represents the goddess – in front of a temple.[277] The temple is indicated by two reed bundles which are the gateposts that must be imagined flanking its entrance, and a series of cult objects behind it, including statues and vessels filled with plenty of food. The ruler is preceded by a nude figure who offers a vessel filled with food to the female figure, and is followed by a servant dressed in a short skirt, who holds the end piece of a textile terminating in a huge tassel.[278] The scene extends over two more registers. The middle one depicts a row of nude figures who, like the one in front of the female figure, carry vessels filled with food and drink. Below follows a row of alternating sheep and goats on top of a row of barley and flax growing on a stream of water. The bottom register illustrates the source of the food provisions carried by the figures above, the animal and grain husbandry, which probably belonged to the temple's estate, while the middle register can be viewed as an expansion of the food carrier in the top register.

This image portrays the ruler providing the gods with food by stocking up the temple's supplies. In view of later sources, the occasion for this event may have been the New Year

---

[272] *AJA* 61 (1957), 55.

[273] Ibidem, 61f.

[274] Börker-Klähn *Bildstelen*, no. 1.

[275] Grönewegen-Frankfort *Arrest and Movement*, 152.

[276] AUE 9 (1993), 81 no. 226.

[277] Whether she wore a distinctive headdress cannot be verified, since an ancient mending obscures the space above her head. At this early period anyway, the visual distinction of divine as opposed to human figures is not yet canonized. That the female figure represented a priestess in the goddess' place is less likely in view of later images, which never show the ruler in front of a priestess, but frequently in front of a deity.

[278] This textile, generally interpreted as part of the ruler's dress, could also be a gift the ruler brought for the goddess, and which his servant helped to carry. On contemporary seal images similar pieces of textiles ending in tassels, perhaps elaborate belts, are part of the gifts brought to the temple in processions, see Rova *Sigilli*, nos. 120, 665, 692, 750–51, 901 (=Amiet *Glyptique Mésopotamienne*, no. 656).

festival.[279] In this case, the image alluded to a particular cult event. At the same time, it epitomizes the ruler's role as the one who communicates with the divine on behalf of the human society, and illustrates the cosmic hierarchy of this society. Abbreviated versions of this scene are depicted on several seal images contemporary with the vase: they include the figures of the ruler and the goddess in conjunction with two large storage vessels.[280] The goddess is usually identified by an isolated gatepost of her temple in the form of a reed bundle, and the ruler may carry a barley plant which clarifies his role as the provider of the storage items.

Encounters between ruler and deity are represented also on the two stelae of Urnanše. The one from Ur (Fig. 24) looks like the truncated top of a registered stela, though it seems to be complete.[281] A presentation scene wraps around three sides of the monument. The enthroned goddess is placed prominently on the broad side with her attendant behind the throne, while the two figures approaching her are seen on the small sides. The stela from al-Hiba (Fig. 25) is more elongated.[282] The broad side with the largest image field is occupied by a similar enthroned goddess. She is approached by five male figures: one on the adjacent small side, Urnanše followed by a servant with a jug on the back side, and two superimposed figures on the other small side. The back side contains below the first image field a second one, which forms a self-contained sub-scene: Urnanše's wife and daughter are seated facing each other and holding each a drinking cup. The combination of the drinking cup with the seated position signifies a banquet.

The text inscribed on the back side of the stela from Ur commemorates a temple construction. The presentation scene can, therefore, be understood as alluding to the divine blessing the ruler received in return for his temple building, and the blessing doubtless represents the climax of the events in a temple construction story. Except for the labels which identify the ruler and his family members, the inscription of the stela from al-Hiba is unfortunately not edited. If the extended presentation scene alluded to a similar event as on the stela from Ur, the banquet may elaborate on the narrative context of the blessing which, according to Gudea's account, took place during the inauguration celebrations for the temple.

The visual commemoration of military victories of Early Dynastic III rulers can combine episodic scenes with a culminating one. The two main panels of the Standard of Ur (Fig. 26) recount episodes of a war and the ensuing victory celebration, and contain the culminating scenes in their top register.[283] On both panels the sequence is from bottom

---

[279] Gudea provides Baba with large amounts of food as well as livestock and other agricultural products on the New Year; see chapter III.E.2.e.

[280] Amiet *Glyptique Mésopotamienne*, nos. 646–49, and 651. Nos. 645 and 650 are probably parts of the same scene, while no. 652 seems to replace the goddess with her statue pedestal, and nos. 653–54 may be parts of a similar scene.

[281] Börker-Klähn *Bildstelen*, no. 15; Braun-Holzinger *Weihgaben*, Stele 4.

[282] Börker-Klähn *Bildstelen*, no. 16; Selz *Bankettszene*, 227–229; Braun-Holzinger *Weihgaben*, Stele 5. My drawing (Fig. 25) is based on high-quality photographs which Bob Biggs generously provided.

[283] Perkins *AJA* 61 (1957), 57. For a schematic illustration of the composition and detailed description see Selz *Bankettszene*, 233 and 332-336. A fresh restoration of the piece is illustrated in Collon *Ancient Near Eastern Art*, 67 fig. 50. Margueron's recent pessimistic contribution in *CPOA* 3 (1996), ignores universal conventions in visual representation, and, as a result, dismisses many clues in the reconstruction of the

to top, and the lower two registers progress from left to right, while the top registers show confronting figures. The bottom register on side A shows four manned chariots: the first one on the left seems to be just entering the battlefield, while the others are seen in action, the equids galloping over wounded or dead enemies, and the combat soldier ready to attack. In the middle register, a troop of foot soldiers wearing helmets and capes follow into the battle; three, who have taken off their cape, fight and/or capture an enemy; and a group of captives is led away from the battle field. The top register shows the culminating episode, the review of the captives by the victorious ruler. He stands in the center of this image field and is larger than the other figures. Behind him follow several of his generals dressed like the chariot warriors and holding their lances, and at the end the ruler's chariot also emphasized by size. The ruler receives several groups of his warriors presenting captives. The captive of the first group, who is dressed in contrast to the other captives, probably represents the defeated enemy leader.

The bottom register of side B depicts a row of figures identified by their dresses and hairdos as foreigners. Two each lead a chariot team, the others carry heavy loads on their shoulders. They are headed by a man of the victorious ruler in civilian dress.[284] This is doubtless a parade of the booty taken during the military campaign represented on side A. The middle register proceeds to the banquet preparations: a row of figures bring life-stock including bulls, caprovines, and fish. That this procession follows upon the booty parade is made clear by the first three figures at the left, which are characterized as foreigners, and thus link this scene to the previous one. The banquet on the top, like the review of captives on side A, can be considered the culmination of the preceding events. The ruler is again identified by his position and larger size. He wears a more elaborate skirt than the other participants, and is attended by his own servant, while another servant caters to the six seated males facing him. The partly broken figure behind him, who is also individually attended, was probably his wife.[285]

The Eannatum Stela (Fig. 27)[286] apparently depicts episodes of a war led by a human king on one side, and its successful completion, epitomized by the icon of the city god[287] returning from battle and displaying the captives in a net, on the other. The episodes are contained in four more or less equally high bands and a smaller top register, while the culminating scenes expand over two much larger registers. The protagonist on side B is engaged in action, while that on side A is shown in a symbolic gesture of dominance. On

narrative.

[284] This figure which belongs at the far right, was erroneously placed in second position in the reconstruction, see Selz *Bankettszene*, 334 note 1.

[285] Selz *Bankettszene*, 272. In the famous "garden scene" on Assurbanipal's palace reliefs, his wife partakes in the banquet celebrating the victory over the Elamites.

[286] For a stimulating discussion of the imagery and composition of this stela see Winter "After the Battle," and for a different interpretation Becker *BaM* 16 (1985), 278–281. Previous literature is given in Winter "King of Kish," 206 note 8, and Braun-Holzinger *Weihgaben*, Stele 7.

[287] The possibility that this figure represents Eannatum rather than Ningirsu, as defended by Becker *BaM* 16 (1985), 284f., cannot be entirely excluded. Littauer and Crouwel *JNES* 32 (1973), convincingly argued that the chariot was more likely pulled by equids than by a hybrid mythological creature, and the presence of a small deity does not exclude that of a ruler. A very similar battle net is held by an Akkadian king on another stela (Fig. 29), and the same skirt is worn by a human figure on the Urnanše Stela form al-Hiba (Fig. 25). Only the Anzu emblem, nowhere else associated with a king, remains problematic.

side A the sequence from bottom to top is suggested by the logical order of return before the display of captives. Indications for the same sequence on side B are the position of the king progressively moving to the center of the register and that of the vultures in the top register. The reconstruction and interpretation of this side, however, remain problematic. Because of the juxtaposition of a burial ritual with three battle scenes, the now lost figure who held the enormous lance pointing at an enemy leader in the bottom register has been taken to be one of Eannatum's predecessors in a scene visualizing one of the battles of the Lagaš-Umma border conflict related in the inscription.[288] The representation of a ruler other than the one who dedicated the stela, however, would be unprecedented. Furthermore, the room for this ruler as well as for the burial mound in the register above is cramped. Were it not for the alignment of the foot on the other side, one would like to move the three fragments at stake to the middle, and perhaps restore the lance holder in a chariot similar to the scene on the third register. Barrelet observed several discrepancies between these fragments and the rest of the stela, and argued that they belonged to another monument with similar imagery,[289] a possibility which cannot be dismissed. The battle scene in the third register shows Eannatum fighting with a lance from his chariot followed by an army shouldering lances, the one in the fourth shows him on foot leading a phalanx of soldiers armed with shields and holding their lances in attacking position, while nude corpses are piled up at the far right. The repetition of the ruler figure suggests that these scenes depicted consecutive episodes – perhaps different moments of the same battle – as on the Standard of Ur.

All extant Akkadian stelae depict military exploits of the kings. The Naramsin Stela (Fig. 28),[290] features a culminating scene extending over the entire carved side of the monument in an extraordinary dynamic composition which glorifies the king's triumph over his enemy. He stands out isolated at the top in a much larger size than all other figures. Although heavily armed, his posture is almost immobile, as though his mere appearance brings about the defeat of the enemy. There is no explicit fighting at all.[291] The Akkadian army moves in three diagonal rows upwards behind its king, while the enemies fall down under his foot. The two enemies in front of the king are dwarfed by his size. One is dying, the other begs for mercy. The inscription mentions Naramsin's campaign in the mountains of the Lullubi.[292] These mountains are apparently indicated by the peak against which the two enemies are depicted. The image then sums up a military campaign in one symbolic image at the moment of victory, the climax of the story. More abbreviated versions of the triumphant king are encountered in a number of

---

[288] Becker *BaM* 16 (1985), 283f., based her interpretation of the back side as a summary of the most important events of the war history related in the text, on the wrong premise that the enemy leader in the bottom register represents the king of Kiš; see Winter *ZA* 76 (1986). Winter "After the Battle," 19f., interpreted the ritual scene as a visualization of Eannatum's dream related in the inscription, which prompts him to wage a war. Such an enigmatic episode does not seem suited for pictorial representation, and Winter herself (ibidem, 23) argued that text and image differ in content and intent.

[289] *JNES* 29 (1970).

[290] For an insightful description see Groenewegen-Frankfort *Arrest and Movement*, 163f., and now also Bänder *Siegesstele*, 171f.

[291] This Mesopotamian image stands in sharp contrast to Egyptian tradition in which the victorious king is epitomized striking down his enenmy, see Davis *Canonical Tradition*, 64–73.

[292] Braun-Holzinger Weihgaben, Stele 13.

rock reliefs dating to the Akkadian and Ur III periods.[293] They depict the king treading on his enemies, at times in front of a warrior deity. Similar scenes or simply prisoners or tributaries are also depicted on pedestals of royal statues.[294]

In contrast, the other Akkadian stelae are organized in registers around several sides of the monument. They illustrate episodes leading to the victory, yet may have contained a culminating scene in the top register. One isolated top register fragment shows a battle net (Fig. 29),[295] similar to the one in the culminating scene of the Eannatum Stela. The figure holding the net as well as that which it confronted are almost entirely lost. The latter is seated and has mace-like objects protruding from the shoulders. It is obviously an enthroned deity, and most probably represented Ištar, the warrior goddess who plays a major role in the inscriptions of the kings of Akkad. In the figure presenting the net to her one would then expect a king, and the remains of the garment accord with the dress Sargon wears on the stela that bears his inscription (Fig. 30).[296]

The Sargon Stela (Fig. 30)[297] preserves a bottom register and half of a second one on three sides. On the bottom register, Sargon, identified by a label, leads a row of soldiers shouldering curved blade axes. A scene of vultures devouring corpses behind them suggests that the army is leaving the battle field. This interpretation is supported by the attendant protecting the king from the sun with a parasol. The second register shows six pairs of combatants. Sargon's soldiers all face right and wear short skirts as opposed to the nudity of the enemies they subjugate. Turning his back to them, another Akkadian soldier drives away in the opposite direction a row of seven nude and bound captives. While the scenes of the second register are comparable to the second register of the Standard of Ur, the bottom one is reminiscent of the king's review of captives on its top register. This sequence of episodes implies that the Sargon Stela was read from top to bottom. The same applies to a fragment which may have belonged to this or a similar stela (Fig. 31):[298] it shows an Akkadian soldier pushing two captives in front of him in the lower register, and parts of two pairs of combatants in the upper register.[299]

The stela from Nasiriya (Fig. 32)[300] preserves parts of three registers. The lowest one shows a row of Akkadian soldiers carrying off booty from an Anatolian campaign,[301] the middle register a row of bound prisoners followed by an Akkadian soldier at the end. The

---

[293] Börker-Klähn *Bildstelen*, nos. 29–34.

[294] Some are known in original, see Moortgat *Art*, figs. 148 and 177f.; others only from descriptions in texts, see Braun-Holzinger *Weihgaben*, 281–290.

[295] Börker-Klähn *Bildstelen*, no. 19; Braun-Holzinger *Weihgaben*, Stele 10; Bänder *Siegesstele*, 116–120 no. 4.

[296] Braun-Holzinger *Weihgaben*, Stele 10, wondered whether the figure represented a god, apparently inspired by the inscription above the shoulder which mentions the god Aba. The fragmentary inscription, however, need not be a label.

[297] Börker-Klähn *Bildstelen*, no. 18; Braun-Holzinger *Weihgaben*, Stele 9; Bänder *Siegesstele*, 99–109 no. 1.

[298] Börker-Klähn *Bildstelen*, no. 20; Bänder *Siegesstele*, 113–116 no. 3.

[299] For additional smaller fragments compatible with the Sargon Stela see Börker-Klähn *Bildstelen*, no. 18, and Bänder *Siegesstele*, 110–112 no. 2.

[300] Börker-Klähn *Bildstelen*, no. 22; Bänder *Siegesstele*, 135–141 no. 8.

[301] Mellink *Anatolia* 7 (1963).

figures of both rows face left, while the lower body of the soldier in the upper register faces right. If the king was the focal point of the captive procession, one would expect him on the lost fourth side. Both scenes succeed the battle. Since the booty procession follows the review of captives on the Standard of Ur, this monument may have been read from top to bottom, like the Sargon Stela.

The stela from Tello,[302] which consists of a fragment of the upper right side with parts of three registers on either side, exhibits a different scenario. The remains on all registers on either side depict individual groups of combatants. Akkadian soldiers defeat their enemies with the bow, the lance, and the battle ax, and capture them. Similar scenes are depicted on contemporary seals,[303] and the stela gives the impression of a compilation of battle scene types, almost like a book of patterns.[304]

The Urnamma Stela[305] was restored at the University Museum in 1932 (Fig. 33a) from fragments found scattered throughout the Nanna precinct at Ur. The restoration was criticized early on by Legrain.[306] Other reconstructions integrating additional fragments[307] have been proposed by Börker-Klähn (Fig. 33b) and Becker (Fig. 33c).[308] In order to examine the precise shape and stone composition of the individual fragments, the stela was disassembled under the supervision of Canby. She has proposed new readings of some scenes (Fig. 33d-f),[309] and will soon publish a full report, including hitherto unpublished fragments from Ur. In view of her observation that not all fragments belonged to the same monument,[310] the effort of integrating as many fragments as possible is futile before the publication of their material analysis is available. I will therefore focus on the imagery of the larger fragments.

The largest top register fragment (Fig. 33c)[311] depicts on either side a hovering goddess pouring water from an overflowing vase and the bust of the king below facing the water

---

[302] Börker-Klähn *Bildstelen*, no. 21; Bänder *Siegesstele*, 122–133 no. 6.

[303] See Bänder Siegesstele, 129f.

[304] For possible Egyptian influence in Akkadian art see Börker-Klähn *WZKM* 74 (1982).

[305] Legrain *MJ* 18 (1927), 75, and *RA* 30 (1933), 113, wanted to attribute the stela not to Urnamma but to his son Šulgi, based on some details of the imagery which he misinterpreted. His thesis found surprisingly wide acceptance. Neither is Šulgi represented in Ningal's lap in the top register on side A, nor does he worship a statue of his father in the bottom register on side B. The figure in the lap is a goddess, as shown below. The identification of Šulgi on the fragment randomly placed in the bottom register is uncertain, and the larger size of the figure of Urnamma there better explained by the use of scale for importance, see chapter IV.D.1.d. Furthermore, the representation of the king at different ages of his life on one and the same monument is unprecedented in Mesopotamian art. The inscription on the wide dividing band commemorates canal diggings which are known to be Urnamma's – see now RIME 3/2 no. 1.1.22 – and there are no royal inscriptions in which a ruler enlists the deeds of his father, unless he appropriates them for himself. Urnamma's authorship of the stela should not be questioned.

[306] Legrain RA 30 (1933). For the history of the discovery and restoration see Canby *Expedition* 29 (1987), 55–58.

[307] UE VI pls. 43A–45.

[308] Börker-Klähn *PKG* 14 (1975), 203f. fig. 37, and *Bildstelen*, §§ 137–154 with pls. G-H; Becker *BaM* 16 (1985), 290–295.

[309] Canby *Expedition* 29 (1987), and *IstM* 43 (1993).

[310] Based on a petrographic analysis, Canby doubts the attribution of the garment fragment with Urnamma's label (personal communication); see now also RIME 3/2 no. 1.1.9.

[311] Börker-Klähn *Bildstelen*, pls. G-H (Fig. 33b), mistakenly placed both obverse and reverse of this fragment on the same side.

flow. On one side he is clearly shown as petitioner with his hand held to the nose, and focusing on an enthroned divine couple. Canby reconstructed the couple based on a similar image depicted on a votive plaque from Tello dedicated for Gudea's life (Fig. 33d).[312] Combining the divine couple with the king facing the opposite direction, however, is unlikely. The condition of the surface is no valid criteria for the assignment to one or the other side. The goddess apparently gestured in the direction of the king, as indicated by a fragment with an arm in front of a jet of water. Another fragment shows a hand in front of a water jet which belonged to a figure facing the opposite direction (Fig. 33a), and may have belonged to a deity in the same position on the other side. That the king on that side poured a libation (Fig. 33d) is not convincing, since it is most unlikely that the water originating from a divine source fed a human libation vessel. Instead, he could have raised his forearm along the line of the break. A fragment preserving a horizontal stream of water above the dividing band (Figs. 33b-c) indicates that the water was flowing on the ground. Although there are remains of four hovering goddesses, there is no compelling reason to reconstruct mirror images in the top registers, be it only because the king faces a divine couple on one side. The king may have been followed by a minor deity. The enthroned divine couple can be identified as Nanna and his consort Ningal.[313] As the divine patron of Ur, Nanna is the most likely candidate to bless the king with prosperity symbolized by the abundance of water, and the stela fragments were found in his temple at Ur. There is a fragment which removes any doubt about the main deity's identity: it depicts a horned crown topped by a moon crescent (Fig. 33c), and must have belonged to a top register because of its size.[314]

The register below the enthroned couple is nearly complete. The king, followed by a Lamma, pours a libation to a seated goddess on the left who stretches out her hand toward him, and another one to a seated god on the right who points a measuring rod and a rope in his direction. The repetition of the king and his escort may be a symmetrical rendering of this party in front of a divine couple seated side by side.[315] The two registers below formed a unit, since they are separated only by a line. They show parts of a construction scene in which the king appears with tools on his shoulder, guided by a god and followed by a servant, while basket carriers approach and climb a ladder leaning against a brick structure.[316] Legrain interpreted the objects in the right hand of the seated god above as builder's tools, and concluded that the libation scene rendered the divine command to build, which was realized in these registers.[317] The measuring rod and the rope, however, are different from the builder's tools carried by the king. They are attested in other encounters between a king and an enthroned deity on the Susa Stela (Fig. 34), the Hammurabi Stela, and the investiture painting in the palace

---

[312] *Expedition* 29 (1987), 60.
[313] So already Legrain *MJ* 18 (1927), 77–83. Börker-Klähn *Bildstelen*, §§ 140 and 150, followed by Becker *BaM* 16 (1985), 292f., saw Enlil legitimizing Urnamma's choice of the crown prince, a thesis based on the outdated interpretation of Legrain *RA* 30 (1933), 112f.; see note 305 above.
[314] UE VI pl. 45a. According to Canby *Expedition* 29 (1987), 61, this fragment cannot be fitted with the couple on side A, and may have belonged to the god on the other side.
[315] Frankfort *Art and Architecture*, 102.
[316] Other fragments including the edge of a recessed temple gate can be assigned to this scene, though their precise location remains uncertain; see chapter IV.B.3, p. 182.
[317] *MJ* 18 (1927), 83–89. Other scholars, including Woolley UE VI 76f., and Börker-Klähn *Bildstelen*, § 141, accepted this interpretation, though not all agreed with Legrain's identification of the deity.

of Zimrilim. Textual sources inform us that they are insignia bestowed upon the king by a deity, usually the patron of his state, as a sign of passing on the right and obligation to rule.[318] Since the Sumerian terms, éš and gi-ninda, which entered the art historian's discussions as ring and rod, originally refer to instruments for the measuring of fields, one cannot exclude that on the Urnamma Stela an allusion to the measuring out, which also occurs in the course of a temple construction, was intended as well.[319]

The back of the libation fragment shows a slaughter scene in the center, as well as the feet of two figures in front of what look like poles with crescents on the right. The register below apparently depicts statues of enthroned deities. The one on the right is attended by a nude servant, who is cleaning its face with a dust-whisk, while holding a towel in his other hand, and the one on the left has figures turning their back on it. In the center various human figures participate in a scene which remains enigmatic.[320] The next register depicts two figures playing a huge drum followed by a cymbalist on the left. The same scene may have been repeated on the right, since there is another fragment with part of a drum.[321] The left side of the register below shows the king followed by a servant in front of a rectangular stand, seemingly empty, and another male figure facing them and holding what looks like a stick or libation vase. Behind, a water jet flows to the ground. The attribution of other fragments to this register remains uncertain.

Groenewegen-Frankfort observed the "momentous climax" in the top registers.[322] The king is rewarded for his successful accomplishment of a task, apparently the construction of a temple. That this was the main topic of the stela is indicated by the prominence given to the construction scene.[323] The other image fields represent episodes of this event. While the construction work dominates the obverse, the scenes on the back seem to be concerned with the temple's inauguration. The musical performance as well as the slaughter fit such a context. The dichotomy of construction and inauguration is evident in Gudea's Cylinder Inscriptions, and can be observed much earlier in imagery, namely on the largest Urnanše plaque (Fig. 37).[324] It is comparable to the dichotomy of battle

---

[318] See Krecher *RlA* (1976–80), 109–114 s.v. Insignien.

[319] So also Becker *BaM* 16 (1985), 291f. Börker-Klähn *Bildstelen*, § 141, acknowledged their meaning as insignia, since they are mentioned in *Urnamma D*, yet dismissed the possibilty that the ones depicted on the stela indeed represented these insignia in favor of Legrain's thesis.

[320] Legrain's interpretation of the group on the left as part of a war-related scene is certainly wrong, since the figures do not wear military outfits. The various cultic interpretations offered by Perkins *AJA* 61 (1957), 60, and by Börker-Klähn *PKG* 14 (1975), 204, *ZA* 64 (1975), and idem *Bildstelen*, §§ 146–148, remain hypothetical, and are not convincing. Canby *Expedition* 29 (1987), 63 fig. 18, saw a wrestling scene in the center.

[321] See also chapter IV.B.5.

[322] *Arrest and Movement*, 167.

[323] Becker *BaM* 16 (1985), 290–95, proposed that side A matches *Urnamma D*, and represented canal diggings. Her thesis is untenable for various reasons. Motifs such as the temple gate have no place in canal diggings, but are found in temple construction scenes such as the one on the Borowski seal and the Gudea fragments; see chapter IV.B.3. There are, to my knowledge, no other visual representations of canal diggings extant. The literal transposition of a text into imagery is un-Mesopotamian (see chapter I.A.2), and the sequence of events does not coincide as clearly as the author contends. Moreover, side B remains unexplained. If compared with a hymn of Urnamma, it should be compared to *Urnamma B* (see Klein *ASJ* 11 (1989) 44–56), which commemorates the construction of Ekur, though the temple construction in the images was that of Nanna's temple in Ur.

[324] See chapter IV.C.2.b, p. 222.

and victory celebration on the Standard of Ur (Fig. 26). The libation scene, in which the king receives the power to act, could either illustrate the successful divination necessary for every temple construction or the preparation for a petition for blessings.[325]

b. Core and Expansion

The notion of core and expansion is crucial for the understanding of early Mesopotamian imagery.[326] Hansen observed it in one of the most popular images in Early Dynastic art: the banquet scene, which occurs in diverse media including stelae, door plaques, inlays, and seals. He defined the "basic theme" as "two seated figures drinking with straws from a large vase or two seated figures with one attendant," and as "elaborated versions" scenes including "several feasting men and women, attendants, musicians, tables, etc."[327] Selz further developed this idea: she distinguished three formal types of banquets – drinking with straws, drinking from cups, or eating indicated by a table – and identified a prototype with reduced and extended versions.[328] Her prototype corresponds to Hansen's basic theme of two figures, though without attendants. Her extended version includes more banquet participants and attendants, which she classified as primary and secondary figures, respectively, while her reduced version is limited to one primary figure who is associated with elements typical of banquet scenes.

Since a banquet, per definition, includes a crowd of participants, I would place the emphasis differently in regard to reduced and extended versions, and view Selz's extended version as the norm, and her prototype as the core components of the scene. The principle of core and expansion in the visual arts is comparable to that in texts: similar to the core of Gudea's building inscriptions which is always combined with optional complements,[329] the core of the banquet scene hardly ever occurs without any optional complements. Abbreviated versions occur mainly in media which are limited in their image field(s), especially seals and door plaques, while media with larger surfaces available show banquets approximating reality. A case in point is the top register on side B of the Standard of Ur (Fig. 26), which includes eight seated participants, three attendants, and two musicians – a lyre player and a singer – at the far right side. A similarly detailed banquet should be expected in the upper register of the Bedre Stela (Fig. 38), the preserved bottom and second registers of which depict scenes usually combined with banquets.

Unlike Hansen, Selz considered all figures and objects that are not strictly banqueters, attendants, or banquet utensils as parts of accompanying scenes (*Nebenszenen*). In this category she distinguished between scenes simultaneous with the banquet, mythological themes, and scenes concerned with the cultic context of the banquet.[330] This classification is based on the premises that all banquets represent one and the same "ritual," and that all motifs combined with a banquet are subordinate to it.[331] I would accept only the

---

[325] See chapter IV.B.6.
[326] For core and expansion in Egyptian art, compare Davis *Canonical Tradition*, 64–73.
[327] *JNES* 22 (1963), 161f.
[328] *Bankettszene*, 14f.
[329] See chapter II.B.
[330] *Bankettszene*, 462–473.
[331] Selz *Bankettszene*, 462f.

second premise, and even that only for her first group, which includes music and dance, wrestling, servants bringing food and drink, servants preparing drinks, and slaughter.[332] Since these elements hardly ever occur in other contexts, I would consider them optional complements of the banquet scene. The mythological themes and motifs occasionally combined with a banquet scene are, in my opinion, unrelated. More frequently they occur independently, and if combined with a banquet, are often formally separated from it, for example, in the second register of two-registered seal images. An exception is the flock of bovines or caprovines, which is not mythological, but probably represents the animals slaughtered on the occasion of the banquet. In the third group, Selz included the well attested boat scene and the row of chariots as well as the one-time combination with a coitus scene, a construction scene, and a harvest scene. She is probably correct in assuming that these scenes hint at the context of the banquet, though this need not be cultic. In the case of the chariots and the construction, I would argue that the banquet is subordinate to the larger context indicated by them.

The interpretation of the relation of the banquet scene with other motifs requires, like the definition of its core, a consideration of the media. Our main source of imagery, the seals, will prove to render the most abbreviated versions, and cannot elucidate all implications inherent in an image. Caution is called for when using them as paradigms also because they are mass-produced, and one cannot expect every such image to make perfect sense in terms of composition and contents. Monuments with larger image field(s) are rare, and often incomplete. An exception is the Standard of Ur (Fig. 26), which elucidates the relation between banquet and military exploits. Although Selz carefully described the links of its two sides,[333] she dismissed the hierarchic superiority of the larger context in which the banquet is tied on this monument. This is doubtless due to her banquet-centric perspective. It is the war theme on side A which occasions the banquet on side B. The banquet in this case is a celebration of a military victory, which remains unidentified in the absence of an accompanying text.[334]

By analogy, the chariots in the bottom register of three-registered door plaques can be understood as alluding to the larger context of a military victory for the banquets represented in their top register. They are not driven but paraded, because the war is over.[335] Two plaques from the Diyala Region show nearly identical imagery (Fig. 35):[336] in the bottom register a chariot with a team of four equids is accompanied by two male figures with whips, one walking behind and holding its reins, the other in front. The image field on the left side of the central hole of the plaque depicts two males transporting a beer jar on a carrying pole, the one on the other side shows male(s) bringing livestock and other hard food. The top register consists of a couple of banqueters with their

---

[332] Strictly speaking, only the first two groups can be considered simultaneous, the last must precede the banquet, while those concerned with food could be repeated in the course of the banquet. For a critique of Selz's first premise see chapter I.A.2, p. 10.

[333] *Bankettszene*, 334

[334] Perkins *AJA* 61 (1957), 56f.

[335] There is no indication such as, for example, a divine emblem, in support of the suggestion by Selz *Bankettszene*, 470, that the chariots are to be dedicated to a city god. For representations of divine chariots, though later in date, see chapter IV.B.4.

[336] Boese *Weihplatten*, AG 2 and CT 2.

attendants, and a harp player entertaining them. A plaque fragment from Ur must have had similar imagery (Fig. 36):[337] its preserved bottom register shows the same elements as the Diyala plaques with the addition of a second male figure behind the chariot. The two pairs of feet facing right in the middle register could belong to men carrying provisions for the banquet. In this case the link between the chariot scene and the larger context of a victory celebration is made explicit by the extra man: he carries a load on a pole, and is reminiscent of the booty carriers on the Standard of Ur (Fig. 26).

The extant Early Dynastic construction scenes are rudimentary. A group of seals,[338] mainly from the Diyala Region, depict a scene, the core of which consists of two figures on either side of a structure, who place a rectangular object on its top. Usually the scene includes a row of figures carrying loads on their heads,[339] who approach that structure, and sometimes involves ladders.[340] Since the latter two elements are typically found in construction scenes of later date,[341] and because the structure is in some cases reminiscent of a ziggurat,[342] this scene has been interpreted as a temple construction.[343] Selz observed the presence of a seated figure associated with typical banquet elements in almost all of these images.[344] In terms of space and the number of elements, the construction clearly dominates over the banquet. A reasonable assumption then would be that the banquet celebrates the completion of the new structure.

The combination of even more abridged versions of a construction and a banquet is depicted on a door plaque of Urnanše from Tello (Fig. 37).[345] The construction is reduced to the icon of the ruler as temple builder, which shows him carrying a basket on his head;[346] the banquet to the image of the seated ruler holding a beaker. An explanation for these extremely truncated versions may be the space made available for the inclusion of Urnanše's children and court members, who are confronting him in both scenes, a phenomenon found only on the monuments of this ruler. At the same time, the abridged rendering with its tendency towards symbolism may have been intentional. The inscription records the construction of more than one temple. The plaque was apparently intended to commemorate a summary of Urnanše's deeds at the particular moment of its dedication, rather than the construction of the temple in which is was installed.

The optional complements of banquet scenes, too, can be more or less detailed. They may consist of a single figure or of configurations which form new sub-units. The borders between element and scene are fluid, and to some degree depend on the subject. Musical

---

[337] Boese *Weihplatten*, U 1.
[338] See Amiet *Glyptique mésopotamienne*, nos. 1441–1465, 1784–1791.
[339] Ibidem, nos. 1442, 1444f., 1450–1453, 1463, 1482, 1784f.
[340] Ibidem, nos. 1446f., 1450, 1458, 1786.
[341] See chapter IV.B.3.
[342] The somewhat indistinct shape and its varying appearance may be due to the rather low quality of these seals.
[343] See Selz *Bankettszene*, 421–423, for older literature. The contention of Amiet *Glyptique mésopotamienne*, 181–186, that these scenes cannot render the construction of a ziggurat, since such buildings did not exist in the Early Dynastic period, needs revision, see Suter *ZA* 87 (1997), 10.
[344] *Bankettszene*, 422f.
[345] Boese *Weihplatten*, T 4.
[346] See chapter II.C.1.b.

entertainment, for example, can be visualized by a single harp player, while wrestling requires a minimum of two combatants. Certain themes lend themselves better to closed units than others: in a wrestling match the combatants naturally confront each other, and thus form a unit, while the provision of food supplies asks for a row of figures, which remains open-ended.

Certain complements of the banquet scene can develop into new series of units. On the Bedre Stela (Fig. 38),[347] for example, the wrestling theme expands over three sides of the second register, each forming a unit: on one broad side three wrestlers, identified by their loin-cloth, sit on the ground with their legs crossed,[348] and holding a long stick which disappears behind their legs; on the narrow side stand two male figures in long skirts, one shaved, the other with long hair and a beard, who hold short sticks; the other broad side depicts two pairs of wrestlers in action. All figures of the first two units face right, i. e. in the direction of the action. On door plaques, wrestling scenes consist of several pairs of combatants in action, or one pair accompanied by a dressed figure with the short stick.[349] This latter figure apparently represents the referee, and thus forms a scene with the wrestlers in action. The two referees on the stela, distinguished by their hairdo, could represent the two competing parties.[350] The cross-legged sitting wrestlers, not attested elsewhere, seem to be waiting to be called into action. If they are identical with the wrestlers in action, the scenes would be consecutive; if they represent additional wrestlers watching the match while waiting, the scenes would be simultaneous. This would be the case also if they represented participants in another kind of contest, which may be indicated by the stick they carry. The bottom register shows two pairs of servants with food provisions – kids and a beer jar, respectively – juxtaposed with two rows of four figures each, who may represent the banquet participants on their way to the banquet. If so, the sequence is from bottom to top.

Core and expansion can be observed in the visualization of other themes. As noted above, the ruler stocking up the temple's supplies depicted in detail on the Uruk Vase (Fig. 23), is reduced to its bare core components on seals. On the Uruk Vase itself, the figures in the lower registers can be considered an expansion of the scene in the top register. With respect to monuments which combine episodic scenes with a culminating scene, one can go even a step further and analyze the episodes as an expansion of the culminating scene. On the Standard of Ur (Fig. 26), for example, the scenes in the lower registers of the main panels can be conceived of as an expansion of those in the top registers. The episodes detail the events which led to the climatic completion of the narrative. Consequently the latter can stand by itself for the whole story. Thus the

---

[347] Börker-Klähn *Bildstelen*, no. 12, and Selz *Bankettszene*, 194f.

[348] The posture of these wrestlers corresponds to that of gatekeeper figures for which we have one three-dimensional rendition, the metal sculpture from Bassetki, which shows the figure sitting with crossed legs; see Braun-Holzinger *Figürliche Bronzen*, no. 61 and p. 24 with note 81.

[349] Boese *Weihplatten*, CN 2 and CS 7+K 7. The two joined fragments in CN 2 do not necessarily belong to the same plaque; see Selz *Bankettszene*, 193 note 4. The left fragment depicts two pairs of combatants, the right may have belonged to a scene as depicted on CS 7+K 7. This configuration is found also on the cylinder seal Amiet *Glyptique mésopotamienne*, no. 1764.

[350] Selz *Bankettszene*, 195.

triumphant victorious king reviewing the captives, displaying them in a net, or treading them can capture an entire military campaign.

c. Image Field and Narrative Unit

The demarcation of the surface used for representation is a vehicle which adds meaning,[351] especially in the case of visual narratives. Any reconstruction proposal of Gudea's stelae must therefore consider the relation of image field and narrative unit in early Mesopotamian art. On the Urnamma Stela (Fig. 33) image fields are delimited by pro-truding dividing bands in horizontal direction and by the uncarved narrow sides in vertical direction. Each image field contains one particular scene which forms a narra-tive unit. This systematic relation between image field and narrative unit is not the norm on earlier monuments. A single image field may contain more than one narrative unit, and a single narrative unit may extend over several image fields. On the Lion-Hunt Stela two consecutive scenes float on the undelimited surface of the stone boulder, while on the Uruk Vase one expanded scene extends over several registered bands. On Urnanše's large plaque (Fig. 37) two scenes are superimposed in one image field, while on his stelae (Figs. 24–25) a presentation scene wraps around all carved sides of the monument. On the larger stela (Fig. 25) the different elements of this scene are contained in irregular window-like image fields, one of which, representing a minimal banquet of Urnanše's wife and daughter, forms a self-contained sub-unit.

Similarly complex relations between image field and narrative unit can be observed on the other Early Dynastic and Akkadian monuments discussed above. A large number of Early Dynastic door plaques are divided into three registers. They contain the core components of a banquet in the top register and optional complements of this scene, as well as elements that imply its occasion (the chariots on Figs. 35–36) in the other registers. The optional complements can be considered sub-events or sub-units, and more than one such unit can occur on the same register. The Bedre Stela (Fig. 38) is organized in registers extending over its four sides, yet each side is framed by a margin band at its edges. The image fields thus generated contain each one sub-unit of the thematic unit confined to one register. Similarly, the Standard of Ur (Fig. 26) has three registers wrapping around its four sides. Yet, the main panels are separated from each other by the mythological contents of the side panels, and they are vertically framed by the same decorative band which horizontally separates them into registers. Each of these panels contains one particular extended scene, and the registers include several sub-units of that scene. The narrative units, in this case, are: entering battle and battle with chariots; entering battle and battle with foot soldiers; making captives; review of captives by the king; parade of booty; procession of food provisions for the banquet; banquet with musical entertainment.

On the Eannatum Stela (Fig. 27) distinct scene types are confined to distinct sides of the monument: the two culminating scenes are contained in two large registers on side A, while the episodic scenes are separated into five registers on side B. Each register on side B contains a distinct scene which begins on the left adjacent, narrow side. In

---

[351] See Meyer Schapiro *Semiotica* 1 (1969).

contrast to the monuments previously described, the imagery on the narrow side does not contain additional sub-units but forms a mere extension of a scene element depicted on side B. On the one-sided Naramsin Stela (Fig. 28) one expanded scene extends over one large image field, while most other Akkadian stelae were apparently four-sided and separated into registers. On the Sargon Stela (Fig. 30), which has rounded edges, the registers continue uninterrupted around the sides. Several scenes can be juxtaposed in the same register, and single scenes can wrap around sides. In contrast, the registers of the Nasiriya Stela (Fig. 32) are vertically delimited by margin bands, though single scenes may equally wrap around a sharp edge. Each register seems to have contained a particular narrative unit.

3. The Stelae of Gudea

a. Formal Characteristics

Like most early Mesopotamian stelae, the stelae of Gudea are curved at the top and divided into registers. If they comprised four or five registers, they must have had an oblong body. Part of an unpublished bottom zone below the imagery, as exhibited by Early Dynastic and Sargonic stelae, seems to be preserved on ST.11 and 12.[352] Only one fragment, ST.28, encompasses a section of an entire rectangular register. It is 38 cm high, and approximates the average height of the rectangular registers on the Urnamma Stela. Other fragments with smaller size figures may have belonged to registers of a height comparable to that of the registers of the Sargon Stela. Whether the rectangular registers of the same stela were of equal height, as seems to be the case on the Akkadian register stelae, or of slightly varying height, as on the Urnamma Stela, cannot be determined with any certainty. The size of figures on top register fragments, compared to other fragments, allows for the possibility that the top registers were twice as high as the other registers, like on the Urnamma Stela, and perhaps already on some Akkadian stelae. Assuming four rectangular registers of equal height, a top register twice as high, and 7 cm high dividing bands, the stela to which ST.28 belonged would have been 2.56 m high, without the bottom zone.

Since no fragment encompasses an entire side, the width and depth of the original monuments are more difficult to assess. The combination of the top register fragments ST.1+2, yields a width of approximately 90 cm for the stela to which they belonged. Completing this top register to a height of 58 cm, and assuming that it had four rectangular registers of half that height, the ratio of the height of this stela to its width would have been 1:2.2, not far from the average ratio of other early Mesopotamian stelae. This stela would have had registers approximately as high as those of the Sargon Stela, yet its width clearly exceeds that of the latter. If its depth was approximately one fourth of the width, as on the Urnamma Stela, and probably also on the Akkadian stela from Tello, which seems to have had similar proportions completing the curvature, it would have been about 22.5 cm deep.

---

[352] According to Börker-Klähn Bildstelen, no. 60, an unpublished fragment in Istanbul preserves the complete height of a bottom zone together with three rows of mountain scales, as depicted on ST.11.

C. About the Reconstruction

Like the post-Sargonic and Urnamma stelae, the corner fragments have sharp edges. Those with imagery on either side suggest that at least some of the stelae of Gudea had four carved sides, like most Akkadian stelae. Margin bands occur on some top registers (ST.1+2, 3, 9), though, as ST.9 shows, not on all sides of the same monument. Labels are used primarily to identify the ruler Gudea in each of his occurrences – nine are inscribed on his garment (ST.1, 12, 30, 32, 42, 43, [44], 46, 47), two next to his head (ST.5, 19) – but once also a raft of cedar (ST.11). One of the three commemorative inscriptions is inscribed in the blank space between figures (ST.22), like the inscriptions on Early Dynastic reliefs, the other two below a register with imagery (ST.20 and 21). Since the lower end of the latter two is not preserved, it remains uncertain whether they were inscribed on a bottom register of the stela, similar to the inscription of the Sargon Stela, or on a large dividing band, such as on the Urnamma Stela.

b. Observations about the Composition

The stelae of Gudea share with the Urnamma Stela the general shape and the main theme of the imagery. Yet, the corner fragments with imagery on either side indicate that the relation between image field and scene was different. If narrative units could wrap around corners, as they do on ST.13 and 14, one expects image fields extending over four sides on each register with one or more narrative units per image field, such as on Akkadian stelae. Moreover, the better preserved scenes which the stelae of Gudea share with that of Urnamma show variations in their composition. In contrast to Urnamma, Gudea never confronts the deity directly in presentation scenes, but is introduced by his personal god. The direct interaction with the divine may reflect the propagation of a more intimate relationship, perhaps inspired by the increased power of Urnamma. Similarly, the libations are poured by a priest in Gudea's presence rather than by Gudea himself. Other scenes not paralleled on the Urnamma Stela show compositional affinities with earlier monuments. The parades of carriers of standards and dedicatory gifts, for example, are comparable to the procession of food carriers or military parades of Early Dynastic and Akkadian monuments. These scenes may wrap around corners or be combined with other scenes on the same register. It seems, therefore, that the composition of the Gudea stelae has more in common with Early Dynastic and Akkadian monuments than with the Urnamma Stela.

With regard to the height of registers and the size of the carved representation in them, any reconstruction attempt must consider the following principles, which the stelae of Gudea share with most early Mesopotamian registered monuments. The dividing bands serve as the ground-line for the representation.[353] In the curved top registers, the figures, usually consisting of the ruler and standing as well as enthroned deities, are larger than in the other register. Their height varies according to their differing status, and their heads do not touch the upper edge (ST.1, 3, 4+5), although a sun-star hovering above (ST.4) may. In contrast, the height of rectangular registers corresponds more or less to the height of the standing figures in them. Some immediately abut the upper edge (ST.53), and the same applies to certain objects (ST.25, 26, 27). Other figures, however,

---

[353] Compare ST.1, 4, 6, 9, 12, 14, 16, 18, 22, 23, 28, 30, 32, 54 for figures, and ST.17, 25, 27, 29, 31, 33 for objects.

are involved with objects exceeding their height as, for example, the standard carriers (ST. 23, 24, 28) or the basket carriers (ST.34), while still others may stand on a ship or a mountainous landscape indicated by three superimposed rows of scales (ST.20). In the case of heads or objects that do not immediately abut the upper edge (ST.22, 30, 33, 49), one can assume that a ruler figure emphasized by size or a tall object in the same register exceeded their height and touched the upper border. Thus the reconstructed height of a fragmentary figure alone does not necessarily yield the height of the register to which it belonged.

The reconstruction of fragmentary figures is complicated by the absence of a realistic canon of proportions for the human body in Gudea's art. The height – width ratio of his statues was determined by the dimensions of the imported stone block.[354] If it was too small for a life-size statue, the superimposed units were reduced only on the vertical axis. A similar scheme seems to be at work on the stelae when the figures are combined with landscape or objects which prevent them from encompassing the entire height of a register. The figure on the ship on ST.12 is clearly reduced in height compared with the figures on the adjacent side, though his feet are not much smaller. Similarly, the Gudea figures on ST.42 and 43 have same-size heads, lower arms, and waists, yet the upper body on ST.43 is clearly much shorter than that on ST.42.

c. The Compatibility of the Fragments

As mentioned above, there are no productive criteria detached from the imagery and carving of the fragments, such as provenience, material, and condition, that would result in clear-cut groups attributable to distinct monuments. This holds true also for the height of complete dividing bands, which ranges between five and seven centimeter, but may vary within a range of one centimeter on the same fragment.[355] The irregularities are too high in relation to the narrow range of values. Similarly, the overlap of the dividing bands over the ground surface of the register can vary from one to one and a half centimeters on the same fragment. The reconstructed height of registers and the size of the carved representation in them may not directly lead to the distinction of different monuments either, since it remains uncertain whether all registers of the same stela were also of the same height. Yet, the comparison of the size and of the figurative representation together with carving quality and iconographical details will allow the determination of fragments which are compatible and may have belonged to the same stela.

---

[354] See chapter II.C.1.a, p. 57.
[355] These heights are exceeded only on ST.19, if we are to believe the dimensions given by its publisher. Located in the Iraq Museum it was not accessible for study.

Table IV.C.2: The Fragments Grouped by the Size of their Figurative Representations[356]

	large stela	*2nd large stela*	*medium stela*	*small stela*
size of top register	78 × 120 × 40 cm		65 × 100 cm	58 × 90 × 22.5 cm
height of other registers	38 cm		34 cm	30 cm
top registers	6–9, 36, 39, 64		3–5	1, 2, 35, 40
standard parades	23–25, 63	27, 28		
shipment of materials	11, 12, 58	20		
construction work	22, 48		18, 34	
temple equipment	9, 29, 55, 59–61	27, 62		13, 14
musical performances	15, 23, 25	53		54
other deities			17+33, 41	
other Gudea figures	42, 43	30, 45	44	32, 46
other human figures	50–52	30, 49		

ST.1 and 2 are compatible in terms of size, depth of relief, and carving quality.[357] They have been restored in one image field in Berlin (Fig. 17), which is 57.5 cm high and 88 cm wide. Börker-Klähn's proposed enlargement of this image field (Fig. 19d) is not productive, since it leaves an unexplained blank space between the seated deity and his minister. If a hovering goddess with an overflowing vase was feeding an overflowing vase held by the seated deity,[358] ST.2 only needs to be moved a few centimeters down and to the right. The scene would be complete, and the image field would have been approximately 58 cm high and 90 cm wide. As Börker-Klähn suggested (Fig. 19d), the divine head ST.40 could have belonged to the enthroned god.

ST.4 and 5 were restored by Unger to a top register measuring 57 × 81.5 cm (Fig. 16). Their combination is likely, though some added details cannot be established beyond doubt, namely the dress worn by the libator, the gender of the deity, its size, and the shape of the throne for which Unger took as a prototype those on the Urnamma Stela.[359] There is no candidate for the deity among the other fragments; ST.35 could fit in terms of its size and carving quality, but the goddess's arm is at an angle too steep to fit with the hand on ST.4. If the enthroned deity is reduced in size, one could imagine an attendant or object behind the throne, which would give the composition a better balance, and would result in an image field only slightly larger than that of the top register in Berlin (Fig. 17). That the two top registers could not have belonged to the same stela is indicated by the place of the label identifying Gudea on his dress on ST.1 but next to his head on

---

[356] The measurements are of course approximate. The stela fragments are referred to by their numbers according to Appendix B.
[357] Börker-Klähn *Bildstelen*, §§ 62–64, produced a list of arguments pro and contra the combination of these fragments without making a decision, yet reconstructed them in one top register on pl. A, against the doubts of Moortgat *Kunst*, 117, and Boehmer *MIO* 13 (1967), 290f. These doubts were based on the impression that the fragments differ in curvature, which may, however, simply be an optical illusion caused by the fragmentary state of the margin band. Boehmer had reasoned that the water jet on ST.1 belonging to Ea's realm could not be combined with the lion throne on ST.2 belonging to Ištar's realm; on ST.17, however, lion throne and overflowing vases are combined.
[358] See chapter IV.B.7, p. 198.
[359] See also Börker-Klähn *Bildstelen*, § 103.

ST.5. This leaves the goddess on ST.35 as a compatible counterpart of the god on ST.2, perhaps presiding a libation scene on the other side of the top register.[360]

Börker-Klähn assigned ST.3 and 39 to the front top register of her "Eninnu Stela" (Fig. 19b), and ST.9, 36, and 64 to its back (Fig. 19a). ST.3, however, is not compatible with the other fragments. Its margin band has only half the thickness of that on ST.9, and the Gudea figure is proportionally much smaller than the head of Ningišzida on ST.39, which is not drawn to scale in her illustration. Furthermore, the front top register field would have been less high than the back one, the edge of which the author did not complete in her drawing, and its ratio of height to width is unrealistic. While ST.3, with a Gudea figure only slightly taller than that on ST.1, could have belonged to the same top register as ST.4+5, the other fragments are compatible with ST.6–8, which have been assigned to another top register field by Unger, followed by Börker-Klähn[361]. They share not only the proportions of the figures, but also the porous quality of the stone, as well as stylistic features as, for example, the full face representation on ST.7 and 36. Furthermore, the dividing bands preserved on ST.6 and 9 are of the same height. It is tempting, therefore, to assign all these fragments to the four sides of the top register of one stela, which would have shown two presentation scenes, one to a god (ST.36 and 64), the other to a goddess (ST.7). The deities are best conceived as a divine couple.[362] Each scene included a divine attendant behind the enthroned deity (ST.8 and 9) and a Gudea figure (ST.6) led by his personal god Ningišzida (ST.6 and 39)[363] into his/her presence, while a Lamma (ST.9) followed behind Gudea on each narrow side. The image fields of the main sides would have measured about 78 cm in height and 120 in width, the narrow side would have been at least 30 cm wide.

Based on these top register fragments, there were at least three different stelae: a large one, to which the fragments just discussed belonged; a smaller one to which ST.3–5 belonged; and third one only slightly smaller than the previous, to which ST.1, 2 and 35 belonged. Assuming that the rectangular registers were half as high as the top register, we can count on a height of about 38 cm for the largest stela, and about 30 cm for the smallest one. The largest had imagery on all four sides, while the number of carved sides of the other stelae remains uncertain. In the following I will consider the compatibility of the remaining fragments with these top registers in the order of the scenes to which they can be assigned.

The fragments that show parts of standards or standard carriers are compatible in size, and all standards face right. The preserved height of the register on ST.28 measures 38 cm. Thus the standard fragments are compatible only with the largest top register. A few differences in details, however, seem to indicate that not all belonged to the same stela. The empty space in front of the carriers on ST.23 and 24 suggests that, if preceded by

---

[360] ST.35 is certainly too large for a lower register of the stela to which ST.1+2 belonged, as Börker-Klähn (Fig. 19d) proposed.
[361] See Börker-Klähn *Bildstelen*, fig. 41b. The right edge of fragment ST.8 is not clearly an edge of a stela, as the restoration of Unger and the reconstruction of Börker-Klähn suggest.
[362] For their identification see chapter IV.B.7.
[363] The break of ST.39 looks almost as if it joined ST.6, were it not for the repetition of the lips with the mustache.

other carriers, these were spaced wider apart than those on ST.28. Further, the streamers on ST.23 and 24 are larger than those on ST.28, while those on ST.63 and 27 are wider than the others; the wings of the bird-man on ST.28 are bigger than those on ST.23 and 24; the head on ST.24 is closer to the upper edge of the register than those of the carriers on ST.23 and 28; the dividing band on ST.27 is larger than those on ST.23-25; and the surfaces of the latter are well preserved, while those of ST.27–28 and 63 are eroded. That the disc carried by the lion on ST.63 is truly spherical and nearly double the size of those on ST.25 and 27 is probably because there was more space available due to its not being carried by a teamster.

Börker-Klähn assigned ST.24, 28, and 63 to the back of her "Eninnu Stela" (Fig. 19a), ST.23 and 25 to her second and larger "Eninnu Stela" (Fig. 19c), and ST.27 to her "Ningirsu-Nanshe Stela" (Fig. 19e). I would group ST.24, which does not join ST.60, with ST.23 and 25, since all three fragments share the same height of the dividing band, and the standard emblems on ST.23 and 24 are practically identical. The taller size of the carrier on ST.24 may be explained by his being the leader of the parade. Nothing speaks against the combination of ST.27 with 28, while ST.63 is closer to ST.25 in the rendering of the lion. If the standards belonged to two different monuments, there must have been two large stelae. An unpublished fragment in Istanbul[364] depicts three standard carriers identical in size, spacing, and iconographical details with the ones depicted on ST.28. This indicates that the parades extended at least over one broad side, and may have continued around the stela.

Two of the three fragments which form part of an importation scene (ST.11 and 12) are clearly compatible, even though they do not join. The third one (ST.20) shows mountain scales of a larger size than those depicted on ST.11, while the workmen pulling the cart must have been of about the same size as the man standing in front of the raft. Since the height of the same dividing band can vary within a range of one centimeter on a single side of a stela, one cannot entirely exclude an attribution of ST.20 to the same stela as ST.11 and 12 based on the differently sized mountain scales, though ST.20 would have to be removed somewhat in space from the other fragments. All three fragments must have belonged to a large stela, if we complete the figures on them. If ST.58 belonged to a shipment scene on a Gudea stela, it would be compatible with a large stela, too.

The candidates for construction scenes vary in size: the man carrying a large coil of rope on ST.18 and the workmen on ST.34 must have belonged to a medium-sized stela, while the field measurer on ST.48 and the workmen on ST.22 are compatible with a large stelae. The man handling ropes on ST.56 could have belonged to a medium-sized or to a large stela, depending on his posture.[365] The assumed transport of a gate lion on ST.29 should be assigned to a large stela because of its large-sized objects and substantial dividing band. The bodies of the figures on ST.22, 29, and 48 are rounder than those on ST.18 and 56, and the relief on the former fragments is at least one centimeter deep, while that on the latter is clearly below one centimeter.

---

[364] The fragment is mentioned by Börker-Klähn *Bildstelen*, no. 68.
[365] The scale of the drawings in Börker-Klähn *Bildstelen*, pl. B (= Fig. 19b) no. 67 (= ST.34), and pl. E (= Fig. 19c) no. 77 (= ST.18), is inaccurate.

The figures that qualify as participants of a procession of dedicatory gift all face left. In terms of size, the ones on ST.55 and 59 must be attributed to a large stela, those on ST.13 and 14 to a small one. Since the latter two have imagery on either side of an edge, at least one small stela had four sides. The fine carving quality as well as the depth of the relief of ST.14 is compatible with the top register ST.1+2. The emblem on ST.26 would fit on top of the chariot on ST.14 in terms of size and direction. The other three fragmentary chariots (ST.27, 61, 62) all face right, and belonged to a large stela according to their dimensions. If they were part of a procession of dedicatory gifts for the divine beneficiary of the stela, as the chariot on ST.14 apparently was, each should be expected on a different stela, unless a second chariot was meant for the consort of Ningirsu.[366] If the chariot on ST.61 was nearly identical in design with that on ST.14, the one on ST.27 had at least a slightly different back part, and its attribution to another stela than the chariot on ST.61 is supported also by the differences in the standard emblems depicted in the lower registers of these two fragments. The poor remains of the chariot on ST.62 are compatible with the one on ST.61. ST.60 depicting a stela and dedicatory weapons is attributable to a large stela, and could be imagined in the center of a gift procession scene.

Moving to the musical performances, the drummers on ST.54 clearly belonged to a small stela, and the one on ST.23 to a large one.[367] The latter must have been of about the same size as the fragmentary drums on ST.9 and ST.25. The remains on ST.25 could be part of the drum on either ST.23, as proposed by Börker-Klähn (Fig. 19c),[368] or ST.9. That at least two drum fragments belonged to the same register is supported by the compatible standard emblems in the lower registers of ST. 23 and 25. The clappers on ST.15 and 53 face right, and must be attributed to large stelae, though the figures on ST.53 are of slightly larger size than those on ST.15, and their heads touch the upper end of the register.

Börker-Klähn placed the parts of a seated deity on ST.17+33 combined with the Isimud figure on ST.41 in the register below ST.1+2 (Fig. 19d). The resulting register, however, is proportionally too large for this top register. Furthermore, the differently shaped thrones speak against the compatibility of these fragments. ST.17+33 and ST.41, if Isimud really appeared on a stela of Gudea, should be assigned to a medium-size stela.

The remaining Gudea figures are of varying size. Those on ST.30, 42 and 43 must have been taller than the Gudea figure on ST.1 and shorter than that on ST.6, and could have belonged to a top register of medium size or a lower register of a large stela. The latter is more likely, since the top registers were apparently reserved for presentation or libation scenes for which neither fragment qualifies. The same holds true for the head ST.45, which must have belonged to a figure of about the same size, since Gudea is usually

---

[366] Börker-Klähn's reconstruction of pairs of chariots in antithetic arrangements (Figs. 19a, c, e) does not make any sense, nor does this composition conform with four-sided monuments.

[367] Börker-Klähn's combination of ST.54 with the large top register fragment ST.9 (Fig. 19a) and ST.13 is unlikely in terms of size as well as composition; the drum of ST.9 is too small in her drawing, and the drawing of the right side of ST.13 inaccurate.

[368] The left side of the upper body of the drummer and the remains of the drum depicted in her drawing are not visible on the original.

bare-headed in the presence of an enthroned deity. In contrast, the figures on ST.32 and 46 are much smaller, and could have belonged to rectangular registers on a small stela, that on ST.44 to a rectangular register on a medium-size one.

If the Gudea figure in the upper register on ST.30 belonged to a rectangular register of a large stela, the libator in its lower register must also have belonged to a large stela. The heads of other human figures on ST.50, 51, and 52 are all compatible with a large stela. The figure on ST.49 is of about the same size as Gudea on ST.1, and may have belonged to a top register of a small stela or a rectangular register of a large one. In the first case, the fragment probably did not belong to a stela of Gudea, since the only human figure expected in a top register is the ruler, and Gudea is never represented with this hairdo.

d. Conceivable Scenarios
If the compatible fragments ST.6–9, 36, 39, and 64 were part of the top register of one large stela (Pl. A), and if ST.11 and 12 belonged to the same monument, this stela showed two presentation scenes in the top register, a scene involving a drum in the register below, and the shipment of material in the bottom register. The placement of a construction preparation at the bottom and a dedicatory gift in the uppermost rectangular register suggest that the imagery was read from bottom to top. The shipment scene on ST.11 and the left side of ST.12 stretches over more than half of a broad side, and may have begun already on the narrow side to the left, where one might imagine people bringing goods for shipment which a scribe is registering before they are loaded. The puzzling figure on ST.58 can tentatively be restored sitting on the ground with writing tools in his hands. On the right side of ST.12, Gudea and another figure, by whom he is preceded, both face the other broad side and form the beginning of a new unit which must have continued there. ST.48 depicting men equipped with tools for measuring is a good candidate for this scene for several reasons: it can be combined with the head in the lower register of ST.22; in the analogous row of figures on ST.10 these men are followed by a ruler figure on the adjacent narrow side; the measuring out of the construction site is one of the preparations that can stand on the same level with the shipment of material; ST.22 shows workmen in its upper register. If ST.22 belonged to this monument, ST.20 should be excluded from it because of the different placement of the commemorative inscription.

The construction scene to which the workmen on ST.22 belong must have filled at least one broad side. (If the mysterious objects in front of which Gudea stands on ST.30 has anything to do with construction that fragment may have belonged to it; the libator in its lower register may then have signified the purification of the construction site before it was measured out.) The only conceivable place left for the parade of standard carriers (ST.23–25) signifying the recruitment of work-force, would be in the second register. Note that the spacing of the standard carriers is similar to that of the workmen on ST.22, and may indicate that there was an inscription between the figures like on ST.22. This inscription would then have stretched over the entire register around the monument. The parade may have extended to the adjacent narrow sides. If there was a place where the standards were stuck in the ground (ST.63) to mark the loam pit, this could have been depicted, for instance, on the narrow side preceding the row of workmen.

This place of the standard parade results in a musical performance in the third register, since a drum fragment and a drummer are depicted on the upper registers of ST.23 and 25, respectively. With the given width of the stela, not more than one large drum would fit on the broad side, and it is, therefore, best placed in the center of this image field, allowing for a combination with the clappers depicted on ST.15. Since the installation of gate lions should precede the inauguration festivities, ST.29 may be placed on the other broad side. If Gudea appeared at least once on each register, and once on each side of the stela, either ST.42 or 43 should be placed on the narrow side to the left of the musical performance.

The drum in the register below the top (ST.9) can now be combined with other dedicatory gifts brought in procession during the inauguration festivities. Possible candidates for this scene are the chariot on ST.61, the display of the gifts on ST.60, and the carriers of gifts on ST.55 and 59. If combined, this scene stretched all around the fourth register. Again one would like Gudea present, and we are left with either ST.42 or 43 as candidate.

Even if not all fragments used in this scenario necessarily belong to the same stela, the attempt to place compatible fragments on one stela has succeeded in a reconstruction proposal which makes sense in terms of the narrative, and agrees with Mesopotamian tradition in the composition of its imagery. Like several Akkadian stelae, this Gudea stela shows one or two scenes per register wrapping around all four sides of the monument. In keeping with Early Dynastic tradition, the imagery is read from bottom to top. The construction and its preparations are depicted on the bottom and second registers, the inauguration – including a musical performance and the dedication of gifts – on the third and fourth register, while the top register culminates in a visualization of Gudea's achievement: he is the one blessed by the divine beneficiaries of the stela in return for his temple building, and his title and status in society are thus legitimated. Another stela of the same size may have shown a similar scenario, since the fragments that remain for it (see Table IV.C.2) duplicate the motifs depicted on this one.

The small stela (Pl. B) showed a presentation scene to Ningirsu in the top register on the front side (ST.1, 2, 40), and perhaps a libation scene to his consort or to his sister Nanše, whom Gudea consulted during the verification of his dream revelation, on the back side (ST.35). The fragments ST.13 and 14, if they belonged to the same monument, indicate that the stela had four sides. In analogy to the scenario of the large stela, these fragments depicting parts of a gift procession, as well as the Gudea figure on ST.46 and the musical scene on ST.54, can tentatively be placed in the first and second register from the top. Note the change of direction in one part of the gift procession (ST. 13 and 14) and in the role of the drummers (ST.54). If the remaining fragment compatible with the small stela (ST.32) depicted the ruler appearing on the construction site, it can be imagined on the register below, where the figures may have faced approaching basket carriers. The other sides of this register and the bottom register could have depicted construction preparations. This proposal for a small stela remains, of course, hypothetical. It is intended to visualize the compatibility of the fragments under discussion in one conceivable scenario.

C. About the Reconstruction

Whether all stelae of Gudea were four-sided is not certain. In fact, the fragment ST.34 which depicts a construction scene extending over two registers on the same side of the stela, analogous to the Urnamma Stela (Fig. 33), speaks for a two-sided monument. The medium-size stela to which it belonged may have included a scene comparable to the second register on the obverse of the Urnamma Stela in terms of contents, for which ST.17+33, 41, and 44 are possible candidates (Pl. C). Note that ST.17 depicts the only niched throne among the Gudea fragments which is comparable to the thrones on the Urnamma Stela. If the compatible top register fragments ST.3-5 belonged to it, ST.3 could have been part of presentation scene on one side, ST.4-5 of a libation scene on the other. The remaining fragment compatible with this stela (ST.18) depicts a gate which could, in analogy to a recent reconstruction proposal of the Urnamma Stela (Fig. 33e-f), be placed to the left of the ladder depicted on ST.34. Like on the Urnamma Stela, the rectangular registers of the other side may have been concerned with the temple's inauguration. This stela would then have followed a different compositional scheme than the above chartered large and small stelae in that the narrative was conceived of two parts, construction and inauguration, each depicted on one side of a two-sided monument.

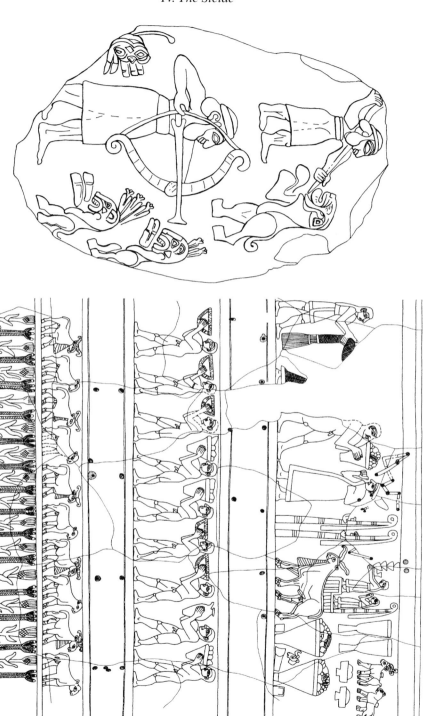

Fig. 22: Lion Hunt Stela at scale 1:8.

Fig. 23: Uruk Vase at scale 1:8.

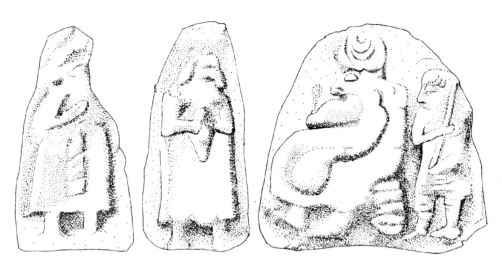

Fig. 24: Urnanše Stela from Ur at scale 1:4.

Fig. 25: Urnanše Stela from al-Hiba at scale 1:10.

Fig. 26: Standard of Ur at scale 1:3.

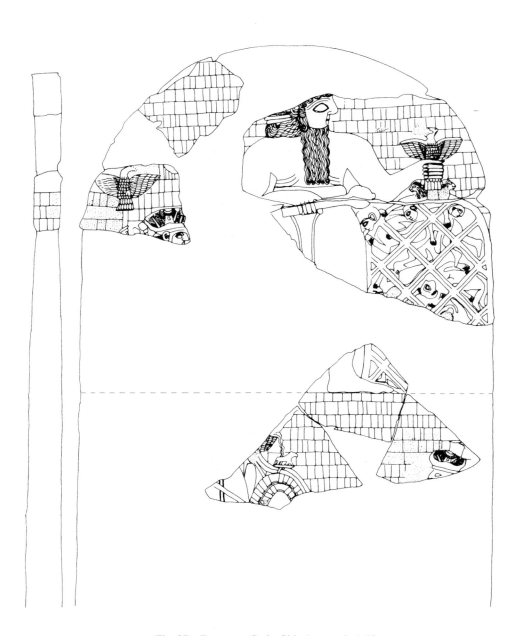

Fig. 27a: Eannatum Stela, Side A, at scale 1:12.

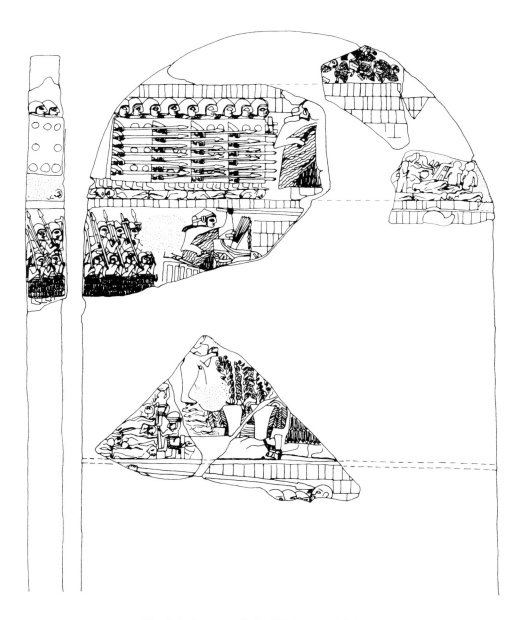

Fig. 27b: Eannatum Stela, Side B, at scale 1:12.

Fig. 28: Naramsin Stela at scale 1:12.

Fig. 29: Sargonic Stela Fragment at scale 1:8.

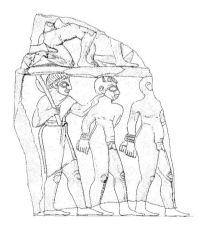

Fig. 31: Sargonic Stela Fragment at scale 1:8.

Fig. 30: Sargon Stela at scale 1:8.

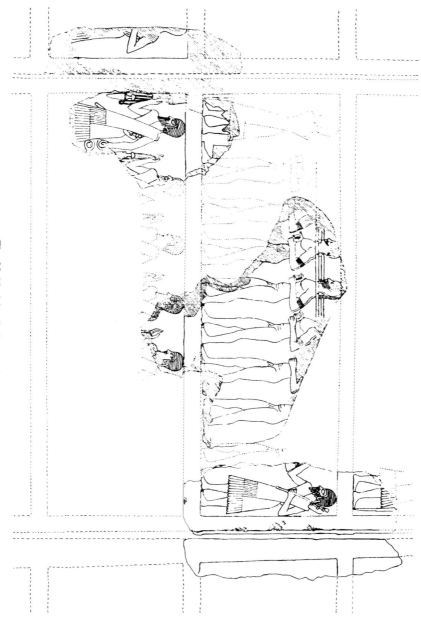

Fig. 32: Nasiriya Stela at scale 1:6.

Fig. 33a: Urnamma Stela,

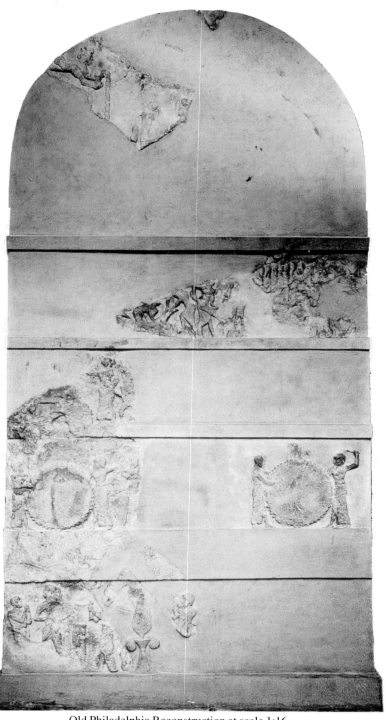

Old Philadelphia Reconstruction at scale 1:16.

Fig. 33b: Urnamma Stela,

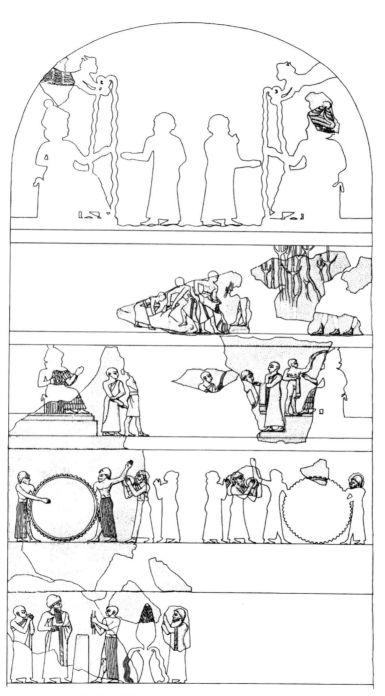

Börker-Klähn's Reconstruction at scale 1:16.

Fig. 33c: Urnamma Stela,

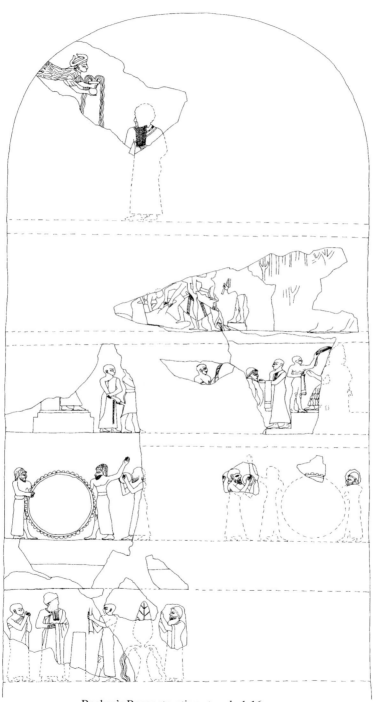

Becker's Reconstruction at scale 1:16.

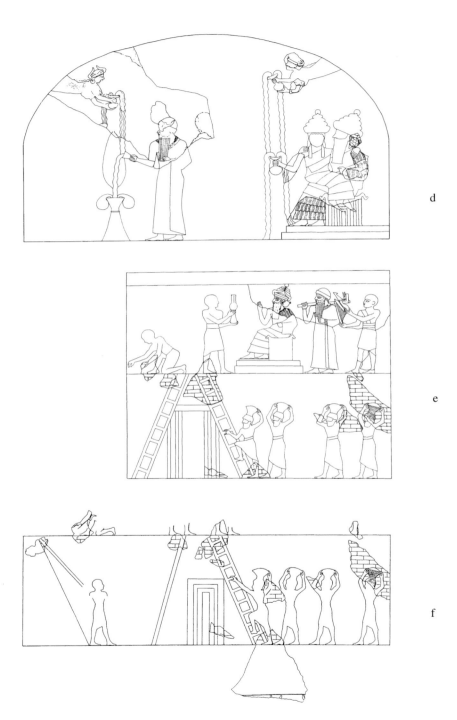

d

e

f

Fig. 33d-f: Urnamma Stela, Canby's Partial Reconstruction at scale 1:16

Fig. 34: Susa Stela at scale 1:10.

Fig. 35: Door Plaque from Tell Agrab at scale 1:3.

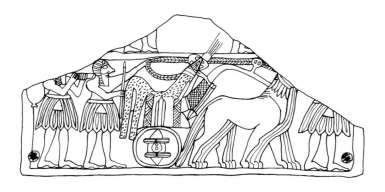

Fig. 36: Door Plaque Fragment from Ur at scale 1:3

Fig. 37: Urnanše Door Plaque at scale 1:4.

Fig. 38: Bedra Stela at scale 1:8.

D.   Analysis of the Narrative

1.   Event Participants

The event participants of the visual narrative depicted on Gudea's stelae consist of a variety of different anthropomorphic figures. They are characterized by a combination of the following features: garments, hair styles, headgear, attributes, gesture, and posture. Only Gudea, the ruler of Lagaš, is identified by a written label. The identity of the others can be inferred on the basis of their features and context, though not all with the same precision. The following discussion explores the visual characterization of these event participants, their identity, and their role in the narrative context as far as preserved.

a. Gudea, the Ruler of Lagaš

The figure of Gudea is labeled on eleven fragments (ST.1, 5, 12, 19, 30, 32, 42, 43, 44, 46, 47), and can be identified by analogy with these representations on three additional ones (ST.3, 6, 45). Gudea always wears the fringed mantle, a ceremonial gown also worn by a few other male figures on the stelae. His head is either bare (ST.1, 3, 5) or covered with a brimmed cap (ST.19, 42, 43, 45). In the Lagaš II and Ur III periods, this cap is worn exclusively by rulers[369] and, therefore, could very well be one of the headgears mentioned in texts as an insignium of rulership.[370] In contrast to the plain brimmed cap of Ur III kings, that of Gudea exhibits a checkered pattern on the stelae. By analogy with the sculpture in the round,[371] each square must be imagined as a spiral, which may represent the curl of a fur. The significance of a cap as opposed to a bare head remains vague, since the scenes in which Gudea wears the cap cannot be clearly identified. That he is always bareheaded in front of enthroned deities on the stelae (ST.1, 3, 5) as well as on the door plaques and the seal (Figs. 9–10), however, may indicate that the cap was worn in scenes in which the ruler participated at the side of other humans, and signified his authority in relation to his subjects. In contrast, Urnamma also wears the cap in front of deities (Fig. 33). If given an attribute, Gudea carries a palm branch on his shoulder (ST.1, 3, 42). This motif was obviously not specific to a particular scene, and could be another royal insignium.[372]

Although many fragments depicting a Gudea figure remain without a clearly identifiable context, it can be surmised that he appeared in a number of different scenes. This is supported by the frequency with which he is depicted, and by comparison with the better-preserved stelae of Eannatum and Urnamma on which the king appears in almost every scene. If Gudea was the leading figure in the narrative and took part in all major events, interacting with gods as well as humans, he was nevertheless not the agent of these events. When presented to an enthroned deity, he is led by Ningišzida who

---

[369]   Boehmer *RlA* 6 (1980–83), 205 s.v. Kopfbedeckung.
[370]   Asher-Greve *AfO* 42–43 (1995–96), 186, tentatively identified it with the aga. See also Waetzoldt *RlA* 6 (1980–83), 197–203 s.v. Kopfbedeckung, especially 197 and 203. For other royal insignia see chapter I.A p. 6f.
[371]   For good detail reproductions see Johansen *Statues of Gudea*, pls. 44–46.
[372]   See chapter V.C.5.

intermediates between him and the higher-ranked deity. Libations are poured by a priest in his presence. In other not clearly identifiable scenes, he seems to attend actions performed by his subjects, since he is represented with his hands resting on his chest.

b. Other Human Beings

The human participants other than Gudea remain anonymous, though they are distinguished by different garments and hair styles. The only female figures are the clappers on ST.15, and possibly ST.53. They wear the same dress, chignon, hair cover and ribbon as statues from Tello that represent female relatives of the rulers of Lagaš.[373] Since garments signify status and rank in many societies, and especially ancient ones, it is not too far-fetched to assume that the clappers on the stelae represent ladies of the court.

Male figures may wear a fringed mantle like that of Gudea, a long skirt combined with a cape, a long pleated skirt on top of a short one, or a short skirt only. Their hair styles include a bare scalp, neck-length curly hair, and long hair tucked up in a double chignon. The latter two are usually combined with a short beard. The fringed mantle is well attested in early Mesopotamian imagery, where it is worn by rulers and high officials on ceremonial occasions.[374] The measuring out of the construction site, in which the figure on ST.48 was an active participant, accords with this tradition, and the figures on ST.23 and 49 are also likely to have participated in some sort of ceremony. The first two are shaved, while the latter wears neck-length curly hair and a beard.

The long skirt combined with a cape, an outfit reminiscent of that of soldiers on other monuments, is exclusively worn by standard carriers (ST.28). Since these conscripts for the temple construction are shaved in contrast to the male figures performing actual labor in other scenes, they may represent their foremen. The long pleated skirt is worn by drummers (ST.23, 54), carriers of dedicatory gifts (ST.13, 14, 59), and most likely also by the figure in front of the temple on ST.18. On the Urnamma Stela (Fig. 33), the same skirt is worn by drummers, and by the figure in front of a stand in the lowest register on side B. The drummers and two dedicatory gift carriers on the stelae of Gudea have a double chignon and a beard; the figure on ST.18 has the same hair style, but no beard. If the pleated skirt and the double chignon were associated with a profession, it may have been with temple employees.

The common short skirt is worn by workmen in importation and construction scenes on ST.20, 22, 34, and can be surmised also for the bare-legged ones on ST.11 and 12. None of them has the head preserved, though the two curls on the shoulder of one worker on ST.34 indicate that he had neck-length curly hair, like the workmen on the Urnamma Stela. Like these, he and his companions were probably bearded. This hair style is attested on two fragments which preserve only a head each (ST.50 and 51).

---

[373] Three inscribed statues wear the same dress: a wife of Gudea (Braun-Holzinger *Weihgaben*, St 132), a wife of the court of Nammahni (ibidem, St 141), and a daughter of Lugirizal, a Lagašite ruler at the time of Šulgi (ibidem, St 153). For a reconstruction of this dress, see Strommenger *APAW* 2 (1971), 50f. no. 13. Their heads are not preserved. The combination of dress and hair style, however, is found in the upper body of a statue from Tello without inscription (DC pl. 24bis: 2); for the hair style compare also a well preserved head from Tello (DC pl. 25:5).

[374] Strommenger *APAW* 2 (1971), 46f. no. 9.

Two bare-chested male figures of whom only the upper body remains exhibit hair styles which differ from other skirted men. The man carrying a foundation deposit on ST.55 is shaved, and the one handling ropes on ST.56 wears a conical cap, perhaps a sort of protection. The libators on ST.4 and 30, whose heads are shaved, may have been nude, as they were in the Early Dynastic period.

The preceding review confirms that garments and hair styles are associated with rank and profession: workmen have curly hair and wear short skirts; drummers and men bringing dedicatory gift, who may have been temple employees, wear a double chignon and a long pleated skirt on top of the short skirt; standard carriers, probably the foremen of the construction workers, are shaved and wear a long skirt and a cape; clappers and field measurers, who probably were part of the ruler's entourage, wear garments covering their entire body; the females have their hair covered, while the males are shaved. All these human figures are stereotypes. Except for the libation priest, they appear in groups, i.e. as a collective. In contrast to Gudea, each type occurs in a limited number of scenes, and performs an action according to its function. The anonymous human beings are the agents in the events.

c. Deities
Deities are distinguished from human beings by their horned crown, which usually consists of four pairs of horns. This headgear functions in images like the divine determinative in texts. In addition, most deities wear a flounced garment never worn by humans. All gods have elaborate long beards, and their hair tucked up in a chignon; the goddesses wear their hair loose in locks falling around their shoulders. While some divine figures exhibit features which permit an identification with a specific deity, the identity of others is not that evident on first sight. Only Gudea's personal god Ningišzida from whose shoulders serpent-dragon heads protrude (ST.1, 6, 39) is depicted with a "physical" feature that establishes his identity.[375] Other deities are characterized by gesture, posture, and attributes, though these do not necessarily establish their precise identity. They designate particular aspects or functions.

The gesture of raising both arms behind the ruler (ST.3 and 9) characterizes Lamma as a protective spirit.[376] She is a personification of a named divine function rather than a specific deity.[377] Her low rank in the pantheon is denoted in her headgear and garment. In contrast to all other divine event participants, she wears a single-horned crown and a pleated, rather than flounced, garment. By analogy with Gudea's basin (Fig. 8) and the Urnamma Stela (Fig. 33), one can surmise the same outfit for the goddess with the overflowing vase, who probably hovered above the enthroned deity in the presentation scene on ST.1+2. She can be interpreted as a personification of prosperity signified by her attribute.[378] These minor goddesses personify concepts, divine protection, and god-

---

[375] See chapter II.C.3.a, p. 66f. Note, however, that the serpent-dragon is not exclusively associated with Ningišzida, but with snake-gods in general; see chapter II.C.2.d. It is the context of Lagaš and the role of leading Gudea that allow an identification as Ningišzida of the figure with serpent-dragons protruding from his shoulders on Gudea's monuments.
[376] See chapter II.C.3.a, p. 67.
[377] Foxvog et al. *RlA* 6 (1980–83), 446–455 s.v. Lamma.
[378] See chapter II.C.1.d.

given prosperity, which are expressed once in a gesture, the other time in an attribute. Similarly, the staff and the position behind the throne characterize the gods on ST.1 and 2 as minister and attendant, respectively, of the enthroned deity.[379] Their precise identity can be established only in relation to their master or mistress, since their attribute and posture designate no more than an office.

Enthroned deities can be male or female. The enthroned position denotes status and authority,[380] and one expects them to be of primary importance and of higher rank in the pantheon than the other divine participants in the same scene. Their identity is not marked by idiosyncratic features such as that adopted for Nanna on the Urnamma Stela (Fig. 33c). Although their attributes and throne decorations give some clues, they cannot settle the question. They are known to be associated with more than one deity and only specify a certain aspect, not unlike the staff denotes the office of the minister. The lions flanking the thrones on ST.2 and ST.17+33 are associated with warrior deities as, for example, Inanna and Ningirsu/Ninurta,[381] and must denote their prowess. The bison-man, who most likely decorated the throne on ST.36, is originally a defeated foe of Utu, but had become a generic trophy of warrior deities by the time of Gudea.[382] Similarly, the overflowing vases on the throne pedestal on ST.17+33, originally signified Enki's attribute, fresh water, but had developed into a generic symbol for prosperity by that time.[383]

In regard to the objects held by enthroned deities, it is important to ask whether they function as attributes characterizing the deity or play a part in the represented event. An object pointed toward an approaching party can be an object of exchange in the interaction taking place, while one held on the chest is more likely an attribute. On Gudea's seal (Fig. 9) Ningirsu offers with his left hand an overflowing vase to the approaching Ningišzida, and on ST.36 the god holds a weapon, a common attribute of warrior deities, on his chest. There are, however, exceptions. On UrDUN's seal (Fig. 21), Ningirsu holds his seven-headed mace, clearly his attribute, towards the approaching party, and on Gudea's seal Ningirsu holds an overflowing vase, clearly an object of exchange in this scene, also in his right hand. Thus, the nature of the object as well as the context of the scene must be taken into consideration when interpreting these objects.

A more conclusive, yet often overlooked, criterion for identifying the enthroned deity lies in the context of the monument.[384] The door plaques of Gudea showed his presentation to the deity to whom they were dedicated.[385] By analogy, one expects the enthroned deity who blesses the ruler in the culminating scene depicted in the top registers of

---

[379] See chapter IV.B.7, p. 198
[380] See Winter *BiMes* 21 (1986), 255 and 260.
[381] For representations of lion thrones of male and female deities see Metzger *Königsthron und Gottesthron*, pl. 65 and 72, and Haussperger *Einführungsszene*, 96 note 509, and 104 note 618.
[382] See chapter IV.B.8.
[383] See chapter II.C.3.a, p. 67.
[384] Similarly, the identification of deities on cylinder seals largely depends on the context of the seal, as was excellently demonstrated by Braun-Holzinger *BaM* 27 (1996).
[385] See chapter II.C.3.a, p. 68.

stelae to be identical with that to whom the stela was dedicated, and in whose temple it stood. Unfortunately, the original location of Gudea's stelae cannot be determined, and what is left of their commemorative inscriptions does not reveal to whom they were dedicated. Yet, there are several indications that the preserved enthroned deities represented Ningirsu and Baba, the divine patron of Lagaš and his consort. Since Ningirsu is the only high-ranked deity in Girsu to be associated with warrior imagery as well as with the function of blessing the ruler with prosperity,[386] he is the best candidate for the enthroned deity on ST.2 and ST.36, and his consort Baba for that on ST.7 and ST.35, if they belonged to the same stelae. This identification is corroborated by the fact that all stela fragments officially excavated at Tello were found near remains of Gudea's Eninnu.[387] The Cylinder Inscriptions confirm that several stelae were dedicated to Ningirsu and Baba in this temple.[388] Moreover, most inscribed objects attributable to Gudea pertain to his (re)construction of Eninnu. In terms of throne decoration the deity who sat on the throne on ST.17+33 could also have been Ningirsu, although the lack of context and its likely place in a lower register leave this unclear. If the Isimud figure on ST.41 belonged with it, for instance, the deity must have been Enki.

The enthroned deities are set on pedestals, like statues. The active role they play in presentation scenes, however, and the participation of other divine figures in the same scene which show no signs of being statues, strongly suggest that more than a simple cult act is represented. The scenes play in a not-entirely-human realm in which the ruler interacted with an animate divine world. This does not exclude the possibility that the imagery was inspired by real-life cult events, as Barrelet has argued in regard to Akkadian seals.[389] Divine statues were conceived of as endowed with life not only in Mesopotamia,[390] but also in many other civilizations.[391] If the ancient beholder recognized the scene as a ritual act performed in front of a statue, he may have imagined the statues to be animate, and understood the inherent message regarding the relationship between ruler and deity. It is interesting to note that the representation of the statue of a seated deity in the third register of side B on the Urnamma Stela (Fig. 33) is not differentiated from the representation of seated deities in presentation scenes on the same stela, and can be identified as a statue only because it is dusted by a servant. A similar ambiguity in regard to the representation of divine figures which are supposed to be statues of a temple and, at the same time, take an active part in the scene playing there can be observed in Attic black figure vase painting.[392]

The deities in the visual narrative thus included high-ranked deities of the Lagašite pantheon – probably Ningirsu and Baba – their attendants and ministers, personifications of divine protection and god-given prosperity, and Gudea's personal god Ningišzida. Most, if not all, deities are confined to presentation and libation scenes. High-ranked deities bless the ruler, commission him with a temple construction, or receive a libation,

---

[386] See chapter III.C.1.b, and compare chapter II.C.3.a, p. 67.
[387] See chapter IV.A.2.
[388] See Appendix C no. 6.
[389] *Or* 39 (1970).
[390] See chapter II.C.1.a.
[391] See Freedberg *Power of Images*.
[392] Connelly "Narrative and Image," 101.

which may be understood as the petition for blessings, or as an allusion to the verification of the commission. Their attendants serve mainly to underline their rank and status. Their minister (ST.1) may announce the approaching party of the ruler to them. The personification of prosperity emphasizes the object of exchange in the event. Lamma protects Gudea. Ningišzida leads him and intermediates for him. In sum, the high-ranked enthroned deities occur both as agents as well as beneficiaries, while the minor deities each appear in one function, much like the stereotypical human beings. With the exception perhaps of Ningišzida, who may have acted on Gudea's behalf, as he does on the seal (Fig. 9), they can be considered part of the setting.

d. Scale and Gesture

A general differentiation among the event participants is communicated through their size in relation to other figures. The use of scale for emphasis is common in Mesopotamian art. A royal figure larger than other human figures in the same scene can be observed on the Standard of Ur (Fig. 26), the Urnanše Plaques (Fig. 37), and the stelae of Eannatum (Fig. 27), Naramsin (Fig. 28), and Urnamma (Fig. 33). On the stelae of Gudea, deities, whether standing or seated, are taller than humans, and higher-ranked ones taller than lower-ranked ones, as can be seen on ST.1+2. That Gudea was taller than other human figures is exemplified in the libation scene on ST.4+5, and suggested by the relative large size of other isolated Gudea figures (ST.30, 42, 43). Humans other than Gudea are usually of the same height, as seen on ST.15, 28, 34, 54.

The most sophisticated scene on the stelae of Gudea is doubtless the culminating scene: the presentation of Gudea to a high-ranked deity that was depicted in most top registers. This scene involves a number of individual figures of different rank and status, most of whom do not occur in other scenes. Moreover, it employs gesture to express their function in the happening and their relationships within the cosmic order. The use of gesture for expression is well documented in Western art, and has also been studied in ancient art,[393] though it has hardly been a topic of investigation in regard to Mesopotamian images. Thus the following observations seem justified here.

The raised forearm with open hand of figures approaching a seated deity (ST.1, 6, 44), as well as of the seated deity itself (ST.4, 35), common in presentation and libation scenes, has been understood as a gesture of greeting.[394] On carved stone monuments and high quality seals the forearm of the seated figure, however, is usually raised at a wider angle than that of approaching figures. This suggests that we are dealing with two different gestures. The gesture of approaching figures recalls the Sumerian term kir$_4$ šu–gál, which literally means "having the hand at the nose."[395] This term occurs in the context of prayers as an introduction to a petition.[396] Thus the gesture is likely to have identified the figure concerned as a petitioner, if for nothing specific, then at least for

---

[393] For example, Gombrich *Image and Eye*, 63–104, and Brilliant *Gesture and Rank*.

[394] Haussperger *Einführungsszene*, 91, 107, 111.

[395] Already Barrelet *CRRA* 19 (1974), 56 sub 1.2.2, and Asher-Greve *Frauen*, 8.

[396] For a recent discussion of the term, more useful for the compilation of sources than their interpretation, see Averbeck *Ritual and Structure*, 463–468. The analogy of presentation scene and prayer has been noticed by Abusch *JAOS* 103 (1983), 13; see also Winter *BiMes* 21 (1986), and Suter *JCS* 43–45 (1991–93), 68.

the recognition by the higher-ranked seated figure. The expression of a petition makes sense in presentations to deities as well as to kings, since it includes an expression of devotion with respect to an authority. It is interesting to note that lexical sources give the reading hubud for KA.ŠU.GÁL, and translate it with Akkadian *balāṣu*,[397] which basically means "to step forward," and is related with Semitic *ʿbd*, "to serve."[398]

If the gesture of the approaching figure signifies a petition, then the forearm raised at a wider angle by the enthroned figure is best understood as expressing the approval of that petition. This approval can be specified by an object held in the hand of the enthroned figure and pointed towards the petitioner. On Gudea's seal (Fig. 9), the object is an overflowing vase, a symbol of prosperity, which Ningišzida receives from Ningirsu on Gudea's behalf; on the stelae of Urnamma (Fig. 33) and later kings (Fig. 34), the seated god points measuring rod and rope, insignia of kingship, toward the king.[399] In the first case, the divine approval is specified as a blessing with prosperity, in the second case as an investiture.[400]

Secondary figures in the scene also exhibit symbolic gestures. Lamma is characterized by her raising of both arms (ST.3 and 9). Since her only function is to protect her protégé,[401] her gesture must signify this protection. Ningišzida holding Gudea by the hand (ST.1, 6, 44) can be conceived of as a gesture expressing the relationship between personal god and man, in which the former intermediates on behalf of the latter *vis-à-vis* a divine authority of higher rank.

Both, the divine attendant and the minister of the seated deity hold their hands on their chest (ST.1 and 2). The same posture is exhibited also by the high-ranked men on ST.10 and 49, and by Gudea figures (ST.5 and 43). While the former position their right hand on the wrist of the left, which is clenched in a fist, Gudea holds the palm of one hand against the back of the other, interlacing the thumbs. The first position of the hands is the one common to the Gudea statues, the second occurs in his Statue M. Both are already attested in the Early Dynastic period.[402] Because statues of human beings with their hands held on the chest are dedicated in temples, they are usually interpreted as representations of worshippers, and their gesture as one of prayer.[403] The various narrative contexts in which the gesture is encountered, however, speak against this thesis, not least because it does not befit deities. The figures exhibiting this gesture are neither agents nor beneficiaries of the depicted events. Considering that we do most of our activities with our hands, this accords with the mere notion that hands resting on the chest are inactive. That the arms do not simply hang down may imply that attentiveness

---

[397] *Diri Ugarit* 1:177, and *Erimhuš* 5:170; personal communication Miguel Civil.
[398] AHw 98.
[399] See chapter I.A.2, p. 7 with note 39.
[400] Alternatively, the gestures, if they were the same, could denote the act of speaking. The petitioner could be imagined presenting his petition in speech, and the grantor proclaiming a sanction or blessings. For a specific gesture denoting the act of speaking in medieval art see Gombrich *Image and Eye*, 66f.
[401] Foxvog et al. *RlA* 6 (1980–83), 446–455 s.v. Lamma.
[402] See Asher-Greve *Frauen*, 68. Colbow's chronological interpretation of the difference, suggesting that the change took place late in Gudea's reign (*Rundplastik*, 91f.), must be abandoned.
[403] Barrelet *CRRA* 19 (1974), 54 § 1.2.1. See also chapter II.C.1.a note 92.

was involved rather than mere passivity.[404] If it was a symbolic gesture, it must have denoted the attentive attendance of an event.

This review shows that gesture signifies the part played in the event by the figure affected, and its relation *vis-à-vis* other participants. In presentation scenes Gudea petitions; Lamma protects him; Ningišzida intermediates between the ruler and the high-ranked deity, and sometimes also petitions on his behalf; the approached high-ranked deity approves of the petitioner, and possibly blesses him; attendant and minister are present in their functions as his or her servants. Gudea's gesture in most, if not all, other scenes demonstrates his attentive attendance in the events and shows that he was the commissioner of the temple construction, rather than the agent carrying out the labor or performing the ritual.

2. The Representation of Space

The common method of rendering space in ancient Near Eastern art can be called paratactic: bodies and their parts are set side by side, and lack corporeality. Groenewegen-Frankfort observed that "the conflict between the three-dimensional object to be rendered and the two-dimensional opportunity given has not been solved in favor of either."[405] As a result, the spatial relation between represented object and observer remains ambiguous. Accustomed to the illusion of space achieved by single-point perspective since the Renaissance, we may conceive of such ancient images as lacking perspective, a conception certainly not shared by ancient viewers. Space in two-dimensional images, whether rendered by a one-point perspective or paratactic method, is always reconstructed in the viewer's mind. Therefore, the perception of space, rather than the "correctness"of spatial representation, should be examined.[406] What clues are given to the viewer for perceiving the intended space? In view of the analysis of narrative, I will be less concerned with the corporeality of bodies than with the arrangement of figures and objects in space, and the identification of the locales.

On Neo-Assyrian palace reliefs organized in registers, there are two basic methods of making the depth of space perceivable: different ground levels are generated either by horizontal overlapping or vertical stacking.[407] In the first case, the figures are on the same ground line, and those closer to the viewer overlap those farther removed in space; in the second, the figures closer to the viewer are on the bottom line, and those farther removed in space are stacked above the former. Both methods are rudimentary in earlier Mesopotamian art. On the Eannatum Stele (Fig. 27), for instance, a phalanx of soldiers is shown once on the same ground line with their heads and swords partly overlapping the heads and shields of other soldiers, while in the register below one row of soldiers is stacked on top of another in such a way that the soldiers of the bottom row overlap the lower bodies of those on top. Stacking without overlaps is employed on the Naramsin

---

[404] Compare Asher-Greve *Frauen*, 68–71.
[405] *Arrest and Movement*, 7.
[406] Russell *Sennacherib's Palace*, 191f.
[407] Russell *Sennacherib's Palace*, 193.

Stela (Fig. 28), on which the marching army climbing a mountain is shown in diagonal rows of soldiers.

In contrast to these earlier monuments, the figures and objects on the stelae of Gudea and Urnamma are placed side by side on the same relief level without overlapping. They are raised from a flat, polished surface, and invariably as deep or slightly less deep than the raised bands which divide the surface into registers, and serve to demarcate the fields for the representation. The registers function as compositional boundaries. They are just high enough to accommodate the standing figures and objects. Their lower borders serve as ground line, their surface as background. The compositional boundaries are an integral part of the space of the representation.[408] But the space, in this case, has no depth.

The perception of spatial depth is also precluded in the two cases in which the figures do not stand on regular dividing bands. The construction scene on ST.34 extends over two image fields of the size of regular registers, joined by a ladder leading from one to the other. The imposition of a fine ground line separating them serves the same purpose as the dividing band in other registers. In the importation scenes on ST.11+12 and 20, the figures stand on mountain lands or on a raft floating on water. These are indicated by three rows of scales and three superimposed beams on wavy lines, respectively. Due to the stacking of one or two horizontal ground zones, the figures on the raft on ST.11+12 are smaller than the figures on the mountain zone, and the latter smaller than those standing on the regular ground line on the adjoining side of the same register, yet no spatial depth is intended or evoked. After the more realistic rendition of landscape on the Naramsin Stela (Fig. 28) and on Akkadian seals, the conventional representation of mountains and water by scales and wavy lines, respectively, must be considered conservative.

The explicit indication of a locale is restricted to importation scenes. The mountains and rivers are not specified further, though the label identifying a cedar raft on ST.11 hints at the "Cedar Mountains," a poetic designation for Amanum, today's Lebanon.[409] The other scenes are staged against a neutral background, the polished relief surface. Their locales can be only inferred from the context. The construction naturally takes place at the construction site. The parade of standards is best imagined on the procession street of Girsu called Girnun,[410] while the presentation of dedicatory gifts, the libations, and the presentation scenes must be imagined in the temple. The same applies to the musical performances, if they took place during the inauguration banquet. Practically all episodes depicted thus take place in the city in which the temple was built, and most of them at the site of the temple itself. Only the provision of materials is staged in remote mountain lands, taking the viewer outside of Girsu.

---

[408] See Meyer Schapiro *Semiotica* 1 (1969).
[409] See CA 15:19, 27, and compare Statue B 5:28 in Table III.E.5.
[410] Falkenstein *Einleitung*, 124 with note 1.

3. *Aspects of Time*

a. Moment and Movement

Since images arrest movement, they can capture only a particular moment of an event, which then arouses in the spectator the memory or imagination of the preceding and succeeding moments to complete and identify the event. Only an illusion of movement through time can be effected by compositional means.[411] A good example of this in early Mesopotamian art is the diagonal on the Naramsin Stela (Fig. 28). The arrangement of images in registers and figures set side by side on the stelae of Gudea, however, does not encourage a dynamic composition. Furthermore, few figures are seen in dynamic postures as, for example, those in the battle scenes on the registered stela of Sargon (Fig. 30). Most stand upright, one foot in front of the other, the body seen almost frontal, and the head in profile. Such "unfunctional" rendering, together with the lack of spatial depth, make movement ambiguous.[412] The figures could be standing still or striding. Whether a differentiation between arrest and movement was intentionally expressed by the spacing of the feet of the figures is not that clear. It is true that the pair of feet of Gudea and Ningišzida in the presentation scenes on ST.1 and 6, for instance, are close together, the toes of one touching the heel of the other, while those of the workmen on ST.22 and 34 are wider apart, leaving a space between them. Yet the same space between a pair of feet also occurs with the drummers on ST.23 and 54, who must be at a halt while playing their instruments.

A single moment is captured in the representation of actions which require a specific arm movement, such as the beating of a drum, the playing of cymbals, the hand clapping in musical performances (ST.15, 53, 54), or the pouring of a liquid from a jug in libation scenes which also show the water flow (ST.4, 30). Similarly, the men handling ropes on ST.18 and 56 are apparently seen at a specific moment of an action, the meaning of which escapes us. The raft on a river on ST.11+12 alludes to movement, yet, since it still abuts land, the scene seems to capture the moment before its departure. In the case of the workmen carrying something on their head on ST.34, an impression of movement is effected by the ladder they leave behind, and must have climbed just a moment before.

The ambiguity of arrest and movement is evident in rows of figures facing the same direction. The row of standard carriers (ST.28) implies a parade, and the figures could be imagined marching as well as standing still while passed in review. The men bringing along dedicatory gifts (ST.13, 14, 55) were probably part of a procession, and could be imagined proceeding to the temple, or standing in front of already-displayed gifts (ST.63). Similarly, the figures carrying measuring tools (ST.48, compare ST.10) could be imagined on their way to the construction site, or standing there ready to perform their task. In presentation scenes in which Gudea is led by the hand by Ningišzida, preceded by a minister god or followed by a Lamma, the procession of the figures and the leading gesture evoke movement, yet the enthroned deity they are approaching suggests arrest.

---

[411] See Gombrich *Image and Eye*, 40–62.
[412] Gronewegen-Frankfort *Arrest and Movement*, 7–11.

The conjunction of figures in movement and figures at a halt is common in Mesopotamian art. On the Standard of Ur (Fig. 26), for example, captives are led off the battle field, and this row of figures continues bustrophedon into the upper register, where it comes to a halt in front of the king reviewing them. Conversely, the chariots proceed from a halt into movement when entering the battle field. While the Standard shows several moments by repeating identical motifs, the ambiguity of the rows of figures on the stelae of Gudea could be intended to capture several moments in one unit: in the case of the standard parade, for example, the parading as well as the review by the ruler; in the presentation scene, the approach of Gudea, his petitioning, and his being blessed by the deity.

The combination of several successive actions in a single image without repeating any individual participant has been recognized as the predominant method of narrative in early Greek art.[413] An oft-cited example in this context is the black-figure cylix ascribed to the Rider Painter, which depicts the blinding of Polyphemos.[414] The scene shows Odysseus and three of his companions in front of the seated cyclops. The latter holds the limbs of one of Odysseus' companions whom he is devouring, while Odysseus hands him a cup which will lead to his drunkenness and subsequent sleep, and at the same time points the stick to his eye with which he will blind him during his sleep. The scene thus captures three successive actions in the attributes of two figures. More than one action in one figure does not seem to occur in Mesopotamian art. Yet, one cannot exclude the possibility that more than one action can be intended in one narrative unit.

The two scenes on the Akkadian seal in Jerusalem (Fig. 20) probably depict successive episodes, though they give the impression of simultaneous actions. The combat consisting of a god who beats another with a mace and the construction scene discussed above[415] are linked by the god next to the victor who raises his arms, probably in jubilation over the victory.[416] While his head is turned back to the combat, his legs are directed toward the construction site. In addition, three of the construction workers turn their heads toward the combat as if they were watching it. That the two scenes render successive events is suggested by the interpretation of the image as two episodes of a mythological story known from texts of a later period.[417] The directedness of the figures must then be understood as an effort to link the two episodes. While the first episode consists of a single action, the second contains six different ones. Although some of these activities are disputable, it is clear that the seated figure and the one with the hoe are engaged in the preparation of building material which the basket carrier carries to the construction

---

[413] Best explained by Weitzmann *Roll and Codex*, 13f., who called it simultaneous, and Snodgrass *Narration and Allusion*, who called it synoptic; see also Connelly "Narrative and Image."

[414] Weitzmann *Roll and Codex*, fig. 1, and Snodgrass *Narration and Allusion*, fig. 5.

[415] See chapter IV.B.3, p. 181.

[416] Opitz *AfO* 6 (1930), 61f. interpreted the gesture as consternation; Wiggermann in Porada *Man and Images*, 79, as the attitude of an atlant.

[417] Opitz *AfO* 6 (1930), 61f., followed by Frankfort *Cylinder Seals*, 131f., interpreted them as the killing of Kingu, and the building of Marduk's palace in the creation epic *Enuma Eliš*. If so, the visual narrative would antedate the earliest written versions by more than a millennium. Wiggermann in Porada *Man and Images*, 79, opted for an earlier version of the creation of mankind (Atrahasis), though this does not explain the combat. Whether one can explains the gap or inconsistency with oral tradition or not, the imagery is evidently mythological, and must have had some underlying story.

site, while the other figures are working on the structure. Thus the activities performed by the different figures in the construction scene can be understood as successive work stages.

With this last example in mind, the possibility can seriously be considered that some scenes on Gudea's stelae compressed successive moments or actions of an event in one narrative unit. The parade of standards, the presentation of dedicatory gifts, and the measuring of the construction site show a group of similar figures simultaneously involved in the same activity, though the precise moment of this activity is ambiguous, and the ambiguity could have been intended to capture more than one moment. The importation and construction scenes, if the former combined the transport of stone with that of lumber, and the latter combined workmen carrying dirt in baskets with others handling ropes, etc., showed several successive actions of the event. The musical performances depict different musicians and clappers playing together for a certain period of time, though only one moment is captured in the image. The libation scene captured the moment during which the liquid was poured, while the presentation scene may have signaled not only the deity blessing the ruler, but also the ruler's approaching the deity and putting forward his petition.

b. Scene and Episode
I have proposed identifying the imagery on the stela fragments of Gudea as parts of scenes which represent different episodes of a temple construction. The combination of several episodes presupposes a temporal sequence, which finds support in the recurring appearance of Gudea. Examining the relation of scene and episode, one should bear in mind that not all parts of an event can be equally well visualized. The artist must choose the moment which best convey(s) the event he wants to visualize, that which enables the spectator to reconstruct it in his mind. Furthermore, the composition of a scene depends on how many agents are involved. The compression of successive episodes in one scene, for example, is possible only if the event involves agents carrying out different actions.

If the standard carriers stand for the recruitment of the work force, as suggested above, the scene captures the parade or review of the conscripts, rather than the recruitment itself, which would have been difficult to visualize. The importation scenes seem to render the transport of materials about to be embarked on the river which will carry them to Girsu. This way, the artist was able to indicate the origin of the material from distant lands. The scenes representing construction work apparently included several construction activities. The equipment of the temple with dedicatory gifts was represented in a procession of figures bringing the gifts along, reminiscent of the rows of figures carrying food supplies to the temple in Early Dynastic images, as well as a display of the gifts. The inauguration festivities were apparently denoted by musical performances. The libation scene could signify the introduction to a prayer in which Gudea communicates with the gods in order to verify the divine commission, or, if in a top register, refer to his prayer petitioning for blessings.

In the context of a temple construction, the presentation scenes are best understood as representing the divine blessing of the ruler in return for his service of (re)constructing the divine house, which guarantees the maintenance of the cult. At the same time, they sum up the ruler's achievement, and situate his deeds on the level of cosmic order. Groenewegen-Frankfort noted this climactic quality in regard to the similar situation on the Urnamma Stela.[418] The presentation scenes are placed at the top of the stela in a much larger image field than all other scenes, and are loaded with conceptual gesture. Not unlike how the victory scene sums up military achievements, the presentation scene can be considered a summation of the ruler's civilian achievements. The maintenance of the cult was a main occupation of the ruler in times of peace. The reception of prosperity from the gods enables him to guarantee prosperity for his people. The culminating scene is staged in a not purely human realm, and occurs in isolation on other monuments. I would argue, therefore, that the stelae of Gudea show culminating scenes in the top registers and successive episodes in the other registers, and that the episodes can be considered an extension of the culminating scenes.

c. The Historicity of the Events

The stelae of Gudea and Urnamma have repeatedly been labeled "cult" stelae in contrast to "historical" stelae that depict military events.[419] This distinction is based on the usually unexplained assumption that a battle or victory scene must refer to a specific historical event, while scenes such as a libation, musical performance, and the like, which cannot be put in place in terms of political history, must refer to generic cult events. Becker attempted to explain the difference with Eliade's concept of sacred and profane time, arguing that "cult" stelae render cyclic, repeatable events, while "battle and victory" stelae render unique, non-recurring events.[420] Such a distinction, however, is unjustified, since a temple construction was viewed by ancient Mesopotamians as much a historical event as a military campaign.[421] Both type of events were undertaken repeatedly, recorded in the same media, and represented by means of a repertoire of stereotyped scenes.

The visual representation of military campaigns is not necessarily more specific than that of temple construction. The scenes on the Eannatum Stela (Fig. 27), for example, cannot be identified with specific battles precisely because they lack any reference to a specific enemy or place. It is only on the basis of the inscription of the stela that they have been interpreted as historical battles.[422] The same applies to Akkadian stelae, except for that of Naramsin (Fig. 28) and the one from Nasiriya (Fig. 32). The former indicates the place, a mountain land, where the campaign took place, and characterizes the enemy by means of ethnic features; the latter specifies the captives and the booty.

In the case of a temple construction, a specification is more difficult to effect, since the temples were built at home. The foreign landscape which may be represented in the context of the provision of building material imported for the construction cannot

---

[418] *Arrest and Movement*, 167.

[419] For example, Börker-Klähn *Bildstelen*, § 34.

[420] Becker BaM 16 (1985), 278–297. This distinction has further led to the wrong assumption that only historical narratives are narrative, a view criticized also by Davis *Masking the Blow*, 243f.

[421] See also Cooper "Mesopotamian Historical Consciousness," 48.

[422] See chapter IV.C.2.a, p. 214f.

identify the main event. Not unlike the inscriptions that accompanied stereotyped battle scenes and identified them with historical events, we can assume that the fragmentary inscriptions on the stelae of Gudea and Urnamma once identified the depicted temple constructions, and thus made them specific historical events. Moreover, these stelae stood in the temples the construction of which they commemorated, and a visual specification would have been redundant. What probably was more important to the commissioner of the stela, was the assurance that a visitor to the temple knew who to credit for its construction.

E. Comparison with the Imagery on Other Objects

In contrast to the extensive visual narrative on the registered stelae, the imagery on other sculpted objects of Gudea is much more allusive and tends toward the symbolic. It is confined to single, isolated scenes and to symbolic figures. They allude to an event in a summary way or epitomize a particular concept.

The repertoire of figures overlaps the one on the stelae and the characterization of the figures is similar. In addition to Gudea, Ningirsu, Baba, Ningišzida, and Lamma occur Ningišzida's minister Alla, the god with the peg, serpent dragons, a human-faced bull, and human warriors and captives. Ningirsu's minister and attendant, and the human figures represented on the stelae, are not attested. As on the stelae, Gudea wears the ceremonial gown in the scenes on the seal, the door plaques, and in statuary (Figs. 3–5, 9, 10), but he also appears dressed in a short skirt (Fig. 6). The label inscription on the shoulder of his statues and on his seal is comparable to the caption on the stelae. He is bareheaded in front of deities (Figs. 9, 10), but wears the brimmed cap in the review of captives (SO.5) and in statuary (Fig. 5). Ningirsu and Ningišzida wear the same flounced garment and multiple-horned crown, and their hair is tucked up in a double chignon (Fig. 9); Ningišzida is equally characterized by serpent dragon heads protruding from his shoulders. Lamma (Fig. 9) and the goddess with the overflowing vase (Fig. 8) wear the same pleated dress and a single-horned crown. Lions that decorate Ningirsu's throne and chariot on the stelae also occur as decorations on a vessel (SV.6) and a mace head (MH.7) dedicated to this god.

Two types of narrative scenes occur: the presentation of the ruler to a deity and the review of captives by the ruler. Both are culminating scenes well documented in early Mesopotamian imagery. The remains of the pedestal SO.5 show parts of a review of captives, as it is represented on numerous Early Dynastic and Akkadian monuments which commemorate military campaigns.[423] This image captures the moment of victory and can be considered the climax of a series of events. Some monuments combine it with other scenes visualizing such episodes, but it also appears in isolation, as on this pedestal. In this case, the review of captives stands for the entire military campaign. Although this event involves by nature human participants different from those of a temple construction, they are stereotyped and remain anonymous, much like those on the stelae, except perhaps for an enemy leader characterized by an unusual hair style, who may have been identified in the now lost part of the inscription.

The presentation scenes on Gudea's seal (Fig. 9) and door plaques (Fig. 10–12) are comparable to the culminating scenes in the top register of the stelae (Pls. A-C). On the seal and the plaques, the scene is reduced to the essentials. For reasons of space neither minister nor attendant of the enthroned deity occur, though the seal includes a Lamma and, no doubt as a decorative filler, the serpent-dragon, the emblem of Ningišzida. Like the stelae, the door plaques commemorate the construction of a particular temple and were dedicated in this temple. The presentation scenes depicted on them are customized

---

[423] See chapter IV.C.2.a, p. 213–217.

for a particular temple, the enthroned deity being the one to whom the temple is built and the plaque dedicated. This explains the appearance of Alla on the plaque dedicated to Ningišzida (Fig. 10). Despite their fragmentary condition, we can surmise that the scenes on the plaques included only the ruler, the enthroned deity, and the deity leading Gudea to it, since the latter two occupy the entire left side of the best preserved plaque (Fig. 10). These are the core elements of the scene. The plaques dedicated to male gods may have included the female consort on the god's lap, as does a plaque dedicated for Gudea's life.[424] On the stelae the ruler's presentation to the god's consort was apparently expanded into a second scene on the back side (Pl. A-B), which repeated the petitioning party.

On a conceptual level, the presentation scene expresses a relationship of authority rooted in the structure of society.[425] In the context of a temple construction, it can be associated with the final episode capturing the climax of the events: the moment when the ruler receives divine blessings in return. On the stelae the events which led to this moment are detailed in the lower registers. In the case of the door plaques, the reception of blessings can be understood as standing for an entire construction account, not unlike how the review of captives stands for an entire military campaign, because the plaques were customized for a particular temple. In contrast to the stelae and plaques, the seal is not part of the equipment of a temple, but a portable instrument used in administration. Therefore I would argue that the message of the seal only conveys the abstract concept that underlies this scene. The enthroned deity who blesses Gudea with prosperity is the chief god of the city-state. He is only associated with the symbol for prosperity, and not with warrior attributes as on the stelae (Pls. A and B), perhaps because the seal expressed the bestowal of blessings in more general terms, and took the god's identity as evident. The petitioning ruler led by his personal god into the presence of the divine patron of the city-state by whom he is blessed does not allude, in this case, to a particular event, but manifests in general terms the ruler's legitimacy in his office.

In addition to the narrative scenes, the imagery on other sculpted objects of Gudea includes several symbolic figures which, with the possible exception of the goddess with the overflowing vase, do not occur in this form on the stelae, although they relate to temple building. Gudea is portrayed with the utensils of an architect drafting the plan of a temple (Fig. 4), in the short skirt of construction workers carrying a basket (Fig. 6), and in the possession of prosperity symbolized by the overflowing vase (Fig. 5); an unidentified god is depicted holding a huge peg between his legs (Fig. 7). These images allude to particular episodes of a construction account. They do not occur on the stelae because the stelae represent these episodes in entire scenes, and therefore had no need or use for symbolic icons. The drafting of the temple plan is implied in the scene that renders the measuring out of the construction site (ST.18?, 48), while the god with the peg probably evoked the divine guidance in this same event. The construction work is visualized in scenes showing Gudea's subjects in the short skirt performing the work (ST.22, 34, 56), while the ruler dressed in his usual gown may have overseen it

---

[424] See chapter IV.C.2.a, p. 218 with note 312.
[425] See chapter IV.B.7, p. 203.

(ST.32). The bestowal of prosperity to Gudea is elaborated in the presentation scenes. The goddess with the overflowing vase personifies prosperity, and alludes to the transfer of prosperity from god to ruler. On the stelae, she may have occurred as a symbol in the scene which depicted that transfer (Pl. B), while on the large basin dedicated to Ningirsu (Fig. 8) she is multiplied in an elaborate frieze. In contrast to the more concrete nature of the narrative scenes on the stelae, which include other participants and specify, for example, who blessed Gudea and who else attended the event, the iconic figures are symbolic and remain largely ideographs. In reality, for instance, we would not expect the ruler to have ever worn the dress of a construction worker.

F.   The Message

1.   Source

It is generally assumed that the stelae, the fragments of which have been discussed above, were commissioned by Gudea, since he is repeatedly identified in the imagery. Unfortunately, the preserved commemorative inscriptions are too fragmentary to confirm this thesis. It is, however, less probable that a successor made them to glorify his forefather posthumously. This possibility was seriously considered by Börker-Klähn, and has also been proposed for the Urnamma Stela, though with no convincing evidence in its support. In the case of the Urnamma Stela, the arguments were based on an unlikely and outdated interpretation of the imagery.[426] In the case of Gudea, Börker-Klähn postulated that the stelae must have been fashioned after the composition of the Cylinder Inscriptions because of the discrepancy between the findspots of the stela fragments and their locations according to the text, and because of the absence on the actual fragments of any remains of the names of the stelae mentioned in the text.[427] Her contention, however, cannot be supported. As I have argued above,[428] the stela fragments were not found at their original location, and the absence of the stela names, an argument *ex silentio*, is explained by the fragmentary preservation of their inscriptions.[429] Börker-Klähn saw further support for her thesis in the similarities between the stelae of Gudea and that of Urnamma.[430] There are, however, also dissimilarities which reveal the heritage Gudea owed to his Early Dynastic and Akkadian predecessors,[431] and the remaining parallels can be explained with the contemporaneity of the two rulers.[432]

Stelae are traditionally royal monuments, and always celebrate the deeds of the ruler who commissioned them.[433] In the text inscribed on the Eannatum Stela (Fig. 27), this late Early Dynastic Lagaš ruler specifically mentioned that he errected it for Ningirsu,[434] and other kings commemorated the erection of stelae in other media.[435] In Lagaš, this tradition documented mostly in texts is more extensive than the preserved monuments suggest. Only two stelae of Urnanše (Figs. 24–25) and one of Eannatum (Fig. 27) have survived, in addition to two anonymous ones of Early Dynastic and Akkadian date, respectively.[436] Yet stelae are regularly mentioned, next to royal statues and other

---

[426] See chapter IV.C.2.a note 305.
[427] *Bildstelen*, § 135.
[428] Chapter IV.A.2.
[429] The stela names mentioned in the Cylinder Inscriptions (Appendix C no. 6) could very well have occurred in the stela inscriptions, since the name is a known component of such inscriptions, and because they consist of the same elements as the names which occur in the inscriptions written on a libation vessel and most statues of Gudea, compare chapters II.B.2.d § 4e, and III.E.2.f. Moreover, the preserved fragments of the stela inscriptions (see chapter IV.A.3) suggest that these texts were more detailed than the short building and dedicatory inscriptions, and resembled in this respect the statue inscriptions which usually include a name.
[430] *Bildstelen*, § 136.
[431] See chapter IV.C.3.a-b.
[432] See chapter I.B.1.
[433] See chapter IV.A.4.
[434] Eannatum 1 rev. 10.
[435] For example, Lugalanda 15 on a brick; or Šu-Sin in the name of his sixth regnal year, see RIME 3 293, and compare ibidem no. 2.1.4.8.
[436] For the latter two see Börker-Klähn *Bildstelen*, nos. 7 and 21.

dedicatory objects, in offering lists from the pre-Sargonic to the Ur III periods.[437] The account of the installation of seven stelae in the Cylinder Inscriptions (CA 22:24-24:7) follows this tradition, and should dispel any doubt about Gudea's being the ultimate source of their message.

Little can be said about the sculptors, material authors of the stelae. Artisans are named only in reference to certain transactions in administrative texts. As authors of their works, they remain anonymous. The Cylinder Inscriptions tell about Gudea's employing artisans in connection with the construction of Eninnu, namely silversmiths (kù-dím) and stone cutters (zadim), next to metal workers (CA 16:25–30).[438] The exact meaning of the term zadim is not sufficiently known to say whether it refers to work on precious stones, to stone quarrying, or to the carving of relief sculpture. The parallelism with kù-dím, and the usage of zadim elsewhere, however, suggest that it denoted someone doing sumptuary work for the temple furnishings.[439] In the Early Dynastic to Ur III periods, this term is the most likely candidate to refer to sculptors. In view of the preciousness of stone in southern Mesopotamia, it is conceivable that those who carved stone were engaged at the same time in other related work to secure their income. Ur III texts from Lagaš suggest that the artisan production in this province was traditionally organized within the temple estates.[440] The profession was apparently hereditary,[441] and artisans were likely members of the middle class.[442] As Neumann suggested, those working with imported materials such as stone were probably of higher standing than those working with domestic products.[443] Only the former are attested as dedicants of gifts to the gods.[444]

While the sculptors must have had authority concerning the composition and style of the imagery on the stelae, it seems safe to assume that their influence on the message was negligible. Like for the Cylinder Inscriptions,[445] one may consider a third party intermediating between the ruler's wishes and the final execution of the reliefs.

2. Contents

In contrast to the stelae of Eannatum and Akkadian rulers, those of Gudea and Urnamma commemorate civilian rather than military deeds, namely temple construction. Due to the fragmentary condition of the stelae of Gudea, it cannot be determined whether all stelae contained all scenes of which fragments have survived. Given that not all of

---

[437] See, for example, de Genouillac TSA 1 ix 1ff.; DP 53 ix 7ff.; DP 48 = Nik 1 27; RTC 247 i 7ff.

[438] For an Akkadian period documentation on large numbers of artisans working on a temple project see Westenholz *Texts in Philadelphia* 2, 24–27, though his interpretation of the data is perhaps too optimistic.

[439] See the discussion by Loding *Craft Archive*, 275–282.

[440] Neumann *Handwerk*, 92–97.

[441] Neumann *Handwerk*, 157 with note 899.

[442] Neumann *Handwerk*, 155–157.

[443] *Handwerk*, 160.

[444] Note especially, a GAL.ZADIM from Early Dynastic Nippur, who dedicated a door plaque and a vessel (AnNip. 24); an Early Dynastic zadim from Lagaš, who dedicated a macehead (AnLag. 15); and two more zadim from there, who dedicated stone vessels for a ruler's life during the Lagaš II period (Gudea 16 and Lagaš 55).

[445] See chapter III.F.1.

Gudea's statue inscriptions account for all episodes of the temple construction in the same detail, and that the phenomenon of core and expansion also existed in the imagery, it is possible that each stela contained only a selection of scenes. Which scenes were included was not vital to the message as a whole, as long as there was a culminating encounter between Gudea and the deity to whom the stela was dedicated in the top register, and a representative selection of episodes of the construction and inauguration of the temple in the lower registers.

The choice of the episodes depicted in lower registers must have depended not only on the importance attributed to particular events, but also on the unusual, striking quality of some. If the circumstances of Gudea's importation of materials from afar, for example, was an innovation in Lagaš made possible perhaps by the communications and trade relations initiated in the Sargonic period, this "new" information was eminently suitable as part of the message. Some scenes, such as the presentation and libation scenes, were evidently customized on particular stelae to suit their divine benefiary. Commemorative inscriptions must have specified that deity as well as the royal dedicant. This information was corroborated by the labels identifying Gudea in the imagery, and by the features characterizing the enthroned deities in the top registers.

3. *Circumstances*

According to the Cylinder Inscriptions, the stelae made for Eninnu were fashioned and installed in one year.[446] Since this event is mentioned between passages relating construction work, the erection of the stelae must have been synchronized with the completion of the construction. This is supported by the description of the finished temple in which the installed stelae are mentioned again (CA 29:1f.). Just how much this report corresponds to reality cannot be determined. It seems reasonable, however, that stelae commemorating a temple construction were made at the same time as the construction, and installed at the inauguration of the temple.

Their place of erection deserves a closer examination because it is related to the functioning of the monument with respect to an audience. Stelae could be erected at the place of a particular event; a victory stela, for example, at the place of the battle or new boundary it commemorated, though an original was always placed in the temple of the deity to whom it was dedicated.[447] Stelae commemorating the construction of a temple were unquestionably set up somewhere in this temple. In the case of Gudea, this is supported by the discovery of the excavated fragments within the area that has been assigned to this ruler's (re)construction of Eninnu, though they were not found *in situ*, and by the written account of the erection of stelae in this temple. Since the topography of the temple complex cannot be established from the excavations, we can only consult the text.

---

[446] CA 22:24–23:4 in Appendix C no. 6.
[447] See chapter IV.A.4.

IV. The Stelae

According to Cylinder A, Gudea installed the seven stelae made for Eninnu in a circle around the temple.[448] Of the six reportedly named and installed,[449] five bear names pertaining to Ningirsu, and were set up in the large courtyard, at Kasurra, at the east front, in front of Šugalam, and in front of EURUga, respectively; the sixth pertains to Baba, and was at the rear of her chambers. All these locations seem to be outdoors: the large courtyard must be the central courtyard of the temple complex; Kasurra and Šugalam were locations near gates, presumably entrances to the temple precinct; the east front may refer to a gate on that side; EURUga may be the side facing the temple of Gatumdug (é-uru-kù-ga); the rear of Baba's chambers was probably the back side of the cella. Since the stelae are said to surround the house, one could imagine them displayed in the area between the central buildings and the precinct wall, perhaps in a park-like environment not unlike that of the precincts of mosques. Outdoor locations were presumably the most public areas within the temple complex. I would suggest, therefore, that the stelae were displayed at strategic locations within the temple area to which the people of Lagaš had access, and not only a privileged group of priests.

4. Receiver

Stelae were dedicated to deities in their temples.[450] If only in terms of royal rhetoric, deities must be considered as receivers of their message. They were regularly informed about royal deeds in texts,[451] and the dedication to them of sculpted objects shows that they were also intended to receive visual messages. Beyond the religious intent, monuments such as stelae express a desire on the part of the ruler to make his existence and deeds known and admired. Since the place where the stelae of Gudea were erected was in all probability public, the citizens of Lagaš can be considered as intended admirers. Whether a determined segment of the population (temple personnel or courtiers) was targeted in particular is not apparent. In terms of "readability," the images carved on the stelae speak for a large audience. They include a limited number of characters, whose identity must have been transparent for an ancient Lagašite who saw the monument in its original context. The only conceptual scenes are the culminating scenes in the top registers. These belonged to the traditional repertoire of Mesopotamian imagery, occurred frequently on seals, and must have been familiar. The episodic scenes in the lower registers, some of which may have been more innovative, render concrete narrative events, and were thus sufficiently explicit.[452]

In contrast to the images, the commemorative inscriptions, which specified who built what for whom, and the labels identifying the representations of Gudea and that of a cedar raft, could be read only by literate people. These inscriptions, however, are not essential for the understanding of the message. They merely lend specifity or historicity to the narrative. For a contemporary of Gudea, who was familiar with the events and

---

[448] The circle is implied by the use of the verb dab₆ in CA 29:1: na 7 é-e dab₆-ba-bi.
[449] CA 23:8–24:7 in Appendix C no. 6.
[450] See chapter IV.A.4.
[451] See chapter III.F.4.
[452] Compare the observations made by Winter *Studies in Visual Communication* 7 (1981) 29, in reference to episodic narrative on Assyrian palace reliefs.

saw the stelae in their original context, i.e. in the temple the construction of which they commemorated, the information provided in the commemorative inscriptions must have been already known, and the labels simply emphasized the figure of the ruler and the imported cedar. These inscriptions may have been intended for a future audience, and future rulers in particular. That the latter were targets of the messages of royal monuments is explicit in the curse section of many of their inscriptions.[453] *Lugal* explicitly expresses the notion of establishing a king's name in future days by means of his images.[454] The desire to attain immortality for one's name and deeds is, of course, universal, and clearly stated, for instance, in Šulgi B 4–6: "this is the praise of his power, this is the song of his strength, this is the lasting record of the accomplishments of the wise one, to be passed down to future generations."

---

[453] For a survey of early Mesopotamian curse formulae see Michalowski and Walker "New Sumerian 'Law Code'," 390–396.
[454] Lines 475–476, see chapter II.C.1.a, p. 60.

V. VERBAL AND VISUAL NARRATIVES: A COMPARISON

A. The Context of the Messages

1. Source

The creation of the cylinders and stelae presupposes in the first place a decision on the ruler's part to have his temple building commemorated in text and imagery. Gudea's decision was conditioned by tradition, if only by a wish to do something more spectacular than his predecessors in Lagaš. Since the Early Dynastic period the commemoration of temple constructions is well documented, though no similarly detailed verbal or visual account has survived. What role courtiers and religious leaders may have played in this decision is now impossible to determine. The execution was by necessity commissioned to skilled personnel: composer(s)/scribe(s) on the one hand, and sculptor(s), on the other. As is almost universally the case in ancient Mesopotamia, these authors remain anonymous. If composers of literary works concerning the ruler belonged to the intelligentsia of the royal court, and sculptors were artisans of higher standing organized within the temple estates, the anonymous authors of verbal and visual accounts originated from different milieus, though both from abodes of power.

2. Channel

The message that Gudea built a temple for his god imparts the same basic information in two quite different expressions: the cylinders and the stelae. It is the channel that constitutes a main difference. Verbal and visual media use different codes, and impact on different senses. The basic requirements for these codes – for one, a system of signs to represent speech; for the other, certain conventions to represent events in imagery – were long established by the time of Gudea. In other words, the source did not invent the encoding systems. There are, of course, more layers to the encoding of the messages under discussion. What was tradition and what innovation, and how do the two media compare in this regard? Even though the cylinders present a unique text in some ways, and the stelae depict scenes for most of which there are few or no parallels, both were composed based on certain traditions. It is also clear that the verbal and visual channels follow different streams of tradition.[1]

Gudea's cylinders apparently were novel in two respects: the commemoration of a royal deed – a temple construction – in the form of a praise song (zà-mi) to a deity, and its extraordinary length and detailed elaboration. Note, however, that Urnamma had his construction of Enlil's Ekur commemorated in a tigi song to Enlil, which is much shorter than Gudea's cylinders, yet similar in outline.[2] Since the reigns of the two rulers

---

[1] This is not unusual, compare, for example, the situation for Maya text and imagery described by Miller "Maya Image and Text," 186f.
[2] For the latest edition of Urnamma B see Klein *ASJ* 11 (1989), 44–56.

overlapped, and because of the absence of precise dates for their constructions, we cannot be entirely sure whether Gudea's cylinders antedate *Urnamma B*.[3] Inscriptions commemorating royal deeds, as well as songs praising deities, exist since Early Dynastic times, and the cylinders rely on this tradition in terms of composition and style.[4] This is manifest in the phraseology, the figures of speech, and the various repetition patterns. Although most literary compositions in which the same features can be observed are preserved only in Old Babylonian copies, it is clear that the composition of such texts, which may have been in part oral, was already undertaken in Early Dynastic times.

Gudea's incentive for introducing the narrative concerned with royal deeds in the form of a song may have been an attempt to reach a wider audience. While commemorative inscriptions were restricted to written transmission addressed mainly to future rulers, songs were performed, and could thus reach a larger, contemporary audience. One could see the "royal hymns" of the Ur III dynasts as a further development of songs concerned with a living ruler. In contrast to Gudea's cylinders, most of them include explicit glorification of the ruler and were introduced into the scribal curriculum for future dissemination.[5] If the cylinders were a draft for a stela, such monumental display of a song may have been another novelty, the earliest evidence for which dates to the Isin period.[6]

The sculpted stela as a vehicle for royal rhetoric can be traced at least to the Early Dynastic period, along with the organization of imagery in registers to be read as a sequence of narrative episodes with a culminating scene at the climax. The formal characteristics and composition of the stelae of Gudea have Early Dynastic and Akkadian antecedents. The visual codes and written captions which characterize and identify represented figures and localities are also established conventions by the time of Gudea. What might have been new, if Gudea's stelae antedated the Urnamma Stela, was the use of the stela for a narrative concerning the ruler's temple building and the detail in which this narrative was told. Early Dynastic rulers and the kings of Akkad used stelae almost exclusively for the representation of their military campaigns (Figs. 26–32), while temple constructions were conveyed in iconic images or culminating scenes in different media, as for example, on the door plaques of Urnanše (Fig. 37). The emphasis on Gudea's civilian, rather than military, deeds may have been a reaction to the kings of Akkad, whose reverse emphasis may have been unpopular in his time.

---

[3] Cf. Klein *ASJ* 11 (1989), 28, who considered the cylinders "the prototype of all later hymns and inscriptions, recording building activities and subsequent dedication ceremonies, including ... Urnammu B," and concluded in "From Gudea to Šulgi," 301, that "it was Gudea, or one of his Lagaš predecessors, who invented the genre of the royal hymns."

[4] Sjöberg *Temple Hymns*, 6, observed that: "The Gudea Cylinders which represent early examples of the Neo-Sumerian category of temple hymns may, when considered in relation to the short temple hymns among the texts from Abu-Salabikh, be the climax of a long tradition of 'Old Sumerian' literature."

[5] Klein "From Gudea to Šulgi," 301.

[6] See chapter III.F.3, p. 157.

V. Verbal and Visual Narratives: a Comparison

3.   Receiver

Both cylinders and stelae seem to target various groups of receivers: deities, future generations, and, even though not specifically mentioned, contemporary audiences. The deities addressed are those the construction of whose temple is narrated. Ningirsu is the object of praise in the doxologies of the cylinders, and the stelae were dedicated to the deities in whose temples they were installed; they must have been named in the now lost parts of the dedicatory inscriptions. If the enthroned deities in the culminating scenes were the ones to whom the stelae were dedicated, that which remains of these scenes points to Ningirsu and his consort Baba. That Ningirsu and, by extension, his consort were the beneficiaries of the stelae is supported by the findspots of the fragments; by the written claim that seven stelae were made for Eninnu; and by the fact that the vast majority of Gudea's inscribed artifacts pertain to this temple. On the divine level then the receiver of the cylinders and stelae is identical.

When it comes to human receivers, the groups targeted seem to differ. The imagery is more likely aimed at the population at large, whereas only educated scribes, a relatively small segment of society, could have been able to read the text. The situation, however, is more complex. The stelae also contain writing, and the cylinders also have a visual aspect, and if they were a draft for a stela, we can be sure that the final product was meant for display. Moreover, the verbal composition was probably recited in some form at least once. Even if only small segments of the population could comprehend and fully appreciate the messages in all their details, they were not exclusively addressed to these groups.

For the illiterate population, the long inscriptions on the two impressive cylinders (or a stela) must have been in themselves a manifestation of power, since writing was the privilege of the ruling class. Those who saw them displayed in the temple, even if they could not read, probably knew from hearsay that they contained the story of Gudea's temple construction. The literary Sumerian in which the text is written may have differed from the vernacular language of the time. If the composition was recited to Gudea's contemporaries, only those accustomed to such performances – perhaps only the educated upper class – would have understood the message in its entirety. It is well-known that the efficacy of religious texts is not a function of its intelligibility. Many Mesopotamian incantations are pure abracadabra, or are written in a pseudo-foreign language, presumably without losing their power, and perhaps even increasing it. Could texts conveying the deed and power of the ruler be similar in this respect? An answer is not easily come by, but the possibility that such a text could have been recited to an uncomprehending audience cannot be completly dismissed. Beyond that, whether the text was retold to a broader audience is doubtful. Although the content was in all likelihood not addressed to scribes only, they may have been an important target group in an effort to foster their loyalty to the ruler.

In the case of the stelae, the sculpted stone monuments were clearly a manifestation of power and geared to impress the masses. Their multiple repetition of identical or similar imagery points to the purpose of manipulating the receiver. Moreover, a much larger segment of the population can be expected to comprehend if not the entire content, at least large parts of it. One can draw a distinction between culminating and episodic scenes. The former are conceptual in nature and require previous knowledge for decoding, while the latter are concrete and therefore easier to read. The presentation scene, however, was a popular image in other media, and must have been discernible for those familiar with it from, for example, cylinder seals. Only the captions and commemorative inscriptions were confined to the literate. These inscriptions may have been addressed mainly to future readers of the monuments, since contemporaries of Gudea probably knew the author and divine beneficiary of Gudea's stelae. One cannot exclude the possibility that contemporary scribes were also addressed to give them some satisfaction of their art. The commemorative inscriptions must have been intelligible to a larger group of literates than the text of the cylinders, since they are much shorter, and less poetic in nature. The caption identifying Gudea were familiar to all those dealing with seals in the administration.

The messages of both media have different layers of information which target different groups. Both cylinders and stelae can be considered manifestations of power, and are as such addressed to everybody. When it comes to content and intelligibility, however, the stelae were clearly intended for a larger audience than the cylinders.

B.   Narrative Components

1.   *Event Participants*

The event participants of the story consist of human and divine beings. Their identification and characterization is naturally achieved by different means in the different
media. The text uses names, epithets, and verbal descriptions, the imagery employs
garments, hair styles, attributes, scale, gesture, and in one case a written caption. Gudea,
the main character, is identified by name, title, and/or epithets in the text, and by a
caption consisting of his name and title in the imagery. The combination of name and
title is obligatory in the short inscriptions, but occurs only four times in the cylinders.
Verbal designations such as "ruler" and "shepherd" have a counterpart in the imagery
in the brimmed cap of the ruler figure, probably a royal insignium, and in the slightly
larger size compared with other human figures. Further characterization of Gudea in
the text emphasizes his relation with the divine world, on one hand, and his function
as competent temple builder, on the other. The first aspect is visualized on the stelae in
the scenes in which Gudea interacts with deities, the second in the scenes in which he
appears as the temple builder. The importance given to the protagonist is evidenced in
his frequent appearance in both text and imagery.

Human beings other than the ruler remain anonymous in both media. The text may
specify their geographical origin, social status, or profession, whereas the imagery
specifies their physical appearance, i.e. garments and hair styles, which probably implied
their social status and profession. Workmen, for example, are bare-chested, while temple
employees wear a long slit skirt over the short skirt, and courtiers a ceremonial dress
covering their entire body. The temple employees are also distinguished by a special
hairdo – the double chignon – which may have been typical of their affiliation with the
temple. It is interesting to note that the only other male figures wearing long hair bound
in a chignon are the gods.

Deities are distinguished from human beings by the horned crown in the imagery, a
visual marker corresponding to the divine determinative preceding their name in the
text. While the text identifies individual deities by name, their identification seems more
complex in the images, but may have been perfectly lucid to an ancient viewer. Only
Ningišzida is specified by an extension of the body, the serpent-dragon heads protruding
from his shoulders. This is perhaps no coincidence, since this god was introduced into
the Lagašite pantheon by Gudea. Although the other deities may be characterized in
general terms by attributes, gesture, and posture, their precise identity relies mainly on
the context of the narrative and the monument. The deity presiding over the presentation
scene in the top register is likely to be the deity residing in the temple in which the stela
is dedicated. The minister of this deity can be recognized by the staff he carries and the
attendant by his position behind the throne, but their precise identity is revealed only
through the identity of their master/mistress. Attributes such as the minister's staff, or
a weapon indicative of the warrior nature of a deity, denote specific aspects similar to
verbal descriptions. The rank of a deity in the pantheon, expressed by epithets in the

text, may have been made explicit in the imagery by the number of horns on the crown, the garment, scale, or by the position relative to other scene participants. Lamma, for example, has only one pair of horns, and wears a pleated dress rather than a flounced garment; the divine attendant on ST.1+2 is smaller than Ningišzida and the minister; and the prominence of Ningirsu in the same scene is indicated by his enthroned position.

Although the identification and characterization of the event participants is achieved by different means in text and imagery, the concepts behind them are similar. The major difference between text and imagery regarding the event participants lies in the role they play in the narrative. The text casts Gudea in the part of the principle agent of the events, and involves the entire Sumerian pantheon, while anonymous people play a secondary role, either as extension of Gudea or mere background. In contrast, the imagery shows Gudea not so much acting as overseeing the actions carried out by his subjects, or else simply present in events enacted by deities. The deities that participate belonged to the local pantheon and occur only in a limited number of scenes. The agents of the actions in the imagery are the anonymous people which populate all episodic scenes. Gudea's role as the initiator, but not necessarily as the agent of the events, is in all likelihood closer to reality, and the imagery is thus more concrete than the text. The more realistic representation of events, the limited number of deities, and the preponderance of human beings in the imagery appear to be geared to the larger audience that the stelae were intended to reach as opposed to the text. The differences between the two media in this respect, therefore, seem to reflect a conscious choice on part of the source.

The prominent role of the temple that is built finds different expressions in text and imagery. In the text Eninnu is named and described by metaphors commonly used in verbal descriptions of Mesopotamian temples as well as others that characterize it as the residence of the warrior god Ningirsu. Moreover, its parts are enumerated at length. On the stelae the temple is never depicted in its entirety, though parts of its equipment occur in various scenes: a temple gate in a construction scene; a gate lion and dedicatory gifts including chariots, weapons, drums, and a stela in scenes concerned with the equipment of the temple; and an offering stand and huge mace as spatial environment of scenes taking place in the temple. Compared with the metaphorical descriptions of Eninnu in the text, the representation of temple parts on the stelae is much more concrete. The temple, the construction of which was told in the visual narrative, was naturally the temple in which the stela was displayed, and must have been named in the commemorative inscription.

2. *Place and Time Indications*

Place indications are restricted almost exclusively to prayers in the text, and hardly exist in the imagery. In both text and imagery it is, rather, the context of an event or a scene which allows inference of its locality. The events pertaining to the construction naturally take place at the construction site, while those pertaining to the inauguration of the temple are likely to happen in that temple. Gudea's construction activity was concentrated at Girsu, which is mentioned in the text, whereas the location of the temple in the imagery was evident in the place where the stela was set up. Specific geographical spheres outside of Girsu occur in the recruitment of manpower and the provision of materials from foreign lands. The Lagašite districts mobilizing for the construction, as well as the foreign lands providing building materials, are identified by name in the text, but by means of emblems and the conventional rendition of mountain landscape, respectively, in the imagery. In contrast to the text, which has some events staged in a purely divine realm, the imagery contains only one scene, the presentation scene, which does not take place in an entirely human realm, though it is not purely divine, either. It may have been conceived of as a temple environment.

Indications concerning the timing of an event, its duration, and its connection with other events are rare and vague in the text, and practically non-existent in the imagery. The placements of the events in historical time seems to be irrelevant to both accounts. Duration is naturally treated differently in text and imagery. In verbal narrative an event can be summarized, scenically described, or even stretched. In visual narrative time is arrested. A single image can capture one or several moments, and in either case evoke an entire event. The sequence of events is linear in the text, and the narration generally complies with their logical order. On the stelae, the scenes are juxtaposed in registers that were apparently read around the monument from bottom to top, except for a candidate of a two-sided stela (Pl. C), on which one side followed the other. The differences concerning place and time in the two accounts reflect differences contingent on the media rather than on a choice of the source.

C. Particular Episodes and Descriptions

1. The Importation of Cedar Logs and Stone Slabs

The importation of cedar logs and stone slabs is a good example of an event represented in both text and imagery. The verbal account in Cylinder A is translated in Appendix C no. 4. The agents are: the ever-present Ningirsu, for two reasons – he is the ultimate beneficiary of the operation, and he has a good knowledge of the mountain regions;[7] Gudea, who will use the wood and stones for the construction of Ningirsu's temple; and unnamed lumberjacks working for Gudea. The objects are six types of wood in raft form, stone slabs, various types of bitumen, and gypsum. The localities include various foreign lands and the harbor of Girsu. The text is structured in two analogous passages, one concerned with the timber, the other with the minerals. Both passages begin with the difficult trip to the mountain lands, allude to the way the goods were transported, and account for their reception in Girsu. In addition, the first passage relates the felling of the cedars. Actions not mentioned but implied are: the felling of the trees other than cedar; the quarrying of the stones and extraction of other minerals; the building of rafts; and the transport of the materials. While the event is related in more detail than others, it could be indefinitely expanded to the point of making up a story by itself.[8] The narration is straightforward with only three circumstantial expansions: the mention of the Šarur weapon for the fashioning of which the cedar will be used; the image of the serpents to describe the rafts winding their way down the river, which elaborates on the transportation technique; and the image of boatloads of grain, which elaborates on the unusual quantity of the imported minerals. The actions take place in the real world, except for the trip to the mountains in which Ningirsu is the guide. Divine guidance legitimates the extraordinary enterprise.[9]

The stelae preserve the representation of a manned cedar raft moored in mountainous lands (ST.11+12), and that of the transport of a stone slab on a wheel-cart by two men in mountainous lands (ST.20). Unfortunately neither scene is complete, and the possibility cannot be excluded that other sub-events of the importation of materials were depicted in addition to these. Yet, in the little that is preserved, one can observe some discrepancies with the text. Several details in the scene with the raft indicate that the focus of that scene was in the mountain lands: the entire crew on the raft faces land; a larger figure stands on ground in front of the raft, and also faces land; the right end of the raft which is seen on water coincides with the right end of the scene. Even if the raft was ready to be set afloat downstream, the action represented is neither the difficult trip to the mountain lands under divine guidance, nor Gudea's reception of the timber in the harbor of Girsu. Similarly, the transport of the slab depicted was apparently that from the stone quarry to a river from which it could be shipped down to Girsu, a sub-event

---

[7] For Ningirsu's relation with the kur, see chapter III.C.1.b.

[8] Compare *Gilgameš and Huwawa*, edited by Edzard ZA 80–81 (1990–91), and *Sargon in Foreign Lands*, edited by Goodnick Westenhold *Legends of the Kings of Akkade*, 78–93.

[9] Another reason for Ningirsu's active role here might have been the effort to keep the Girsu-centric perspective of the events, see chapter III.C.2.b.

which is not specifically mentioned in the verbal narrative. That Ningirsu or Gudea appeared in the visual narrative is at least questionable. It seems rather that these scenes showed only human workmen performing the action. Whether other materials occurred is equally questionable. The stone slab is certainly the material most suitable for visual representation among the minerals mentioned in the text and may also have been chosen because the stelae were made of limestone which was transported in slabs just like the one seen on the cart.[10] The cedar is the most prominent of the woods in the text, since it is the one used for the fabrication of the Šarur. Moreover, the cedar logs and the stone slabs are the first entry in each group listed in the text.

Although the two fragments are of differing dimensions, one could conceive of a composite image in which a stone slab was transported to a raft for embarkation. That the raft served as a means of transport as well as a building material is not a problem, since such double use of logs is common practice.[11] If this scenario is correct, the two episodes, kept separately in the text, were coalesced into one image on the stelae. If it is complete, the visual account reduced each sub-event in the text to one material standing as *pars pro toto* for a group of materials of the same kind, timber and minerals, or perhaps for all importations.[12] As a result of the coalescence of two episodes, there is only one location, the river in the mountain lands. While the text names the types of timber and minerals, and specifies the foreign lands from which they were imported, the image depicts mountains and river in a generic way by the conventional scales and wavy lines. As for materials, the cedar raft is identified by a written label, since there is no other way to visually specify a particular type of logs, while the stone slab is differentiated by its shape and volume from other types of minerals such as clay, pebbles, bitumen and gypsum. In contrast to the circumstantial expansions in the text, which are metaphorical or foreshadow a future event, the imagery adds concrete elements: we learn that a raft was made of several logs bound together with ropes and was steered with an oar; or that stone slabs were transported on wheel-carts pulled by men with ropes.

The visualization of the event can be considered more concrete than its verbal counterpart. It shows actions performed by human workmen in mountain lands rather than relating Ningirsu's guiding the way to the mountains and Gudea's reception of the materials. It is also clear that the imagery does not include all the materials mentioned in the texts, but only some of them; and that it captures the event with sub-events not specifically mentioned in the text, but more suited to the identification of the episode on part of the viewer. The comparison shows that the image is not dependent on the text, but that both text and imagery relate the same event in their own way. This is substantiated by a second written account of the importation of building materials for the construction of Eninnu, related in the context of the equipment of the temple in Statue B.[13] This much more factual account lacks some of the materials mentioned in Cylinder A, adds others,

---

[10] While the fashioning of the stelae is separated from the importation of the stone slabs in Cylinder A 22:24–23:7, the two are immediately linked in Statue B 6:3–12.

[11] For example, in the river trade in Iraq at the beginning of this century, described by Musil *Middle Euphrates*, 2 and 53.

[12] The text passage discussed here is a sub-event among other importations, see chapter III.B.4 section 4.3. It stands out from the others by the analogous frame of its two parts, see III.D.2.d.

[13] See chapter III.E.2.d.

and differs in the order and grouping of the entities. It represents yet another version of the same event. The fact that cedar and limestone are both included and used for the fashioning of the Šarur and the stelae, respectively, confirms the importance given to these entities.

2. *Gudea's Divine Escorts*

An example which points to the difference of verbal and visual traditions concerns Gudea's divine escorts. In the Cylinder Inscriptions, Gudea is led by Ningišzida as well as Lugalkurdub and Igalim on his way to the construction site when he is about to make the bricks, and escorted by Lamma and Udug in his petition to invite Ningirsu into the new temple. The passages read as follows:

CA 18:13	^{d}lugal-kur-dúb igi-šè mu-na-gin	Lugalkurdub went in front of him,
CA 18:14	^{d}ig-alim-ke$_4$ gír mu-na-gá-gá	Igalim was guiding his step,
CA 18:15	^{d}nin-giš-zi-da dingir-a-ni	Ningišzida, his deity,
CA 18:16	šu mu-da-gál-gál	was holding him by his hand.
CB 2:9	ú-dug$_4$ sag$_9$-<ga>-ni igi-šè mu-na-gin	His good Udug went in front of him,
CB 2:10	^{d}lamma sag$_9$-ga-ni egir-ni im-ús	his good Lamma followed behind him.

On the stelae, Gudea is led by the hand by his personal god Ningišzida and sometimes followed by a Lamma in presentation scenes (ST.6 and 39 on Pl. A; ST.1 on Pl. B; ST.3 and 44 on Pl. C). The only complete scene depicted on his seal (Fig. 9) shows both. Once Ningišzida is preceded by Ningirsu's minister (ST.1), perhaps Šagan̄šegbar.[14]

The divine escorts appear in specific episodes in the text, but in a more generic and conceptual context – the culminating scene – in the imagery. Not only is the context different, but cylinders and stelae also vary in the identity and composition of the divine escorts. Lugalkurdub and Igalim, Ningirsu's war general and chief prosecutor,[15] respectively, were apparently not represented on the stelae. Nor is there evidence for the depiction of an Udug. Moreover, the visual account combines in one scene Ningišzida and Lamma, who occur in different episodes in the verbal account. These discrepancies can be explained with the different streams of tradition of the two media. In literary tradition, Lamma and Udug usually occur as a pair.[16] They embody protection, not unlike Judeo-Christian guardian angels. In fact, the Sumerian terms designate more a function than a particular deity, since individual deities as well as the Anunna can assume their role.[17] In the visual arts until the end of the Ur III period Lamma alone takes on the

---

[14] See chapter IV.B.7, p. 198.

[15] See chapter III.B. 8.2.1 and 3.

[16] *Lugalbanda I* 232f.; *Lugalbanda II* 330f.; *Inanna & Bilulu* 112, 116, 123, 127; *Nanše A* 176f.; *Nungal Hymn* 87; *Uruk Lament* 2.21'; *Urnammu A* 176f.; *Šulgi D* 221 and 337; *Lipit-Ištar C* 48; *Išme-Dagan A* 115, 149f., and *A1* 109. As a pair, they are also mentioned in the prayer to Gatumdug in Cylinder A 3:20f., in which Gudea asks the goddess to provide the divine escort for his trip to Ningin. The passage is formulated analogous to that in Cylinder B: "may your good Udug walk in front of me, may your good Lamma walk behind me." See also Foxvog et al. *RlA* 6 (1980–83), 447f. § 2.

[17] Foxvog et al. *RlA* 6 (1980–83), 447f. s.v. Lamma. In Cylinder B 2:1, Gudea addresses the Anunna as

role of divine protector,[18] and her appearance in narrative is confined to the presentation scene. She may intercede between a human petitioner and a seated deity, or simply stand behind her human protégé with both arms raised. The latter position and gesture, which becomes standard in the Ur III period, is attested for the first time under Gudea.[19] Lamma's relegation behind her protégé is obviously related to Gudea's introduction of his personal god Ningišzida as intermediary.

The visual account follows pictorial tradition in as far as Lamma occurs in presentation scenes and a(nother) deity leads the ruler by the hand, but it is customized concerning that deity. The verbal account follows literary tradition in regard to Lamma and Udug, but it is customized in regard to the deities that lead Gudea on his way for making the brick. Ningišzida's appearance in this episode is understandable. It coincides with this deity's role in the imagery. Note that in the statue inscriptions, Gudea follows behind Ningišzida in the delivery of Baba's bridewealth, and Ningišzida addresses the ensuing petition for blessings to the goddess on behalf of the ruler.[20] Both events can be imagined in the form of a presentation scene. Lugalkurdub and Igalim, on the other hand, do not occur as divine escorts elsewhere, and may be mentioned only to give this episode more importance.[21] Since Urnamma is preceded by a god in the construction scene on his stela (Fig. 33), the possibility cannot be entirely excluded that Gudea, too, may have appeared under divine guidance in a similar scene. ST.32 is a possible candidate. If so, he was not guided by the three gods mentioned in the text, but was led by Ningišzida and followed by Lamma, as in presentation scenes.

3. The Chariots

Chariots occur both in the verbal and in the visual account. In the Cylinder Inscriptions, Gudea twice presents Ningirsu with a chariot. One is bestowed in the course of the verification process to prompt Ningirsu for a communication (Appendix C no. 2), the other during the inauguration festivities as a gift and equipment for the new temple (Appendix C no. 7: CB 13:18–20). In the first event, the chariot's fabrication and consecration are described twice in detail: when Nanše instructs Gudea how to make it (CA 6:15–7:2) and when Gudea carries out the instruction (CA 7:9–29). From these passages we learn that the chariot was made of wood and adorned with silver and lapis lazuli; that it was equipped with donkeys, an emblem on which Ningirsu's name was written, and weapons including arrows, a quiver, and the ankar; and that it was brought to the temple accompanied by the (sound of) the drum called "Dragon of the Country." The chariot presented during the inauguration festivities is named "Subjugator of the Foreign Lands" (kur mu-gam), characterized as awe-inspiring, and is pulled by donkeys

---

Lamma of all lands.

[18] Udug may be represented in the "god with the mace," as Wiggermann *JEOL* 29 (1985–86), 23–27, suggested. This figure is popular on Old Babylonian seals, and not attested before the Isin-Larsa period.

[19] See chapter II.C.3.a.

[20] Statue G 2:1–16, and E 7:22–8:15; see chapters III.E.2.e-f.

[21] The accumulation of several deities leading a human figure recalls presentation scenes on Akkadian seals in which two or three are quite common, though the one closest to the seated deity can be – and sometimes clearly is – the minister of the seated deity; compare Boehmer *Glyptik*, figs. 350, 376, 445, 453, 455, 523, 537, 538, 539, 541, 572.

described as a roaring storm.[22] It occurs as the first item in a list of gifts followed by various weapons (CB 13:21–14:8). A second parallel passage enlists cult vessels (CB 14:9–18). The subsequent passage includes metaphorical descriptions of Ningirsu on the chariot (CB 16:7–16) and of the vessels in use (CB 17:4–11).

Four stela fragments represent parts of a similar chariot of the type of a straddle car (ST. 14, 27, 61, and 62). It is pulled by donkeys and equipped with arrows in a quiver attached to the back of the car. The casing is elaborately decorated with bison-men flanking its sides, a stylized palm in the center, and an Anzu clenching its claws into the back of a pair of lions on top. The elements of this decoration can be identified as trophies of Ningirsu; they are enumerated in Cylinder A when installed in the temple in the course of the construction. For reasons outlined above,[23] the chariots depicted on the stelae are best associated with the consecration of dedicatory gifts, not least because the verification process was visualized on the stelae only in a very allusive way, if at all.[24]

A comparison of the way the chariots are characterized in the two accounts reveals correspondences as well as discrepancies:

	verbal description	*visual description*
name	"Subjugator of the Foreign Lands"	—
material	mes and oak wood, lapis lazuli, silver	[colors]?
appearance	"brings fear, rides awesomely"	form of a straddle car
draught animals	donkeys: "panthers chosen for their speed"/ "a roaring storm"	two equids
emblem	with Ningirsu's name written on it	double-headed Anzu
accessories	arrows, quiver, ankar	arrows in quiver attached at back
decoration	–	bison-men, palm, pair of lions

Both media agree in general terms regarding the nature of the draught animals, the presence of an emblem, and certain weapons. The verbal account specifies the animal's species, and describes their nature in mythical terms, while the visual account specifies their number, and depicts them as equids. The emblem is not described in the text, which mentions only that it was inscribed with the god's name, while the image inevitably has to give it a shape, but lacks a written label, probably because the shape identifies the emblem as Ningirsu's. The weapons are the same, except that the text adds the ankar, and the image specifies where they were in relation to the chariot. Each media specifies additional features absent in the other: the text names the chariot and the materials it is made of, while the image depicts decoration not mentioned in the text. This decoration is based on mythical tradition (Ningirsu's trophies), which is documented in the text in another context (installation of Ningirsu's trophies in the temple). The verbal description

---

[22] The donkeys of the first chariot were described as pirig kas$_4$-e pà-da, "panthers chosen for their speed" (CA 7:20).

[23] Chapter IV.B.4, p. 188f.

[24] See chapter IV.B.6.

of the chariot's general appearance is abstract in nature, while the visual depiction is by necessity concrete.

If we ask about the source of inspiration for the two descriptions, it would seem that both draw on common mythical tradition as well as the visual experience of their makers, namely chariots of the gods that must have been seen in procession on certain religious festivals. The materials mentioned in the text, for instance, are concrete, while the decoration in the image is inspired by myth. The difference then is a question of degree: the text relies more on mythical tradition, the image more on concrete reality. This apparently reflects a choice made by the source of the messages, since the image could very well have represented, for example, the draught animals as mythical creatures, like on Akkadian seals depicting gods on chariots.

Although a comparison of the representation of the event in which the chariots occurred in the two media is somewhat hampered by the fragmentary preservation of the stelae, it can be argued that in this respect, too, the text is marked by literary elaboration, while the image reflects a less sophisticated and more concrete actuality. In addition to a chariot and weapons, the text mentions cult vessels, while the stelae depict a drum (ST.9 and 13 on Pls. A-B), perhaps a foundation deposit carried in the procession (ST.55 on Pl. A), and the display of a stela flanked by weapons (ST.60 on Pl. A). The gifts in the text accord with Ningirsu's self-portrait given as a response to Gudea's dream incubation. Chariot and weapons on the one hand, and cult vessels on the other, are required for Ningirsu to perform his functions in the divine world as the warrior of Enlil and the išib of An.[25] In contrast, the stelae apparently showed a more random assortment of dedicatory gifts, and may have coalesced in one scene the bringing to the temple and their installation there (Pl. A). Furthermore, the text accounts for the presentation of economic produce after the dedicatory gifts for which there is no pictorial parallel on the stelae.[26] Like for the importation of building materials, the authors of the stelae chose some items as *pars pro toto*, and in this case only some correspond to those mentioned in the text. Moreover, the text simply states that Gudea bestowed gifts upon the temple and enumerates them, while the stelae show anonymous men bringing the gifts. This is a typical instance in which Gudea is the agent in the text, whereas anonymous humans act in the imagery. One cannot exclude the possibility that Gudea was present in the scene, and was considered the initiator of the event. In either case, the image accords better with the actual event, while the text abstracts it, using the poetic devices of parallelism and enumeration. It is interesting to recall that in contrast to the second chariot episode, the first alluded to a procession and mentioned a drum.

---

[25] CA 9:20–10:13; see chapter III.B.9.1.
[26] Chapter III.B.9.3. Two anonymous door plaque fragments from Tello (Boese *Weihplatten*, T 20–21), however, depict what might have been part of a procession bringing economic products to the temple: one shows a man with a bull, the other a bull followed by a ram.

4. The Šarur

On the top register fragment ST.9, a huge mace is erected behind an attendant god who stood behind the throne of a seated deity (Pl. A). The mace can thus be located in the temple as a requisite characterizing the warrior aspect of the deity residing in it. Given its size and prominent position in the top register, it must have been a significant object. It is tempting to identify it with Ningirsu's weapon Šarur which is given a certain importance in the Cylinder Inscriptions.[27] Šarur is first mentioned in Ningirsu's speech, prompted by Gudea's dream incubation, in which the patron of Eninnu provides the temple builder with detailed information for his project:

CA 09:20 gá ᵈnin-gír-su a huš gi₄-a	I am Ningirsu who stops the fierce waters,[28]
CA 09:21 ur-sag gal ki-ᵈen-líl-ká-ka	the great warrior of Enlil's realm,
CA 09:22 en gaba-ri nu-tuku	the lord without adversary.
CA 09:23 é-mu é-50 gá en kur-ra ab-diri-a	My house is Eninnu. I am the lord who prevails over any foreign land.
CA 09:24 tukul-mu šár-ùr kur šu-šè gar-gar	My weapon, Šarur, controls any foreign land.
CA 09:25 igi huš-a-mu kur-re nu-um-íl	My fierce glare no foreign land can bear.
CA 09:26 da-úš-a-mu lú la-ba-ta-è	My sling no man can escape.
CA 10:1 a-ugu₄-mu nam-gal-ki-ág-da	My own father, in great love, named me:
CA 10:2 lugal a-ma-ru ᵈen-líl-lá	"king, deluge of Enlil,
CA 10:3 igi huš-a-ni kur-da nu-íl	whose fierce glare no foreign land can bear,
CA 10:4 ᵈnin-gír-su ur-sag ᵈen-líl-lá	Ningirsu, warrior of Enlil."
CA 10:5 mu-šè mu-sa₄	

The Šarur is listed here as one of the essential paraphernalia of Ningirsu. Next, it is mentioned in the passage discussed above in connection with the importation of cedar for its fabrication. Then we learn about its installation in the account of the construction:

CA 22:20 ᵍⁱˢšár-ùr-bi urì-gal-gin₇ lagaš^{ki}-da im-da-si	He installed its Šarur like a big pole in Lagaš,
CA 22:21 šu-ga-lam ki huš-ba im-mi-ni-gar	set it up in Šugalam's awesome place.
CA 22:22 su-zi bí-du₈-du₈ bára-gír-nun-na ki di-ku₅-ba	It was causing terror. On the dais of Girnun, the place of judgment,
CA 22:23 ú-a lagaš^{ki} gu₄ gal-gin₇ á ba-íl-íl	the caretaker of Lagaš was raising the horns like a great bull.

The last two events are also recorded in Statue B 5:37–38, and the last alone in the name given to the sixth regnal year of Gudea,[29] though in less poetic style. Finally, Šarur is mentioned in the speech of Ningirsu during the inauguration banquet, where it is described as follows:[30]

---

[27] That Šarur might have been a huge mace was proposed already by Edzard *CRRA* 20 (1975), 160.

[28] This epithet is understood as an allusion to the dam which Ningirsu/Ninurta built in the mountains according to *Lugal* 349–361, see also ibidem 705.

[29] RTC 201: mu ᵍⁱˢšár-ùr-ra ba-dù-a.

[30] The passage is restored from fragment 2 ii, see chapter III.B.10.4.

CB 22:3′ é ^dnin-gír-su gù di-dè im-ma-gub	Ningirsu stood there to call upon the house:
CB 22:4′ dim an-né mu-dù-a-bi	"The pillar which is erected by An,
CB 22:5′ urì-gal lagaš^{ki}-da si-ga-bi	the pole which is installed in Lagaš,
CB 22:6′ ^{giš}šár-ùr-bi me[n] kù-gin₇ sig₄- [é]-ke₄ sag [an-šè íl]	its Šarur which ov[erlooks] the [house's] brick(work) like a pure crown, ...

Šarur is Ningirsu/Ninurta's main weapon not only in Gudea's Cylinder Inscriptions, but also in other compositions. In the enumeration of Ninurta's weapons in *Angim* 129–130, it is the first item of the list, and in *Lugal* it is personified and plays a major role as servant and companion of its master.[31] The intimate relationship of the hero with his weapon recalls the medieval epics in which Excalibur, the sword of King Arthur, and Durandel, the sword of Roland, play similar roles.

The different treatment of Šarur in text and imagery exemplifies the wealth of detail and poetic elaboration of secondary events developed throughout the text versus the concrete, and at the same time much more allusive, nature of the imagery. The text relates the fashioning and installation of Šarur, and the surrounding circumstances, and at the same time invokes its mythological dimensions. The imagery depicts the weapon as a requisite in the temple which helps identifying the deity residing there. Although the visual representation could have evoked the information provided in the text for anyone familiar with it, it does not make it explicit.

5. *The Palm Frond*

As a last particular, I will explore a pictorial detail which has no obvious counterpart in texts and exemplifies the difficulties that impose themselves for the modern scholar when interpreting certain attributes in images despite their concrete nature. On three fragments Gudea carries a palm frond in his right hand. Two of them (ST.1 and 3) are parts of presentation scenes, while the third (ST.42) was part of another scene which cannot be identified, but was not a presentation scene. Since the palm frond does not occur in all presentation scenes, and is once attested in another scene, it is more likely a descriptive attribute of its carrier than an object essential for a particular event. Heuzey's identification of it as a symbol of victory, based on the mutilation of Gudea's face on the two fragments known to him (ST.1 and 42) which he associated with the revenche of the Elamites in retaliation for Gudea's campaign against them,[32] is not convincing. To my knowledge, no other figure in early Mesopotamian art carries a comparable attribute.[33]

Date palms are mentioned in different contexts in written sources. They usually refer to an entire tree, rather than one branch. The date palm that was Ningirsu's trophy, for instance, can be excluded as a candidate, not only because it is inconceivable that Gudea carries a divine trophy, but also because this trophy is represented as a whole tree on the chariots. The statement uttered by the Date Palm in the Debate between Tamarisk

---

[31] See Cooper's comments in *Return of Ninurta*, 122f. Šarur occurs in Cylinder B as an epithet of the war generals of Ningirsu: Lugalkurdub is called "Šarur of battle subjugating the Mountain" (CB 7:19), and the second general "Šarur, deluge of battle" (CB 8:2).
[32] NFT 293.
[33] So already Barrelet *CRRA* 19 (1974), 56.

and Date Palm:[34] "where I am not present, the king does not libate," obviously refers to the plant onto which libations are poured, as depicted on the stelae of Gudea and Urnamma and in many other images.[35] The artificial date palms that decorated temples must be imagined as whole trees as well. A cedar pole encased in bronze, and embossed with a scale-like design reminiscent of a palm tree was found near a doorway of the Neo-Assyrian temple of Sin at Khorsabad.[36] This kind of decoration goes back to earlier times, as evidenced in the second year of Gungunum:[37] "year in which he (the king) brought two copper date palms to the temple of Utu," and apparently in two clay tags attributable to UruKAgina of Lagaš which mention "a date palm on the right side" brought or planted (mu-DU) by the king.[38]

None of the above references elucidates the meaning of the palm frond in Gudea's hand. As a last possibility, one could consider the term gidru, usually translated "scepter." This term designates a royal insignium frequently mentioned in texts which seems to be conspicuously absent in the visual images of rulers.[39] It occurs in the description of the functions of Igalim in Cylinder B 6:16: "to place a long lasting scepter into the (ruler's) hand." Gidru, written ^{giš}PA, can be derived from giš + duru₅ "fresh/green branch," since the sign name of PA is gešṭuru. A direct correlation between scepter and branches is made in Šulgi D:

391: gidri-zu nì-nam-nun-na hé-em   May your scepter be everything pertaining to princeship,
392: pa-mul-bi an-dùl-le-éš hu-mu-ù-ak   May its exuberant branches be like a canopy.

Based on the above evidence, it is tempting to identify the palm frond with the royal insignium usually translated "scepter." It is interesting that the canonical list *Lu* I 34 uses "palm tree" as a metaphoric term for king.[40] This example shows that attributes in images such as the palm frond cannot speak to someone unfamiliar with the mental background of the culture which created them. Their explication cannot be sought in verbal descriptions of royal images only or the verbal counterpart of the scene in which they occur, but must appeal to a much wider range of resources.

---

[34] According to the Old Babylonian version, see Lambert BWL 156:9 and 160:2. The Emar version is phrased slightly different, see Wilcke ZA 79 (1989), 175:38'.
[35] See chapter IV.B.6.
[36] Place *Ninive* I, 120–122; III pl. 73; Loud *Khorsabad* I, 97ff.
[37] mu 2 ^{giš}nimbar^{urudu} é ^dutu-šè i-ni-in-k[u₄-ra]. Thureau-Dangin RA 15 (1918), 52 i 6, and Ungnad RlA 2 (1938), 150 and 155 s.v. Datenlisten. A copper date palm is mentioned also in Hh XI 415, see MSL 7 146.
[38] UruKAgina 36–37, see Steible *Altsumerische Bau- und Weihinschriften*, 175f.
[39] So Krecher RlA 5 (1976–80), 113 s.v. Insignien. For textual references to the royal insignium gidru, see also Wiggermann JEOL 29 (1985–86), 13 note 41.
[40] MSL 12 94.

D. The Relation between Text and Image

The same core message – the ruler built a temple for his god – is conveyed in words in Gudea's cylinders and in images on his stelae. In a limited scale it is commemorated also in his building inscriptions on various elements of the construction, such as bricks, clay nails, etc., and in most statue inscriptions, while some foundation figurines and statues actually represent the ruler as temple builder, and the culminating scene on door plaques alluded to a temple construction. In contrast to the brief building inscriptions, the Cylinder Inscriptions recount the event in detail. They delineate not only the main event in its constituents, but also expand on the initial circumstances and final results. Compared with this detailed verbal account, the imagery on the stelae, though much more narrative than the culminating scene on door plaques or the temple builder icons, consists of relatively few scenes which represent or evoke selected episodes of the story.

Despite their fragmentary condition, it is possible to deduce which events were visualized on the stelae and which were not, based in part on the repetition of scene elements, and in part on the comparison with the known iconography concerning temple construction. The visualized events include the parade of the work-force; the provision of building materials; the surveying of the construction site; construction work; the furnishing of the temple with dedicatory gifts; and musical performances, probably as a *pars pro toto* for the inauguration banquet. In addition, libation scenes may have alluded to the verification of the commission, and presentation scenes to the final and culminating event, the divine blessing of the ruler. Compared with the verbal account in the Cylinder Inscriptions, the entire verification process (sections 2-3) is condensed in one scene; the construction preparations (section 4) in three scenes; the construction itself (section 5) in one scene, perhaps with sub-scenes; the presentation of gifts in one scene (section 9), and the banquet (section 10) in two. The transmission of the divine commission (section 1), the inauguration preparations (section 6), and the induction of the deities (section 7-8) are not visualized.

This comparison shows that the visual account avoids events that do not occur in the "real" world, except for the presentation scene which was inspired by real life ritual, yet establishes a connection with the divine sphere. Hence, the text includes the entire Sumerian pantheon, while the imagery involves but a small number of local deities. To some degree the choice of episodes in the imagery is comparable to the choice of events that are detailed in the construction account of some statue inscriptions. Like the imagery on the stelae, these more factual verbal accounts elaborate on the construction preparations and on the equipment of the temple, and involve only a small number of local deities. In addition to the different degree of detail and the different emphasis of events, the verbal and visual accounts have a different hierarchy of events. The text focuses on the action of the construction, the imagery on the completion of the story. Some variations in the representation of certain events also point to a different agenda. Some dedicatory gifts, for example, occur in both text and imagery, while others occur only in one or the other media. Not only are certain details preferred over others, but some can be completely eliminated. There is, for example, a gate lion on a stela fragment, while the text does not mention gate lions, although it recounts the construction in much more detail than the imagery.

The verbal and visual media have their own traditions in telling what is, in essence, the same story. Neither is dependent on the other. Rather than a linear dependency of the type: *event → verbal account → visual account* or: *event → visual account → verbal account*, the relationship just described must be conceived as a tree-like structure:

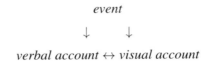

event

↓   ↓

verbal account ↔ visual account

The differences in the accounts of the two media are rooted in the differences of the senses that perceive them and on the different audiences they try to reach, and are conditioned by the different traditional "rhetoric" of text and image. Generally speaking, the imagery is less specific in terms of the identity of event participants and locations, while the text is less specific in terms of their physical appearances. The imagery is more concrete in the sense that the representation is fairly close to the real events, while the text makes abundant use of metaphors, contains many mythological allusions, and involves the divine world to a much higher degree than the imagery. Both surround the core message with an underlying message about the ruler's rank and status in Sumerian society. It is their strategies toward that end that differ: the text centers on the action of the temple construction, while the imagery operates with a few select episodes and a climax in view. The core of the text conveys that Gudea built Eninnu for Ningirsu, and the culminating scene recapitulates the primary ideological message: the concern for and the authority to construct temples is a royal prerogative, and it is divinely sanctioned.[41]

---

[41] Michalowski "Early Mesopotamian Communicative Systems," 62, in regard to the Hammurabi Law Code.

APPENDIX A

Catalogue of the Minor Sources

This catalogue includes the presently known artifacts attributable to Gudea on the basis of their inscriptions, except for the cylinders and stelae. Attribution to Gudea is understood in the sense that he can be identified as the agent in the text. Objects dedicated, some for Gudea's life, by his wives or other individuals of his court[1] and uninscribed objects associated with this ruler on uncertain grounds[2] are not included. Steible's assignment of fragmentary inscriptions, in which Gudea's name is not or only partly preserved, are included and accepted unless stated otherwise.[3] Objects commissioned by Gudea, especially clay nails, have found their way into innumerable museums and private collections all over the world, and continue to be published.[4] In view of their repetitiousness, new discoveries are not likely to add significant new information. The catalogue is arranged by object categories, for which the following sigla are used in this order:

CN = clay nail
BS = brick stone
DS = door socket
DT = stair step
FT = foundation tablet
FG = foundation figurine representing a kneeling god
FK = foundation figurine representing a basket carrier
FB = foundation figurine representing a bull
GL = gate lion
DP = door plaque
SO = pedestal or stand
SV = stone vessel
MH = mace head
CS = cylinder seal
UI = unidentified object

---

[1] Gudea 1–3, 16, 21f., 41, 71, 81, 84f., 90, Statue R.
[2] Scholars who, like Parrot *Tello*, 147–207, attributed uninscribed objects to Gudea usually did not explain their reasoning for doing so. Their attribution seems to be based merely on the fact that this ruler left a wealth of inscribed objects compared with other Lagaš II rulers, and is thus a more likely candidate. The corpus of artifacts of other Lagaš II rulers is not substantial enough for drawing clear distinctions. An exception has been made only for some foundation figurines with unpublished or illegible inscriptions (FG.29–31 and FK.1–5) which can be assigned to Gudea based on their shape, see chapter II.C.2.b–c.
[3] The foundation figurine AO 311 listed under Gudea 51G is excluded, because it bears Urbaba's inscription, see DC 241 pl. 8bis:1; Parrot *Tello*, 144 fig. 44b; Rashid *Gründungsfiguren*, no. 80. Moreover, it is bigger than the Gudea pieces and of a higher quality in modeling.
[4] The Oriental Institute of the University of Chicago, for example, houses one hundred and thirty-two unpublished clay nails attributed to Gudea as well as a door socket and a foundation tablet, all purchased, which Miguel Civil brought to my attention. The door socket and foundation tablet are catalogued under DS.20 and FT.41.

For the statues, interposed between mace heads and cylinder seal, the traditional designation by letters has been maintained. To avoid a cumbersome and repetitious enumeration of thousands of clay nails and hundreds of bricks, these two categories are given one entry per text and category. In other words, all clay nails with the same inscription received one entry, the bricks with that same text another. All remaining artifacts are catalogued individually. The catalogue contains the following information:

- museum number, or excavation number in parentheses if the former is unknown, for individually catalogued objects.
- provenance, designating the place where the object was found or is said to come from,[5] followed by the quantity of objects in parentheses for those not individually catalogued.
- brief description for sculpted objects.
- name of divine beneficiary and of construction recorded in the inscription.
- bibliographical reference to:
  - the excavation report(s), or the first publication of the object if not legally excavated, for individually catalogued objects.
  - the catalogue in Rashid *Gründungsfiguren* for foundation figurines.
  - the edition of the inscribed text in Steible *Neusumerische Bau- und Weihinschriften*.
  - the catalogue in Braun-Holzinger *Weihgaben* for dedicatory objects.
  - more recent publications.[6]
- cross-reference to the chapter(s) in which the object is discussed.

Clay Nails

CN.1
Provenance unknown (2).
Baba: bàd-uru-kù-ga.
  Steible *Neusumerische Bau- und Weihinschriften*, Gudea 5.
Chapter I.B.2 no. 4.

CN.2
Tello (20); al-Hiba (1); Provenance unknown (6).
Baba: é-uru-kù-ga.
  Steible *Neusumerische Bau- und Weihinschriften*, Gudea 7D-L.
Chapter I.B.2 no. 4.

CN.3
Tello (12); Uruk (1); Ur (1); Provenance unknown (21).
Dumuziabzu: é-gír-su^ki.
  Steible *Neusumerische Bau- und Weihinschriften*, Gudea 10.
  Cavigneau *UVB* 31–32 (1973–74), 55 no. W23651.
Chapter I.B.2 no. 9.

---

5 For the problems concerning the provenance of the Gudea material see chapter II.A.2.
6 RIME 3/1 appeared after this catalogue was completed, and is not referenced here.

CN.4
Ur (1).
Enki: é-gú-^{id}idigna.
>Steible *Neusumerische Bau- und Weihinschriften*, Gudea 11.
Chapter I.B.2 no. 21.

CN.5
Tello (28); Provenance unknown (13).
Gatumdug: é-uru-kù-ga.
>Steible *Neusumerische Bau- und Weihinschriften*, Gudea 15D-L.
Chapter I.B.2 no. 7.

CN.6
Tello (23); Provenance unknown (13).
Igalim: é-me-huš-gal-an-ki.
>Steible *Neusumerische Bau- und Weihinschriften*, Gudea 19E-L.
Chapter I.B.2 no. 5.

CN.7
Tello (3); Provenance unknown (6).
Inanna: é-an-na-gír-su^{ki}.
>Steible *Neusumerische Bau- und Weihinschriften*, Gudea 24C-D.
Chapter I.B.2 no. 8.

CN.8
Tello (7).
Inanna: é-an-na-gír-su^{ki}.
>Steible *Neusumerische Bau- und Weihinschriften*, Gudea 25.
Chapter I.B.2 no. 8.

CN.9
Tello (2).
Inanna: é-gír-su^{ki}.
>Steible *Neusumerische Bau- und Weihinschriften*, Gudea 26.
Chapter I.B.2 no. 8.

CN.10
Tello (19); Provenance unknown (12).
Meslamtaea: é-gír-su^{ki}.
>Steible *Neusumerische Bau- und Weihinschriften*, Gudea 28B-G.
Chapter I.B.2 no. 11.

CN.11
Tello (2); al-Hiba (2); Zurghul (22); Umm Chatil (1); Uruk (1); Ur (2); Provenance unknown (7).
Nanše: é-sirara$_6$.

Steible *Neusumerische Bau- und Weihinschriften*, Gudea 29G-O.[7]
Cavigneau *UVB* 31–32 (1973–74), 56 no. W23724.[8]
Chapters I.B.2 no. 18; II.A.2.b.

CN.12

Provenance unknown (1).
Nanše: é.
Steible *Neusumerische Bau- und Weihinschriften*, Gudea 32.
Chapter I.B.2 no. 18.

CN.13

Ur (2); Provenance unknown: purchased in Tell Jidr (1).
Nanše: é-an-gur$_{22}$-zú-lum^{ki}.
Steible *Neusumerische Bau- und Weihinschriften*, Gudea 33.
Chapter I.B.2 no. 22.

CN.14

Tello (69); Uruk (2); Larsa (1); Provenance unknown (79).
Nindara: é-gír-su^{ki}.
Steible *Neusumerische Bau- und Weihinschriften*, Gudea 36E-W and 38.[9]
Arnaud *Syria* 48 (1971), 293 no. L.7013.[10]
Snell *Stovall Museum*, 5 nos. 1–2.
Chapter I.B.2 no. 13.

CN.15

Zurghul (1); Uruk (3); Provenance unknown (1).
Nindub: é.
Steible *Neusumerische Bau- und Weihinschriften*, Gudea 39A-E.[11]
Chapters I.B.2 no. 20; II.A.2.b.

CN.16

Tello (39); Provenance unknown (24).
Ningirsu: é-PA.
Steible *Neusumerische Bau- und Weihinschriften*, Gudea 46B-J.
Chapter I.B.2 no. 2.

CN.17

Tello (1033); al-Hiba (1); Medain (1); Provenance unknown (102).
Ningirsu: é-50.

---

[7] Gudea 29I is not from Tello, but from al-Hiba.
[8] Whether this text is a duplicate of Gudea 29 or 30 cannot be determined.
[9] The text Gudea 38 duplicates Gudea 36.
[10] The inscription on this unpublished clay nail, identified as I Rawl. pl. 5 no. 23 by Arnaud, could be either Gudea 38 or 39, since I Rawl. pl. 5 no. 23 is a joint copy of two different British Museum texts; see Steible *Neusumerische Bau- und Weihinschriften*, Gudea 38A.
[11] Gudea 39B is Biggs *BiMes* 3 no. 63, one clay nail, not the 12 exemplars mentioned ibidem p. 12 which Steible listed twice: once correctly under Gudea 29K, another time under 39B.

Steible *Neusumerische Bau- und Weihinschriften*, Gudea 48S-ZZ, bb-cc.[12]
Black *ASJ* 17 (1995), 319 no. 1.
Snell *Stovall Museum*, 5f. nos. 3–4.
Chapter I.B.2 no. 1.

CN.18
Provenance unknown (1).
Ningirsu: é-50.
Steible *Neusumerische Bau- und Weihinschriften*, Gudea 49a.
Chapter I.B.2 no. 1.

CN.19
Provenance unknown (2).
Ningirsu: é-50.
Steible *Neusumerische Bau- und Weihinschriften*, Gudea 50.
Chapter I.B.2 no. 1.

CN.20
Tello (277); Zurghul (1); Provenance unknown (37).
Ningirsu: é-50.
Steible *Neusumerische Bau- und Weihinschriften*, Gudea 51M-T, X.[13]
Chapter I.B.2 no. 1.

CN.21
Ur (1).
Ningirsu: é-50.
Steible *Neusumerische Bau- und Weihinschriften*, Gudea 52G.
Chapter I.B.2 no. 1.

CN.22
Tello (13); al-Hiba (1).
Ningirsu: abul-ká-sur-ra.
Steible *Neusumerische Bau- und Weihinschriften*, Gudea 56A-E.
Chapter I.B.2 no. 3.

CN.23
Tello (2); Provenance unknown (26).
Ningišzida: é-gír-su^ki.
Steible *Neusumerische Bau- und Weihinschriften*, Gudea 64C-E.
Chapter I.B.2 no. 14.

CN.24
Tello (17); Provenance unknown (68).
Ningišzida: é-gír-su^ki.

---

[12] Gudea 48Z: VA 3062 is from al-Hiba, not from Zurghul.
[13] Gudea 51R: VA 3060 is from Zurghul, not from al-Hiba.

Steible *Neusumerische Bau- und Weihinschriften*, Gudea 67B-M, O.
Snell *Stovall Museum*, 6 no. 5.
Chapter I.B.2 no. 14.

CN.25
Tello (2).
Ninhursag: é.
    Steible *Neusumerische Bau- und Weihinschriften*, Gudea 69.
Chapter I.B.2 no. 15.

CN.26
Tello (5); Provenance unknown (2).
Ninhursag: é-gír-su^{ki}.
    Steible *Neusumerische Bau- und Weihinschriften*, Gudea 70.
Chapter I.B.2 no. 15.

CN.27
Provenance unknown (1).
NinmarKI: bàd-gú-ab-ba-TÙR^{ki}/é.
    Steible *Neusumerische Bau- und Weihinschriften*, Gudea 72.
Chapter I.B.2 no. 24.

CN.28
Tello (6).
Ninšubur: é.
    Steible *Neusumerische Bau- und Weihinschriften*, Gudea 74.
Chapter I.B.2 no. 16.

CN.29
Tello (12); Provenance unknown (12).
Šulšaga: é-ki-tuš-akkil-lí.
    Steible *Neusumerische Bau- und Weihinschriften*, Gudea 75D-H.
Chapter I.B.2 no. 6.

CN.30
Provenance unknown (1).
Ninazu: é-gír-su^{ki}.
    Steible *Neusumerische Bau- und Weihinschriften*, Gudea 92.
Chapters I.B.2 no. 12; II.B.2.a § 1.c note 38.

CN.31
Uruk (1).
[...]: é-[...].
    Steible *Neusumerische Bau- und Weihinschriften*, Gudea 99.
Excluded from discussion because attribution to Gudea is uncertain.

Brick Stones

BS.1
Tello (3); Tell Jidr (1); Provenance unknown (1).
Baba: é-uru-kù-ga.
   Steible *Neusumerische Bau- und Weihinschriften*, Gudea 7A-C.
Chapter I.B.2 no. 4.

BS.2
Provenance unknown (3).
Baba: é-uru-kù-ga.
   Steible *Neusumerische Bau- und Weihinschriften*, Gudea 8.
Chapter I.B.2 no. 4.

BS.3
Tello (1); al-Hiba (3); Provenance unknown (1).
Gatumdug: é-uru-kù-ga.
   Steible *Neusumerische Bau- und Weihinschriften*, Gudea 15A-C.
Chapter I.B.2 no. 7.

BS.4
Tello (1).
Gatumdug: é-uru-kù-ga.
   Steible *Neusumerische Bau- und Weihinschriften*, Gudea 15a.
Chapter I.B.2 no. 7.

BS.5
Tello (2).
Inanna: é-gír-su^{ki}.
   Steible *Neusumerische Bau- und Weihinschriften*, Gudea 23, 24E.[14]
Chapter I.B.2 no. 8.

BS.6
Tello (1).
Meslamtaea: é-gír-su^{ki}.
   Steible *Neusumerische Bau- und Weihinschriften*, Gudea 28A.
Chapter I.B.2 no. 11.

BS.7
Tello (4); Zurghul (4); Larsa (1); Provenance unknown (3).
Nanše: é-sirara$_6$.
   Steible *Neusumerische Bau- und Weihinschriften*, Gudea 29A-F, 30A, 39F.[15]
   Arnaud *Syria* 48 (1971), 293 no. L.7088.
Chapters I.B.2 no. 18; II.A.2.b.

---

[14] I take Gudea 24E as identical with 23B, see Steible ibidem.
[15] Gudea 30A is identical with Gudea 29A (See BS.7); Gudea 39F is identical with Gudea 29E.

BS.8
Provenance unknown (1).
Nanše: é-sirara$_6$.
  Steible *Neusumerische Bau- und Weihinschriften*, Gudea 30B.[16]
Chapter I.B.2 no. 18.

BS.9
Tello (4); Provenance unknown (3).
Nindara: é-gír-su^{ki}.
  Steible *Neusumerische Bau- und Weihinschriften*, Gudea 36A-D.
Chapter I.B.2 no. 13.

BS.10
Tello (1).
Ningirsu: é-PA.
  Steible *Neusumerische Bau- und Weihinschriften*, Gudea 45.
Chapter I.B.2 no. 2.

BS.11
Tello (2).
Ningirsu: é-PA.
  Steible *Neusumerische Bau- und Weihinschriften*, Gudea 46A.
Chapter I.B.2 no. 2.

BS.12
Tello (13+); Provenance unknown (3).
Ningirsu: é-ánzu^{mušen}-bábbar/a-ga-eren.
  Steible *Neusumerische Bau- und Weihinschriften*, Gudea 47.
Chapters I.B.2 no. 1; II.A.2.a; III.A.1 note 5.

BS.13
Tello (73); Tell Jidr (1); Provenance unknown (12).
Ningirsu: é-50.
  Steible *Neusumerische Bau- und Weihinschriften*, Gudea 48A-O, ff.
  Black *ASJ* 17 (1995), 320 nos. 2–3.
Chapter I.B.2 no. 1.

BS.14
Tello (1).
Ningirsu: é-50.
  Steible *Neusumerische Bau- und Weihinschriften*, Gudea 49.[17]
Chapter I.B.2 no. 1.

---

[16] Gudea 30B is not from Girsu, but of unknown provenance.
[17] Gudea 49B is excluded here because its attribution to Gudea is uncertain, compare Nammahni 8 1:6–2:2.

BS.15

Tello (2); Provenance unknown (6).
Ningirsu: é-50.
    Steible *Neusumerische Bau- und Weihinschriften*, Gudea 52A-E.
Chapter I.B.2 no. 1.

BS.16

Tello (7); Provenance unknown (1).
Ningirsu: é-50.
    Steible *Neusumerische Bau- und Weihinschriften*, Gudea 53.
Chapter I.B.2 no. 1.

BS.17

al-Hiba (32); Provenance unknown (1).
Ningirsu: é-ba-gára.
    Steible *Neusumerische Bau- und Weihinschriften*, Gudea 58.
Chapters I.B.2 no. 17; II.A.2.b.

BS.18

Tello (2).
Ningišzida: é-gír-su^ki.
    Steible *Neusumerische Bau- und Weihinschriften*, Gudea 64A-B.
Chapter I.B.2 no. 14.

BS.19

Tello (4).
Ningišzida: é-gír-su^ki.
    Steible *Neusumerische Bau- und Weihinschriften*, Gudea 67A.
Chapter I.B.2 no. 14.

BS.20

Provenance unknown (1).
Ningišzida: é-gír-su^ki.
    Steible *Neusumerische Bau- und Weihinschriften*, Gudea 68A.
Chapter I.B.2 no. 14.

BS.21

Tello (3).
(é-50-^dnin-gír-su-ka).[18]
    Steible *Neusumerische Bau- und Weihinschriften*, Gudea 76.
Chapter II.B.1 note 36.

---

[18] This is a label inscription in which Gudea is specified as the builder of the temple named in parentheses.

BS.22
Tello (1).
Inanna: é.
    Steible *Neusumerische Bau- und Weihinschriften*, Gudea 91.
Chapter I.B.2 no. 8.

Door Sockets

DS.1: BM 90849.
Tello (?).[19]
Nanše: é-sirara$_6$.
    CT 21 pl. 38; King *History*, pl. XXVII.
    Steible *Neusumerische Bau- und Weihinschriften*, Gudea 31.
Chapter I.B.2 no. 18.

DS.2: BM 105108.
Provenance unknown.
Ningirsu: é-PA.
    Anonymous *British Museum Guide* (1922), 59 no. 22.
    Steible *Neusumerische Bau- und Weihinschriften*, Gudea 46K.
Chapter I.B.2 no. 2.

DS.3: AO 103.
Tello: Tell A.
Ningirsu: é-50.
    Parrot *Tello*, 201.
    Steible *Neusumerische Bau- und Weihinschriften*, Gudea 48aa.
Chapters I.B.2 no. 1; II.A.2.a.

DS.4: AO 104.
Tello: Tell A, gate M.
Ningirsu: é-50.
Parrot *Tello*, 201.
    Steible *Neusumerische Bau- und Weihinschriften*, Gudea 48aa.
Chapters I.B.2 no. 1; II.A.2.a.

DS.5: AO 110.
Tello: Tell A, entrance of palace.
Ningirsu: é-50.
Parrot *Tello*, 201.
    Steible *Neusumerische Bau- und Weihinschriften*, Gudea 48aa.
Chapters I.B.2 no. 1; II.A.2.a.

---

[19] As noted by Sollberger *Syria* 52 (1975), 76 note 10, King's provenance of this door socket as Tello (CT 21 p. 8) is not trustworthy.

DS.6: AO 112.
Tello.
Ningirsu: é-50.
Parrot *Tello*, 201.
  Steible *Neusumerische Bau- und Weihinschriften*, Gudea 48aa.
Chapter I.B.2 no. 1.

DS.7: AO 116.
Tello.
Ningirsu: é-50.
Parrot *Tello*, 201.
  Steible *Neusumerische Bau- und Weihinschriften*, Gudea 48aa.
Chapter I.B.2 no. 1.

DS.8: AO 109.
Tello: Tell J.
Ningirsu: é-50.
  DC 67 pl. 27:3; Parrot *Tello*, 201.
  Steible *Neusumerische Bau- und Weihinschriften*, Gudea 51U.
Chapters I.B.2 no. 1; II.A.2.a.

DS.9: AO 105.
Tello: Tell G.
Ningirsu: é-50.
  Parrot *Tello*, 201.
  Steible *Neusumerische Bau- und Weihinschriften*, Gudea 51V.
Chapters I.B.2 no. 1; II.A.2.a.

DS.10: AO 106.
Tello: Tell A.
Ningirsu: é-50.
  Parrot *Tello*, 201.
  Steible *Neusumerische Bau- und Weihinschriften*, Gudea 51V.
Chapters I.B.2 no. 1; II.A.2.a.

DS.11: AO 107.
Tello: Tell A, courtyard A.
Ningirsu: é-50.
  Parrot *Tello*, 201.
  Steible *Neusumerische Bau- und Weihinschriften*, Gudea 51V.
Chapters I.B.2 no. 1; II.A.2.a.

DS.12: AO 108.
Tello.
Ningirsu: é-50.
  Parrot *Tello*, 201.

Steible *Neusumerische Bau- und Weihinschriften*, Gudea 51V.
Chapter I.B.2 no. 1.

DS.13: AO 111.
Tello.
Ningirsu: é-50.
   Parrot *Tello*, 201.
   Steible *Neusumerische Bau- und Weihinschriften*, Gudea 51V.
Chapter I.B.2 no. 1.

DS.14: AO 114.
Tello.
Ningirsu: é-50.
   Parrot *Tello*, 201.
   Steible *Neusumerische Bau- und Weihinschriften*, Gudea 51V.
Chapter I.B.2 no. 1.

DS.15: AO 115.
Tello.
Ningirsu: é-50.
   Parrot *Tello*, 201.
   Steible *Neusumerische Bau- und Weihinschriften*, Gudea 51V.
Chapter I.B.2 no. 1.

DS.16: BM 90831.
Tello.
Ningirsu: é-50.
   CT 21 pl. 39 (copy of inscription).
   Steible *Neusumerische Bau- und Weihinschriften*, Gudea 51W.
Chapter I.B.2 no. 1.

DS.17: IM (4H7).
al-Hiba: 4H-T2.
Ningirsu: é-ba-gára.
   Crawford *JCS* 29 (1977), 200–202 (with photo).
   Steible *Neusumerische Bau- und Weihinschriften*, Gudea 61A.
Chapters I.B.2 no. 17; II.A.2.b; B.2.d § 4b.

DS.18: IM (4H17).
al-Hiba: 4H-T6.
Ningirsu: é-ba-gára.
   Crawford *JCS* 29 (1977), 203.
   Steible *Neusumerische Bau- und Weihinschriften*, Gudea 61B-C.[20]
Chapters I.B.2 no. 17; II.A.2.b; B.2.d § 4b.

---

[20] Gudea 61C is identical with Gudea 61A or B.

DS.19: AO 113.
Tello.
Ningišzida: é-gír-su^{ki}.
    Parrot *Tello*, 201.
    Steible *Neusumerische Bau- und Weihinschriften*, Gudea 67N.
Chapter I.B.2 no. 14.

DS.20: Oriental Institute, Chicago A6150.
Provenance unknown.
Ningirsu: é-PA.^{21}
Chapter I.B.2 no. 2.

Stair Steps

DT.1: Whereabouts unknown; left at Tello?
Tello: Tell A/B.
Ningirsu: é-50/gi-gunu$_4$.
    NFT 66, 280 (with drawing).
    Steible *Neusumerische Bau- und Weihinschriften*, Gudea 57.
Chapters I.B.2 no. 1; IV.A.2 note 7.

Foundation Tablets

FT.1: YBC 2160.
Provenance unknown.
Baba: bàd-uru-kù-ga.
    YOS IX 16 (copy of inscription).
    Steible *Neusumerische Bau- und Weihinschriften*, Gudea 4.
Chapter I.B.2 no. 4.

FT.2: IM 18647.
Tello.
Baba: é-uru-kù-ga.
    FT II pl. XXXIX (copy of inscription).
    Steible *Neusumerische Bau- und Weihinschriften*, Gudea 6A.
Chapter I.B.2 no. 4.

FT.3: Israel Museum, Jerusalem.
Provenance unknown.
Baba: é-uru-kù-ga.
    Merhav *Glimpse into the Past*, 48 no. 25 (with photo).
    Steible *Neusumerische Bau- und Weihinschriften*, Gudea 6B.
Chapter I.B.2 no. 4.

---

^{21} The inscription of this stone fragment, most likely from a door socket, duplicates Gudea 46.

FT.4: VA 4859.
Provenance unknown.
Baba: é-uru-kù-ga.
  Jakob-Rost *Sumerische Kunst*, pl. 32.
  Steible *Neusumerische Bau- und Weihinschriften*, Gudea 9A.
Chapter I.B.2 no. 4.

FT.5: AO 12772.
Tello.
Gatumdug: é-gír-su^{ki}.
  FT II 135.
  Steible *Neusumerische Bau- und Weihinschriften*, Gudea 14.
Chapter I.B.2 no. 7.

FT.6: VA 2339.
Provenance unknown; purchased in Zurghul.
Hendursag: é.
  VAS I 13 (copy of inscription).
  Steible *Neusumerische Bau- und Weihinschriften*, Gudea 17.
Chapter I.B.2 no. 19.

FT.7: MNB 1369.
Tello.
Igalim: é-me-huš-gal-an-ki.
  Steible *Neusumerische Bau- und Weihinschriften*, Gudea 19C.
Chapter I.B.2 no. 5.

FT.8: MNB 1381.
Tello.
Igalim: é-me-huš-gal-an-ki.
  Steible *Neusumerische Bau- und Weihinschriften*, Gudea 19C.
Chapter I.B.2 no. 5.

FT.9: AO 26665.
Tello.
Igalim: é-me-huš-gal-an-ki.
  Steible *Neusumerische Bau- und Weihinschriften*, Gudea 19C.
Chapter I.B.2 no. 5.

FT.10: AO 26666.
Tello.
Igalim: é-me-huš-gal-an-ki.
  Steible *Neusumerische Bau- und Weihinschriften*, Gudea 19C.
Chapter I.B.2 no. 5.

FT.11: Public Library, New York X-1.
Provenance unknown.
Igalim: é-me-huš-gal-an-ki.
    Schwarz *BNYPL* 44 (1940), 807 no. 11.
    Steible *Neusumerische Bau- und Weihinschriften*, Gudea 19D.
Chapter I.B.2 no. 5.

FT.12: MNB 1375.
Tello.
Inanna: é-an-na-gír-su^{ki}.
    DC pl. XXXI (transliteration of inscription).
    Steible *Neusumerische Bau- und Weihinschriften*, Gudea 24B.
Chapter I.B.2 no. 8.

FT.13: BM 135994.
Zurghul.
Nanše: é-sirara$_6$.
    Sollberger *Syria 52* (1975), 177f. figs. a-b.
    Steible *Neusumerische Bau- und Weihinschriften*, Gudea 30D.
Chapters I.B.2 no. 18; II.A.2.b.

FT.14: BM 119012.
Ur: Ningal temple.
Nindara: é-lál-túm-ki-ès-sá^{ki}.
    UET I 28 (copy of inscription).
    Steible *Neusumerische Bau- und Weihinschriften*, Gudea 37.
Chapter I.B.2 no. 23.

FT.15: Rijksmuseum, Leiden A1951/6.2.
Provenance unknown.
Ningirsu: é-PA.
    Römer *OMRO* 56 (1975), pl. I:3–4.
    Steible *Neusumerische Bau- und Weihinschriften*, Gudea 45a.
Chapter I.B.2 no. 2.

FT.16: AO 26640.
Tello.
Ningirsu: é-50.
    Steible *Neusumerische Bau- und Weihinschriften*, Gudea 48Q.
Chapter I.B.2 no. 1.

FT.17: Collection E. T. Hoffmann 115.
Provenance unknown.
Ningirsu: é-50.
    EBH 195 (transliteration of inscription).
    Steible *Neusumerische Bau- und Weihinschriften*, Gudea 48R.
Chapter I.B.2 no. 1.

FT.18: Whereabouts unknown.

Provenance unknown.

Ningirsu: é-50.

> Lenormant *Choix*, no. 4.
>
> Steible *Neusumerische Bau- und Weihinschriften*, Gudea 48ee.

Chapter I.B.2 no. 1.

FT.19: AO 257A.

Tello.

Ningirsu: é-50.

> DC pl. 29:2.
>
> Steible *Neusumerische Bau- und Weihinschriften*, Gudea 51H.

Chapter I.B.2 no. 1.

FT.20: MNB 1372.

Tello.

Ningirsu: é-50.

> Steible *Neusumerische Bau- und Weihinschriften*, Gudea 51I.

Chapter I.B.2 no. 1.

FT.21: AO 259.

Tello.

Ningirsu: é-50.

> Steible *Neusumerische Bau- und Weihinschriften*, Gudea 51I.

Chapter I.B.2 no. 1.

FT.22: AO 26641.

Tello.

Ningirsu: é-50.

> Steible *Neusumerische Bau- und Weihinschriften*, Gudea 51I.

Chapter I.B.2 no. 1.

FT.23: AO 26667.

Tello.

Ningirsu: é-50.

> Steible *Neusumerische Bau- und Weihinschriften*, Gudea 51I.

Chapter I.B.2 no. 1.

FT.24: AO 26668.

Tello.

Ningirsu: é-50.

> Steible *Neusumerische Bau- und Weihinschriften*, Gudea 51I.

Chapter I.B.2 no. 1.

FT.25: BM 91007.
Provenance unknown.
Ningirsu: é-50.
    CT 21 pl. 34 (copy of inscription).
    Steible *Neusumerische Bau- und Weihinschriften*, Gudea 51J.
Chapter I.B.2 no. 1.

FT.26: BM 91008.
Provenance unknown.
Ningirsu: é-50.
    CT 21 pl. 34 (copy of inscription).
    Steible *Neusumerische Bau- und Weihinschriften*, Gudea 51J.
Chapter I.B.2 no. 1.

FT.27: BM 91060.
Provenance unknown.
Ningirsu: é-50.
    CT 21 pl. 34 (copy of inscription).
    Steible *Neusumerische Bau- und Weihinschriften*, Gudea 51J.
Chapter I.B.2 no. 1.

FT.28: Nationalmuseum, Copenhagen 5709.
Provenance unknown.
Ningirsu: é-50.
    Jacobsen *Copenhagen* no. 75 (copy of inscription).
    Steible *Neusumerische Bau- und Weihinschriften*, Gudea 51K.
Chapter I.B.2 no. 1.

FT.29: Eremitage, S. Petersburg 14399.
Provenance unknown.
Ningirsu: é-50.
    Šilejko *Votivnyia*, pl. I:1.
    Steible *Neusumerische Bau- und Weihinschriften*, Gudea 51L.
Chapter I.B.2 no. 1.

FT.30: Eremitage, S. Petersburg 14400.
Provenance unknown.
Ningirsu: é-50.
    Šilejko *Votivnyia*, pl. I:1.
    Steible *Neusumerische Bau- und Weihinschriften*, Gudea 51L.
Chapter I.B.2 no. 1.

FT.31: Eremitage, S. Petersburg 8068.
Provenance unknown.
Ningirsu: é-ba-gára.
    Šilejko *ZVO* 25 (1921), 139 (copy of inscription).

Steible *Neusumerische Bau- und Weihinschriften*, Gudea 59.
Chapter I.B.2 no. 17.

FT.32: Nationalmuseum, Copenhagen.
Provenance unknown.
Ningišzida: é-gír-su^{ki}.
    Jacobsen *Copenhagen* no. 74 (copy of inscription).
    Steible *Neusumerische Bau- und Weihinschriften*, Gudea 68B.
Chapter I.B.2 no. 14.

FT.33: Collection Chandon de Briailles.
Provenance unknown.
Ningišzida: é-gír-su^{ki}.
    Lambert *RA* 47 (1953), 83 fig. 1.
    Steible *Neusumerische Bau- und Weihinschriften*, Gudea 68C.
Chapter I.B.2 no. 14.

FT.34: VA 8789.
Provenance unknown.
Ningišzida: é-gír-su^{ki}.
    Marzahn *AoF* 14 (1987), 25 no. 3 (copy of inscription).
    Steible *Neusumerische Bau- und Weihinschriften*, Gudea 68D.
Chapter I.B.2 no. 14.

FT.35: IM 13678.
Provenance unknown.
Ningišzida: é-gír-su^{ki}.
    Steible *Neusumerische Bau- und Weihinschriften*, Gudea 68E.
Chapter I.B.2 no. 14.

FT.36: NBC 2518.
Uruk.
Ninšubur: é.
    BIN II 12 (copy of inscription).
    Steible *Neusumerische Bau- und Weihinschriften*, Gudea 73.
Chapter I.B.2 no. 16.

FT.37: MNB 1366.
Tello.
Šulšaga: é-ki-tuš-akkil-lí.
    DC pl. 29:1 and XXXII.
    Steible *Neusumerische Bau- und Weihinschriften*, Gudea 75A.
Chapter I.B.2 no. 6.

FT.38: MNB 1366.
Tello.
Šulšagana: é-ki-tuš-akkil-lí.
DC pl. XXXII note 2.
Steible *Neusumerische Bau- und Weihinschriften*, Gudea 75B.
Chapter I.B.2 no. 6.

FT.39: (TG 505).
Tello.
Šulšaga: é-ki-tuš-akkil-lí.
FT II pl. XL (copy of inscription).
Steible *Neusumerische Bau- und Weihinschriften*, Gudea 75C.
Chapter I.B.2 no. 6.

FT.40: AO 26661.
Tello.
[...]: bàd-gír-su^{ki}.
Steible *Neusumerische Bau- und Weihinschriften*, Gudea 82, pl. V.

FT.41: Oriental Institute, Chicago A6151.
Provenance unknown.
Nindara: é-gír-su^{ki}.[22]
Chapter I.B.2 no. 13.

Foundation Figurines Representing a Kneeling God[23]

FG.1: MNB 1362.
Tello.
Igalim: é-me-huš-gal-an-ki.
DC 243f.; Parrot *Tello*, 202–204.
Rashid *Gründungsfiguren*, no. 94.
Steible *Neusumerische Bau- und Weihinschriften*, Gudea 19A.
Chapters I.B.2 no. 5; II.C.1.c.

---

[22] The inscription of this foundation tablet duplicates Gudea 36.
[23] Unfortunately the excavation reports of Tello, where most of these figurines were found, ususally treat them as a group of uncertain number and indistinguishable examplars, and thus make it impossible to precise the findspot or inscription of individual pieces. Due to corrosion – all foundation figurines are made of copper – many inscriptions have become nearly or entirely illegible. Steible *Neusumerische Bau- un Weihinschriften*, did not include all figurines known by the time of his publication, and collated only the pieces housed today in the Louvre and in the British Museum. Yet he assigned twenty-seven figurines of kneeling gods, including one of Urbaba (see note 3 above), to texts commemorating Gudea's construction of Eninnu (Gudea 51A-G and 52F). This attribution is doubtful in view of the fact that not more than six-teen of the forty-one stone tablets known today, which were originally buried each with a figurine in a foundation box, are destined for Eninnu (FT.15–30). The remaining twenty-four (FT.1–14, 31–41) record the construction of various other buildings. In this catalogue, Steible's attribution to Eninnu of foundation figurines the inscriptions of which have either not been identified in previous publications or have said to be illegible received a question mark.

FG.2: AO 312.
Tello.
Igalim: é-me-huš-gal-an-ki.
  DC 243f.; Parrot *Tello*, 202–204.
  Rashid *Gründungsfiguren*, no. 92.
  Steible *Neusumerische Bau- und Weihinschriften*, Gudea 19B.
Chapters I.B.2 no. 5; II.C.1.c.

FG.3: AO 76 (Fig. 7).
Tello.
Ningirsu: é-50.
  DC 243f.; Parrot *Tello*, 202–204.
  Rashid *Gründungsfiguren*, no. 89.
  Steible *Neusumerische Bau- und Weihinschriften*, Gudea 51G.
Chapters I.B.2 no. 1; II.C.1.c; IV.E.

FG.4: AO 77.
Tello.
Ningirsu: é-50 (?).
  DC 243f.; Parrot *Tello*, 202–204.
  Rashid *Gründungsfiguren*, no. 90.
  Steible *Neusumerische Bau- und Weihinschriften*, Gudea 51G.
Chapters I.B.2 no. 1; II.C.1.c.

FG.5: AO 260.
Tello.
Ningirsu: é-50.
  DC 243f. pl. 28:4; Parrot *Tello*, 202–204.
  Rashid *Gründungsfiguren*, no. 91.
  Steible *Neusumerische Bau- und Weihinschriften*, Gudea 51G.
Chapters I.B.2 no. 1; II.C.1.c.

FG.6: AO 25581.
Tello.
Šulšaga: é-ki-tuš-akkil-lí.[24]
  DC 234f. pl. 28:3; Parrot *Tello*, 202–204
  Rashid *Gründungsfiguren*, no. 93.
  Steible *Neusumerische Bau- und Weihinschriften*, Gudea 51G.
Chapter I.B.2 no. 6; II.C.1.c.

FG.7: MNB 1365.
Tello.
Ningirsu: é-50 (?).
  DC 243f.; Parrot *Tello*, 202–204.

---

[24] The identification of this inscription follows Heuzey DC 243.

Rashid *Gründungsfiguren*, no. 95.
Steible *Neusumerische Bau- und Weihinschriften*, Gudea 51G.
Chapters I.B.2 no. 1; II.C.1.c.

FG.8: MNB 1380.
Tello.
Ningirsu: é-50 (?).
DC 243f.; Parrot *Tello*, 202–204.
Rashid *Gründungsfiguren*, no. 96.
Steible *Neusumerische Bau- und Weihinschriften*, Gudea 51G.
Chapters I.B.2 no. 1; II.C.1.c.

FG.9: MNB 1384.
Tello.
Ningirsu: é-50 (?).
DC 243f.; Parrot *Tello*, 202–204.
Rashid *Gründungsfiguren*, no. 97.
Steible *Neusumerische Bau- und Weihinschriften*, Gudea 51G.
Chapters I.B.2 no. 1; II.C.1.c.

FG.10: EŞEM 1524.
Tello.
Ningirsu: é-50.
DC 243 note 2 or NFT 66, 282; Parrot *Tello*, 202–204.
Rashid *Gründungsfiguren*, no. 81.
Steible *Neusumerische Bau- und Weihinschriften*, Gudea 51E.
Chapters I.B.2 no. 1; II.C.1.c.

FG.11: EŞEM 1572.
Tello.
Ningirsu: é-50 (?).
DC 243 note 2 or NFT 66, 282; Parrot *Tello*, 202–204.
Rashid *Gründungsfiguren*, no. 82.
Steible *Neusumerische Bau- und Weihinschriften*, Gudea 51E.
Chapters I.B.2 no. 1; II.C.1.c.

FG.12: EŞEM 1574.
Tello.
Ningirsu: é-50 (?).
DC 243 note 2 or NFT 66, 282; Parrot *Tello*, 202–204.
Rashid *Gründungsfiguren*, no. 83.
Steible *Neusumerische Bau- und Weihinschriften*, Gudea 51E.
Chapters I.B.2 no. 1; II.C.1.c.

FG.13: EŞEM 1721.
Tello.
Ningirsu: é-50 (?).
    DC 243 note 2 or NFT 66, 282; Parrot *Tello*, 202–204.
    Rashid *Gründungsfiguren*, no. 84.
    Steible *Neusumerische Bau- und Weihinschriften*, Gudea 51E.
Chapters I.B.2 no. 1; II.C.1.c.

FG.14: EŞEM 492.
Tello.
Ningirsu: é-50 (?).
    DC 243 note 2 or NFT 66, 282; Parrot *Tello*, 202–204.
    Rashid *Gründungsfiguren*, no. 85.[25]
    Steible *Neusumerische Bau- und Weihinschriften*, Gudea 51E.
Chapters I.B.2 no. 1; II.C.1.c.

FG.15: EŞEM 491.
Tello.
Ningirsu: é-50 (?).
    DC 243 note 2 or NFT 66, 282; Parrot *Tello*, 202–204.
    Rashid *Gründungsfiguren*, no. 86.
    Steible *Neusumerische Bau- und Weihinschriften*, Gudea 51E.
Chapters I.B.2 no. 1; II.C.1.c.

FG.16: EŞEM 6024.
Tello.
Ningirsu: é-50 (?).
    DC 243 note 2 or NFT 66, 282; Parrot *Tello*, 202–204.
    Steible *Neusumerische Bau- und Weihinschriften*, Gudea 51E.
Chapters I.B.2 no. 1; II.C.1.c.

FG.17: EŞEM 6504.
Tello.
Ningirsu: é-50 (?).
    DC 243 note 2 or NFT 66, 282; Parrot *Tello*, 202–204.
    Rashid *Gründungsfiguren*, no. 87.
    Steible *Neusumerische Bau- und Weihinschriften*, Gudea 51E.
Chapters I.B.2 no. 1; II.C.1.c.

FG.18: IM 6954.
Tello: Tell A, under courtyard A.
Ningirsu: é-50 (?).
    FT II 10, 89f. pl. 87:1; Parrot *Tello*, 204.

---

[25] This figurine cannot be identical with the one reported by de Genouillac in FT II pl. 87:3, as suspected by Rashid, because it is in Istanbul, and the finds from de Genouillac's excavations were divided between the Louvre and the Iraq Museum.

Rashid *Gründungsfiguren*, no. 88.
Steible *Neusumerische Bau- und Weihinschriften*, Gudea 51B.
Chapters I.B.2 no. 1; II.C.1.c.

FG.19: (TG 16).
Tello: Tell A, under courtyard A.
[...]: [...].
FT II 10, 89f. pl. 87:2; Parrot *Tello*, 204.
Chapter II.C.1.c.

FG.20: (TG 17).
Tello: Tell A, under courtyard A.
[...]: [...].
FT II 10, 89f. pl. 87:3; Parrot *Tello*, 204.
Chapter II.C.1.c

FG.21: AO or TG 445.
Tello.
Ningirsu: é-50 (?).
Rashid *Gründungsfiguren*, no. 98.
Steible *Neusumerische Bau- und Weihinschriften*, Gudea 51G.
Chapters I.B.2 no. 1; II.C.1.c.

FG.22: BM 91056.
Provenance unknown.
Ningirsu: é-50.
Anonymous *British Museum Guide* (1908), 145 no. 17 (with photo).
Rashid *Gründungsfiguren*, no. 99.
Steible *Neusumerische Bau- und Weihinschriften*, Gudea 51F.
Chapters I.B.2 no. 1; II.C.1.c.

FG.23: BM 91057.
Provenance unknown.
Ningirsu: é-50.
Anonymous *British Museum Guide* (1908), 145 no. 18; van Buren *Foundation Figurines*, pl. VI:10.
Rashid *Gründungsfiguren*, no. 100.
Steible *Neusumerische Bau- und Weihinschriften*, Gudea 51F.
Chapters I.B.2 no. 1; II.C.1.c.

FG.24: BM 91058.
Provenance unknown.
Ningirsu: é-50.
Anonymous *British Museum Guide* (1908), 145 no. 19; King *History*, pl. XXVI
Rashid *Gründungsfiguren*, no. 101.
Steible *Neusumerische Bau- und Weihinschriften*, Gudea 51F.
Chapters I.B.2 no. 1; II.C.1.c.

FG.25: BM 96566.

Provenance unknown.

Ningirsu: é-50.

> Anonymous *British Museum Guide* (1922), 84 no. 54; van Buren *Foundation Figurines*, pl. VI:11.
> Rashid *Gründungsfiguren*, no. 102.
> Steible *Neusumerische Bau- und Weihinschriften*, Gudea 51F.

Chapters I.B.2 no. 1; II.C.1.c.

FG.26: BM 102613.

Provenance unknown.

Ningirsu: é-50.

> Anonymous *British Museum Guide* (1908), 145 no. 20; van Buren *Foundation Figurines*, pl. VII:12.
> Rashid *Gründungsfiguren*, no. 103.
> Steible *Neusumerische Bau- und Weihinschriften*, Gudea 52F.

Chapters I.B.2 no. 1; II.C.1.c.

FG.27: VA 3023.

Provenance unknown.

Ningirsu: é-50.

> Meyer *Sumerier und Semiten*, 56 no. 7 (with photo).
> Rashid *Gründungsfiguren*, no. 104.
> Steible *Neusumerische Bau- und Weihinschriften*, Gudea 51A.

Chapters I.B.2 no. 1; II.C.1.c.

FG.28: VA 3056 (lost during the War).

Provenance unknown.

Ningirsu: é-50 (?).

> Meyer Sumerier und Semiten, 56 no. 7.
> Rashid *Gründungsfiguren*, no. 105.
> Steible *Neusumerische Bau- und Weihinschriften*, Gudea 51A.

Chapters I.B.2 no. 1; II.C.1.c.

FG.29: Museo Barracco, Rome no. 45.

Provenance unknown.

Ningirsu: é-50.

> Anonymous *Collection Hakky Bey*, 22 pl. 5:10 no. 213.
> Rashid *Gründungsfiguren*, no. 106.
> Steible *Neusumerische Bau- und Weihinschriften*, Gudea 51D.

Chapters I.B.2 no. 1; II.C.1.c.

FG.30: The Pierpont Morgan Library, New York 2388.[26]
Provenance unknown.
[...]: [...].
  Buchanan *Archaeology* 15 (1962), 274 (with photo).
  Rashid *Gründungsfiguren*, no. 107 = 109.
Chapter II.C.1.c

FG.31: Walters Art Gallery, Baltimore 54.790.
Provenance unknown.
[...]: [...].
  Hill *Fertile Crescent*, 9f. fig. 8.
  Rashid *Gründungsfiguren*, no. 108.
Chapter II.C.1.c; IV.E.

FG.32: Israel Museum, Jerusalem 71.23.299 (previously Collection Brummer).
Provenance unknown.
[...]: [...].
  Merhav *Jan Mitchel Gift*, 69–70 (with photo).
  Rashid *Gründungsfiguren*, no. 110.
Chapter II.C.1.c.

FG.33: Musée de Mariemont 139.
Tello.
Ningirsu: é-50 (?).
  Goossens *Mariemont*, pl. 64:3.
  Steible *Neusumerische Bau- und Weihinschriften*, Gudea 51C.
Chapters I.B.2 no. 1; II.C.1.c.

Foundation Figurines Representing a Basket Carrier

FK.1: AO 75.
Tello: Tell T.
Šulšaga: é-ki-tuš-akkil-lí.[27]
  DC 73, 244f. pl. 28:2; Parrot *Tello*, 204.
  Rashid *Gründungsfiguren*, no. 111.
Chapters I.B.2 no. 6; II.C.1.b.

FK.2: AO 258.
Tello.
Ningirsu: é-50.[28]

---

[26] Buchanan's erroneous attribution of this piece to the Yale Babylonian Collection was corrected by Schlossmann "Two Foundation Figurines," 9f. note 2.
[27] The identity of divine beneficiary and construction are inferred from FT.37 which was found together with this figurine.
[28] According to the excavation reports, "the best preserved one" of the three basket carriers from Tello now

DC 244f.; Parrot *Tello*, 204.
    Rashid *Gründungsfiguren*, no. 112.
Chapters I.B.2 no. 1; II.C.1.b.

FK.3: AO 26678 (Fig. 6).
Tello.
[...]: [...].
    DC 244f.; Parrot *Tello*, 204.
    Rashid *Gründungsfiguren*, no. 113.
Chapter II.C.1.b; IV.E.

FK.4: EŞEM 6506.
Tello: Tell B.
[...]: [...].
    NFT 66, 282; Parrot *Tello*, 204.
    Rashid *Gründungsfiguren*, no. 114.
Chapter II.C.1.b.

FK.5: YBC 2188.
Provenance unknown.
[...]: [...].
    Dougherty *AASOR* 5 (1923–24), 34 note 42; Clay *Yale Babylonian Collection* 2 (1929), 11 fig. 11.
    Rashid *Gründungsfiguren*, no. 115.
Chapter II.C.1.b.

Foundation Figurines Representing a Bull

FB.1: MNB 1374.
Tello: Tell M.
Inanna: é-an-na-gír-su^{ki}.
    DC 69, 245 pl. 28:5; Parrot *Tello*, 204.
    Rashid *Gründungsfiguren*, no. 116.
    Steible *Neusumerische Bau- und Weihinschriften*, Gudea 24A.
Chapters I.B.2 no. 8; II.C.2.b.

FB.2: MNB 1377.
Tello: Tell M.
Inanna: é-an-na-gír-su^{ki}.
    DC 69, 245; Parrot *Tello*, 204 fig. 44a.
    Rashid *Gründungsfiguren*, no. 117.
    Steible *Neusumerische Bau- und Weihinschriften*, Šulgi 13B.[29]

---

in the Louvre (FK.1–3) commemorates the construction of Eninnu; likely candidates for the text are Gudea 48 and 51 both of which occur on foundation tablets.
[29] There has been some confusion in the literature regarding the three (not two!) foundation pegs surmounted by a lying bull. All are from Tello and now in the Louvre. Two are nearly identical in shape (FB.1–2), were found *in situ* on tell M, and record Gudea's construction of Inanna's Eanna. The third one (Rashid

Chapters I.B.2 no. 8; II.C.2.b.

FB.3: BM 135993.
Zurghul.
Nanše: é-sirara$_6$.
    Sollberger *Syria* 52 (1975), 178ff. pl. IX.
    Rashid *Gründungsfiguren*, no. 118.
    Steible *Neusumerische Bau- und Weihinschriften*, Gudea 30C.
Chapters I.B.2 no. 18; II.A.2.b; C.2.b.

Gate Lions

GL.1: AO 69.
Tello.
Limestone; back of crouching lion; 25 cm high.
Gatumdug: é-uru-kù-ga.
    DC 231 pl. 24:2; Parrot *Tello*, 195 fig. 42l.
    Steible *Neusumerische Bau- und Weihinschriften*, Gudea 13.
    Braun-Holzinger *Weihgaben*, T 7.
Chapters I.B.2 no. 7; II.C.2.a; IV.B.4 note 103.

GL.2: IM (W 24717).
Uruk: Nd XXIII:1.
Diabase; front of crouching lion; 25,5 cm high.
Ningirsu: abul-ká-sur-ra.
    Boehmer *BaM* 16 (1985), 141–145 pls. 21–22; Kessler ibidem, 149f.
    Steible *Neusumerische Bau- und Weihinschriften*, Gudea 94.
    Braun-Holzinger *Weihgaben*, T 8.
Chapters I.B.2 no. 3; II.C.2.a; IV.B.4 note 103.

Door Plaques

DP.1: AO 59 (Fig. 12).
Tello: Tell A, room 4.
Limestone; upper edge with horn crown; 13,6 × 15 × 5 cm.
Ningirsu [...].
    DC 35, 215 pl. 26:9; Parrot *Tello*, 173.
    Steible *Neusumerische Bau- und Weihinschriften*, Gudea 62.
    Braun-Holzinger *Weihgaben*, W 26.
Chapters I.B.2 p. 25; II.A.2.a; C.3.a; IV.E.

Gründungsfiguren, no. 132) has a much longer and slimmer peg, a bull turning his head up and to the side, and records Šulgi's construction of Nanše's Ešeššešegarra. It was erroneously attributed to Gudea, as observed by Sollberger *Syria* 52 (1975), 180 note 2. While Rashid corrected the error in his catalogue, Steible erroneously attributed FB.2 to Šulgi as well.

DP.2: AO 12764 (Fig. 11).

Tello: Tell A.

Limestone; upper edge with two hands and the head of a serpent dragon; 21,5 × 13 × 4 cm.

[...]: é-uru-kù-ga.[30]

> FT II 34; Parrot *Tello*, 184.
>
> Steible *Neusumerische Bau- und Weihinschriften*, Gudea 9B.
>
> Braun-Holzinger *Weihgaben*, W 25.

Chapters I.B.2 no. 4; II.A.2.a; C.2.d. note 141; 3.a; IV.E.

DP.3: AO 12763 (Fig. 10).

Tello: Tell V.

Limestone; left side with two figures facing right; 42 × 36,5 × 5 cm.

Ningišzida: [é].[31]

> FT II 35 pl. 84:1; Parrot *Tello*, 159, 184 fig. 38a.
>
> Steible *Neusumerische Bau- und Weihinschriften*, Gudea 66.
>
> Braun-Holzinger *Weihgaben*, W 27; idem "Bote des Ningišzida," 41f. pl. 14:2.

Chapters I.B.2 no. 14; II.A.2.a; C.3.a; IV.B.7 note 242; IV.D.1.a; E.

Pedestals and Stands

SO.1: AO 20152.

Provenance unknown; purchased in 1951 from Curzy-Géjou.[32]

Steatite; front of stand in the shape of human-headed bison; 11,3 × 7 cm.

Hendursag [...].

> Parrot *RA* 46 (1952), 203f. (with photo).
>
> Steible *Neusumerische Bau- und Weihinschriften*, Gudea 18.
>
> Braun-Holzinger *Weihgaben*, T 13.

Chapters I.B.2 p. 25; II.C.2.c.

SO.2: AO 26639A-B.

Tello.

Black stone; two fragments of stand; a: 7,5 × 4,6; b: 9,3 × 3,3.

Ningirsu: é-50.

> Steible *Neusumerische Bau- und Weihinschriften*, Gudea 60, pl. IV.
>
> Braun-Holzinger *Weihgaben*, Ständer 5.
>
> André-Salvini *SMEA* 30 (1992), 272 pls. IIIh-i, IVd-e.

Excluded from discussion because the two fragments do not belong to the same object, and if taken apart the attribution of either fragment to Gudea becomes uncertain.

---

[30] Steible assigned this plaque to Baba, noting that his attribution remains uncertain. Both the epithet nin-a-ni and the construction é-uru-kù-ga are attested for Baba as well as for Gatumdug.

[31] By analogy with the other plaque inscriptions, the text should be restored as a building inscription rather than as two labels; see Braun-Holzinger who restored lines 6–8: [...], [é-a]-ni, ⌜mu-na-dù⌝.

[32] Braun-Holzinger questioned the authenticity of this piece based on its close resemblance with an uninscribed exemplar in the Louvre (AO 2752).

SO.3: NBC 2517.

Provenance unknown.
Limestone; fragment of cylindrical stand; 6,3 cm, diameter 5,5 cm.
[...].
> BIN II 8 (copy of the inscription).
> Steible *Neusumerische Bau- und Weihinschriften*, Gudea 93.
> Braun-Holzinger *Weihgaben*, Ständer 6.

SO.4: Lowie Museum, Berkeley UCLM 9–1794.

Provenance unknown.
Marble; cylindrical pedestal; 12,8 cm, diameter 18,4 cm.
Ningišzida.
> Foxvog RA 72 (1978), 41 Gudea 4.
> Steible *Neusumerische Bau- und Weihinschriften*, Gudea 65C.
> Braun-Holzinger *Weihgaben*, Sockel 5.

Chapters I.B.2 p. 25; II.B.1 note 34.

SO.5: AO 26428 (previously AO 57).

Tello: between Tell I-I' and J.
Limestone; seven fragments of pedestal with review of captives (?); a: 10 × 8,2 cm; b: 5,2 × 14 cm; c: 6,5 × 4,3 cm; d: 7 × 5 cm; e: 6 × 6 cm; f: 6 × 6,7 cm; g: 7 × 5,5 cm.
[...].
> DC 68, 221f. pl. 26:10a-b (a-b); Parrot *Tello*, 177 figs. 35i-j (a-b).
> Steible *Neusumerische Bau- und Weihinschriften*, Gudea 95 (a).
> Braun-Holzinger *Weihgaben*, Sockel 6 (a-d).

Chapters II.A.2.a; C.3.b; IV.E.

Stone Vessels

SV.1: BM 116450.

Ur: Enunmah.
Obsidian fragment; 4,5 × 2 cm.
Baba [...].
> Steible *Neusumerische Bau- und Weihinschriften*, Gudea 9C.
> Braun-Holzinger *Weihgaben*, G 247.

Excluded from discussion because attribution to Gudea is uncertain.

SV.2: EŞEM 5213.

Nippur: Ekur.
Dolerite; cylindrical basin; 66 cm, diameter 45 cm.
Enlil.
> Hilprecht *Explorations*, 296, 462, 473f.; Unger *PKOM* 1 (1916), 29ff. pl.1–2.
> Steible *Neusumerische Bau- und Weihinschriften*, Gudea 12.
> Braun-Holzinger *Weihgaben*, G 248.

Chapters I.B.2 p. 25; II.A.2.b; B.2.d § 4b.

SV.3: AO 26638.
Tello.
Alabaster fragment; $10 \times 6,5 \times 2$ cm.
Inanna.
  Steible *Neusumerische Bau- und Weihinschriften*, Gudea 27, pl. III.
  Braun-Holzinger *Weihgaben*, G 249.
Chapter I.B.2 p. 25.

SV.4: YBC 2332.
Provenance unknown.
Limestone bowl; 6,1 cm, diameters 13,6/4 cm.
Nindara.
  YOS IX 106, pl. XLIV.
  Steible *Neusumerische Bau- und Weihinschriften*, Gudea 35B.
  Braun-Holzinger *Weihgaben*, G 250.
Chapters I.B.2 p. 25; II.B.1 note 34.

SV.5: AO 196.
Tello.
Stone bowl fragment; 8×26 cm, original diameter 50 cm.
Ninegal.
  Steible *Neusumerische Bau- und Weihinschriften*, Gudea 40.
  Braun-Holzinger *Weihgaben*, G 251.
Chapter I.B.2 p. 25.

SV.6: AO 73.
Tello: Tell A, passage F.
Limestone; basin fragment with crouching lion; $14 \times 42 \times 32$ cm.
Ningirsu: é-50.
  DC 26, 231f. pl. 24:3; Parrot *Tello*, 195 fig. 42k.
  Steible *Neusumerische Bau- und Weihinschriften*, Gudea 42.
  Braun-Holzinger *Weihgaben*, G 252.
Chapters I.B.2 no. 1; II.A.2.a; C.2.a; IV.E.

SV.7: AO 67 + EŞEM 5555 (Fig. 8).
Tello: Tell A and B.
Limestone; several fragments of large basin with goddesses holding overflowing vases; restored: $67 \times 118 \times 57$ cm.
Ningirsu.
  DC 16; 216–218 pl. 24:4 (AO 67); Parrot *Tello*, 195 fig. 42c.
  Steible *Neusumerische Bau- und Weihinschriften*, Gudea 43.
  Braun-Holzinger *Weihgaben*, G 253.
Chapters I.B.2 p. 25; II.A.2.a; B.2.d § 4.a; C.1.d; IV.A.2 note 13; B.7; D.1.c; E.

SV.8: YBC 16412.
Tello.
Diorite; bowl fragment; $7 \times 13 \times 1,4$ cm.

Ningirsu.
  FT II 133 pl. XXXIX (copy of the inscription).
  Steible *Neusumerische Bau- und Weihinschriften*, Gudea 55.
  Braun-Holzinger *Weihgaben*, G 254.
Chapter I.B.2 p. 25.

SV.9: AO 190.
Tello: Tell V.
Steatite; libation vessel with serpents and serpent dragons; 23 cm, diameter 8/12 cm.
Ningišzida.
  DC 234f. pl. 44:2; Parrot *Tello*, 198 pl. XXI.
  Steible *Neusumerische Bau- und Weihinschriften*, Gudea 65A.
  Braun-Holzinger *Weihgaben*, G 255.
Chapters I.B.2 p. 25; II.A.2.a; B.1 note 34; C.2.d; IV.B.6 note 195; 7 note 212; 8 note 247; E.

SV.10: AO 12921.
Tello.
Limestone bowl; 9,5 cm, diameter 39 cm.
Ningišzida.
  FT II 118, 135; Parrot *Tello*, 200.
  Steible *Neusumerische Bau- und Weihinschriften*, Gudea 65B.
  Braun-Holzinger *Weihgaben*, G 256.
Chapters I.B.2 p. 25; II.B.1 note 34.

SV.11: AO 26644.
Tello.
Marble; bowl fragment; 11 × 12 cm.
[...].
  Steible *Neusumerische Bau- und Weihinschriften*, Gudea 86.
  Braun-Holzinger *Weihgaben*, G 260.

SV.12: AO 305.
Tello.
Steatite; fragment of libation vessel; 9 cm.
Ninizimua.
  DC 381 pl. 44bis:3; Parrot *Tello*, 200.
  Steible *Neusumerische Bau- und Weihinschriften*, Gudea 89.
  Braun-Holzinger *Weihgaben*, G 261.
Chapter I.B.2 p. 25; B.2.d § 4e.

SV.13: AO 167.
Tello.
Limestone; bowl fragment; 4,5 × 7,5 cm, original diameter 17 cm.
[...].

Steible *Neusumerische Bau- und Weihinschriften*, Gudea 96, pl. VI.
Braun-Holzinger *Weihgaben*, G 262.

SV.14: AO 12108E.

Tello.
Alabaster; fragment of cylindrical vessel; 9,5 × 7,5 cm, original diameter 11 cm.
[...].
    FT II 117, 129, pl. XL (copy of inscription).
    Steible *Neusumerische Bau- und Weihinschriften*, Gudea 97.
    Braun-Holzinger *Weihgaben*, G 263.

Mace Heads

MH.1: AO 130.

Tello.
Granite; 12 cm, diameter 16 cm.
Igalim.
    DC pl. 26:2; Parrot *Tello*, 198 fig. 42j.
    Steible *Neusumerische Bau- und Weihinschriften*, Gudea 20A.
    Braun-Holzinger *Weihgaben*, K 40.
Chapters I.B.2 p. 25; II.B.1 note 34.

MH.2: BM 22468.

Provenance unknown.
Diorite fragment; 10,1 cm, original diameter 10 cm.
Igalim.
    CT 10 pl. 2 (copy of inscription).
    Steible *Neusumerische Bau- und Weihinschriften*, Gudea 20B.
    Braun-Holzinger *Weihgaben*, K 41.
Chapters I.B.2 p. 25; II.B.1 note 34.

MH.3: AO 262.

Tello.
Marble; diameter 20 cm.
Nindara.
    DC pl. 26bis:3; Parrot *Tello*, 198 fig. 42f.
    Steible *Neusumerische Bau- und Weihinschriften*, Gudea 34A.
    Braun-Holzinger *Weihgaben*, K 44.
Chapters I.B.2 p. 25; II.B.1 note 34.

MH.4: AO 26663.

Tello.
Marble fragment; 11,5 × 12 cm, original diameter 28 cm.
[...].
    Steible *Neusumerische Bau- und Weihinschriften*, Gudea 34B, pl. III.

Braun-Holzinger *Weihgaben*, K 46.
Chapter II.B.1 note 34.

MH.5: EŞEM.
Tello.
Stone; 13,5 cm, diameter 17 cm.
Nindara.[33]
    Braun-Holzinger *Weihgaben*, K 45.
Chapters I.B.2 p. 25; II.B.1 note 34.

MH.6: YBC 2249.
Provenance unknown.
Diorite; 14,4 cm, diameter 19 cm.
Nindara.
    YOS IX 102.
    Steible *Neusumerische Bau- und Weihinschriften*, Gudea 35A.
    Braun-Holzinger *Weihgaben*, K 47.
Chapters I.B.2 p. 25; II.B.1 note 34.

MH.7: AO 133B.
Tello.
Limestone; with three lion heads; 9 cm, diameter 14 cm.
Ningirsu.
    DC 229 pls. 25bis:1a-b, LIX; Parrot *Tello*, 196 fig. 42h.
    Steible *Neusumerische Bau- und Weihinschriften*, Gudea 44.
    Braun-Holzinger *Weihgaben*, K 48.
Chapters I.B.2 p. 25; II.B.2.d § 4a; C.2.a; IV.E; Appendix C no. 7 note 3.

MH.8: AO 132.
Tello: Tell A, under courtyard A.
Limestone fragment; 10 cm.
Ningirsu.
    DC 48 pl. 26:7; Parrot *Tello*, 198 fig. 42e.
    Steible *Neusumerische Bau- und Weihinschriften*, Gudea 63.
    Braun-Holzinger *Weihgaben*, K 49.
Chapters I.B.2 p. 25; II.A.2.a.

MH.9: AO 14124.
Tello.
Stone fragment; 7 cm.
[...].
    FT II 135.
    Steible *Neusumerische Bau- und Weihinschriften*, Gudea 79.
    Braun-Holzinger *Weihgaben*, K 52.
Excluded from discussion because attribution to Gudea is uncertain.

---

[33] The inscription duplicates Gudea 34.

MH.10: AO 12108G.
Tello.
Marble fragment; 5,5 × 4,5 cm.
[...].
> FT II 120, 128 pl. XL (copy of inscription).
> Steible *Neusumerische Bau- und Weihinschriften*, Gudea 98.
> Braun-Holzinger *Weihgaben*, K 51.

MH.11: IM 20639.
Tello.
Limestone; with curled up snake.
DN unknown.
> Parrot *Tello*, 198.
> Braun-Holzinger *Weihgaben*, K 53.

MH.12: Whereabouts unknown.
Tello: Tell A/B.
Stone; half with two lion heads; diameter 25 cm.
DN unknown.
> NFT 296.
> Braun-Holzinger *Weihgaben*, K 54.
Chapters II.A.2.a; IV.A.2 note 13.

Statues

Statue A: AO 8 (Fig. 3).
Tello: Tell A, courtyard A.
Diorite; standing; headless; 124 cm.
Ninhursag: é-gír-su^{ki}.
> DC 44, 134f. pls. 15:5, 20, VI-VII; Parrot *Tello*, 160 pl. XIIIa.
> Steible *Neusumerische Bau- und Weihinschriften*, Gudea Statue A.
> Braun-Holzinger *Weihgaben*, St 107.
Chapters I.B.2 no. 15; II.A.2.a; B.2.e; C.1.a; IV.E.

Statue B: AO 2 (Fig. 4).
Tello: Tell A, courtyard A.
Diorite; sitting with plan on lap; headless; 93 cm.
Ningirsu: é-50/gi-gunu$_4$.
> DC 45, 138ff. pls. 15:1, 16–19, VII-XV; Parrot *Tello*, 161 pl. XIVb.
> Steible *Neusumerische Bau- und Weihinschriften*, Gudea Statue B.
> Braun-Holzinger *Weihgaben*, St 108.
Chapters I.B.2 no. 1; II.A.2.a; B.2.e; C.1.a; IV.B.4 note 99; E.

Statue C: AO 5.
Tello: Tell A, courtyard A.
Diorite; standing; headless; 140 cm.
Inanna: é-an-na-gír-su^ki.
    DC 45, 132f. pls. 10, 13:1, XVI-XVII; Parrot *Tello*, 161 pl. XIIIb.
    Steible *Neusumerische Bau- und Weihinschriften*, Gudea Statue C.
    Braun-Holzinger *Weihgaben*, St 109.
Chapters I.B.2 no. 8; II.A.2.a; B.2.e; C.1.a.

Statue D: AO 1.
Tello: Tell A, room N.
Diorite; sitting; head and right shoulder broken; 158 cm.
Ningirsu: é-50/gi-gunu₄.
    DC 4, 135f. pls. 9, XVII-XIX; Parrot *Tello*, 162 pl. XIVa.
    Steible *Neusumerische Bau- und Weihinschriften*, Gudea Statue D.
    Braun-Holzinger *Weihgaben*, St 110.
Chapters I.B nos. 1, 2; II.A.2.a; B.2.e; C.1.a; IV.B.4 note 99.

Statue E: AO 6.
Tello: Tell A, courtyard A.
Diorite; standing; headless; 140 cm.
Baba: é-sila-sír-sír(-uru-kù-ga).
    DC 45, 131f. pls. 11, 13:2, XIX-XXIII; Parrot *Tello*, 162 pl. XIIIc.
    Steible *Neusumerische Bau- und Weihinschriften*, Gudea Statue E.
    Braun-Holzinger *Weihgaben*, St 111.
Chapters I.B.2 no. 4; II.A.2.a; B.2.e; C.1.a.

Statue F: AO 3.
Tello: Tell A, courtyard A.
Diorite; sitting with tablet and ruler on lap; headless; 86 cm.
Gatumdug: é-uru-kù-ga.
    DC 45, 136f. pls. 14, 15:2, 15:4, XXIII-XXV; Parrot *Tello*, 163 pl. XIVc-d.
    Steible *Neusumerische Bau- und Weihinschriften*, Gudea Statue F.
    Braun-Holzinger *Weihgaben*, St 112.
Chapters I.B.2 no. 7; II.A.2.a; B.2.e; C.1.a; IV.B.4 note 99.

Statue G: AO 7.
Tello: Tell A, courtyard A.
Diorite; standing; head and right shoulder broken; 133 cm.
Ningirsu: é-PA.
    DC 44f., 133 pls. 13:3, XXV-XXVIII; Parrot *Tello*, 163f.
    Steible *Neusumerische Bau- und Weihinschriften*, Gudea Statue G.
    Braun-Holzinger *Weihgaben*, St 113.
Chapters I.B.2 no. 2; II.A.2.a; B.2.e; C.1.a.

Statue H: AO 4.
Tello: Tell A, courtyard A.
Diorite; sitting; head and right shoulder broken; 77 cm.
Baba: é-sila-sír-sír(-uru-kù-ga).
    DC 45, 136 pls. 13:4, XXVIII; Parrot *Tello*, 164 pl. XIIId.
    Steible *Neusumerische Bau- und Weihinschriften*, Gudea Statue H.
    Braun-Holzinger *Weihgaben*, St 114.
Chapters I.B.2 no. 4; II.A.2.a; B.2.e; C.1.a; IV.B.4 note 99.

Statue I: AO 3293 + 4108.
Tello: Tell V.
Diorite; sitting; 45 cm.
Ningišzida: é-gír-su^{ki}.
    DC 330, 448 pl. 21bis:1; NFT 21–28, 232f. pl. I; Parrot *Tello*, 165 pl. XVa.
    Steible *Neusumerische Bau- und Weihinschriften*, Gudea Statue I.
    Braun-Holzinger *Weihgaben*, St 115.
Chapters I.B.2 no. 14; II.A.2.a; B.2.e; C.1.a; IV.B.4 note 99.

Statue K: AO 10.
Tello: Tell A, gate L.
Diorite; standing; upper body and feet broken; 124 cm.
Ningirsu: é-50.
    DC 23f., 133f.; Parrot *Tello*, 164.
    Johansen *Statues of Gudea*, 9 pl. 17–18.
    Steible *Neusumerische Bau- und Weihinschriften*, Gudea Statue K.
    Braun-Holzinger *Weihgaben*, St 116.
Chapters I.B.2 p. 25; II.A.2.a; B.2.e; C.1.a.

Statue L see UI.7.

Statue M: Detroit Institute of Art 82.64 (previously Collection P. R. Stocklet).
Provenance unknown; purchased from Feuardent Frères through J. E. Géjou.
Paragonite; standing; feet broken; 41 cm.
Geštinanna: é-gír-su^{ki}.
    Scheil *RA* 22 (1925), 41–43 pl. 1–2.
    Steible *Neusumerische Bau- und Weihinschriften*, Gudea Statue M.
    Braun-Holzinger *Weihgaben*, St 117.
Chapters I.B.2 no. 10; II.A.2.a; B.2.e; C.1.a.

Statue N: AO 22126 (Fig. 5).
Provenance unknown; purchased from J. E. Géjou.
Calcite; standing with overflowing vase in hands; 62 cm.
Geštinanna: é-gír-su^{ki}.
    Scheil *RA* 27 (1930), 162f. pl. 1–2.
    Steible *Neusumerische Bau- und Weihinschriften*, Gudea Statue N.
    Braun-Holzinger *Weihgaben*, St 118.
Chapters I.B.2 no. 10; II.A.2.a; B.2.e; C.1.a; IV.E.

Statue O: Ny Carlsberg Glyptotek, Copenhagen 840.
Provenance unknown; purchased from J. E. Géjou.
Steatite; standing; 63 cm.
Geštinanna: é-gír-su^ki.
  Thureau-Dangin *Monuments Piot* 27 (1924), 97ff. pl. VIII.
  Steible *Neusumerische Bau- und Weihinschriften*, Gudea Statue O.
  Braun-Holzinger *Weihgaben*, St 119.
Chapters I.B.2 no. 10; II.A.2.a; B.2.e; C.1.a.

Statue P: Metropolitan Museum, New York 59.2 (previously Collection J. E. Géjou).
Provenance unknown.
Diorite; sitting; 44 cm.
Ningišzida: é-gír-su^ki.
  Scheil *RA* 27 (1930), 163 pl. 3–4.
  Steible *Neusumerische Bau- und Weihinschriften*, Gudea Statue P.
  Braun-Holzinger *Weihgaben*, St 120.
Excluded from discussion because it is an obvious fake: its inscription is identical with that of Statue I except for the name, which duplicates that of Statue C (iii 18-iv 1).

Statue Q: IM 2909 + CBS 16664.
Provenance unknown.
Diorite; sitting; 30 cm.
Ningišzida.
  Langdon *JRAS* (1927) 765–68 pl. IV (body); Legrain *MJ* 18 (1927) 241 (head).
  Steible *Neusumerische Bau- und Weihinschriften*, Gudea Statue Q.
  Braun-Holzinger *Weihgaben*, St 121.
Chapters I.B.2 p. 25; II.A.2.a; B.2.e; C.1.a; IV.B.4 note 99.

Statue S: EŞEM 5215.
Tello: Tell H.
Limestone; 18 fragments restored; standing.
[...].
  DC 60f., 330 pl. 21ter:5; Parrot *Tello*, 170f.
  Unger *RA* 51 (1957) 170–176 pls. I-II (reconstruction).
  Steible *Neusumerische Bau- und Weihinschriften*, Gudea Statue S.
  Braun-Holzinger *Weihgaben*, St 123.
Chapters II.A.2.a; B.2.e; C.1.a.

Statue T: Collection Golénišev 5144,1.5 (body); UM L.29.212 (head).
Nippur: Ekur.[34]
Dolerit; two body fragments and a head; head: 65 × 55 cm.
Nisaba [é ... ?].

---

[34] According to Haynes' diary quoted in Legrain *MJ* 18 (1927), 245, the head was found in 1899 near the findspot where the body had been found in 1896.

Hilprecht *Bêl Temple*, 52 fig. 33 (head); idem *Explorations*, 473 (head).
Steible *Neusumerische Bau- und Weihinschriften*, Statue T.
Braun-Holzinger *Weihgaben*, St 124.
Excluded from discussion because attribution to Gudea is uncertain.

Statue U: BM 92988.

Tell Hammam.
Dolerite; fragmentary body of standing statue; 101 cm.
Nanše: [...]/gi-gunu$_4$.[35]

Loftus *JRGS* 26 (1856), 144f.; Sollberger *RA* 62 (1968), 142–145 figs. 1–2.
Steible *Neusumerische Bau- und Weihinschriften*, Gudea Statue U.
Braun-Holzinger *Weihgaben*, St 125.
Chapters II.A.2.b; B.2.e; C.1.a.

Statue V: BM 122190.

Provenance unknown; purchased in 1931.
Dolerite; standing upper body; 73.6 cm.
[...].

ILN 21th March (1931), 473 (with photo).
Steible *Neusumerische Bau- und Weihinschriften*, Gudea Statue V.
Braun-Holzinger *Weihgaben*, St 126.
Excluded from discussion because inscription not preserved, and probably a fake.

Statue W: AO 20.

Tello: Tell A, room 30.
Diorite; neck fragment; 16 × 11 cm.
Ningirsu: é-50.

DC 23, 148 pl. 13:5; Parrot *Tello*, 171.
Steible *Neusumerische Bau- und Weihinschriften*, Gudea Statue W.
Braun-Holzinger *Weihgaben*, St 127.
Chapters I.B.2 no. 1; II.A.2.a; B.2.e.

Statue X: AO 26646.

Tello.
Diorite fragment; 5 × 9 × 3 cm.
Meslamtaea [...].

Steible *Neusumerische Bau- und Weihinschriften*, Gudea Statue X, pl. XX.
Braun-Holzinger *Weihgaben*, St 128.
Chapters I.B.2 p. 25; B.2.e.

---

[35] If Sollberger's generally accepted attribution of this statue to Nanše is correct, then the gi-gunu$_4$ must be that of Nanše's not Ningirsu's temple, as Steible suggested. The construction of the gi-gunu$_4$ was probably preceded by an account of the construction of the entire temple.

Statue Y: AO 26633.
Tello.
Limestone fragment; 11 × 6 × 4 cm.
Ningirsu [...].
  Steible *Neusumerische Bau- und Weihinschriften*, Gudea Statue Y.
  Braun-Holzinger *Weihgaben*, St 129.
Chapters I.B.2 p. 25; B.2.e.

Statue Z: AO 26637.
Tello.
Diorite fragment; 9,3 × 9 × 5,3 cm.
[...].
  Steible *Neusumerische Bau- und Weihinschriften*, Gudea Statue Z, pl. XX.
  Braun-Holzinger *Weihgaben*, St 130.
Chapter B.2.e

Statue AA see UI.8.

Statue BB: AO 26635 + 26670.[36]
Tello.
Limestone fragments; AO 26635: 7 × 17,5 × 9,5, AO 26670: 7 × 9 × 8 cm.
Baba.
  Steible *Neusumerische Bau- und Weihinschriften*, Gudea 88.
  Braun-Holzinger *Weihgaben*, St 134.
Chapters I.B.2 p. 25; B.2.e.

Cylinder Seals

CS.1: AO 3541 and 3542 (Fig. 9).
Tello.
Two clay sealings preserving the complete image of a seal which was 2,7 cm high and had 0,3 cm thick metal caps. Engraved was a presentation scene and an inscription containing Gudea's name and title.
  DC 293f. fig. K; Parrot *Tello*, 201f. fig. 43f.
  Delaporte *Catalogue Louvre* I, T.108.
Chapters II.B.1 note 36; C.2.d. note 141; 3.a; IV.B.7; D.1.a; c; d; E; V.C.2.

---

[36] Braun-Holzinger identified these fragments as part of a statue, contra Steible's identification as a stela. The last three preservered lines of the inscription may be restored: [alan-(n)a-ni] mu-[tu] ^{d}b[a-ba$_6$], and Baba in the last line explained as the beginning of the statue's name.

Appendix A

Unidentified Objects

UI.1: Public Library, New York T-2.

Provenance unknown.

"Polished piece of steatite."[37]

Gatumdug: [...].

    Schwarz *BNYPL* 44 (1940), 808 no 23.

    Steible *Neusumerische Bau- und Weihschriften*, Gudea 15M

Chapter I.B.2 p. 25.

UI.2: Birmingham City Museum 589'65.

Provenance unknown.

"Limestone block."

Ningirsu: é-50.

    George *Iraq* 41 (1979), 122 no. 22.

    Steible *Neusumerische Bau- und Weihinschriften*, Gudea 48P.

Chapter I.B.2 no. 1.

UI.3: AO 22500.

Tello.

Agate cone.[38]

Ningirsu.

    Nougayrol *RA* 41 (1947), 26f. fig. 2 (as AO 16653).

    Steible *Neusumerische Bau- und Weihinschriften*, Gudea 54.

Chapters I.B.2 p. 25; II.B.1 note 36.

UI.4: AO 12733.

Tello.

Limestone fragment; 96 × 82 cm.

Ningirsu: abul-ká-sur-ra.

    FT II 133 pl. XXXIX (copy of inscription).

    Steible *Neusumerische Bau- und Weihinschriften*, Gudea 56F.

Chapter I.B.2 no. 3.

UI.5: AO 12781.

Tello.

Clay cylinder fragment.

Ningirsu: gi-gunu$_4$.

    FT II 130f pl. XLVIII (copy of inscription).

    Steible *Neusumerische Bau- und Weihinschriften*, Gudea 78.

Chapter I.B.2 no. 1.

---

[37] The description of this piece – no photo is available – makes one wonder whether it is half of a foundation tablet with the break polished by a dealer wanting to sell it as a complete piece.

[38] Nougayrol described it as a "cabochon d'agate affectant à peu près la forme d'une balle Lebel, mais d'un calibre sensiblement plus fort," and provided a drawing.

UI.6: Netherlands Institute of the Near East, Leiden LB 17–19.
Provenance unknown.
Several fragments of clay tubes.
[...].

 De Liagre Böhl *Oorkonden*, 12f.
 Steible *Neusumerische Bau- und Weihinschriften*, Gudea 87.

UI.7: AO 28.
Tello: Tell A.
Diorite fragment; 52 × 22 × 19 cm.
[...].

 DC 152; Parrot *Tello*, 164 (statue K).
 Steible *Neusumerische Bau- und Weihinschriften*, Gudea Statue L.
Excluded from discussion because attribution to Gudea is uncertain.

UI.8: AO 26630.[39]
Tello.
Limestone fragment; 6 × 15 × 7 cm.
[...].

 Steible *Neusumerische Bau- und Weihinschriften*, Gudea Statue AA.
 Braun-Holzinger *Weihgaben*, St 131.

---

[39] As Braun-Holzinger pointed out, the physical appearance of this fragment does not recommend Steible's identification as a statue: the surface is flat. The inscription does not follow the scheme of simple building or dedicatory inscriptions, but is not readily identifiable as a statue inscription either. More elaborate inscription also occur on stelae, see chapter IV.A.3; yet, they encompass not more than one column of text in their present condition.

APPENDIX B

Catalogue of the Stela Fragments

This catalogue comprises sixty-four limestone fragments which have been or may be assigned to stelae of Gudea. Except for *Bildstelen* nos. 91–92,[1] all pieces previously catalogued by Börker-Klähn are included. Nine fragments and a few new joins have been added.[2] Joining fragments received one entry. The catalogue numbers are preceded by the siglum ST to distinguish this category of objects from those catalogued in Appendix A. Each entry provides the following information:

- museum number(s).
- provenance, followed by the excavator's name in parentheses if officially excavated.[3]
- description of shape and measurements.[4]
- bibliographical reference to:
  - the Tello excavation report(s) or the first publication if illicitly excavated.
  - the catalogue in Börker-Klähn *Bildstelen*, which contains a detailed bibliography up to 1982.
  - the edition of the inscribed text in Steible *Neusumerische Bau- und Weihinschriften*.
  - more recent publications.
- cross-reference to the chapter(s) in which the fragment is discussed.
- drawing by the author at the ratio 1:4 of the original, with three exceptions: ST.10, the largest fragment, is drawn at the ratio 1:6; the drawing of ST.19, not available for examination, is after Levy; ST.47, not available for examination either, remains unpublished.

---

[1] No. 91, a poorly preserved stone fragment depicting the head of a quadruped, is apparently lost. Its low-quality reproduction in DC 374 does not permit a classification of the original artifact to which it belonged nor a chronological attribution. Heuzey *Réstitution*, 20f., tentatively attributed it to the Eannatum Stela. No. 92 is the pedestal fragment SO.5 in Appendix A.

[2] The fragments ST.16, 19, 21, 30, 31, 37, 46, 47, 48, and joins in ST.9, 13, 20. Two inscribed but unsculpted limestone fragments from Tello identified as stela parts by Steible *Neusumerische Bau- und Weihinschriften*, Lagaš 48–49, have not been included, since they probably belonged to statues; for the first see Braun-Holzinger *Weihgaben*, Stele 19; the other (ibidem, Stele 20) is written in two columns, and parallels a passage in Gudea Statue B 3:6–9 and E 1:18–20.

[3] For fragments not mentioned in the excavation reports, this information was obtain from the catalogues of the Louvre in Paris and the Archaeological Museum of Istanbul, respectively.

[4] My measurements often diverge from those of Börker-Klähn *Bildstelen*, nos. 35–90. Absolute precision is almost impossible when measuring irregular stone fragment, and I do not claim that my measurements are invariably more accurate. The imagery is described in detail in chapter IV.B.

ST.1

ST.1: VA 2796a (Pl. B).
Provenance unknown.
Left side of top register; 65 × 46 × 12,2 cm.
    Meyer *Sumerier*, 43–51 pl. 7.
    Börker-Klähn *Bildstelen*, no. 35.
    Steible *Neusumerische Bau- und Weihinschriften*, Gudea 77B.
Chapters II.C.2.d note 141; 3.a note 152; IV.A.2 note 2; 3; B.7; C.3.a; b; c; d; D.1.a; c; d; 3.a; V.B.1; C.2; 5.

ST.2

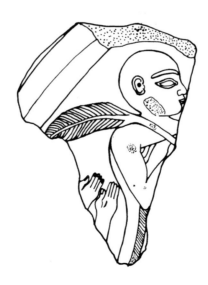

ST.3

ST.2: VA 2796b and c (Pl. B).
Provenance unknown.
Right side of top register; b: 24,5 × 22 × 11,8 cm; c: 11 × 11,6 cm.
  Meyer *Sumerier*, 43–51 pl. 7.
  Börker-Klähn *Bildstelen*, no. 37.
Chapters II.C.3.a note 152; IV.A.2 note 2; B.4; 7; 9; C.3.a; c; d; D.1.c; d; V.B.1.

ST.3: AO 10867 (Pl. C).
Provenance unknown; purchased from J. E. Géjou (alias M. David) in 1926.
Left edge of top register; 26,5 × 19 × 8,5 cm.
  Contenau *Manuel* I, 134 fig. 78.
  Börker-Klähn *Bildstelen*, no. 73.
  Spycket *WO* 14 (1983), 249.
Chapters IV.A.2 note 2; B.7; C.3.a; b; c; d; D.1.a; c; d; V.C.2; 5.

ST.4

ST.4: AO 4585 + EŞEM 6002 + 6101 (Pl. C).
Tello: Tell A/B (Cros).
Center of top register; 64 × 55 × 14 cm.
    NFT 294 fig. 7 (AO 4585).
    Parrot *Tello*, 179 (AO 4585).
    Unger *ZDPV* 77 (1961), 81f. pl. 5B.
    Börker-Klähn *Bildstelen*, nos. 81–83.
    Seidl *Or* 55 (1986), 322.
Chapters IV.A.2; 5 note 35; B.6; C.3.b; c; d; D.1.b; d; 3.a.

ST.5

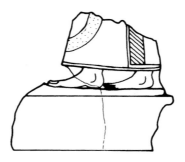

ST.5: EŞEM 5976 (Pl. C).

Tello (Cros).

Right side of top register; a: 30 × 16 × 8 cm; b: 14 × 16 × 8 cm.

    Unger *ZDPV* 77 (1961), 81f. pl. 5B.

    Börker-Klähn *Bildstelen*, no. 84.

    Steible *Neusumerische Bau- und Weihinschriften*, Gudea 77G.

Chapters IV.A.2; 3; 5 note 35; B.6; C.3.a; b; c; d; D.1.a; d.

ST.6

ST.6: EŞEM 6087 + 6089 + 12383 (Pl. A).
Tello (Cros).
Fragment with lower divider; 47 × 34,8 cm.
    Börker-Klähn *Bildstelen*, no. 41.
    Seidl *Or* 55 (1986), 321f.
Chapters II.C.2.d note 141; IV.A.2; 5 note 35; B.7; C.3.b; c; d; D.1.a; c; d; 3.a; V.C.2.

ST.7

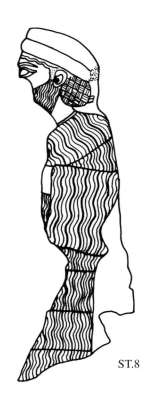

ST.8

ST.7: EŞEM 1533 (Pl. A).
Tello: Tell A, entrance of palace (de Sarzec).
Fragment; 25,5 × 19 cm.
    DC 212–214 pl. 8bis:4.
    Parrot *Tello*, 176 fig. 35b.
    Börker-Klähn *Bildstelen*, no. 41.
Chapters IV.A.2 with note 15; 5 note 35; B.7; C.3.c; d; D.1.c.

ST.8: EŞEM 6106 (Pl. A).
Tello (Cros).
Fragment; 39 × 13 cm.
    Börker-Klähn *Bildstelen*, no. 41.
Chapters IV.A.2; 5 note 35; B.7; C.3.c; d.

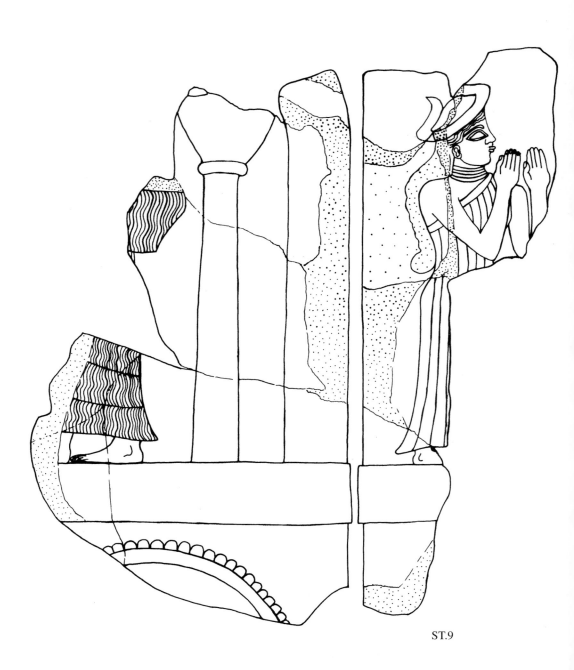

ST.9

ST.9: AO 4573 + 4580 + EŞEM 5837 + 6117 (Pl. A).
Tello: Tell A/B (Cros).
Corner with parts of top and second register; 64 × 34 × 21 cm.
    NFT 285f. fig. 2, pl. IX:2–3 (AO 4573 + 4580).
    Parrot *Tello*, 179f. fig. 37 (AO 4573 + 4580).
    Börker-Klähn *Bildstelen*, no. 89 (AO 4573 + 4580).
Chapters IV.A.2; 5 note 35; B.5; 7; C.3.a; b; c; d; D.1.c; d; V.C.3; 4.

ST.10

ST.10: AO 52.
Tello: Tell A, near gate M (de Sarzec).
Corner with parts of three registers; $125 \times 60 \times 20$ cm.
   DC 37, 219f. pl. 23.
   Parrot *Tello*, 174–176 pl. XXa.
   Börker-Klähn *Bildstelen*, no. 90.
Chapters IV.A.2; B.3; 5; 9; D.1.d; 3.a.

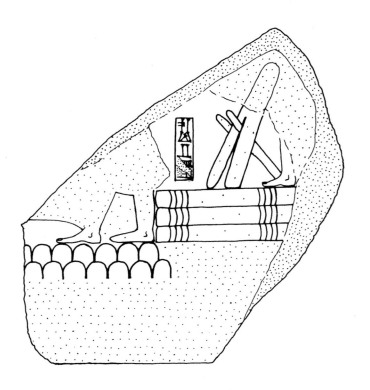

ST.11

ST.11: EŞEM 5842 (Pl. A).[5]
Tello: Tell A/B (Cros).
Fragment (of bottom register?); 37 × 34 × 27 cm.
    NFT 296.
    Börker-Klähn *Bildstelen*, no. 58.
    Braun-Holzinger *Weihgaben*, Stele 21.
Chapters IV.A.2; 3; B.2; C.3.a; c; d; D.1.b; 2; 3.a; V.C.1.

---

[5] When I inspected this fragment, its surface was more eroded than on the reproduction in Börker-Klähn. My drawing represents the condition when first published.

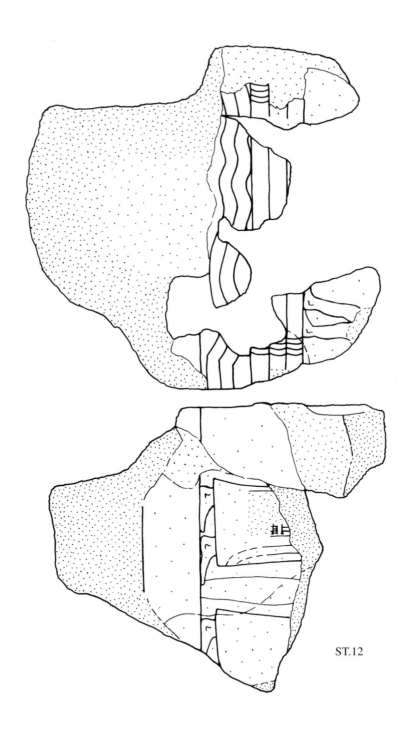

ST.12

ST.12: EŞEM 6016 (Pl. A).
Tello (Cros).
Corner fragment (of bottom register?); 37 × 37.6 × 30 cm.
 Unger *RlV* 7 (1926), pl. 145a.
 Börker-Klähn *Bildstelen*, no. 59.
 Steible *Neusumerische Bau- und Weihinschriften*, Gudea 77F.
Chapters IV.A.2; 3; 5 note 35; B.2; 9; C.3.a; b; c; d; D.1.a; b; 2; 3.a; V.C.1.

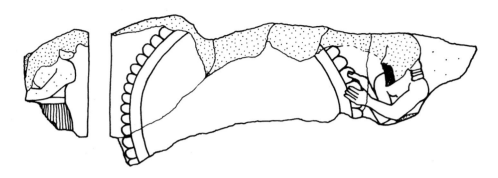

ST.13

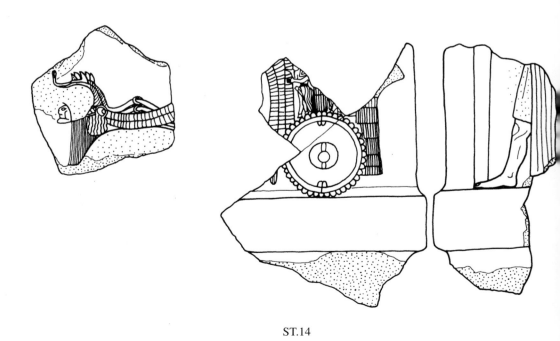

ST.14

ST.13: AO 4579 + EŞEM 5805 (Pl. B).
Tello: Tell A/B (Cros).
Corner fragment; 17 × 7 × 39 cm.
    NFT pl. IX:5 (AO 4579).
    Parrot *Tello*, fig. 36g (AO 4579).
    Börker-Klähn *Bildstelen*, no. 65.
Chapters IV.A.2; 5 note 35; B.5; 9; C.3.b; c; d; D.1.b; 3.a; V.C.3.

ST.14: VA 2902 + 2903 and 2904 (Pl. B).
Provenance unknown.
Corner fragment with lower divider; 2902–3: 29 × 22 × 13 cm; 2904: 16,5 × 15 × 3,5
cm.
    Meyer *Sumerier*, 52f. pl.8.
    Börker-Klähn *Bildstelen*, no. 45.
Chapters IV.A.2 note 2; B.4; 5; 7; C.3.b; c; d; D.1.b; 3.a; V.C.3.

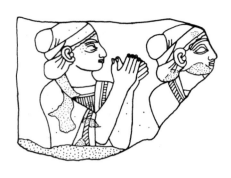

ST.15

ST.16

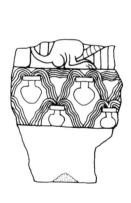

ST.17

ST.18

ST.15: AO 10235 (Pl. A).
Provenance unknown; purchased from J. E. Géjou in 1925.
Left edge fragment; $16 \times 21,5 \times 8,5$ cm.
>Parrot *Tello*, 185.
>Börker-Klähn *Bildstelen*, no. 88.

Chapters IV.A.2 note 2; B.5; C.3.c; d; D.1.b; d; 3.a.

ST.16: AO 63.
Tello: Tell A, courtyard A (de Sarzec).
Right edge fragment; $9 \times 9,8 \times 5$ cm.
>DC 48, 218 pl. 25:6.
>Parrot *Tello*, 176 fig. 35d.

Chapters IV.A.2; B.9; C.3.b.

ST.17: AO 4584 (Pl. C).
Tello (Cros): Tell H, tomb.
Right edge fragment with lower divider; $15,5 \times 12 \times 5,5$ cm.
>NFT 131 pl. VIII:2.
>Parrot *Tello*, 182 fig. 36c.
>Börker-Klähn *Bildstelen*, no. 39.

Chapters IV.A.2; B.4; 7; C.3.b; c; d; D.1.c.

ST.18: EŞEM 6000 (Pl. C).[6]
Tello: Tell A/B (Cros).
Right edge fragment with lower divider; $36 \times 28 \times 16$ cm.
>NFT 294 pl. X:7.
>Parrot *Tello*, 182 fig. 36a.
>Börker-Klähn *Bildstelen*, no. 77.

Chapters IV.A.2; 5 note 35; B.3; C.3.b; c; d; D.1.b; 3.a; E.

---

[6] The surface of this fragment has clearly suffered since the first published photograph was taken; compare the reproductions in NFT and Börker-Klähn *Bildstelen*. The additional fragment on the lower right seen in the latter was not attached when I inspected the piece, and may in fact have been a false join. My drawing represents the condition as preserved in the reproduction in NFT, yet with the addition of the doubtless join of the right edge completing the rope in the hand of the represented figure.

ST.19

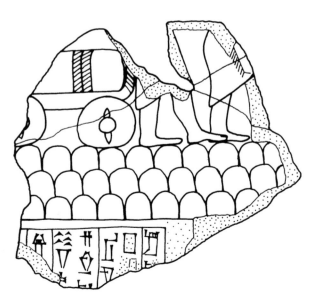

ST.20

ST.19: IM 14178.[7]
Provenance unknown.
Fragment with upper divider; 22 × 32 × 20.
   Levy *AfO* 11 (1936), 152 (with drawing).
   Steible *Neusumerische Bau- und Weihinschriften*, Gudea 77A.
Chapters IV.A.2 note 2; 3; B.9; C.3.a; c note 355; D.1.a.

ST.20: EŞEM 5843 + 5851 + 5989.
Tello: Tell A/B (Cros).
Fragment; 29 × 30 × 3 cm.
   NFT 296.
   Börker-Klähn *Bildstelen*, no. 60 (EŞEM 5843 + 5989).
   Braun-Holzinger *Weihgaben*, Stele 22.
Chapters IV.A.2; 3; 5 note 35; B.2; C.3.a; b; c; d; D.1.b; 2; V.C.1.

---

[7] This fragment could not be examined and no photograph has been made available. The drawing is after that provided by its publisher.

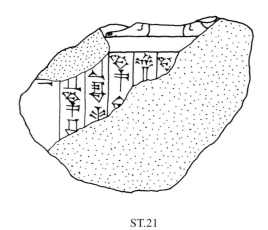

ST.21

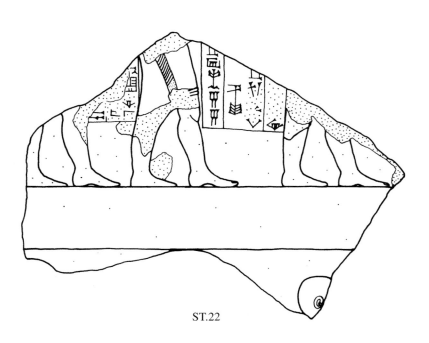

ST.22

ST.21: AO 26634 (previously AO 56).
Tello (de Sarzec).
Fragment; 19 × 26 × 6 cm.
 Steible *Neusumerische Bau- und Weihinschriften*, Gudea 80, pl. XXI.
 Braun-Holzinger *Weihgaben*, Stele 17.
Chapters IV.A.2; 3; B.9; C.3.a.

ST.22: AO 16649 (Pl. A).
Tello: Tell Y (Parrot).
Fragment with parts of two registers; 31 × 41 × 9,5 cm.
 Parrot *Tello*, 184 fig. 38b.
 Börker-Klähn *Bildstelen*, no. 87.
 Spycket *WO* 14 (1983), 250.
 Steible *Neusumerische Bau- und Weihinschriften*, Lagaš 39.
 Braun-Holzinger *Weihgaben*, Stele 18.
Chapters IV.A.2; 3; B.3; 9; C.3.a; b; c; d; D.1.b; 3.a; E.

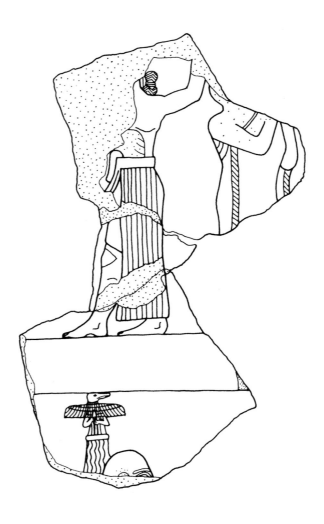

ST.23

ST.23: EŞEM 5811 (Pl. A).
Tello: Tell A/B (Cros).
Fragment with parts of two registers; 50 × 31,2 × 16 cm.
  NFT 290 fig. 6d, 295 fig. 10.
  Parrot *Tello*, 182 fig. 36l (upper part).
  Börker-Klähn *Bildstelen*, nos. 67 and 79.
Chapters II.C.3.b; IV.A.2; 5 note 35; 5 note 37; B.1; 5; 9; C.3.b; c; d; D.1.b; 3.a.

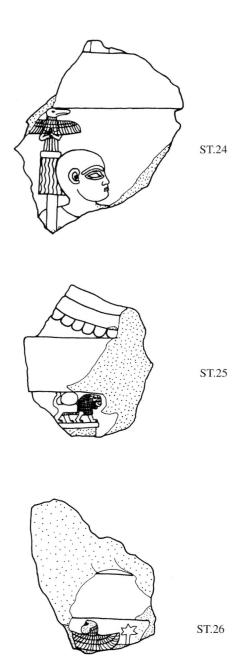

ST.24

ST.25

ST.26

ST.24: AO 4576 (Pl. A).
Tello: Tell A/B (Cros).
Fragment with upper divider; 21 × 18 × 7,5 cm.
   NFT 290 fig. 6c, pl. X:2.
   Parrot *Tello*, 180 fig. 37.
   Börker-Klähn *Bildstelen*, no. 69.
Chapters II.C.3.b; IV.A.2; B.1; C.3.b; c; d.

ST.25: AO 4577 (Pl. A).
Tello: Tell A/B (Cros).
Fragment with parts of two registers; 17 × 14 × 4 cm.
   NFT 290f. fig. 6a, pl. IX:6.
   Parrot *Tello*, 180 fig. 37.
   Börker-Klähn *Bildstelen*, no. 66.
Chapters IV.A.2; B.1; 5; 9; C.3.b; c; d.

ST.26: EŞEM 5810.
Tello: Tell A/B (Cros).
Fragment with upper divider; 21 × 13 × 12 cm.
   NFT 290 fig. 6e, pl. XI:1 (part).
   Parrot *Tello*, 180.
   Börker-Klähn *Bildstelen*, no. 71.
Chapters IV.A.2; 5 note 37; B.1; C.3.b; c.

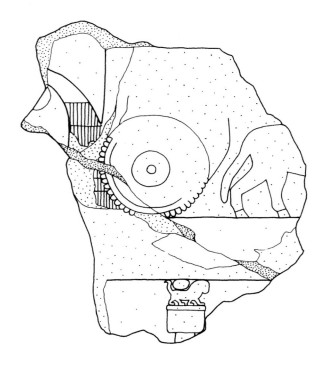

ST.27

ST.27: AO 4586 + EŞEM 5808 + 6150.
Tello: Tell A/B (Cros).
Fragment with parts of two registers; $36 \times 30 \times 6,5$.
  NFT 293f. fig. 3 (AO 4586).
  Parrot *Tello*, 182 (AO 4586).
  Börker-Klähn *Bildstelen*, no. 61.
Chapters IV.A.2; 5 note 35; B.1; 4; C.3.b; c; V.C.3.

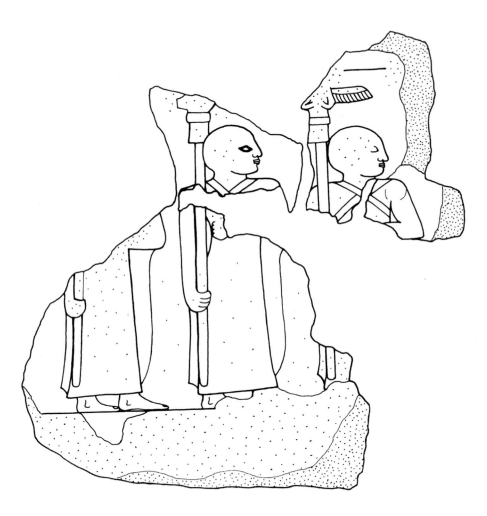

ST.28

ST.28: EŞEM 5824.
Tello: Tell A/B (Cros).
Fragment with lower divider; 52 × 49 × 15 cm.
   Börker-Klähn *PKG* 14 (1975), fig. 36.
   Börker-Klähn *Bildstelen*, no. 68.
Chapters II.C.3.b; IV.A.2; 5 note 35; B.1; C.3.a; b; c; D.1.b; d; 3.a.

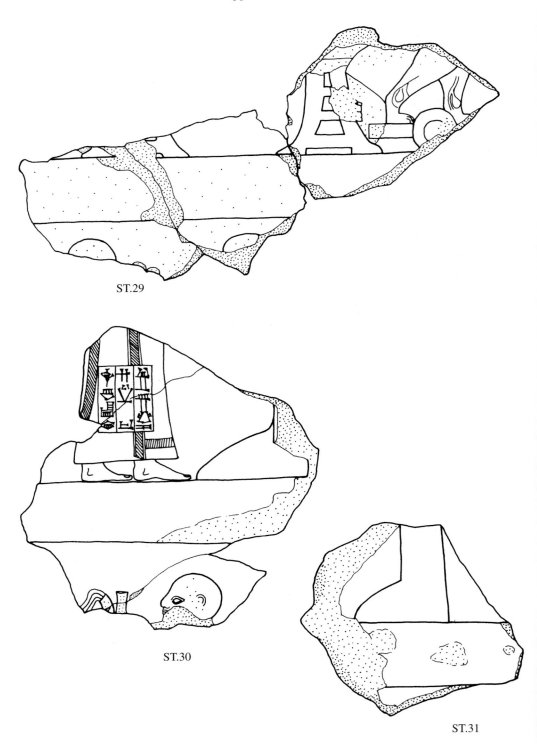

ST.29

ST.30

ST.31

ST.29: AO 4587 + EŞEM 6115 (Pl. A).
Tello: Tell A/B (Cros).
Fragment with parts of two registers; 27 × 51 × 17,5 cm.
  NFT 295 fig. 10 (AO 4587).
  Parrot *Tello*, 182 fig. 36k (AO 4587).
  Börker-Klähn *Bildstelen*, no. 78.
Chapters IV.A.2; 5 note 35; B.4; 5; 9; C.3.b; c; d.

ST.30: EŞEM 6088.
Tello (Cros).
Fragment with parts of two registers; 33,5 × 32 × 6 cm.
  Börker-Klähn *Bildstelen*, § 114.
Chapters IV.A.2; 3; B.6; 9; C.3.a; b; c; d; D.1.a; b; d; 3.a.

ST.31: EŞEM 6025.
Tello (Cros).
Fragment with lower divider; 21 × 23 × 7 cm.
  Börker-Klähn *Bildstelen*, § 114.
Chapter IV.A.2; B.9; C.3.b.

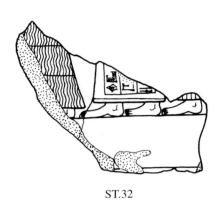

ST.32

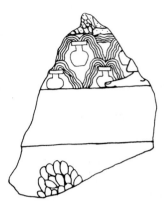

ST.33

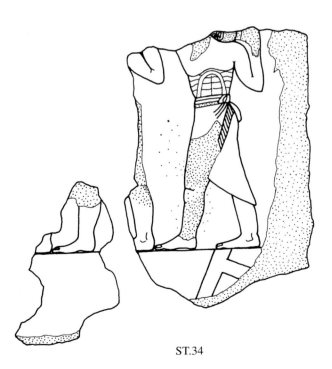

ST.34

ST.35

ST.32: VA 2892 (Pl. B).
Provenance unknown.
Fragment with lower divider; 17,5 × 20 × 4,8 cm.
  Börker-Klähn *Bildstelen*, no. 51.
  Steible *Neusumerische Bau- und Weihinschriften*, Gudea 77E.
Chapters II.C.2.d note 141; IV.A.2 note 1; 3; B.7; C.3.a; b; c; d; D.1.a; E; V.C.2.

ST.33: BM 95477 (Pl. C).
Provenance unknown.
Fragment with parts of two registers; 20 × 16 × 6,6 cm.
  King *History*, pl. opposite p.72.
  Börker-Klähn *Bildstelen*, no. 40.
Chapters IV.A.2 note 2; B.6; 7; C.3.b; c; d; D.1.c.

ST.34: EŞEM 5999 + 6001 (Pl. C).
Tello: Tell A/B (Cros).
Fragment; 35 × 31,5 × 12 cm.
  NFT 292 pl. X:6 (EŞEM 6001).
  Parrot *Tello*, 180f. fig. 37 (EŞEM 6001).
  Börker-Klähn *Bildstelen*, no. 62.
Chapters IV.A.2; 5 note 35; B.3; 9; C.3.b; c; d; D.1.b; d; 2; 3.a; E.

ST.35: AO 4572 (Pl. B).
Tello: Tell A/B (Cros).
Fragment; 16,5 × 20 × 7,5 cm.
  NFT 295f. pl. IX:7.
  Parrot *Tello*, 182 fig. 36h.
  Börker-Klähn *Bildstelen*, no. 48.
Chapters IV.A.2; B.6; C.3.c; d; D.1.c; d.

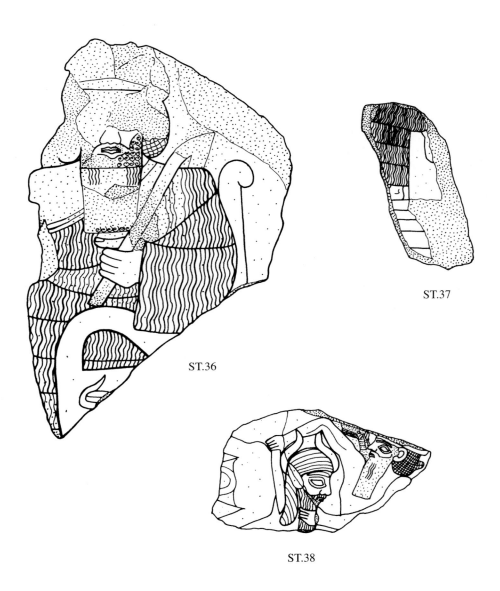

ST.36

ST.37

ST.38

ST.36: AO 53 (Pl. A).
Tello: Tell A, entrance of palace (de Sarzec).
Fragment; 44 × 27,5 × 11 cm.
   DC 211f. pl. 22:5.
   Parrot *Tello*, 173 fig. 35e.
   Börker-Klähn *Bildstelen*, no. 42.
Chapters IV.A.2; B.7; C.3.c; D.1.c.

ST.37: AO 60.
Tello: Tell A (de Sarzec).
Fragment; 18 × 12 × 6,5 cm.
   DC 215f.
   Parrot *Tello*, 174 note 135.
   Boese *Weihplatten*, 206.
Chapters IV.A.2; B.7.

ST.38: VA 2905.
Provenance unknown.
Fragment; 13,5 × 22 × 6 cm.
   Meyer *Sumerier*, 52 note 2.
   Opitz *AfO* 5 (1928–29), 81–89 pl. 11:1.
   Börker-Klähn *Bildstelen*, no. 44.
   Seidl *Or* 55 (1986), 321.
Chapters IV.A.2 note 2; B.8.

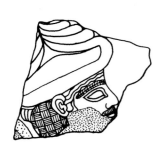

ST.39

ST.40

ST.41

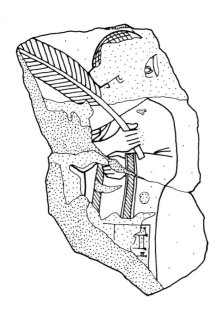

ST.42

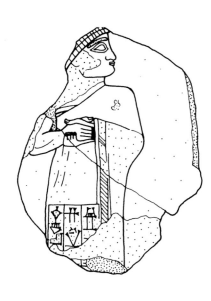

ST.43

ST.39: AO 4571 (Pl. A).
Tello: Tell A/B (Cros).
Fragment; 13 × 15 × 10 cm.
  NFT 284 pl. IX:1.
  Parrot *Tello*, 179 fig. 37.
  Börker-Klähn *Bildstelen*, no. 36.
Chapters II.C.2.d note 141; IV.A.2; B.9; C.3.c; d; D.1.c; V.C.2.

ST.40: VA 2894 (Pl. B).
Provenance unknown.
Fragment; 9,2 × 7,2 × 3 cm.
  Meyer *Sumerier*, 51f. (with photo).
  Börker-Klähn *Bildstelen*, no. 38.
Chapters IV.A.2 note 2; B.9; C.3.c; d.

ST.41: VA 2890 (Pl. C).
Provenance unknown.
Fragment; 14,5 × 9,6 × 3,5 cm.
  Meyer *Sumerier*, 55 (with photo).
  Börker-Klähn *Bildstelen*, no. 49.
Chapter IV.A.2 note 2; B.7; C.3.c; d; D.1.c.

ST.42: AO 4575 (Pl. A).
Tello: Tell A/B (Cros).
Fragment; 29,5 × 21 × 6 cm.
  NFT 293 pl. X:4.
  Parrot *Tello*, 179 fig. 37.
  Börker-Klähn *Bildstelen*, no. 74.
  Steible *Neusumerische Bau- und Weihinschriften*, Gudea 77D.
Chapters IV.A.2; 3; 5 note 37; B.9; C.3.a; b; c; d; D.1.a; d; V.C.5.

ST.43: AO 4574 (Pl. A).
Tello: Tell A/B (Cros).
Fragment; 26,5 × 19,5 × 8 cm.
  NFT 293 pl. X:3.
  Parrot *Tello*, 179 fig. 36d.
  Börker-Klähn *Bildstelen*, no. 75.
  Steible *Neusumerische Bau- und Weihinschriften*, Gudea 77C.
Chapters IV.A.2; 3; B.9; C.3.a; b; c; d; D.1.a; d.

ST.44

ST.45

ST.46

ST.48

ST.49

ST.44: VA 2891 (Pl. C).
Provenance unknown.
Fragment; 22,5 × 13,6 × 1,8 cm.
  Meyer *Sumerier*, 50–52 (with photo).
  Börker-Klähn *Bildstelen*, no. 50.
Chapters II.C.2.d note 141; IV.A.2 note 1; 3; B.7; C.3.a; c; d; D.1.a; d; V.C.2.

ST.45: AO 4574bis.
Tello: Tell A/B (Cros).
Fragment; 7,1 × 6,5 × 1,7 cm.
  NFT 293 pl. VIII:1.
  Parrot *Tello*, 177 fig. 36b.
  Börker-Klähn *Bildstelen*, no. 76.
Chapters IV.A.2; B.9; C.3.c; D.1.a.

ST.46: AO 6966 (Pl. B)
Tello (Cros).
Fragment; 7,5 × 5,5 × 2 cm.
  Steible *Neusumerische Bau- und Weihinschriften*, Gudea 77I, pl. VI.
Chapters IV.A.2; 3; B.9; C.3.a; c; d; D.1.a.

ST.47: AO 457L.
Tello (de Sarzec).
Fragment.[8]
  Steible *Neusumerische Bau- und Weihinschriften*, Gudea 77H.
Chapters IV.A.2; 3; B.9; C.3.a; D.1.a.

ST.48: EŞEM 1558 (Pl. A).
Tello (de Sarzec).
Fragment; 21 × 17,5 × 10 cm.
  DC 379.
Chapters IV.A.2; B.3; C.3.c; d; D.1.b; 3.a; E.

ST.49: AO 4582.
Tello: Tell A/B (Cros).
Fragment; 22,5 × 16,5 × 6 cm.
  NFT 292 pl. X:5.
  Parrot *Tello*, 180 fig. 37.
  Börker-Klähn *Bildstelen*, no. 55.
Chapters IV.A.2; B.3; 9; C.3.b; c; D.1.b; d.

---

[8] This fragment could not be found during my visit in Paris. According to Steible, it preserves the lower part of a garment, which, based on its inscription, evidently belonged to a Gudea figure.

ST.50   ST.51   ST.52

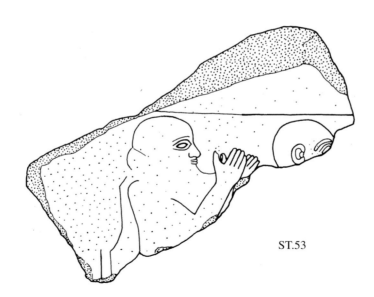

ST.53

ST.50: AO 243A (Pl. A).
Tello (de Sarzec).
Fragment; 6 × 5 × 1,5 cm.
   DC 378.
   Börker-Klähn *Bildstelen*, no. 56.
Chapters IV.A.2; B.3; 9; C.3.c; D.1.b.

ST.51: AO 243B.
Tello (de Sarzec).
Fragment; 4,5 × 5,7 × 0,6 cm.
   DC 378.
   Börker-Klähn *Bildstelen*, no. 57.
Chapter IV.A.2; B.9; C.3.c; D.1.b.

ST.52: AO 52B (Pl. A).
Tello: Tell A, entrance of palace (de Sarzec).
Fragment; 6 × 6 × 1,7 cm.
   DC 221 pl. 22:4.
   Parrot *Tello*, 176.
   Börker-Klähn *Bildstelen*, no. 72.
Chapters IV.A.2; B.9; C.3.c.

ST.53: AO 55.
Tello: Tell A, entrance of palace (de Sarzec).
Fragment with upper divider; 28 × 35 × 12 cm.
   DC 221 pl. 22:6.
   Parrot *Tello*, 177 fig. 35h.
   Börker-Klähn *Bildstelen*, no. 80.
Chapters IV.A.2; B.5; C.3.b; c; D.1.b; 3.a.

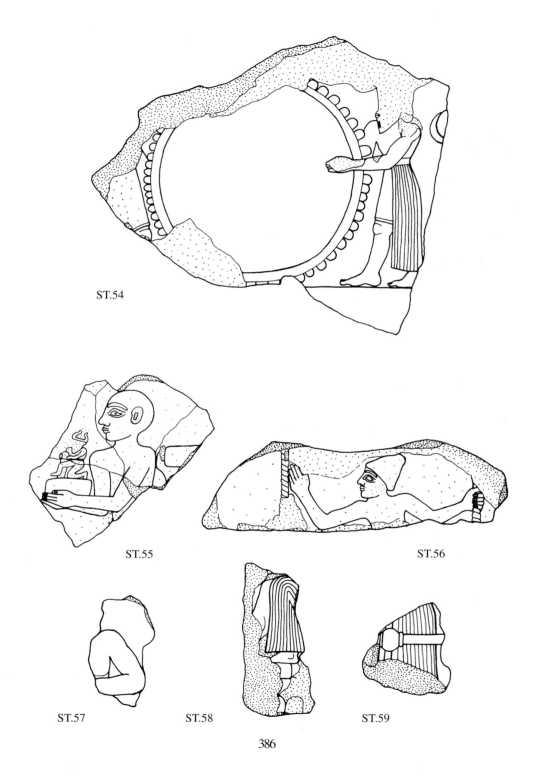

ST.54

ST.55

ST.56

ST.57

ST.58

ST.59

ST.54: AO 4578 (Pl. B).
Tello: Tell A/B (Cros).
Fragment with lower divider; 32 × 38,5 × 8 cm.
    NFT 286–290 fig. 4, pl. IX:4.
    Parrot *Tello*, 180 fig. 37.
    Börker-Klähn *Bildstelen*, no. 64.
Chapters IV.A.2; B.5; 9; C.3.b; c; d; D.1.b; d; 3.a.

ST.55: AO 4581bis (Pl. A).
Tello: Tell A/B (Cros).
Fragment; 19 × 19,5 × 4 cm.
    NFT 294 fig. 8.
    Parrot *Tello*, 182 fig. 36f.
    Börker-Klähn *Bildstelen*, no. 85.
Chapters IV.A.2; B.4; C.3.c; d; D.1.b; 3.a; V.C.3.

ST.56: AO 10236.
Provenance unknown; purchased from J. E. Géjou in 1925.
Fragment; 9,5 × 34 × 12 cm.
    Parrot *Tello*, 185.
    Börker-Klähn *Bildstelen*, no. 86.
Chapters IV.A.2 note 2; B.3; C.3.c; D.1.b; 3.a; E.

ST.57: VA 2893.
Provenance unknown.
Fragment; 12,2 × 7,2 × 7,5 cm.
    Börker-Klähn *Bildstelen*, no. 52.
Chapters IV.A.2 note 2; note 15; B.9.

ST.58: VA 2896 (Pl. A).
Provenance unknown.
Fragment; 16,5 × 7,8 × 5 cm.
    Börker-Klähn *Bildstelen*, no. 53.
Chapters IV.A.2 note 2; B.2; C.3.c; d.

ST.59: VA 2897 (Pl. A).
Provenance unknown.
Fragment; 10 × 9,5 × 4 cm.
    Börker-Klähn *Bildstelen*, no. 54.
Chapters IV.A.2 note 2; B.4; C.3.c; d; D.1.b.

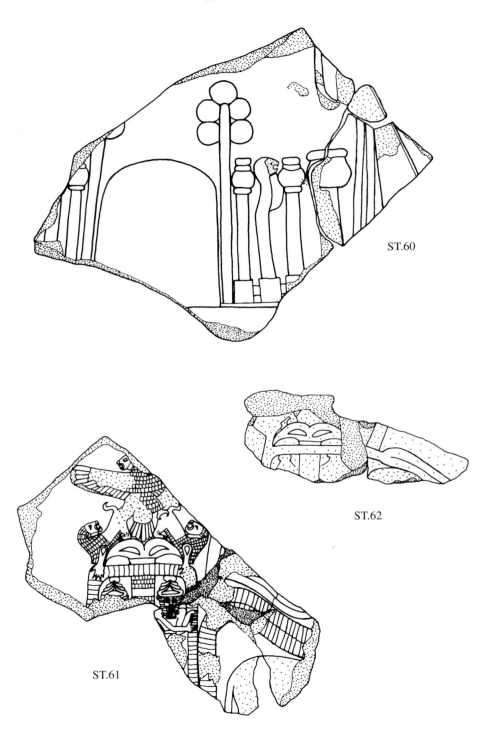

ST.60

ST.62

ST.61

ST.60: AO 4581 + EŞEM 5802 (Pl. A).
Tello: Tell A/B (Cros).
Fragment; 34,4 × 43 × 19,5 cm.
    NFT 283f. pl. X:1 (AO 4581).
    Parrot *Tello*, 179 fig. 36i (AO 4581).
    Börker-Klähn *Bildstelen*, no. 63.
Chapters IV.A.2; 5 note 35; B.4; 7; C.3.c; d; V.C.3.

ST.61: AO 4583 + EŞEM 5847 (Pl. A).
Tello: Tell A/B (Cros).
Fragment; 29 × 30 × 7 cm.
    NFT 296 pl. VIII:3 (AO 4583).
    Parrot *Tello*, 182 fig. 36e (AO 4583).
    Börker-Klähn *Bildstelen*, no. 46.
Chapters IV.A.2; 5 note 35; B.1; 4; 7; 8; C.3.c; d; V.C.3.

ST.62: EŞEM 5988 + 6148.
Tello: Tell A/B (Cros).
Fragment; 10 × 24 × 9 cm.
    Börker-Klähn *PKG* 14 (1975), fig. 36.
    Börker-Klähn *Bildstelen*, no. 47.
Chapters IV.A.2; 5 note 35; B.4; C.3.c; V.C.3.

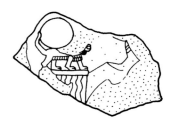

ST.63

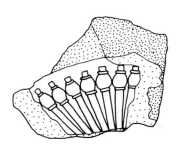

ST.64

ST.63: EŞEM 5828 (Pl. A).
Tello: Tell A/B (Cros).
Fragment; 10,8 × 14,8 × 1,5 cm.
    NFT 290 fig. 6b.
    Börker-Klähn *Bildstelen*, no. 70.
Chapters IV.A.2; 5 note 37; B.1; C.3.c; d; D.3.a.

ST.64: VA 2901 (Pl. A).
Provenance unknown.
Fragment; 12,6 × 17,5 × 6,2 cm.
    Meyer *Sumerier*, 27f. (with photo), 52.
    Börker-Klähn *Bildstelen*, no. 43.
Chapters IV.A.2 note 2; B.4; 7; C.3.c; d.

APPENDIX C

Selected Passages of the Cylinder Inscriptions

1. The Project

CA 01:01	u$_4$ a[n-k]i-a nam tar-[ra-(a)-d]a	When destinies had to be decreed in the universe,
CA 01:02	laga[š^{ki}]-e me gal-la [sag] an-šè mi-ni-íb-íl	Lagaš excelled regarding the great mes.
CA 01:03	^{d}en-líl-e en ^{d}nin-gír-su-šè igi zi mu-ši-bar	Enlil looked approvingly at lord Ningirsu.
CA 01:04	uru me-a níg-ul pa nam-è	In our city an everlasting thing appeared.
CA 01:05	šà gú-bi nam-gi$_4$	The heart was satisfied.
CA 01:06	šà ^{d}en-líl-lá gú-bi nam-gi$_4$	Enlil's heart was satisfied.
CA 01:07	šà gú-bi nam-gi$_4$	The heart was satisfied.
CA 01:08	a-gi$_6$-uru$_{16}$ nam-mul ní íl-íl	The mighty flood sparkled, inspiring respect.
CA 01:09	šà ^{d}en-líl-lá-ke$_4$ ^{id}idigna-àm a dùg-ga nam-túm	Enlil's heart, like the Tigris, carried pleasant water.
CA 01:10	é-e lugal-bi gù ba-dé	The house has been chosen by its master.
CA 01:11	é-50 me-bi an-ki-a pa-è mu-ak-ke$_4$	He will make Eninnu's mes visible in the universe.
CA 01:12	ensí lú geštú dagal-kam geštú ì-gá-gá	The ruler, a man of vast intelligence, will apply his mind.
CA 01:13	níg-gal-gal-la šu mi-ni-mú-mú	He will foster something truly grand.
CA 01:14	gud du$_7$ ⌈máš⌉ du$_7$-de$_6$ si im-sá-sá-e	He will direct perfect bulls and perfect kids.
CA 01:15	sig$_4$ nam-tar-ra sag mu-ši-íb-íl	He will carry the destined brick on (his) head.
CA 01:16	é kù dù-dè gú-bi mu-ši-íb-zi	He will strive to build the pure house.
CA 01:17	lugal-ni-ir u$_4$-NE maš-gi$_6$-ka	It was at day in a revelation dream
CA 01:18	gù-dé-a en ^{d}nin-gír-su-ra igi mu-ni-du$_8$-àm	that Gudea saw his master, lord Ningirsu.
CA 01:19	é-a-ni dù-ba mu-na-dug$_4$	He spoke to him about the building of his house.
CA 01:20	é-50 me-bi gal-gal-la-àm	He showed him Eninnu's very great mes.
CA 01:21	igi mu-na-ni-gar	

2. A Chariot for Ningirsu

CA 07:09	sipa zi gù-dé-a	The good shepherd Gudea
CA 07:10	gal mu-zu gal in-ga-túm-mu	knows great things, and also accomplishes great things.
CA 07:11	inim ^{d}nanše-e mu-na-dug$_4$-ga-aš	He heeded the words Nanše spoke to him.
CA 07:12	sag-sig ba-ši-gar	
CA 07:13	é-níg-ga-ra-na kišib bí-kúr	He broke the seal on his storehouse,
CA 07:14	giš im-ma-ta-gar	took out some wood from there.
CA 07:15	gù-dé-a giš a mu-DU-DU	Gudea ... the wood,
CA 07:16	giš-e mí im-e	took good care of the wood.
CA 07:17	^{giš}mes-e sag bí-sag$_9$	The mes-wood was hewed,
CA 07:18	^{giš}ha-lu-úb-ba gín bí-bar	the oak-wood was split with an ax.
CA 07:19	^{giš}gigir za-gìn-šè mu-na-a-DI	He made a chariot (adorned?) with lapis lazuli for him,
CA 07:20	du$_{24}$-ùr-bi pirig kas$_4$-e pà-da	harnessed to it its donkey stallions, panthers
CA 07:21	im-ma-ši-lá-lá	chosen for their speed,
CA 07:22	šu-nir ki-ág-ni mu-na-dím	fashioned his beloved emblem for him,
CA 07:23	mu-ni im-mi-sar	(and) wrote his name on it.
CA 07:24	balag ki-ág-e ušumgal kalam-ma	With his beloved drum, Great-Dragon-of-the-Country,
CA 07:25	^{giš}gù-di mu-tuku níg ad-gi$_4$-gi$_4$-ni	the famous roaring instrument, his consultant,
CA 07:26	ur-sag níg-ba-e ki-ág-ra	he presented it to the gift-loving warrior,
CA 07:27	lugal-ni en ^{d}nin-gír-su-ra	his master, lord Ningirsu
CA 07:28	é-50-anzu-babbar-ra	in Eninnu, White-Anzu.

CA 07:29   mu-na-da-ku$_4$-ku$_4$

3. Recruitment of Work Force

CA 14:07 u$_4$-ba ensí-ke$_4$ kalam-ma-na zi-ga ba-ni-gar	At that time the ruler made a conscription in his country.
CA 14:08 ma-da gú sag šár-šár-ra-na	In his provinces among all his numerous people,
CA 14:09 gú-edin-na ^{d}nin-gír-su-ka-ka	in Ningirsu's Guedinna,
CA 14:10 zi-ga ba-ni-gar	he made a conscription.
CA 14:11 uru dù-a á-dam gar-ra-na	In his fortified cities and settled hamlets,
CA 14:12 gú giš-bar-ra ^{d}nanše-ka	in Nanše's Gugišbarra,
CA 14:13 zi-ga ba-ni-gar	he made a conscription.
CA 14:14 gud huš zi-ga gaba-gi$_4$ nu-tuku	Aroused-Bison-Bull-without-Opponent-
CA 14:15 ^{giš}erin babbar-ra lugal-bi-ir dab$_5$-ba	Dragging-white-Cedars-for-its-Master
CA 14:16 im-ru-a ^{d}nin-gír-su-ka-ka	mobilized for him in Ningirsu's district;
CA 14:17 zi-ga mu-na-gál	
CA 14:18 šu-nir mah-bi lugal-kur-dúb sag-bi-a mu-gub	its huge standard, Lugalkurdub, marched at its head.
CA 14:19 peš$_{10}$-gál gaba-gál a-ta è-a	What-is-on-Banks-and-Shores-Emerging-from-
CA 14:20 íd mah a diri hé-gál-bi barà-barà	the-Water-Huge-Rivers-and-Surplus-Waters-
CA 14:21 im-ru-a ^{d}nanše-ka	Spreading-their-Abundance
CA 14:22 zi-ga mu-na-gál	mobilized for him in Nanše's district;
CA 14:23 u$_5$ kù šu-nir ^{d}nanše-kam sag-bi-a mu-gub	the sacred gull, Nanše's standard, marched at its head.
CA 14:24 gu máš anše edina-na lá-a	The-Net-Catching-Animals-of-the-Steppe-
CA 14:25 ni-is-ku erín mu-tuku erín ^{d}utu ki-ág	the-Famous-Choice-Yoke-Team-the-Yoke-Team-Loved-by-Utu
CA 14:26 im-ru-a ^{d}inanna-ka zi-ga mu-na-gál	mobilized for him in Inanna's district;
CA 14:27 aš-me šu-nir ^{d}inanna-kam sag-bi-a mu-gub	the disk, Inanna's standard, marched at its head.
CA 14:28 é ^{d}nin-gír-su-ka dù-dè	To build Ningirsu's house
CA15:1-3 [...]	[...]

4. Importation of Timber and Minerals

CA 15:19 kur ^{giš}erin-na lú nu-ku$_4$-ku$_4$-da	In the impenetrable Cedar Mountains,
CA 15:20 gù-dé-a en ^{d}nin-gír-su-ke$_4$	lord Ningirsu established roads for Gudea.
CA 15:21 gír mu-na-ni-gar	
CA 15:22 ^{giš}erin-bi gín-gal-e im-mi-ku$_5$	Its cedars were cut with huge axes;
CA 15:23 šár-ùr á-zi-da lagaš^{ki}-a	for the Šarur, the reliable strength of Lagaš,
CA 15:24 tukul a-ma-ru lugal-la-na-šè	the deluge weapon of his master, they were hewed.
CA 15:25 gín im-ma-bar	
CA 15:26 muš-mah-àm a-e im-ma-diri-ga-àm	Like huge serpents floating downstream:
CA 15:27 hur-sag ^{giš}erin-<ta> ad ^{giš}erin-na	cedar rafts from the Cedar Mountains,
CA 15:28 hur-sag ^{giš}šu-úr-me-ta	cypress rafts from the Cypress Mountains,
CA 15:29 ad ^{giš}šu-úr-me	
CA 15:30 hur-sag ^{giš}za-ba-lum-ma-ta	juniper rafts from the Juniper Mountains,
CA 15:31 ad ^{giš}za-ba-lum	
CA 15:32 ^{giš}ù-<suh$_5$> gal-gal ^{giš}tu-lu-bu-um	and many large rafts of large pines, sycamores,
CA 15:33 ^{giš}e-ra-núm	and oaks,
CA 15:34 ad gal-gal-bi diri-diri-ga-bi	
CA 15:35 kar mah ká-sur-ra-ke$_4$	at the great harbor of Kasurra
CA 16:01 [gù-dé-a en ^{d}nin-gír-su-ra]	[Gudea moored for lord Ningirsu.]
CA 16:02 [im-ma-na-ús]	
CA 16:03 [kur ...]	[In the ... Mountains]
CA 16:04 [gù-dé-a] en ⌐^{d}⌐[nin-gír]-su-[ke$_4$]	lord Ningirsu established roads for Gudea.
CA 16:05 gír mu-[na-ni-gar]	
CA 16:06 na gal-gal-bi lagab-ba mi-ni-túm	Its large stones were brought from there in the form of slabs;

CA 16:07	má h[a]-⌜ù?⌝-na más na lu-a	boatloads of dark clay and pebbles (?),[1]
CA 16:08	esír-a-ba-al esír igi-esír im-babbar-ra	various types of bitumen,[2] and gypsum
CA 16:09	hur-sag má-ad-ga-ta	from the Madga mountains,
CA 16:10	níg-ga má še gán DU-a-gin$_7$	(all these) goods, like boats carrying the field's harvest,
CA 16:11	gù-dé-a en ^{d}nin-gír-su-ra	Gudea moored for lord Ningirsu.
CA 16:12	im-ma-na-ús	

5. The Foundation

CA 20:24	gù-dé-a lú é-dù-a-ke$_4$	Gudea, the house-builder,
CA 20:25	é-a dubsig-bi men kù sag-gá mu-ni-gál	put the basket for the house (like) a pure crown on his head.
CA 20:26	uš mu-gar á-gar ki im-mi-tag	He laid the foundation; set the wall on the ground.
CA 20:27	sá mu-sì sig$_4$-ga gu bí-dúb	He marked a square; the chalk line was snapped on the bricks.
CA 21:01	é-a sá 2-nam nam-mi-sì	He marked the second square of the house:
CA 21:02	gu dug-ba sag gál-la-àm	it is a string (marking) a heaped up (measuring) vessel.
CA 21:03	é-a sá 3-àm nam-mi-sì	He marked the third square of the house:
CA 21:04	anzu^{mušen} amar a ti^{mušen}-àm	it is an Anzu (and?) the young of a father eagle?.
CA 21:05	é-a sá 4 nam!-mi-sì	He marked the forth square of the house:
CA 21:06	nemúr pirig huš-a gú-da lá-a-àm	it is a young panther embracing a fierce lion.
CA 21:07	é-a sá 5-àm nam-mi-sì	He marked the fifth square of the house:
CA 21:08	AN.SAR su-lim íl-la-àm	it is a blue sky carrying brilliance.
CA 21:09	é-a sá 6-àm nam-mi-sì	He marked the sixth square of the house:
CA 21:10	u$_4$ sá-dug$_4$-ga hi-li gùr-àm	it is an arriving sun laden with splendor.
CA 21:11	é-a sá 7 nam-mi-sì	He marked the seventh square of the house:
CA 21:12	é-50 ì-ti u$_4$-zal-la kalam si-àm	Oh Eninnu! It is a moonlight at dusk fulfilling the country.

6. The Stelae

CA 22:24	na gal-gal lagab-ba mi-ni-DU-a	The great stones which he had brought in their slabs
CA 23:01	mu 1-a mu-DU mu 1-a mu-ak	he brought in one year, (and) worked (them) in one year.
CA 23:02	u$_4$ 2 u$_4$ 3 nu-ma-da-ab-zal	Two days, three days did not pass.
CA 23:03	á u$_4$-da 1-ta mu-dù	In one day's work he erected each one.
CA 23:04	u$_4$ 7-kam-ma-ka é-e im-mi-dab$_5$	On the seventh day he had them surround the house.
CA 23:05	na da-bi kun-šè mu-ná	The stones' sides he laid down as stairs,
CA 23:06	[Š]IM-šè mu-dím-dím	fashioned them into basins,
CA 23:07	é-a mi-ni-šu$_4$-šu$_4$	and had them stand in the house.
CA 23:08	na kisal-mah-a mi-dù-a-na	The stone which he erected in the huge courtyard,
CA 23:09	na-rú-a lugal-kisal-si	the stele of Lugalkisalsi,

---

[1] Thureau-Dangin SAKI 107, and Lambert and Tournay *RB* 55 (1948), 416, understood má ha-ù-na má na lu-a in this line as boatloads of two different types of stones, while Falkenstein SAHG 153, and *Grammatik* I, 106, and Jacobsen *Harps*, 407, took the terms as two types of boats. The orignal understanding is preferable, based on the comparison with Statue B 6:57–63: ^{im}ha-um im-ta-e$_{11}$ hur-sag bar-me-ta ^{na_4}na lu-a má gal-gal-a im-mi-si-si úr é-50-ka mu-na-ni-gur. This passage immediately follows the import of bitumen. For ^{im}ha-um (with variant ha-ù-n) = *hāpu* = "dark clay," see CAD 6, 86. As Steible *Neusumerische Bau- und Weihinschriften* 2, 26, tentatively suggested, lu in ^{na_4}na lu-a should be derived from lu = *dešû* = innumerable; innumerable ashlars (Kalksteinquader), however, are not only absent in the archaealogical record, but also a less likely fill material for foundations than pebbles.

[2] For ésir a-ba-al, a bitumen extracted from the water, probably a river, see PSD 2, 10 ad 1.2; for igi-ésir, perhaps "surface crude bitumen," see Civil *NABU* (1989) 40 no. 62. The ésir between these two terms may simply be plain bitumen.

CA 23:10	gù-dé-a en ^dnin-gír-su-ke₄	that stone he named
CA 23:11	gír-nun-ta mu-zu	"Lord Ningirsu recognized Gudea from Girnun."
CA 23:12	na-ba mu-šè im-ma-sa₄	
CA 23:13	na ká-sur-ra bí-dù-a	The stone which was erected at the Kasurra,
CA 23:14	lugal a-ma-ru ^den-líl-lá	that stone he named
CA 23:15	gaba šu-gar nu-tuku	"The king, the deluge of Enlil without rival,
CA 23:16	gù-dé-a en ^dnin-gír-su-ke₄	lord Ningirsu looked at Gudea approvingly."
CA 23:17	igi zi mu-ši-bar	
CA 23:18	na-ba mu-šè im-ma-sa₄	
CA 23:19	na igi u₄ è-a bí-dù-a	The stone which was erected in front of the rising sun,
CA 23:20	lugal u₄ gù-di ^den-líl-lá	that stone he named
CA 23:21	en gaba-ri nu-tuku	"The king, the roaring storm of Enlil,
CA 23:22	gù-dé-a en ^dnin-gír-su-ke₄	the lord without adversary,
CA 23:23	šà kù-ge bí-pà	lord Ningirsu chose Gudea in pure heart."
CA 23:24	na-ba mu-šè im-ma-sa₄	
CA 23:25	na igi šu-ga-lam-ma-ka bí-dù-a	The stone which was erected in front of Šugalam,
CA 23:26	lugal mu-ni-šè kur-ku-ku-e	that stone he named
CA 23:27	gù-dé-a en ^dnin-gír-su-ke₄	"The king at whose name the foreign land trembles,
CA 23:28	gu-za-ni mu-gi	lord Ningirsu made Gudea's throne firm."
CA 23:29	na-ba mu-šè im-ma-sa₄	
CA 23:30	na igi é-URU×A-ga-ka bí-dù-a	The stone which was erected in front of the EU-RUga,
CA 24:01	gù-dé-a en ^dnin-gír-su-ke₄	that stone he named
CA 24:02	nam dùg mu-ni-tar	"Lord Ningirsu decreed a sweet destiny for Gudea."
CA 24:03	na-ba mu-šè im-ma-sa₄	
CA 24:04	na a-ga ^dba-ba₆-ka bí-dù-a	The stone which was erected in Baba's rear chamber,
CA 24:05	é-50 igi an-na-ke₄-zu	that stone he named
CA 24:06	^dba-ba₆ zi-šà-gál gù-dé-a	"An's eyes recognizing Eninnu,
CA 24:07	na-ba mu-šè im-ma-sa₄	Baba (is) Gudea's power of life."

7. *Inauguration Presents*

CB 13:11	agrig kalag-[ga] ^dnanše-ke₄	The strong steward of Nanše,
CB 13:12	sipa gú-tuku ^dnin-[g]ír-su-⌈ka⌉-ke₄	the prudent shepherd of Ningirsu,
CB 13:13	gal mu-zu gal ì-g[a]-túm-mu	knows great things, and also accomplishes great things.
CB 13:14	é-e lú ⌈é⌉ dù-a-ke₄	For the house, the one building the house,
CB 13:15	gù-dé-a ensí	Gudea, the ruler of Lagaš,
CB 13:16	lagaš^{ki}-ke₄	
CB 13:17	sag im-rig₇-ge	is going to offer gifts:
CB 13:18	^{giš}gigir kur mu-gam su-zi íl ní-gal u₅-a	the chariot Subjugator-of-the-Foreign-Lands which brings fear, and rides frightfully,
CB 13:19	^{anše}du₂₄-ùr-bi u₄ gù dùg-dùg-ga	whose donkey stallions, a very well roaring storm,
CB 13:20	gìr ba-si-ga-da	will be at its service,
CB 13:21	šitá sag 7 tukul huš mè	the seven-headed mace, the frightful weapon in battle,

CB 13:22	tukul ub¹ 2-e nu-íl ᵍⁱˢnagà mè	the weapon the ... cannot bear, the crusher in battle,
CB 13:23	mi-tum tukul nìr (ZA.NIM) sag pirig	the mace, the weapon made of *hulalu*-stone with lion heads,³
CB 14:01	kur-da gaba nu-gi₄	which has no rival in any foreign land,
CB 14:02	ᵍⁱˢKA×GÍR gír šunir 9	the sword blades, nine emblems,
CB 14:03	á nam-ur-sag-gá	the strength of the warrior class,
CB 14:04	ᵍⁱˢpan tir mes-gin₇ KA-gar-ra-ni	his bow which wails like a mes-forest,
CB 14:05	ti-šúr mè-a nim-gin₇ gír-da-ni	his furious arrows which flash like lightning in battle,
CB 14:06	é-mar-uru₅ ug pirig muš-huš-šè	his quiver, panthers and lions
CB 14:07	eme è-dè-da-ni	sticking their tongues at an enraged snake,
CB 14:08	á mè me nam-lugal si-si-a-da	the strength of battle, to direct the mes of king-ship.
CB 14:09	ensí lú é dù-a-ke₄	The ruler building the house,
CB 14:10	gù-dé-a ensí	Gudea, the ruler of Lagaš,
CB 14:11	lagašᵏⁱ-ke₄	
CB 14:12	sag im-mi-íb-rig₇-ge	is going to offer gifts for it:
CB 14:13	⌜é⌝ an-na lagab za-gìn-na kù-NE gug-gi-rin me-luh-ha-da	Copper, tin, lapis lazuli slabs, ... silver, flower-red carnelian from Meluhha,
CB 14:14	urudušen mah uruduURI mah	huge copper pots, huge copper kettles,
CB 14:15	uruduéš-da kù uru dubur kù an-né túm	pure copper cups, pure copper bowls fit for An,
CB 14:16	anzumušen-ga-ke₄	were [set up] at the place of the sá-[dug₄](-offering)
CB 14:17	banšur kù an-na íl-la-da	for Anzu to carry the offering table up to holy An.
CB 14:18	ki sá-[dug₄-ga] bí-[gub]	
CB 14:19	dnin-gí[r-su]-ke₄ uru-ni	Ningirsu was given a pleasant residence
CB 14:20	lagašᵏⁱ-⌜e x⌝ ki dùg ba-sum	by his city and Lagaš.
CB 14:21	é ki-ná-a ki ní-te é-a-ba	In the sleeping quarters, the place of rest in the house,
CB 14:22	ná mu-ni-gub	he made (his) bed.
CB 14:23	kur-kur-re mušen-gin₇ sila-a dumu den-líl-lá-da	All the lands, like birds on their journey,
CB 14:24	ní mu-da-ab-te-te	are resting with Enlil's son.
CB 14:25	íd-dè a-zal-le si-a-da	The rivers full of running water,
CB 14:26	ambar-ra HI-suhurku₆ suhur ku₆ gál-la-da	the marshes having carps and barbs,
CB 15:01	enkud kù-gál-bi zag-ba gub-ba-da	the fish wardens and water masters in charge of them,
CB 15:02	a gal-gal-e še si-si-a	the great fields filled with grain,
CB 15:03	gur₇-du₆-gur₇ maš ki lagašᵏⁱ-ke₄	the massive grain piles of Lagaš piled up,
CB 15:04	gú-gur-gur-ra-da	
CB 15:05	tùr dù-a-da a-maš dù-a-da	the (newly) built cattle pens, the (newly) built sheepfold,
CB 15:06	u₈ zi-da sila₄ ⌜dù-dù-a⌝-da	the good ewes producing lambs,
CB 15:07	udu-nita u₈ zi-bi šu-ba-ba-ra-da	the rams mounting (?) their good ewes,
CB 15:08	áb zi-da amar gub-gub-ba-da	the good cows putting down calves,
CB 15:09	šà-ba gud nindá gù-nun-bi di-da	the seed bull roaring in their midst,
CB 15:10	gud-e šu₄-dul₅-la si-sá-a-da	the oxen directed under the yoke,
CB 15:11	engar gud-rá-bi zag-ba gub-ba-da	the farmers and ox-drivers in charge of them,
CB 15:12	anše šá-dul₅-bi íl-a-da	the donkeys bearing their yoke,
CB 15:13	á-KU še si-bi egir-bí ús-sa-⌜da⌝	its sacks (?) full of grain following behind,
CB 15:14	DUN-e uruda ha-⌜x⌝ mah lá-a-da	the young men equipped with huge copper axes,
CB 15:15	é-kinkin mah íl-la-da	the highly productive mills,
CB 15:16	ᵍⁱˢda-gá GAD.TAK₄.DU₈ é gemé-tur ⌜dnin-gír-su⌝-[ka]-ke₄	... the house of Ningirsu's young female servants
CB 15:17	[...]-⌜x⌝-gin₇ [...]-a?-a-da	[...] ...,
CB 15:18	[...-g]e en níg-e si-⌜sá⌝-a-da [...] ...,	

---

³ It is tempting to identify this weapon with the mace head MH.7 in Appendix A, which Gudea dedicated to Ningirsu, since it has three lion heads and is said to be made of *hulalu*-stone.

CB 15:19	é sa 50 ⌈x⌉ húl-la si-a-da	Eninnu's courtyard filled with joy,
CB 15:20	si-im-da á-lá balag nam-nar šu-du₇-a	tambourines, tympana, and drums perfecting the music,
CB 15:21	balag ki-ág-ni ušumgal kalam-ma	his beloved drum Great-Dragon-of-the-Country
CB 15:22	sag-ba gin-na-da	marching at its (the parade's) head,
CB 15:23	ensí é mu-dù-a	the ruler who built Eninnu,
CB 16:01	gù-dé-a en ᵈnin-gír-su-ra	Gudea, presented (all that) for lord Ningirsu.
CB 16:02	mu-na-da-ku₄-ku₄	

8. Divine Blessings of Gudea

CB 23:10′	sila-sír-sír [ki] á-[ág-ba]	[At] the Silasirsir, [its place of] assi[gnment,]
23:11–16	[...]	(undecipherable traces)
CB 23:17	ᵍⁱˢgu-za gub-ba-bi lú nu-kúr-e	The throne which stands (there) no one will reverse.
CB 23:18	dingir-zu en ᵈnin-giš-zi-da dumu-KA an-na-kam	Your deity is lord Ningišzida, eldest child of An.
CB 23:19	dingir ama-zu ᵈnin-sún-na ama-gan numun zi-da	Your divine mother is Ninsun, the mother of good seed,
CB 23:20	numun-e ki-ág-gá-àm	beloved by her seed.
CB 23:21	áb zi-dè munus ba-tu-da-me	You were born by the good cow, the woman.
CB 23:22	mes zi ki lagašᵏⁱ è-a	You are Ningirsu's good young man emerging [from]
CB 24:01	ᵈnin-gír-su-ka-me	Lagaš.
CB 24:02	sig-ta nim-šè [m]u-zu hé-gál	Your name shall extend from south to north.
CB 24:03	[g]ù-dé-a [dug₄]-ga-za	Gudea, your [wo]rds are outstanding.
CB 24:04	[sag]-bi-šè ⌈x⌉-na-DU	
CB 24:05	[x] ⌈x⌉ KA guruš [(x)] an-né zu-me	You are [...], the youth recognized by An.
CB 24:06	[en]sí ⌈zi⌉ é-e nam-tar-ra-me	You are the [good ru]ler destined by the house.
CB 24:07	[g]ù-dé-a [du]mu ᵈnin-giš-zi-da-ka	[G]udea, [s]on of Ningišzida,
CB 24:08	nam-ti [h]a-mu-ra-sù	may life be long for you!"

BIBLIOGRAPHY

Abusch, Tzvi. "The Form and Meaning of a Babylonian Prayer to Marduk." *JAOS* 103 (1983): 3–15.

—. "Ishtar's Proposal and Gilgamesh's Refusal: An Interpretation of the Gilgamesh Epic, Tablet 6, Lines 1–79." *History of Religions* 26 (1986): 143–187.

—. "Gilgamesh's Request and Siduri's Denial. Part I: The Meaning of the Dialogue and its Implications for the History of the Epic." in *The Tablet and the Scroll: Near Eastern Studies in Honor of William W. Hallo*, eds. Mark E. Cohen et al. 1–14. Bethesda, Maryland: CDL Press, 1993.

al-Gailani Werr, Lamia. *Studies in the Chronology and Regional Style of Old Babylonian Cylinder Seals*. BiMes, 23. Malibu: Undena Publications, 1988.

Alster, Bendt. *Dumuzi's Dream: Aspects of Oral Poetry in a Sumerian Myth*. Mesopotamia, 1. Copenhagen: Akademisk Forlag, 1972.

—. *Studies in Sumerian Proverbs*. Mesopotamia, 3. Copenhagen: Akademisk Forlag, 1975.

—. "Interaction of Oral and Written Poetry in Early Mesopotamian Literature." in *Mesopotamian Epic Literature: Oral or Aural?*, eds. Herman L. J. Vanstiphout and Marianna E. Vogelzang. 23–69. Lampeter: Edwin Mellen Press, 1992.

Alster, Bendt and Aage Westenholz. "The Barton Cylinder." *ASJ* 16 (1994): 15–46.

Amiet, Pierre. *Glyptique susienne des origines à l'époque des perses achéménides*. MDP, 43. Paris: Paul Geuthner, 1972.

—. *L'Art d'Agadé au Musée du Louvre*. Paris: Éditions des musées nationaux, 1976.

—. *The Art of the Ancient Near East*. New York: Harry N. Abrams, 1980.

—. *La Glyptique mésopotamienne archaïque*. Paris: Editions du CNRS, 1980 (2nd edition).

—. "The Mythological Repertory in Cylinder Seals of the Agade Period (ca. 2335–2155 B.C.)." in *Art in Ancient Seals*, ed. Edith Porada. 35–60. Princeton: Princeton University Press, 1980.

André-Salvini, Béatrice. "À propos d'un objet cultuel de l'époque de Gudéa (AO 29931)." *SMEA* 30 (1992): 267–273.

Anonymous. *British Museum Guide to the Babylonian and Assyrian Antiquities*. London: Trustees, ²1908 and ³1922.

—. *Catalogue des antiquités composant la Collection Hakky Bey*. Paris, 1906.

Arnaud, Daniel. "Catalogue des textes trouvés au cours des fouilles et explorations régulières de la mission française à tell Senkereh-Larsa en 1969 et 1970." *Syria* 48 (1971): 289–93.

Asher-Greve, Julia M. *Frauen in altsumerischer Zeit*. BiMes, 18. Malibu: Undena Publications, 1985.

—. "The Oldest Female Oneiromancer." *CRRA* 33 (La femme dans le Proche Orient antique) (1987): 27–32.

—. "Review of Selz, Die Bankettszene." *BiOr* 44 (1987): 787–795.

—. "Observations on the Historical Relevance of Visual Imagery in Mesopotamia."

Cahiers du Centre d'Etude du Proche-Orient Ancient 5 (1989): 175–195.

—. "Reading the Horned Crown." *AfO* 42–43 (1995–96): 181–189.

Attinger, Pascal. *Eléments de linguistique sumérienne: La construction de du₁₁/e/di 'dire'*. Orbis Biblicus et Orientalis, Sonderband. Göttingen: Vandenhoeck & Ruprecht, 1993.

Averbeck, Richard E. *A Preliminary Study of Ritual and Structure in the Cylinders of Gudea*. Ann Arbor, Michigan: University Microfilms International, 1988.

Azarpay, Guitty. "The Neo-Sumerian Canon of Proportions in Art." in *Archaeologia Iranica et Orientalis: Miscellanea in Honorem Louis Vanden Berghe*, eds. L. de Meyer and E. Haerinck. 163–170. Gent: 1989.

—. "A Canon of Proportions in the Art of the Ancient Near East." in *Investigating Artistic Environments in the Ancient Near East*, ed. Ann C. Gunter. 93–103. Madison: University of Wisconsin Press, 1990.

—. "A Photogrammetric Study of Three Gudea Statues." *JAOS* 110 (1990): 660–665.

Baer, André. "Goudéa cylindre B colonnes XVIII à XXIV: Essai de restauration." *RA* 65 (1971): 1–14.

Bänder, Dana. *Die Siegesstele des Naramsîn und ihre Stellung in Kunst- und Kulturgeschichte*. Beiträge zur Kunstgeschichte, 103. Idstein: Schulz-Kirchner Verlag, 1995.

Barrelet, Marie-Thérèse. "Etudes de glyptique akkadienne: L'imagination figurative et le cycle d'Ea." *Or* 39 (1970): 213–251.

—. "Peut-on remettre en question la 'Restitution matérielle de la stèle des vautours'?" *JNES* 29 (1970): 233–258.

—. "La 'figure du roi' dans l'iconographie et dans les textes depuis Ur-Nanše jusqu'à la fin de la Ire dynastie de Babylone." *CRRA* 19 (Le palais et la royauté) (1974): 27–138.

Barthes, Roland. "An Introduction to the Structural Analysis of Narrative." *New Literary History* 6, 2 (1975): 237–272.

Barton, George A. *The Royal Inscriptions of Sumer and Akkad*. New Haven: Yale University Press, 1929.

Bauer, Josef. "Zum Totenkult im altsumerischen Lagasch." *ZDMG Supplementa* 1 (1969): 107–114.

Becker, Andrea. "Neusumerische Renaissance? Wissenschaftsgeschichtliche Untersuchungen zur Philologie und Archäologie." *BaM* 16 (1985): 229–316.

Behm-Blancke, Manfred R. *Das Tierbild in der altmesopotamischen Rundplastik*. BaF, 1. Mainz: Philipp von Zabern, 1978.

Behrens, Hermann. *Enlil und Ninlil: Ein sumerischer Mythos aus Nippur*. Studia Pohl: Series Major, 8. Rome: Biblical Institute Press, 1978.

Berlin, Adele. *Enmerkar and Ensuhkešdanna: A Sumerian Narrative Poem*. Occasional Publications of the Babylonian Fund, 2. Philadephia: University Museum, 1979.

—. "Parallel Word Pairs: A Linguistic Explanation." *UF* 15 (1983): 7–16.

—. *The Dynamics of Biblical Parallelism*. Bloomington: Indiana University Press, 1985.

Bernbeck, Reinhard. "Siegel, Mythen, Riten: Etana und die Ideologie der Akkadzeit." *BaM* 27 (1996): 159–213.

Bible Lands Museum Jerusalem: Guide to the Collection. Jerusalem: R. Sirkis, 1992.

Biggs, Robert D. and Miguel Civil. "Notes sur les textes sumériens archaïques." *RA* 60 (1966): 1–16.

Black, Jeremy A. "Review of Klein, Three Šulgi Hymns." *AfO* 29–30 (1983–84): 110–113.

—. "The Slain Heroes: Some Monsters of Ancient Mesopotamia." *SMS Bulletin* 15 (1988): 19–25.

—. "A Note on Zurghul." *Sumer* 46 (1989–90): 71–74.

—. "Eme-sal Cult Songs and Prayers." *AulaOr* 9 (1991): 23–36.

—. "Some Structural Features in Sumerian Narrative Poetry." in *Mesopotamian Epic Literature: Oral or Aural?*, eds. Herman L. J. Vanstiphout and Marianna E. Vogelzang. 71–101. Lampeter: Edwin Mellen Press, 1992.

—. "Inscriptions of Gudea in Montevideo." *ASJ* 17 (1995): 319–320.

Blanchard, J. M. "The Eye of the Beholder: On the Semiotic Status of Paranarratives." *Semiotica* 22 (1978): 235–268.

Boehmer, Rainer Michael. *Die Entwicklung der Glyptik während der Akkad-Zeit.* Berlin: Walter de Gruyter, 1965.

—. "Die Datierung des Puzur/Kutik-Inšušinak und einige sich daraus ergebende Konsequenzen." *Or* 35 (1966): 345–376.

—. "Review of Meyer, Altorientalische Denkmäler." *MIO* 13 (1967): 289–291.

—. "Isimu." *RlA* 5 (1976–80): 179–181.

—. "Früheste altorientalsche Darstellungen des Wisents." *BaM* 9 (1978): 18–21.

—. "Kopfbedeckung." *RlA* 6 (1980–83): 203–210.

—. "Uruk-Warka XXXVII: Survey des Stadtgebietes von Uruk, VI: Kleinfunde no.142." *BaM* 16 (1985): 141–145.

—. "Ein früher neusumerischer Wisent aus Uruk." *IBK* 24 (1986): 25–30.

Boese, Johannes. *Altmesopotamische Weihplatten: Eine sumerische Denkmalsgattung des 3.Jt. v.Chr.* UAVA, 6. Berlin: Walter de Gruyter, 1971.

—. "Zur absoluten Chronologie der Akkad-Zeit." *WZKM* 74 (1982): 33–55.

Borger, Rykle. "Gottesbrief." *RlA* 3 (1957–71): 575f.

Börker-Klähn, Jutta. "Šulgi badet." *ZA* 64 (1975): 235–240.

—. "Neusumerische Flachbildkunst." *PKG* 14 (1975): 197–206.

—. *Altvorderasiatische Bildstelen und vergleichbare Felsreliefs.* BaF, 4. Mainz: Philipp von Zabern, 1982.

—. "Die Reichsakkadische Kunst und Ägypten." *WZKM* 74 (1982): 57–94.

Borowski, Elie. "Introduction to the History of the Seal Collection of the Bible Lands Museum Jerusalem." in *Seals and Sealing in the Ancient Near East*, ed. Joan Goodnick Westenholz. 11–22. Jerusalem: Bible Lands Museum, 1995.

Bottéro, Jean. "Das erste semitische Grossreich." *FWG* 2 (1965): 91–128.

—. *Mesopotamia: Writing, Reasoning, and the Gods.* Chicago: University of Chicago Press, 1992.

Braun-Holzinger, Eva. *Figürliche Bronzen aus Mesopotamien.* Prähistorische Bronzefunde I.4. München: C.H. Beck, 1984.

—. "Löwenadler." *RlA* 7 (1987): 94–97.

—. *Mesopotamische Weihgaben der frühdynastischen bis altbabylonischen Zeit.* HSAO, 3. Heidelberg: Heidelberger Orientverlag, 1991.

—. "Der Bote des Ningišzida." in *Von Uruk nach Tuttul: Eine Festschrift für Eva*

Strommenger, eds. Barthel Hrouda et al. 37–43. München: Profil Verlag, 1992.

—. "Verschleppte Bau- und Weihinschriften der Herrscher von Lagaš." *ASJ* 19 (1997): 1–18.

Brilliant, Richard. *Gesture and Rank in Roman Art: The Use of Gestures to Denote Status in Roman Sculpture and Coinage*. Memoires of the Connecticut Academy of Arts and Science, 14. New Haven: Connecticut Academy of Arts and Science, 1963.

Brinkman, John A. "Kudurru." *RlA* 6 (1980–83): 268–277.

Buccellati, Giorgio. "Through a Tablet Darkly: A Reconstruction of Old Akkadian Monuments Described in Old Babylonian Copies." in *The Tablet and the Scroll: Near Eastern Studies in Honor of William W. Hallo*, eds. Mark E. Cohen et al. 58–71. Bethesda, Maryland: CDL Press, 1993.

Buchanan, Briggs. "Ancient Near Eastern Art in the Yale Babylonian Collection." *Archaeology* 15 (1962): 267–275.

—. *Early Near Eastern Seals in the Yale Babylonian Collection*. New Haven: Yale University Press, 1981.

Calmeyer, P. "Zur Rekonstruktion der 'Standarte' von Mari." *CRRA* 15 (La civilisation de Mari) (1967): 161–169.

Campbell, Jeremy. *Grammatical Man: Information, Entropy, Language, and Life*. New York: Simon and Schuster, 1982.

Canby, Jeanny Vorys. "A Mounumental Puzzle: Reconstructing the Urnammu Stele." *Expedition* 29 (1987): 54–64.

—. "The Doorway on the Ur Nammu Stele." *IstM* 43 (1993): 147–150.

Carroué, François. "La situation chronologique de Lagaš II: Un élément du dossier." *ASJ* 16 (1994): 47–75.

Castellino, Giorgio R. *Testi Sumerici e Accadici*. Torino: Tipografia Torinese, 1977.

Cavigneaux, Antoine. "Die Inschriften der XXXII. Kampagne." *UVB* 31–32 (1973–74): 54–57.

—. "L'essence divine." *JCS* 30 (1978): 177–185.

Chatman, Seymour. *Story and Discourse: Narrative Structure in Fiction and Film*. Ithaca, New York: Cornell University Press, 1978.

Christian, Viktor. *Altertumskunde des Zweistromlandes von der Vorzeit bis zum Ende der Achämenidenherrschaft*. Leipzig: K. W. Hiersemann, 1940.

Civil, Miguel. "Šu-Sîn's Historical Inscriptions: Collection B." *JCS* 21 (1967): 24–38.

—. "Note lexicographique sur SUHUR/KA." *RA* 61 (1967): 63–68.

—. "The Sumerian Writing System: Some Problems." *Or* 42 (1973): 21–33.

—. "Les limites de l'information textuelle." in *L'archéologie de l'Iraq du début de l'époque néolithique à 333 avant notre ère: Perspectives et limites de l'interprétation anthropologique des documents. Paris, 13–15 juin 1978*, ed. Marie-Thérèse Barrelet. 225–232. Colloques Internationaux du CNRS, 580. Paris: Editions du CNRS, 1980.

—. "An Early Dynastic School Exercise from Lagaš (Al-Hiba 29)." *BiOr* 40 (1983): 559–566.

—. "Enlil and Ninlil: The Marriage of Sud." *JAOS* 103 (1983): 43–66.

—. "On Some Literary Texts Mentioning Ur-Namma." *Or* 54 (1985): 27–45.

—. "Feeding Dumuzi's Sheep: The Lexicon as a Source of Literary Inspiration." *AOS* 67 (1987): 37–55.

—. "Sumerian Riddles: A Corpus." *AulaOr* 5 (1987): 17–37.

—. "The Statue of Šulgi-ki-ur₅-sag₉-kalam-ma, Part One: The Inscription." in *DUMU-E₂-DUB-BA-A: Studies in Honor of Åke W. Sjöberg*, eds. Hermann Behrens et al. 49–64. Occasional Publications of the Samuel Noah Kramer Fund, 11. Philadelphia: University Museum, 1989.

—. "On Mesopotamian Jails and Their Lady Warden." in *The Tablet and the Scroll: Near Eastern Studies in Honor of William W. Hallo*, eds. Mark E. Cohen et al. 72–78. Bethesda, Maryland: CDL Press, 1993.

—. "Sumerian Poetry." *NPEPP* (1993): 1233–1234.

—. *The Farmer's Instructions: A Sumerian Agricultural Manual*. AulaOr Supplementa, 5. Sabadell, Barcelona: Editorial Ausa, 1994.

—. "From the Epistolary of the Edubba." in *Fs. Lambert* (in press).

—. *Sumerian Debates and Dialogues*. (forthcoming).

Clay, Albert T. *Collections of Yale University 2: The Yale Babylonian Collection*. New Haven, no date.

Cohen, Gillian. "Visual Imagery in Thought." *New Literary History* 7 (1976): 513–523.

Cohen, Mark E. *The Cultic Calendars of the Ancient Near East*. Bethesda, Maryland: CDL Press, 1993.

Colbow, Gudrun. *Zur Rundplastik des Gudea von Lagaš*. Münchener Vorderasiatische Studien, 5. München: Profil Verlag, 1987.

Collon, Dominique. *First Impressions: Cylinder Seals in the Ancient Near East*. London: British Museum Publications, 1987.

—. *Ancient Near Eastern Art*. London: British Museum Press, 1995.

Connelly, Joan Breton. "Narrative and Image in the Attic Vase Painting: Ajax and Kassandra at the Trojan Palladion." in *Narrative and Event in Ancient Art*, ed. Peter J. Holliday. 88–129. Cambridge: Cambridge University Press, 1993.

Contenau, George. *Manuel d'archéologie orientale depuis des origines jusqu'à l'époque d'Alexandre*. Paris: A. Picard, 1927–47.

—. *Paris: Musée national du Louvre: Monuments mésopotamiens nouvellement acquis ou peu connus*. Paris: Editions d'art et de l'histoire, 1934.

Cooper, Jerrold S. *The Return of Ninurta to Nippur: an-gim dím-ma*. AnOr, 52. Rome: Biblical Institute Press, 1978.

—. *The Curse of Agade*. Baltimore: John Hopkins University Press, 1983.

—. "Medium and Message: Inscribed Cones and Vessels from Presargonic Sumer." *RA* 79 (1985): 98–114.

—. "Mesopotamian Historical Consciousness and the Production of Monumental Art in the Third Millenium B.C." in *Investigating Artistic Environments in the Ancient Near East*, ed. Ann C. Gunter. 39–51. Madison: University of Wisconsin Press, 1990.

—. "Babbling on Recovering Mesopotamian Orality." in *Mesopotamian Epic Literature: Oral or Aural?*, eds. Herman L. J. Vanstiphout and Marianna E. Vogelzang. 103–122. Lampeter: Edwin Mellen Press, 1992.

Crawford, Vaughn E. "Inscriptions from Lagash, Season 4, 1975–76." *JCS* 29 (1977): 189–222.

Cros, Gaston et al. *Mission française de Chaldée: Nouvelles fouilles de Tello*. Paris: Ernest Leroux, 1910.

Davis, Whitney. *The Canonical Tradition in Ancient Egyptian Art*. Cambridge: Cambridge University Press, 1989.

—. *Masking the Blow: The Scene of Presentation in Late Prehistoric Egyptian Art*. Berkeley: University of California Press, 1992.

de Genouillac, Henri. *Fouilles de Tello II: Epoques d'Ur IIIe dynastie et de Larsa*. Paris: Paul Geuthner, 1936.

de Liagre Böhl, Franz Marius Theodor. *Oorkonden uit de periode der rijken van Sumer en Akkad (3000–2000 v. Chr.)*. Mededeelingen uit te Leidsche verzameling van spijkerschrift-inscripties, 1. Amsterdam: Noord-Hollandsche uitgeversmaatschappij, 1933.

de Miroschedji, Pierre. "Vases et objets en stéatite susiens du musée du Louvre." *DAFI* 3 (1973): 9–79.

Delaporte, Louis Joseph. *Musée national du Louvre: Catalogue des cylindres, cachets et pierres gravées de style oriental*. Paris: Hachette, 1920–23.

de Sarzec, Ernest et al. *Découvertes en Chaldée*. Paris: Ernest Leroux, 1884–1912.

Diakonoff, Igor M. "The Inscriptions of Gudea of Lagash." *MIO* 15 (1969): 525–532.

Dittmann, Reinhard. "Glyptikgruppen am Übergang von der Akkad- zur Ur III-Zeit." *BaM* 25 (1994): 75–117.

Dolce, Rita. *Gli Intarsi Mesopotamici dell'epoca Proto-dinastica*. Serie Archeologica, 23. Rome: Istituto di studi del Vicino Oriente, Universita, 1978.

Donbaz, Veysal and A. K. Grayson. *Royal Inscriptions on Clay Cones from Ashur now in Istanbul*. RIME Supplement, 1. Toronto: University of Toronto Press, 1984.

Dougherty, Raymond P. "Parallels to Solomon's Provisioning System." *AASOR* 5 (1923–24): 23–65.

—. "Searching for Ancient Remains in Lower 'Irâq." *AASOR* 7 (1925–26): 1–93.

Dunham, Sally S. *A Study of Ancient Mesopotamian Foundations*. Ann Arbor, Michigan: University Microfilms International, 1980.

—. "Bricks for the Temples of Šara and Ninurra." *RA* 76 (1982): 27–41.

—. "Sumerian Words for Foundation: Part I: Temen." *RA* 80 (1986): 31–64.

Edzard, Dietz Otto. "Die Einrichtung eines Tempels im älteren Babylonien: Philologische Aspekte." *CRRA* 20 (Le temple et le culte) (1975): 156–163.

—. "Königsinschriften (A. Sumerisch)." *RlA* 6 (1980–83): 59–65.

—. "Deep-Rooted Skyscrapers and Bricks: Ancient Mesopotamian Architecture and its Imagery." in *Figurative Language in the Ancient Near East*, eds. Markham Geller et al. 13–24. London: School of Oriental and African Studies, University of London, 1987.

—. "Literatur." *RlA* 7 (1987): 35–48.

—. "Selbstgespräch und Monolog in der akkadischen Literatur." *HSS* 37 (1990): 149–162.

—. "Gilgameš and Huwawa A." *ZA* 80/81 (1990/91): 165–203/165–233.

—. "Irikagina (Urukagina)." *AulaOr* 9 (1991): 77–80.

—. "Metrik." *RlA* 8 (1993): 148f.

—. "Private Frömmigkeit in Sumer." in *Official Cult and Popular Religion in the Ancient Near East*, ed. Eiko Matsushima. 195–208. Heidelberg: Universitätsverlag Carl Winter, 1993.

—. "The Names of the Sumerian Temples." in *Sumerian Gods and their Representations*, eds. I. L Finkel and M. J. Geller. 159–165. Cuneiform Monographs, 7. Groningen: Styx, 1997.

Edzard, Dietz Otto et al. *Ergänzungsheft zu A. Falkenstein, Grammatik der Sprache des Gudea von Lagaš*. AnOr, 29A. Rome: Biblical Institute Press, 1978.

Ellis, Richard. *Foundation Deposits in Ancient Mesopotamia*. YNER, 2. New Haven: Yale University Press, 1982 (2nd edition).

Falkenstein, Adam. *Grammatik der Sprache Gudeas von Lagaš I: Schrift- und Formenlehre*. AnOr, 28. Rome: Biblical Institute Press, 1949.

—. *Grammatik der Sprache Gudeas von Lagaš II: Syntax*. AnOr, 29. Rome: Biblical Institute Press, 1950.

—. "Die Anunna in der Sumerischen Überlieferung." *AS* 16 (1965): 127–140.

—. *Die Inschriften Gudeas von Lagaš: Einleitung*. AnOr, 30. Rome: Biblical Institute Press, 1966.

—. " 'Wahrsagung' in der sumerischen Ueberlieferung." *CRRA* 14 (La divination en Mésopotamie ancienne) (1966): 45–56.

—. "Zum sumerischen Lexikon." *ZA* 58 (1967): 5–15.

—. "Girsu (A.Philologisch)." *RlA* 3 (1957–71): 385–391.

—. "Gudea (A.Philologisch)." *RlA* 3 (1957–71): 676–679.

Farber, Getrud. "me." *RlA* 7 (1987–90): 610–613.

—. "Konkret, kollektiv, abstrakt?" *AulaOr* 9 (1991): 81–90.

Fischer, Claudia. "Gudea zwischen Tradition und Moderne." *BaM* 27 (1996): 215–228.

Foster, Benjamin R. "The Sargonic Victory Stele from Telloh." *Iraq* 47 (1985): 15–30.

Foster, Benjamin R. and Karen Polinger Foster. "A Lapidary's Gift to Geštinanna." *Iraq* 40 (1978): 61–65.

Foxvog, Daniel et al. "Lamma/Lammassu (A. Mesopotamien, Philologisch)." *RlA* 6 (1980–83): 446–453.

Frankfort, Henri. *Cylinder Seals: A Documentary Essay on the Art and Religion of the Ancient Near East*. London: Macmillan & Co., 1939.

—. *Kingship and the Gods: A Study of Ancient Near Eastern Religion as the Integration of Society and Nature*. Chicago: University of Chicago Press, 1948.

—. *The Art and Architecture of the Ancient Orient*. Harmondsworth: Penguin Books, 1985 (4th edition).

Frayne, Douglas. "New Light on the Reign of Išbi-Erra." *CRRA* 28 (AfO Beiheft 19) (1982): 25–32.

Freedberg, David. *The Power of Images: Studies in the History and Theory of Response*. Chicago: University of Chicago Press, 1989.

Fuhr-Jaeppelt, Ilse. *Materialien zur Ikonographie des Löwenadlers Anzu-Imdugud*. München: Scharl & Strohmeyer, 1972.

Gelb, Ignace J. "The Double Names of the Hittite Kings." *Rocznik Orientalistyczny* 17 (1953): 146–154.

—. "The Names of Ex-Voto Objects in Ancient Mesopotamia." *Names* 4 (1956): 65–69.

Gelb, Ignace J. et al. *Earliest Land Tenure Systems in the Near East: Ancient Kudurrus*.

OIP, 104. Chicago: Oriental Institute, 1991.

Geller, Markham J. "Review of Gibson (ed.), The Organization of Power." *ZA* 81 (1991): 144–146.

Genette, Gérard. *Figure III*. Paris: Editions du Seuil, 1972.

George, Andrew R. "Cuneiform Texts in the Birmingham City Museum." *Iraq* 41 (1979): 121–140.

—. *House Most High: The Temples of Ancient Mesopotamia*. Winona Lake: Eisenbrauns, 1993.

Glassner, Jean-Jacques. "Chronologie." *NABU* (1994): no. 9.

Gombrich, Ernst H. *The Image & the Eye: Further Studies in the Psychology of Pictorial Representation*. London: Phaidon Press, 1982.

Gomi, Tohru. "Shulgi-Simti and her Libation Place (KI-A-NAG)." *Orient* 12 (1976): 1–14.

Goodnick Westenholz, Joan. "Heroes of Akkad." *JAOS* 103 (1983): 327–336.

—. "Enheduanna, En-Priestess, Hen of Nanna, Spouse of Nanna." in *DUMU-E$_2$-DUB-BA-A: Studies in Honor of Åke W. Sjöberg*, eds. Hermann Behrens et al. 539–556. Occasional Publications of the Samuel Noah Kramer Fund, 11. Philadelphia: University Museum, 1989.

—. "The Clergy of Nippur: The Priestess of Enlil." *CRRA* 35 (Nippur at the Centennial) (1992): 297–310.

—. "Oral Traditions and Written Texts in the Cycle of Akkade." in *Mesopotamian Epic Literature: Oral or Aural?*, eds. Herman L. J. Vanstiphout and Marianna E. Vogelzang. 123–154. Lampeter: Edwin Mellen Press, 1992.

—. *Legends of the Kings of Akkad: The Texts*. Winona Lake: Eisenbrauns, 1997.

Goossens Godefroy. *Les antiquités égyptienne, grèques, étrusques, romaines et gallo-romaines du Musée de Mariemont*. Bruxelles, 1952.

Gragg, Gene B. "The Keš Temple Hymn." in *The Collection of the Sumerian Temple Hymns*, Åke W. Sjöberg and Bergmann S. J. 155–188. TCS, 3. Locust Valley, New York: J. J. Augustin Publisher, 1969.

—. "A Class of 'When' Clauses in Sumerian." *JNES* 32 (1973): 124–134.

—. "The Fable of the Heron and the Turtle." *AfO* 24 (1973): 51–72.

Grayson, A. K. "Review of Salonen, Hausgeräte." JAOS 90 (1970): 528–529.

—. "Old and Middle Assyrian Royal Inscriptions–Marginalia." in *Ah Assyria ...: Studies in Assyrian History and Ancient Near Eastern Historiography Presented to Hayim Tadmor*, eds. Mordechai Cogan and Israel Eph'al. 264–266. Jerusalem: Magnes Press, 1991.

Greengus, Samuel. "Bridewealth in Sumerian Sources." *HUCA* 61 (1990): 25–88.

Gressmann, Hugo. *Altorientalische Texte und Bilder zum Alten Testament*. Berlin: Walter de Gruyter, 1926–27.

Groenewegen-Frankfort, Henrietta A. *Arrest and Movement: Space and Time in the Art of the Ancient Near East*. Cambridge: Harvard University Press, 1987.

Hallo, William W. *Early Mesopotamian Royal Titles*. AOS, 43. New Haven: American Oriental Society, 1957.

—. "Gutium." *RlA* 3 (1957–71): 708–720.

—. "The Cultic Setting of Sumerian Poetry." *CRRA* 17 (1970): 116–134.

—. "The Royal Correspondance of Larsa I: A Sumerian Prototype for the Prayer of

Hezekiah." *AOAT* 25 (1976): 209–224.

—. "Toward a History of Sumerian Literature." *AS* 20 (1976): 181–203.

—. "The Limits of Skepticism." *JAOS* 110 (1990): 187–199.

Hansen, Donald P. "New Votive Plaques from Nippur." *JNES* 22 (1963): 145–166.

—. "Al-Hiba: A Summary of Four Seasons of Excavation (1968–1976)." *Sumer* 34 (1978): 72–85.

—. "Lagaš." *RlA* 6 (1980–83): 419–430.

Harper, Prudence O. et al. (eds.). *The Royal City of Susa: Ancient Near Eastern Treasures in the Louvre.* New York: The Metropolitan Museum of Art, 1992.

Hartmann, Henrike. *Die Musik der sumerischen Kultur.* Frankfurt: Universitätsverlag, 1960.

Haussperger, Martha. *Die Einführungsszene: Entwicklung eines mesopotamischen Motivs von der altakkadischen bis zum Ende der altbabylonischen Zeit.* Münchener Vorderasiatische Studien, 11. München: Profil Verlag, 1991.

Heisel, Joachim P. *Antike Bauzeichnungen.* Darmstadt: Wissenschaftliche Buchgesellschaft, 1993.

Heimpel, Wolfgang. *Tierbilder in der sumerischen Literatur.* Studia Pohl, 2. Rome: Biblical Institute Press, 1968.

—. "Observations on Rhythmical Structure in Sumerian Literary Texts." *Or* 39 (1970): 492–495.

—. "The Nanshe Hymn." *JCS* 33 (1981): 65–139.

—. "Gudea's Fated Brick." *JNES* 46 (1987): 205–211.

—. "Libation." *RlA* 7 (1987–90): 1–5.

Heuzey, Léon. *Paris: Musée national du Louvre: Catalogue des antiquitées Chaldéenne.* Paris: Librairies-imprimeries réunis, 1902.

—. "Le sceau de Gudea: Nouvelles recherches sur quelques symboles Chaldéens." *RA* 5 (1902): 129–139.

—. "Une des sept stèles de Goudéa." *Monuments et Mémoires* 16 (1909): 5–24.

Heuzey, Léon and François Thureau-Dangin. *Réstitution matérielle de la stèle de Vautours.* Paris: Leroux, 1909.

Hill, D. K. *The Fertile Crescent.* Baltimore: Trusties, 1944.

Hilprecht, H. V. *Explorations in Bible Lands during the 19th Century.* Philadelphia: A. J. Hollman & Co., 1903.

Hunger, Hermann. "Kolophone." *RlA* 6 (1980–83): 186f.

Huot, Jean-Louis. "The Man-Faced Bull." *Sumer* 34 (1978): 104–113.

Hurowitz, Avigdor. *I Have Built You An Exalted House: Temple Building in the Bible in Light of Mesopotamian and Northwest Semitic Writings.* JSOT/ASOR Monograph Series, 5. Sheffield, England: JSOT Press, 1992.

Invernizzi, A. "Review of Börker-Klähn, Altvorderasiatische Bildstelen." *Mesopotamia* 18–19 (1983–84): 239–245.

Jacobsen, Thorkild. *Cuneiform Texts in the National Museum Copenhagen, Chiefly of Economic Contents.* Copenhagen: C.T. Thomsens, 1939.

—. "La géographie et les voies de communication du pays de Sumer." *RA* 52 (1958): 127–129.

—. *Toward the Image of Tammuz and Other Essays on Mesopotamian History and Culture.* HSS, 21. Cambridge: Harvard University Press, 1970.

—. "The Stele of the Vultures Col.I-X." *AOAT* 25 (1976): 247–259.

—. *The Harps that Once ...: Sumerian Poetry in Translation*. New Haven: Yale University Press, 1987.

—. "The Asakku in Lugal-e." in *A Scientific Humanist: Studies in Memory of Abraham Sachs*, eds. Erle Leichty et al. 225–232. Occasional Publications of the Samuel Noah Kramer Fund, 9. Philadelphia: University Museum, 1988.

—. "The Term Ensí." *AulaOr* 9 (1991): 113–121.

Jakob-Rost, Liane. *Die Sumerische Kunst aus den Staatlichen Museen zu Berlin*. Leipzig, 1966.

Jastrow, Morris. *Bildermappe zur Religion Babyloniens und Assyriens*. Giessen: A. Töppelmann, 1912.

Jeremias, Alfred. *Handbuch der altorientalischen Geisteskultur*. Leipzig: Hinrichs, 1929 (2nd edition).

Johansen, F. *Statues of Gudea: Ancient and Modern*. Mesopotamia, 6. Copenhagen: Akademisk Forlag, 1978.

Jones, Tom B. "Sumerian Administrative Documents: An Essay." *AS* 20 (1976): 41–61.

Kessler, Karlheinz. "Uruk-Warka XXXVII: Survey des Stadtgebietes von Uruk, VII: Die Löweninschrift Gudeas." *BaM* 16 (1985): 149f.

King, Leonard William. *A History of Sumer and Akkad*. London: Chatto & Windus, 1923.

Kirk, G. S., *Myth: Its Meanings and Functions in Ancient & Other Cultures*. Cambridge: University Press, 1970.

Klein, Jacob. "Building and Dedication Hymns in Sumerian Literature." *ASJ* 11 (1989): 27–67.

—. "From Gudea to Šulgi: Continuity and Change in Sumerian Literary Tradition." in *DUMU-E$_2$-DUB-BA-A: Studies in Honor of Åke W. Sjöberg*, eds. Hermann Behrens et al. 289–302. Occasional Publications of the Samuel Noah Kramer Fund, 11. Philadelphia: University Museum, 1989.

–. "Šulgi and Išmedagan: Originality and Dependence in Sumerian Royal Hymnology." in *Bar-Ilan Studies in Assyriology dedicated to Pinhas Artzi*, eds. Jacob Klein and Aaron Skaist. 65–136. Ramat-Gan: Bar-Ilan University Press, 1990.

Kobayashi, Toshiko. "On the Meaning of the Offerings for the Statue of Entemena." *Orient* 20 (1984): 43–65.

—. "A Study of the Peg Figurine with the Inscription of Enannatum I." *Orient* 24 (1988): 1–17.

—. "Ninazu, The Personal Deity of Gudea." *Orient* 30–31 (1995): 142–157.

Köcher, Franz. "Der babylonische Göttertypentext." *MIO* 1 (1953): 57–107.

Koldewey, Robert. "Die altbabylonischen Gräber in Surghul und El Hibba." *ZA* 2 (1887): 403–430.

Kramer, Samuel Noah. *The Sacred Marriage Rite: Aspects of Faith, Myth, and Ritual in Ancient Sumer*. Bloomington: Indiana University Press, 1969.

—. "The Ur-Nammu Law Code: Who was Its Author?" *Or* 52 (1983): 453–456.

—. "The Temple in Sumerian Literature." in *Tempel in Society*, ed. Michael V. Fox. 1-16. Winona Lake, Indiana: Eisenbrauns, 1988.

Krecher, Joachim. "Das sumerische Phonem /g̃/." in *Festschrift L. Matouš*, eds. B. Hruška and G. Komoroczy. 7–73. Budapest: Eötvös Loránd University, 1978.

—. "Sumerische Literatur." in *Altorientalische Literaturen*, ed. Wolfgang Röllig. 100–150. Neues Handbuch der Literaturwissenschaft, 1. Wiesbaden: Akademische Verlagsgesellschaft Athenaion, 1978.

—. "Insignien." *RlA* 5 (1976–80): 109–114.

Lackenbacher, Sylvie. *Le roi bâtisseur: Les récits de construction assyriens des origines à Tiglatphalasar III*. Paris: Editions Recherche sur les civilisations, 1982.

Lafont, Bertrand. "Review of Steible, Neusumerische Bau- und Weihinschriften." *BiOr* 50 (1993): 675–681.

Lafont Bertrand and Fatma Yildiz. *Tablettes cunéiformes de Tello au Musée d'Istanbul datant de l'époque de la III dynastie d'Ur*. Uitgaven van het Nederlands Historisch-Archeologisch Instituut te Istanbul, 55. Istanbul: Nederlands Historisch-Archeologisch Instituut, 1989.

Lambert, Maurice. "Deux texts de Gudea." *RA* 47 (1953): 83–84.

Lambert, Maurice and R. Tournay. "Le cylindre A de Gudéa." *RB* 55 (1948): 403–437.

—. "Le cylindre B de Gudéa." *RB* 55 (1948): 520–543.

—. "Review of Parrot, Ziggurats et Tour de Babel." *RA* 45 (1951): 33–40.

Lambert, Wilfred G. "Ancestors, Authors, and Canonicity." *JCS* 11 (1957): 1–14.

—. "Gilgamesh in Literature and Art: The Second and First Millenia." in *Monsters and Demons in the Ancient and Medieval Worlds: Papers Presented in Honor of Edith Porada*, eds. Ann E. Farkas et al. 37–52. Main: Philipp von Zabern, 1987.

—. "The Sumero-Babylonian Brick-God Kulla." *JNES* 46 (1987): 203f.

—. "The Reading of Uru-KA-gi-na Again." *AulaOr* 10 (1992): 256–258.

Landsberger, Benno. "Einige unerkannt gebliebene oder verkannte Nomina des Akkadischen, 2." *WZKM* 57 (1961): 1–23.

—. "Einige unerkannt gebliebene oder verkannte Nomina des Akkadischen, 3." *WO* 3 (1964): 48–79.

Legrain, Léon. "The Stela of the Flying Angels." *MJ* 18 (1927): 75–98.

—. "Restauration de la stèle d'Ur-Nammu." *RA* 30 (1933): 111–115.

Levy, Selim. "A Statue of Gudea in the Iraq Museum in Baghdad." *AfO* 11 (1936–37): 151f.

Limet, Henri. *L'anthroponymie sumérienne dans les documents de la 3e dynastie d'Ur*. Bibliothèque de la Faculté de Philosophie et Lettres de l'Université de Liège, 180. Paris: Les Belles Lettres, 1968.

Littauer Mary Aiken and Joost H. Crouwel. "The Vulture Stela and an Early Type of Two-Wheeled Vehicle." *JNES* 32 (1973): 324–329.

—. *Wheeled Vehicles and Ridden Animals in the Ancient Near East*. Handbuch der Orientalistik, I, 2.B. Leiden: E. J. Brill, 1979.

Liverani, Mario. "Memorandum on the Approach to Historiographic Texts." *Or* 42 (1973): 178–194.

—. "Model and Actualizaion: The Kings of Akkad in the Historical Tradition." in *Akkad: The First World Empire*, ed. Mario Liverani. 41–67. HANE 5. Padova: Sargon srl, 1993.

Loding, Darlene. *A Craft Archive from Ur III*. Ann Arbor: University Microfilms International, 1974.

Longman III, Tremper. *Fictional Akkadian Autobiography. A Generic and Comparative Study*. Winona Lake, Indiana: Eisenbrauns, 1991.

Lotman, Jury M. "The Discrete Text and the Iconic Text: Remarks on the Structure of Narrative." *New Literary History* 6 (1975): 333–338.

Loud, G. *Khorsabad I: Excavations in the Palace and at a City Gate*. OIP, 38. Chicago: Oriental Institute, 1936.

Ludwig, Marie-Christine. *Untersuchungen zu den Hymnen des Išme-Dagan von Isin*. SANTAG, 2. Wiesbaden: Otto Harrassowitz, 1990.

Maeda, Tohru. "Two Rulers by the Name of Ur-Ningirsu in Pre-Ur III Lagash." *ASJ* 10 (1988): 19–35.

Margueron, J.-C. " 'L'Étandard d'Ur': Récit historique ou magique?" in *Collectanea Orientalia: Études offertes en hommage à Agnès Spycket*, eds. H. Gasche et B. Hrouda. 159-169. CPOA, I 3. Neuchâtel: Recherches et Publications, 1996.

Martin, Wallace. *Recent Theories of Narrative*. Ithaca and London: Cornell University Press, 1986.

Marzahn, Joachim. "Sumerische Inschriften des Vorderasiatischen Museums zu Berlin." *AoF* 14 (1987): 21–40.

Mayer-Opificius, Ruth. "Gedanken zur Bedeutung frühdynastischer Rundbilder." in *Ad bene et fideliter seminandum: Festgabe für Karl-Heinz Deller zum 21. Februar 1987*, eds. Gerlinde Mauer and Ursula Magen. 247–268. AOAT, 220. Neukirchen-Vluyn: Neukirchner Verlag, 1987.

—. "Feldzeichen." in *Collectanea Orientalia: Études offertes en hommage à Agnès Spycket*, eds. H. Gasche et B. Hrouda. 213–226. CPOA, I 3. Neuchâtel: Recherches et Publications, 1996.

Maxwell-Hyslop, K. R. "The Goddess Nanše: An Attempt to Identify her Representation." *Iraq* 54 (1992): 79–82.

Meissner, Bruno. *Grundzüge der babylonisch-assyrischen Plastik*. AO, 15, 3–4. Leipzig: Hinrichs, 1915.

Mellink, Machteld. "An Akkadian Illustration of a Campaign in Cilicia?" *Anatolia* 7 (1963): 101–115.

Merhav, Rivka et al. *The Jan Mitchell Gift to the Israel Museum: Past and Present*. Jerusalem: Israel Museum, 1974.

—. *A Glimpse into the Past: The Joseph Ternbach Collection*. Jerusalem: Israel Museum, 1981.

Metzger, Martin. *Königsthron und Gottesthron: Thronformen und Throndarstellungen in Aegypten und im Vordern Orient im 3. und 2. Jt. v. Chr. und deren Bedeutung für das Verständnis von Aussagen über den Thron im Alten Testament*. AOAT, 15. Neukirchen-Vluyn: Neukirchner Verlag, 1985.

Meyer, Eduard. *Sumerier und Semiten in Babylonien*. Berlin: Königliche Akademie der Wissenschaften, 1906.

Michalowski, Piotr. "The Death of Shulgi." *Or* 46 (1977): 220–225.

—. "History as a Charter: Some Observations on the Sumerian King List." *JAOS* 103 (1983): 237–248.

—. *The Lamentation over the Destruction of Sumer and Ur*. Mesopotamian Civilizations, 1. Winona Lake, Indiana: Eisenbrauns, 1989.

—. "Early Mesopotamian Communicative Systems: Art, Literature, and Writing." in *Investigating Artistic Environments in the Ancient Near East*, ed. Ann C. Gunter. 53–69. Madison: University of Wisconsin Press, 1990.

—. "Charisma and Control: On Continuity and Change in Early Mesopotamian Bureaucratic Systems." in *The Organization of Power: Aspects of Bureaucracy in the Ancient Near East*, eds. McGuire Gibson and Robert D. Biggs. 45–57. SAOC, 46. Chicago: Oriental Institute, 1991 (2nd edition).

—. "Orality and Literacy and Early Mesopotamian Literature." in *Mesopotamian Epic Literature: Oral or Aural?*, eds. Herman L. J. Vanstiphout and Marianna E. Vogelzang. 227–245. Lampeter: Edwin Mellen Press, 1992.

—. "Sailing to Babylon, Reading the Dark Side of the Moon." in *The Study of the Ancient Near East in the Twenty-First Century*, eds. Jerrold S. Cooper and Glenn M. Schwartz. 177-193. Winona Lake, Indiana: Eisenbrauns, 1996.

Michalowski, Piotr and C. B. F. Walker. "A New Sumerian 'Law Code'." in *DUMU-E_2-DUB-BA-A: Studies in Honor of Åke W. Sjöberg*, eds. Hermann Behrens et al. 383–396. Occasional Publications of the Samuel Noah Kramer Fund, 11. Philadelphia: University Museum, 1989.

Miller, Arthur G. "Comparing Maya Image and Text." in *Word and Image in Maya Culture: Explorations in Language, Writing, and Representation*, eds. William F. Hanks and Don S. Rice. 176–188. Salt Lake City: University of Utah Press, 1989.

Mitchell, W. J. T. *Iconology: Image, Text, Ideology*. Chicago: University of Chicago Press, 1986.

Monaco, Salvatore F. "Two Notes on ASJ 10, 1988." *ASJ* 12 (1990): 89–105.

Moortgat, Anton. *Die Kunst des Alten Mesopotamien I: Sumer und Akkad*. Köln: DuMont, 1982 (2nd edition).

Müller-Karpe, Michael. *Metallgefässe im Iraq: Von den Anfängen bis zur Akkad-Zeit*. Prähistorische Bronzefunde, II 14. Stuttgart: Franz Steiner Verlag, 1993.

Muscarella, Oscar White (ed.). *Ladders to Heaven: Art Treasures from the Lands of the Bible*. Toronto: McClelland & Stewart, 1981.

Musil, Alois. *The Middle Euphrates*. Oriental Explorations and Studies, 3. New York: American Geographical Society, 1927.

Neumann, Hans. *Handwerk in Mesopotamien: Untersuchungen zu seiner Organisation in der Zeit der III. Dynastie von Ur*. Schriften zur Geschichte und Kultur des alten Orients, 19. Berlin: Akademie-Verlag, 1987.

Nougayrol, Jean. "Textes et documents figurés." *RA* 41 (1947): 23–53.

Nunn, Astrid. "Die Mehrgesichtigkeit oder die Weisheit." in *Von Uruk nach Tuttul: Eine Festschrift für Eva Strommenger*, eds. Barthel Hrouda et al. 143–149. München: Profil Verlag, 1992.

Oelsner, Joachim. "Ein Zikkurrat-Grundriss aus Nippur." *FB* 24 (1984): 63–65.

Opificius, Ruth. "Girsu (B. Archäologisch)." *RlA* 3 (1957–71): 391–401.

Opitz, D. "Der geschlachtete Gott." *AfO* 5 (1928–29): 81–89.

—. "Studien zur altorientalischen Kunst." *AfO* 6 (1930): 59–65.

Oppenheim, A. Leo. *The Interpretation of Dreams in the Ancient Near East with a Translation of an Assyrian Dream-Book*. TAPS, 46,3. Philadelphia: American Philosophical Society, 1956.

—. *Ancient Mesopotamia: Portrait of a Dead Civilization*. Chicago: University of Chicago Press, 1977 (2nd edition).

Panofsky, Erwin. *Studien zur Ikonologie: Humanistische Themen in der Kunst der Renaissance*. Köln: Dumont, 1980.

411

Parrot, André. *Tello: Vingt campagnes de fouilles 1877–1933*. Paris: Editions Albin Michel, 1948.

—. "Taureau androcéphale au nom de Gudéa (AO 20152)." *RA* 46 (1952): 203f.

—. *Glyptique mésopotamienne: Fouilles de Lagash et de Larsa (1931–1933)*. Paris: Paul Geuthner, 1954.

—. *Sumer: The Dawn of Art*. New York: Golden Press, 1961.

Perkins, Ann. "Narration in Babylonian Art." *AJA* 61 (1957): 54–62.

Picchioni, Sergio Angelo. "La direzione della scrittura cuneiforme e gli archivi di Tell Mardikh-Ebla." *Or* 49 (1980): 225–251.

Place, Victor. *Ninive et l'Assyrie*. Paris: Imprémerie impériale, 1867–70.

Pongratz-Leisten, Beate. "Mesopotamische Standarten in literarischen Zeugnissen." *BaM* 23 (1992): 299–340.

Porada, Edith. "True or False? Genuine and False Cylinder Seals at Andrews University." *Andrews University Seminary Studies* 6 (1968): 134–149.

—. *Man and Images in the Ancient Near East*. Anshen Transdisciplinary Lectureships in Art, Science and the Philosophy of Culture, 4. Wakefield: Moyer Bell, 1995.

Postgate, J. N. "Text and figure in ancient Mesopotamia: match and mismatch." in *The Ancient Mind: Elements of Cognitive Archaeology*, eds. C. Renfrew and E. B. W. Zubrow. 176–184. Cambridge: University of Cambridge Press, 1994.

Price, Ira Maurice. *The Great Cylinder Inscriptions A and B of Gudea*. Leipzig: Hinrichs, 1899–1927.

Prince, Gerald. *A Grammar of Stories: An Introduction*. De Proprietatibus Litterarum: Series Minor, 13. The Hague: Mouton, 1973.

Propp, Vladimir. *Morphology of the Folktale*. Austin, Texas: University of Texas Press, 1968 (2nd edition).

Raisbeck, Gordon. *Information Theory: An Introduction for Scientists and Engineers*. Cambridge, Mass.: M.I.T. Press, 1965.

Rashid, Subhi Anwar. *Gründungsfiguren im Iraq*. München: C. H. Beck, 1983.

—. *Musikgeschichte in Bildern II, 2: Mesopotamien*. Leipzig: Deutscher Verlag für Musik, 1984.

Renger, Johannes M. "Untersuchungen zum Priestertum der altbabylonischen Zeit (1)." *ZA* 58 (1967): 110–188.

—. "The Daughters of Urbaba: Some Thoughts on the Succession to the Throne during the 2. Dynasty of Lagash." *AOAT* 25 (1976): 367–369.

Rittig, Dessa. *Assyrisch-babylonische Kleinplastik magischer Bedeutung vom 13.-6. Jh. v. Chr.* Münchener Vorderasiatische Studien, 1. München: Profil Verlag, 1970.

Rosengarten, Yvonne. *Sumer et le sacré: Le jeu des prescriptions (me), des dieux, et des destins*. Paris: Editions E. de Boccard, 1977.

Roth, Martha. *Law Collections from Mesopotamia and Asia Minor*. Atlanta: Scholars Press, 1995.

Rova, Elena. *Ricerche sui sigilli a cylindro vicino-orientali del periodo di Uruk/Jendet Nasr*. Orientis Antiqui Collectio, 20. Roma: Istituto per l'Oriente, 1994.

Russell, John M. *Sennacherib's Palace without Rival at Nineveh*. Chicago: University of Chicago Press, 1991.

Sallaberger, Walther. *Der Kultische Kalender der Ur III Zeit*. UAVA, 7. Berlin: Walter de Gruyter, 1993.

Sauren, Herbert. "Die Einweihung des Eninnu." *CRRA* 20 (Le temple et le culte) (1975): 95–103.

Schapiro, Meyer. "On Some Problems in the Semiotics of Visual Art: Field and Vehicle in Image Signs." *Semiotica* 1 (1969): 223–242.

Schlossman, Betty L. "Two Foundation Figurines." in *Ancient Mesopotamian Art and Selected Texts: The Pierpont Morgan Library*. 9–21. New York: The Pierpont Morgan Library, 1976.

—. "Portaiture in Mesopotamia in the Late Third and Early Second Millenium B.C." *AfO* 26 (1978–79): 56–65.

Schwarz, Benjamin. "Votive Inscriptions from Lagash in the Eames Babylonian Collection." *Bulletin of the New York Public Library* 44 (1940): 807–810.

Seidl, Ursula. "Review of Börker-Klähn, Altvorderasiatische Bildstelen." *Or* 55 (1986): 320–327.

Selz, Gebhard. "Eine Kultstatue der Herrschergemahlin Šaša: Ein Beitrag zum Problem der Vergöttlichung." *ASJ* 14 (1992): 245–268.

—. *Untersuchungen zur Götterwelt des altsumerischen Stadtstaates von Lagaš*. Occasional Publications of the Samuel Noah Kramer Fund, 13. Philadelphia: The University Museum, 1995.

—. "The holy Drum, the Spear, and the Harp. Toward an understanding of the problems of deification in the third millennium Mesopotamia." in *Sumerian Gods and Their Representations*, eds. I. L Finkel and M. J. Geller. 167–213. Cuneiform Monographs, 7. Groningen: Styx, 1997.

—. "TÙN = tùn bei Gudea" *NABU* (1997): no. 36.

Selz, Gudrun. *Die Bankettszene. Entwicklung eines "überzeitlichen" Bildmotivs in Mesopotamien, Teil 1: Von der frühdynastischen bis zur Akkad-Zeit*. FAOS, 11. Stuttgart: Franz Steiner Verlag, 1983.

Seux, M.-J. *Epithètes royales akkadiennes et sumériennes*. Paris: Letouzey et Ané, 1967.

Sigrist, Marcel & Tohru Gomi. *The Comprehensive Catalogue of Published Ur III Tablets*. Bethesda: CDL Press, 1991.

Sjöberg, Åke W. "Götterreisen." *RlA* 3 (1957–71): 480–483.

—. "Die göttliche Abstammung der sumerisch-babylonischen Herrscher." *OrSuec* 21 (1972): 87–112.

—. "Three Hymns to the God Ningišzida." *StOr* 46 (1975): 301–322.

Sjöberg, Åke W. and Bergmann S. J. *The Collection of the Sumerian Temple Hymns*. TCS, 3. Locust Valley, New York: J. J. Augustin Publisher, 1969.

Snell, Daniel C. "Cuneiform Inscriptions." in *Classical Antiquities: The Collection of the Stovall Museum of Science and History*, ed. A. J. Heisserer. 5–11. Norman: University of Oklahoma Press, 1986.

Snodgrass, A. M. *Narration and Allusion in Archaic Greek Art*. J. L. Myres Memorial Lecture, 11. London: Leopard's Head Press, 1982.

Sollberger, Edmond. "Sur la chronologie des rois d'Ur et quelques problèmes connexes." *AfO* 17 (1954–56): 10–48.

—. "The Rulers of Lagash." *JCS* 21 (1967): 279–291.

—. "Note sur Gudea et son temps." *RA* 62 (1968): 137–143.

—. "A Foundation Deposit from the Temple of Nanše." *Syria* 52 (1975): 175–180.

Solyman, Toufic. *Die Entstehung und Entwicklung der Götterwaffen im alten Mesopotamien und ihre Bedeutung*. Beirut: H. Abdelnour, 1968.

Spycket, Agnès. "La déesse Lamma." *RA* 54 (1960): 73–84.

—. *Les statues de culte dans les textes mésopotamiens des origines à la Ire dynastie de Babylone*. Cahiers de la Revue Biblique, 9. Paris: J. Gabalda, 1968.

—. *La statuaire du proche-orient ancien*. Handbuch der Orientalistik, I, 2. Leiden: E. J. Brill, 1981.

—. "Lamma/Lammassu (B. Archäologisch)." *RlA* 6 (1980–83): 453–455.

—. "Review of Börker-Klähn, Altvorderasiatische Bildstelen." *WO* 14 (1983): 247–250.

Stamm, Johann Jakob. *Die Akkadische Namengebung*. Darmstadt: Wissenschaftliche Buchgesellschaft, 1968.

Steible, Horst. *Die altsumerischen Bau- und Weihinschriften*. FAOS, 5. Stuttgart: Franz Steiner Verlag, 1982.

—. *Die neusumerischen Bau- und Weihinschriften*. FAOS, 9. Stuttgart: Franz Steiner Verlag, 1991.

—. "Versuch einer Chronologie der Statuen des Gudea von Lagaš." *MDOG* 126 (1994): 81–104.

Steinkeller, Piotr. "The Date of Gudea and his Dynasty." *JCS* 40 (1988): 47–53.

—. "Early Semitic Literature and the Third Millennium Seals with Mythological Motifs." in *Literature and Literary Language at Ebla*, ed. Pelio Fronzaroli. 243–275. Quaderni di Semitistica, 18. Firenze: Universita di Firenze, Dipartimento di Linguistica, 1992.

Stephens, Ferris J. *Votive and Historical Texts from Babylonia and Assyria*. YOS, 9. New Haven: Yale University Press, 1937.

Strommenger, Eva. "Statuen und ihr Datierungswert." *ZA* 53 (1959): 27–50.

—. "Das Menschenbild in der Altmesopotamischen Rundplastik von Mesilim bis Hammurapi." *BaM* 1 (1960): 1–103.

—. *Fünf Jahrtausende Mesopotamien*. München: Hirmer, 1962.

—. "Gudea (B.Archäologisch)." *RlA* 3 (1957–71): 680–687.

—. "Mesopotamische Gewandtypen von der Frühsumerischen bis zur Larsa-Zeit." *APAW* 2 (1971): 37–55.

—. "Herrscher (B. Bildkunst)." *RlA* 4 (1972–75): 345–351.

Suter, Claudia E. "A Shulgi Statuette from Tello." *JCS* 43–45 (1991–93): 63–69.

—. "Gudeas vermeintliche Segnungen des Eninnu." *ZA* 87 (1997): 1–10.

—. "A New Edition of the Lagaš II Royal Inscriptions Including Gudea's Cylinders." *JCS* 50 (1998): 67–75.

Šilejko, Vladimir K. *Votivnyja nadpisi šumerijskih pravitelej*. Petrograd: M. A. A. Aleksandrova, 1915.

—. "Tituly SAL, NIN i SAL.ME LUGAL ve dokumentakh XXVIII-XXIV vekov." *ZVO* 25 (1921): 133–144.

Tadmor, Hayim. "The Historical Inscriptions of Adad-Nirari III." *Iraq* 35 (1973): 141–150.

Tallon, Françoise. "Review of Börker-Klähn, Altvorderasiatische Bildstelen." *Syria* 62 (1985): 187–190.

–. "Art and the Ruler: Gudea of Lagash." *Asian Art* 5 (1992): 31–51.

Thomsen, Marie-Louise. *The Sumerian Language: An Introduction to its History and Grammatical Structure*. Mesopotamia, 10. Copenhagen: Akademisk Forlag, 1984.

Thureau-Dangin, François.*Die sumerischen und akkadischen Königsinschriften.* Leipzig: Hinrichs, 1907.

—. "La chronologie de la dynastie de Larsa." *RA* 15 (1918): 1–58.

—. *Les cylindres de Goudéa découverts par Ernest de Sarzec à Tello.* TCL, 8. Paris: Paul Geuthner, 1925.

Tinney, Steve. *The Nippur Lament: Royal Rhetoric and Divine Legitimation in the Reign of Išme-Dagan of Isin.* Occasional Publications of the Samuel Noah Kramer Fund, 16. Philadephia: University Museum, 1996.

—. "On the Poetry for King Išme-Dagan." *OLZ* 90 (1995): 5–26.

Todorov, Tzvetan. *The Poetics of Prose.* Ithaca, New York: Cornell University Press, 1977.

Toscanne, Paul. *Inscriptions cunéiformes du Muséée du Louvre: Les cylindres de Gudéa.* Paris: Librairies-imprimeries réunis, 1901.

Unger, Eckhard. *Zwei babylonische Antiken aus Nippur.* PKOM, 1. Konstantinopel: A. Ihsan & Co., 1916.

—. "Das Weihbecken des Gudea an Ningirsu." *AOTU* II, 3 (1921): 27–121.

—. "Kunst, E: Vorderasien." *RlV* 7 (1926): 169–177.

—. *Sumerische und akkadische Kunst.* Breslau: F. Hirt, 1927.

—. "Die Wiederherstellung des Weihbeckens des Gudea von Lagasch." *Istanbul Asariatika Müzeleri Neşriyati* 8 (1933): 11–16.

—. "Kinematographische Erzählungsform in der altorientalischen Relief- und Rundplastik." *AfO Beiheft* 1 (1933): 127–133.

—. "Kalksteinstatue des Gudea von Lagasch in Paris und Istanbul." *RA* 51 (1957): 169–176.

—. "Die Erde als Stern des Kosmos im 4. Jt. am Toten Meer." *ZDPV* 77 (1961): 72–86.

Ungnad, Anton. "Datenlisten." *RlA* 2 (1938): 131–194.

Uspensky, Boris. *A Poetics of Composition: The Structure of the Artistic Text and Typology of a Compositional Form.* Berkeley: University of California Press, 1973.

Vallat, François. "La date du règne de Gudea." *NABU* (1997): no. 1.

van Buren, Elizabeth Douglas. *Foundation Figurines and Offerings.* Berlin: Hans Schötz, 1931.

—. *The Flowing Vase and the God with Streams.* Berlin: Hans Schötz, 1933.

van Dijk, Jan J. *Sumerische Götterlieder II.* Abhandlungen der Heidelberger Akademie der Wissenschaften, Philosophisch-historische Klasse, 1. Heidelberg: Universitätsverlag Carl Winter, 1960.

—. *LUGAL UD ME-LÁM-bi NIR-GÁL: Le récit épique et didactique des Travaux de Ninurta, du Déluge et de la Nouvelle Création.* Leiden: E. J. Brill, 1983.

van Driel, G. "Review of Ellis, Foundation Deposits." *JAOS* 93 (1973): 67–74.

Vansina, Jan. *Oral Tradition: A Study in Historical Methodology.* Chicago: Aldine Publishing Company, 1965.

Vanstiphout, Herman L. J. "Some Thoughts on Genre in Mesopotamian Literature." *CRRA* 32 (Keilschriftliche Literaturen) (1986): 1–11.

—. "Repetition and Structure in the Aratta Cycle: Their Relevance for the Orality Debate." in *Mesopotamian Epic Literature: Oral or Aural?*, eds. Herman L. J. Vanstiphout and Marianna E. Vogelzang. 247–264. Lampeter: Edwin Mellen Press, 1992.

—. "The Banquet Scene in the Mesopotamian Debate Poems." *Res Orientales* 4 (1992): 9–22.

—. "'Verse Language' in Standard Sumerian Literature." in *Verse in Ancient Near Eastern Prose*, eds. Johannes C. de Moor and Wilfred G. E. Watson. 305–329. Neukirchen-Vluyn: Neukirchener Verlag, 1993.

Vanstiphout, Herman L. J. and Marianna E. Vogelzang, eds. *Mesopotamian Epic Literature: Oral or Aural?* Lampeter: Edwin Mellen Press, 1992.

Volk, Konrad. "Improvisationsmusik im alten Mesopotamian?" in *Improvisation II*, ed. Walter Fähndrich. 160–202. Winterthur: Amadeus, 1994.

—. *Inanna und Šukaletuda: Zur historisch-politischen Deutung eines sumerischen Literaturwerkes.* SANTAG, 3. Wiesbaden: Harrassowitz, 1995.

Waetzoldt, Hartmut. "Kopfbedeckung." *RlA* 6 (1980–83): 197–203.

Ward, W. H. *Seal Cylinders of Western Asia.* Washington, DC.: Carnegie Institution, 1910.

Watson, P. J. *Catalogue of Cuneiform Tablets in Birmingham City Museum I: Neo-Sumerian Texts from Drehem.* Teddington House: Aris and Phillips, 1986.

Weitzmann, Kurt. *Illustrations in Roll and Codex: A Study of the Origin and Method of Text Illustration.* Studies in Manuscript Illumination, 2. Princeton, New Jersey: Princeton University Press, 1970 (2nd edition).

Westenholz, Aage. *Old Sumerian and Old Akkadian Texts in Philadelphia 2: The 'Akkadian' Texts, the Enlilemaba Texts, and the Onion Archive.* CNI Publications, 3. Copenhagen: Museum Tusculanum Press, 1987.

Wiggermann, F. A. M. "Exit Talim! Studies in Babylonian Demonology, I." *JEOL* 27 (1981–82): 90–105.

—. "The Staff of Ninšubura: Studies in Babylonian Demonology, II." *JEOL* 29 (1985–86): 3–34.

—. *Mesopotamian Protective Spirits: The Ritual Texts.* Cuneiform Monographs, 1. Groningen: Styx & PP Publications, 1992.

—. "Mischwesen (A. Philologisch)." *RlA* 8 (1994): 222–246.

—. "Mušhuššu." *RlA* 8 (1995): 455–462.

—. "Transtigridian Snake Gods." in *Sumerian Gods and their Representations*, eds. I. L Finkel and M. J. Geller. 33–55. Cuneiform Monographs, 7. Groningen: Styx, 1997.

Wilcke, Claus. "Sumerische Kultlieder." *Kindlers Literaturlexikon* VI (1965): 2126–2135.

—. "Der aktuelle Bezug der Sammlung der sumerischen Tempelhymnen und ein Fragment eines Klageliedes." *ZA* 62 (1972): 35–61.

—. "Hymne (A. Nach sumerischen Quellen)." *RlA* 4 (1972–75): 539–544.

—. "Formale Gesichtspunkte in der Sumerischen Literatur." *AS* 20 (1976): 205–316.

—. "Zum Geschichtsbewusstsein im Alten Mesopotamien." in *Archäologie und Geschichtsbewusstsein*, ed. H. Müller-Karpe. 31–52. Kolloquien zur allgemeinen und vergleichenden Archäologie, 3. München: Verlag C. H. Beck, 1982.

—. "Die Emar-Version von Dattelpalme und Tamariske." *ZA* 79 (1989): 161–190.

—. "Genealogical and Geographical Thought in the Sumerian King List." in *DUMU-E$_2$-DUB-BA-A: Studies in Honor of Åke W. Sjöberg*, eds. Hermann Behrens et al. 557–571. Occasional Publications of the Samuel Noah Kramer Fund, 11. Philadelphia: 1989.

Wilson, E. Jan. *The Cylinders of Gudea: Transliteration, Translation and Index*. AOAT, 244. Neukirchen-Vluyn: Neukirchner Verlag, 1996.

Winter, Irene J. "Royal Rhetoric and the Development of Historical Narrative in Neo-Assyrian Reliefs." *Studies of Visual Communication* 7, 2 (1981): 2–38.

—. "The Program of the Throneroom of Assurnasirpal II." in *Essays on Near Eastern Art and Archaeology in Honor of Charles Kyrle Wilkinson*, eds. Prudence O. Harper and Holly Pittman. 15–31. New York: Metropolitan Museum of Art, 1983.

—. "Review of Spycket, La statuaire du proche-orient ancien." *JCS* 36 (1984): 102–114.

—. "After the Battle is Over: The Stele of the Vultures and the Beginning of Historical Narrative in the Art of the Ancient Near East." in *Pictorial Narrative in Antiquity and the Middle Ages*, eds. H. L. Kessler and M. S. Simpson. 11–32. Studies in the History of Art, 16. Washington: National Gallery of Art, 1985.

—. "Eannatum and the 'King of Kiš'?: Another Look at the Stele of the Vultures and 'cartouches' in early Sumerian art." *ZA* 76 (1986): 205–212.

—. "The King and the Cup: Iconography of the Royal Presentation Scene on Ur III Seals." *BiMes* 21 (1986): 253–268.

—. "Women in Public: The Disk of Enheduanna, the Beginning of the Office of EN-Priestess and the Weight of Visual Evidence." *CRRA* 33 (La femme dans le Proche-Orient antique) (1987): 189–201.

—. "The Body of the Able Ruler: Toward an Understanding of the Statues of Gudea." in *DUMU-E$_2$-DUB-BA-A: Studies in Honor of Åke W. Sjöberg*, eds. Hermann Behrens et al. 573–584. Occasional Publications of the Samuel Noah Kramer Fund, 11. Philadelphia: University Museum, 1989.

—. "Legitimation of Authority through Images and Legend: Seals Belonging to Officials in the Administrative Bureaucracy of the Ur III State." in *The Organization of Power: Aspects of Bureaucracy in the Ancient Near East*, eds. McGuire Gibson and Robert D. Biggs. 59–99. SAOC, 46. Chicago: Oriental Institute, 1991 (2nd edition).

—. " 'Idols of the King:' Royal Images as Recipients of Ritual Action in Ancient Mesopotamia." *Journal of Ritual Studies* 6, 1 (1992): 13–42.

Witzel, Maurus. "Der Gudea-Zylinder A in neuer Übersetzung mit Kommentar." *Keilschriftliche Studien* 3 (1922): 1–97.

—. *Gudea Inscriptiones: Statuae A-L, Cylindri A et B*. Rome: Biblical Institute Press, 1932.

Wrede, Nadija. "Katalog der Terrakotten der Archäologischen Oberflächenuntersuch-ungen des Stadtgebietes von Uruk (Uruk 35–37)." *BaM* 21 (1990): 215–301.

Yoffee, Norman. *The Economic Role of the Crown in the Old Babylonian Period*. BiMes, 5. Malibu: Undena Publications, 1977.

—. "On Studying Old Babylonian History." *JCS* 30 (1978): 18–32.

—. "The Late Great Tradition in Ancient Mesopotamia." in *The Tablet and the Scroll: Near Eastern Studies in Honor of William W. Hallo,* eds. Mark E. Cohen et al. 300–308. Bethesda, Maryland: CDL Press, 1993.

Zervos, Christian. *L'art de la Mésopotamie de la fin du quatrième millénaire au XVe siècle avant notre ère*. Paris: Cahiers d'Art, 1935.

Zettler, Richard L. "Sealings as Artifacts of Institutional Administration in Ancient Mesopotamia." *JCS* 39 (1987): 197–240.

—. "Written Documents as Excavated Artifcats and the Holistic Interpretation of the Mesopotamian Archaeological Record." in *The Study of the Ancient Near East in the Twenty-First Century*, eds. Jerrold S. Cooper and Glenn M. Schwartz. 81–101. Winona Lake, Indiana: Eisenbrauns, 1996.

CONCORDANCES

A.   Museum Numbers

Archaeological Museum, Istanbul

EŞEM 491	FG.15
EŞEM 492	FG.14
EŞEM 1721	FG.13
EŞEM 1524	FG.10
EŞEM 1533	ST.7
EŞEM 1558	ST.48
EŞEM 1572	FG.11
EŞEM 1574	FG.12
EŞEM 5213	SV.2
EŞEM 5215	Statue S
EŞEM 5555	SV.7
EŞEM 5802	ST.60
EŞEM 5805	ST.13
EŞEM 5808	ST.27
EŞEM 5810	ST.26
EŞEM 5811	ST.23
EŞEM 5824	ST.28
EŞEM 5828	ST.63
EŞEM 5837	ST.9
EŞEM 5842	ST.11
EŞEM 5843	ST.20
EŞEM 5847	ST.61
EŞEM 5851	ST.20
EŞEM 5976	ST.5
EŞEM 5988	ST.62
EŞEM 5989	ST.20
EŞEM 5999	ST.34
EŞEM 6000	ST.18
EŞEM 6001	ST.34
EŞEM 6002	ST.4
EŞEM 6016	ST.12
EŞEM 6024	FG.16
EŞEM 6025	ST.31
EŞEM 6087	ST.6
EŞEM 6088	ST.30
EŞEM 6089	ST.6
EŞEM 6101	ST.4
EŞEM 6106	ST.8

EŞEM 6115	ST.29
EŞEM 6150	ST.27
EŞEM 6117	ST.9
EŞEM 6148	ST.62
EŞEM 6504	FG.17
EŞEM 6506	FK.4
EŞEM 12383	ST.6
EŞEM NN	MH.5

Birmingham City Museum

589'65	UI.2

British Museum, London

BM 22468	MH.2
BM 90831	DS.16
BM 90849	DS.1
BM 91007	FT.25
BM 91008	FT.26
BM 91056	FG.22
BM 91057	FG.23
BM 91058	FG.24
BM 91060	FT.27
BM 92988	Statue U
BM 95477	ST.33
BM 96566	FG.25
BM 102613	FG.26
BM 105108	DS.2
BM 119012	FT.14
BM 116450	SV.1
BM 122190	Statue V
BM 135993	FB.3
BM 135994	FT.13

Collection Chandon de Briailles

NN	FT.33

Collection Golénišev

5144,1.5	Statue T

Collection Hoffmann

115	FT.17

Detroit Institute of Art		AO 3	Statue F
82.64	Statue M	AO 4	Statue H
		AO 5	Statue C
Eremitage, S. Petersburg		AO 6	Statue E
8068	FT.31	AO 7	Statue G
14399	FT.29	AO 8	Statue A
14400	FT.30	AO 10	Statue K
		AO 20	Statue W
Iraq Museum, Baghdad		AO 28	UI.7
IM 2909	Statue Q	AO 52	ST.10
IM 6954	FG.18	AO 52B	ST.52
IM 14178	ST.19	AO 53	ST.36
IM 13678	FT.35	AO 55	ST.53
IM 18647	FT.2	AO 56	= AO 26634
IM 20639	MH.11	AO 57	= AO 26428
IM NN	DS.17	AO 59	DP.1
IM NN	DS.18	AO 60	ST.37
IM NN	GL.2	AO 63	ST.16
		AO 67	SV.7
Israel Museum, Jerusalem		AO 69	GL.1
71.23.299	FG.32	AO 73	SV.6
NN	FT.3	AO 75	FK.1
		AO 76	FG.3
Lowie Museum, Berkeley		AO 77	FG.4
UCLM 9–1794	SO.4	AO 103	DS.3
		AO 104	DS.4
Nationalmuseum, Copenhagen		AO 105	DS.9
5709	FT.28	AO 106	DS.10
NN	FT.32	AO 107	DS.11
		AO 108	DS.12
Netherlands Institute of the Near		AO 109	DS.8
East, Leiden		AO 110	DS.5
LB 17–19	UI.6	AO 111	DS.13
		AO 112	DS.6
Ny Carlsberg Glyptotek, Copenhagen		AO 113	DS.19
840	Statue O	AO 114	DS.14
		AO 115	DS.15
Metropolitan Museum of Art, New York		AO 116	DS.7
59.2	Statue P	AO 130	MH.1
		AO 132	MH.8
Musée de Mariemont		AO 133B	MH.7
139	FG.33	AO 167	SV.13
		AO 190	SV.9
Musé du Louvre, Paris		AO 196	SV.5
AO 1	Statue D	AO 243A	ST.50
AO 2	Statue B	AO 243B	ST.51

AO 257A	FT.19	AO 20152	SO.1
AO 258	FK.2	AO 22126	Statue N
AO 259	FT.21	AO 22500	UI.3
AO 260	FG.5	AO 25581	FG.6
AO 262	MH.3	AO 26428	SO.5
AO 305	SV.12	AO 26630	UI.8
AO 312	FG.2	AO 26633	Statue Y
AO 445?	FG.21	AO 26634	ST.21
AO 457L	ST.47	AO 26635	Statue BB
AO 3293	Statue I	AO 26637	Statue Z
AO 3541	CS.1	AO 26638	SV.3
AO 3542	CS.1	AO 26639A-B	SO.2
AO 4108	Statue I	AO 26640	FT.16
AO 4571	ST.39	AO 26641	FT.22
AO 4572	ST.35	AO 26644	SV.11
AO 4573	ST.9	AO 26646	Statue X
AO 4574	ST.43	AO 26661	FT.40
AO 4574bis	ST.45	AO 26663	MH.4
AO 4575	ST.42	AO 26665	FT.9
AO 4576	ST.24	AO 26666	FT.10
AO 4577	ST.25	AO 26667	FT.23
AO 4578	ST.54	AO 26668	FT.24
AO 4579	ST.13	AO 26670	Statue BB
AO 4581	ST.60	AO 26678	FK.3
AO 4581bis	ST.55	MNB 1362	FG.1
AO 4583	ST.61	MNB 1365	FG.7
AO 4584	ST.17	MNB 1366	FT.37–38
AO 4585	ST.4	MNB 1369	FT.7
AO 4586	ST.27	MNB 1372	FT.20
AO 4587	ST.29	MNB 1374	FB.1
AO 4580	ST.9	MNB 1375	FT.12
AO 4582	ST.49	MNB 1377	FB.2
AO 6966	ST.46	MNB 1380	FG.8
AO 10235	ST.15	MNB 1381	FT.8
AO 10236	ST.56	MNB 1384	FG.9
AO 10867	ST.3		
AO 12108E	SV.14	**Nies Babylonian Collection, New Haven**	
AO 12108G	MH.10	NBC 2517	SO.3
AO 12733	UI.4	NBC 2518	FT.36
AO 12763	DP.3		
AO 12764	DP.2	**Oriental Institute, Chicago**	
AO 12772	FT.5	A6150	DS.20
AO 12781	UI.5	A6151	FT.41
AO 12921	SV.10		
AO 14124	MH.9	**Public Library, New York**	
AO 16649	ST.22	T-2	UI.1

X-1	FT.11	VA 2894	ST.40
		VA 2896	ST.58
Museo Barracco, Rome		VA 2897	ST.59
45	FG.29	VA 2901	ST.64
		VA 2902	ST.14
Pierpont Morgan Library, New York		VA 2903	ST.14
2388	FG.30	VA 2904	ST.14
		VA 2905	ST.38
Rijksmuseum, Leiden		VA 3023	FG.27
A1951/6.2.	FT.15	VA 3056	FG.28
		VA 4859	FT.4
University Museum, Philadelphia		VA 8789	FT.34
CBS 16664	Statue Q		
UM L.29.212	Statue T	**Walters Art Gallery, Baltimore**	
		54.790	FG.31
Vorderasiatisches Museum, Berlin		**Yale Babylonian Collection, New Haven**	
VA 2339	FT.6	YBC 2160	FT.1
VA 2796a	ST.1	YBC 2188	FK.5
VA 2796b-c	ST.2	YBC 2249	MH.6
VA 2890	ST.41	YBC 2332	SV.4
VA 2891	ST.44	YBC 16412	SV.8
VA 2892	ST.32		
VA 2893	ST.57		

B. DC

fig. K	CS.1	pl. 15:5	Statue A	pl. 26:2	MH.1
pl. 8bis:4	ST.7	pl. 16–19	Statue B	pl. 26:7	MH.8
pl. 9	Statue D	pl. 20	Statue A	pl. 26:9	DP.1
pl. 10	Statue C	pl. 21bis:1	Statue I	pl. 26:10a-b	SO.5
pl. 11	Statue E	pl. 21ter:5	Statue S	pl. 26bis:3	MH.3
pl. 13:1	Statue C	pl. 22:4	ST.52	pl. 27:3	DS.8
pl. 13:2	Statue E	pl. 22:5	ST.36	pl. 28:2	FK.1
pl. 13:3	Statue G	pl. 22:6	ST.53	pl. 28:3	FG.6
pl. 13:4	Statue H	pl. 23	ST.10	pl. 28:4	FG.5
pl. 13:5	Statue W	pl. 24:2	GL.	pl. 28:5	FB.1
pl. 14	Statue F	pl. 24:3	SV.6	pl. 29:1	FT.37
pl. 15:1	Statue B	pl. 24:4	SV.7	pl. 29:2	FT.19
pl. 15:2	Statue F	pl. 25:6	ST.16	pl. 44:2	SV.9
pl. 15:4	Statue F	pl. 25bis:1a-b	MH.7	pl. 44bis:3	SV.12

C. NFT

pl. I	Statue I	pl. IX:1	ST.39	pl. IX:6	ST.25
pl. VIII:1	ST.45	pl. IX:2–3	ST.9	pl. IX:7	ST.35
pl. VIII:2	ST.17	pl. IX:4	ST.54	pl. X:1	ST.60
pl. VIII:3	ST.61	pl. IX:5	ST.13	pl. X:2	ST.24
pl. X:3	ST.43	pl. X:4	ST.42	pl. X:5	ST.49

| pl. X:6 | ST.34 | pl. X:7 | ST.18 | pl. XI:1 | ST.26 |

D. FT II

| pl. 84:1 | DP.3 | pl. 87:1 | FG.18 | pl. 87:2 | FG.19 | pl. 87:3 | FG.20 |

E. Parrot Tello

fig. 35b	ST.7	fig. 36l	ST.23	fig. 42j	MH.1
fig. 35d	ST.1	fig. 37	ST.24	fig. 42k	SV.6
fig. 35e	ST.36	fig. 37	ST.25	fig. 42l	GL.1
fig. 35h	ST.53	fig. 37	ST.9	fig. 43f	CS.1
fig. 35i-j	SO.5	fig. 37	ST.34	fig. 44a	FB.2
fig. 36a	ST.18	fig. 37	ST.39	pl. XIIIa	Statue A
fig. 36b	ST.45	fig. 37	ST.42	pl. XIIIb	Statue C
fig. 36c	ST.17	fig. 37	ST.49	pl. XIIIc	Statue E
fig. 36d	ST.43	fig. 37	ST.54	pl. XIIId	Statue H
fig. 36e	ST.61	fig. 38a	DP.3	pl. XIVa	Statue D
fig. 36f	ST.55	fig. 38b	ST.22	pl. XIVb	Statue B
fig. 36g	ST.13	fig. 42c	SV.7	pl. XIVc-d	Statue F
fig. 36h	ST.35	fig. 42e	MH.8	pl. XVa	Statue I
fig. 36i	ST.60	fig. 42f	MH.3	pl. XXa	ST.10
fig. 36k	ST.29	fig. 42h	MH.7	pl. XXI	SV.9

F. Steible *Neusumerische Bau- und Weihinschriften*

Gudea 4	FT.1	Gudea 19B	FG.2	Gudea 31	DS.1
Gudea 5	CN.1	Gudea 19C	FT.7–10	Gudea 32	CN.12
Gudea 6A	FT.2	Gudea 19D	FT.11	Gudea 33	CN.13
Gudea 6B	FT.3	Gudea 19E-L	CN.6	Gudea 34A	MH.3
Gudea 7A-C	BS.1	Gudea 20A	MH.1	Gudea 34B	MH.4
Gudea 7D-L	CN.2	Gudea 20B	MH.2	Gudea 35A	MH.6
Gudea 8	BS.2	Gudea 23	BS.5	Gudea 35B	SV.4
Gudea 9A	FT.4	Gudea 24A	FB.1	Gudea 36A-D	BS.9
Gudea 9B	DP.2	Gudea 24B	FT.12	Gudea 36E-W	CN.14
Gudea 9C	SV.1	Gudea 24C-D	CN.7	Gudea 37	FT.14
Gudea 10	CN.3	Gudea 24E	BS.5	Gudea 38	CN.14
Gudea 11	CN.4	Gudea 25	CN.8	Gudea 39A-E	CN.15
Gudea 12	SV.2	Gudea 26	CN.9	Gudea 39F	BS.7
Gudea 13	GL.1	Gudea 27	SV.3	Gudea 40	SV.5
Gudea 14	FT.5	Gudea 28A	BS.6	Gudea 42	SV.6
Gudea 15A-C	BS.3	Gudea 28B-G	CN.10	Gudea 43	SV.7
Gudea 15D-L	CN.5	Gudea 29A-F	BS.7	Gudea 44	MH.7
Gudea 15M	UI.1	Gudea 29G-O	CN.11	Gudea 45	BS.10
Gudea 15a	BS.4	Gudea 30A	BS.7	Gudea 45a	FT.15
Gudea 17	FT.6	Gudea 30B	BS.8	Gudea 45A	BS.11
Gudea 18	SO.1	Gudea 30C	FB.3	Gudea 46B-J	CN.16
Gudea 19A	FG.1	Gudea 30D	FT.13	Gudea 46K	DS.2

Gudea 47	BS.12	Gudea 53	BS.16	Gudea 75A	FT.37
Gudea 48A-O	BS.13	Gudea 54	UI.3	Gudea 75B	FT.38
Gudea 48P	UI.2	Gudea 55	SV.8	Gudea 75C	FT.39
Gudea 48Q	FT.16	Gudea 56A-E	CN.22	Gudea 75D-H	CN.29
Gudea 48R	FT.17	Gudea 56F	UI.4	Gudea 76	BS.21
Gudea 48S-ZZ	CN.17	Gudea 57	DT.1	Gudea 77A	ST.19
Gudea 48aa	DS.3–7	Gudea 58	BS.17	Gudea 77B	ST.1
Gudea 48bb-cc	CN.17	Gudea 59	FT.31	Gudea 77C	ST.43
Gudea 48ee	FT.18	Gudea 60	SO.2	Gudea 77D	ST.42
Gudea 48ff	BS.13	Gudea 61A	DS.17	Gudea 77E	ST.32
Gudea 49	BS.14	Gudea 61B-C	DS.18	Gudea 77F	ST.12
Gudea 49a	CN.18	Gudea 62	DP.1	Gudea 77G	ST.5
Gudea 50	CN.19	Gudea 63	MH.8	Gudea 77H	ST.47
Gudea 51A	FG.27–28	Gudea 64A-B	BS.18	Gudea 77I	ST.46
Gudea 51B	FG.18	Gudea 64C-E	CN.23	Gudea 78	UI.5
Gudea 51C	FG.33	Gudea 65A	SV.9	Gudea 79	MH.9
Gudea 51D	FG.29	Gudea 65B	SV.10	Gudea 80	ST.21
Gudea 51E	FG.10–17	Gudea 65C	SO.4	Gudea 82	FT.40
Gudea 51F	FG.22–25	Gudea 66	DP.3	Gudea 86	SV.11
Gudea 51G	FG.3–9, 21	Gudea 67A	BS.19	Gudea 87	UI.6
Gudea 51H	FT.19	Gudea 67B-M	CN.24	Gudea 88	Statue BB
Gudea 51I	FT.20–24	Gudea 67N	DS.19	Gudea 89	SV.12
Gudea 51J	FT.25–27	Gudea 67O	CN.24	Gudea 91	BS.22
Gudea 51K	FT.28	Gudea 68A	BS.20	Gudea 92	CN.30
Gudea 51L	FT.29–30	Gudea 68B	FT.32	Gudea 93	SO.3
Gudea 51M-T	CN.20	Gudea 68C	FT.33	Gudea 94	GL.2
Gudea 51U	DS.8	Gudea 68D	FT.34	Gudea 95	SO.5
Gudea 51V	DS.9–15	Gudea 68E	FT.35	Gudea 96	SV.13
Gudea 51W	DS.16	Gudea 69	CN.25	Gudea 97	SV.14
Gudea 51X	CN.20	Gudea 70	CN.26	Gudea 98	MH.10
Gudea 52A-E	BS.15	Gudea 72	CN.27	Gudea 99	CN.31
Gudea 52F	FG.26	Gudea 73	FT.36	Lagaš 39	ST.22
Gudea 52G	CN.21	Gudea 74	CN.28	Šulgi 13B.2	FB.2

G. Braun-Holzinger *Weihgaben*

G 247	SV.1	G 260	SV.11	K 48	MH.7
G 248	SV.2	G 261	SV.12	K 49	MH.8
G 249	SV.3	G 262	SV.13	K 51	MH.10
G 250	SV.4	G 263	SV.14	K 52	MH.9
G 251	SV.5	K 40	MH.1	K 53	MH.11
G 252	SV.6	K 41	MH.2	K 54	MH.12
G 253	SV.7	K 44	MH.3	Sockel 5	SO.4
G 254	SV.8	K 45	MH.5	Sockel 6	SO.5
G 255	SV.9	K 46	MH.4	St 107	Statue A
G 256	SV.10	K 47	MH.6	St 108	Statue B

St 109	Statue C	St 121	Statue Q	Ständer 6	SO.3
St 110	Statue D	St 123	Statue S	Stele 17	ST.21
St 111	Statue E	St 124	Statue T	Stele 18	ST.22
St 112	Statue F	St 125	Statue U	Stele 21	ST.11
St 113	Statue G	St 126	Statue V	Stele 22	ST.20
St 114	Statue H	St 127	Statue W	T 13	SO.1
St 115	Statue I	St 128	Statue X	T 7	GL.1
St 116	Statue K	St 129	Statue Y	T 8	GL.2
St 117	Statue M	St 130	Statue Z	W 25	DP.2
St 118	Statue N	St 131	UI.8	W 26	DP.1
St 119	Statue O	St 134	Statue BB	W 27	DP.3
St 120	Statue P	Ständer 5	SO.2		

H. Rashid *Gründungsfiguren*

81	FG.10	91	FG.5	101	FG.24	111	FK.1
82	FG.11	92	FG.2	102	FG.25	112	FK.2
83	FG.12	93	FG.6	103	FG.26	113	FK.3
84	FG.13	94	FG.1	104	FG.27	114	FK.4
85	FG.14	95	FG.7	105	FG.28	115	FK.5
86	FG.15	96	FG.8	106	FG.29	116	FB.1
87	FG.17	97	FG.9	107	FG.30	117	FB.2
88	FG.18	98	FG.21	108	FG.31	118	FB.3
89	FG.3	99	FG.22	109	FG.30		
90	FG.4	100	FG.23	110	FG.32		

I. Börker-Klähn *Bildstelen*

35	ST.1	49	ST.41	63	ST.60	77	ST.18
36	ST.39	50	ST.44	64	ST.54	78	ST.29
37	ST.2	51	ST.32	65	ST.13	79	ST.23
38	ST.40	52	ST.57	66	ST.25	80	ST.53
39	ST.17	53	ST.58	67	ST.23	81–83	ST.4
40	ST.33	54	ST.59	68	ST.28	84	ST.5
41	ST.6–8	55	ST.49	69	ST.24	85	ST.55
42	ST.36	56	ST.50	70	ST.63	86	ST.56
43	ST.64	57	ST.51	71	ST.26	87	ST.22
44	ST.38	58	ST.11	72	ST.52	88	ST.15
45	ST.14	59	ST.12	73	ST.3	89	ST.9
46	ST.61	60	ST.20	74	ST.42	90	ST.10
47	ST.62	61	ST.27	75	ST.43		
48	ST.35	62	ST.34	76	ST.45		

INDICES

A. Sumerian Texts Quoted

B.   General